Environmental Law and Policy

Environmental Law and Policy

Edited by
Chitta Ranjan Gogoi

Delta Book World
New Delhi-110 002

First Published in 2018
ISBN 978-93-85719-06-6

Published by **Abhishek Goel** on behalf of

Delta Book World
G-4, Prahlad House
4832/24, Ansari Road
New Delhi - 110 002 (India)

Tel.: 011-4707 2321
E-mail: deltabookworld@gmail.com

PRINTED IN INDIA

Dedicated to

My Father Jogat Chandra Gogoi

and

Father in Law Hari Chandra Baruah

Preface

The present book is an attempt to study the various aspects of environmental law and policy in India. Indeed, the environmental problems are posing dangerous threat to the human civilization. Environmental pollution, global warming and man-animal conflict are some of the emerging problems faced by the mother earth in the present time. As majority of the environmental problems are caused by human beings, spreading awareness among the people regarding the need of conservation of environment is must.

The authors of the book have presented their insight to the various environmental problems and suggested remedies for eradicating the problems. The book will be of great help for the students, faculty members, and NGO's and policy makers. Suggestions from the readers are welcome and will be greatly acknowledged.

Any creative work is not possible without the help and encouragements of other people. Through this small piece of acknowledgment, I would like to thank and acknowledge the help that I have received from various sources. I would like to thank the esteemed authors for their valuable contributions on different aspects of environmental law and policy. I am thankful to Dr. Sudhansu Ranjan Mohapatra, Dean, School of Law, Sambalpur University, Sambalpur University, Odisha, for his constant encouragement and help in carrying out academic pursuit. I extend my sincere thanks and love to my wife Jyotirmoyee Baruah for her constant support, encouragement and patience. I take this opportunity to express my gratitude to Abhishek Goel and entire staff of M/s. Delta Book World for publishing the book.

Chitta Ranjan Gogoi
Assistant Professor,
Centre for Juridical Studies
Dibrugarh University,
Dibrugarh, Assam, India.

Contents

1

Role of Judiciary in Protection of the Forests in India

Dr. Asha Verma*

INTRODUCTION

The forests are home to some of the world's signature fauna, including the Bengal tiger and Asian elephant, as well as a diverse tropical flora unique to the subcontinent.[1] The forests also contain vast reserves of natural resources, like timber products and minerals.[2] With its population growing, demanding more resources, and consuming more, Indian forests face possible degradation. Forest helps in keeping air and water fresh and climate good. The Indian Forest Act 1927 and State legislation relating to forest impose Governmental control over forests by classifying them into reserved forests, protected forests and village forests.

Forest was in abundance in ancient India. The religion culture and tradition of ancient India favoured protection of flora and fauna. Only rational utilization of forest resources for human needs and welfare was made. However imperial control over Indian forest initiated by Indian rulers and continued by the British regime brought out a revenue oriented policy towards forest. The Forest Acts of 1865, 1878 and 1927 were instrumental in achieving that object. Even after independence

* Faculty, Amity Institute of Advanced Legal Studies, Amity University, Noida (UP).

the revenue oriented policy towards exploitation of forest was not changed and the Indian Forest Act 1927 continued to be in force in Indian territories states.

The Supreme Court of India interpreted Article 21 which guarantees the fundamental right to life and personal liberty, to include the right to a wholesome environment and held that a litigant may assert his or her right to a healthy environment against the State by a writ petition to the Supreme Court or a High Court.

The Apex Court in ***Union of India v Abdul Jalil***[3] observed that the word 'reserved' has not been defined in the Indian Forest Act 1927. The Allahabad High Court in ***State v Avaid***[4] viewed that a grove is not a forest. In ***Laxman Iccharam v Divisional Forest Officer***[5], the Nagpur High Court has held that the term '***forest***' having not been defined in the Forest Act, the meaning given in the Shorter Oxford English Dictionary may be applied, which is extensive tract of land covered with trees and undergrowth, sometimes intermingled with pasture.

The forests are threatened by many reasons. Like:

- biotic damaging agents such as insects and diseases, wildlife and grazing
- a biotic damaging agents such as fire, storm, wind, snow, drought, mudflow, avalanches and depositions of air pollutants
- Human-induced damaging factors such as damage from harvesting operations, fire or impacts of air pollution and climate change.

Often, these agents act in combination, e.g. forests damaged by fire or storm are more susceptible to insect or fungi attack or, vice versa, forests attacked by insects or fungi are more susceptible to storm or snow break. Thus, it is difficult to assign damaged forest areas to one specific agent.

Forests not only provide wood but they directly control floods, drought, soil erosion etc. Conservation of Forests is of vital importance for India. Environmental scientists have calculated what a mature tree of gives to the environment:

1. Releases Oxygen,
2. Checks air pollution,
3. Control moisture and prevents water pollution,
4. Prevents soil erosion and increases soil fertility,
5. Provides shelter to birds and nests.

Many existing international treaties contain provisions that aim to regulate certain activities related to forests. However, there is no global legal instrument in which forests are the main subject; there is no international treaty in which all environmental, social and economic aspects of forest ecosystems are included.

There is great necessity for conserving forests. With the increase in the Indian population, the area under forest is gradually decreasing. To ensure ecological stability, at least thirty percent of the nation's area should be under adequate forest cover. There was large scale deforestation and the forest cover dwindled to less than eighteen percent. Originally, the forests were placed on the State List whereby the States alone could make legislation concerning forests. By 1976, the forests were placed under the Concurrent List and the Parliament also could make legislations on that subject. Despite the major steps taken by the Governments, the deforestation continued unabatedly. In 1996, Supreme Court issued sweeping directions to oversee the enforcement of Forest Laws across the nation. In ***T.N. Godavarman Thirumulpad vs Union of India***[6], the Supreme Court to give effect to the provision of National Forest Policy 1988. The Court gave notice to the Union Government and State Governments. Forest must be understood according to its dictionary meaning and the description covers all statutory recognized forest, whether designated as 'reserved', 'protected' or not, including any area recorded in Government records as forest.

Forest Conservation Law has also been significantly been impacted through another case, ***Centre for Environmental Law (WWF) India v. Union of India***[7] concerning national parks and sanctuaries. While hearing this case, the Supreme Court through one of its interim orders on 13-11-2000 has restrained all State Governments from de-reserving national parks, sanctuaries and forests.

The impact of both these judgments has been that: all on-going activities must be stopped – without prior approval of the Central Government. There would be complete ban on felling of trees. Feeling of trees in all forests is to remain suspended except in accordance with the working plans of the State Government, as approved by Central Government. Where permit system is in vogue, the Department of Forests or State Forest Corporation alone can cut trees. There shall be complete ban on movement of cut trees and timber from the North Easter States to other parts of the country, either by rail, road or waterways. Workers in the wood-based industries should be paid their usual wages. Ecologically-sensitive area is to be found out and totally excluded from exploitation.

HISTORICAL DEVELOPMENT OF FOREST LAWS IN INDIA

The Britishers were the first to realize the importance of forests in India. And soon they made a proper strategy and policies regarding forest in India. In 1855, a memorandum was issued whose main aim was to maintain and regulate the movements of forests dwellers having British Rule. The following sequence speaks about the historical background of forest laws in India:

YEAR	DEVELOPMENT
1855	Memorandum to regulate the movements of forest dwellers within the forests
Forest Act of 1865	Empowered the colonial Government to appropriate to itself any land covered with trees
Indian Forest Act 1878	Created an absolute state monopoly over forests and forest resources/produce

Forest Policy 1894	Management of forests for the general well-being of the country and maintenance of adequate forests to preserve climatic and physical conditions of the country and to fulfill needs of the people
Indian Forest Act 1927	Industry friendly and responsible for a serious depletion of forest cover in the country
Forest (Conservation) Act 1980	Restriction on the use of forest land for a non-forest purpose and prevention the de-reservation of forests

The Indian Forest Act 1927 created an absolute State monopoly over forests and forest resources. This regime of forests control sought to restrain private extraction of raw materials for the railways[8] and some other industries as well. Then the Forest Policy in1894 was made with this approach:

(a) "The sole object to which the management of forests is to be directed is to promote the general well-being of the country; and

(b) The maintenance of adequate forests is dictated primarily for the preservation of climatic and physical conditions of the country and, to fulfill the needs of the people".[9]

CONSTITUTIONAL PERSPECTIVE TOWARDS FORESTS

1. Seventh Schedule of the Constitution: In the Concurrent List, 42nd Amendment inserted.

(a) Entry 17-A, providing for forests.

(b) Entry 17-B, for the protection of wild animals and birds.

(c) Entry 20-A, providing for population control and family planning.

2. Eleventh Schedule of the Constitution: This new schedule is added by the Constitution 73rd Amendment Act, 1992. This schedule has 8 entries (2, 3, 6, 7, 11, 12, 15 and 29) providing for environmental protection and conservation.

3. **Twelfth Schedule of the Constitution:** The entry number 8 of this schedule added to the constitutional text by the 74th Amendment Act 1992 provided for the Urban Local bodies, with the function of environment and promotion of ecological aspects to them.

List I (Union List) entries:

52. Industries,

53. Regulation and development of oil fields and mineral oil/resources,

54. Regulation of mines and mineral development,

56. Regulation and development of inter-state rivers and river valleys,

57. Fishing and fisheries beyond territorial waters.

List II (State List) entries:

6. Public health and sanitation;

14. Agriculture protection against past and prevention of plant diseases;

18. Land& Colonization etc;

21. Fisheries;

23. Regulation of Mines and Mineral development subject to the provisions;

24. Industries subject to the provisions.

List III (Common or Concurrent List) entries:

17-A Forests;

17-B Protection and wild animals and birds;

20. Economic and social planning;

20-A Population control and family planning.

To comply with the principles of the Stockholm Declarations adopted by the International Conference on Human Environment, the Government of India, by the Constitution 42nd Amendment Act, 1976 made the express provision for the protection and promotion of the environment, by the introduction of Article 48-A and 51- A (g) which form the part of Directive Principles of State Policy and the Fundamental Duties respectively.[10]

Article 48-A: Protection and improvement of environment and safeguarding of forests and wild life: "*The State shall endeavour* *to protect and improve the environment and to safeguard the forest and wildlife of the country*".

Article 51-A (g): "*It shall be the duty of every citizen of India to protect and improve the natural environment including forests, lakes, rivers and wildlife and to have compassion for living creatures*"

INTERNATIONAL COMMITMENT TO PRESERVE THE FORESTS

There is currently no comprehensive legally binding instrument on forests. International negotiations explicitly aimed at a global forest convention were initiated in 1990, proposed and endorsed by the G-7, the group of seven major industrialized states. At that time it was thought that it would be feasible to conclude a forest convention in 1992, when the United Nations Conference on Environment and Development (UNCED) would be held in Rio de Janeiro, Brazil. But during the negotiations in Rio it became apparent that the international community was far from reaching consensus on the contents of a forest convention. There was even disagreement about whether such a convention should be negotiated at all. Instead, the juridically lame "Non-Legally Binding Authoritative Statement of Principles for a Global Consensus on the Management, Conservation and Sustainable Development of all Types of Forests" (Forest Principles) was adopted. Since a statement is, by its nature, non-legally binding, the title's inclusion of these words shows that this non-binding aspect needed extra emphasis, demonstrating the great divergence of views during the UNCED negotiations.[11]

The United Nations Conference on Human Environment held on in June, 1972 at Stockholm placed the issue of the protection of biosphere on the official agenda of international policy and law. The agenda of the conference consisted of the following:

(a) Planning and management of human settlements for environmental quality.

(b) Environmental aspects of natural resources management.

(c) Identifications and control of pollutants and nuisances of broad international significance.

(d) Educational, Information, Social and cultural aspects of environmental issues.

(e) Development and environment.

(f) International Organizational implications of action proposals.

The Stockholm Conference agendas, proclamations, principles and subsequent global, environment protection efforts shows the words realization of the need to preserve and protect the natural environment. The Conference acclaimed man's fundamental right to adequate conditions of life in an environment of a quality that permitted a life off dignity and well-being.

UNITED NATIONS FRAMEWORK CONVENTION ON CLIMATE CHANGE

There is a close relationship between climate and forests. Forests act as reservoirs by storing carbon in biomass and soils and as carbon sinks when their area or productivity is increased, which results in greater uptake of atmospheric carbon dioxide (CO2), the most important greenhouse gas. Various forestry practices have a significant role in helping to slow down the accumulation of CO2 in the atmosphere. Conversely, forests are a source of greenhouse gases when biomass burns or decays. Some practices involved in plantation development, forest management and agro-forestry, such as tilling and use of natural fertilizers, can release greenhouse gases.

UNFCCC was adopted as a consequence of the worldwide concern over global warming. The ultimate objective of the convention is to limit human-induced disturbances to the global climate system by seeking to achieve a stable level of greenhouse gases in the atmosphere. In 1997 the COP adopted an additional legally binding commitment, the Kyoto Protocol, which sets out emission reduction targets and methods.

United Nations Convention to Combat Desertification in those Countries Experiencing Serious Drought and/or Desertification, particularly in Africa.

UNCCD aims at combating desertification, mitigating the effects of drought and contributing to sustainable development.

This involves long-term strategies that focus on improved productivity of land and on the rehabilitation, conservation and sustainable management of land and water resources, leading to improved living conditions for people. Protection and expansion of forests are important elements in UNCCD, since forests have significant ecological functions that mitigate effects of drought and prevent desertification. Strategies to deal with desertification are likely to mitigate forest loss as well, and vice versa. Intact forest ecosystems help stabilize the soil; consequently, deforestation fosters both desertification and land degradation. Deforestation has serious consequences in terms of water runoff, soil erosion and loss of soil fertility.

Ramsar Convention on Wetlands of International Importance Especially as Waterfowl Habitat (Ramsar Convention)

The objective of the Ramsar Convention is the conservation and wise use of wetlands through national action and international cooperation. More than a thousand sites, totaling over 80 million hectares, are designated as wetlands of international importance. Some of these sites contain forest ecosystems, such as mangroves, although the exact number cannot be established, as forests as such are not identified under the convention.

Convention for the Protection of the World Cultural and Natural Heritage (World Heritage Convention)

The World Heritage Convention (WHC) aims to establish a system of collective protection of cultural and natural heritage of outstanding universal value. States recognize their duty to ensure the protection, conservation and transmission to future generations of their cultural and natural heritage. Forests can be considered as natural heritage, defined as "natural sites or precisely delineated areas of outstanding universal value from the point of view of science, conservation or natural beauty" (Article 2).

Convention on International Trade in Endangered Species of Wild Fauna and Flora (CITES)

CITES is aimed at protecting certain endangered species of wild fauna and flora from overexploitation through international trade, via a system of import/expert permits. The convention focuses exclusively on trade and is premised on the view that the control of international markets will contribute to the preservation of endangered species. CITES operates by listing endangered species in one of its three appendices, which constitute different levels of control in international trade. Numerous forest animal species are included in the appendices, but at present only 16 tree species have been listed, mainly species used for timber.

Vienna Convention for the Protection of the Ozone Layer (Vienna Convention)

The convention establishes a framework for the adoption of measures to protect "human health and the environment against adverse effects ... from human activities which modify ... the ozone layer"(Article 2). The main relevance of the ozone regime for forests is the link between depletion of the ozone layer and the possible adverse effects this might have on forests (Article 1.2). For commercial forests, tree breeding and genetic engineering may be used to improve tolerance of ultraviolet-B (UV-B) radiation, but for unmanaged or natural forests these methods are not an option. While many forest tree species appear to be UV-B tolerant, there is some evidence that detrimental UV-B effects can slowly accumulate in trees from year to year.

Convention Concerning Indigenous and Tribal Peoples in Independent Countries (ILO Convention No. 169)

The International Labour Organization (ILO) convention, which may also be cited as the Indigenous and Tribal Peoples Convention, also aims to protect the social, economic and cultural rights of indigenous peoples. Parties assume the responsibility for undertaking action to protect their rights, with the participation of the peoples concerned, and to guarantee respect for their integrity.

Indigenous peoples are often closely associated with forests; forests provide habitat and are important to them for economic, social and cultural reasons. Concerns about conserving and managing forests often coincide with concerns about the survival and integrity of the cultures and knowledge of indigenous peoples.

Relevant articles in the convention are to be found in the section that considers land rights (Articles 13 to 19), such as:

- Article 14, which states that "the rights of ownership and possession of the peoples concerned over the lands which they traditionally occupy shall be recognised";
- Article 15, which provides that the rights of people "to the natural resources pertaining to their lands shall be specially safeguarded", including the right "to participate in the use, management and conservation of these resources" including sharing of benefits and receiving "fair compensation" for damages.

AGREEMENT ESTABLISHING THE WORLD TRADE ORGANIZATION (WTO)

WTO forms the administrative and institutional framework of the revised 1994 General Agreement on Tariffs and Trade (GATT) and related instruments. The GATT/WTO regime is intended to support and ensure the proper functioning of free trade, while taking into account the protection of the environment. The most important provision in this regard is GATT Article XX, which includes exceptions to all trade rules for certain purposes such as the protection of animal or plant life and the conservation of exhaustible natural resources, subject to the condition that they will not be "applied in a manner which would constitute a means of arbitrary or unjustifiable discrimination ... or a disguised restriction on international trade".

The GATT/WTO regime is of relevance to forests since it regulates all trade, including timber and timber products, and since trade liberalization can have both positive and negative effects on the exploitation of natural resources. A range of provisions in WTO can accommodate the use of trade measures needed for environmental purposes, as are often included in other environmental treaties.

POLICIES TOWARDS PRESERVATION/PROTECTION OF FORESTS

Forest policies are drafted in India to provide a direction to legislative and executive action with respect to conservation, exploitation and utilization of forests and forest resources. The first forest Policy in India was framed in 1894. It provided right of the state to exclusive control over forest protection, production and management. This policy was drafted to strengthen the colonial approach to forestry.[12]

The India State Forest Report 2015[13] showed that the country's carbon stock has increased by 103 million tonnes. Some positive points from the forest report are:

- India follows a policy of keeping one-third of the country's total land area under forest and tree cover.
- The forest cover of India has increased by 21.34 percent in the last two years.
- Very dense forests in India cover 2.61 percent of the total forest area, moderately dense forests account for 9.59 percent while open forests stand at 9.14 percent.
- Among all the states and Union Territories, Mizoram has the highest forest cover with 88.93 percent of the total area, followed by Lakshadweep.
- However, northeastern states have experienced a decline in forest cover except Manipur.
- The Andaman and Nicobar Islands have gained around 1,930 square kilometre of very dense forests, Uttar Pradesh has added 572 square kilometre of very dense forest cover and Tamil Nadu has reported a net gain of 100 square kilometre of very dense forest cover.
- The mangrove cover in India has increased by 112 square kilometre following acute conservation in the Sundarbans and Bhitarkanika forest.

SOME DOWNSIDES OF THE FOREST REPORT:

- Although the total forest cover has seen an increase, around 2,510 square kilometre of very dense and mid-dense forests have been wiped out since 2013.
- States of Jammu and Kashmir, Uttarakhand, Meghalaya, Kerala, Arunachal Pradesh, Karnataka and Telangana have suffered huge loss of forest cover.

- Around 2,254 square kilometre of mid-dense forest cover has turned into non-forest lands in the past two years.

PUBLIC INTEREST LITIGATION

Public Interest Litigation (PIL) is permitted by the Supreme Court and High Courts under writ jurisdiction at the instance of public spirited citizens for the enforcement of constitutional and other legal rights of any person or groups of persons who because of their disadvantageous position are unable to approach the court for relief. The Supreme Court under Article 32 and the High Courts under Article 226 can be moved by any public spirited citizen or by NGOs for the prevention of environmental pollution. Justice PN Bhagwati has rightly said, "*The Court has to innovate new methods and strategies to provide access to justice to large masses of people who are denied basic human rights, to whom freedom and liberty have no meaning.*"[14]

The judicial activism has always been instrumental in addressing the environmental cause through PILs. It was because of this that the Supreme Court included the Right to Healthy environment, a fundamental right under Article 21. The Court has issued notices and directives to the Central and State Governments on multiple environmental issues, such as freezing production licenses granted to manufacturers of endosulfan pesticide, relocating hazardous industries from the National Capital Region, issuing guidelines for the prevention of noise pollution, and requiring civic bodies to file affidavits detailing measures to manage plastic waste.[15]

JUDICIAL APPROACH TOWARDS THE PROTECTION OF FORESTS

The courts in India have played a dynamic role in preserving the environment and eco-system. In a series of cases, the superior courts of India issued various directions and orders to prevent the environmental degradation. To understand the role of the courts in this regard, the structure of the judicial system and also the constitutional and statutory provisions are to be taken note of.

The judiciary has contributed to the forest conservation in

India by widening the scope of *locus standi* and entertaining Public Interest Litigation in India, enunciating a web of doctrines and interpreting Constitutional law from environmental perspectives. The Court had firmly disallowed the non-forest activities and granting of lease for non forest activities in forests. Renewal of stone crushing lease without prior permission from the Central Government[16] was considered a serious breach of duty in the case ***Dhirendra Agrawal v. State of Bihar.***[17] The use of forest land for non forest purpose was clearly denied by the court in the case of ***State of Bihar v. Banshi Ram Modi.***[18] Similarly excavations of iron ore[19] and tourism[20] in forest were highly criticised by the Supreme Court. In ***UP Legal Aid & Advise Board v State of UP***[21], it was held that the Forest Settlement Officer is under legal obligation to inquire into all claims including those, existence of which can be ascertained from the records of Government and from records of any person who is fully acquainted with such claim. In ***State v District Judge, Bijnor***[22], the Allahabad High Court held that no person can carry on fishing within the reserved forest without the permission of the Forest Settlement Officer or State Government. The fish found in a channel or pond in reserved forest is a forest produce.

In ***State of MP v SP Sales Agencies & others***[23], the Supreme Court held that launching of criminal prosecution is not necessary. Mere commission of forest produce is sufficient to initiate confiscation proceedings. In ***M/s. Laxmi Viroja Udyog Chitai v Divisional Forest Officer, Almora,***[24] the Allahabad High Court has held that where the highest bidder in auction of the forest produce failed to pay bid amount then on re-auction, difference cannot be recovered from that highest bidder as a means of land revenue under Section 82 of the Indian Forest Act 1927.

Playing a pro-active role in the matters involving environment, the judiciary in India has read the right to life enshrined in Article 21 as inclusive of right to clean environment. It has mandated to protect and improve the environment as found in a series of legislative enactments and held the State duty bound to ensure sustainable development where common natural resources were properties held by the Government in trusteeship for the free and unimpeded use of the general public as also for the future generation. The Court has consistently expressed concern about impact of pollution on ecology in present and in future and the obligation of the State to anticipate, prevent and attach the causes of environmental degradation and the responsibility of the State to secure the health of the people, improve public health and protect and improve the environment.[25]

TN Godavarman Thirumulkpad v. Union of India[26]

This case has been instrumental in forest conservation in India. This case, also known as the "forest case", is an example of the judiciary overstepping its constitutional mandate. The Court has effectively taken over the day-to-day governance of Indian forests leading to negative social, ecological and administrative effects. The Godavarman case represents the single biggest judicial intervention in administration of forest in the country. This case was initially instituted to address timber felling in the *Nilgiri* range of Tamil Nadu. But subsequently, when several cases of similar nature were brought before the Court, they were tagged with the Godavarman case.[27]

The Supreme Court, in this case, has innovatively utilized several methods of resolving the conflicts presented before it which have a bearing on the entire country. In its numerous orders, the attempt to define 'Forest' and 'Forest land', the appointment of various committees and commissions, reliance on experts' opinion on technical issues beyond the competence of the judiciary, the creative use of *Amicus Curiae* are several such methods which the Court has utilized in the interest of justice. The case has emerged as the largest judicial forum on all aspects of forest management including definition of forest, working plans, saw mills, dams, mining, infrastructure projects, use of forest land, encroachment, across the country and is not limited to any specific location or State. The case has also resulted in creation of new structures for example the National Level Committee on Forestry popularly known as the Central Empowered Committee (CEC) which has been created under the Environment Protection Act.

Goa Foundation v. Conservator of Forests[28]

The petitioners filed the petition under Article 226 of the Constitution that the Corporation should be compelled to procure environment clearance for the alignment passing through the State of Goa from the Ministry of Environment and Forests, Government of India, and until such clearance is secured all the work in respect of providing railway line should be withheld. The grievance of the petitioners is that the proposed alignment has been planned and undertaken without an adequate Environment Impact Assessment (E.I.A.) and an Environment Management Plan (E.M.P.). The petitioners claim that the proposed alignment is wholly destructive of the environment and the eco-system and violate the citizens' rights under Article 21 of the Constitution. The petitioners also claim that even though the ecological damage will not be felt immediately, such damage will be gradual and will lead to the deterioration of the land quality and will affect large number of people. The petitioners further claim that as the proposed alignment passes across the rivers, creeds, basins and backwaters, the Corporation cannot proceed to carry out the work without obtaining the statutory clearance required under the provisions of the Environment (Protection) Act, 1986.

Kamaruddin N. Sheikh v. State of Maharashtra[29]

The petitioner was in possession of land which was declared as a private forest by an order passed by the Sub-Divisional Officer, Bombay. He contented to protect his property interests. He filed an appeal before the Maharashtra Revenue Tribunal. That appeal was dismissed by the Tribunal. He received a letter later on from the Divisional Forest Officer, Borivali, directing to stop quarrying operations and to pay royalty to Forest Department. The Maharashtra Revenue Tribunal after remand allowed the appeal and arrived at the conclusion that the land in question was not a forest land. It was held by the High Court that the land was a private forest which vests in the State Government under the Maharashtra Private Forests (Acquisition) Act, 1975.

Sri Ram Saha v State of West Bengal[30]

In this petition the contention of the petitioner was not to be prevented him from felling down some of the existing trees standing on his ralyati land which has been recorded in the records of right under the classification *Bagan* (garden). He contended that at no point of time the said land was a forest of any nature and the same has never been converted from an earlier forest. The concerned trees intended to fell down are unproductive mango trees and they are very old trees and have lost their fruit-bearing ability and the petitioner has been incurring heavy financial loss every year and the trees have been affected with parasites and other uncontrollable worms so much so that any further standing of the trees would jeopardize the fruit-bearing ability of the other adjacent trees and they are urgently needed to be uprooted and accordingly, the petitioner has decided to cut down the said affected unproductive old trees of the garden for renovation of the garden by plantation of saplings therein. The Supreme Court directed that each State Government should constitute within one month an Expert Committee to identify areas which are forests. Irrespective of whether they are so notified, recognized or classified under any law, and irrespective of the ownership of the land of such forest, and identify areas which were earlier forests but stand degraded, denuded or cleared and also identify areas covered by plantation trees belonging to the Government and those belonging to private persons.

The SC also held that the Forest Conservation Act, 1980 was enacted with a view to check deforestation which ultimately results in ecological imbalance; and therefore, the provisions made therein for the conservation of forests and for matters connected therewith, must apply to all forests irrespective of the nature of ownership or classification thereof.

Bhagwan Bhoi v State of Orissa[31]

In this case the landwas shown as forest and in possession of the Forest Department. The only question was as to whether petitioner can carry on Saw Mill on the forest land. It was stated that since the petitioner was not granted license for Saw Mill after 1997, so cannot be renewed. The Supreme Court while considering the question about the object and purpose of the enactment of Forest (Conservation) Act, 1980 issued some guidelines which is as follows:

> "In view of the meaning of the word "forest" in the Act, it is obvious that prior approval of the Central Government is required for any non-forest activity within the area of any "forest". In accordance with Section 2 of the Act, all ongoing activity within any forest in any State throughout the country, without the prior approval of the Central Government, must cease forthwith. It is therefore, clear that the running of Saw Mills of any kind including veneer or ply wood mills, and mining of any mineral are non-forest purposes and are, therefore, not permissible without prior approval of the Central Government. Accordingly, any such activity is prima facie violation of the provisions of the Forest Conservation Act, 1980. Every State Government must promptly ensure total cessation of all such activities forthwith."

Shri Bhagwati Tea Estates v Government of India[32]

The Kerala Private Forests (Vesting and Assignment) Act, (Act 26 of 1971) was enacted by the Kerala Legislature to acquire forest lands held on *janmam* right as a measure of agrarian reform. The Act did not provide for any compensation being paid to the owners of these private forests. The forest lands so vesting in government were intended to be assigned to landless agriculturists and agricultural labourers for cultivation. Soon after the Act was made, which had the effect of vesting the ownership and possession of private forests in the government, the affected owners filed writ petitions in the Kerala High Court challenging the constitutional validity of the enactment.

Lafarge Umiam Mining Pvt. Ltd. v Union of India[33]

This case was in the context of the National Forest Policy 1988 where the Central Government has been explicitly identified as the regulator (decide on applications for the diversion of forest land for non-forest purposes). In this case the Court had ordered the Central Government to set up the National Regulator under Section 3(3) of the Environment (Protection) Act, 1986 for appraising projects, enforcing environmental conditions, for approvals and to impose penalties on polluters. The basic objectives of the National Forest Policy 1988 include positive and pro-active steps to be taken.

If we look at the environmental movements in India, especially during the 1980s era, many unconventional judgments were given by the judiciary. During this period environmental conflicts entered into the halls of the judiciary. When Public Interest Litigations were allowed as an innovative mechanism of bringing matters of public importance to the Court's attention by anyone, not necessarily an affected party, several environment matters were brought to the Supreme Court. And the Supreme Court not only played an important role in the implementation of environmental laws but also interpreted the right to life under Article 21.

When we are dependent so much on the natural resources like water, air, forests etc., then it becomes more important for us to conserve and preserve these resources. Forest conservation has become a worldwide concern, so the time has come to protect them for us and our future generations and should not be solely dependent on the decisions of Courts or policies by the governments.

The above chart[34] shows the environmental offences committed and the consequences later on.

NOTES

1. Shalini Bhutani & Ashish Kothari, The Biodiversity Rights of Developing Nations: A Perspective from India, 32 GOLDEN GATE U. L. REV. 587, 588 (2002) (discussing the mega biodiversity of India).
2. National Forest Policy, 1998, pmbl., No. 3-1/86-FP (India), available at http://moef.nic.in/divisions/fp/nfp.htm. accessed on 10th October 2016.
3. AIR 1965 SC 147.

4. AIR 1977 All. 192.
5. AIR 1953 Nag. 51 (FB).
6. (1996) 9. S.C.R. 982.
7. (2013) 8 SCC 234.
8. Rangarajan M., Fencing the Forests, Ist edn., Oxford University Press (1996) New Delhi, p. 29.
9. India's Forests-Forests Policy and Legislative Framework, MoEF, available online at http://ifs.nic.in/rt/book/page3.pdf, accessed on 15th October 2016.
10. Kagzi, M.C. Jain "The Constitutional of India" Vol.1.New Delhi: India Law House, 2001.
11. http://www.fao.org/docrep/003/y1237e/y1237e03.htm accessed on 25th October 2016.
12. This policy was drafted on the advice of the German agriculturist Volcker. Commercial production of the timber was the main thrust of the policy. Acquisition of wood for meeting the defence requirements of the Imperial army as well as for other purposes, such as the construction of railways et al was the main purpose of the policy.
13. http://indiatoday.intoday.in/education/story/forest-report/1/540270.html accessed on 25th October 2016.
14. SP Gupta v Union of India,AIR 1982 SC 149.
15. http://thediplomat.com/2014/01/the-indian-supreme-court-as-environmental-activist/accessed on 22th October 2016.
16. It is mandatory under section 2 of FCA, 1980.
17. AIR 1993 Pat 109.
18. AIR 1985 SC 814.
19. B V Joshi v State of Andhra Pradesh AIR 1989 AP 122.
20. Union of India v Kamath Holiday Resorts Pvt. Ltd. AIR 1996 SC 1040.
21. AIR 199 All. 281.
22. AIR 1981 All. 205.
23. AIR 2003 SC 2088.
24. AIR 2000 All. 146.
25. http://www.tnsja.tn.nic.in/article/Role%20of%20Crts%20in%20Prot%20of%20HR%20PSJ.pdf accessed on 10th October 2016.
26. AIR 1997 SC 1228.

27. See order dated 22.07.1996. In W. P. (C) 202 of 1995 where another case titled Environmental Awareness Forum vs State of J&K W. P.(C) 171 of 1996 was tagged with the Godavarman Case (Unreported order)
28. 1992 (2) Bom. CR 695.
29. 1996 (4) Bom. C. Rep. 209.
30. (1999) 1 Cal LT 399 (HC).
31. 2003 SCC OnLine Jhar 125.
32. AIR 1996 SC 209.
33. (2011) 7 SCC 338.

2

Historical Growth of Wildlife Protection Laws in India:

A Critical Analysis

Sree Krishna B.H.*

INTRODUCTION

The Indian subcontinent boasts of serving as the natural habitat of a large and varied wildlife. We can find some of the most magnificent as well as the rarest wildlife species of the world in the country. The beauty and variety we see in the jungles of India is difficult to be expressed in words. However, the past few decades have seen the greed and negligence of human beings working to the detriment of this rich wildlife. Large-scale poaching, habitat destruction and conflict with humans have resulted in a rapid decline in the population of most of the wild animals and birds. Conservation of Indian wildlife was not given the requisite importance for a long time. However, the government as well as the people slowly and gradually understood their responsibility in this context. Today, efforts are being made towards wildlife conservation in India, to preserve this natural wealth. Numerous wildlife conservation projects have been undertaken in India, both at the government as well as the individual level, to protect the rich wildlife of the subcontinent.[1]

---

* Research Scholar, National Law School of India University, Bengaluru

1.2 Threats to Wildlife

The major threats being faced by the wildlife in India are:

- The problem of overcrowding is one of the major reasons for the depleting population of wild animals in India. The wildlife sanctuaries of India have become overcrowded and their capacity has decreased to quite an extent.
- Tourism in the national parks of the country is increasing day by day. One of the reasons for this is a rise in the popularity of eco-tourism and adventure tourism. This has led to a growth in vehicle pollution and wildlife road fatalities, apart from leading to a damage of the natural habitat of birds and animals.
- With the increase in tourism, the parks have witnessed an increase in wildfires also. Innocent campfires started by visitors have, more often than not, led to menacing wildfires. These fires not only kill animals, but also destroy their natural habitat.
- The wildlife of coastal areas is constantly disturbed by personal watercrafts, like jet skis or wave runners. These personal watercrafts enter shallow waters and expel nesting birds from their roosts. Such activities are disturbing the mating pattern of birds.
- Releasing of chemicals and other toxic effluents into the water bodies has led to poisoning of the water. The animals and birds drinking such water face a fatal threat. Even the population of fish, living in such water bodies, is declining at a fast pace.
- The climate changes taking place in the world today, are affecting not only humans, but also the wildlife. The natural habitat as well as migration patterns of the animals and birds is experiencing disturb patterns.
- Last but not the least, the threat of poaching has been haunting the wildlife of India since ages. Even after the establishment of wildlife sanctuaries and national parks, the threat of poaching has not been totally eliminated.[2]

1.3 Ancient History of Indian Wildlife

Wildlife in India has been surviving since the Vedic Period dating back to 1500 BC to 500 BC, and records of nearly 250 species of birds which existed during that time have been obtained. The blackbuck was quite common in 'Aryavarta' or the land of the Aryans which were present in the northern part of the Vindhya Mountains and even those which extended till the south. The House Crow and Indian Koel were commonly noticed at that time. Information about wildlife belonging to this period have been existent in the medical treatises of Sushruta and Charaka. The 2000-year-old 'Gajashastra' which was written in Pali script contains references of the training of elephants which were often captured. Several animal bones have been discovered in the sites of Indus Valley Civilisation which existed prior to 1700 BC and they include the bones of Elephants, Chital, Jackal, Hare and Rhinoceros. Clay tablets of this period have depicted a particular species of Elephant and Rhinoceros which are presently extinct and a tiger seal of 3000 BC have been unearthed from Harappa. An animal known as 'Zebu' has completely disappeared today, from the Indus basin and western India, probably on account of breeding with domestic cattle and the consequent loss of natural habitat. Elephants were the earliest known Indian animals which were employed to be mounted upon during battles, a raised platform used in hunting and also as a status symbol during the age of Harappan Civilization.[3]

The Rig Veda highlighted the potentialities of nature in controlling the climate, increasing fertility and improvement of human life emphasizing on intimate kinship with nature. Atharva Veda considered trees as abode of various gods and goddesses. Yajur Veda Emphasized that the relationship with nature and the animals should not be that of dominion and subjugation but of mutual respect and kindness. Many animals and plants were associated with Gods and Goddesses so that they were preserved for the future generations. As they were associated with supernatural powers, no one dared to misuse the resources and therefore there was a check on the excess utilization of resources. King Ashoka of the Mauryan Empire did as much as he could to protect environment. He made several laws for the preservation of the ecology of India.[4]

During the 3rd and the 4th centuries BC, the rulers of Maurya Dynasty altered their attitudes towards wild beasts who made attempts to protect animals of forests. Elephants were emphasized upon the most, as they served innumerable purposes for the rulers, particularly during wars. Apart from horses, elephants were also treated royally, for this reason. Elephants and horses played crucial role in defeat of Alexander's general Seleucus. One can derive information about them in Kautilya's 'Arthashastra'. Vast number of Lions, Tigers and Elephants were protected by the Mauryas. However. King Ashoka, after he had embraced Buddhism implemented laws for the conservation of wild animals. The edicts of Ashoka claim that he made a rule which fined 100 'panas' to people who poached deer inside the royal hunting grounds.[5]

1.4 Medieval History of Indian Wildlife

Jahangir and Babur were amongst the Mughal emperors who made regular observations of the amount of wildlife in their kingdoms in their journals. Certain books suggest that Lesser Rhinoceros survived during that time especially near Mahanadi River and Sunderbans, close to Bengal and also near the Rajmahal Hills near Ganges River. Many of these animals were killed near Kolkata and Babur was fond of hunting them down. Jahangir recorded the number of animals hunted by him and from his age of 12 till 48, he had hunted about 28,532 animals by his own efforts. About 35 Swamp Deer or 'Mhaka', 889 Blue Bulls, nine Foxes, Otters, Hyenas and Leopards and 86 Tigers were included in that list. It is believed that UstadMansur who was a court artist of Jahangir in the 17th century, had painted a wonderful portrait of a Siberian Crane. The Dodo was introduced in his court through the Portuguese who was governing Goa during that time. An unsigned painting of this creature which is said to have been accomplished by Mansur.

1.5 Modern History of Indian Wildlife

Various species of beautiful and rare insects were brought to this country during the pre-colonial and post-colonial era, free of cost. The various broad surveys of the past clearly illustrate that across the centuries, the forest has been seen by rulers in various ways. Like for instance, it was seen as a place of scenic beauty; or as the site of great hunts, with their close similarities to warfare. But for many more people, the vast grassland and forests were also a home and a resource catchment area. Two clear events mark the history of Indian wildlife. Firstly the impacts of the British, whose intrusions into the world of the wild were far more extensive than those of their predecessors.And second one was the unleashing of widespread destructive forces, including the state-sponsored slaughter of certain wild animals and the harnessing of the forest for industrial raw material and military supplies. Some of these were not new, however the scale and intensity of the impact was without any equivalent. As a result, about a hundred years ago, even species that were a well-known part of the landscape in large areas of the country began to recede into plain memory. The second major event in the history of Indian wildlife was the creation of legal and governmental apparatus to administer large stretches of forest, eventually totalling around a fifth of India's total land area.[6]

With the independence of the country a dominant group emerged with a kinder and gentler approach to nature. However, the legacy of the control system remained despite major changes. The vast history of Indian wildlife signifies that much of the future relies on the reforms or restructures of the system and protection of nature's heritage.

1.5.1 Pre-independence

The British government started control over forest in the year 1806 when a commission was appointed to enquire into the availability of teak in Malabar and Travancore by way of appointment of Conservator of Forest. This moved failed to conserve forest as the appointed conservator plundered the forest wealth instead of conserving it. Consequently, the post of conservator of forest was abolished in the year 1823.[7]

On 3 August 1855, Lord Dalhousie, the governor general of India, reversed previous laissez-faire policy to establish the India Forest Department and annex large areas of sparsely populated lands in India. These lands were declared protected areas and staffed by foresters, fireguards, rangers, and administrators. Over the next decades, forestry in India became an international profession with global specialists ruling an empire of trees and grasslands. The new environmental policies served in turn to support British imperialism in India. Unlike the conservative French and English royal forests reserved for hunting by the privileged elite, or the later American concept of total protection in national parks, the new colonial environmentalism was intended to generate income for the imperial British state through strict control of India's natural resources. Lord Dalhousie's new forest policies greatly expanded British authority over the land and people of India, a colonial empire that the British had procured piecemeal over the course of several centuries of mercantile and military exploitation. Thus, environmentalism and imperialism have a shared past, and the newly protected forests marked a symbiotic alliance of environmental concern with expansion of state power in India.[8]

Lord Dalhousie's tenure as governor-general from 1848 to 1856 saw the acquisition of territory and implementation of administrative reforms for which posterity dubbed Dalhousie "the great Proconsul." Dalhousie's support for conservation was unapologetically imperialist. Upon reaching the capital at Calcutta for his inauguration in 1848, he proclaimed, "we are Lords Paramount of India, and our policy is to acquire as direct a dominion over the territories in possession of the native princes, as we already hold over the other half of India." The British government in India made it clear that "all the forests are the property of Government, and no general permission to cut timber therein will be granted to anyone."[9]

The second half of the 19th century marked the beginning of an organized forest management in India with some administrative steps taken to conserve forest; the formulation of forest policy and the legislations to implement the policy decision. The systematic management of forest resources began with the appointment of the First Inspector General of Forest in 1964. Dietrich Brandis was the first Inspector General of India. Lord Canning appointed Dietrich Brandis as the first inspector general of the India-wide Indian Forest Department, a post he held from 1864 to 1883. The immediate task of the forest department was under the supervision of Inspector General was that of exploration of resources, demarcation of reserves, protection of the forest from fire and assessment of the growing stock in valuable reserve by sample enumeration and prescription of yields which could be sustained. The objective of management of forest thus changed from obtaining of timber for various purposes to protecting and improving forests and treating them as a biological growing entity. Forest conservators had already been appointed in Bombay (1847), Madras (1856), and the United Burma Provinces (1857); Brandis in turn appointed forest conservators to the Northwestern Provinces and Central Provinces in 1860, Oudh in 1861, Punjab in 1864, Coorg and Bengal in 1864, Assam in 1868, and Berar in 1868. By the end of 1868, the Forest Department had administrators in every province of the subcontinent. In 1871, the Forest Department was placed under the newly established Department of Revenue and Agriculture, itself under the umbrella of the Home Department.[10]

The first step of the British Government to assess state monopoly right over the forest was the enactment the Forest Act, 1865. The act was revised after about thirteen years later in 1878 and extended to most of the territories under the British rule. It also expanded the powers of the state by providing for reserved forest, which were closed to the people and by empowering the forest administration to impose penalties for any transgression of the provision of the Act. Yet the latter act was passed only after a prolonged and biter debate within the protagonist of the earlier debate put forth arguments strikingly similar to those advanced by participants in the contemporary debate about the environment of India. Hurriedly drafted, the 1865 act was passed to facilitate the acquisition of those forest areas that were earmarked for railway supplies. It merely sought to establish the claims of the state to the forests in immediately required, subject to the proviso that existing rights would not be abridged. Almost immediately, the search commenced for a more stringent and inclusive piece of legislation. A preliminary draft, prepared by Brandis in 1969, was circulated among the various presidencies. A conference of forest officers, convened in 1874, then went into defects of the 1865 act and the details of the new one. The British Government declared its first Forest Policy by a resolution on the 19th October 1884.[11]

The 1865 Forest Act empowered the government to appropriate any land covered with trees. However, notification could only be effected if the existing rights of individuals and communities were not impinged upon. It is, of course, quite another story how many of these people had the awareness and the wherewithal to come forward and have their rights acknowledged and recognised.The Forest Act of 1865 was superseded by the Indian Forest Act of 1878 which was designed to facilitate strict state control over forest resources, and was distinctly 'annexationist' in nature. This Act sought to do away with all privileges and rights that were not explicitly granted by the state. Through a single piece of legislation, a centuries-old system of rights and privileges for forest-inhabiting and forest-dependent communities was terminated.The Indian Forest Act of 1878 radically changed the nature of common property and made it state property. The rights of people over forest lands and produce were later regarded as concessions. According to the 1878 Forest Act, forests were categorised into three types: reserved, protected, and village forests. Reserved forests were deemed the most commercially valuable and amenable to sustained exploitation. Overall state control of reserved forests was sought, involving either the relinquishing or transfer of other claims and rights. Very occasionally, limited access to these forests was granted. Legally, the process of reservation of forests could be challenged though rural communities had little experience with legal procedures, and illiterate villagers were often unaware that a survey and demarcation was in progress.[12]

Protected forests were similarly state-controlled, but some concessions were granted conditional to the reservation of commercial tree species when they became valuable. Protected forests could also be closed to fuelwood collection and grazing, whenever it was deemed necessary to do so. As demand for timber increased, many protected forests were re-designated reserved forests so that the state could exercise complete control over them.This Act also provided for the classification of forests as village forests, apparently to meet the needs of people residing in villages so that they could be kept away from commercially valuable reserved and protected forests. The mapping of forests allowed the implementation of scientific management. There is no denying hat the British introduced the concept of scientific management of forests in India, but its dominant paradigm very evidently was to pursue maximum sustainable yields and management practices were organised around this principle.[13]

To implement the Forest policy of 1884, the Forest act of 1927 was enacted. Till 1935, the government of India enacted the Forest Act. In 1935, the British Parliament through the Government of India created provincial legislature and the subject of the forest as included in the provincial legislature list. Thereafter, several provinces made their own laws to regulate forest. Most of these laws were within the framework laid down in the 1927 Act. The British all along their reign in India formed many other Acts from time to time.[14]

The Indian Forest Act of 1927 consolidated all the previous laws regarding forests that were passed before the 1920s. The Act gave the Government and Forest Department the power to create Reserved Forests, and the right to use Reserved Forests for Government use alone. It also created Protected Forests, in which the use of resources by local people was controlled. Some forests were to be controlled by the village community, and these were called village Forests. The Act remained in force till the 1980s when it was realized that protecting forests for timber production alone was not acceptable. The other values of protecting the services that forests provide and its valuable assets such as biodiversity began to overshadow the importance of their revenue earnings from timber.[15]

This led to the Forest Conservation Act of 1980 and its amendment 1988. India's first Forest Policy was enunciated in 1952. Between 1952 and 1988, the extent of deforestation was so great that it became essential to formulate a new policy on forests and their utilization. The earlier forest policies had focused only on revenue generation. In the 1980's it became clear that forests must be protected for their other functions such as the maintenance of soil and water regimes centered on ecological concerns. It also provided for the use of goods and services of the forest for its local inhabitants.

The new policy framework made conversion of forests into other uses much less possible. Conservation of the forests as a natural heritage finds a place in the new policy, which includes the preservation of its biological diversity and genetic resources.

It also values meeting the needs of local people for food, fuel wood, fodder and Non-Timber Forest Produces (NTFPs). It gives priority to maintaining environmental stability and ecological balances. It expressly states that the network of Protected Areas should be strengthened and extended.

The Forest Conservation Act of 1980 was enacted to control deforestation; it ensured that forestlands could not be de-reserved without prior approval of the Central Government. This was created as some states had begun to de-reserve the Reserved Forests for non-forest use.

These states had regularized encroachments and resettled 'project Affected people' from development projects such as dams in these de-reserved areas. The need for a new legislation became urgent. The Act made it possible to retain a greater control over the frightening level of deforestation in the country and specified penalties for offenders.

PENALTIES

Penalties for offences in Reserved Forests:

No person is allowed to make clearing or set fire to a reserved forest. Cattle are not permitted to trespass into the reserved forest, cutting, collecting of timber, bark or leaves, quarrying or collecting any forest products is punishable with imprisonment for a term of six months or with a fine which may extended to Rs. 500 or both.

Penalties for offences in protected Forests:

(a) A person who commits any of the following offences like cutting of trees, stripping the bark or leaves of trees, set fire to such forests or permits cattle to damage any tree, shall be punishable with imprisonment for a term which may extended to six months or with a fine which any extended to Rs. 500 or both.

(b) Any forest officer even without an order from the magistrate or a warrant can arrest any person against whom a reasonable suspicion exists.

1873 – The Madras Act was passed to prevent the indiscriminate destruction of wild elephants. This was the first Act under the British regime for regional protection of wild life.

1887 – The Wild Birds Protection Act No 10 of 1887 was passed which enabled the British government to frame rules prohibiting possession or sale of any kind of specified wild birds only during breeding Season. Also this Act was only applicable to those areas, which were under the control and supervision of Municipalities and cantonments under the British regime.

1912 – The Wild Birds and Animals Protection Act No 8 of 1912 was passed. For the first time, a codified law was enacted prohibiting the killing and capturing of wild animals and the disobedience of which entailed a penal offence. The Act was also comprised scheduled animals, which listed birds and animals which could not be killed, captured or sold.

1935 – The Wild Birds and Animals Protection Act No 27 of 1935 was enacted. This was a land mark year in the history of wild life as it was for the first time that the provincial government, could by notification, set aside an area to be a sanctuary for protection and growth of wild animals and birds.

1935- This year also witnessed the passing of the government of Indian Act 1935 in which the legislative powers were distributed between federal and provincial legislatures.

Other main laws include:

WATER POLLUTION:

The Shore Nuisance (Bombay and Kolaba) Act, 1853

The Orient Gas Company Act, 1857

Indian Penal Code, 1860

The Serais Act, 1867

The North India Canal and Drainage Act, 1873

The Obstruction in Fairways Act, 1881

The Indian Easement Act, 1882

The Indian Fisheries Act, 1897

The Indian Ports Act, 1908

The Indian Steam Vessels Act, 1917

The Poison Act, 1919

The Indian Forest Act, 1927

The Orient Gas Company Act, 1857

The Serais Act, 1857

The Northern India Canal and Drainage Act, 1873

The Obstruction in Airways Act, 1881

The Indian Fisheries Act, 1897

The Indian Ports Act, 1901

The Bengal Smoke Nuisance Act, 1905

The Explosives Act, 1908

The Bombay Smoke Nuisance Act, 1912

The Inland Stream Vessel Act, 1917

The Mysore Destructive Insects & Pests Act, 1917

The Poison Act, 1919

The Andhra Pradesh Agricultural, Pest & Diseases Act, 1919

The Indian Boilers Act, 1923

The Workmen's Compensation Act, 1923

The Indian Forest Act, 1927

The Motor Vehicles Act, 1939

The Bihar Wastelands (Reclamation, Cultivation & Improvement) Act, 1946.

Air Pollution Acts

Indian Penal Code, 1860

The Indian Boilers Act, 1923

Motor Vehicle Act, 1939 (Repealed by Act No.59 of 1988)

The Poison Act, 1919

Municipality Laws

Uttar Pradesh Municipality Laws, 1916

Bihar and Orissa Municipality Laws, 1922

Wildlife Protection Acts

Forest Act of Madras 1873

Elephant Preservation Act, 1879

World Birds Protection Act, 1887

World Birds and Animal Protection Act, 1912

Hailey National Park Act,1936 (Now Called Corbett National Park)

Miscellaneous Acts

The Indian Fisheries Act, 1897

The Indian Forest Act, 1927

Criminal Procedure Code, 1893

1.5.2 Post-independent India

The India Constitution, as adopted in 1950, did not deal with the subject of environment or prevention and control of pollution as such (until 1976 Amendment). The original text of the Constitution under Article 372(1) has incorporated the earlier existing laws into the present legal system and provides that notwithstanding the repeal by this Constitution of enactments referred to in Article 395, but subject to other provisions of the other provisions of the Constitution, all laws in force immediately before the commencement of the Constitution shall remain in force until altered, repealed or amended by a competent legislature or other competent authority. As a result, even after five decades of independence, the plethora of such laws is still in operation without any significant charge in them. The post-independence era, until 1970, did not see much legislative activity in the filed of environmental protection. Two early post-independence laws touched on water pollution. The Factories Act of 1948 required all factories to make effective arrangements for waste disposal and empowered State Governments to frame rules implementing this directive. Under the River Boards Act of 1956, river boards established are empowered to prevent water pollution of inter-state rivers. To prevent cruelty to animals, the Prevention of Cruelty of Animals Act was framed in 1960.[16]

Some States took initiative in the field of environmental protection, viz., Orissa River Pollution Prevention Act, 1953, and, Maharashtra Prevention of Water Pollution Act, 1969. While the Orissa Act was confined only to rivers, the Maharashtra Act extended to rivers, watercourses, whether flowing or for the time being dry, inland water both natural and artificial, and subterranean streams. Thus, there were scattered provisions for checking pollution of air, water, etc., but there was no unified effort in developing any policy concerning the pollution emanating from these areas. This position went up to the seventies. Meanwhile concern arose over, inter-alia, population increase, greater pollution levels; human impact on animal populations and natural landscapes and other aspects of resource depletion. It was the Stockholm Declaration of 1972 which turned the attention of the Indian Government to the boarder perspective of environmental protection. The government made its stand well known through five year plans as well as the legislations enacted subsequently to curb and control environmental pollution. After 1970, comprehensive (special) environmental laws were enacted by the Central Government in India.[17]

Post-Independence, there has been a growing concern about the decline of wildlife populations and the necessity of conservation and preservation of India's wildlife. This led to the enactment of the Wild Life (Protection) Act (WLPA) in 1972. By an amendment in 2003, the objective of the WLPA, reads as follows, "An act to provide for the protection of wild animals, birds, plants and for matters connected therewith or ancillary and incidental thereto with a view to ensuring the ecological and environmental security of the country." Thus wildlife conservation is acknowledged as integral to ecological and environmental security of our country rather than being limited to conservation of certain species of plants, animals and birds or their habitats. The establishment of Protected Areas has been the major effort to secure wild species and their habitats across the country. Protected Areas include Sanctuaries and National Parks but following an amendment to the WLPA in 2006, the new categories of Conservation and Community Reserves are also included as PAs. In 1998, the country had 426 PAs including 54 National Parks and 372 Wildlife Sanctuaries extending over 3.34 % of the geographical area of the country. By 2009, this had grown to a network of 661 PAs comprising 100 National Parks, 514 Wildlife Sanctuaries, 43 Conservation Reserves and 4 Community Reserves in different biogeographic zones, extending to about 4.9 % of the geographical area of the country.[18]

1952 – The first wildlife authority, in the form of an advisory board, was set up in 1952 called the Central Board for Wild Life renamed as Indian Board for Wildlife.

1972 – The Wild Life protection Act 1972 (Act No 53 of 1972) was passed. It was the first comprehensive Act passed for the protection of wild animals. However, subject to licences, hunting was permitted for certain purposes such as special, big and small games. Further the Act also permitted trade of trophies of scheduled animals under a licence.

1973 – The project Tiger was launched. Subsequently, several other schemes were initiated for protection of specific habitats and to save threatened species such as the Asiatic Lion in Gujarat, Barasigha in Madhya Pradesh, Hangul in Kashmir and many more.

1976 – The constitution (forty-second Amendment) Act 1976 was passed in which art 48A was Inserted in the Directive principles of state policy, which read as under – The state shall Endeavour to protect and improve the environment and to safeguard the forests and Wildlife of the country. A separate chapter IVA was incorporated where art 51A (g) states – Its shall be the duty of every citizen of India to protect and improve the natural environment including forests, lakes, rivers and wildlife and to have compassion for living creatures. Also the protection of wild animals and birds was transferred as 17B in the concurrent list of the constitution. In this manner, the state undertook upon itself an obligation to protect wildlife with a corresponding duty on the citizens for protection and improvement of wildlife among other things. Constitution sanctity was bestowed to the process of protection of wild fauna and flora for the first time.

1976 – Ratification of the convention on International Trade in Endangered species of Wild fauna and flora (CITES) by India on October 18.

1976/77 – A separate Directorate of wildlife Education and Research was established.

1980 – The Forest Conversation Act 1980 was passed, which is interalia, also aimed to preserve the natural habitat of Indian wildlife.

1982 – In the Amendment Act No 23 of 1982, sections 11 and 12 of wild life Act 1972 were amended which permitted the capture and translocation of wild animals for scientific management and introduction of endangered species in alternative suitable habitat. The 47 licensing practice for carrying out business in trophies and an animal article was also amended in Section 44 of the WLPA.

1982 – The Wildlife Institute of India was established whose prime objective was to provide a professional and scientific support to the management and development of wildlife in India.

1983 – The National Wildlife Action Plan was adopted by the Indian board for wildlife which was inspired by the World Conversation Strategy and the Bail Action Plan. The Chairperson of IBWL, Smt. Indira Gandhi, the then Prime Minister of India, outlined a board framework and strategy for wildlife preservation of India.

1986 – A Major step was taken to enforce the provision of CITES under art 253 of the Constitution of India. A separate Chapter V-A was inserted in the WLPA, which prohibited trade and commerce in trophies, animal articles derived from animals listed in the scheduled of the Act.

CONCLUSION

There are various laws to protect the environment in India but still the one can have a look at his surroundings and say that these laws have failed. The failure can be attributed to many reasons such as failure to implement the provisions of the law effectively, lack of actions from the government, illiteracy among the masses etc. Therefore, the first thing that needs to be done is changing the mindset of the people by making them understand the importance of wildlife in India. Only when people understand, they can make the change. Government also needs to take strong measures to protect the wildlife in India.

REFERENCES

1. Wildlife conservation in India, available at: http://www.iloveindia.com/wildlife/wildlife-conservation.html (last visited on: march 18, 2016)
2. wildlife conservation efforts in india, available at: http://rockonfanz.blogspot.in/2010/03/wildlife-conservation-efforts-in-india_13.html (last visited on: march 17, 2016)

3. History of Indian Wildlife, available at: http://www.indianetzone.com/50/history_indian_wildlife.htm (last visited on: march 18, 2016)
4. National Policies of Indian Government Pre and Post Independence, available at: http://shodhganga.inflibnet.ac.in/bitstream/10603/6868/9/10_chapter%205.pdf (last visited on: march 17, 2016)
5. Abhimanyu Singh, Environmentalism, available at: http://www.slideshare.net/abhimanyunusrl/environmentalism-comparative-analysis-of-preindependent-and-postindependent-india (last visited on: march 19, 2016)
6. Bharat Budholai, Environment Degradation, available at: http://www.legalserviceindia.com/articles/brenv.htm (last visited on: march 18, 2016)
7. ArchanaVaidya, a history of forest regulation, available at: http://infochangeindia.org/environment/backgrounder/a-history-of-forest-regulations.html (last visited on: march 18, 2016)
8. PoojaMoundyal, Summary of Forest Protection Act (1927) of India, available at: http://www.yourarticlelibrary.com/law/acts/summary-of-forest-protection-act-1927-of-india/30188/ (last visited on: march 20, 2016)
9. Environmental Legislation India, available at: http://shodhganga.inflibnet.ac.in/bitstream/10603/6565/9/09_chapter%204.pdf (last visited on: march 19, 2016)
10. Ministry of Environment and Forests, Report of the working group on wildlife, ecotourism and animal welfare, available at: http://planningcommission.gov.in/aboutus/committee/wrkgrp12/enf/wg_wild.pdf (last visited on: march 17, 2016)

NOTES

1. Wildlife conservation in India, available at: http://www.iloveindia.com/wildlife/wildlife-conservation.html (last visited on: march 18, 2016)
2. wildlife conservation efforts in india, available at: http://rockonfanz.blogspot.in/2010/03/wildlife-conservation-efforts-in-india_13.html (last visited on: march 17, 2016)
3. History of Indian Wildlife, available at: http://www.indianetzone.com/50/history_indian_wildlife.htm (last visited on: march 18, 2016)
4. National Policies of Indian Government Pre and Post Independence, available at: http://shodhganga.inflibnet.ac.in/bitstream/10603/6868/9/10_chapter%205.pdf (last visited on: march 17, 2016)

5. *Supra* note 3.
6. *Ibid.*
7. Supra note 4
8. Abhimanyu Singh, Environmentalism, available at: http://www.slideshare.net/abhimanyunusrl/environmentalism-comparative-analysis-of-preindependent-and-postindependent-india (last visited on: march 19, 2016)
9. Supra note 4.
10. Bharat Budholai, Environment Degradation, available at: http://www.legalserviceindia.com/articles/brenv.htm (last visited on: march 18, 2016)
11. *Ibid.*
12. ArchanaVaidya, a history of forest regulation, available at: http://infochangeindia.org/environment/backgrounder/a-history-of-forest-regulations.html (last visited on: march 18, 2016)
13. Ibid.
14. Supra note 4.
15. PoojaMoundyal, Summary of Forest Protection Act (1927) of India, available at: http://www.yourarticlelibrary.com/law/acts/summary-of-forest-protection-act-1927-of-india/30188/(last visited on: march 20, 2016)
16. Environmental Legislation India, available at: http://shodhganga.inflibnet.ac.in/bitstream/10603/6565/9/09_chapter%204.pdf (last visited on: march 19, 2016)
17. *Ibid.*
18. Ministry of Environment and Forests, Report of the working group on wildlife, ecotourism and animal welfare, available at: http://planningcommission.gov.in/aboutus/committee/wrkgrp12/enf/wg_wild.pdf (last visited on: march 17, 2016)

3

The Custom of *Jallikattu* in Law and Practice in India: Need For a Jurisprudential Shift

Mini Srivastava*
Ms. Shivangi Yadav**

INTRODUCTION

This paper opens by exploring the competing jurisprudences in environmental law. It endeavors to answer a very important question – Why should we respect the environment? There can be two possible answers - for ourselves (and our future generations) or for environment's sake. Most of the people go by the first approach while some rational and sensitive people, who have enlightened vision of environment, would adopt the second approach. It would be interesting to assess the rationale of the lawmakers, internationally and nationally, while making the environmental legislations particularly in reference to animal welfare. Thereafter, this paper would give an account of the prevailing animal sports in India and the competing justifications from both sides. Lastly, it would discuss the very significant yet controversial practice of *Jallikattu* and the 2014 Supreme Court Judgment and the latest 2017 amendment to Prevention of Cruelty Act in relation to the sport.

* Assistant Professor, Amity Law School, Amity University
** Student of BALLB, Amity University

COMPETING JURISPRUDENCES IN ENVIRONMENTAL LAW

The relationship between Man and Environment can be viewed from two perspectives: The first perspective places man in the central position and environment takes a secondary position. The second approach accords primary importance to environment and keeps human interest in the periphery. These perspectives are known as Anthropocentrism and Eco-centrism respectively. Anthropocentrism is derived from two Ancient Greek words 'ánthrôpos' meaning human being and 'kéntron' meaning centre, thus Anthropocentrism means 'human centered'. It is a viewpoint that all environment responsibility is derived from human interests alone and places human beings at the center of the Universe vis-à-vis experiences and the value of human. Any other entity has a value only pertaining to the interests of humans. Thus, an anthropocentric would value environment or for that matter anything for the joy/pleasure that it provides to human beings and not for what it independently is. Hence, the environment would be valued as important for the benefit that it provides to us and thus we have an obligation (indirect) towards it.[1]In the strong sense, Anthropocentrism implies assigning of an inherent value to human beings alone, whereas, when interpreted in a weaker sense, any act of protection of the interests of human beings at the expense of nature or any other living entity is justified by the greater amount of inherent value assigned to humans.[2]

The idea of Anthropocentrism has been reflected in the works of scholars like Aristotle, Immanuel Kant, William Baxter, etc. Aristotle (*Politics*, Bk. 1, Ch. 8)[3]maintains that "nature has made all things specifically for the sake of man" and that the value of non-human things in nature is merely instrumental. Generally, anthropocentric positions find it problematic to articulate what is wrong with the cruel treatment of non-human animals, except to the extent that such treatment may lead to bad consequences for human beings. Immanuel Kant("Duties to Animals and Spirits", in *Lectures on Ethics*)[4], for instance, suggests that cruelty towards a dog might encourage a person to develop a character which would be desensitized to cruelty towards humans. From this standpoint, cruelty towards non-human animals would be instrumentally, rather than intrinsically, wrong.[5] Further, Anthropocentrism in itself has been seen through a prism, emanating from which are cornucopian[6] point of view and prudential or enlightened anthropocentrism.[7]

With the emergence of the environmental ethics, a new stream of ideology developed which confronted the anthropocentric approach on environment. A new consciousness developed that places intrinsic value on all living organisms and their natural environment, regardless of their perceived usefulness or importance to human beings. This ideology came to be known as Eco-centrism. It is derived from two Greek word 'oikos' meaning house (nature) and 'kéntron' meaning center. Thus, Eco-centrism is a nature centered approach. Aldo Leopold's *A Sand County Almanac* (1949)[8], in particular, advocated the adoption of a "land ethic" by stating, "That land is a community is the basic concept of ecology, but that land is to be loved and respected is an extension of ethics...A thing is right when it tends to preserve the integrity, stability, and beauty of the biotic community. It is wrong when it tends otherwise. (Leopold 1949: 224-25)".[9]

Thus, nature as a whole has an innate value, independent of the human interests. Human needs do not determine the value of any part of nature. The basic premises on which this approach is founded are that *first*, the resources on Earth are limited, *second*, Earth is for all species including animals, plants and humans and *last but not the least*, there should be minimum disturbance of natural processes.[10]

Eco-centrism is often linked with other environmental theories like Deep Ecology and Gaia Hypothesis.[11]Thus, all the above theories revolve around the idea the Earth's Environment holds a larger value than human beings.

CHANGING APPROACES IN INTERNATIONAL ENVIRONMENTAL LAW

This chapter, in particular, analyses the various international environmental law related treaties and conventions pertaining to animal welfare from the prism of the above mentioned philosophies to assess the master value behind them.

A paradigm shift has been seen in the approaches adopted by the International Environment law. Earlier, it was founded upon the philosophy of anthropocentrism, but with the advent of time, it started to recognize the eco-centric approach. This shift, in relation to animal welfare, can be elucidated in three stages[12], which are as under:

The First Stage was that of Protection of environment vis-à-vis human self-interest. The international treaties and conventions were directly based on the canons of Anthropocentrism. There are certain instruments which followed this theory, viz., The Declaration of the Protection of Birds Useful to Agriculture (1875), Convention Designed to Ensure the Protection of Various Species of Wild Animals which are Useful to Man or Inoffensive (1900), Convention for the Regulation of Whaling (1931) which had the objective of ensuring the health of the whaling industry rather than conserving or protecting the whale species.

The Second Stage saw the development of the concept of Inter-generational equity/rights wherein, the treaties were extended to not only to meet the requirements of present generation but future generations also, anthropocentrism was not considered in its true sense. For example, the 1946 Whaling Convention which built upon the 1931 treaty mentioned in the preamble that "it is in the interest of the nations of the world to safeguard for future generations the great natural resource represented by the whale stocks". Similarly, the Stockholm Declaration of the UN embodied this shift in thinking, stating that "man... bears a solemn responsibility to protect and improve the environment for present and future generations" and subsequently asserts that "the natural resources of the earth.... must be safeguarded for the benefit of present and future generations through careful planning and management". Other documents expressed this shift in terms of sustainability and sustainable development.

During the Third Stage, it started pure recognition of the principles of Eco-centrism through multinational treaties. UNEP

Biodiversity Convention (1992) "Conscious of the intrinsic value of biological diversity and of the ecological, genetic, social, economic, educational, cultural, recreational and aesthetic values of biological diversity and its components.... [we have] agreed as follows: ......". The World Charter for Nature (1982) proclaims that "every form of life is unique, warranting respect regardless of its worth to man." The Charter uses the term "nature" in preference to "environment" with a view to shifting to non-anthropocentric human-independent terminology. In 2000, a Universal Declaration on Animal Welfare[13] was designed by World Society for the Protection of Animals. This Declaration encourages governments to increase awareness and promote activities for the welfare of animals, thereby propagating the view of Eco-centrism. In 2011, the Declaration of Animal Rights[14], clearly established the worldwide acceptance of the ideologies of Eco-centrism.

STATE'S APPROACHES *QUA* ENVIRONMENT PROTECTION

Constitution and Environment

The Indian Constitution through various provisions aim at protecting environment. Environmental law in India emanates from various Articles and schedules of the Constitution. The Directive Principles of State Policy and Fundamental Duties[15] specifically provides for provisions on protection of environment. Article 48A[16]directs the state "to protect and improve the environment and to safeguard the forests and wildlife of the country". Article 51(A)(g) imposes a duty on every citizen of India "to protect and improve the natural environment including forest, lakes, rivers and wildlife, and to have compassion for living creatures. The above two Articles can be interpreted to have an Eco-centric approach; however, they are not enforceable on their own. All the three lists mentioned in the 7th Schedule of the Indian Constitution, also deals with the subjects related to the environment as well as animal welfare. List III: Concurrent List specifically deals with Entries with subjects like Prevention of Cruelty[17], Forests[18], Protection of wild animals and birds[19], and population control and family planning[20].

Legislature and Environment

Both Union and State Legislature are empowered to make laws, rules and regulations on Environment under the above Articles. The Environmental Protection Act, 1986, umbrella legislation, was enacted by the Parliament under Article 253 of the Indian Constitution after the environmental debacle in Bhopal.

Animal welfare has been a part of the culture of the sub-continent. India has been the abode of many religious practices which advocated compassion towards animals. Legislature, from 1960 has passed many laws on animal welfare, thereby, promoting the interest of animals. The Principal Legislation, vis-à-vis Animal welfare, is the Prevention of Cruelty Act, 1960. This Act aspires to prevent the infliction of unnecessary pain or suffering on animals and for that purpose to amend the law relating to the prevention of cruelty to animals. However, a special mention must be done for Section 28 of the Prevention of Cruelty of Animals Act, 1960 which states that killing of any animal in a manner provided by the religion of any community would not be an offence under this Act. This Act, which is otherwise Eco-Centric, through Section 28 has given more impetus to human interests vis-à-vis animal interests. Such attitude has an anthropocentric approach inherent in it.

Executive and Environment

Under the aegis of the Prevention of Cruelty Act, 1960, there have been various Rules[21] passed which are as follows:

1) The Prevention of Cruelty to Draught and Pack Animals Rules, 1965: It provides for the maximum load for draught animals, like bullock, pony, mule, donkey and camel.
2) The Prevention of Cruelty to Animals (Licensing of Farriers) Rules, 1965: These Rules require every Farrier[22] to obtain a license before using cattle[23] for carrier purposes.
3) The Performing Animals Rules, 1973: Central government, through these rules, makes it mandatory for every person desirous of exhibiting or training any performing animal[24], to seek registration.

4) The Transport of Animals, Rules 1978: It requires every person to obtain a certificate from a qualified veterinary surgeon to the effect that the animals, namely, dogs, cats, monkeys, cattle, equines, sheep and goats, are in a fit condition to travel by rail; road or sea and are not suffering from any infectious or contagious disease or diseases shall accompany each consignment. 2001 Amendment of these Rules included Poultry and Pigs also.

5) The Prevention of Cruelty to Animals (Application of Fines) Rules, 1978: Through these Rules, Central Government, lays down the procedure of the application of fines.

6) The Prevention of Cruelty to Animals (Registration of Cattle Premises) Rules, 1978: Every person owning or in charge of premises in which not less than five heads of cattle are kept for the purpose of profit, shall apply and acquire the registration of the premises.

7) The Prevention of Cruelty (Capture of Animals) Rules, 1979: These Rules required that no animal (excluding birds) shall be captured for purposes like sale, export or for any other purpose.

8) Ban on exhibition/training of five performing animals, 1998: Central Government, through this notification specified that the following five animals are forbidden from any activity which requires training/exhibition, whatsoever: Bears, Monkeys, Tigers, Panthers and Lions

9) Prevention of Cruelty to Animals (Transport of Animals on foot), 2000: These Rules require every person to attain a health certificate of each animal from a verified veterinary doctor and to follow all the other requirements specified.

10) Prevention of Cruelty to animals (Slaughter house) Rules, 2001: It specified all the do's and dont's, while opening a slaughter house. Rule 3 (2) prohibits (a) a pregnant animal, (b) animal which has an offspring less than three months old, (c) animal under the age of three, and (d) animal which has not been certified by a veterinary doctor that it is in a fit condition to be slaughtered, from being slaughtered.

11) Prevention of Cruelty to animals (establishment and regulation of societies for prevention of cruelty to animals) rules, 2001: Central Government through these Rules require every state to establish a Society for prevention of cruelty to animals (SPCA).

12) Animal birth control (dogs) rules, 2001: Dogs, under these rules, are to be properly sterilized and immunized.

13) Breeding of and Experiments on Animals (Control and Supervision) Rules, 1998[25]: It sets forth the general requirements for breeding and using animals or research, including rules governing facilities, personnel, and procedures. 2001 Amendment of this rule simplifies the definition of Experimentation and registration requirements. 2006 Amendment, further, added *inter alia,* animals should first be used 'lowest on the phylogenetic scale and the experimenters should give justification for not using any non-animal alternatives.

Other than the above rules, there have been certain Regulations and Rules made by the Central Government under other legislations *qua* animal welfare

1) The Establishment of Medical College Regulations, 2013 (Amendment): The Medical Council of India is empowered to make this regulation under Section 33 of the Indian Medical Council Act, 1956. This amendment required all the Medical Colleges to use computer assisted modules instead of animals, to study physiology and pharmacology.[26]

2) The Education (Amendment) Regulations, 2014: The Pharmacy Council of India made and amendment in the above regulation which forbid the experimentation on animals for the purpose of imparting knowledge.[27]

3) Drugs and Cosmetics Rules, 1945: Regulation 148 C[28] and 135 B[29] were added by way of Central Government's notification which prohibited the testing of cosmetics on animals and their import, respectively.

Thus, the State Executive, by means of the above Rules and Regulations has depicted an eco-centric approach in theory. The practice of these rules which is more eco-centric in nature as it has placed the welfare of animals at a position which cannot be compromised. Whether these rules are applied also with eco-centric approach is a question of research, beyond the purview of this paper.

Judiciary and Environment

Over the period of time, the Indian Judiciary, through its activism, has enlarged the boundaries of Article 21 of the Indian Constitution by interpreting it to have been extended to the right to live with the basic human dignity.[30] Right to the wholesome environment was recognized to be a part of Article 21, by the Supreme Court in *Charan Lal Sahu vs. Union of India And Ors.*[31] Animal welfare is an integral part of the Indian Environmental law and jurisprudence. Indian Judiciary has, from time to time, through it active role, strengthened the animal law. The Supreme of India has adopted the Eco-Centric approach in cases pertaining to animal welfare.[32]

The Kerala High Court in *N.R. Nair vs. Union of India*[33]recognized the right of animals to exist with basic dignity without any abuse. In *State of Gujarat v. Mirzapur Moti Kureshi Kassab Jamat* andOrs.[34], the Supreme Court of India held that by enacting Article51A(g) and giving it the status of a fundamental duty, one of the objects sought to be achieved by Parliament is to ensure that the spirit and message of Articles 48 and 48Aare honored as a fundamental duty of every citizen. Article 51A(g), therefore, enjoins that it was a fundamental duty of every citizen "to have compassion for living creatures", which means concern for suffering, sympathy, kindliness etc., which has to be read along with Sections 3, 11(1)(a) & (m), 22 etc. of Prevention of Cruelty to Animals Act.[35] Moreover, in *People For Ethical Treatment Of ... vs. Union Of India & Others,* Bombay High Court ruled that, if a film has any animal performing in it, has to obtain a certificate from the Animal Welfare Board of India. Through the cases above, it is clear that judiciary has taken resort to the principles of Eco-Centrism while dealing with issues of animal welfare.

ANIMAL SPORTS IN INDIA AND COMPETING JUSTIFICATIONS

India, from time immemorial, has been an abode to many sports involving animals. They form an indispensable part of the culture and celebrations of various factions of the society. Most of the times these sports are a part of tradition, which eventually becomes a Custom. Some of these sports are explained below:

Jallikattu

Jallikattu is a traditional animal sport practiced as part of the Pongal celebrations, prevalent in the state of Tamil Nadu. Jallikattu is derived from two Tamil words, 'jalli' meaning gold or silver coins and 'kattu' meaning tied. Therefore, it a sport which requires the taming of a berserk bull in order to win the prize tied with the horns of the bull. Jallikattu is not only dangerous to human beings but also to the bull. The Jallikattu controversy highlighted various other animal sports[36]practiced in various part of the country, which are:

Cock-Fight

It is a sport played during the festival of Sankranti in Andhra Pradesh. Two roosters (specially bred for this purpose) are made to fight in a ring called a cockpit. At times, knives or metal spurs are attached to the legs of the birds. Although it has been banned the High Court of Andhra Pradesh in 2017, it is still practiced illegally in the state.

Kambala

It is an annual Buffalo Race held in coastal areas of Karnataka. The race rakes place between two pairs of buffaloes in wet fields, controlled by a whip-lashing. The high court of Karnataka has passed an interim order of stay on all activities related to Kambala.

Bail Gadi Shariat (Bull Cart Race)

It is a recreational race between two bullock carts prominent in Maharashtra and Punjab. The bullocks are kept not for commercial purpose but for races like such. The Supreme Court has banned this sport but due to political support and loose implementation, it is still practiced but illegally in Maharashtra.

Camel Race

Pushkar Fair is considered incomplete without the camel race. The winner of the camel race receives a cash prize from the government of Rajasthan. Although this race does not have any religious importance but it is held to reflect the significance of camel in the desert.

Dog Fight

These blood fights between dogs are held mainly for entertainment purposes. Dog fights are eminent amongst the rich class suburban in Indian, prevalent in Delhi, Haryana etc. Like many, this practice is also banned but illegally held.

Bulbul Fight

This fight is organized during the festival of Makar Sankranti in the Hayagriva-Madhava Temple in Hajo, Assam. The ban on this sport was heavily protested by the temple authorities.

The above are few animal sports which have been frequently in limelight. There are many other animal sports still practiced in India without any check.

Competing justifications for animal sports

The supporters of these animal sports justify the continuation of such sports for the reason that religious sentiments are attached to them. Traditions, customs, rituals are inherent in each religion, therefore they help in the formation of a unique religious identity with which various people associate. Thus, ban on such sports would be against the tradition. Whereas, the Environmentalists detest the practice of using animal as a part of a sport. Traditions, customs, etc. cannot be the rationale behind the ill-treatment of other living creature. They equally have a right to sustain in a friendly environment, which becomes impossible when such cruelty inducing sports exist.

JALLIKATTU AMENDMENT (2017) *QUA*

Animal Welfare Board of India Case (2014)[37]

A petition was filed by the Animal Welfare Board of India in the Supreme Court of India to ban the cruel sport of Jallikattu. The Supreme Court, however, permitted the Government of Tamil Nadu to continue the practice of Jallikattu for five months under the supervision of District Collectors. While the above case was pending, Ministry of Environment and Forests (MOEF) issued a notification wherein bull was prohibited from being used as Performing animals, thus banning the practice. Despite the above notice, this practice continued under the Tamil Nadu Regulation of Jallikattu Act, 2009.

In May, 2014, Supreme Court by virtue of Section 3, 11(1)(a), 11(1)(m)(ii) of Prevention of Cruelty to Animals Act, 1960 abolished the state law and banned Jallikattu from being practiced because of the cruelty inherent in it. It declared that the rights guaranteed to the Bulls under Section 3 and 11 of Prevention of Cruelty to Animals Act, 1960 read with Articles 51A(g) and (h) cannot be curtailed, except under Sections 11(3) and 28 of Prevention of Cruelty to Animals Act, 1960.

In January, 2016, Ministry of Environment and Forests, again issued a notification which allowed the practice to be continued. However, on the petition of the Animal Welfare Board and People for the Ethical Treatment of Animals, the Supreme Court in January, 2016, issued a stay on the above notification and upheld the ban on Jallikattu. There were several protests held against the ban across the State of Tamil Nadu. The primary demands of such protests were to remove the bulls from the list of performing animals in the Prevention of Cruelty to Animal Act, 1960, safeguard the practice through an Act and to ban People for the Ethical Treatment of Animals.

Due to these protests, the Governor of Tamil Nadu on 21st January, 2017, passed an ordinance under Article 213 (1) of the Constitution of India, which allowed the continuation of Jallikattu. This ordinance was further transformed into the Prevention of Cruelty to Animals (Tamil Nadu Amendment) Act, 2017 in January, 2017, thereby amending the provisions of the Prevention of Cruelty to Animals Act, 1960 for the state of Tamil Nadu.

In response to the judgment of the Supreme Court in *Animal Welfare Board of India v. A. Nagaraja and Ors*, Tamil Nadu Government, amended the Prevention of Cruelty to Animals Act,

1960 (herein referred as Principal Act). Section 2 of the Prevention of Cruelty to Animals (Tamil Nadu Amendment) Act, 2017 added clause (dd) to Section 2 of the Principal Act, which defined Jallikattu as "an event involving bulls conducted with a view to follow tradition and culture on such days from the months of January to May of a calendar year and in such places, as may be notified by the State Government, and includes "manjuviratu", "vadamadu" and "erudhuvidumvizha". It has been asserted by the above Act that Jallikattu is a practice, followed to promote the tradition and culture, and to ensure the preservation of native bulls.[38]

Section 4 of the above Amendment Act, added clause (f) to sub-section (3) of section 11 of the Principal Act, which made Jallikattu an exception under the above section, thereby, diluting the effects of Supreme Court judgment. It further added Section 28 A to the Principal Act which decriminalized the event of Jallikattu, altogether. [39]

On the passage of the Prevention of Cruelty to Animals (Tamil Nadu Amendment) Act, 2017, a relief was seen amongst the people of Tamil Nadu, who were against the ban of the sport. The Supreme Court of India has reserved its judgment on the Prevention of Cruelty to Animals (Tamil Nadu Amendment) Act, 2017, as of now.

The rationale behind the Amendment was that Jallikattu helps in the preservation of the native breeds of the bulls and without such practice it would be difficult for farmers in Tamil Nadu to raise the native livestock.[40] The sport is a mark of pride for all the people who practice it, it is inseparable. Such primitive method of preserving the native breeds of bull should not be adopted anymore. Recourse must be taken to practices which are less harmful to the animal.

CONCLUSION

There is no doubt that the humans are increasingly becoming literate with each passing day. However, the question that we must ponder upon is that are we really becoming educated in true sense? Is our education according to ourselves the utmost importance and thereby making us insensitive *qua* all other species of the eco-system particularly in case of conflict between the human interests and interests of other species. Also, another important aspect worth considering is that are we still becoming silent in the matters of animal cruelty when the practices are backed by religion, culture or tradition. If yes, then our value system needs a serious re-evaluation. Our forefathers were probably less literate than us, but were far more educated in respecting the Mother Nature and its various species. We must develop the eco-centrism in us and should not have any fallacious belief that we are most superior and significant species and thus have the illimitable liberty of altering it for our needs and greeds.

The eco-centrism teaches us to distribute equal interest to all the living beings and nature. Thus, we must bring change in our conscience and the value system and should be wise enough to differentiate between the cruel and harmless practices of animal sports like Jallikattu and carry on only those practices which are harmless to other species, as much as possible. Only then, we will truly deserve to be called the most intelligent species on the planet.

NOTES

1. Anthropocentrism vs. Biocentrism, available at: https// www.coursehero.com/file/16303345/Anthropocentrism-vs-Biocentrism-2doc/ (Last visited on March 20, 2017).
2. Brennan, Andrew and Lo, Yeuk-Sze, "Environmental Ethics", *The Stanford Encyclopedia of Philosophy* (Winter 2016 Edition), Edward N. Zalta (ed.), URL = https://plato.stanford.edu/archives/win2016/entries/ethics-environmental/ (Last visited on March 20, 2017).
3. Aristotle. Politics, translated by E. Barker, OUP, Oxford, 1948.
4. Immanuel Kant, *Lectures on Ethics*, translated by P. Heath, (eds.) P. Heath and J.B. Schneewind, Cambridge University Press, Cambridge, 1997.
5. Supra note 2
6. It comes from the word 'Cornucopia' which according to Greek Mythology means 'horn of plenty' which is a symbol of abundance.
7. The former outlook believes that the Earth's resources are inexhaustible and earth has the capacity to hold the unchecked growth of human

population. While the latter holds the view that humans have an ethical obligation towards the nature but only in relation with other humans, Sara E. Boslaugh, Anthropocentrism Philosophy, Encyclopedia Britanica.URL= https://www.britannica.com/topic/anthropocentrism (Last visited on March 20, 2017).

8. Aldo Leopold, A Sand County Almanac, OUP, Oxford, 1949.
9. Supra note 2.
10. Environmental Value System: What are Eco-centrism, Anthropocentrism and Techno centrism Worldviews?, available at: http://misakienvsystems.blogspot.in/2013/01/environmental-philosophies-what-are.html
11. The theory of deep ecology maintains that humans are only part of a larger ecosphere, and we should seek to understand how the environmental system operates as a whole. The other theory, that is, Gaia Hypothesis, propagates the view that Earth, a single ecosystem, has a feedback mechanism through which it maintains its state of equilibrium without adversely affecting the life on it. Supra note 1.
12. *Animal Welfare Board of India v. A. Nagaraja* & Ors (2014)7 SCC 547
13. It is a proposal of inter-governmental agreement to recognize the rights of animals.
14. Declaration of Animal Rights is a public campaign of international animal rights and planet conservation group Our Planet. This Declaration is open for public to sign for.
15. *Inserted* by the Constitution (42nd Amendment) Act, 1976.
16. Ibid.
17. Entry 17, List III.
18. Entry 17A, List III.
19. Entry 17B, List III.
20. Entry 20A, List III.
21. The Prevention of Cruelty to animals Act, 1960, available at: https://awbi.org/awbi-pdf/Act%20&%20Rules%20-%20English.pdf
22. Rule 2 (b), "Farrier" means a person who carrier on the business of shoeing cattle.
23. Rule 2 (a), "Cattle" means buffaloes, bullocks, horses, mules, or donkeys and includes other animals used for draught, pack or carriage purpose, which require shoeing.
24. Rule 2 (c), The Performing Animals Rules, 1973, "Performing animal"

means any animal which is used at, or for the purpose of any entertainment to which the public are admitted through sale of tickets.

25. India legislation & animal welfare oversight, available at: http://alttox.org/mapp/regulatory-policy/india-programs-policies/india-legislation-animal-welfare-oversight/ (Last modified January 25, 2016).

26. Regulation 3.

27. Regulation 2.

28. "148-C. prohibition of testing of cosmetics on animals. –No person shall use any animal for testing of cosmetics."

29. "135-B. Prohibition of import of cosmetics tested on animals. - No cosmetic that has been tested on animals after the commencement of the Drugs and Cosmetics (Fifth Amendment) Rules, 2014 shall be imported into the country.

30. See Also, Maneka Gandhi vs. Union of India, 1978 SCR (2) 621; Francis Coralie vs. Union Territory of Delhi, 1981 AIR 746, 1981 SCR (2) 516; Bandhua Mukti Morcha vs. Union of India, 1984 AIR 802, 1984 SCR (2) 67; Peoples Union for Democratic Rights vs. Union of India, 1982 AIR 1473, 1983 SCR (1) 456; Chandra Raja Kumar vs. Police Commissioner Hyderabad, AIR 1998 AP 302; State of Maharashtra vs. Chandrabhan, 983 AIR 803, 1983 SCR (3) 327.

31. 1989 SCR Supl. (2) 597; Rural Litigation Entitlement Kendra Dehradun vs. State of U.P. AIR 1985 SC 652; Damodar Rao vs. Municipal Corporation AIR 1987 SC 171; M. C. Mehta vs. Union of India (Ganga Pollution Case) AIR 1988 SC 111; M. C. Mehta vs. Union of India (Oleum gas Leak Case) AIR 1987 SC 965.

32. *T.N. Godavarman* Thirumulpad vs. Union of India and Ors. (2012) 4 SCC 362; Centre for Environmental Law World Wide Fund-India vs. Union of India and Ors. (2013) 8 SCC 234.

33. (2000) 2 KLT 625.

34. (2005) 8 SCC 534.

35. *Anim*al Welfare Board of India vs. A.Nagaraja and Ors. (2014)7 SCC 547.

36. TasneemKutubuddin, Know About The 7 Disputed Animal Sports In India Which Are Similar To Jallikattu, available at: https://thelogicalindian.com/story-feed/sports/animal-sports-india/37(2014)7 SCC 547.

38. Prevention of Cruelty to Animals (Tamil Nadu Amendment) Act, 2017, Sections 4, 6,7.

39. Section 28-A. Saving in respect of 'Jallikattu'.– Nothing contained in

this Act shall apply to 'Jallikattu' conducted to follow and promote tradition and culture and such conduct of 'Jallikattu ' shall not be an offence under this Act."

40. Himakiran Anugula, "Banning Jallikattu Will Undermine Tamil Nadu's Indigenous Cattle Breeds", available at: https://thewire.in/19157/banning-jallikattu-will-decimate-indias-indigenous-cattle-breeds/ (Last Modified January 10, 2017).

4 Economic Growth of India and Environmental Degradation: An Empirical Study

Divya Gupta*

INTRODUCTION

While economic growth has produced many benefits – raising standards of living and improving quality of life across the world – it has also resulted in the depletion of natural resources and the degradation of ecosystems. There has been much debate over whether or not it is possible to achieve economic growth without unsustainably degrading the environment, and a growing realisation that economic growth at the current rate of depletion and degradation of environmental assets cannot continue indefinitely. For example, the increase in CO2 levels in the atmosphere as a result of human activity means that the world is already locked into some climate change, and faces a major challenge to keep global temperature rises to below two degrees.

In the context of environmental resources more generally, the Millennium Ecosystem Assessment (2003) found that 15 out of the 24 ecosystems services it examined were being degraded or used unsustainably, and the use and consumption of natural resources such as minerals and metals continues at an increasing

---

*Assistant Professor, Economics Department, Daulat Ram College, University of Delhi, Delhi

pace. Some take the view that the finite resources of the Earth place limits on the extent to which economies can keep expanding in the long-term. Others believe that using environmental resources sustainably is consistent with continued economic growth, with the costs of inaction likely to be far greater than the cost of acting now.

The question of sustaining the economic growth without despoiling environment, resource constraint, steady state of income and environmental quality is an issue for both social and natural science scholars. The growth in economy requires more capital and other resources which in turn generates larger quantity of wastage including emission to the environment. The accumulation of wastage and pollutant due to the extraction of resources could lead to degradation of environment, loss of human welfare, with rising in economic growth. When the accumulation of wastage and pollution due to continuous extractions of resources can run beyond the carrying capacity of the environment the whole economic activity will fall at risk.

The causal relationship between economic development and different indicators of environmental quality has been extensively explored in the recent years by the Environmental Kuznets Curve (EKC) models globally, regionally or country wise by several authors. In 1991, the EKC hypothesis was first introduced by Grossman and Krueger for different environmental indicators, including the carbon dioxide emissions as well. The EKC hypothesis stated an inverted U-shape relation between various indicators of environmental quality and per capita income.

ENVIRONMENTAL KUZNETS CURVE (EKC)

EKC is an inverted-U-shaped relationship between economic growth (per capita income) and measured pollution indicators (indicators of environmental quality). In fact EKC hypothesis summarizes a dynamic process of change; as income of an economy grows over time, emission level grows first, reaches a peak and then starts declining after a threshold level of income has been achieved. The EKC hypothesis actually summarizes an essentially dynamic process of change; as income of an economy grows over time, emission level grows first, reaches a peak and then starts declining after a threshold level of income has been crossed.

The relationship between economic growth and CO2 emissions reveals that, initially economic growth is linked with high CO2 emissions tends to decrease as an economy attain turning point on threshold level of economic growth. Environmental Kuznets Curve (EKC) model represents the structural change of economy with economic growth as economic growth is linked to continuous structural transformation and change. Structural changes reflects the changes in the shares of agriculture, industry and services have broadly followed by the same time pattern with the changes in growth rate but the content of change have varied from period to period. By changing the composition of economic activity to the sectors it affects environmental quality with higher or lower pollution intensity. The first and most common explanation of an inverted-U Kuznets relationship is the stages of economic growth economies go through as they make a transition from agriculture to industry and then post industrial service-based systems. As pointed out by Panayotou (1993, p. 14), environmental degradation tends to increase as the structure of the economy changes from rural to urban and from agricultural to industrial as mass production and consumption grow. It then starts falling with the second structural change from energy-intensive heavy industry to services and technology-intensive industry due to the lower environmental impact of service industries.

At lower levels of income, the dominant shift is from agriculture to industry and pollution intensity increases as waste and pollution generates as mass production and consumption grow in the economy due to greater use of natural resources, more emission of pollutants, emphasize to increase in material output. At higher incomes, economic development progresses, the dominant shift is for industry to post-industrial or service economy as the share of industry will go down as services goes up because of increased environmental awareness, higher environmental expenditures, efficient technologies and increased demand for environmental quality.

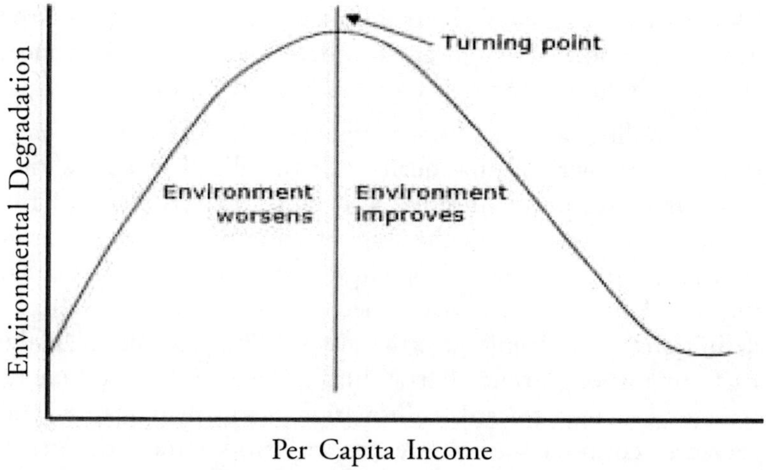

Figure 1: Environmental Kuznet's curve (EKC)

Specifically:

- At low incomes, pollution abatement is undesirable as individuals are better off using their limited income to meet their basic consumption needs;
- Once a certain level of income is achieved, individuals begin considering the trade-off between environmental quality and consumption, and environmental damage increases at a lower rate; and
- After a certain point, spending on abatement dominates as individuals prefer improvements in environmental quality over further consumption, and environmental quality begins to improve alongside economic growth.

Since 1991 the issues of environmental Kuznets curve have become a standard feature in technical literature of environment and economic interaction. The view is that the initial economic activity inevitably hurts the environment. The assumptions are based on static technology, tastes and environmental investments.

It states that as incomes rise, the demand for improvements in environmental quality will increase, as well the resources available for investment. And concludes although economic growth usually leads to environmental degradation in the early stages of the process, the only – way to attain a decent environment in most countries is to become rich (Perman and Stern, 1999).

According to the traditional argument the issues of economic growth and environmental qualities are conflicting ideas. With a state of constant technology and constant structure of the economy, pure growth in the scale of the economy would result in a proportional growth in pollution and other environmental impacts. This traditional view reflects the scale effect alone in its definitions of economic growth sources. The proponents of the EKC hypothesis argue that at higher levels of development, structural change towards information intensive industries and services, coupled with increased environmental awareness, enforcement of environmental regulations, better technology and higher environmental expenditures, result in leveling off and gradual decline of environmental degradation (Panayotou, 1993, p 1).

A number of studies have developed theoretical models about how preferences and technology might interact to result in different time paths of environmental quality. The different studies make different simplifying assumptions about the economy. Most of these studies can generate an inverted U shape curve of pollution intensity. Selden and Song (1995) assume infinitely lived agents, exogenous technological change and that pollution is generated by production and not by consumption. McConnell (1997) develops models based on overlapping generations where pollution is generated by consumption rather than by production activities as Stokey (1998) allows endogenous technical change. So, the result depends on the assumptions made and the value of particular parameters.

The proximate variables may in turn be driven by changes in underlying variables such as environmental regulation, awareness, and education in the course of economic development.

Ming-Feng and Daigee (2006) for Taiwan finds the inverted U – shaped relationships between NO2 and CO2 with economic growth. As income increase NO2 and CO2 increases later on start to decline with increase in income. Philip and Adeyemi (2013) find absence of ECK hypothesis in Nigeria and failed to attain reasonable turning point. Abesha (2009) studied Domestic Energy Consumption and Deforestation in Hareri region Assessment of Students' Awareness and Views in Ethiopia. And the study finds the views about environmental problems resulted from unsustainable dependence of biomass energy and Air pollution, is a serious environmental problem in developed nation is considered by more than half of students.

(a) Changes in Economic Structure and Trends of carbon dioxide (CO_2) Emissions with GDP per capita of India and

(b) To observe the existence of EKC relationship between CO_2 emissions and economic growth (GDP per capita) of India.

RESEARCH METHODOLOGY & ANALYSIS

This paper uses World Bank data to see the trends and patterns of CO_2 emissions (metric tons per capita) according to GDP per capita (current US $) for the year of 2005 to the year of 2016 for India.

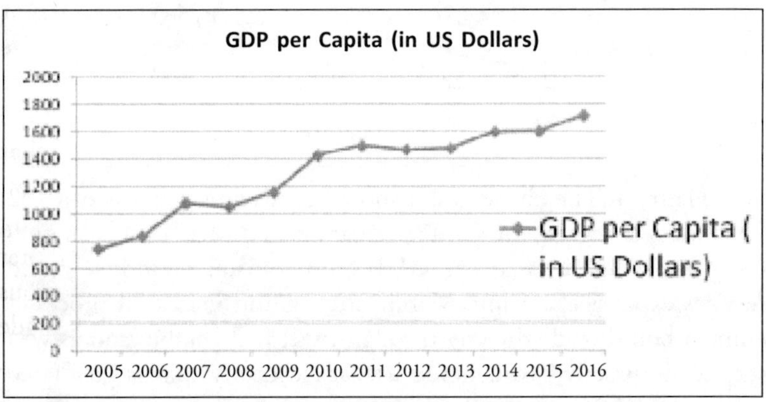

Figure 2 shows that GDP per capita is rising between 2005-16

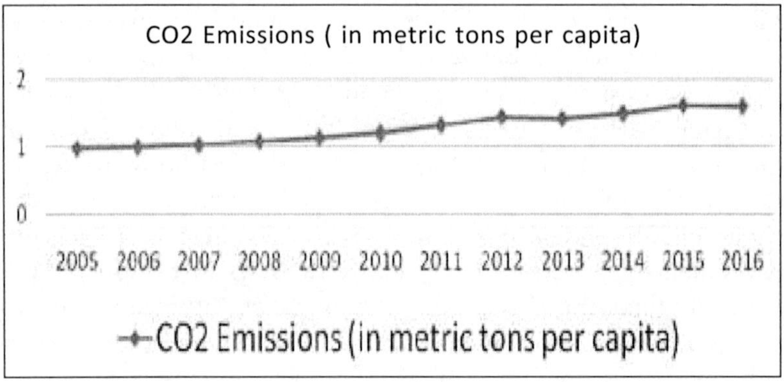

Figure 3: Shows that CO_2 emission has been consistently rising. Carbon dioxide emissions have grown dramatically in the past century because of human activities, mainly by the use of fossil fuels as well as changes in land use.

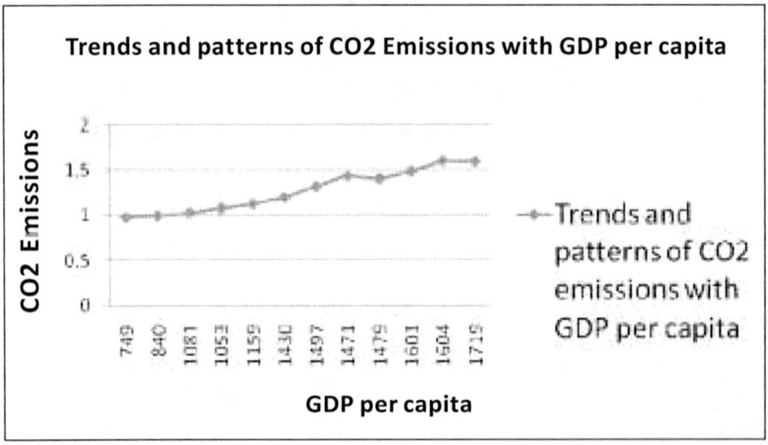

Figure 4: The above graph shows trends and patterns of CO2 emissions as regards of GDP per capita of India. It is seen that CO2 emissions increase as GDP contribution of industry and services expansively rising. Manufacturing and industrial processes emit carbon dioxide directly through fossil fuel combustion as well services indirectly through the use of electricity that is generated using fossil fuels all combine to produce large amounts of each type of greenhouse gas but specifically large amounts of CO2.

RESULTS

- Between 2005-2016, India witnessed increase in economic growth (measured by GDP per capita)
- Between 2005-2016, there is also a consistent increase in CO_2 emissions.
- As GDP increases, the carbon dioxide emissions rise
- We were unable to prove the existence of a reasonable turning point and thus no Environmental Kuznets curve (EKC) inverted "U" shape was obtained.

CONCLUSION

By examining GDP change over 2005-2016 of India it is clear that, the country is not capable to reduce CO2 emissions. For this reason we also unable to prove the existence of EKC shape (inverted-U shape) by estimating the period of 2005 to 2016. As CO2 is global pollutant not local pollutant and effects are not restricted by country boundaries so global cooperation are needed to reduce CO2 emissions. The study reveals us that environmental awareness, environmental policy, global cooperation, improved and polluting abatement technologies are needed in order to direct the environment–growth relationship toward a downward trend. Like India, developing countries should take better technical personnel and wider budgets for monitoring and enforcement activities to implement environmental policy.

REFERENCES

Baldwin, R., 1995. Does sustainability require growth? In: Goldin, I., Winters, L.A. (Eds.), The Economics of Sustainable Development. Cambridge Univ. Press, Cambridge, UK, pp. 19-47.

Dinda.S, 2004, Environmental Kuznets Curve Hypothesis: A Survey, Elsevier, Ecological Economics 49 (2004) 431– 455.

Huang.W, Lee.G, Wu.C, 2007, GHG emissions, GDP growth and the Kyoto Protocol: A revisit of Environmental Kuznets Curve hypothesis, Elsevier, Energy Policy 36 (2008) 239–247.

McConnell, K.E., 1997. Income and the demand for environmental quality. Environment and Development Economics 2, 383– 399.

Panayotou T. 1993. Empirical test and policy analysis of environmental degradation at different stages of economic development, WP 238. Technology and Employement Program. International labour office. Geneva.

Pezzey, J.C.V., 1989. Economic analysis of sustainable growth and sustainable development. Environment Department working paper 15. World Bank.

Selden, T., Song, D., 1994. Environmental quality and development: is there a Kuznets Curve for air pollution emissions? Journal of Environmental Economics and management 27, 147– 162.

5

Global Climate Change: Perspective from Power Shift in International Politics

Alok Kumar*

INTRODUCTION

Since emergence of the nation-state in 16th century, power politics has always remained important in *International Politics* which includes interactions, policies and behaviours of states. Their capacity reflects through their decisions, in other words, *what kinds of capacity they have which reflects through making process.* The *Super Powers* have capacity to take decisions to influence behaviour of world politics. Great Powers have capacity to make pressure on *Super Powers* to take few decisions to fulfil the objectives of them. However, the small powers are not have capacity to take independent decisions.[1]

European Countries colonised the world by their power politics. They colonised most of countries in the world but at the same time, the process of decolonization had also started by other states like US which got independence in 1776.[2] This was an example, people got inspirations from this, they make plans or strategies how can they free from colonial process. In the architecture of colonial process that was not easy, but due to

---

*School of International Studies, Central University of Gujarat , Gandhinagar, Gujarat, India

existing forces in the colonial states which had challenged the *European imperialism.*[3] As the result this challenge, few states got independence after World War-II that was signal for imperialist states which would not able to maintain their hegemony till long period but *any how they were trying to their maintain dominance or preserve their powers* by using different methods.[4] After World War-II, several countries got independence and tried to influence the behaviour of world politics by their presence.[5] Now newly independence states were raising their voices at the global level. By end of World War-II, two countries US and USSR had emerged major player in global politics and they were trying to spread their ideologies (capitalism and communism), which had became cause of the conflict between them.[6] Since 1945 to 1990, massive industrialization occurred in not only European Countries but also Non-European countries which had reflected their internal growth and capacity. All countries were focusing on the rapid industrialization which resulted global warming and environment decline. That time, this issue continued neglected by the most responsible countries like US and England. But today, this issue is highly concerned by the developing and least developing countries because they are highly affected of global climate change and they are raising their voices their voices and taking stands to criticise developed world.

AFRICAN COUNTRIES

The African continent is second most popular continent of the world. It is the land where the first human lived that mean that the generation of human existence started from this continent. It contains more than fifty countries and second largest population of the world. According to 2016, Nigeria is having largest population while Saint Helena, Ascension and Tristan da Cunha (UK) is having very less problem. The people are black who are native and white are outsiders. These countries are colonised by the European countries to exploit their natural resources.[7] Michel Doyal defines colonialism when one state controlled to others by economic, military, cultural, social and political sphere. Basically this is the act of accumulation and acquisition, stated by Edward W. Said.[8] These countries are having rich natural resources like gas, gold, iron, diamond, petroleum, silver, bauxite, copper, uranium and cobalt. During 17th to mid-19th century, these countries are exploited by the European countries. To fulfill trade interests, European powers had divided Africa into 40 new states by 1913.[9] But due to movements in different countries, these countries had started to demand their independence. By 1950, four African countries, South Africa, Egypt, Ethiopia and Liberia got independence. Nigeria is the most popular states where more than 250 different languages and religious divide the Muslim North and Christianity South. Botswana produces 35% of Arica's diamonds and other natural resources like nickel, soda ash, copper and gold. The diamond is the main industry for its economy.[10] The Republic of Congo produces 34% diamond and 13% copper of Africa.[11] South Africa is the world's largest producer of platinum, manganese, chrome, vermiculite and second largest producer rutile, palladium, manganese and zirconium.[12] Tanzania is the highest gold producer country in Africa. And it also produces iron ore, nickel, diamond, silver, copper and cobalt.[13] Namibia produces the largest uranium and it contributed highest level in its economy.[14] Zambia supplies 65 to 77 percent copper to the industries.[15] Because of the exploitation of the huge amount of natural resources, several African countries are facing serious security challenges. For example, Guinea Bissau is facing serious challenges like water security, decreased agricultural yields and soil degradation. Therefore, it needed technical support from the developed countries. Sierra Leone is threatened by climate change floods, storms, droughts, heatwaves, landslides and rain fall patterns. Here, the highly rainfall, the issue of food and water security, and burn land conversion for cattle grazing. The people from South Sudan do not know when rain comes. The most of population depend on the agriculture but due to draughts, this sector is going to damage. Nigeria is facing changing rainfall patterns, temperature shifts, storms sea-level and the space of desert is growing continue.[16] Therefore, the critical question in front of the common people of African countries that, they want to oppose foreign companies from their countries but they are not have other alternatives to exploit their natural resources. The larger part of their economy depends on the natural resources but they are thinking that the impacts of the exploitation of natural resources can dangerous their future generations. Therefore, the students, intellectuals and scientists are opposing the policies of the western countries specially the discriminatory role of United States. In July 2015, a conference held in Paris, there were very les participants from the African Countries. The few people were protesting in the conference hall and demanding to sing on UN Framework Convention on Climate Change. Those states are not ready to implement the policies of global climate, actually they are giving "death sentence" African Nations, they said. Environmental Scientists argued that Africa would face serious challenges of global warming.[17] The most affected countries of global warming were trying to make pressure on US and China to reduce the production of emission gases. Therefore, by 2014 the US President Barak Obama and Chinese President Xi Jinping announced that they would restrict the coal industries at the larger level because which are producing larger amount of CO2 emission that for dangerous for our next generations.[18]

ASIA COUNTRIES

The People of Asia celebrates their diversity on basis of religion, region, languages, culture and ethnicity. This region is having highest population of the world. China, India, Russia, Iran, Saudia Arbia, Japan are major countries which are playing the crucial role in global politics. These are giving challenge to the hegemonic nature of global politics specially the western domination. Middle-East Region is the hub of natural resources where local and multinational companies are exploiting the natural resources for their benefits which are not considering the issue of climate change. In South Asia Region is popularly known for diverse culture. Here, the local and multinational companies are exploiting the natural resources to get their maximum benefits as well as fulfil the demands of people. According to the report, India 1.3%, Russia 11.23%., Japan 8.64%, South Korea 10.89%, Iran 6.94%, Saudi Arabia 18.56% , Thailand 3.80%, Kazakhstan 12.02%, United Arab Emirates 40.31%, Singapore 34.59%, Malaysia 5.32%, Pakistan 0.77%, Hong Kong 12.19%, Kuwait 31.52%, Qatar 79.82% Sri Lanka 0.60%, Burma 0.24%, Maldives 2.31% and Bhutan 0.48% are producing carbon dioxide emissions per capita.[19] The those countries are producing less amount of carbon dioxide emissions which are affecting more as compare to which are producing more carbon dioxide emissions. For example, in October 2009, the Government of Maldives had organised a meeting in the sea which tried to give a message to the global community that if the world community would not able to consider the issue of global warming that would dangerous for next generations. The world will face serious security challenges, they added.[20] Since 1994 to 2014, Pakistan, Myanmar, Bangladesh, Philippines and Vietnam are most affected countries in Asia. For example, Myanmar have lost $ 1256 million dollar and 7137people lost their lives in 41 natural disasters. Philippines lost $ 2786.28 million dollar and 933 people lost their lives in 328 events. Bangladesh lost $ 3128.80 million dollar and 228 people lost their lives in 228 events. Pakistan lost $ 3988 million dollars and 456 people lost their lives by 141 events. Vietnam lost $ 2918 million dollars and 391 people lost their lives by 216 events.[21] Developed countries argued that the policies of global climate implement equally. However, the major economies of Asia India, China, Japan, South Korea, Russia, India and Saudi Arabia stated that now they are not in binding climate change policies because it can be affect their economies. They added that first developed countries would reduce the production of greenhouse gases. Now they are able to raise to question on western countries which was not possible Mid-20th century.

NORTH AMERICA COUNTRIES

This continent posses 23 independent nations and estimated 7.5% world population. Each country is having diversity but the colour of people is white and the temperature is between 20 to

50 °C. The most of people speak English, Spanish and French languages. The US, Canada, Mexico are major leading economy in global sphere. All countries are facing the serious challenges of global climate change like increase in inundations, sea level rise, storm surge flooding, increase the risk of death to due heat waves, degraded water quality increase in inundations and vector-borne infectious diseases. In 2013, the US President Barak Obama said that we need to think seriously how we can deal the issue of climate change. And he stated that the US Congress should research market based solution to climate change. National Oceanic and Atmospheric Administration stated that the year 2013 has proved highest heat year since 1950s. And Shipping in Mississippi River was closed due to lack of water. Few villages in Alaska like Kivalina forced to shift from one place to others due to rise sea waters. The rising of sea level in Washington is the serious issue therefore Quileute and Hoh tribes are losing reserve land. For this particular issue, legislation passed by Cantwell and Patty Murray for providing the facility to the tribes. NOAA reported that eight inches sea level rise over last century in San Francisco. And billion dollars of US property lose very year in floods. And in 2012, around 1,000 tornadoes were confirmed by the US. In the same, 118 people die and 3,000 infected by Nile Virus and the Texas and Oklahoma burnt and heat due to global warming.[22] North American countries produces carbon like US 17.67%, Mexico 3.99%, Brazil 2.11%, Cuba 2.65%, Jamaica 4.29%; Kenya 0.29%, Guatemala 0.85%, Panama 4.60%, Honduras 1.1%, Dominica 1.93%, Saint Lucia 2.57% and Barbados 4.87%.[23] The million dollars lost by the different countries. For example, since 1993 to 2013, Honduras lost $813.56 trillion, Guatemala $477.79 trillion and Mexico $3622.85 trillion.[24] And the US lost $ 881.2 billion dollars since 1980-2011 in several natural disasters like droughts, Heatwaves, severe Local Storms, Non-Tropical Floods, Winter Storms, Wildfires and Freezes.[25] The National Academy of Sciences released a report in 2010 which stated that the US should reduce emissions of heat-trapping gases by 2030 and should generate alternatives

energy resources. NSA recommended that the US should promote renewal energy, reduces coal emissions, uphold greening transportation and also should help developing countries by giving affordable technologies.[26]

SOUTH AFRICA

This continent possesses more than ten countries, and the people are enjoying the diversity of culture. They believe in the different culture and faith. The major countries of this continent are Brazil, Argentina, Colombia, Peru, Uruguay and Venezuela. The most production of this continent based on ecosystem. The impact of climate change has also seen in the major sectors like forests, wetlands, water resources, agriculture, costal zones and human health by surface of high temperature. The drought, floods and freezes has become common things in the Southern Part of the continent that is the result of Atmospheric circulation which is also affects the extensive deserts in Northern Mexico, Bolivia, Chile, Peru and Argentina. The socio-economic factors also influenced due to climate change in Brazil and Peru which have reduced the disruption in Agricultural. The rainfall and intensity also seen in Chile and Western Argentina, there is problem of limited fresh water. This continent has largest number of generic resources in the world while it produces fewer amounts of greenhouse gases, which is approximately 4% only. However, the impact of global climate is larger level on agriculture based productions. On contrary some studies suggested that countries should use advance technology to reduce the production of greenhouses gases. This region has capacity to balance ecosystem by having approximately 27% global forest coverage.[27] This region has strong capacity to reduce greenhouses gases. The fourth countries of this region, namely, Brazil, Argentina, Mexico and Venezuela produce highest level of co2 emitters. So that rage of climate changes can be seen like problem of drinking water, floods, Andes Mountains and crop yield.[28] The most of countries of this region is facing the problem of the heat, extreme droughts, melting glacier that is cause of floods and extensive droughts.

Along with these issues, migration is a serious problem which has observed by the experts. Those people have low social and economic status; they are migrated to the megacities. They are creating the demographic problem in the cities. According to the report in 2010, 83% population is living in the cities that will be 86% by 2020. In Argentina, 70% migrants thought to reside in the megacities cities, in Chile 65% reside in the Metropolitan area of Santiago. Therefore, people are living in these cities are facing the problem of drinking water, scarcity of natural resources, pollution and health. The level of sea is rising so that population which is living the megacities are affecting. The availability of water is continuing decreasing in the Bolivia so that rural people is migrating from their places to the cities. In Quito, five people died and 130 families forced to move other places.[29]

EUROPEAN COUNTRIES

This continent contains more than 50 countries and people speak more than 200 languages. Basically, the people believe in multicultural society and enjoy the virtue of cultural values. According to the modern knowledge system, the democratic values had started from this continent. Thousands inventions had taken place here; they are highly technological advance today. They believe in individual rights and dignity. Because of highly technocratic society and rapid industrialization today, they are facing serious challenges from the global climate change. Jacqueline McGlade EEA Executive Director stated that climate change is a reality around the world, and extend and speed of change is becoming more evident.[30] A report studied the issue of climate change in the European countries during 2002-11. This report has observed certain issues. Like, 1.3c temperature increased, ten thousand people have lost their lives due to heat waves, increasing river floods in Northern Europe, flow of draughts noticed in Southern Europe, recorded low level sea ice and melting Greenland ice sheet and increasing sea level. The seal level is increasing 1.7mm in 20th century and 3.mm in current decade. The several new diseases are increasing in the continent. And the many studied have found several changes in the pants and animal characteristics. The less availability of water in the Southern Europe is creating problems for agriculture production. The costal zones and regional seas are facing certain problems like rising sea level, increase sea surface temperatures, increase the ocean acidity, northward expansion of fish and plankton species, changes in phytoplankton communities and increasing risk for fish stock. In Northwest Europe is increasing river flow, decreasing energy demand for heating and increasing the risk of river and coastal flooding. In Mediterranean Region, the rise of temperature, increasing the risk of biodiversity loss, decreasing the crop yields, increasing risk for forest fire, decrease the capacity of hydropower potential and increase risk of desertification. In Northern Europe, the temperature is rising much larger than global average, decrease the snow, lake and river ice cover, decreasing energy demand for heating and increasing damage risk in winter storms. In Central and Eastern Europe is increasing the water temperature, increasing risk for fire and decreasing economic values of forests.[31]

ANTARCTICA

This region is covered by the Iceland. In over period of time, the heat waves are increased so that ice melting very fast. In every decade, the average of temperature is increasing so that more than 70 meter increase around the world. Sea water is going to fresh water that is disturbing biological diversity and physical environment.

POWER SHIFT AND VOICES OF EMERGING ECONOMIES

In contemporary world politics, India, Russia, Brazil China and South Africa are emerging new economies at the global level which are giving challenge to existing hegemonic world order. With help of others, these countries wanted to make a new global order to fulfill their interests. BRICS is one of the examples where the members are trying to build up a new world order to govern the world politics. They tried to show "the leadership of third world countries".[32] India argued that first developed countries should reduce the emission of greenhouses gases because India has produced only 6% annul global emission while the US is 27%. In 2015, Indian Prime Minister, Narendra Modi strongly stated that those states are living with luxury of choices should sharply reduce emissions. He wanted that states should implement comprehensive equitable and durable agreement. Over the years, Developed countries have been major polluters and they should assume to play greater role in fighting global warming by giving affordable technologies to the developing countries.[33] India never stated such kinds of statement in the past. This shows that now India has capacity to comment on developed world which was not possible before 1990s. That time, India was not able take clear stand and the give such kinds of statements. China blamed that western countries are responsible for climate change. First they should work on it rather than expect from new emerging economies by stating that developed countries should bear an unshirkable responsibility. Therefore it was not ready to sign on Paris agreement but later on the US and China both decided to sign on Paris Agreement.[34-35] This shows that China does not believe in "words" while believe in "practices". Today, China is second powerful country in the world therefore it has capacity to criticise them who are wrong. Developing countries stated that western countries are more polluter countries, and interesting thing is that they are more discussing on global climate change but they do not want to reduce to emission of greenhouse gases.[36] Since debate was started on global climate change, the US was not ready to reduce the emissions of greenhouse gases due to threat of its economic growth but now the US has geared up to reduce the emission of greenhouse gases that is positive symbol for world community. In 2015, President Vladmir V. Putin of Russia stated that climate change has become one of the gravest challenges for humanity therefore Russia has decided to reduce 70% greenhouse gases by 2030.[37] Brazil is also major producer of greenhouse gases but due to threat of economic growth it is not ready to binding in environment laws similarly other countries but it promised that it would work to reduce the greenhouse gases by using different methods.[38] Therefore, it has rectified Paris Agreement in September, 2016 to reduce 1.3 billion tonnes carbon dioxide emissions by 2025.[39] However, Japan has serious concern on the global climate change therefore it is doing so many things to reduce the emission of the greenhouses gases by introducing the renewal energy, solar plants and increase wind and geothermal resources. It promised to reduce the 26% greenhouse gases emissions by 2030. In 2010, Cancun Climate Conference in Mexico, it agreed to give $ 100 billion aid to developing countries in tackling the climate change by 2020. It has also given $ 1.5 billion aid to the Green Climate Fund to assisting least developing and developing countries, Small Island and countries in Africa. In 2014, Innovation for Cool Earth forum started by Abe to provide the platforms for academicians, industrialists and environmental scientists for discussing the problem of climate change issue. The objective of this forum is how the innovations or new technologies can deal the problem of environmental change. provide low-carbon technologies for developing countries, Japan will promote the Joint Crediting Mechanism with help of other countries.[40] New emerging countries are taking decisions against those developed countries which are not taking seriously global climate issue. They are putting their voices against developed world that are responsible more global warming as compare to the developing and the least developing countries that was 20 years back in world politics.

CONCLUSION

Power is capacity to influence the behaviour of others by using different methods. It has to be found that not only developing countries are facing the serious challenges of the climate change but also developed world. That mean, entire world is facing of the challenges of global climate change. So that it is responsibility of the world community to deal this issue seriously otherwise it will face the serious impacts. On contrary, the facts that we cannot denied that almost all developed countries exploited the natural resources across the world by using different methods. Since 17th century to mid 20th century, European countries exploited the natural resources in colonises. Even today, most of multinational companies from the western world are exploiting the natural resources. Along with this, other companies from the major countries like Russia, Japan, India, South Africa and China are exploiting the natural resources that we to be recognised. The issue of climate change not only raising by the developed countries but also it is concerning by the developing and least developing countries but there is a contractions between "words" and "works". The developed world arguing to resolve the issue of global climate change by only "words" they do not want the cut down their emission of greenhouse gases due to their economic threat. The most affected countries of global climate change like Japan, India, and Maldives are demanding to "work" on it. They believe that without full support of developed world, the issue of global climate change will not resolve. If the world community will not take it seriously, we will face the serious impacts of global climate change. So we need to think on it seriously. Developing and least developing countries believe that first developed countries should reduce the emission of greenhouses gases then other countries which are emerging will reduce the emission of greenhouses. Now, new emerging economies are giving direct challenge to the developed countries. Developing countries argued that developed countries are more polluters as compare to developing countries so that first they should start and preserve the world by giving financial aid and affordable technologies to whom not have. The voices from new powers cannot ignore by the developed world today because all countries of world who knows, who is more responsible for global climate change as compare to others. The important question is not here who is more responsible or who is less responsible. The important thing is that all countries are responsible for global climate that we cannot ignore.

NOTES

1. Nossal, Kim Richard (1999), "Lonely Superpower on Unapologetic Hyperpower", *Presented Paper*, South African Political Studies Association, Western Cape.
2. Beard, Charles A., Beard, Maryr (2005), History of the United States, New York: The Macmillan Company.
3. Anderson, Dale (2005), The American Colonies Declare Independence, New York: World Almanac Library.
4. Fanon, Frantz (1952), Black Skin, White Masks, London: Pluto Press. (Translated by Charles Lam Markmann).
5. Waltz, Kenneth (2000), "Structural Realism after the Cold War", International Security, 25, 1, 5-41.
6. Leffler, Melvyn and Painter, David S. (1994), Origin of Cold War An International History, New York: Routledge.
7. BBC News, available at http://www.bbc.co.uk/worldservice/africa/features/storyofafrica/14chapter4.shtml accessed on 15 Sep. 2016.
8. Said, Edward W. (1994), Culture and Imperialism, New York: Knopf Press.
9. History of Africa, available at http://www.our-africa.org/history-war-and-politics accessed on 20 September 2016.
10. AFK Insider (2015), "10 Most Mineral-Rich Countries in Africa", available at http://afkinsider.com/67750/africas-mineral-rich-countries/2/ accessed on 20 September 2016.
11. AFK Insider (2015), "10 Most Mineral-Rich Countries in Africa", available http://afkinsider.com/67750/africas-mineral-rich-countries/3/ accessed on 20 September 2016.
12. AFK Insider (2015), "10 Most Mineral-Rich Countries in Africa", available http://afkinsider.com/67750/africas-mineral-rich-countries/4/ accessed on 20 September 2016.
13. AFK Insider (2015), "10 Most Mineral-Rich Countries in Africa", available http://afkinsider.com/67750/africas-mineral-rich-countries/6/ accessed on 20 September 2016.
14. AFK Insider (2015), "10 Most Mineral-Rich Countries in Africa", available http://afkinsider.com/67750/africas-mineral-rich-countries/6/ accessed on 20 September 2016.
15. AFK Insider (2015), "10 Most Mineral-Rich Countries in Africa", available http://afkinsider.com/67750/africas-mineral-rich-countries/5/ accessed on 20 September 2016.

16. Information available https://shift-magazine.net/2015/11/17/10-countries-most-affected-by-climate-change/ accessed on 20 September 2016.
17. Winsor, Morgan (2015), "Climate Change in Africa: African Global Warming Role Smart but Crucial To Crisis Solution Experts", available at http://www.ibtimes.com/climate-change-africa-african-global-warming-role-small-crucial-crisis-solution-2008048 accessed on 25 September 2016.
18. Burck, Jan, Marten, Franziska & Bals, Christoph (2015), The Climate Change Performance Index Results 2015, Belgium: German Watch.
19. "World Carbon dioxide emissions data by country: China speeds ahead of the rest", The Guardian News Paper, available at https://www.theguardian.com/news/datablog/2011/jan/31/world-carbon-dioxide-emissions-country-data-co2 accessed on 1 October 2016.
20. Foreign Services (2009), "Maldives Government Highlights the impacts of climate change", available at http://www.dailymail.co.uk/news/article-1221021/Maldives-underwater-cabinet-meeting-held-highlight-impact-climate-change.html#ixzz4O5Yk0HVT accessed on 02 October 2016.
21. Burck, Jan, Marten, Franziska & Bals, Christoph (2015), The Climate Change Performance Index Results 2015, Belgium: German Watch.
22. Indian Country (2013), "The 7 Most Alarming Effects of Climate Change on North America", available at http://indiancountrytodaymedianetwork.com/2013/02/22/seven-most-alarming-effects-climate-change-north-america-2013-edition-147835?page=0%2C1 accessed on 2 October 2016.
23. "World Carbon dioxide emissions data by country: China speeds ahead of the rest", The Guardian News Paper, available at https://www.theguardian.com/news/datablog/2011 /jan/31/world-carbon-dioxide-emissions-country-data-co2 accessed on 1 October 2016.
24. Burck, Jan, Marten, Franziska & Bals, Christoph (2015), The Climate Change Performance Index Results 2015, Belgium: German Watch.
25. Smith, Adam B. And Katz, Richard W. (2013), US Billion-Dollar Weather and Climate Disaster: Data Sources, Trends, Accuracy and Biases", available https://www.ncdc.noaa.gov/monitoring-content/billions/docs/smith-and-katz-2013.pdf accessed on 05 October 2016.
26. Union Concerned Scientists (2008), "Solutions to Global Warming in North America", available at http://www.climatehotmap.org/global-warming-solutions/north-america.html accessed on 05 October 2016.

27. Watson, R.T., Zinyowera, M.C., Moss, R.H. (1997), The Regional Impacts of Climate Change: An Assessment of Vulnerability, England: Cambridge University Press.
28. Union Concerned Scientists (2008), "Solutions to Global Warming in North America", available at http://www.climatehotmap.org/global-warming-solutions/north-america.html accessed on 05 October 2016.
29. Warn, Elizabeth & Adamo B., Susan (2014), The Impact of Climate Change: Migration and Cities in South America, Geneva: World Metrological Organization.
30. The European Environment Agency (2016) ,"Climate Change evident across Europe, confirming urgent and need for adoption", available at http://www.eea.europa.eu/media/newsreleases/climate-change-evident-across-europe accessed on 20 September 2016.
31. Information available at http://www.eea.europa.eu/soer-2015/europe/climate-change-impacts-and-adaptation/climate-change-impacts-in-europe/ accessed on 25 September 2016.
32. Sang-seek, Park (2012), "New world Order Emerging as US hegemony weakens, available at http://www.conectas.org/arquivos-site/New%20world%20order%20emerging%20as%20US%20hegemony%20weakens.pdf accessed on 20 September 2016.
33. Chauhan, Chetan (2015), "Climate Change is not of our Making: Modi at Paris Summit", New Delhi, 01 December 2015.
34. Dickie, Mure (2007), "China blames the west for global warming", Financial Times, New Delhi, 6 February, 2007.
35. The Guardian (2016), "Breakthrough as US and China agree to ratify Paris Climate Deal", New Delhi, 3 September 2016.
36. Tierney, Laura (2009), "Developing versus Developed", The Politics of Climate Change, available at https://www.mtholyoke.edu/ ~tiern20l/classweb/climatechange/development.html accessed on 25 September 2016.
37. Davenport, Coral (2015), "A Change in Tone for Vladimir Putin's Climate Change Pledges" The New York Times, New York, 1 December 2015.
38. Robinson, Kaleigh (2010), "Brazil Global Warming Agenda", Washington, World Resource Institute.
39. India Live Today (2016), "Brazil Ratifies Paris Agreement on Climate Change", Bangalore, 13 September, 2016.
40. Oike, Atsuyuki (2015), "Japan's action plan to fight climate change", *The Japan Times,* 30 July, Tokyo.

6 Deforestation-Forestation: Analyzing Symbiotic Relationship of the Ttribes in Conservation of Biodiversity and Ecological Restoration

Vikram Singh*

INTRODUCTION

> The thinning, changing, and elimination of forests – deforestation, no less – is not a recent phenomenon; it is as old as the human occupation of the earth, and one of the key processes in the history of our transformation of its surface. (Williams, 2002)

Deforestation is one of the most volatile environmental issues of the present time that attracted debates over its pros and cons from various scholars of multiple disciplines. Half of the worlds original forests has been destructed by 2011, majority being in the last 50 years (FAO, 2011). The problem of deforestation is more acute in the tropics i.e. in the developing and underdeveloped world. There are some reasons to relate deforestation to human society than the nature. Deforestation accelerated during in the nineteenth and early twentieth century's. During the most intense colonial exploitation of timber resources, from 1850 to 1920, as much as 33 million hectares of forest was

---

*Assistant Professor, Department of Social Work, Guru Ghasidas University (A Central University), Koni, Bilaspur; Chhattisgarh: India-495009 Mobile No: +91-8962231719 Email Id: vsvikkysingh@gmail.com

cleared in India (Williams, 2002); today 68 million hectares of forest remains. Destruction of biotic potential of land leads to desertification. Such problem arises due to overgrazing indiscriminate falling of trees and over exploitation of land resources the devastating effect of deforestation in India include soil, water and wind erosion estimated to cost over 16400 crore every year. Deforestation has a major impact on productivity of our crop land. Some other statistics:

- About half of the world's tropical forests have been cleared (FAO).
- Forests currently cover about 30 percent of the world's land mass (National Geographic).
- Forest loss contributes between 6 percent and 12 percent of annual global carbon dioxide emissions (Nature Geo-science).
- About 36 football fields worth of trees lost every minute (World Wildlife Fund (WWF).

Deforestation is not an abrupt or discrete process. Its vigor and extensiveness is achieved through a complex and dynamic socio-cultural interface played between the natural forest system and different tribal communities. The objectives and attitudes of the tribes to the forest resource utilization, conservation and ecological restoration are of particular importance. So, it is necessary to consider the emergence of deforestation process through the changing social perspective of tribe's central India.

Tribal population is around 8.6 per cent of India's total population (Census 2011). Most of the tribal's are concentrated in the central belt of the country comprising of Gujarat, Maharashtra, Rajasthan, Madhya Pradesh, Andhra Pradesh, Orissa, Bihar and West Bengal.

The symbiotic relationship of the tribal's with forests is a trite fact. Tribals derive both directly and indirectly a substantial amount of their livelihood from the forests. They are talented to build their houses with timber, bamboo and reeds and practices cottage crafts with the help of local raw materials, which they procure from their forest environment. They also obtain herbs and medicinal plants, which have therapeutic value, both curative and preventive. Their religion, folklore and world-view are also woven round the spirits and deities of the forests.

REVIEW OF LITERATURE

Nirmal Kumar Basu (1968): provided extensive details on the livelihood patterns, economic and cultural life of the Santhal tribe. Dilip Kumar Goswami (2004) gave a detailed history of the ancient dynasties. Basha (1992) in 'Impact of Forest Policies on Tribal Life,' explains the various Forests Acts and Policies of India.

The tribal once enjoyed absolute freedom in the forests and used the natural resources prudently. The forest policies and the appurtenant forest laws of the British Colonial period did not help to better their lot economically and socially. Tribal life in Central India is an excellent instance of the blending of rural & urbanity with conservation and ecological restoration of Forests.

Tribes of Madhya Pradesh classified under the group of scheduled tribes, with other sub-groups of tribes are also making their presence felt. Madhya Pradesh likes to concentrate wholly upon their festivities and celebrations. Tribes of Chhattisgarh primarily consist of a significant number that even surpasses the urban population (Encyclopedia of India, 2012).

The problem of deforestation is more acute in the tropics i.e. in the developing and underdeveloped world. There are some reasons to relate deforestation to human society than the nature. Firstly there is a debate over the actual definition of the term. While some intended to include any kind of forest clearing by cutting and/or burning as deforestation, some others are more interested in conversion of the forest lands into non-forest uses (Mayhew, 1997). Governed by an elitist bureaucracy it rules almost one third land of India by virtue of the power incurred to them through a series of draconian forest laws (Biswas, 2002).

INCEPTION OF THE PAPER

Although the Census of 2011 enumerates the total population of Scheduled Tribes at 10, 42, 81,034 persons, constituting 8.6 per cent of the population of the country, the

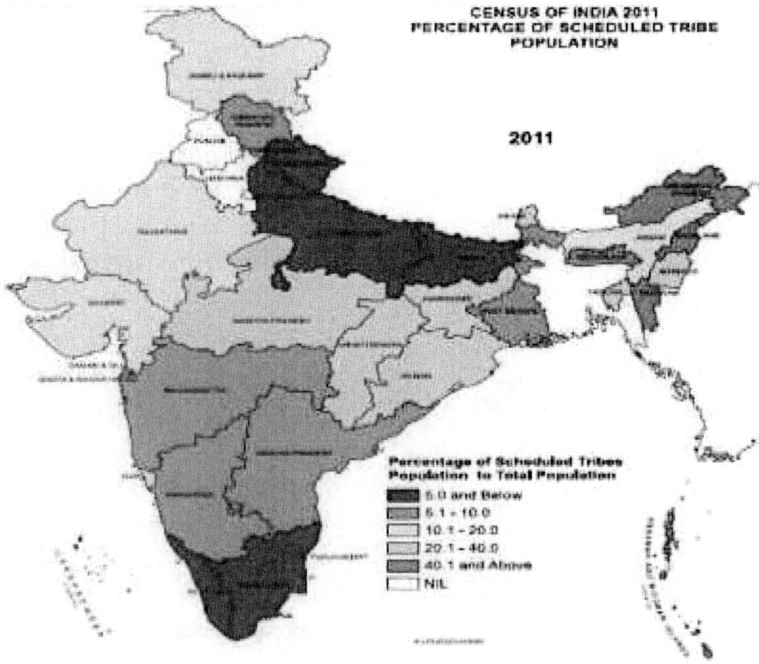

tribal communities in India are enormously diverse and heterogeneous. There are wide ranging diversities among them in respect of languages spoken, size of population and mode of livelihood. The number of communities that find their place in the list of the Schedule of the Indian constitution is reflective of this diversity. The Government of India, in its Draft National Tribal Policy, 2006 records 698 Scheduled Tribes in India. As per the Census of India 2011, the number of individual groups notified as Scheduled Tribes is 705. Central India Region constituted by the States of Bihar, Jharkhand, West Bengal, Orissa and Madhya Pradesh and Chhattisgarh, where more than 55 per cent tribal people of India live. A majority of tribal groups work in the primary sector, and are heavily dependent on agriculture either as cultivators or as agricultural labourers via Forest resources. At the same time, a number of Scheduled Tribes no longer follow their traditional occupations and work as labourers on plantations or in mines and factories (in many cases, since the nineteenth-century).

AREA PROFILE

Achanakmar biosphere reserve has very high concentration of tribal population. Some of the major tribal communities found in the region are Gonds and their sub tribes like Madia, Mudia, Gurva, Agariya and Rajgond. Other tribes are Baigas, Kol, Kanwar and Pradhans.

Total population of the area is 3, 38,738 (2011 Census), of which 54.11% and 6.90% are Schedule Tribes (ST) and Schedule Castes, respectively. Thus tribal population dominates the area. The common tribes are Gonds (Maria, Mudia,Gurva, Agariya and Rajgond sub tribes) and Baiga, Kol, Kawar and Pradhans.

The Population density in the Biosphere Reserve is 177 sq. km. Sex ratio in the area is far above than the national average figure as 976/1000 male. The literacy rate is far below as 25.0 (Male-37 & Female-13).The of majority of population occupied in agriculture but it is still primitive. The cultivation is mainly rain-fed type in view of unavailability of irrigation facilities in the area. Flow irrigation is absolutely lacking in the region. The occupational pattern in the region clearly depicts that about 88% of population is directly and/or indirectly depend on Primary sector of agriculture, which further sub divided in to cultivators (69.25%) and agricultural labours (27.3%). The secondary and tertiary sectors support only 4.0% and 8.2% of population requires immediate attention for its further development.

OBJECTIVES

The objectives of the proposed research are as follows:

1. To understand the underlying causes of forest deforestation by using site-specific case studies.
2. To know status of Deforestation in Central region of India.
3. To understand the mechanism of deforestation vis-a vis its relation with tribes.

4. To analyse the changes has been brought due to Forest Right Act on deforestation.

RESEARCH METHODOLOGY

Study Area

The Achanakmar Biosphere Reserve is one of the premium biosphere reserves in India. The reserve covers a huge area of 3835.5189sq. km. and it falls in almost northern part of bio-geographic zone of 6 and Bio-geographic province 6a (Deccan peninsula, Central highlands). About 68.10% out of the total area of these reserves lies in the Bilaspur district in Chhattisgarh.

Achanakmar Biosphere Reserve

CENTRAL ZONE

Study area is described in detail by (EPCO, 1999). The Achanakmar Biosphere Reserve are located between 22'15' to

22'85' N latitude and 81'25'to 82'5' E longitude. The land use analysis made by RSAC, Bhopal indicates that 63.19% of the area is occupied by the forest. Major problem in the area are illicit grazing by cattle, expansion of agriculture, increased mining, over exploitation of NTFP's, medicinal plants, alienation of tribes from their land.

The climate of the reserve is tropical and the year is distinctly divisible in to winter (November-February), summer (April-June) and a warm rainy season (July-September), Mean monthly minimum temperature within the annual cycle ranges from 10.9° to 25.6 ° C and mean monthly maximum temperature from 24.1to 42.° C. The annual rainfall average 1322 mm. (mean monthly range is 6.63 mm to 359. 88 mm) of which about 85% occurs during the period mid June to September. The soil of the study area that varies greatly depending upon the parent rocks and topography is red lateritic, nutrient poor (lacking N and P) and characterized by excessive amounts of iron oxide (Prakash 1992).

RESEARCH DESIGN & SAMPLING TECHNIQUE

The research design employed for the present study was Non-Experimental Longitudinal study. Under this trend methods have been used hence data has been collected two times within interval to find out the transition in Deforestation and its impact among tribes. Using probability - sampling method around 68 households was selected for final study.

SOURCE OF DATA COLLECTION

The tribal community people were interviewed to understand their changing source of livelihoods. The scope of the interviews was wide-ranging covering different cultural practices and indigenous knowledge related to the conservation of biodiversity and ecological restoration. Separate and joint focused group interviews were conducted for the old people. Based on repeated survey of the area, representative sites of pure Sal forest were selected for where initially tribes have their habitat and after two year of interval when they alienated from the land. The forest vegetation was analyzed within the representativeness and non-representativeness using the particular species. The vegetation data were quantitatively analyzed for frequency, density and abundance. An importance value inbox (IVI) was calculated as the sum total of relative frequency, relative density and relative dominance (Phillips 1959).

RESULT AND DISCUSSION

A total of 101 species that belongs to 46 families' preservation were recorded of study area. The result showed that the greater number a species degraded after these families left the area.

Table 1: Comparison of Species structure of the Forest (Year 2013 and 2015)

Species	2013			2015		
	Density (stems ha^{-1})	Basal cover (m^2 ha^{-1})	IVI	Density (stems ha^{-1})	Basal cover (m^2ha^{-1})	IVI
1	2	3	4	5	6	7
Shorea robusta Gaertn f. Dipterocarpacear (SAL)	350	14.24	84.97	233	15.66	104.23
Terminalia tomentosa Wt & Agn. Combretaceae (ASNA)	140	4.98	37.43	133	7.96	67.9

contd...

1	2	3	4	5	6	7
Diospyros melanoxylon Roxb. Ebenaceae(TENDU/KENDU)	117	2.0	24.84	27.0	3.23	19.11
Embelia robusta C.B. Clarke non Roxb. Myrsinaceae (BHINGI)	143.0	1.59	21.43	-	-	-
Miliusa tomentosa (Roxb.) J. Sinclair, Annonaceae (Dom-Sal)	107.0	0.73	20.52	90.0	0.64	31.76
Pterocarpus marsupium Roxb. Fabaceae (Benga)	40.0	3.31	18.78	7.0	0.12	3.54
Buchanania lanan Spreng, Anacardiaceae (Chironji)	80.0	1.32	17.97	27.0	0.47	11.58

contd...

1	2	3	4	5	6	7
Woodfordia fruticosa Lythraceae (Red Bell Bush)	10.0	1.73	6.17	-	-	-
Eugenia cumini Druce, Myrtaceae(Jamun)	17.0	0.80	6.10	-	-	-
Ougeinia oojeinensis (Roxb.) Hochr. Fabaceae(Panan)	23.0	0.44	5.61	10.0	0.22	4.31
Lannea grandis Engl. Anacardeaceae(India Ash Tree)	13.0	0.9	5.45	7.0	0.14	3.60
Emblica officinalis Gaertn, Euphorbiaceae(Amla)	27.0	0.19	5.26	7.0	0.28	4.31
Dendrocalamus strictus Nees Poaceae (Male/Solid Bamboo)	17.0	0.32	4.79	-	-	-

Table one show the drastic degradations or total banishments in the vegetations species after these tribal families left the area. With this data it can be analysed that the Deforestation through displacement programs, are believed that deforestation does not have altered socio-cultural elements such as domestic economy, household income, education, religious beliefs and cultural practices including food practices of tribal communities vis-à-vis it also affected conservation of biodiversity and ecological restoration.

CONCLUSION

Therefore, on the basis of the analysis of the issues on environmental degradation in the tribal regions there is an urgent need to prevent environmental degradation by stopping deforestation and over exploitation of natural resources in tribal regions of India in general and from the tribal region. Therefore, from every angles emphasis should be made to initiate and revive the spirit among the people to preserve the existing forest wealth, bring more land under forest and maintain the ecological balance throughout the country and particularly in the tribal regions of India. The proposed strategies and action plans of the study are protection of forests by the local people and making alternative strategies for employment in the rural areas, controlling out migration and displacement of the tribals from their regions, enhancement of social forestry and creating awareness among the rural people.

SUGGESTIONS

1. Protection of forests by the people for the people.
2. Quick growing planted forests for cheap fuel wood would be encouraged.
3. Enhancement of social forestry.
4. Conserving natural heritage by preserving the remaining forests leaving it to their natural owners.
5. Increasing substantially the forest cover in the country through massive afforestation and social forestry programmes especially on denuded and unproductive lands.

6. Meeting the requirements of fuel wood, fodder and minor forest produce of the rural and tribal populations through agro forestry programmes.
7. Creating a massive people's movement for achieving these objectives and to minimize pressure on existing forests.

REFERENCES

1. Basu, N.K. (1968). Tribes of India. New Delhi: National Book Trust,
2. Biswas, A. (2002). Forests and people of India: special notes on West Bengal. Changing environmental scenario of Indian sub-continent. Kolkata: acb publications.
3. Curtis, J.T. and McIntosh, R.P. 1950. The interrelations of certain analytic and synthetic phytosociological characters. Ecology 31: 434-455.
4. Dashora, J.L, 1992, The Vanishing Tribal Culture, Quarterly Report Journal, 24 (1).
5. EPCO, 1999. Amarkantak Biosphere Reserve; Project Document. Environmental Planning and Coordination Organization, Bhopal.
6. FAO. 2010a. Criteria and indicators for sustainable woodfuels. FAO Forestry Paper No. 160. Rome. www.fao.org/docrep/012/i1673e/i1673e00.htm.
7. FAO. 2011a. Forests for improved nutrition and food security. Rome. www.fao.org/forestry/27976-02c09ef000fa99932eefa37c22f76a 055.pdf.
8. FAO. 2011b. Looking ahead in world food and agriculture. Perspectives to 2050, by P. Conforti. Rome. www.fao.org/docrep/014/i2280e/i2280e00.htm.
9. FAO. 2011c. State of the World's Forests 2011, Rome. www.fao.org/docrep/013/i2000e/i2000e00.htm.
10. FAO. 2011d. The State of Food and Agriculture 2010–2011: Women in agriculture – closing the gender gap for development, Rome. www.fao.org/ docrep/013/i2050e/i2050e.pdf.
11. Mayhew, S. (1998). Dictionary of Geography, Londan; Oxford University press.
12. Misra, R. 1986. Ecology Workbook, Oxford and IBH Publishing. Calcutta.
13. Mukherjee, 0., 1995, Acculturation Among the Kanikars of Travancore, Geographical Review of India, 17 (1), p. 6- 1 8.

14. Phillips, E.A. 1959. methods of Vegetation Study, Holt, Rinehart and Winston, New York.
15. Pielou, E.C. 1966. the measurement of diversity in different types of biological collections. Journal of Theoretical Biology 13: 131-144.
16. Prakash, R. 1992. Wild Life Working Plan. IInd Preliminary Proposal. Forest Department, Govt. of M.P., Bhopal.
17. Sagar, R and Singh, J.S. 1999. Species diversity and its measurement. The Botanica 49: 9-16.
18. Shannon,C.E. and Weaver, W. 1963. The Mathematical Theory of Communications. University of Illinios Press, Urbana.
19. Shashi, S.S, ed., 1995, Social Customs of the Kanikkars, Encyclopedia of Indian Tribes Series, Tribes of Kerala, Ammol Publications Pvt. Ltd., New Delhi, p. 75-98.
20. Simpson. E.H. 1949. Measurement of diversity Nature 168-688.
21. Smith, R.L. 1974. Ecology and field Biology. Harper and Row, New York.
22. Whittaker, R.H. 1972. Evolution and measurement of species diversity. Taxon 21: 213-251.
23. Williams, M. 2002. Deforesting the earth: from prehistory to global crisis. Chicago, USA, University of Chicago Press.

7

Animal Rights:
An Aurora for the Brute

Mayuri Gogoi*
Tanjima Arafat Hussain*

"Rights? Are you really claiming for animal rights? I wonder how and what rights could a dog possibly have?"

"Rights for monkeys? Why not! Why don't you claim that they should even receive other social rights or say, right to free education? And maybe even the right to vote?"

These are the phrases often heard by the animal rights activist, who's ever acted to promote animal rights.

Animal Rights! Doesn't that sound atrocious? The very thought that strikes our mind is that what is the necessity to provide rights to the creatures who don't even possess intellectuality? They could not be even made aware that they have got certain rights. Then, what's the inexorableness of these rights? Now, here the relation between the terms 'suffering' and 'living creatures' can be brought to light to take a stand where the question claim of these rights for the brute arises. Living creatures, here, includes both humans and non-humans. Are we humans not provided a bucketful of rights to protect us from sufferings?

---

*BALLB(H) 6th Semester, Centre for Juridical Studies, Dibrugarh University, Assam.

Yes! We have got enough rights to avoid sufferings and agonies, which if weighed, shall even result in 'micro' or may be less than that. Still, we don't drop a single chance to claim our rights once the pain hit us. Reason- "we are living creature and any kind of suffering or pain should not be tolerated. So, rights are of utmost importance on this feet." When we humans claim our rights so desperately, taking the stand of 'being the living creatures', then why not the animals should be provided only a mug-full of rights? The rights provided to the animals are comparatively very less in number than that of the rights provided to the humans. Still, then the so-called 'intellectual-ones' continuous to harm the non-intellectual innocent brutes. Sometimes only for their self-satisfaction. Are they really humans? Despite of all their inhumane activities, can they be called the most intellectual living creatures on this earth? And if this is to be answered very simply, then it's a 'no'. If they use their intellectuality in harming the non-intellectual ones, then there is nothing that keeps them different.

Since time immemorial animals are provided certain rights, in which some, or all, non-human animals are entitled to the possession of their own lives and that their most basic interests- like that of their need to avoid pain and suffering, should be afforded the same consideration as similar interests of human beings. These rights, literally, seems like an aurora in the lives of the brutes. But, does it only seems as this or it actually is? These rights though seems to be available, are actually not enjoyed by the unaware innocent non-human animals. Their exploitation is in good pace as it was, in one way or the other. Animals are exploited in different ways like using the animals in entertainment, for experimentation of cosmetics and used in Research laboratories, kept as workers, used for the craze of humans for meat, for clothing purposes such as using the skin for leather, fur for the woolen products and numerous other ways. This exploitation in continuing all over the world despite the existence of different animal welfare and rights protecting organizations, different welfare and maintenance programmes and other related legislations.

If mention is made of these inhuman practices in India, it is no less in this regard. Though India is home to several religious traditions advocating non-violence and compassion towards animals, a country where lakhs of God and Goddesses are worshipped whose 'vahana' happened to be an animal and has passed a number of animal welfare reforms since 1960, but India is also one of the world's leading producers of animal products. India still bears some so-called intellectual ones who are involved in some inhuman practices which causes harm to the animals and even strictly prohibited by the Prevention of Cruelty to Animals Act, 1960[1] and Wild Life Protection Act, 1972, and other legislations and even falls under the roof of punishable offence.

As per the recent report (New Delhi), one of the policy decisions of India to declare a ban on the testing of cosmetics and their ingredients on animals and use of captive dolphins for public entertainment being banned anywhere in the country, make it more advance in the race of progressiveness than the United States on matters of animal rights. Despite of such advancement in taking initiatives for the protection of animal rights, why is India still lagging behind in respect of enforcement of these rights is a matter of great concern today.

Since here, India context is taken into account, a mention can be made about the *Jallikattu ban incident.* PETA, the global animal rights group had actively campaigned for restrictions against Jallikattu to which the Tamil Nadu Government passed an ordinance promulgating to circumvent the 2014 SC ban on the traditional and popular bull-taming sport. And eventually, PETA and other animal rights activists have become targets for those protesting against the Jallikattu ban.

As we see, that the protection of animals from the cruelty is a necessary step towards the natural balance, the Indian Government like many other countries has put forwarded some important notable legislations for the same purpose. But regardless of this fact animals are still continuing to face cruelty. This is because the general people are unaware of these particular legislations or are still continuing to violate these legislations. So, along with the enactment of these legislations, the awareness for the same must be put into notice by the Government.

(i) **The Prevention of Cruelty to Animals Act,1960** was constituted mainly with the objective of "preventing the infliction of unnecessary pain or suffering on animals." In this respect the central Government has established an "Animal Welfare Board of India"[2] for the promotion, welfare and protection of animals from being subjected to unnecessary pain or suffering.

The Act defines the term 'cruelty' to animals in a wide sense under Chapter III. Precisely, cruelty to animals is when any person beats, kicks, over-rides, over-drives, over-loads, tortures, mutilate, administer an injurious substance, or cruelly kill an animal. It is also illegal to employ an unfit animal, transport cruelly, chain, confine, tether an animal, give it little or no food or water, yelling and scaring it or leaving it outside in cold or hot weather for long period of time. It is a violation to engage animals in fighting or shooting competitions in which animals are released from captivity to be shot.

Any form of cruelty to animals in punishable under this Act. If the offence is convicted for the first time, one can be punished with fine which shall not be less than Rs.10 and extend to Rs.50; and if the offence is convicted for subsequent/second time within three years of the previous offence, with fine which shall not be less than Rs.25 and may extend to Rs.100 or with imprisonment which may extend to a period of 3 months or with both.

In *K. Muniasamythevar v. Supdt. of Police,*[3] the Madras High Court held that 'rekla race' of the bullock cannot be permitted as the cart man would be whipping the bullock in order to win the race. Such whipping amounts to "treating animals cruelly."

The Act has established a Committee for the Purpose of Control and Supervision of Experimentation on Animals. The Committee is supposed to help in the implementation of good laboratory practices and ensure that animal testing is carried out under proper conditions. The Committee may authorise its officer or any other person to enter and inspect such institutions or places where experiments on animals are carried out. If any person contravenes any order so made by the Committee, or violates any condition imposed on the person/institution, he/the institution shall be punished with fine upto Rs.200 and the person in-charge of such institution shall also be deemed guilty of this offence.

(ii) In 1972, the Indian Parliament passed a comprehensive national law- the **Wild Life (Protection) Act, 1972**. The sole aim of this Act was protecting wildlife, birds and plants and for matters connected thereto or ancillary or incidental thereto with a view to ensuring the ecological and environmental security of the country[4]. The Act prohibits hunting and also created protected areas and controls trade of wildlife and wildlife products. The Act has created a separate and independent authority to protect and improve wildlife.

The Act under Chapter III-A has specified provisions for the protection of specified plants of sanctuaries, national parks, forests or areas specified by notification.

These specified plants are considered to be the property of the State and the Central Government and therefore, to commence or carry on business or occupation as a dealer in specified plants, a person must have a license from the CWW or other officer. And cultivation, dealing in, or possession of specified plants without a license has also been declared to be a punishable act.

This Act has also banned the purchase, sale, capture of any wild animal, animal article, trophy or meat, etc., without a valid license from the designated authority.[5]

The Act also prohibits transportation of any wild animal, trophy, animal article, etc. (other than vermin) without a valid license under section 48-A.

Similarly, purchase from an unlicensed dealer of an animal, animal article, trophy, etc. is also not permitted under the Act.[6]

Directive Principles of State Policy in Part IV of the Constitution of India bears certain provisions relating to the protection and organization of animals in a proper manner.

As per Art.48, the Constitution of India requiring the State to take necessary steps for the purpose of preserving and also with the intent to improve the breeds, and restraining the slaughter of cows and calves in other milch and draught cattle. As per Art. 48 A, the Constitution imposes a duty on the shoulder of the State to endeavor to protect and take initiative to improve the environment and to safeguard the forests and wildlife of the country.

If a reference is made to the Fundamental Duties mentioned in Art. 51A of Part IV A, then as per this article, the Constitution places a duty on every citizen to "protect and improve the natural environment including forests, lakes, rivers and wildlife and to have compassion for living creatures."

JUDICIAL PROCEEDINGS

1. *People For Ethical Treatment of Animals v. Union of India*

Bombay High Court in 2006 held that any film maker willing to use any animal in their films need to obtain a "No Objection Certificate" from the Assam Welfare Board of India stating that the provisions of the performing Animals (Registration) Rules, 2001 have been duly met. The exploitation of animals in the name of entertainment was controlled by this law.

2. *Shri Ajay Madhusudan Marathe v. New Sarvodaya CHS Ltd.*

The complainant here was bared to use the lift of the society with his pet by the society authority with the lame excuse that, if dog uses the lift it will spread diseases. The Consumer Court Delhi held in favor of the complainant that as a consumer of co-housing society he can use the facilities with the pet provided the pet should be vaccinated and recognized by kennel club of India License.

3. *Ozair Hussain v. Union of India*

The Supreme Court of India held that the food and cosmetic companies should mention the identification of ingredients used in making, whether it is vegetarian or non-vegetarian. And the

Red circle dedicates non-vegetarian and Green circle dedicates vegetarian.

4. *Gauri Maulekhi v. Union of India and Ors*

The Supreme Court of India in 2004 held that all the cattle smuggling across the border for Gadhimai festival held in Nepal was prohibited.

5. *Nair, N.R. and Ors v. Union of India and Ors.*

When the notification of the Kerala High Court that bears, monkeys, tigers, panthers and lions shall not be exhibited or trained as performing animals, was challenged in the Supreme Court of India, the court held that animals suffer cruelty as they are abused and caged to them perform, and therefore, this contravenes the PCA Act, 1960.

From the above discussion we can conclude that, in the words of Mahatma Gandhi "The greatness of a nation and its moral progress can be judged by the way its animals are treated." The words of this Great personality clearly indicates that the reason-lacked animals though not born as humans, but the innocent brute deserve to be treated with canonize and nurture an should be provided all the essential rights that are required to avoid suffering. As finest of the laws and regulations are provided for the welfare of the animals, so necessary steps and stratagem should be taken for the enforcement of those laws and protection of their rights.

NOTES

1. This Act repealed the Prevention of Cruelty to Animals Act, 1890.
2. Per S. 4 of the Act.
3. AIR 2006 Mad 225
4. Incorporated by the Amendment Act, 2002.
5. S. 48.
6. S. 49

8

Environment and Role of Women: A Critical Appraisal

Dr. Ritamoni Das*

INTRODUCTION

The dictionary meaning of the word environment is surroundings; external conditions influencing development or growth of people, animals or plants; living or working conditions etc. Environment consists of the sum total of the stimulation that the individual receives from conception in the mother's womb to death. The word environment has been derived from the French word 'Environner' meaning encircling or surrounding. According to Anastasi, "The environment is everything that affects the individual except his genes." According to section 2(a) of the Indian Environment (Protection) Act, 1986, the term "Environment" includes water, air and land and human beings, other living creatures, plants, micro-organism and property. Environment is the source of life on earth and it not only directs but also determines the existence, growth and development of mankind and all its creativities. It is the subject which is global in nature. It has two types- natural environment and man-made environment. Under the natural environment any change in the system caused due to natural processing is counter balanced by

*Assistant Professor, Damdama College, Kulhati Kamrup, Assam. Email: ritamoi4@gmail.com

the change in the other components of the environment. Man made environment is created by men such as industrial revolution, communication network like telephone, fax, agricultural apparatus, satellite and energy sources like thermal, hydro energy and atomic energy etc.

Women constitute half of the human capital in the world. In India, they are popularly termed as "adhi-abadi" of the nation. Mostly in all the courtiers, only women have the primary responsibility for nutrition, child care and household management. In the developing countries, women play a major role as farmer, animal tender, water and fuel collector etc. They are also active in environmental issues. Women have good knowledge of use of local flora and fauna like herbal medicines, food, fuel etc. They play a vital role not only in conservation of natural resources but also make contribution to the economic development. If we try to find that who are more closely found to related in protection and conservation of environment, it is the women. Women living in rural areas and mountain areas are more near to environment. In every day life they are dealing with environment. It is in their heart. So women can play a very positive role in conservation of mother earth. As they are in the direct contact with the environment they get deep knowledge about it. Thus women have served as agriculturalists, water resource manager, and traditional scientists, among others. Dankelman and Davidson (1998) observed that women play a key role in managing their natural surroundings and adopt several mechanisms to deal with the kinds of environmental crisis they face. They, however observe that the responses of governments have not been significant and as a result women, men, and children continue to face problems including pollution, poor services, human waste pollution, fumes from household fuel, and the consequences of soil erosion and flooding.

As rightly noted by Dashe (1919), without the enhanced perception of a gendered analysis to guide in to the future environmental management programs, a crash is inevitable. Therefore, there is the need to understand the various ways women have actively participated in environmental protection and management with a view to integrate them in to environmental management programs. According to the world bank in 1991, " women play an essential role in the management of natural resources , including soil, water, forests and energy. And often have a profound traditional and contemporary knowledge of the natural world around them." Mexico City, where 'women and environment issue' was brought in to the public consciousness by the Indian Physicist Vanndana Singha.

With the word environment now a day's degradation word is closely related. In the present society environmental degradation is a burning issue. Our environment is degrading day by day because of so may reason. Developed countries are observing controlled evirometal pollution but the condition of other countries is pathetic. Though the sources of the environmental pollution are multi dimensional, but the following are the major source of environmental pollution or degradation –

Population growth – the growth of uncontrolled human population is the most responsible factor for environmental pollution. It is caused due to unmindful human activities. There by ecological balance is disturbed. India is the second largest country in the world. The government has sponsored so may family planning programmed but it has failed to achieve it goals to because of poverty, lack of education and conservation approach of certain communities.

Deforestation – it has harmful effect on human life because poisonous carbon-dioxide is taken by trees and plants only. Deforestation has direct adverse impact on soil sand land because of exposure of ground surface to high intensity of rain fall. One major cause for deforestation is the conversion of forest lad into agricultural land that is why rate of erosion of soil has rapidly increased in the recent time, which has generated environmental degradation. The national forest policy was adopted by the parliament in 1988 shortly before the passage of the amendment to the forest (conservation) act but the undue exploitation of forest could not be checked.

Industrial development – industries are emitting carbon-dioxide, carbon-monoxide ad other toxic gases thus the natural gaseous composition of atmosphere is rapidly changing and toxic gases are affecting human health, aquatic life and also plans and trees. Such ecological imbalance may cause skin cancer and other dangerous diseases.

Unplanned urbanization – it is one of the most important reason for degradation of environment. Over population helps unplanned urbanization. Because of unplanned urbanization quality of life of the people decrease day by day. Over population in the cities creates some another problems like air pollution, water pollution, noise pollution etc. Developing intention for living in a city, attraction for high quality life etc. leads to unplanned urbanization.

Technological development – technology leads development of a country. But use of technology creates pollution like air pollution, noise pollution, land pollution, water pollution etc.

Lack of environmental awareness – lack of environmental awareness is another reason for environmental degradation. If people does not aware about it, if they does not have the knowledge of their own role regarding environment then degradation will happen in environment.

Chemical effluents – effluents are another by products of industries which poses threat to the environment. Petroleum industries and chemical manufacturing industries etc. creates major waste products which pollute river and aquatic life.

Natural causes – natural causes like quakes storms, tidal waves creates a log resulting degradation to human life and environment. Human can not be blamed for these natural causes of environmental degradation.

Role of Women in Conservation of Environment – More than 70% of the Indian population are in rural areas. Always it has been seen that the principal conservers of bio-diversity are women. Even today they perform duties such as seed selection, multiplication and conservation. The on-farm conservation traditions of rural and tribal women, with reference to agro-biodiversity are well known. Unfortunately, current food security systems depend on too few crops. It is important to expand the basis of food security by including large numbers of species and varieties of food plants still maintained by tribal and rural families.

Traditionally, women have dealt with non-monetized biomass based subsistence economy of the household i.e. firewood, cow dung, crop wastes, organic manure, etc. The fact is that women work as unpaid labourers on family farms with a greater role than men in operational decision making. Because of over population pressure has increased on male migration and it again increase the work load of women.It means that women's responsibilities extend from the household duties to working in the fields.

In developing countries women are regarded as primary users of natural resources because they are the ones who are responsible for gathering food, fuel and fodder. Although in these countries, women mostly can't own the land and farms but, they are the ones who spend most of their time working on the farms to feed the household. Because of technological development male involvement with land decrease, many of them leave the farm to go to cities to find jobs; so women become increasingly responsible for an increasing portion of farm tasks. These rural women tend to have a closer relationship with land and other natural resources, which promotes a new culture of respectful use and preservation of natural resources and the environment, ensuring that the following generations can meet their needs. Besides considering how to achieve appropriate agricultural production and human nutrition, women want to secure access to the land. Women's perspectives and values for the environment are somewhat different than men's. Women give greater priority to protection of and improving the capacity of nature, maintaining farming lands, and caring for nature and environment's future. Repeated studies have shown that women have a stake in environment and this stake is reflected in the degree to which they care about natural resources. Ecofeminism refers to women's and feminist perspectives on the environment – where the domination an exploitation of women, of poorly resourced peoples and of nature is at the heart of the ecofeminist movement.

Today, women struggle against alarming global trends, but they are working together to effect change. By establishing domestic and international non-governmental organizations, many women have recognized themselves and acknowledge to the world that they no only have the right to participate in environmental dilemmas but they have different relationship with environment including different needs, responsibilities, and knowledge about natural resources. This is why women are affected differently than men by environmental degradation, deforestation, pollution and over pollution. According to United Nations Chronicle journal researchers have found an association between breast cancer and the pesticide DDT and its derivative DDE; and also one study by the World Health Organization has found that women who are exposed to pesticides face a higher risk of abortion. These kinds of health problems cause women to feel more responsible regarding environmental issues. some have said that women would protect the Earth better than men if in power. Although there is no evidence for this hypothesis, recent movements have shown that women are more sensitive to the earth and its problems. They have created a special value system about environmental issues. While it is true that poor women continue to suffer various kinds of deprivation, discrimination and atrocities, the country has mounted a concerted on slaught against these problems through various development/empowering strategies to include confidence among women, bring an awareness of their own potential and to ensure their participation in their own development, an empowering strategy has been advocated by the Government based on promotion of literacy and education, credit, employment and income generation. Though the Government of India is working towards an environmentally sound and sustainable quality of life, the problems, challenges and issues are multi-faceted. However, women in India are playing a crucial role in protection and conservation of environment. Women in India have brought a different perspective to the environment debate, because of their different experience base. Poor women in our country have brought a different perspective to the environment debate, because of their different experience base. Poor women's lives are not compartmentalized and they see the issues in a broad and holistic perspective. They understand clearly that economics and environment are compatible. Their experience reveals to them that soil water and vegetation, necessary for their day-to-day living, requires, care and good management. Environmental degradation is related not only to the biosphere alone, but to the social sphere as well.

Throughout history men have looked at natural resources as commercial entities or income generating tools, while women have tended to see the environment as a resource support their basic needs. As an example, rural Indian women collect the dead branches which are cut by storm for fuel wood to use rather than cutting the live trees. Since African, Asian and Latin American women use the land to produce food for their family, they acquire the knowledge of the land/soil conditions, water, and other environmental features. Any changes in the environment on these areas, like deforestation, have the most effect on women of that area, and cause them to suffer until they can cope with these changes.

An example of female predominance in the defense of natural forests comes from India in 1906. As forest clearing was expanding conflict between loggers and government and peasant communities increased. To thwart resistance to the forest cleaning, the men were diverted from their villages to a fictional payment compensation site and loggers were send to the forests. The women were left in the villages, however, they protested by physically hugging themselves to the trees to prevent their being cut down and this is now called now called the Chipko movement.

Chipko movement – One of the first environmentalist movements which were inspired by women was the Chipko movement (Women tree-huggers in India). "Its name comes from a Hindi word meaning to stick" (as in glue). The movement was an act of defiance against the state government's permission given to a corporation for commercial logging. Women of the village resisted, embracing trees to prevent their felling, to safeguard their lifestyles which were dependent on the forests. Deforestation could qualitatively change the lives of all village residents but it was the women who agitated for saving the forests. Organized by a non-governmental organization that Chandi Prasad led, The Chipko movement adopted the slogan "ecology is permanent economy."

Green Belt Movement – Another movement, which is one of the biggest in women and environment history, is the Green Belt movement. Nobel Prize winner Wangari Maathai founded this movement on the World Environment Day in June 1977. The starting ceremony was very simple a few women planted seven trees in Maathai's backyard. By 2005, 30 million trees had been planted by participants in the Green Belt movement on public and private lands. The Green Belt movement aims to bring environmental restoration along with society's economic growth. This movement led by Maathai focused on restoration of Kenya's rapidly diminishing forests as well as empowering the rural women through environmental preservation. This conflict started because men wanted to cut the trees to use them for industrial purposes while women wanted to keep them since it was their food resource and deforestation was a survival matter for local people.

Rachel Carson – One of the outstanding women environmentalists is Rachel Carson. Rachel Carson (1907-1964) was a scientists, writer, and ecologist. Rachel, Carson went to the Pennsylvania College for Women, majoring in English, but she was inspired by her biology teacher so she switched her major to biology. She became more interested and focused on the sea while she was working at the Marine Biological Laboratories in Massachusetts. Her eloquent prose let to the publication of her first book, Under the Sea-Wind: a Naturalists' Picture of Ocean Life, in 1941. In 1949 she became chief editor of the Fish and Wildlife Service (FWS). Her second book, The Sea Around us, won the National Book Awarded sold more than 200,000 copies. After that she retired from FWS and became a full time writer. After her third book about the sea 'The Edge of the Sea' Carson focused on effects of chemicals and pesticides on the environment. That is when she wrote her book about environment, Silent Spring. The book was about what man has done to the nature and eventually to him and started a modern environmental movement. Carson believed that human and nature are mutually dependent on each other. She argued that industrial activities such as pesticides use can damages the earth ecosystem and will have far-reaching ecological consequences such as future human health problems. Today, scientific studies have demonstrated these consequences.

Maria Cherkasova – Maria Cherkasova (1938) is a journalists, ecologist, and director of Centre for Independent Ecological Programs (CIEP). She is famous because of coordinating a 4-year campaign to stop construction of hydro-electric dam on the Katun River. After Cherkasova involvement in the student movement on environmental protection in 1960's, she began to work for the Red Data Book for the Department of Environmental Protection in 1960's. She began to work for the Red Data Book for the Department of Environmental Protection Institute. She researched and preserved rare species until she became the editor of USSR Red Data Book. Sheco founded the Socio-Ecological Union which has become the largest ecological NGO in the former Soviet Union. In 1990, she became director of CIEP which arrange and drives activities in an extensive range of ecologically related areas on both domestic and international fronts. It is common knowledge throughout the world that the growth of technology and the processes of commercialization, industrialization, and globalization affect men and women differently. The world realizes, clearly today that real development cannot take roots if it by-passes women. Therefore, India embarks on bold and sweeping economic reforms, concern for women and efforts to bring them in main stream occupying the Centre stage. India has been a relentless champion of the success of women at all spheres in international and national forums. The women's movement in India continuously interacts with and informs public opinion. The Indian Parliament has been a front-runner in progressive legislation upholding the status of women. India has the distinction of running one of the world's largest primary health care systems and the largest child development program. India has set up a National Commission for Women through an Act of Parliament to serve as a kind of ombudsman for women's issues in the country and the day is not far off when the Parliament opens its doors for one third of its strength to women.

Relevant legal provision on environment – India is one of the few countries of the world that have made a specific reference in the constitution of to the need for environmental protection, control and preservation. The constitution (42nd Amendment) Act of 1976 has made it a Fundamental duty to protect and improve the natural environment. Article 51 (a) provides that it shall be the duty of every citizen of India to protect and improve the natural environment including forests, lakes, rivers and wild life and have compassion for living creatures. Article 21 of Constitution guarantee the right to life; a life of dignity, to be lived in a proper environment, free from danger of disease and infection. Besides there are number of Directive Principles which give indirect emphasis for protection of environment. In addition to Indian Constitutional aspect, certain special legislations are also available in India for Environmental protection such as –

1. The Air (Prevention and control of pollution) Act, 1981
2. The Water (Prevention and control of Pollution) Act, 1974.
3. The Wildlife (Protection) Act, 1972.
4. The India Forest Act, 1927.
5. The Forest (Conservation) Act, 1980 and the comprehensive legislation.
6. Environmental protection Act, 1986

CONCLUSION

In this paper women's participation in environmental protection, how they are conscious about environment, how they are closely attached to environment etc are discussed. Women can develop their role when society will support them properly. In this regard women education can play a very great role as education is the strongest weapon to any struggle. NGO'S also can help by providing some training regarding how women can help to decrease the environmental degradation, how can they protect the environment etc, to women. The critical role of women, as resource managers, as community activists, as environmental advocates, must be recognized when strategies for the protection of the environment are being developed. Women should be allowed to participate at the local, regional, national, and international levels on environmental issues. In the words of Maye (1994), this participation, to be meaningful, should go beyond tokenism. To make a significant impact on decision making, women should be present in equal numbers to men (or at least on a 40:60 proportional split of genders). As resource managers, women should be consulted and supported in what they are already doing to protect the environment. Specifically, more women should be involved in decision making with regard to policies programs, or funding of environment.

REFERENCES

Agrawal, A (1989). *Women in Rural Society.* Allahabad: Vohra Pub & Distributors.

Tripathi, S.C. (2004). *Environmental Law* . Allahbad: Central Law Publication.

Sarma, R.A (2010). *EnvironmentalEducation.* Meerut: Surya Publication.

9

Role of Judiciary in Protecting and Promoting the Environment: An Analysis

Meghali Saikia*

INTRODUCTION

A healthy environment leads to a healthy mind, which result in the all around development of the human being as well as of the society or nation at large. Since time immemorial, people across the world have always made efforts to preserve and protect the natural resources like air, water, plants, flora and fauna. Ancient scriptures of different countries, our sages and saints always preached and also taught the people to worship earth, sky, rivers, seas plants, trees and every form of life. Majority of people still consider it as their sacred duty to protect the plants, trees, rivers, wells etc. But with the passage of time, things are changing day by day. The main objective behind this research is to identify the present scenario and study the nature and extent of developments in various environmental statuses through various statutes, law and convention and various issues regarding the court decisions and judicial pronouncements.

The natural resources of the earth, including the air, water, land, flora and fauna and especially representative samples of

*LLM 4th Semester, Centre for Juridical Studies, Dibrugarh University, Dibrugarh, Assam

natural ecosystems, must be safeguarded for the benefit of present and future generations through careful planning or management as appropriate.[1] The concept of ecological protection and preservation is not new. It has been intrinsic to many ancient civilizations. Ancient Indian texts highlights that it is the dharma of each individual in the society to protect nature and the term 'nature' includes land, water, trees and animals which are of great importance to us.[2] At the same time, new innovations like, thermal power, atomic plant and so on without any sufficient natural assurance pose another danger to the situations which results in issues like global warming, climate change, acid rain, etc. Therefore, there arises a need for a comprehensive analysis of the protection of the environment. Public Interest Litigation (PIL) has been prominently relied upon to tackle environmental problems, and this considered as an important tool in this regard.

MEANING OF ENVIRONMENT

The English term 'Environment' is derived from the French term 'Environer', Latin 'in-viron' which means to surround, to encircle, or to from a ring around. It is accepted that the term environment in ecology was introduced by a biologist Jacob Van Uerkal.[3] The word "environment" relates to surroundings. It includes virtually everything. It can be can defined as anything which may be treated as covering the physical surroundings that are common to all of us, including air, space, land, water, plants and wildlife. According to the Webster Dictionary, it is defined as the "Aggregate of all the external condition and influences affecting the life and development of an organism.[4]"

The Environment (Protection) Act, 1986 Section 2(a) environment "includes water, air and land and the inter-relationship which exists among and between water, air and land, and human beings, other living creatures, plants, micro-organism and property."

Thus, after analyzing all the above definitions, the basic idea that can be concluded is that environment means the surroundings in which we live and is essential for our life. Environment is the wellspring of life on earth like water, air, soil, etc., and determines the presence, development and improvement of humanity and all its activities.

INTERNATIONAL INSTRUMENTS

Declaration of the United Nations Conference on the Human Environment:

It was in the mid 1970s that the Indian States showing interest in the protection of environment after the Stockholm Conference in 1972. The first of the 26 principles enunciated in the Declaration illuminates the fundamental change in attitude.

The United Nations Conference on the Human Environment, having met at Stockholm from 5 to 16 June 1972, having considered the need for a common outlook and for common principles to inspire and guide the peoples of the world in the preservation and enhancement of the human environment.

It proclaims that Man is both creature and moulders of his environment, which gives him physical sustenance and affords him the opportunity for intellectual, moral, social and spiritual growth. In the long and tortuous evolution of the human race on this planet a stage has been reached when, through the rapid acceleration of science and technology, man has acquired the power to transform his environment in countless ways and on an unprecedented scale. Both aspects of man's environment, the natural and the man-made, are essential to his well-being and to the enjoyment of basic human rights the right to life itself. The protection and improvement of the human environment is a major issue which affects the well-being of peoples and economic development throughout the world. It is the urgent desire of the peoples of the whole world and the duty of all Governments.

The Conference calls upon Governments and peoples to exert common efforts for the preservation and improvement of the human environment, for the benefit of all the people and for their posterity.[5]

Other Related International Treaties and Conventions

- Convention on Long-Range Transboundary Air Pollution, Geneva, 1979
- Chicago Convention on International Civil aviation, Montreal, 1981
- Espoo Convention, 1991
- Framework Convention on Climate Change (UNFCCC), New York, 1992, including the Kyoto Protocol, 1997, and the Paris Agreement, 2015
- Arhus Convention, 1998
- Vienna Convention for the protection of the Ozone Layer, Vienna, 1985
- Convention on the Protection and Use of Transboundary Watercourses and International Lakes, Helsinki, 1992
- Minamata Convention on Mercury, Minamata 2013
- Stockholm Convention on Persistent Organic Pollutants Stockholm, 2001
- Convention on the Prevention of Marine Pollution by Dumping of Waste and Other Matter (London Convention), London, 1972
- Protocol on Preparedness, Response and Co-operation to Pollution Incidents by Hazardous and Noxious Substances, London 2000
- Barcelona Convention, 1976
- United Nations Convention on the Law of the Sea, Montego Bay, 1982

NATIONAL GREEN TRIBUNAL ACT, 2010 (NGT)[6]

National Green Tribunal is an Act of the Parliament of India which enables creation of a special tribunal to handle the expeditious disposal of the cases pertaining to environmental issues. It draws inspiration from the India's constitutional provision of Article 21, which assures the citizens of India the right to a healthy environment.

During the Rio de Janeiro summit of United Nations Conference on Environment and Development in June 1992,

India vowed the participating states to provide judicial and administrative remedies for the victims of the pollutants and other environmental damage.

There lie many reasons behind the setting up of this tribunal. After India's move with Carbon credits, such tribunal may play a vital role in ensuring the control of emissions and maintaining the desired levels. This is the first body of its kind that is required by its parent statute to apply the "polluter pays" principle and the principle of sustainable development.

This court can rightly be called 'special' because India is the third country following Australia and New Zealand to have such a system.

JURISDICTION

The Tribunal has Original Jurisdiction on matters of "substantial question relating to environment" (i.e. a community at large is affected, damage to public health at broader level) & "damage to environment due to specific activity" (such as pollution). The powers of tribunal related to an award are equivalent to Civil court and tribunal may transmit any order/award to civil court have local jurisdiction. However, the tribunal does not follow civil law. It follows principles of natural justice. The Bill specifies that an application for dispute related to environment can be filled within six months only when first time dispute arose (provide tribunal can accept application after 60 days if it is satisfied that appellant was prevented by sufficient cause from filling the application).

Also Tribunal is competent to hear cases for several acts such as Forest (Conservation) Act, Biological Diversity Act, Environment (Protection) Act, Water & Air (Prevention & control of Pollution) Acts etc. and also have appellate jurisdiction related to above acts after establishment of Tribunal within a period of 30 days of award or order received by aggrieved party. The Bill says that decision taken by majority of members shall be binding and every order of Tribunal shall be final. Any person aggrieved by an award, decision, or order of the Tribunal may appeal to the Supreme Court within 90 days of commencement of award but Supreme Court can entertain appeal even after 90 days if appellant satisfied SC by giving sufficient reasons.

A division bench of the Madras high court comprising Justice N Paul Vasanthakumar and Justice P Devadass on February 2014 held that high courts did have jurisdiction to entertain appeals against the orders of the NGT as in Section 29 of the NGT Act 2010, which deals with bar of jurisdiction of civil courts the jurisdiction of the high court under Article 226/227 is not ousted.

NOTABLE CASES DECIDED BY THE TRIBUNAL:

Yamuna Conservation Zone

On 25 April 2014, the NGT said that the health of Yamuna will be affected by the proposed recreational facilities on the river. The NGT also recommended the Government to declare a 52 km stretch of the Yamuna in Delhi and Uttar Pradesh as a conservation zone.[11]

Coal Blocks in Chhattisgarh Forests

The National Green Tribunal has cancelled the clearance given by the then Union Environment and Forests Minister, Jairam Ramesh, to the Parsa East and Kante-Basan captive coal blocks in the Hasdeo-Arand forests of Chhattisgarh, over ruling the statutory Forest Advisory Committee.

The forest clearance was given by Mr. Ramesh in June 2011, overriding the advice of the Ministry's expert panel on the two blocks for mining by a joint venture between Adani and Rajasthan Rajya Vidyut Utpadan Nigam Limited. The blocks requiring 1,989 hectares of forestland fell in an area that the government had initially barred as it was considered a patch of valuable forest and demarcated as a 'no-go' area.

The order is bound to have a more far-reaching impact, with the tribunal holding that "mere expression of fanciful reasons relating to environmental concerns without any basis, scientific study or past experience would not render the advice of FAC – a body of experts – inconsequential. Under the Forest Conservation

Act, 1980, the FAC is required to appraise projects that require forestlands and advise the Environment Ministry to grant approval or reject the proposals.

But in this case, the NGT noted, the Minister had taken all of one day and relied upon his "understanding and belief" without any "basis either in any authoritative study or experience in the relevant fields." The Minister, while clearing the coal blocks, had given six reasons for doing so, including that the coal blocks are linked to super-critical thermal power plant, which is imperative to sustain the momentum generated in the XI Plan for increasing power production. These 'anthropocentric' considerations, the NGT held, were not valid to evaluate the project.

JUDICIAL REMEDIES FOR ENVIRONMENT POLLUTION[7]

The remedies available in India for environmental protection comprise of tortuous as well as statutory law remedies. The tortuous remedies available are trespass, nuisance, strict liability and negligence. The statutory remedies incorporates: Citizen's suit, e.g.,

- an activity brought under Section 19 of the Environmental (Protection) Act, 1986,
- an activity under area 133, Criminal Procedure Code, 1973.and
- and activity brought under the Section 268 for open irritation, under Indian Penal Code,1860

Apart from this, a writ petition can be filed under Article 32 in the Supreme Court of India or under Article 226 in the High Court.

Tortious liability:

The Indian judiciary has developed the following tortuous remedies:

Damage: In the recent case of *Shriram Gas Leak*, involving a leakage of Oleum gas which resulted in substantial environmental harm to the citizens of Delhi, the Apex court held that the quantum of damages awarded must be proportionate to the capacity and magnitude of the polluter to pay. However, the Apex Court has deviated from this test in the *Bhopal Gas Tragedy.*

Injunction: The purpose of injunction is to prevent continuous wrong. The grant of perpetual injunction is governed by Sec.37 to 42 of the Specific Relief Act, 1963.

Nuisance: Nuisance means the act which creates hindrance to the enjoyment of the person in form of smell, air, noise, etc. According to Stephen, nuisance is anything done to hurt or annoyance of lands, tenements of another and not amounting to trespass. Nuisance can be divided into two categories:

> **Private Nuisance:** It is a substantial and unreasonable interference with the use and enjoyment of one's land.
>
> **Public Nuisance:** It is an unreasonable interference with a general right of the public.

Trespass: It means intentional or negligent direct interference with personal or proprietary rights without lawful excuses. The two important requirements for trespass are:

1) There must be an intentional or negligent interference with personal or proprietary rights.
2) The interference with the personal or proprietary rights must be direct rather than consequential.

Negligence: It connotes failure to exercise the care that a reasonably prudent person would exercise in like circumstances.

Strict Liability: The rule enunciated in *Rylands v. Fletcher* by Blackburn J. is that the person who for his own purpose brings on his land and collects and keeps there anything likely to be a mischief, if it escapes, must keep it as its peril, and if he does not do so is prima facie even though, he will be answerable for all the damage which is the natural consequence of its escape. The doctrine of strict liability has considerable utility in environmental pollution cases especially cases dealing with the harm caused by the leakage of hazardous substances.

SOME REMARKABLE PRINCIPLES AND DOCTRINES PROPOUNDED BY THE INDIAN JUDICIARY:

1. Doctrine of Absolute Liability

The Bhopal Case: *Union Carbide Corporation* v. *Union of India*[8]. In this case, the court held that, where an enterprise is occupied with an inherently dangerous or a hazardous activity and harm results to anybody by virtue of a mishap in the operation of such dangerous or naturally unsafe movement coming about, for instance, in getaway of poisonous gas, the enterprise is strictly and completely obligated to repay every one of the individuals who are influenced by the accident and such risk is not subject to any exemptions. Accordingly, Supreme Court created another trend of Absolute Liability without any exemption.

2. Polluter Pays Principles

> "*If anyone intentionally spoils the water of another ... let him not only pay damages, but*
>
> *Purify the stream or cistern which contains the water...*" – Plato

Polluter Pays Principle has become a very popular concept lately. 'If you make a mess, it's your duty to clean it up '- this is the fundamental basis of this slogan. It should be mentioned that in environment law, the 'polluter pays principle' does not allude to "fault." Instead, it supports a remedial methodology which is concerned with repairing natural harm. It's a rule in international environmental law where the polluting party pays for the harm or damage done to the natural environment. Vellore Citizens Welfare Forum v. Union of India.[9]

The Supreme Court has declared that the polluter pays principle is an essential feature of the sustainable development.

3. Precautionary Principle

The Supreme Court of India, in Vellore Citizens Forum Case, developed the following three concepts for the precautionary principle:

> Environmental measures must anticipate, prevent and attack the causes of environmental degradation; Lack of scientific certainty

should not be used as a reason for postponing measures; Onus of proof is on the actor to show that his action is benign.

4. Public Trust Doctrine

The Public Trust Doctrine primarily rests on the principle that certain resources like air, water, sea and the forests have such a great importance to people as a whole that it would be wholly unjustified to make them a subject of private ownership. *M.C. Mehta v. Kamal Nath and Other.*[10] The public trust doctrine, as discussed by court in this judgment is a part of the law of the land.

5. Doctrine of Sustainable Development

The World Commission on Environment and Development (WCED) in its report prominently known as the 'Brundtland Report' named after the Chairman of the Commission Ms. GH Brundtland highlights the concept of sustainable development. As per Brundtland Report, Sustainable development signifies "development that meets the needs of the present without compromising the ability of the future generations to meet their own needs". There is a need for the courts to strike a balance between development and environment.

Rural Litigation and Entitlement Kendra v. State of UP[11]

The court for the first time dealt with the issue relating to the environment and development; and held that, it is always to be remembered that these are the permanent assets of mankind and or not intended to be exhausted in one generation.

Vellore Citizen's Welfare Forum[12]

In this case, the Supreme Court observed that sustainable development has come to be accepted as a viable concept to eradicate poverty and improve the quality of human life while living within the carrying capacity of the supporting eco- system.

THE CONSTITUTIONAL ASPECTS ON ENVIRONMENTAL LAW:

The Indian Constitution is amongst the few in the world that contains specific provisions on environment protection. The chapters directive principles of state policy and the fundamental duties are explicitly enunciated the nation commitment to protect and improve the environment. It was the first time when responsibility of protection of the environment imposed upon the states through Constitution (Forty Second Amendment) Act, 1976.

Article 48-A[13] the provision reads as follows: "The State shall endeavour to protect and improve the environment and to safeguard the forest and wildlife of the country." The Amendment also inserted Part VI-A (Fundamental duty) in the Constitution, which reads as follows:

Article 51-A (g)[14] "It shall be duty of every citizen of India to protect and improve the natural environment including forests, lakes and wildlife and to have compassion for living creature."

In *Sachidanand Pandey* v. *State of West Bengal*[15], the Supreme Court observed "whenever a problem of ecology is brought before the court, the court is bound to bear in mind Article 48-A and Article 51-A (g).

ENVIRONMENTAL PROTECTION: THE JUDICIAL APPROACH

There are numbers of the following judgments which clearly highlight the active role of judiciary in environmental protection these are follows:

(a) The right to a wholesome environment

Charan Lal Sahu Case

The Supreme Court in this case said, the right to life guaranteed by Article 21 of the Constitution includes the right to a wholesome environment.

Damodhar Rao v. S. 0. Municipal Corporation Hyderabad

The Court resorted to the Constitutional mandates under Articles 48A and 51A(g) to support this reasoning and went to the extent of stating that environmental pollution would be a violation of the fundamental right to life and personal liberty as enshrined in Article 21 of the Constitution[16].

(b) Public nuisance: the judicial response

Ratlam Municipal Council v. Vardhichand[17]

The judgment of the Supreme Court in instant case is a land mark in the history of judicial activism in upholding the social justice component of the rule of law by fixing liability on statutory authorities to discharge their legal obligation to the people in abating public nuisance and making the environmental pollution free even if there is a budgetary constraints., J. Krishna Iyer observed that, "social justice is due to and therefore the people must be able to trigger off the jurisdiction vested for their benefit to any public functioning." Thus he recognized PIL as a Constitutional obligation of the courts.

(c) Judicial relief encompasses compensation to victims

Delhi gas leak case: *M.C. Mehta v. Union of India*[18]

In instant case, the Supreme Court laid down two important principles of law:

1) The power of the Supreme Court to grant remedial relief for a proved infringement of a fundamental right (in case if Article-21) includes the power to award compensation.
2) The judgment opened a new frontier in the Indian jurisprudence by introducing a new "no fault" liability standard (absolute liability) for industries engaged in hazardous activities which has brought about radical changes in the liability and compensation laws in India. The new standard makes hazardous industries absolutely liable from the harm resulting from its activities.

(d) Fundamental right to water

The fundamental right to water has evolved in India, not through legislative action but through judicial interpretation. In *Narmada Bachao Andolan v. Union of India and Ors.*, the Supreme Court of India upheld that "Water is the basic need for the survival of human beings and is part of the right to life and human rights as enshrined in Article 21 of the Constitution of India ... and the right to healthy environment and to sustainable development are fundamental human rights implicit in the right to life.[19]

human beings are never satisfied with what
these activities the boundaries of the wildlife
g the wild animals to come out of their area
ment, and in order to save themselves from
art to kill them and in retaliation the wild
harm to them.

ed human beings despite knowing the
t would arise once the conflict occurs and the
ded situations that have to be faced by the homo-
of the retaliation of the beast in their veins of
en the intellectual ones ricochet with their reason
er.

ted Hindustan Times recently on a report provides
t shows that 1360 peoples were killed in man animal
elephants and tigers in the last few years, which is
an the human fatalities in Maoist Red Zones. It was
about 20%-25% as compared to the previous three
-2013) by the two dominant species. The conflict zone
to new areas in Madhya Pradesh, Tamil Nadu, Odisha,
ttisgarh. The animals like leopard reach the bigger cities,
phants and tigers are confined to small areas like villages
towns. To name a few these animals have been spotted
ential areas in Gurgaon, Mumbai, Nainital, Meerut and
.[1] The Data also shows that for every four people killed in
nimal conflicts, an endangered animal also loss.

According to a latest government data, as many as 187
hants and around 110 tigers were killed in such conflicts.
y animals were captured and summarily sentenced to a life
de enclosures, which animal and activist say in the cruelest
m of punishment to be given to animals born free.[2]

If a mention is made in context of Northeastern Zone, the
egion is no lesser in its involvement of man animal conflict. In
pecial reference to one of the part of Northeast, 1024 persons
lost their lives in this conflict from 2001-2016 following a man-
elephant conflict in Assam which is the home of Asian Pachydern.

CONCLUSION

As per the Declaration of the United Nations Conference on Human Environment we know that man has the fundamental right to freedom, equality and adequate conditions of life, in an environment of a quality that permits a life of dignity and well-being, and he bears a solemn responsibility to protect and improve the environment for present and future generations. In this respect, policies promoting or perpetuating apartheid, racial segregation, discrimination, colonial and other forms of oppression and foreign domination stand condemned and must be eliminated. The natural resources of the earth must be safeguarded for the benefit of present and future generations through careful planning or management. In recent years, there has been a sustained focus on the role played by the higher judiciary in devising and monitoring the implementation of measures for pollution control, conservation of forests and wildlife protection. Many of these judicial interventions have been triggered by the persistent incoherence in policy-making as well as the lack of capacity-building amongst the executive agencies. The Supreme Court is, at the present time, stretching the different legal provisions for environmental protection. In this way, the judiciary tries to fill in the gaps where there is laciness of the legislation which open the numerous approaches to help the country. In India, the courts are extremely cognizant and cautious about the special nature of environmental rights, considering that the loss of natural resources can't be renewed. There are some recommendations which need to be considered.

NOTES

1. Declaration of the United Nations Conference on the Human Environment, Stockholm, 16th June 1972.
2. MC Mehta, Growth of Environmental Jurisprudence in India, p.71, 1999.
3. P.K. Pandey, Environmental Studies, Mahaveer Publication, Dibrugarh, p13, 2016.
4. R.M. Lodha, Environmental Ruin: The Crises of Survival, p.364, New Delhi: Indus Publishing Company, (1993).

5. Available at http://www.unep.org/documents.multilingual/default.asp?documentid=97&articleid=1503 accessed on 20th November 2016 at 10pm.
6. Available at http://www.greentribunal.gov.in accessed on 22nd November, 2016 at 10pm.
7. Available at http://www.lawctopus.com/academike/role-indian-judiciary-protection-environment-india accessed on 20th November 2016 at 8pm.
8. AIR 1990 SC 273.
9. AIR 1996 SCC 212.
10. (1997)1 SCC 388.
11. AIR 1987 SC 1037.
12. AIR 1996 5 SCC 647.
13. The Constitution of India, 1950, Article 48-A.
14. 1950, Article 51-A (g).
15. AIR 1987 SC 1109.
16. C. M. Abraham and Sushila Abraham, The Bhopal Case and the Development of Environmental Law in India, p. 362, Vol. 40 International and Comparative Law Quarterly April 1991 available at http://heinonline.org
17. AIR 1980 SC 1622.
18. AIR 1987 SC 965.
19. Vrinda Narain, Water as a Fundamental Right: A Perspective from India, Vol. 34 available at www.vjel.org/docs/Narain_Water_Draft.pdf

10

From the very primiti
is prevailing but it turning o
time. Man had to depend on
come into contact with the w
takes place. It also occurs when
overlaps with the established wild
negative impact on people's resou
The conflict between man and wild
loss of life or competition for scarce

Since the human population is g
needs are also increasing parallel. In or
they are affecting the wildlife in one way or
population is occupying the natural wildl
fulfill of various needs: such as woods, rubber,
and many other such desires. Human beings
deforestation process or in the destruction of t
of the animals because their selfish crave for thei
a reason for a self satisfying themselves, as it is a v

BALLB (H) 6th Semester, Centre for Juridical Studies, Dibrugar
Dibrugarh, Assam

As per the government records in 2016 approximately 61elephants were killed across the state due to train hits, poaching, poisoning, electrocution.[3] Similarly, approximately 65 human lives were also lost in this year in different parts of the state due to elephant attacks on human settlements.[4]

The above data shows the number of persons died in passing few years. With the loss of 118 lives, in the year 2015 recorded the maximum number of death due to man-elephant conflict in Assam.

LEGAL FRAMEWORK FOR CONSERVATION OF WILDLIFE IN INDIA

1. The Wildlife (Protection) Act, 1972

The Wildlife (Protection) Act, 1972 (WLPA) is an oldest and one of the important statute that provides a powerful legal framework for the wildlife conservation in India. It was last amended in 2006. The main objects of the Act are to promote measures in prohibition of hunting, protection and management of habitats of wildlife, establishment of protected areas for Wildlife, management of zoos etc.

This Act of 1972 provides several categories of protected areas/reserves in India like National Parks, Wildlife sanctuaries, Tiger Reserves, Conservation Reserves and Community Reserves.

The WLPA strictly prohibits grazing and private tenurial rights in National Parks, but at the discretion of Chief Wildlife Warden it can be allowed to Sanctuaries. Some of the protected areas/reserves like National Parks and Tiger Reserves are strictly protected by the laws and no human activities are allowed there except which is in the interest of wildlife conservation or for the betterment of those areas.

This act includes two new categories of protected areas i.e. Community Reserves and Conservation Reserves. These two categories provide a greater role for the local communities, stakeholders and civil society, and also introduced some new opportunities to protect many areas of conservation which may not consist of lager areas like national parks and sanctuaries and so are not designated under strict categories.

Along with the establishment of protected areas, the WLPA includes some other important aspects like appointment of state wildlife authorities, procedure of appointment and wildlife boards, the regulation of trade in wildlife products and prevention, detection and punishment for violation of the act.

The amended act of WLPA in 2006 introduced a new chapter (IV B) for establishment of the National Tiger Conservation Authority and notification of Tiger Reserves. The Wildlife Crime Control Bureau (WCCB) was constituted vide the 2006 amendment to monitor and control the illegal trade in wildlife products.

The WLPA provides investigation and prosecution of offences in a court of law by authorized officers of forest department and police officers.

2. National Wildlife Action Plan (2002-2016)

The National Wildlife Action Plan (NWAP) (2002-2016) is a revised plan of first NWAP of 1983. In the need for a change to the increasing commercial use of natural resources, continuous growth of human and livestock population and change in consumption pattern. The plan focuses on strengthening and enhancing the protected area network, on the conservation of endangered wildlife and their habitats and on controlling trade in wildlife products and on research education and training.

The plan favors two new protected area categories – conservation reserve and community reserve allowing greater participation of local communities in the management of protected areas through traditional or cultural conservation practice. To fulfill the needs of local communities living outside the protected areas and drafting the need for relocation and rehabilitation of villages within protected areas. Recognizing the need to reduce human wildlife conflict the plan establishes effective compensation mechanism. As a key objective, plan includes the restoration of degraded habitats outside the protected areas.

JUDICIAL INTERPRETATION:

Green Cross World Environment Protection Action Group vs. Union of India and others

Here a Writ Petition was filed as a PIL, which questions the killing of a tiger by the officials of the forest department of the state and pray for an investigation on this matter to the Central Bureau of Investigation. Later the Court held that, to direct the respondents to take effective and speedier measures in the light of standard operating procedure and take such necessary actions as requires to inform and educate all its officials so that the incident which took place never repeat.

T.N. Godavarman Thirumlpad vs. Union of India and others

In this case the court directed the State of Chhattisgarh to give full effect to the central scheme-"the Integrated Development of Wildlife Habitats to save the wild buffalo from extinction. The State was also directed to take immediate steps to prevent inter breeding between wild and domestic buffalos and to maintain genetic purity of wild species. The State was asked to intensive research and monitors the population of wild buffalo in Udanti Wildlife Sanctuary and other areas. Moreover the state is also directed to initiate wildlife training programmes for the officials of State Forest Department. An Annual Plan of operations detaining the proposed course action as per the "Integrated Development of Wildlife Habitats is to be submitted to central government within a period of 3month.

In the case *A.R Gokulakrishnan (social activist)* v. *The Secretary to Forest and Environment and others*, the hon'ble Chief Justice ordered to the filing Public Interest Litigation by directing to take the remedial measures to prevent the manance of wild bears which were destroying crops.

CONCLUSION

Difficult things are done at once, impossible takes a little longer. To completely abolish conflict between man and animal is almost impossible now. The only thing that can be done is a firm step that needs to be taken by human beings. The more static the law is, more stronger it is. The greatest criticism faced by Indian laws is its proper implementation. On the one hand, where there exist innumerable laws and legislations, the other hand the issue is turning to be bigger and greater in the present time.

NOTES

1. http://googleweblight.com/i?u=http%3A%2F%2Fm.hindustantimes.com%2Findia-news%2Fman-animal-conflict-on-the-rise-over-living-space%2Fstory-NVUYgygBKfi2wjPXohqEmK.html&grqid=yNeFYF7B&hl=en-IN
2. Ibid
3. http://www.newsbharati.com/Encyc/2016/12/27/Man-elephant-conflict-in-Assam
4. Ibid

CONCLUSION

As per the Declaration of the United Nations Conference on Human Environment we know that man has the fundamental right to freedom, equality and adequate conditions of life, in an environment of a quality that permits a life of dignity and well-being, and he bears a solemn responsibility to protect and improve the environment for present and future generations. In this respect, policies promoting or perpetuating apartheid, racial segregation, discrimination, colonial and other forms of oppression and foreign domination stand condemned and must be eliminated. The natural resources of the earth must be safeguarded for the benefit of present and future generations through careful planning or management. In recent years, there has been a sustained focus on the role played by the higher judiciary in devising and monitoring the implementation of measures for pollution control, conservation of forests and wildlife protection. Many of these judicial interventions have been triggered by the persistent incoherence in policy-making as well as the lack of capacity-building amongst the executive agencies. The Supreme Court is, at the present time, stretching the different legal provisions for environmental protection. In this way, the judiciary tries to fill in the gaps where there is laciness of the legislation which open the numerous approaches to help the country. In India, the courts are extremely cognizant and cautious about the special nature of environmental rights, considering that the loss of natural resources can't be renewed. There are some recommendations which need to be considered.

NOTES

1. Declaration of the United Nations Conference on the Human Environment, Stockholm, 16th June 1972.
2. MC Mehta, Growth of Environmental Jurisprudence in India, p.71, 1999.
3. P.K. Pandey, Environmental Studies, Mahaveer Publication, Dibrugarh, p13, 2016.
4. R.M. Lodha, Environmental Ruin: The Crises of Survival, p.364, New Delhi: Indus Publishing Company, (1993).

5. Available at http://www.unep.org/documents.multilingual/default.asp?documentid=97&articleid=1503 accessed on 20th November 2016 at 10pm.
6. Available at http://www.greentribunal.gov.in accessed on 22nd November, 2016 at 10pm.
7. Available at http://www.lawctopus.com/academike/role-indian-judiciary-protection-environment-india accessed on 20th November 2016 at 8pm.
8. AIR 1990 SC 273.
9. AIR 1996 SCC 212.
10. (1997)1 SCC 388.
11. AIR 1987 SC 1037.
12. AIR 1996 5 SCC 647.
13. The Constitution of India, 1950, Article 48-A.
14. 1950, Article 51-A (g).
15. AIR 1987 SC 1109.
16. C. M. Abraham and Sushila Abraham, The Bhopal Case and the Development of Environmental Law in India, p. 362, Vol. 40 International and Comparative Law Quarterly April 1991 available at http://heinonline.org
17. AIR 1980 SC 1622.
18. AIR 1987 SC 965.
19. Vrinda Narain, Water as a Fundamental Right: A Perspective from India, Vol. 34 available at www.vjel.org/docs/Narain_Water_Draft.pdf

10

Man Animal Conflict and Law: An Analysis

Jamini Chetia and Sanjukta Sharma*

From the very primitive age, conflict between man and animal is prevailing but it turning out to be a burning issue in the present time. Man had to depend on nature for their needs. So when they come into contact with the wildlife the conflict between them takes place. It also occurs when the growing human population overlaps with the established wildlife territory, which results to a negative impact on people's resources, wildlife or their habitat. The conflict between man and wild life also results to injury or loss of life or competition for scarce resources for both of them.

Since the human population is growing very rapidly their needs are also increasing parallel. In order to fulfill their needs they are affecting the wildlife in one way or the other. The growing population is occupying the natural wildlife territory for their fulfill of various needs: such as woods, rubber, production of paper, and many other such desires. Human beings get involved in the deforestation process or in the destruction of the natural habitat of the animals because their selfish crave for their own wants and a reason for a self satisfying themselves, as it is a very transparent

---

BALLB (H) 6th Semester, Centre for Juridical Studies, Dibrugarh University, Dibrugarh, Assam fact that the so-called human beings are never satisfied with what they have and due to these activities the boundaries of the wildlife is shrinking , resulting the wild animals to come out of their area to the human settlement, and in order to save themselves from the wildlife they start to kill them and in retaliation the wild animal also cause harm to them.

The so-called human beings despite knowing the consequences that would arise once the conflict occurs and the worst of the dreaded situations that have to be faced by the homo-sapiens because of the retaliation of the beast in their veins of revenge, still then the intellectual ones ricochet with their reason launched critter.

The reputed Hindustan Times recently on a report provides a data where it shows that 1360 peoples were killed in man animal conflict by elephants and tigers in the last few years, which is higher in than the human fatalities in Maoist Red Zones. It was increasing about 20%-25% as compared to the previous three years (2010-2013) by the two dominant species. The conflict zone also spread to new areas in Madhya Pradesh, Tamil Nadu, Odisha, and Chhattisgarh. The animals like leopard reach the bigger cities, while elephants and tigers are confined to small areas like villages or small towns. To name a few these animals have been spotted in residential areas in Gurgaon, Mumbai, Nainital, Meerut and Bhopal.[1] The Data also shows that for every four people killed in man animal conflicts, an endangered animal also loss.

According to a latest government data, as many as 187 elephants and around 110 tigers were killed in such conflicts. Many animals were captured and summarily sentenced to a life inside enclosures, which animal and activist say in the cruelest form of punishment to be given to animals born free.[2]

If a mention is made in context of Northeastern Zone, the region is no lesser in its involvement of man animal conflict. In special reference to one of the part of Northeast, 1024 persons lost their lives in this conflict from 2001-2016 following a man-elephant conflict in Assam which is the home of Asian Pachydern.

11

Environmental Impact Assessment: A Brief Overview

Bichitra Das*

INTRODUCTION

The term Environmental Impact Assessment or EIA, simply refers to the examination or deep scrutiny of any proposed projects or developmental works before its initiation, so that its impact on the environment can be forecasted, which would thereby help the concerned organisations to stop anything in course of those on-going projects, that may lay adverse and damaging effects to the environmental surroundings around it. It is a very powerful tool in the present scenario, since it gives the concerned organisation to help preserve the natural resources, to provide prior protection to humans, lands and animals, and to maintain a balanced and a healthy ecosystem.

EIA first came to being after the Second World War, when a group of countries were much concerned about the protection of the environment and had collectively agreed to conserve the natural resources in the long run, which would serve human needs in the days to come. USA became the first country to enact legislation

---

BALLB(H) 6th Semester, Centre for Juridical Studies, Dibrugarh University, Dibrugarh,Assam on EIA. The United Nations Conference on the Environment in Stockholm in 1972 and subsequent conventions formalized EIA.

NEED FOR EIA

The significance of EIA can be well understood by considering the very example of the increasing global population. Reasons obscuring to it can be many. Nevertheless there needs to be adequate availability of fresh living lands to help sustain life and livelihood. While the former is a matter of laying down tiring efforts towards protection, the latter is equally responsible for holding a firm grip so as not to let the deeds of substantial damage, slip away from the hold. With the advancement of science and technology, the number of various types of industries has largely sprung up. Thus, associated sophisticated projects have found way to be implemented in insanely different ways. What remains untouched is the awareness of the undesired and unwanted bi-products of progressive damage. Thus, EIA proves to be the best instrument to screen out what needs to be done and what isn't.

THE UNITED NATIONS ENVIRONMENT PROGRAMME:

The United Nations Environment Programme (UNEP) is the overall coordinating environmental organization of the United Nations system. Its mission is to provide leadership and encourage partnerships in caring for the environment by inspiring, informing and enabling nations and people to improve their quality of life without compromising that of future generations. UNEP's Economics and Trade Branch (ETB) is one of the branches of the Division of Technology, Industry and Economics (DTIE). Its mission is to enhance capacities of countries, particularly developing countries and countries with economies in transition, and to integrate environmental considerations in development planning and macroeconomic policies, including trade policies. The work programme of the Branch consists of three main components: economics, trade and financial services. The Economics component of the programme focuses on enhancing the capacities of countries, particularly developing countries and countries with economies in transition, to develop and implement assessment tools and economic instruments. UNEP's work on assessments includes the further development and promotion of environmental impact assessment as an effective tool to integrate environmental considerations at the project, programme and policy levels to achieve sustainable development.

PHASES OF ENVIRONMENTAL IMPACT ASSESSMENT

The first phase of an environmental assessment is called an Initial Environmental Examination (IEE) and the second is Environmental Impact Studies (EIS) or simply detailed EIA.

a) Initial Environmental Examination (IEE)

IEE is carried out to determine whether potentially adverse environmental effects are significant or whether mitigation measures can be adopted to reduce or eliminate these adverse effects. The IEE contains a brief statement of key environmental issues, based on readily available information, and is used in the early phase of project planning. The IEE also suggests whether in-depth studies are needed. When an IEE is able to provide a definite solution to environmental problems, an EIA is not necessary. IEE also requires expert advice and technical input from environmental specialists so that potential environmental problems can be clearly defined.

b) Environmental Impact Assessment (EIA)

EIA is a procedure used to examine the environmental consequences or impacts, both beneficial and adverse, of a proposed development project and to ensure that these effects are taken into account in project design. The EIA is therefore based on predictions. These impacts can include all relevant aspects of the natural, social, economic and human environment. The study therefore requires a multi-disciplinary approach and should be done very early at the feasibility stage of a project. In other words, a project should be assessed for its environmental feasibility.

EIA IN DIFFERENT COUNTRIES

United States

The National Environmental Policy Act of 1969 (NEPA), enacted in 1970, established a policy of environmental impact assessment for federal agency actions, federally funded activities or federally permitted/licensed activities that in the U.S. is termed "environmental review" or simply "the NEPA process. The law also created the Council on Environmental Quality, which promulgated regulations to codify the law's require-ments. Under United States environmental law and Environmental Assessment (EA) is compiled to determine the need for an *Environmental Impact Statement* (EIS). Federal or federalized actions expected to subject or be subject to significant environmental impacts will publish a Notice of Intent to Prepare an EIS as soon as significance is known. Certain actions of federal agencies must be preceded by the NEPA process. Contrary to a widespread misconception, NEPA does not prohibit the federal government or its licensees/permittees from harming the environment, nor does it specify any penalty if an environmental impact assessment turns out to be inaccurate, intentionally or otherwise. NEPA requires that plausible statements as to the prospective impacts be disclosed in advance. The purpose of NEPA process is to ensure that the decision maker is fully informed of the environmental aspects and consequences prior to making the final decision.

United Kingdom

The process of Environmental Impact Assessment is governed by the Town and Country Planning (Environmental Impact Assessment) Regulations 2011 as amended. These regulations apply the EU directive "on the assessment of the effects of certain public and private projects on the environment" to the planning system in England.

The regulations only apply to certain types of development and/or projects. They can even apply to 'permitted development' which is development for which you do not need to get planning permission. They do not apply to development consented under other regimes which are subject to separate Environmental Impact Assessment regulations.

India

The Environmental Impact Assessment (EIA) experience in India indicates that the lack of timely availability of reliable and authentic environmental data has been a major bottle neck in achieving the full benefits of EIA. The environment being a multi-disciplinary subject, a multitude of agencies is involved in collection of environmental data. However, no single organization in India tracks available data from these agencies and makes it available in one place in a form required by environmental impact assessment practitioners. The main laws in action are the Water Act (1974), the Indian Wildlife (Protection) Act (1972), the Air (Prevention and Control of Pollution) Act (1981) and the Environment (Protection) Act (1986), Biological Diversity Act (2002). The responsible body for this is the Central Pollution Control Board. Environmental Impact Assessment (EIA) studies need a significant amount of primary and secondary environmental data. Primary data are those collected in the field to define the status of the environment (like air quality data, water quality data etc.). Secondary data are those collected over the years that can be used to understand the existing environmental scenario of the study area. The environmental impact assessment (EIA) studies are conducted over a short period of time and therefore the understanding of the environmental trends, based on a few months of primary data, has limitations. Ideally, the primary data must be considered along with the secondary data for complete understanding of the existing environmental status of the area. In many EIA studies, the secondary data needs could be as high as 80% of the total data requirement. EIC is the repository of one stop secondary data source for environmental impact assessment in India.

CONCLUSION

The very existence of this world is based on the fact of how well we are being able to take care of the surreal environment around us. No matter how long we advance and create the best of the gizmos and gadgets, we still have to carry alongside us, the notion of not harming or negatively influencing the natural surrounding around us. The importance and application of EIA is boundless. Yet, every hour that passes by, sadly records the status of a precious part of the environment somewhere in the world, being degraded away. The sole responsibility of EIA is not sufficient to mitigate the losses, possibly to be incurred. We need to initially spread awareness of the concerns, which sooner or later would recur, providing us another challenging task to deal with.

Emphasis should be laid on the key factors, most of which runs in the list of the 'basic amenities of life' in accordance to a living being. These include safety to lands, water, air, ecosystem, atmosphere, etc.

Though most of the developed and developing nations have already implemented the different aspects of assessing the environment of their domain via different appointed agencies, yet care must be taken to ensure the best of the services in the form of keen scrutiny that would mean the progressive sinking slope of the curve of damage.

All persons associated with the EIA in their respective countries must selflessly render their services as this is not for their own country, but a service to the entire race of humans. Care must be taken so as to not adulterate the true reports, which otherwise would lead to more number of tasks to be performed, the worse of which can be the substantial isolation of the project, taken at hand to be assessed for environmental safety.

12

Climate Change Law and its Significance in India

Binita Bania and Prinjee Baruah*

INTRODUCTION

We, the human beings are regarded as the most superior species in the world having the capacity of thinking rationally. But to what extent do we apply the ability of taking a rational decision is a matter of question. When it comes to follow the laws and regulations, humans hardly comply with them even though they are in written forms, in statutes, in Constitution and so on. Human beings are somewhere lost being more materialistic, more competitive and less sensitive. In the mean time we even are losing the ability to think about the relationship we have with the nature. Somewhere we are over utilizing and over exploring whatever nature has gifted to us. Human activities have almost resulted in the death of environment causing what is known to be environmental degradation. Climate change is one among them.

So what is the solution? Of course we cannot totally stop the change in climatic condition as is backed by many other reasons as well. But appropriate steps if taken by people, will bring a devastating effect to at least bring it in control. How much

* BALLB(H) 6th Semester, Centre for Juridical Studies, Dibrugarh University, Dibrugarh, Assam

impact can a small step by every single State will have, can be known from different attempts by nations made through various conventions and treaties. A non-binding treaty like the Paris Climate Deal is gaining importance by almost all the countries of the world and even impelled President Donald Trump to roll back Obama-era climate policies. The sooner we realize, the safer humanity and humankind will be.

When nuclear acquisition has become so necessary in the 21st century by the nations, it has caused great threat to the human civilization. As was said by Stephen Hawking, humanity has only around 1000 years left. The introduction of Paris-climate agreement is an effort to restrain each country's greenhouse gas emission which will help combat climate change. After China, India has world's deadliest air pollution and the two nations together contribute 83% to world's climate change.

The present paper is an attempt to put light upon the existing laws on climate change in India and their significance in the present time.

Human activity has resulted to cause increase rate of carbon dioxide produced by the use of fossil fuel. Pollution caused to air and water is regarded as one of main cause of climate change and when India is growing rapidly, green house emission from energy is also increasing. Climate change affects the whole biodiversityin total and is a slow poison to the human kind.

INTERNATIONAL LAW OF CLIMATE CHANGE

Until Second World War, no important laws or conventions to environment protection was framed. But a few protocols, treaties and conventions can be regarded as a turning point to the development of environment protection laws globally. Some among them are:

1. Kyoto Protocol, 1997
2. The Antarctic Treaty, 1959
3. Convention For Conservation of Antarctic Seal,1972
4. The Montreal Protocol on Substances that Deplete the Ozone Layer

5. Protocol to the Vienna Convention for the protection of Ozone Layer,1987

The answer as to why international norms or principles is necessary for environment protection is obvious from the fact that there is race for power among nations which include possession of nuclear weapon. In the due course, they fail to recognize the most important problem of climate change and tend to ignore it. Environmental Law incorporates a number of principles which are violated by nuclear weapons.

Above mentioned are only a few of the landmark steps taken towards climate change issue. In the recent years, most of the developed counties along with some other developing counties like India and China are struggling to find a solution to the problem. The Paris Climate Deal is one among them. If it is ratified by all nations, it will definitely bring a change to the system in total.

LEGAL FRAMEWORK ON ENVIRONMENTAL PROTECTION IN INDIA

The year 1860 is regarded as the landmark period in the history of legal control of environmental pollution. Attempts were made in this year for the first time to impose criminal sanction to those involved in polluting environment mainly to air and water.

Chapter XIV of **The Indian Penal Code** under Sections 268 to 294 deals with offences which affect the public health, safety, convenience and morals and impose penalty to those who threaten the life of the people by polluting the environment.

Some of the preventive measures for the protection of our environment is mentioned in **The Code of Criminal Procedure.** Chapter X, Part B having Section 133 to 143 and Part C containing Section 144 can be most effective and speedy remedy for preventing and controlling public nuisance which cause air and water pollution.

A. Air Protection

1. The Air (Prevention and Control of Pollution) Act of 1981, No. 14, 29 March 1981, to provide for the prevention, control and abatement of air pollution.

2. The Ozone Depleting Substances (Regulation and Control) Rules, 17 July 2000, to enact rules for regulating ozone depleting substances.

B. Energy

1. The Energy Conservation Act of 2001, No. 52, 29 September 2001, to provide for efficient use of energy and its conservation and for matters connected therewith or incidental thereto.

2. Energy Conservation (Amendment) Act, 2010, No. 28, 24 August 2010, to amend the Energy Conservation Act of 2001 Electricity Act 2003, Amended 2007, to better coordinate development of the power sector by providing a comprehensive framework for power development.

C. Forests

1.The Indian Forest Act of 1927, No. 16, 21 September 1927, to consolidate the law relating to forests, the transit of forest produce and the duty livable on timber and other forest produce.

2. Forest Conservation Act of 1980, No. 69, 27 December 1980, to provide for the conservation of forests and for matters connected therewith or ancillary or incidental thereto.

Various other Acts has been initiated in the present days trying to control and protect the environment from destruction.[1]

INDIAN CONSTITUTION AND CLIMATE CHANGE

Although no direct mention is made in the Indian Constitution regarding climate change, but the Fundamental Duties typifies some of the measures or steps that have been taken to control the growing problem of climate change. The fundamental duties as mentioned, imposes duty upon the citizens to protect environment and control environmental pollution. Article 51-A (g) reads as follows- "It shall be the duty of every citizen of India to protect and improve the natural environment including forests, lakes, rivers and wildlife and to have compassion for living creatures".

State's responsibility with regard to environment protection has been laid down under Article 48-A of Indian Constitution. The Article mentions that "the state shall Endeavour to protect and improve the environment and to safeguard the forest and wildlife of the country".[2]

Environmental case laws and legislations are important because they regulate and define the activities of humans upon the geological and biological systems that are affected by contact. Issues such as ecology, sustainability, responsibility and stewardship are often causes for legal actions and urgent judicial intervention is required. A research in the field of environment and climate change is as important in field of law as is for the scientist indulged in it.

Importance of climate change laws can be presumed through various cases decided by the apex court.

Decided Cases

1. M.C. Mehta v. Union of India "Ganga Pollution" Case (1988)

The main principle laid down was that water pollution problems, particularly discharging noxious, poisonous and polluting matter into rivers should be dealt with strictly. It must be stopped altogether as water is the elixir of life and river valleys have been the cradles of civilization. The cost of checking pollution is irrelevant looking to the widespread ramification of water borne-disease.[3]

2. In Subba Rao v. State of Himachal Pradesh

The Supreme Court ordered the closure of a bone factory which was polluting the environment by its pungent smell and making the life of the people miserable. The Court held that no person can make money in the name of public health.[4]

IMPORTANCE OF TORT LAW AND PUBLIC INTEREST LITIGATION

Most of the Jurists are of the view that those involved in polluting the environment cause a civil wrong and must be held liable for compensation. In the case of M.C. Mehta *v.* Kamal

Nath, (2000) 6 SCC213 Saghir Ahmed J rightly observed thatif a person is guilty of causing pollution can be held liable to pay exemplary damages so that it may act as a deterrent for others not to cause pollution in any manner. Application of tort law could have played a very vital role in controlling pollution but in a country like India, people pay less interest to approach the court in small cases like trespass, nuisance, negligence and so on. Otherwise, the concept of Absolute Liability from the case M.C Mehta *v.* Union of India is a perfect remedy to control pollution and the growing concern of climate change.

Human caused greenhouse gas emission is the main reason behind the increase of global temperature which will affect both natural system and human wellbeing. Although there exist many natural causes for change in the climate which include volcanic activities, ocean currents etc., human's contribution to climate change is no less. So the importance of climate change law is of great concern in the present time.

A strict law is of great significance in the present time which imposes high penalty on those attempting to harm the nature. In India where people are mostly ignorant to the terms like "climate change", "pollution", "deforestation" etc., imposing sanction will at least curb pollution to some extent.

Climate change laws help put reasonable restrictions and thereby protecting the environment, preserving the flora and fauna and controlling the pollution coming out from various sources.

LOOPHOLES OF CLIMATE CHANGE LAWS IN INDIA

The present government has taken various initiatives in the present time for protecting the environment. India's National Action Plan on Climate Change is one among them. But to achieve those goals is the crux of the matter. Most scientist claim climate change to be a continuous process that can never be stopped but there are several ways to at least put it on control. Laws are made in abundance but proper implementation has never been possible from the very primitive time.

Imposing high penalty to those involved in such activities is important as well. Initiatives must also be taken to make amendments to the existing laws punishing those involved.

India lacks in taking initiatives and encouraging the different sectors like industries to participate in Clean Development Mechanism and also in participating for other treaties, conventions to meet the challenges of sustainable development, climate change, etc.

CONCLUSION

Evidence proves to the reality of enthropogenic global warming. Either in war or perilous climatic condition, human beings have a great role to play. The role is to control oneself from polluting the environment and putting stress to the need of awareness. Global awareness to the aspect of climate change is crucial. Ultimately human has to protect the humanity from destruction.

Developed country plays greater role in climate change but it is high time for developing countries like India as well, to take effective steps regarding it. Lawyers need to take equal initiatives in the matter as in the coming years they will have to face much more climate change issues. Science and technology and cooperation among nations will lead to a transformation in the field of environment and curbing the problem as well.

NOTES

1. S.N. Myneni, Environmental Law: Asia Law House, New edition 2008, p. 615 to 638.
2. Ibid.
3. Prof.Satish C. Shastri, Environmental Law: Luckhnow, Eastern Book Company, 2012, p. 451.
4. https://lawupdaterblog.wordpress.com/2016/09/07/article-on-importance-of-environmental-laws-in-india/

13

Sustainable Development and Indian Judicary: A Critical Study

Chitta Ranjan Gogoi*

INTRODUCTION

The process of industrialization, technological advancement and urbanization has a profound impact upon the relationship of man with nature. The nature is being disturbed, degraded day by day because of the evils of men. In one hand one cannot deny the role of industrialization, urbanization and technological advancement, on the other hand one cannot deny the value of environment for human being. The notion that development and nature is not antithesis is being now promoted to save the nature as well as human civilization. The concept of sustainable development is a part and parcel of the notion that environment and development is not antithesis. The growing concern for the notion has not only been recognized at international level but also in the municipal law. The Indian judiciary has been instrumental in developing certain principles, doctrines and guidelines which promote sustainable development. Here an attempt has been

*Assistant Professor, Centre for Juridical Studies, Dibrugarh University, Assam

made to analyze the role played by the judiciary in promoting the idea of sustainable development.

BASICS OF SUSTAINABLE DEVELOPMENT

The concept of sustainable development can be seen in Stockholm Declaration and it has further been developed by the Brundtland Commission. The present concept of sustainable development has been developed by Rio declaration but the same has found its recognition in international legal instruments and national laws. In 2002, UN conference namely "World Summit on Sustainable Development" was held which also focused on sustainable development.

Sustainable development aims at well being of individual by integrating social development, economic development, and environmental conservation and protection. The most popular definition of the sustainable development is the one given by Brundtland Commission in the following words "development that meets the needs of the present without compromising the ability of future generations to meet their own needs." In Narmada Bachao Andolan v. Union of India[1] 2000 (10) SCC 664, the honourable Supreme Court of India observed that "sustainable development means what type or extent of development can take place, which can be sustained by nature ecology with or without mitigation." In other words, sustainable development is that development which promotes equitable benefits, regenerates environment. The very concept of sustainable development aims at development which protects environment while leading any developmental process. Philippe Sands has mentioned the following components of sustainable development:[2]

1. The need to take into consideration the needs of the present and future generations (the principle of inter generational equity).
2. The acceptance, on environment protection grounds, of limits placed upon the use and exploitation of natural resources. (the principle of sustainable use).
3. Role of equitable principles in allocation of the rights and obligations between various states.

4. The need to integrate all aspects of environment and development (principle of integration).

INTERNATIONAL LAW ON SUSTAINABLE DEVELOPMENT

International sustainable development law refers to the sum total of international legal principles and treaties which address the common areas between international economic law, international environmental law and international social law which aims at development that can last long.

As per Stockholm declarations principle 21, states have the sovereign right to exploit their own resources pursuant to their own environmental policies and responsibility to ensure that activities within their jurisdiction or control do not cause damage to the environment of other states or of areas beyond the limits of national jurisdiction. In 1995., the expert group meeting on identification of principles of international law for sustainable development came out with 19 principles and divided the concepts of international law for sustainable development into five categories:

1. Principles of interrelationship and integration
2. Principles and concepts relating to environment and development
3. Principles and concepts of international cooperation
4. Principles of participation , decision making and transparency
5. Principles and concepts of dispute avoidance and resolution procedures , monitoring and compliance.

The New Delhi Declaration of Principles of International Law Relating to Sustainable Development, 2002[3] came out with 7 key principles which are as follows:

1. duty of states to ensure sustainable use of natural resources;
2. equity and the eradication of poverty;
3. The principle of common but differentiated responsibilities.
4. The principle of the precautionary approach to human health, natural resources and ecosystems

5. The principle of public participation and access to information and justice
6. The principle of good governance.
7. integration and interrelationship, in particular in relation to human rights and social, economic and environmental objectives.

In 2005, Kyoto Protocol entered into force. It is an international treaty which extends the 1992 United Nations Framework Convention on Climate Change (UNFCCC) that commits State Parties to reduce greenhouse gas emissions, based on the scientific consensus.

In 2010, 10th Conference of Parties to the Convention on Biodiversity was held in Nagoya. It resulted in adoption of a strategic plan to preserve biodiversity and creation of an Intergovernmental Science Policy Platform on Biodiversity and Ecosystem Services (IPBES).

In 2012, the UN Conference on Sustainable Development (UNCSD) was conducted on two themes namely the green economy in the context of sustainable development and the institutional framework for sustainable development.

The Indian initiative on sustainable development can be grouped into few stages:

1. The first stage is of 1972-1983 . At this stage main focus was on environment and its protection. After the international development in the form of Stockholm Conference, 1972, India amended the Constitution to incorporate provisions regarding environment.
2. The second stage is of 1984-1997. It mainly focused on environment and its protection. But India embarked upon social justice and equity after the enactment of Public Liability Insurance Act, 1991.
3. The third stage is of 1998-2004. The main focus of this stage was reconciling the economic imperative with the environment and social imperatives. At this stage, keeping in mind the mandate of Convention on Biological Diversity India enacted the Bio-diversity Act, 2002.

4. The fourth stage is of 2005 and beyond. This phrase has seen the pro-active rights based approach to social welfare, justice and equity. Further, it has seen a high degree of integration between the different pillars of sustainable development.

INDIAN JUDICIARY AND SUSTAINABLE DEVELOPMENT

The Indian judiciary being the protector of the rights of people has contributed to a great extent in respect of environmental protection. The role of judiciary got its momentum when the concept of public interest litigation was introduced in India. It will not perhaps be wrong to say that in Indian environmental jurisprudence, the role of public interest litigation comes first. It is though the series of public interest litigation the judiciary has played an important role in environmental protection. The role of courts in promoting sustainable development lies in the development of principles, guidelines sand certain doctrines.

Supreme Court's concern for sustainable development can be traced back to the Vellore Citizens Forum v. Union of India[4] case. In this case recognizing the need of sustainable development it has been observed "the traditional concept that development and ecology are opposed to each of her, is no longer acceptable. Sustainable development is the answer." It was further observed that "the Precautionary Principles and the Polluter Pays Principles are essential features of sustainable development."

In Indian Council for Enviro-Legal Action v. Union of India & ors[5], the Supreme Court of India dealing with the polluter pays principles held that "the polluter pays principle means that absolute liability of harm to the environment extends not only to compensate the victims of pollution, but also to the cost of restoring environmental degradation. Remediation of damaged environment is part of the process of sustainable development."

In M C Mehta v. Kamal Nath[6], the Supreme Court of India developed the doctrine of Public Trust. The Court in this case remarked that state as a trustee under a duty to protect the environment for its beneficiaries namely people. In the words of the court "our legal system based on English common law includes the public trust doctrine as part of its jurisprudence. The state is the trustee of all natural resources which are by nature meant for public use and enjoyment. Public at large is the beneficiary of the seashore, running waters air, forests and ecologically fragile lands. The state as trustee is under a legal duty to protect the natural resources. These resources meant for public use cannot be converted into private ownership."

In T Damodar Rao v. S O Municipal Corporation, Hyderabad[7], the Andhra Pradesh High Court confronted with a question that whether the land provided as an open space in the city improvement scheme, could be allowed to be used for constructing residential quarters. The court held that owners of the area concerned can only use their property in accordance with and in conformity with provisions of the development plan.

In M.P. Ramababu v. District Forest Officer[8] held that deep underground soil and water belong to the state in the sense that the doctrine of public trust extends to them. If a person uses land in order to pollute the underground water or soil, state can interfere in the absence of any specific law.

In Association for Environment Protection v. State of Kerala[9], the Supreme Court directed that hotel/restaurant constructed on the banks of Periyar River in absence of environmental impact assessment as per condition mandated in the GO dated 13-1-1978 or obtaining clearance from Environmental Planning and Coordination Committee.

The above mentioned are a few cases decided by the higher judiciary in India which have a direct or indirect bearing upon sustainable development. It is seen that the judiciary has played a proactive role in promoting sustainable development. In India, there are plethoras of laws which deal with sustainable development. However, it is a matter of irony that the implementation of the laws relating to sustainable development is poor. The awareness among the people regarding preservation of the environment is also less. Some of the suggestions may be put forwarded in order to strengthen the sustainable development in India. These are as follows:

1. The concept of restitution as has been prevalent in many countries like USA may be incorporated under environmental statutes. The polluter pays principle to a great extent has filled up the gap that has been created for nonexistence of restitution in India. But one has to keep in mind that the role of judiciary is always case specific. Restitution measures like social service, compulsory labour may be employed to correct the damage caused to the environment by the accused convicted person. This measure can be linked to the corporate social responsibility. If any corporate body commits environmental crime then restitution measures may be employed.
2. A National legal literacy mission may be created by the Union government in coordination with state governments and local authorities to impart the basic knowledge of rights and duties of citizens under environmental laws as well as other laws. It has the potentiality to reduce the environmental degradation.
3. Environmental impact assessment should be made compulsory before establishing any industrial plant, dams etc.
4. The Government should emphasize on the generation of renewable sources of energy instead of non renewable sources of energy. It will reduce the environmental degradation to a great extent.

CONCLUSION

From the above analysis, it appears that the higher judiciary has played a significant role in the development, promotion of sustainable development perhaps, it is not an exaggeration to state that it is the judiciary's creative role through which seed of sustainable development has been sowed. In order to save the nature for us and coming generations, a concerted effort on the part of the people, executive and judiciary is need of the hour. We need to look forward keeping in mind that "man is nature's best promise and worst enemy" as has been stated by Honourable Justice V R Krishna Iyer.

NOTES

1. 2000 (10) SCC 664.
2. Quoted from G S Tiwari, Sustainable Devlopment as a Socio-economic growth strategy: Expanding Horizons of Environmental Law in India available at http://14.139.60.114:8080/jspui/bitstream/123456789/12424/1/018_Sustainable%20Development%20as%20a%20Socio-Economic%20Growth%20Strategy_Expanding%20Horizons%20of%20Environmental%20Law%20in%20India%20(435-452).pdf
3. Available at http://cisdl.org/tribunals/pdf/NewDelhiDeclaration.pdf (Last accessed on 23rd June, 2017).
4. AIR 1996 SC 2718.
5. AIR 1996 SC 1446.
6. (1997) 1 SCC 388.

14

Electronic Waste: A Growing Concern in Today's Environment; Its Implications, Regulations & Management in India

Rajitna Balakrishnan*

INTRODUCTION

Electronic waste or **e-waste** describes discarded electrical or electronic devices. Used electronics which are destined for reuse, resale, salvage, recycling, or disposal are also considered e-waste. Informal processing of e-waste in developing countries can lead to adverse human health effects and environmental pollution. Electronic scrap components, such as CPUs, contain potentially harmful components such as lead, cadmium, beryllium, or brominated flame retardants. Liquid and atmospheric releases end up in bodies of water, groundwater, soil, and air and therefore in land and sea animals – both domesticated and wild, in crops eaten by both animals and human, and in drinking water. The different categories of electrical and electronic equipment's are:

1. Large household appliances
2. Small household appliances
3. IT and telecommunications equipment
4. Consumer equipment

---

*Assistant Professor, Centre for MBA, Kannur University, Nileswar

5. Lighting equipment
6. Electrical and electronic tools (with the exception of large-scale stationary industrial tools)
7. Toys, leisure and sports equipment
8. Medical devices (with the exception of all implanted and infected products)
9. Monitoring and control instruments
10. Automatic dispensers.

The manufacturing of Electrical and Electronic Equipment (EEE) is one of the emerging global activities. The main factors identified to be responsible for the increased consumption and productions of electrical and electronic equipment are rapid economic growth, coupled with urbanization and industrialization. The Indian Information Technology (IT) sector is one of the major contributors to the global economy. At the same time, it is responsible for the generation of the bulk of E-waste or Waste Electrical and Electronic Equipment (WEEE) in India. Although the global E-waste problem has been able to attract attention across the world, not much emphasis has been given to the E-waste engendered in developing countries. Developing countries like India, today, is burdened with the colossal problem of E-waste which is either locally generated or internationally imported, causing serious menace to human health and environment. The hazardous components in electrical and electronic equipment are a major concern during the waste management phase. In the context of India, recycling of Waste Electrical and Electronic Equipment is not undertaken to an adequate degree.

COMPOSITION OF E-WASTE

E-waste consists of all waste from electronic and electrical appliances which have reached their end- of- life period or are no longer fit for their original intended use and are destined for recovery, recycling or disposal. It includes computer and its accessories monitors, printers, keyboards, central processing units; typewriters, mobile phones and chargers, remotes, compact discs, headphones, batteries, LCD/Plasma TVs, air conditioners, refrigerators and other household appliances.

The composition of e-waste is diverse and falls under 'hazardous' and 'non-hazardous' categories. Broadly, it consists of ferrous and non-ferrous metals, plastics, glass, wood and plywood, printed circuit boards, concrete, ceramics, rubber and other followed by plastics (21%), non-ferrous metals (13%) and other constituents. Non-ferrous metals consist of metals like copper, aluminium and precious metals like silver, gold, platinum, palladium and so on. The presence of elements like lead, mercury, arsenic, cadmium, selenium, hexavalent chromium, and flame retardants beyond threshold quantities make e-waste hazardous in nature. It contains over 1000 different substances, many of which are toxic, and creates serious pollution upon disposal. Obsolete computers pose the most significant environmental and health hazard among the e-wastes items. Iron and steel constitute about 50% of the waste.

E-WASTE ISSUES IN INDIA

The production of electronic waste or e-waste is one of the busiest and the fastest growing in the global industry. In Indian context, the electronics industry has emerged as the fastest growing segment of Indian industry both in terms of production and exports. Rapid economic growth, coupled with urbanization and a mounting demand for consumer goods, has increased both the consumption and the production of e-waste. The introduction of innovative electronic gadgets and appliances has become part of our daily lives, that without it, we almost that think we can never be productive or efficient. These gadgets provide us with the comfort, health and security and with easy access to information and exchange. However, this knowledge that the society has is creating its own toxic footprints.

The Information Technology Revolution of the early 1990s intensified the problem of E-waste in India. Sixty-five cities in India generate more than 60% of the total E-waste generated in India. Ten states generate 70% of the total E-waste generated in

India. Maharashtra ranks first followed by Tamil Nadu, Andhra Pradesh, Uttar Pradesh, West Bengal, Delhi, Karnataka, Gujarat, Madhya Pradesh and Punjab in the list of E-waste generating states in India. Among the top ten cities generating E-waste, Mumbai ranks first followed by Delhi, Bangalore, Chennai, Kolkata, Ahmedabad, Hyderabad, Pune, Surat and Nagpur (Guidelines for Environmentally Sound Management of E-waste, 2008).

One of the major concerns related to E-waste, particularly in developing countries like India and China, are dumping of E-waste from some developed countries. Large quantities of used electronics are typically sold to countries like India, China and other countries in the Asia Pacific region. These electronics have very high repair capability and high raw material demand. This can result in high accumulations of residue in poor areas without strong environmental laws. Major reasons for these exports are cheap labour and lack of environmental and occupational standards in Asia.

The main sources of electronic waste in India are the government, public and private (industrial) sectors, which account for almost 70 per cent of total waste generation. The contribution of individual households is relatively small at about 15 per cent; the rest being contributed by manufacturers. Though individual households are not large contributors to waste generated by computers, they consume large quantities of consumer durables and are, therefore, potential creators of waste. An Indian Market Research Bureau (IMRB) survey of 'E-waste generation at Source' in 2009 found that out of the total e-waste volume in India, televisions and desktops including servers comprised 68 per cent and 27 per cent respectively. Imports and mobile phones comprised of 2 per cent and 1 per cent respectively.

The recycling of E-waste is a major concern in India. The workers in the recycling sector are dominated by the urban poor with very low literacy levels and hence they have very little awareness regarding the potential hazards of E-waste. Among the urban poor, there are a substantial number of women and children engaged in various recycling activities which further exaggerate the problem of E-waste as they are more vulnerable to the hazards from this kind of waste. One of the major concerns related to E-waste, particularly in developing countries like India and China, are dumping of E-waste from some developed countries. Large quantities of used electronics are typically sold to countries like India, China and other countries in the Asia Pacific region. These electronics have very high repair capability and high raw material demand. This can result in high accumulations of residue in poor areas without strong environmental laws. Major reasons for these exports are cheap labour and lack of environmental and occupational standards in Asia. In this way the toxic effluent of the developed nations would flood towards the world's poorest nations.

MAGNITUDE OF THE PROBLEM WITH RESPECT TO THE INDIAN SCENARIO

In Indian context, the electronics industry has emerged as the fastest growing segment of Indian industry both in terms of production and exports. The Information Technology Revolution of the early 1990s intensified the problem of E-waste in India. Sixty-five cities in India generate more than 60% of the total E-waste generated in India. Ten states generate 70% of the total E-waste generated in India. Maharashtra ranks first followed by Tamil Nadu, Andhra Pradesh, Uttar Pradesh, West Bengal, Delhi, Karnataka, Gujarat, Madhya Pradesh and Punjab in the list of E-waste generating states in India. Among the top ten cities generating E-waste, Mumbai ranks first followed by Delhi, Bangalore, Chennai, Kolkata, Ahmedabad, Hyderabad, Pune, Surat and Nagpur (Guidelines for Environmentally Sound Management of E-waste, 2008).

The recycling of E-waste is a major concern in India. The workers in the recycling sector are dominated by the urban poor with very low literacy levels and hence they have very little awareness regarding the potential hazards of E-waste. Among the urban poor, there are a substantial number of women and children engaged in various recycling activities which further exaggerate the problem of E-waste as they are more vulnerable to the hazards from this kind of waste.

One of the major concerns related to E-waste, particularly in developing countries like India and China, are dumping of E-waste from some developed countries. Large quantities of used electronics are typically sold to countries like India, China and other countries in the Asia Pacific region. These electronics have very high repair capability and high raw material demand. This can result in high accumulations of residue in poor areas without strong environmental laws. Major reasons for these exports are cheap labour and lack of environmental and occupational standards in Asia. In this way the toxic effluent of the developed nations would flood towards the world's poorest nations.

ENVIRONMENTAL & HEALTH IMPLICATIONS OF E-WASTE

Pollutants or toxins in e-waste are typically concentrated in circuit boards, batteries, plastics, and LCDs (liquid crystal displays). The waste from electronic products include toxic substances such as cadmium and lead in the circuit boards; lead oxide and cadmium in monitor cathode ray tubes (CRTs); mercury in switches and flat screen monitors; cadmium in computer batteries; polychlorinated biphenyls in older capacitors and transformers; and brominated flame retardants on printed circuit boards, plastic casings, cables and PVC cable insulation that releases highly toxic dioxins and furans when burned to retrieve copper from the wires.

- Many of these substances are toxic and carcinogenic. The materials are complex and have been found to be difficult to recycle in an environmentally sustainable manner even in developed countries
- Most electronic goods contain significant quantities of toxic metals and chemicals like mercury, which is currently being phased out in the developed countries. Mercury is mobile and poisonous in any form - inorganic, organic or elemental. Its organic compound methyl mercury has been scientifically proved to be a neuro-toxicant that damages the brain. It is geno-toxic too as it passes through the placental and the blood brain barrier, putting the foetus at risk.

- Mercury is known to cause severe and permanent damage to the central nervous system, lungs and kidneys. It can trigger depression and suicidal tendencies and cause paralysis, Alzheimer's disease, speech and vision impairment, allergies, hypospermia and impotence. Mercury bio-accumulates (builds up in organisms) and biomagnifies (moves up the food chain). According to the United Nations Environment Programme's (UNEP) Global Mercury Assessment Report, even minuscule increases in methyl mercury exposures can affect the cardiovascular system.
- E-waste typically contains complex combinations of materials and components down to microscopic levels. The wastes are broken down in not just for recycling but for the recoverable materials such as plastic, iron, aluminium, copper and gold. However, since e-waste also contains significant concentration of substances that are hazardous to human health and the environment, even a small amount of e-waste entering the residual waste will introduce relatively high amount of heavy metals and halogenated substances. Such harmful substances leach into the surrounding soil, water and air during waste treatment or when they are dumped in landfills or left to lie around near it. Sooner or later they would adversely affect human health and ecology.

E-WASTE MANAGEMENT

There are basically four ways in which e-waste has been treated till date. But none has been found to be fully satisfactory. The most common one has been storing e-wastes in landfills, but it is replete with all the dangers of leaching described earlier. The hazardous effects are far worse in the older or less stringently maintained landfills or dumpsites. In the US, about 70 per cent of heavy metals (including mercury and cadmium) found in landfills come from electronic discards. Because of its hazardous nature, dumping in landfills have been banned in most of the states in the US and European Union.

Another method commonly used has been to incinerate or burn the goods concerned, but this process releases heavy metals such as lead, cadmium and mercury into the atmosphere.

Municipal incinerators have been some of the largest point sources for dioxins in the US and Canadian environments and of heavy metal contamination of the atmosphere. Reusing and recycling are the other ways of dealing with e-wastes. They have been preferable because they increase the lifespan of the products and therefore imply less waste over time. Re-use constitutes direct second hand use, or use after slight modifications are made to the original functioning equipment like memory upgrades, etc. However, they end up as waste eventually as they have limited life span. The reuse of second-hand electronic goods in the developing world including India falls in this category, where the waste ends up locally and where there is no adequate facility and competence to deal with them appropriately. While recycling appears to be a safe method to utilize or dispose e-wastes, it can be a misleading characterization of disparate practices-including dismantling, shredding, burning, exporting, etc. which are mostly unregulated and often create additional hazards itself. "Recycling" of hazardous wastes, even under the best of circumstances, has little environment benefit as it simply moves the hazards into secondary products that eventually have to be disposed of. One view says that unless the goal is to redesign the product to use non-hazardous materials, recycling may be a false solution. On the other hand, the Toxics Link, NGO based in Delhi holds that recycling isn't just good for the environment but also good business practice. Recycling is therefore an important solution, especially if we consider that e-waste contains many valuable and rare materials.

E-WASTE LEGISLATION

The issue of electrical and electronic equipment disposal, import and recycling has become the subject of serious discussion and debate among the Government organizations, environmentalist groups and the private sector manufacturers of computers and consumer electronic equipment's. E-waste is going to be a big problem in the future due to modern life style and increase in the living standards of people and augmentation of economic growth. The issue was brought to the notice of Parliament and Government on 23 December 2005, a Private Member's Bill on 'The Electronic Waste (Handling and Disposal) Bill, 2005' was introduced in Rajya Sabha by Shri Vijay J. Darda, Hon'ble Member from Maharashtra. It may be mentioned that after the enactment of the Environment Protection Act, 1986, the Central Pollution Control Board (CPCB) was delegated the functions to implement rules on hazardous wastes, bio-medical wastes, municipal solid wastes and plastic wastes. Under the purview of the CPCB, the Division of Hazardous Waste Management has been overseeing the management of e-waste. According to the CPCB, there are 36,165 industries in the country generating about 6.2 million MT hazardous waste every year, of which land fillable waste is 2.7 million MT, incinerable waste 0.41 million MT and recyclable hazardous waste 3.08 million MT.109. Besides, as per the Department of Commerce, Ministry of Commerce and Industry, Government of India, over 10,000 items, including hazardous items, are imported to India The Hazardous Waste (Management and Handling) Rules, 2003.

In 1986, India enacted its first comprehensive environmental law, namely, the Environmental (Protection) Act, 1986 (EPA) after the Bhopal Gas tragedy and as a commitment under the Stockholm Conference in 1972. Section 3 of the Environment (Protection) Act, 1986, gives all encompassing powers of setting standards, laying down procedures and supervision on the Central Government. The Rules under the EPA bestows upon the Union Government comprehensive powers to take all such measures as is necessary or expedient for the purposes of protecting and improving the quality of environment and preventing, controlling and abating environmental pollution.

However, some provisions contained in some specific policies enable import of e-waste. For instance, India's EXIM (export-import) policy allows import of the second hand computers not more than 10 years old, besides letting computers in as donations. The Foreign Trade (Development and Regulation) Act, 1992 provides for import of computers and peripherals from zones which have been set up primarily for export, i.e. Export Oriented Units (EOU), Exports Processing Zones (EPZ), Software Technology Parks (STP) and Electronics Hardware Technology Parks (EHTP) at a zero custom duty. These computers can be donated to the recognized non-commercial educational institutions, registered charitable hospitals, public libraries, public-funded research and development establishments and organizations of the Government.

POLICY LEVEL INITIATIVES IN INDIA

In view of the ill-effects of hazardous wastes to both environment and health, several countries exhorted the need for a global agreement to address the problems and challenges posed by hazardous waste. However, the policy level initiatives regarding E-waste in India needs immediate attention. Following are some of the policy level initiatives in India regarding E-waste.

THE HAZARDOUS WASTES (MANAGEMENT AND HANDLING) AMENDMENT RULES, 2003

Under Schedule 3, E-waste is be defined as "Waste Electrical and Electronic Equipment including all components, sub-assemblies and their fractions except batteries falling under these rules".

GUIDELINES FOR ENVIRONMENTALLY SOUND MANAGEMENT OF E-WASTE, 2008

This guideline was a Government of India initiative and was approved by Ministry of Environment and Forest and Central Pollution Control Board.

THE E-WASTE (MANAGEMENT AND HANDLING) RULES, 2011

This is the very recent initiative and the only attempt in India meant solely for addressing the issues related to E-waste. According to this regulation, 'electrical and electronic equipment' means equipment which is dependent on electric currents or electro-magnetic fields to be fully functional and 'e-waste' means waste electrical and electronic equipment, whole or in part or rejects from their manufacturing and repair process, which are intended to be discarded. These rules are meant to be applied to every producer, consumer or bulk consumer involved in manufacturing, sale purchase and processing of electrical and electronic equipment, collection centers, dismantlers and recyclers of e-waste.

CONCLUSION

Electronic equipment and therefore e-waste are everywhere in our society. The pollution caused by their irregular management substantially degraded the environment mostly in poorer countries, receiving them for recycling and recovery of their valuable metals. Environmental activists opine that environment protection laws in India are not stringent enough to address the issues relating to either domestic waste or imports of hazardous waste including e-waste. We also do not have appropriate technology to ascertain the quantum and quality of wastes in the imported items. Considering the future scenario, it is imperative that the safe management of waste is done in an organized manner with sufficient resources and sustainable recycling technologies on the one hand and effective legislations and monitoring mechanisms on the other.

REFERENCES

Amit Jain, 'Global e-waste growth' in Rakesh Johri, e-waste: Implications, regulations and management in India and current global best practices, TERI, New Delhi, 2008.

Alexander Janz and Bernd Bilitewski, 'Hazardous substances in waste electrical and electronic equipment' in Rakesh Johri, e-waste: Implications, regulations and management in India and current global best practices, TERI, New Delhi, 2008.

Baldev Singh (ed.), Jawaharlal Nehru on Science & Society. A collection of his writings and speeches, Nehru Memorial Museum & Library, New Delhi, 1988.

M.P.Ram Mohan, Iti Garg and Gayatri Kumar 'Regulating E-waste: a review of the international and national legal framework on E-waste' in Rakesh Johri, e-waste: Implications, regulations and management in India and current global best practices, TERI, New Delhi, 2008.

Sagata Sarkar, 'Current Status & Challenges of the e-Waste Industry', Presentation at the National Forum on e-Waste, Organized by CII & MoEF, 26 May, 2010, India Habitat Centre, New Delhi.

Satish Sinha, 'Dark shadows of digitization on Indian horizon' in Rakesh Johri, E-waste: Implications, regulations and management in India and current global best practices, TERI, New Delhi, 2008.

TN Khoshoo and John S Moolakkattu, Mahatma Gandhi and the Environment, The Energy and Resources Institute, New Delhi, TERI Press, 2010.

Tzvi Levinson, Christina Folman, and Julia Lietzmann, 'e-waste legislation in the European Union and the Basel Convention' in Rakesh Johri, E-waste: Implications, regulations and management in India and current global best practices, TERI, New Delhi, 2008.

15

Adopting Rural Extension and Environmental Friendly Farming Technologies for Realising Environmental Sustainability

Surabhila P*

INTRODUCTION

Addressing the common need for food, feed, fibre and fuel requires a global action plan to increase agricultural output in an environmentally sustainable, economically feasible and socially responsible manner. At the heart of the solution are farmers. They are the ones who grow our crops, manage the land, and safeguard biodiversity. The global population has almost tripled since 1950. By 2030, there will be an additional 1.7 billion mouths to be fed, most of who are from developing countries. To cope with this reality, the farmers need to double or even triple food production by 2050. However, the farming policies have neglected the critical role the farmers have, especially small holder farmers, must play in making sustainable development a reality. The development pressure is acute. The ratio of arable land to population is expected to decline to 55% by 2030. By 2025, 1.8 million people will be living with acute water scarcity. Simultaneously, climate change

---

*Asst.Director, Centre for MBA, Kannur University, Nileswaram Campus

will put regional and global food supplies at risk. The basic livelihoods of hundreds of millions of people will be threatened.

Majority of Indian population inhabits rural areas and 80% of the population depends on agriculture for their livelihood. Paradoxically, a national household survey established that poverty is concentrated in rural areas in general and agricultural areas in particular. This is because agriculture, as a dominant land rule and economic activity, is a double edged sword, necessary for daily livelihood but not giving escape from poverty. Where poverty and food insecurity are dominant, they provoke short term behavior and attitude towards natural resources in pursuit of basic survival which is inimical to environmental integrity. Such interactions might result in undesirable consequences like poor farming practices as survival need conflict with protection of viable agricultural ecosystems. Shortage, high cost of labour and low returns are forcing farmers and even householders to resort to the use of weedicides. This suggests that agriculture, poverty and environmental degradation are linked to insufficiency of knowledge and skills, awareness of the market possibilities and the basics of land management. This further affirms the need to educate farmers, connect farmers' community throughout the country who have access to information on market demand, prices, good agricultural practices, quality agricultural inputs supported by a technology enabled robust transaction platform that facilitates all their offline activities should also focus on creation of alternative to the existing practice of agricultural trade.

OBJECTIVES OF THE STUDY

- To dwell into the myriad of undesirable agricultural practices in India.
- To explain the ecological problems associated with undesirable agricultural practices.
- To determine the measures for Sustainable Farm Management.
- To explore the way forward for environmental sustainability through agricultural development.

THE EXTEND OF UNDESIRABLE AGRICULTURAL PRACTICES IN INDIA

The use of weedicides rose from 27.26 tonnes during 2011-12 to 140.36 tonnes during 2013-14. Their use dipped to 22.45 tonnes during 2012-13. With increasing incidence of life-threatening diseases in the country being linked to pesticide residues in agricultural produce, India is taking too big a risk. The use of chemical pesticides in food crops in the country has to come down. Eco-friendly methods, including bio-controls need to find acceptance among farmers in the country. Sources reveals that costs of new pesticides are prohibitive and farmers tend to use cheaper pesticides such as lambdacyhalothrin, quinalphos, cypermethrin, fenvalarate and glyphosate, which is a widely-used weedicide. Studies on the issue of pesticide residue in vegetables showed that Kerala alone consumed 65 tonnes of the insecticide chlorpyriphos between 2011-12 and 2013-14. Use of quinalphos, another insecticide, during the same period was 59 tonnes. During the same period, 52 tonnes of new pesticide, chlorantraniliprole (Green category), was used.

THE HAZARDS OF TOXIC PESTICIDES ON ENVIRONMENT

Fertilizers and pesticides both have definite pros and cons associated with their use. Both types of chemical tend to increase yields, and thus make a significant difference in food production, particularly in countries that struggle periodically with famines. On the other hand, they both can cause water pollution when erosion carries the chemicals off of farms along with eroded soils after each rainfall.

The impact of pesticides consists of the effects of pesticides on non-target species. Pesticides are chemical preparations used to plant fungal or animal pests. Over 98% of sprayed insecticides and 95% of herbicides reach a destination other than their target species, because they are sprayed or spread across entire agricultural fields. Runoff can carry pesticides into aquatic environments while wind can carry them to other fields, grazing areas, human settlements and undeveloped areas, potentially affecting other species. Other problems emerge from poor production, transport and storage practices. Over time, repeated application increases pest resistance, while its effects on other species can facilitate the pest's resurgence. Each pesticide or pesticide class comes with a specific set of environmental concerns. Such undesirable effects have led many pesticides to be banned, while regulations have limited and/or reduced the use of others. Over time, pesticides have generally become less persistent and more species-specific, reducing their environmental footprint. However, the global spread of pesticide use, including the use of older/obsolete pesticides that have been banned in some jurisdictions, has increased overall.

Soil is another critical area where investments are needed. Due to poor organic matter incorporation, organic carbon in soil is below the required level in most parts of India. Indiscriminate use of chemical fertilizers has further eroded soil health. Many methods of soil enrichment including: recycling of organic matter and converting "waste to wealth", have been demonstrated on the ground by scientists as well as farmers. The task at hand is to scale up these for greater farmer uptake. This would also mean a reframing of the current fertilizer subsidy regime, which is heavily biased in favour of synthetic chemical fertilizers. Though there is a growing awareness about the harmful effects of chemical pesticides on environment and human beings, the fact still remains that chemical pesticide use has gone up over the years. The pesticides used in India are more harmful than those in many other parts of the world. There is an urgent need to promote alternative ways of pest management, such as Non-pesticidal Management (NPM) practices to eventually phase out the use of synthetic pesticides and make agriculture chemical free. It is critically important that agricultural cropping systems be complementary to maintaining healthy productive ecosystems, which are essential to human well-being.

USE OF FERTILIZERS, MANURES AND PESTICIDES FOR SUSTAINABLE FARM MANAGEMENT

Optimum crop production depends on inputs of commercial fertilizer and herbicides. Today's technology-based agricultural practices have had a huge effect on increased food production across the prairies. Generally, the economic effects of increased production have been very positive; however, the ecological effects are not always as positive.

Commercial fertilizers and animal manure are used to increase crop yields and to replace soil nutrients removed with harvested crops. Both have been valuable in reversing the trend of declining soil productivity and soil nutrients. Research across western Canada has clearly shown that added fertilizer not only increases crop yields, but also builds soil organic matter when more crop residue and root matter are returned to the soil.

SAFEGUARD NATURAL RESOURCES

Land management should be improved through the widespread adoption of sustainable practices of land use.

- Conservation agriculture can be used to prevent soil erosion and land degradation.
- Manage watersheds and water use more efficiently.
- Protect wildlife habitat and biodiversity through an integrated ecosystems approach.
- Provide incentives for improving ecosystem services.

NEED FOR BROAD-BASED, KNOWLEDGE-CENTRED APPROACH TO AGRICULTURAL DEVELOPMENT

Innovative mechanisms have been introduced to supplement agriculture. Passing on relevant knowledge and skills to enhance how farmers use their land to increase productivity and fertility has been typically been performed through agriculture extension. Failures in rural land uses have been linked to inadequacies in the extension function. Where extension has been effective, case studies show a positive outcome. This suggests that extension can enhance sustainable land use, if adapted to support stewardship alongside uses like agriculture.

Although not only one reason, failures in agricultural research and extension services are identified as important causes of environmental and productivity decline. Extension is means of transmission of knowledge and skills to farmers to enable them to improve the productivity of the land. Falling productivity is linked to the ineffectiveness or implementation of inappropriate extension methods, limited use of science, poor land and husbandry practices, and week research extension – farmer linkages. The need to revamp environmental and land use standards, and in turn reverse poverty trend for the population implies the system must take initiative to embrace land stewardship as a tool to achieve sustainability.

The approach starts with focusing on farmers and the tools and information they need to steward land, grow crops, bring in their harvest and then get it to market. While modern agricultural technologies and management approaches have doubled the production of world food calories over the past half-century, many smallholder farmers struggle to achieve even the most basic level of subsistence. New investments, incentives and innovations are needed to achieve greater sustainability, while delivering increased agricultural production. These benefits must be made available to all farmers, recognising their role as guardians of our shared environment, biodiversity, and ecosystems. There is a need for a radical shift in thinking which places the farmer at the centre of sound and sustainable agricultural practices.

This approach – delivering productivity and sustainability - must also lead to a more equitable and efficient production system. Combined with better functioning markets, an enhanced farming system will contribute to improved economic development, providing food security, fair prices and improved land management. To succeed, any new approach must be based on a stable policy environment within which farmers can work and invest. This, in turn, requires us to establish stable, long-term policy and regulatory frameworks for the development of agriculture; to enhance national financial allocations; to direct international development assistance towards the agricultural sector in developing countries; and to undertake comprehensive stakeholder consultation processes in the design and implementation of agricultural programs.

Here comes the role of ICT – ICT with its role of providing knowledge, and skills to land users, will a provide means for the farmers to be empowered with knowledge and sensitized to keep adapting to the changing situation. The objectives of the mission are: Bridging farmer centricity and service orientation to the programs, enhancing reach and impact of extension services, improving access of farmers to information and services throughout crop-cycle, enhancing and integrating the existing ICT initiatives of Centre, and States, enhancing efficiency and effectiveness of programs through process redesign and more effective management of schemes of DAC Promoting a common framework across states.

CONCLUSION

Farming first provides a call-to-action for policy-makers and practitioners to develop a locally sustainable value chain for global agriculture. It emphasises the need for knowledge networks and policies centred on helping subsistence farmers to become small-scale entrepreneurs. Good governance is perhaps the single most important factor in eradicating poverty and promoting development. The Approach Paper to the Twelfth Plan emphasizes the need to redouble our efforts to ensure that 4% average annual agricultural growth rate is achieved, if not more. In this context Government's commitment to good governance in agriculture can significantly contribute to achieve 4% average annual growth. This is because the concern of good governance has its genesis in the sustainability of big agricultural projects that are funded by the Government through budgetary resources and/or financed by the Rural Financial Institutions through mobilizing resources from customers and the market to achieve specific objectives along with measureable development indicators. While governance acknowledges the facts that all farmers should have equal opportunity to sustainably develop agriculture for their livelihoods, food and nutritional security and poverty-alleviation, there need to have a broad and long-term perspective on good governance along with a sense of what is needed that can contribute to agricultural growth leading to environmental protection. Besides, there should be proper understanding of the historical, cultural and socio-economic complexities on which that perspective can be founded. For rural India to be vibrant, the way forward is to address the twin challenges of reviving the dynamism of the farm sector by building its climate resilience and integrating effective extension to remedy current situation.

REFERENCES

1. Annamalai, K. and Rao, S. (2003) What Works: ITC's e-Choupal and Profitable Rural Transformation. University of Michigan, Ann Arbor, MI, USA: World Resources Institute, Digital Dividend Project.
2. Anderson, J., Van Crowder, L., Dion, D. and Truelove, W. (1998) Applying the lessons of participatory communication and training to rural telecentres. In: Richardson. D. and Paisley, L. (eds) The First Mile of Connectivity. Rome: Food and Agriculture Organization. www.fao.org/docrep/x0295e/x0295e00.htm
3. African Connection Program (2003) Rural ICT Toolkit for Africa. www.infodev.org/projects/telecommunications/351africa/Rural%20ICT%20To olkit%20-%20DRAFT3.doc
4. Dr. Sanjay Kumar Dwivedi, Ajay Kumar Bharti, E-Governance in India: Problems and Acceptability, Journal of Theoretical and Applied Information Technology.
5. Nidhi Srivastava, "E-Governance in Rural India", Nidhi Srivastava / (IJCSIT) International Journal of Computer Science and Information Technologies, Vol. 6 (1) , 2015, 741-744, ISSN: 0975-9646.
6. NCAER (2005) Agriculture Sector, National Council of Applied Economics Research, New Delhi. 14. NCAER(2006) Liberalizing Domestic Agricultural Markets in India, National Council of Applied Economic Research, New Delhi.
7. Note on AGRISNET, Department of Agriculture and Co-operation, Government of India, http://agricoop.nic.in/conten1.htm#c15, last accessed on 10.9.2007.
8. Planning Commission (2007a) Draft Report of Sub-Committee of National Development Council on Agriculture and Related Issues, Planning Commission, Government of India, New Delhi.
9. Prof. T.P. Rama Rao, ICT and e-Governance for Rural Development, Governance in Development: Issues, Challenges and Strategies" organized by Institute of Rural Management, Anand, Gujarat, December, 2004

10. Sushil (2005) A Flexible Strategy Framework for Managing Continuity and Change, International Journal of Global Business and Competitiveness, 1(1), pp.22-32. 25.
11. Sushil (2007) Principles of Flowing Stream Strategy, Working Paper.
12. Tripathi R.K. and Sadamate V.V. (2002), Research-Extension Linkages through Agricultural Technology Management(ATMA) under NATP and Involvement of Krishi Vigyan Kendras in Samanta R.K. and Gowda M.J.C.(Ed.) Krishi Vigyan Kendrs- The Capacity Builder of Farmers, B.R.Publishing Corporation, Delhi.
13. Varma S.P. (1978) Indian Constitution and Government, A Textbook for Class XII, National Council of Educational Research and Training, New Delhi.
14. Volderba H. (1998) Building the Flexible Firm: How to Remain Competitive, Oxford University Press, Oxford.
15. Sunil Soni, "E- Governance in India", International Journal of Research in IT, Management and Engineering, IJRIME Volume3, Issue3, ISSN: 2249-1619.

16

Major Environmental Movements in India: An Overview

Shahana T*

INTRODUCTION

An environmental movement can be defined as a social or political movement, for the conservation of environment or for the improvement of the state of the environment. It is an international movement, represented by a range of organizations, from the large to grassroots and varies from country to country. Due to its large membership, varying and strong beliefs, and occasionally speculative nature, the environmental movement is not always united in its goals. The movement also encompasses some other movements with a more specific focus, such as the climate movement. At its broadest, the movement includes private citizens, professionals, religious devotees, politicians, scientists, non-profit organizations and individual advocates.

The origins of the environmental movement lay in response to increasing levels of smoke pollution in the atmosphere during the industrial revolution due to the emergence of great factories and the concomitant. Britain's Alkali Acts, 1863, the first large-scale modern environmental laws came to regulate the deleterious

---

*Assistant Professor, Centre for MBA, Nileswar, Kannur University

air pollution (gaseous hydrochloric acid) given off by the Leblanc process, used to produce soda ash.

The modern conservation movement was first manifested in the forests of India, with the practical application of scientific conservation principles. The conservation ethic that began to evolve included three core principles: that the human activity damaged the environment, that there was a civic duty to maintain the environment for future generations, and that scientific, empirically based methods should be applied to ensure this duty was carried out. Sir James Ranald Martin was prominent in promoting this ideology. The Madras Board of Revenue started local conservation efforts in 1842, headed by Alexander Gibson, a professional botanist who systematically adopted a forest conservation program based on scientific principles. This was the first case of state management of forests in the world.Eventually, the government under Governor-General Lord Dalhousie introduced the first permanent and large-scale forest conservation program in the world in 1855, a model that soon spread to other colonies, as well the United States.

The late 19th century saw the formation of the first wildlife conservation societies. The zoologist Alfred Newton published a series of investigations into the Desirability of establishing a 'Close-time' for the preservation of indigenous animals between 1872 and 1903. His advocacy for legislation to protect animals from hunting during the mating season led to the formation of the Plumage League (later the Royal Society for the Protection of Birds) in 1889. It is the first environmental protection society formed worldwide. For most of the century from 1850 to 1950, however, the primary environmental cause was the mitigation of air pollution. The Coal Smoke Abatement Society was formed in 1898 making it one of the oldest environmental NGOs. It was founded by artist Sir William Blake Richmond, frustrated with the pall cast by coal smoke. Systematic and general efforts on behalf of the environment only began in the late 19th century; it grew out of the amenity movement in Britain in the 1870s, which was a reaction to industrialization, the growth of cities, and worsening air and water pollution. In 1893 Hill, Hunter and Rawnsley agreed to set up a national body to coordinate environmental conservation efforts across the country; the "National Trust for Places of Historic Interest or Natural Beauty" was formally inaugurated in 1894.

In the 20th century, environmental ideas continued to grow in popularity and recognition. In 1916 the National Park Service was founded by US President Woodrow Wilson. The major literary force in the promotion of the environmental movement was Rachel Carson's "Silent Spring" about declining bird populations due to DDT, an insecticide, pollution and man's attempts to control nature through use of synthetic substances. The first Earth Day was celebrated on 22 April 1970. Its founder, former Wisconsin Senator, Gaylord Nelson was inspired to create this day of environmental education and awareness after seeing the oil spill off the coast of Santa Barbara in 1969. Greenpeace was created in 1971 as an organization that believed that political advocacy and legislation were ineffective or inefficient solutions and supported non-violent action. In 1972, the United Nations Conference on the Human Environment was held in Stockholm, and for the first time united the representatives of multiple governments in discussion relating to the state of the global environment. This conference led directly to the creation of government environmental agencies and the UN Environment Program.

FACETS OF ENVIRONMENTAL MOVEMENTS

- The conservation movement seeks to protect natural areas for sustainable consumption, as well as traditional (hunting, fishing, trapping) and spiritual use.
- Environmental health movement dates at least to Progressive Era, and focuses on urban standards like clean water, efficient sewage handling, and stable population growth. Environmental health could also deal with nutrition, preventive medicine, aging, and other concerns specific to human well-being.
- Environmental justice is a movement that began in the U.S. in the 1980s and seeks an end to environmental racism and prevent low-

income and minority communities from an unbalanced exposure to highways, garbage dumps, and factories. The Environmental Justice movement seeks to link "social" and "ecological" environmental concerns, while at the same time preventing de facto racism, and classism.

- Ecology movement could involve the Gaia Theory, as well as Value of Earth and other interactions between humans, science, and responsibility.
- Bright green environmentalism is a currently popular sub-movement, which emphasizes the idea that through technology, good design and more thoughtful use of energy and resources, people can live responsible, sustainable lives while enjoying prosperity.
- Deep Ecology is an ideological spinoff of the ecology movement that views the diversity and integrity of the planetary ecosystem, in and for itself, as its primary value.
- The anti-nuclear movement opposes the use of various nuclear technologies. The initial anti-nuclear objective was nuclear disarmament and later the focus began to shift to other issues, mainly opposition to the use of nuclear power. There have been many large anti-nuclear demonstrations and protests. Major anti-nuclear groups include Campaign for Nuclear Disarmament, Friends of the Earth, Greenpeace, International Physicians for the Prevention of Nuclear War, and the Nuclear Information and Resource Service.

MAJOR ENVIRONMENTAL MOVEMENTS IN INDIA

A large number of environmental movements have emerged in India especially after 1970s. These movements have grown out of a series of independent responses to local issues in different places at different times. The emergence of environmental movements is not restricted to any particular part of the country. As pointed out by Karan, P. P. (1994: 32-33): the environmental movements have emerged from the Himalayan regions of Uttar Pradesh to the tropical forests of Kerala and from Gujarat to Tripura. The main environmental movements are Chipko Andolan, Save the Bhagirati and Stop Tehri Project Committee in Uttar Pradesh, Save the Narmada Movement (Narmada Bachao

Andolan) in Madhya Pradesh and Gujarat, youth organizations and tribal people in the Gandhamardan Hills whose survival is directly threatened by development of bauxite deposits, the opposition to the Baliapal and Bhogarai test range in Orissa, the Appiko Movement in the Western Ghats, groups opposing the Kaiga Nuclear Power Plant in Karnataka, the campaign against the Silent Valley Project, the Rural Women's Advancement Society, formed to reclaim waste land in Bankura district and the opposition to the Gumti Dam in Tripura. Local movements are working against deforestation, water-logging, salinization and desertification in the command areas of dams on the Kosi, Gandak and Tungabhadra rivers and in the canal-irrigated areas of Punjab and Haryana. Some other local movements like Pani Chetna, Pani Panchyat and Mukti Sangharsh advocate ecological principals for water use.

Some of the best known environmental movements in India have been briefly described below:

1. Bishnoi Movement:

This movement was led by Amrita Devi in which around 363 people sacrificed their lives for the protection of their forests. This movement was the first of its kind to have developed the strategy of hugging or embracing the trees for their protection.

2. Chipko Movement:

Another landmark in the history of India's environmental movement was the Chipko Andolan movement or tree hugging movement. It was started in 1973 in 1973 in the Chamoli district of Uttaranchal, was against deforestation. Sunderlal Bahueguna, Gauri Devi & Chandi Prasad Bhatt were prominent leaders of this movement. It was people revolt against mindless deforestation and they did it simply by hugging trees in when the woodmen came to axe them. Like Khejri Movement, it was also a nonviolent resistance against large-scale tree felling. Large number of tribal women, under the leadership of Bachani Devi took part in the movement. Their slogan was "Chipko, Chipko" which means hug. These acts of the people finally forced the axe men to withdraw.

The Chipko movement succeeded to enforce a stoppage of tree felling for 10 years in the region.

3. Appikko Movement:

The Appiko movement was a revolutionary movement based on environmental conservation in India. It was inspired by Chipko movement. It inspired the villagers of Uttara Kannada district of Kannada district of Kannada state in southern India to launch similar movements to save their forests. In September 1983, led by Panduranga Hedge, men, women, and children of Salkani hugged the trees in Kalase forest. Appiko is the local term for hugging in Karnataka. Appiko movement gave birth to a new awareness all over South India. It is organized by Pandu Ram Hedge of Karnataka.

4. Narmada Bachao Andolan:

The most popular movement in the environmental history of India is the movement against the Narmada River Valley Project. The Narmada is the largest west-flowing river on the Indian peninsula.It is a movement against building multi – purpose dam over Narmada river which will ultimately result in flood and water logging in large area covered about 100000 people. The movement was led by Medha Patekar, Baba Amte, and Arundhati Roy. The movement used various tools of protest such as Satyagraha, Jal Samarpan, Rasta Roko, Gaon Bandh, demonstrations and rallies, hunger strikes and blockade of projects.

5. Tehri Dam Conflict:

The protest was against the displacement of town inhabitants and environmental consequence of the weak ecosystem. Tehri dam attracted national attention in the 1980s and the 1990s. The major objections include, seismic sensitivity of the region, submergence of forest areas along with Tehri town etc. Despite the support from other prominent leaders like Sunderlal Bahuguna, the movement has failed to gather enough popular support at national as well as international levels.

6. Jungle Bachao Andholan:

It began in Bihar and later spread to states like Jharkhand and Orrissa. The tribals of Singhbhum district of Bihar hubbled up a protest when the government decided to replace the natural sal forests whicth highly priced teak, a move that was termed as "a greed game, political populism".

7. Baliyapal Movement:

It is a movement against testing of missiles on the land of Baliyal villagers which may lead to infertility of soils.

8. Save Ganga Movement:

Save Ganga movement is a wide spread Gandhian non – violent movement supported by saints and popular activists across the Indian states Uttarpradesh and Bihar in support of a free Ganga. The movement is supported by Ganga Seva Abhiyanam, Pune – based National women's organization besides those of many others like – minded organizations and with the moral support from many religious leaders, spiritual and political, scientists, environmentalists, writers and social activist.

ENVIRONMENTALISM IN KERALA

The first environmental movement in Kerala traced back to the protest against water pollution caused by the discharge of chemical effluents by Grasim Industries at Vazhakkad in 1964. Vazhakkad, is a village on the banks of river Chaliyar. K.A. Rahman was the leader of this first environmental agitation in the state of Kerala. Moreover, the traditional workers in this area had also staged an unsuccessful struggle against the river pollution under the banner of Chaliyar Kakka Malsya Thozhilali Union (A union for traditional fish workers in Chaliyar). Either of these agitations produced any notable result.

The history of modern environmental activism in Kerala could be traced back Malayalam literature. The affinity with nature has been a feature of Malayalam literature since long. The literary works of prominent writers like G Sankara Kuruppu,

Vyloppilli Sreedharan Menon, P. Kunhiraman Nair, Changapuzha Krishnapilla, N.V. Krishna Varier, Edasseri Govindhan Nair, N.N. Kakkad etc, seem to play a key role in the making of environmental awareness among the people of Kerala. The nomenclature Marakkavikal (tree poets) itself indicates the dominance of environmental aesthetics in Malayalam literature. Dr. Rathi Menon's Nishabda Vasantham, the translation of 'Silent spring' was another attraction of Malayalam literary ecology.(Madhusoodhanan, 2011).

John C Jacob played a remarkable role in the history of environmental activism in Kerala. He is mainly remembered for his educational programmes among the students. In 1972, he formed Zoological Club, the first environmental organization for the students in entire south India. He had maintained good relationship with World Wild Life Fund India, which helped him to organize the first nature study camp (1974) in Kerala at Ezhimala, in Kannur district. 40 Students and 20 teachers participated in this camp. When his college authorities put some restrictions on the off campus programmes of Zoological Club, Johncy went on with an idea of forming "Society for Environment Education in Kerala", popularly known as SEEK which developed into a centre of environmental activism with unique educational programmes. People from different parts of the state were attracted to the nature study programmes organized by SEEK. Johncy had developed his own medium for environmental communication. There were two environment related magazines to his account. The first one, Soochimughi, was started in 1981 and the second, Ankh, in 1986. John C. Jacob is also closely associated with silent valley campaigning. His farsightedness actually led to the formations of large number of nature clubs in schools and colleges. The SEEK, Zoological Clubs and newly formed nature clubs collectively mobilized the support for the silent valley movement. He was in the forefront of the first protest march against the silent valley project held in 1979 at Payyannur. M.K Prasad, the well known environmentalist in Kerala, has acknowledged his role in mobilizing student support for the silent valley movement. His image as a 'man of controversy' became more significant with his decision to embrace Hinduism (Civic, 2008).

The formation of Kerala Sastra Sahithya Parishad (KSSP), 1962, popularly known as Parishad was another important event in the history of Kerala environment movement. Devagiri College in Calicut, an institution run by Catholic Church, turned to be the birthplace of KSSP. The main contribution of KSSP is in the field of science education. The campaign programmes carried out with the strong support of art and literature exerted significant influence on the process of political development in Kerala. It was through these campaigning programmes, people of Kerala conceived, the importance of environment protection, community health, public education system, energy preservation, food security, rational thinking and so on.

SAVE SILENT VALLEY MOVEMENT

The protest was against the destruction of forest, an opposition to ecologically unsustainable development, and above all, maintenance of the ecological balance. It was M.K Prasad, a teacher of Botany and an active member of KSSP, who spearheaded the Silent Valley movement. He had realized that many of Kerala's environmental problems were the result of cutting down of trees in the Western Ghats. In 1978, he unsuccessfully moved a resolution against the proposed Silent Valley Project in the annual conference of KSSP held at Kottayam. It was in this crucial juncture he built up an alliance with his fellow activists outside KSSP like John C Jacob for launching an effective campaigning against the project. He was successful in using the organizational framework of Zoological Club, SEEK and various nature clubs in different parts of the state. The first demonstration against Silent Valley project was organized at Payyannur under the leadership of Johncy Jacob. This was followed by s series of protest movements across the state. Meanwhile, a section of Marxist theoreticians like C.P. Narayanan and M.P. Parameswaran came up to support the environmentalist and produced literature on Marxian ecology. It was in this context, in spite of the difference of opinion within the organization, the KSSP decided to go ahead with its campaign against the project. It had an impressive membership of 7000 thinking people, which was effectively used for mobilizing public opinion on the need to save Silent Valley. In this connection, it collected signature of teachers, prominent citizens, students and send a memorandum to the government of Kerala. The street plays, exhibitions, seminars, discussions and debates became common in the state. The jatha organized by KSSP covered about 400 villages and the way it interacted with the common people added another chapter in the history of environment communication in Kerala. Influenced by their teachers who constituted a major part of the KSSP membership, teenagers in large number came out on the street to protest against Silent Valley project. It also succeeded to mobilize the support of opinion leaders like Dr. Salim Ali, eminent ornithologist and personal acquaintance of Mrs. Indira Gandh, K.P.S Menon, former ambassador to the Soviet Union, M.G.K. Menon, Dr. Swaminathan and several others. M.K. Prasad has acknowledged the role of these prominent individuals in the success of Silent Valley struggle. The Swaminathan Committee, appointed by the central government, finally recommended abandonment of the project, which the state government accepted in 1983.

ANTI ENDOSULFAN MOVEMENT

Leelakumari, an agricultural assistant, firstly started the struggle against Endosulfan. The agony caused by the premature death of her elder brother, due to exposure to Endosulfan induced her to work for hundreds of people poor villagers living in worst affected areas in Kazargode district. Her main contribution was in the field of litigation in which she received unprecedented support from SEEK and Thanal, two important nongovernmental organizations working in the field of environment protection. The unreceptive attitude of scientific community towards the health hazards, reported from the affected areas, and the absence of an effective legal framework to deal with the environmental impact of human activities seems to be the main problems in managing the Endosulfan issue. Sree Padhre is of the opinion that entomologist generally support industry. When the village people formed 'Endosulfan Spraying Protest Action Committee', for registering their protest, the entire Pesticide industries came together to form a common platform called Pesticides Manufacturers and Formulated Association of India (PMFA). The influence exerted by this powerful pressure group seems to delay the rehabilitation process (Sreedhar, 2011). The anti Endosulfan movement has explored the vulnerability of state when it exposed to capitalism. The response of Plantation Corporation (PCK), a public sector undertaking fully controlled by the government of Kerala, towards the agitations was suspicious. The negative attitude of many government agencies, at regional and national levels, strongly supports this argument.

CONCLUSION

From the analysis it is very clear that India has rich tradition of environmental movements in India. And we have a list of notable environmentalist who continuously fights against rising environmental issues in India. As pointed out above, a large number of environmental movements have emerged in India especially after 1970s. These movements have grown out of a series of independent responses to local issues in different places at different times. The emergence of environmental movements is not restricted to any particular part of the country.

17

Fundamental Duty of Citizen to Protect Environment in India: An Appraisal

Dhwajen Sonowal*

INTRODUCTION

We must remind the jural relation between right and duty as established by Salmond. According to him, there can be no right without a corresponding duty or duty without corresponding right. In other words, every duty must be a duty towards some person or persons, in whom, therefore, a correlative right is vested. And conversely every right must be a right against some persons, upon whom, therefore, a correlative duty is imposed (Myneni, 2010, p. 205). The rights and duties are two sides of the same coin which have correlatives between them. Now the present days, pollution free environment is a fundamental right and this can be enforced before the court of law but at the same time we have correlative duty to maintain the purity of such environment. Through this paper, it is tried to establish that every citizen has legal as well as moral obligation to protect the natural environment which is recognized by our Constitution and the judiciary of India.

*Assistant Professor, Centre for Juridical Studies, Dibrugarh University, Assam

MEANING OF ENVIRONMENT

The word 'environment' is originated from French term '*environner*' which means '*to surround*'. Etymologically, it means a sum of all social, economic, biological, physical and chemical factors, which constitute the surroundings of man, who is both creator and moulder of his own environment (Myneni, 2010, p.1).

Section 2(a) of Environmental Protection Act, 1986 of India provides the definition of the said term that it includes air water and land and the inter-relationship which exists among and between air water and land and human beings, other living creatures, plants, micro-organism and property. Similarly, Section 1(2) of Environmental Protection Act, 1990 of U.K. provides the definition of environment that it consist of all or any of the following media, namely, air, water and land; and the medium or air includes the air within the buildings and the air within other natural or man-made structures above or below ground.

DUTY TO PROTECT ENVIRONMENT IN ANCIENT INDIA

If we trace back the ancient Indian history, we will find Indian law on environment protection in Kautilya's *Arthashastra.* At that time, law was '*dharma*' and it was the *dharma* of all individual to protect the nature in the society. The people worshiped the objects of nature, such as, trees, water, land and animals etc. which gained important position at that time (Jariwala, 1992, p.1). Similarly, we may remind the cardinal principle of *Ahimsa* of Buddhism. This principle teaches us that we have moral obligation to conserve and protect natural environment and it should come from our heart. Man should not exploit natural resources and should not kill animals. It shows the love of flora and fauna.

Since the time immemorial, the Indian society has been conscious the importance of protecting environment and ecology. The main goal of social life is to live harmony with nature. The sages and saints of India lived in forests and their preachings contained in Vedas, Upanishads, Smritis, etc. are ample evidence of the society's respect for plants, trees, earth, sky, air, water and every form of life. It was regarded as a sacred duty of everyone to protect them (Jaswal and Jaswal, 2009, p.5). The Indian Judiciary has also recognised that in those days, people worshipped trees, rivers and sea which were treated as belonging to all living creatures. The children were educated by their parents and grandparents about the necessity of keeping the environment clean and protecting earth, rivers, sea, forests, trees, flora, fauna and every species of life (*Fomento Resorts and Hotels Ltd. v. Minguel Martins*, 2009, 3 SCC 57). Thus, it is the obligation of the individual or individuals but the society as a whole accepted its obligation to protect the environment (*T.N. Godaverman v. Union of India*, 2002, 10 SCC 606).

PRESENT SCENARIO OF DUTY TO PROTECT ENVIRONMENT

So far as the healthy or pollution free environment/ecology is concern, it is a fundamental right as envisages Article 21 of the Constitution of India. The constitutional courts have been interpreting that '*pollution free environment*' is the '*right to life*' in the light of Article 21, 47, 48A of the Constitution and developing environmental jurisprudence day by day. The Supreme Court held that *hygienic environment* is an integral facet of *right to healthy life* and it would be impossible to live with human dignity without a *humane and healthy environment* (*M.C. Mehta v. Union of India*, 1999, 6 SCC 9). On the other hand, enjoyment of life and its attainment, including the right to live with human dignity, encompasses within its ambit, the protection and preservation of environment, ecological balance, free from pollution of air and water, sanitation without which life cannot be enjoyed (*Virender Gaur v. State of Haryana*, 1999, 2 SCC 577).

It is admitted that the constitutional courts of India has established that right to healthy environment is a fundamental right but at the same time being a responsible citizen of India, we have a corresponding duty to preserve and protect our natural environment and to established ecologically civilized society. Duty may be both moral and legal.

The 42nd Constitution Amendment Act, 1976 has inserted Part IV-A, i.e. *Fundamental Duties* of the Constitution on the recommendation of the Swaran Singh Committee to bring in line with Article 29(1) of the Universal Declaration of Human Rights, 1948 (Jaswal & Jaswal, 2009, p.45). Before inserting the said Part, P.V. Kane has criticized that the Constitution of India has ignored the Indian tradition of duties and spoke only the rights (Kane 1962, p. 1664). Besides, the Supreme Court has also criticized in *Chander Bhawan v. State of Mysore* (AIR 1970 SC 2042) and held that it was a fallacy to think that under our constitution, there were only rights and no duties. Part IV enabled the legislatures and the Government to impose various duties on citizen.

The fundamental duties consist of Gandhian noble principles. It is obligation on the part of every citizen who seeks the enforcement of his fundamental rights not to violate the right of any other person. The then Prime Minister, Indira Gandhi said that the Chapter of Fundamental Duties has been introduced not to smother rights but to establish democratic balance. Our Constitution was notable for highlighting the Directive Principles of State Policies along with fundamental rights and neither can bear flower and fruit without performance of the duties (Morje, 1977, p.25). The Parliament of India has inserted this innovative idea of fundamental duties with a view to encapsulate the jurisprudential lacunae in the maxim that '*law is not merely right alone; the only real right of man in the society is to do his duty*' (Sud, 1977, p. 88).

FUNDAMENTAL DUTY TO PROTECT ENVIRONMENT

The fundamental duties are defined as the moral obligations of all citizens to help, promote a spirit of patriotism and to uphold the unity and integrity of India. The citizens are morally obligated by the Constitution to perform those duties. However, these duties are intended to create psychological consciousness among the citizens and are of merely educative value. They also have legal value in the sense that any laws which implement fundamental duties cannot be invalid on the ground of conflict with the fundamental rights unless such conflict is irreconcilable (Shukla, 2015, p.392). So, this obligation reminds every citizen that while enforcing his fundamental rights, he must also conscious of his duties. In other words, he cannot enforce his fundamental rights without adhering to the fundamental duties as enshrined Article 51-A (Kumar, 2010, p. 482). Thus, the Constitution and its scheme of fundamental duties are reminding us to become responsible citizen of India (Shukla, 2015, p.392).

In 1970's, due to global consciousness for the protection of environment, Stockholm Conference and other increasing awareness programme of the environmental crisis prompt the Government of India has inserted the fundamental duty to protect natural environment under Article 51-A(g) the Constitution. This Article provides the duty of every citizen of India to protect and improve the natural environment including forests, lakes, rivers and wildlife and to have compassion for living creatures. And at the same time, we can relate the Article 51-A(j) which provides individual as well as collective activity of citizen to raise the nation constantly to higher levels of endeavour and achievements.

The fundamental duty with respect to environment is intend to promote peoples participation in the protection of environment (Myneni, 2010, p.622). The protection of environment is a matter of constitutional priority. The environmental problem is the concern of every citizen and neglect of it is an invitation of disaster (*V. Lakshmipathy v. State*, AIR 1992 Kant. 57 at 66). According to M.P. Jain, the Indian citizen ought to perform their duties in an excellent manner and not half heartedly (Jain, 2009, p.1396).

ENFORCEMENT OF FUNDAMENTAL DUTY TO PROTECT ENVIRONMENT

So far as the enforceability is concern, the status of the fundamental duties are similar to that of the Directive Principles of State Policies; the former are addressed to the citizens while latter are addressed to the State, without any legal sanction for their violation. In other words, these duties are not enforceable by using judicial weapon, i.e. writ of *mandamus* or any other legal remedy. Thus, the Constitution does not make any provision to enforce this duty to protect the natural environment. However, it is expected that if a law is enacted by the legislature to enforce this provision, it shall not be declared unconstitutional on the ground of its inconsistency with the provisions of Article 14 and that of 19 (Chandrahasa, 2016, p.132).

In *A.I.I.M.S. Student's Union v. A.I.I.M.S.*, the Supreme Court of India made it clear that fundamental duties though not enforceable by law but these duties are providing valuable guidance and aid to interpretation and resolution of constitutional and legal issues. Thus, it serves as a guide not only for redressing the issue but also for constructing or moulding the relief to be given by the courts.

It is already mentioned that the fundamental duties are not addressed to the State, hence, a citizen cannot claim that he must be properly equipped by the State so that he may perform his duties under Article 51-A. However, the Hon'ble Supreme Court has issued a number of directions to the States for implementation of Article 51-A(g) in *M.C. Mehta v. Union of India*, (1988 SC 1115). In the instant case, the Court has directed the Central Government as follows:

a. To provide all educational institutions throughout the territory of India to give weekly lessons in the first ten classes, relating to the protection and improvement of the natural environment including forest, lake, rivers and wild life;

b. To get textbook written for the said purpose and to distribute them free of cost among the students;

c. To introduce short term training courses for the teachers who teach this subject;

d. Not only the Central Government but also State Government and local authorities are to introduce cleanliness weeks when all citizens including the members of state instrumentalities, such as the executive, the legislature and the judiciary should render free personal service to keep their local areas free form pollution of land, water and air.

JUDICIARY INITIATIVES TO PROTECT ENVIRONMENT AS FUNDAMENTAL DUTY

The Judiciary of India plays an important role for protecting the environment and recognized the obligations of every citizen to protect it. It is a legal duty and shall be enforce it by law. In *L.K. Koolwal v. State* (AIR 1988 Raj. 2), the Rajasthan High Court held that Article 51A assigns the duty of citizens but at the same time the State has to perform obligations and primary duties in accordance with the law of the land. If the State fails to perform such obligatory or primary duty, then the citizen has right to move before the court for enforcement of the duty cast on state instrumentalities, agencies, departments, local bodies and statutory authorities created under the particular law of the State. The Court has pointed out Salmond's jural co-relative that right and duty co-exist. There cannot be any right without any duty and there cannot be any duty without any right.

For the first time the Bombay High Court (*Goa Foundation v. State of Goa*, AIR 2001, Bom. 318 at 319) examined the question of *locus standi* from the angle of fundamental duties under the Constitution of India. In the instant case, the Court held that the Goa Foundation was a registered society and its members were citizen of India and they had a obligation to protect and improve natural environment under Article 51-A(g). The Court further held that the petitioner society had a *locus standi* to move to the Court to prevent ecological degradation, to formulate and implement programmes for rehabilitation of environment and to restore ecological balance.

In *K.M. Chinnappa and Ors. v. Union of India* (30th Oct. 2002), the Court held that the term 'environment' is of broad spectrum which brings within its ambit 'hygienic atmosphere and ecological balance'. Therefore, it is not only duty of the State but also duty of every citizen to maintain hygienic environment. The State, in particular has duty in that behalf and to shed its extravagant unbridled sovereign power and to forge in its policy to maintain ecological balance and hygienic environment.

In *sitaram Chhaparia v. State of Bihar* (AIR 2002 Pat. 134) the Patna High Court held that protecting the environment is a fundamental duty under Article 51-A(g) of the Constitution of India and the respondent company was directed to wind up the industry and the State respondents were obliged to ensure that.

When it comes down to protecting mother-nature, the protection of environment and ecology, there are no competing equalities. Law will not encourage nor protect any ecological imbalance and Courts should not decide on it. The theme is better understood to preserve it and not to violate. If anyone violate this duty then the Courts steps in to protect. It is the spirit of the Constitution of India under Article 51-A, ordaining fundamental duties to protecting environment and preserve ecological balance. Hence, blasting hills for quarrying is the antithesis of it (*Suprendra Singh v. State of Bihar And Ors.* 11 May, 2004).

The need to conserve and protect the natural resources in nationwide was recognized by Supreme Court in *State of Tamilnadu v. Hind Stone* (AIR 1981 SC 711). The Court further recognized that rivers, forests and minerals and such other resources constitute *natural wealth*. These wealth should not fritted away or exhausted by any generation. It is the moral obligation of every generation to develop and conserve the natural resources of the nation for the future generation in best possible way. In other words, we can say that it is the pious obligation which extends from present generation to future generation.

In *Kinkari Devi v. State* (AIR 1988 HP 4) Justice P.D. Desai remarked that there is both a constitutional pointer to the State and a constitutional duty of the citizens not only to protect but also to improve the environment and to preserve and safeguard the forest, the flora and fauna, the rivers and the lakes and all other water resources of the country. The neglect or failure to abide by the pointer or to perform the duty is nothing short of betrayal of the fundamental law which the state and indeed the very Indian is bound to uphold and maintain.

Being a best animal of this Earth, we should not confer upon the government rather every citizen must undertake the prevention of environment and maintain ecological balance. Besides, it is the social obligation and let us remind every Indian Citizen that it is his fundamental duty as enshrined in Article 51-A(g) of the Constitution (*Rural Litigation and Entitlement Kendra v. State of Uttar Pradesh*, AIR 1987 SC 359 at p. 364).

CONCLUSION

Today the whole global village is crying due to environmental destruction and pollution. It directly affects to human life, health and livelihood. We must not forget that the environment is the clearest example that all human activities on this earth are interconnected. Thus, it is morally indefensible to establish ecologically civilized society for the common good and to maintain its purity and sustainability for the future generation.

REFERENCES

1. Myneni, S.R. (2010). *Jurisprudence (Legal theory).* Asia Law House, Hyderabad.
2. Myneni, S.R. (2010). *Environmental Law.* Asia Law House, Hyderabad.
3. Jariwala, C.M. (1992). Changing Dimensions of Indian Environmental Law. In P. Leelakrishnan (Ed.), *Law and Environment.* New Delhi.
4. Jaswal, P.S. & Jaswal, N. (2009). *Environmental Law.* Allahabad Law Agency, Faridabad.
5. Kane, P.V. (1962). *History of Dharmasastra.* Vol. V, Bhandarkar Oriental Research Institute, Poona.
6. Morje, M.N. (1977, March). *The Fundamental Duties.* Yojana, Vol. 21.
7. Sud Arun (1977). *Our Fundamental Duties.* Journal of Political Studies, Vol. 10 No.1
8. Shukla, V.N. (2015). *Constitution of India.* Eastern Book Company, Lucknow.
9. Kumar, N. (2010). *Constitutional Law of India.* Allahabad Law Agency, Faridabad.
10. Jain, M.P. (2009). *Indian Constitutional Law.* Lexis Nexis Butterworths Wadhwa, Nagpur.

11. Chandrahasa, (2016). Enforcement of Fundamental Duties of Citizens. *International Research Journal of Management Sociology & Humanity*, Vol. 7 Issue 5.

Index

ALLE ZEIT WACH 1842

Communications and Control Engineering Series

Editors: A. Fettweis · J. L. Massey · M. Thoma

Scientific Fundamentals of Robotics 5

M. Vukobratović
D. Stokić
N. Kirćanski

Non-Adaptive and Adaptive Control of Manipulation Robots

With 111 Figures

Springer-Verlag
Berlin Heidelberg New York Tokyo

D. Sc., Ph. D. MIOMIR VUKOBRATOVIĆ, corr. member of
Serbian Academy of Sciences and Arts

Ph. D. DRAGAN STOKIĆ
Ph. D. NENAD KIRĆANSKI
Institute »Mihailo Pupin«, Belgrade
Volgina 15, POB 15, Yugoslavia

ISBN-13: 978-3-642-82203-2 e-ISBN-13: 978-3-642-82201-8

DOI: 10.1007/978-3-642-82201-8

Library of Congress Cataloging in Publication Data.

Vukobratović, Miomir.
Non-adaptive and adaptive control of manipulation robots.
(Scientific fundamentals of robotics ; 5)
(Communications and control engineering series)
Includes bibliographies and index. 1. Robotics. 2. Manipulators (Mechanism)
I. Stokić, D. (Dragan) II. Kirćanski, N. (Nenad), 1953– . III. Title. IV. Series.
V. Series: Communications and control engineering series.
TJ211.V845 1985 629.8'92 85–17340

Softcover reprint of the hardcover 1st edition 1985

Bookbinding: Lüderitz & Bauer, Berlin
2161/3020 5 4 3 2 1 0

Preface

The material presented in this monograph is a logical continuation of research results achieved in the control of manipulation robots. This is in a way, a synthesis of many-year research efforts of the associates of Robotics Department, Mihailo Pupin Institute, in the field of dynamic control of robotic systems. As in Vol. 2 of this Series, all results rely on the mathematical models of dynamics of active spatial mechanisms which offer the possibility for adequate dynamic control of manipulation robots.

Compared with Vol. 2, this monograph has three essential new characteristics, and a variety of new tasks arising in the control of robots which have been formulated and solved for the first time.

One of these novelties is nonadaptive control synthesized for the case of large variations in payload parameters, under the condition that the practical stability of the overall system is satisfied. Such a case of control synthesis meets the actual today's needs in industrial robot applications.

The second characteristic of the monograph is the efficient adaptive control algorithm based on decentralized control structure intended for tasks in which parameter variations cannot be specified in advance. To be objective, this is not the case in industrial robotics today. Thus, nonadaptive control with and without a particular parameter variation is supplemented by adaptive dynamic control algorithms which will certainly be applicable in the future industrial practice when parametric identification of workpieces will be required.

The third characteristic of this monograph is the presentation of a package for the synthesis and verification of control laws for manipulation robots with up to six degrees of freedom. Announced in Vol. 2 of the Series, this package is described in detail in the present volume. These details include: robot data entry and specification of control task, synthesis of trajectories, verification of the practical stability of the complete nonlinear robot model, simulation of the overall system, final selection of an adequate control law and microcomputer implementation. To this new quality of the monograph one should add the result relating to a detailed analysis of the numerical complexity of both nonadaptive and adaptive control. Among other points, this has also permitted formulation of the concept of a general controller for dynamic control of manipulation robots.

The monograph contains five chapters. Computer-assisted generation of dynamic robot models in analytical form is presented in Chapter 1. To permit efficient application of the models of robot mechanism dynamics to the synthesis of control algorithms, analytical representation of the variables of dynamic models and construction of real-time program code are described. It should be stated that the construction of real-time dynamics of manipulation robots is treated in detail in Vol. 4 of this Series, and only a brief description is repeated here to give autonomy to this text.

The task of nonadaptive control of manipulation robots with variable parameters is considered in Chapter 2. In contrast to Vol. 2, the problem solved in this monograph is the control robust to large payload variation - the most commonly used parameter in industrial manipulation. This chapter also provides a survey of nonadaptive control algorithms and an insight into various techniques employed in control synthesis, including the optimal regulator, "inverse problem" technique, force feedback, and decoupled and decentralized control. Algorithms for the synthesis of local controllers are described in detail. Particular attention is devoted to optimal servosystems, robust servoregulators, and regulators based on pole-placement method. A method for analyzing the practical stability of robots with variate parameters when only local controllers are applied is developed. Global control is also introduced either via force feedback or via on-line calculated dynamic robot model. Algorithms for the synthesis of both local and global control which are directly applicable to the computer-aided control synthesis as presented in Chapter 4, are described in detail.

Chapter 3 is devoted to the adaptive control of manipulators. Two concepts are considered, one based on the centralized and the other on the decentralized robot model. The application of self-tuning control strategy, algorithms based on hyperstability theory, and some quasigradient algorithms based on Lyapunov's theory are discussed within the first concept. However, the algorithms for decentralized control are much more important for practical application, because of the considerably lower numerical complexity.

Chapter 4 gives a description of the software package for robot control synthesis based on the theoretical results presented in previous chapters. All blocks of the software package, such as specification of kinematic and dynamic parameters of the mechanism, parameters of actuators, manipulation task, etc., are described in detail.

Chapter 5 is devoted to the implementation of control algorithms on today's low-cost microcomputers. The concept of a general-purpose controller, i.e., a controller capable of automatic generation of the model for a specified robot, is described. Examples of robot parameter identification by the control system are also presented. Numerous results obtained on a real manipulator are given at the end to illustrate the flexibility of control laws described in Chapters 2 and 3. They allow the readers to obtain an insight into the possibilities for realizing various types of control as well as into the advantages achievable by introducing dynamic control of robots.

This monograph is intended for all researchers in applied and theoretical robotics, robot designers, and for post graduate students of robotics. The background required for following the text includes a knowledge of the basic results from linear and nonlinear systems theory as well as a fundamental knowledge of mechanisms dynamics. Although the procedures from modern theory of large-scale nonlinear systems are used and developed in the monograph, the book has been conceived so as to allow easy following of the text and application of results to readers who are not very familiar with this theory.

The authors are grateful to Miss G. Aleksić for her help in preparing English version of this book. Our special appreciation goes to Miss V. Ćosić for her careful and excellent typing of the whole text.

May 1985
Belgrade, Yugoslavia

The Authors

Contents

Chapter 1
Computer-Assisted Generation of Robot Dynamic Models in Analytical Form

1.1 Introduction

The application of general control theory to complex mechanical systems, such as robots, aircrafts, complex hydraulic systems, etc., represents an extremely difficult problem because of the prominent nonlinearity and complexity of mathematical models of these systems. With industrial robots, which will be treated in this book, the application of such theory and the development of new control algorithms are unavoidable in order to achieve high positioning speed and accuracy. Several control concepts employing partially simplified or even exact mathematical models in on-line operation have so far been brought to an advanced level. In on-line control, the calculation of model equations must be repeated very often, preferably at sampling frequency which is not lower than 50 Hz, since the resonance frequency of most mechanical manipulators is about 10 Hz. However, the problem of forming the dynamic equations of manipulators in real time, i.e. after each 20ms or less, by means of today's microcomputers is rather difficult and complex.

In explaining a new path to solve this problem, which we have followed in this chapter, let us first mention some results in robot modelling achieved to date. It is possible to systematize these results according to different criteria. So, methods may be divided with respect to the laws of mechanics on the basis of which motion equations are formed. Taking this as a criterion, one may distinguish methods based on Lagrange's, Newton-Euler's, Appel's and other equations. The property of whether the method permits the solution of the direct or of the inverse problem of dynamics may represent another criterion. The direct problem of dynamics refers to determining the motion of the robot for known driving forces (torques), and the inverse problem of dynamics to determining the driving forces for known motion. Clearly, the methods allowing both problems of dynamics to be solved are of particular importance. The number of floating-point multiplications (divisions)/additions (subtractions) required to form the model is yet another criterion for comparing the methods. This criterion is certainly the most important one from the point of view of their on-line applicability.

The first result in the class of Lagrange's methods, which are used to solve either the direct or the inverse problem of dynamics, was reported by J.J.Uicker, [1]. Since the method referred mostly to certain classes of closed-loop mechanisms, M.Kahn [2] elaborated an algorithm for the modelling of open kinematic chains. The method was modified and preformulated by L.Woo and F.Freundenstein [3] through introducing screw-calculus, and by A.Yang [4]. N.Orlandea and T.Berenui gave a program implementation of this method [5] in the form of a program package for dynamic analysis of robots. Improved versions of this method in the sense of a reduced number of numerical operations were developed by S. Mahil [6] and M.Renaud [7]. A property common to these algorithms is that they do not employ recursive relations but closed-form expressions for the elements of model matrices. However, J.Hollerbach showed [8] that the number of multiplications/additions in these methods depended on n^4 (n - the number of degrees of freedom) and that over 5000 multiplications and approximately as many additions were required for manipulators with 3 degrees of freedom. The number of operations for manipulators with 6 degrees of freedom was more than 10 times larger. It is easy to show that these methods can hardly be implemented on today's microcomputers in real time. Namely, an average up-to-date 16-bit microcomputer (with an arithmetic processor or appropriate floating-point hardware support), can realize one multiplication and one addition in about 0.1ms. This, in turn means that about 200 floating-point multiplications and additions are implementable in 20 ms, and this is considerably less than the number of operations required in the above-mentioned methods.

M.Vukobratović and V.Potkonjak [9] developed an algorithm which employs recursive expressions for the construction of matrices of dynamic models. Although the number of operations was thus reduced by a number of times in comparison with Kahn-Uicker's method, even this method could hardly be implemented in real time, since it required several thousands of floating-point operations for a typical manipulator structure.

As may be seen from the preceding text, the algorithms based on Lagrange's equations, which permit either the direct or the inverse problem of dynamics to be solved, require too many computer efforts to be real-time implementable. This is why R.Waters and J.Hollerbach developed algorithms for solving only the inverse problem of dynamics on the basis of Uicker-Kahn's method. These procedures allow the determination of driving forces (torques) for a given known motion. The number of floating-point multiplications/additions was thus reduced to dependence on n^2 [10], or n [8]. These savings result from the fact that the inertia matrix of manipulator model is not explicitly calculated, i.e., the second derivatives of internal coordinates implicitly figure in manipulator equations. Therefore, such algorithms are not applicable to all control concepts (e.g. in [11]). In addition, regardless of the dependence of the number of multiplications on n, these methods were also shown to be hardly implementable in real time. So, in spite of the advanced preformulation of the algorithm, Hollerbach obtained that the number of floating-point multiplications amounted to 412n - 277, which gives about 1000 floating-point multiplications for manipulators with 3 degrees of freedom.

The application of Newton-Eulers' dynamic equations to modelling of joint-connected rigid bodies may be found in papers by T.Kane [12]. Kane derived dynamic equations not restricting his attention to robotic systems, but for a somewhat broader class including space vehicles (satellites) with several joint-connected rigid bodies. R.Huston made a concretization of Kane's results for robotic systems [13] and elaborated its program implementation. These algorithms permit either the direct or the inverse problem of dynamics to be solved using closed-form expressions for the elements of matrices of mathematical model. However, similarly to Kahn-Uicker's method, the number of operations required to form the model by these algorithms is very large. A much more efficient computer method was elaborated by M.Vukobratović and J. Stepanenko [14] through introducing recursive relations into the solution of either the direct or the inverse problem of dynamics. It was shown that the number of floating-point multiplications required to be performed in this method was $1.5n^3 + 18n^2 + 223.5n$. This means that even about 900 multiplications are required for a manipulator with 3 degrees of freedom. Walker and Orin [15] gave a new organization of the calculation of this method and thus reduced the number of operations to dependence on n^2. However, the number of operations was still not sufficiently reduced to make the method suitable for real time applications. A special case of Newton-Euler's method which allows the solution to the inverse problem of dynamics was treated by Luh, Walker and Paul [16]. By expressing the equations of motion of each link exclusively in local coordinate systems, they obtained a procedure much more efficient than preceding ones. According to this algorithm, the number of floating-point multiplications is 150n - 48, and this makes about 400 operations for manipulators with 3 degrees of freedom. In addition, as already noted for Hollerbach's method [8], this algorithm is not applicable to all control concepts, since it does not give the inertia matrix of the system but only driving forces and moments. Employing the preceding algorithm, J.Luh and S.Lin [17] developed, a procedure for the computation of driving forces by parallel calculation on a computer with several central processor units. The procedure was illustrated by the example of a six-degree-of-freedom Stanford manipulator controlled by 6 processor units. It was shown that the computation of the forces (torques) of actuators required about 20 floating-point multiplications and additions per one processor unit.

It follows from the preceding text that even real-time control of manipulators with no more than 3 degrees of freedom is implementable only by using several processor units in parallel operation. This is why an essential question arises as to whether the number of floating-point operations in previous methods, is really minimal. Before answering the question, let us note a property common to all mentioned methods. The described methods are independent of the type of manipulator structure and encompass the general laws of kinematics and dynamics of a system of rigid bodies, which permit the construction of mathematical models or the calculation of driving forces. One can recognize that, for a given type of manipulator configuration, the actual analytical model comprises a considerably smaller number of numerical operations. Certain indications about the validity of this hypothesis were given by M.Aldon [18], M.Vukobratović and N.Kirćanski [19, 20] and M.Renaud [20]. For example, it was shown [19] that the construction of the model of an anthropomorphic manipulator with 3 degrees of freedom required no more than 44 floating-point multiplications and 23 additions, and this is over 10 times less than in any of the above-mentioned methods. Only 352 multiplications were shown to be required for a manipulator with 5 degrees of freedom [21]. However, none of the mentioned papers gives a solution to the problem of computer-aided generation of the analytical model for an arbitrary, given type of manipulator configuration. This problem is considered in detail in the volume 4 of the series "Scientific Fundamentals of Robotics", [22], and in the paper [26]. Here, it will be presented shortly.

In the algorithm for automatic generation of the analytical model, we will assume that the parameters of a manipulator (lengths, masses, inertias, etc.) are known and will treat them as constants. Joint coordinates (angles or linear displacements corresponding to rotational or linear degrees of freedom, respectively), as well as their derivatives will be treated as independent variables, i.e., as symbols. Moreover, for the construction of matrices of dynamic model (inertia matrix, matrices of Coriolis and centrifugal effects, of gravity vector), it will be shown in Paragraph 1.2. that only joint coordinates may be taken as independent variables. Accordingly, all quantities participating in the construction of the mathematical model will be treated as functions of joint coordinates. Lagrange's method (e.g., Uicker-Kahn's) or Newton-Euler's methods (Huston-Kane's algorithm) can be used to form the matrices of the dynamic model. However, the partial derivatives of transient matrices and the inertia tensors of links figure in Lagranges's methods. Of course, it would be much more convenient if only the main moments of inertia were used instead of inertia tensors, and the appropriate closed-form expressions instead of the derivatives of transient matrices. This is why Paragraph 1.2. contains a preformulation of these methods which gives very compact expressions for the elements of dynamic model matrices. Since the procedure for this preformulation was considered in detail in [22], only the obtained closed-form expressions will be given.

Formalism for manipulating the analytical expressions using a computer will be described in Paragraph 1.3. It will be shown that any analytical expression participating in the construction of the mathematical model of a manipulator can be represented by a polynomial or by a corresponding matrix. Since these matrices provide exact descriptions of the structure of analytical expressions, i.e. polynomials, they will be referred to as "polynomial matrices".

Further on, operations between polynomial matrices allowing the construction of all elements of the dynamic model matrices will be described. It will be shown that it is very simple to implement these operations on digital computers, and, accordingly, to construct the analytical models of manipulators by means of a computer. After that, the procedure for optimal calculation of the obtained analytical model in the sense of a minimal number of floating-point multiplications/additions will be presented. Previous results have provided a basis for constructing an "EXPERT PROGRAM" which generates a program for calculating the analytical model in a desired computer language (FORTRAN, assembler, etc.). This program-code can now be implemented on the microcomputer of the control system of the robot for which the model is formed.

Operation of the described program package will be illustrated in the next paragraph using the example of Stanford manipulator with 6 degrees of freedom. It will be shown that the generated analytical model comprises a very small number of numerical operations, which, in turn, allows very short calculation time to be achieved.

1.2 A Closed Form Dynamic Model of a Robotic Manipulator

To permit precise definition of the variables participating in the construction of the mathematical model of a robot, we will first give definitions of the main notions describing the physical model of a robot mechanism. We will give the definitions of a link, kinematic and dynamic variable, joint coordinate, etc.

We consider a mechanism comprising n rigid bodies (links) interconnected by rotational or prismatic joints, where one degree of freedom of motion exists between each two bodies. The first joint performs the motion of the first link with respect to the fixed coordinate system Oxyz attached to the support.

A link of a manipulator represents a rigid body whose parameters are determined by a set $C_i(\mathcal{K}_i, \mathcal{D}_i)$, where $\mathcal{K}_i$ denotes the set of kinematic and $\mathcal{D}_i$ the set of dynamic parameters. The index i denotes the serial number of the link in the chain, counting from the support to the end-effector.

Sets $\mathcal{K}_i$ and $\mathcal{D}_i$ can be defined in different ways. For example, in most Lagrange's methods the kinematic parameters are defined with respect to local coordinate frames assigned to manipulator links. In each frame one axis coincides with the joint axis and the other with the common normal between the axes of the two adjacent joints. This is Denavit-Hartenberg's formalism [23] which is very convenient for kinematic analysis. In contrast to this approach, in Newton-Euler's methods [14] local frames are most often attached to mass centers of the links, and the axes are directed along the main axes of inertia. The parameters defined with respect to such coordinate systems are more convenient for dynamic analysis. Following the second approach the sets $\mathcal{K}_i$ and $\mathcal{D}_i$ are defined as

$$K_i = \left(\tilde{e}_i,\ \underset{\sim}{e}_{i+1},\ \tilde{r}_{ii},\ \tilde{r}_{i,i+1}\right)$$

$$D_i = \left(m_i,\ \tilde{J}_i\right)$$

$\tilde{e}_i$ denotes the unit vector of the axis of the ith joint,

$\underset{\sim}{e}_{i+1}$ is the unit vector of the (i+1)-st axis in the ith frame,

$\tilde{r}_{ik}$ denotes the vector from the center of the kth joint to the mass center of the ith link,

m_i denotes the mass of the ith link,

$\tilde{J}_i = \text{diag}\left(J_{i1}, J_{i2}, J_{i3}\right)$ is the diagonal 3×3 matrix comprising the main moments of inertia of the ith link.

The sign ~ denotes that the corresponding vector is expressed with respect to the local coordinate frame. Thus, $\tilde{e}_i$ and $\tilde{r}_{ik}$ are expressed with respect to the local coordinate frame assigned to the link i. As pointed out, ith frame is a Cartesian coordinate system attached to the mass center of the link, with the axes aligned along the main axes of inertia. Unit vectors of these axes will be denoted as $\vec{q}_{i1}$, $\vec{q}_{i2}$ and $\vec{q}_{i3}$. An example of a link is shown in Figure 1.1. The second link of an Elbow manipulator is chosen for illustration.

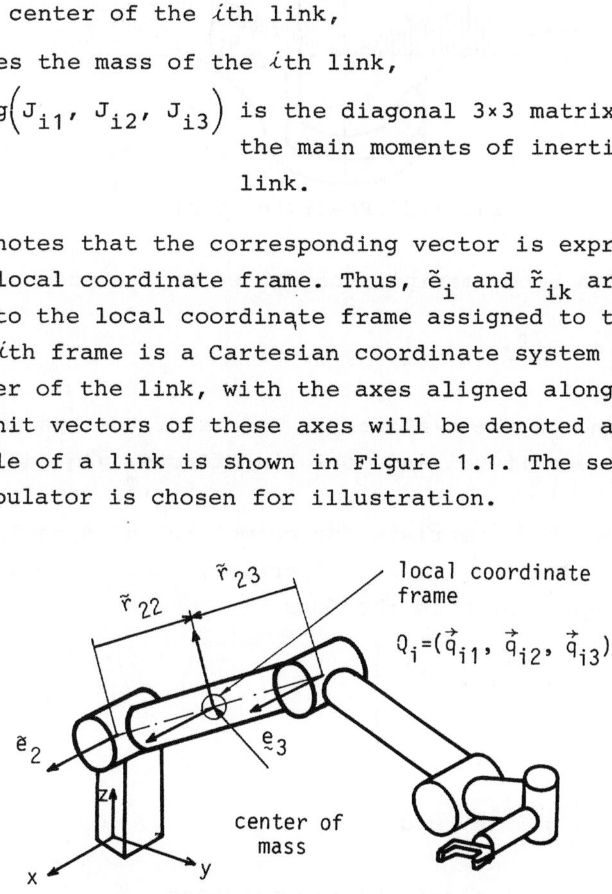

Fig. 1.1. The characteristic vectors for the second link of the Elbow manipulator

Relative position of the links is determined by joint coordinates $q_1, \ldots, q_n$. In the case of a rotational joint, q_i is defined as the angle between the projections of vectors $\vec{r}_{i-1,i}$ and $\vec{r}_{ii}$ onto the plane perpendicular to the axis of the i-th joint $\vec{e}_i$, Figure 1.2. In a sliding joint, q_i represents the linear displacement of the ith link with respect to the (i-1)-st link. The positive sense of rotation for revolute joints or displacement for prismatic joints is determined by the direction of the joint axes.

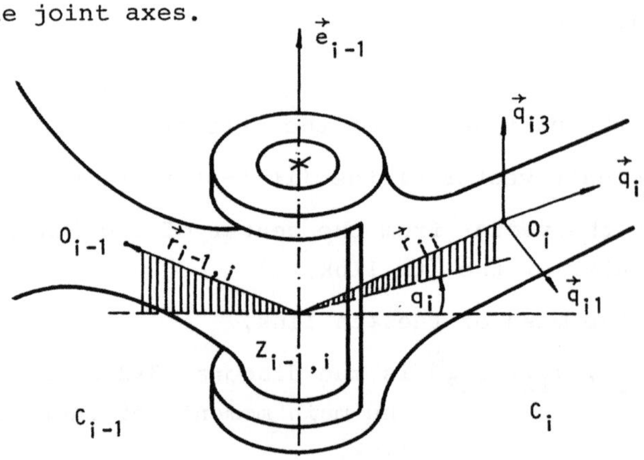

Fig. 1.2. Revolute joint

Dynamic model of a robot manipulator can be represented as [24]:

$$P = H(q, d)\ddot{q} + \dot{q}^T C(q, d)\dot{q} + g(q, d) \tag{1.2.1}$$

where $H(q, d)$ denotes the $n\times n$ inertia matrix of the system, $C(q, d)$ the $n\times n\times n$ matrix of centrifugal and Coriolis effects, $g(q, d)$ the n-dimensional gravitational vector, and $q = [q_1 \cdots q_n]^T$ - the joint coordinates vector. Vector d comprises the geometric and dynamic parameters of the mechanism (lengths, masses, inertias, etc.). The second term in (1.2.1) may be represented in the form

$$\dot{q}^T C(q, d)\dot{q} = \begin{bmatrix} \dot{q}^T C^1(q, d)\dot{q} \\ \vdots \\ \dot{q}^T C^n(q, d)\dot{q} \end{bmatrix} \tag{1.2.2}$$

where $C^i(q, d)$, $i=1,\dots,n$ are the $n\times n$ matrices.

We have seen that the matrices of dynamic model depend on joint coordinates and parameters only. This is a very important property for obtaining an efficient algorithm for forming the analytical models of robots. It should be noted that a large number of robot modelling methods referred to in the preceding paragraph do not enable obtaining the model in form (1.2.1). For example, in some methods [9, 14] the model is obtained in form $P = H(q, d)\ddot{q} + h(q, \dot{q}, d)$ where joint velocities figure implicitly. Moreover, some methods provide only the solution of inverse dynamics problem, i.e., give the model in the form $P = P(q, \dot{q}, \ddot{q}, d)$, where all variables figure implicitly [8, 10, 17].

The dynamic model matrices obviously depend on kinematic variables $K_i = \left(Q_i, \vec{e}_i, \vec{e}_{i+1}, \vec{r}_{ii}, \vec{r}_{i,i+1}\right)$ and on dynamic parameters $\mathcal{D}_i$. In addition, vectors from the set of kinematic variables depend on the instantaneous manipulator configuration, i.e., on joint coordinates $q_1,\dots,q_n$. Determination of the elements of the dynamic model matrices therefore requires these vectors to be calculated with respect to the reference coordinate system Oxyz. This is a kinematic problem solvable in different ways. We will present a simple solution to this problem using the well known formula for finite rotations of vectors. Let us assume that the mechanism is in an initial configuration in which all joint angles are equal zero. Let the unit vectors of the link coordinate systems in this position be known, and let us denote them by $\vec{q}^{\,o}_{ij}$, $(j=1,2,3)$, $i=1,\dots,n$. Now we perform rotation of all mechanism links about axis $\vec{e}_1$ by angle q_1. After that, we perform motion of all of mechanism links, except for the first, by angle q_2 about axis $\vec{e}_2$. This procedure is repeated to the (i-1)-th joint. In this spatial position the joint coordinates vector is $q = \left(q_1,\dots,q_{i-1}, 0,\dots 0\right)$. Let us now perform a rotation of the mechanism part which comprises links i, i+1,...,n by angle q_i about axis $\vec{e}_i$ (Fig. 1.3).

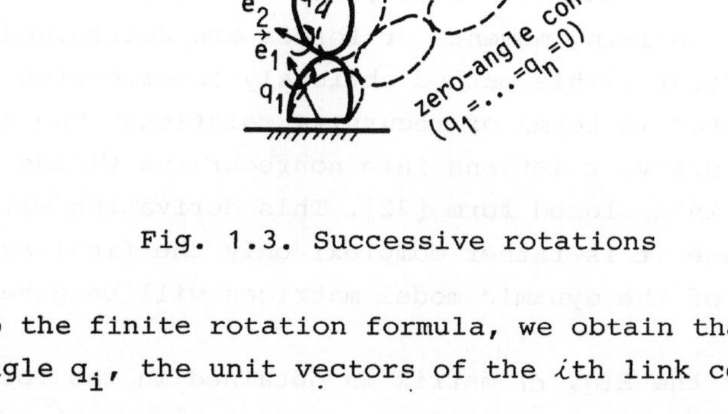

Fig. 1.3. Successive rotations

According to the finite rotation formula, we obtain that, after the rotation by angle q_i, the unit vectors of the ith link coordinate frame become

$$\vec{q}_{ij} = \vec{q}_{ij}^{(1)} \cos q_i + \vec{q}_{ij}^{(2)} \sin q_i + \vec{q}_{ij}^{(3)}, \quad j=1,2,3 \tag{1.2.3}$$

with

$$\vec{q}_{ij}^{(1)} = \vec{e}_i \times \left(\vec{q}'_{ij} \times \vec{e}_i\right)$$

$$\vec{q}_{ij}^{(2)} = \vec{e}_i \times \vec{q}'_{ij}$$

$$\vec{q}_{ij}^{(3)} = \left(\vec{e}_i \cdot \vec{q}'_{ij}\right)\vec{e}_i$$

where $\vec{q}'_{ij}$ denotes the unit vector of the *j*th axis of the *i*th link coordinate frame before the rotation by angle q_i. If the *i*th joint is a prismatic one, $\vec{q}'_{ij} = \vec{q}_{ij}$ will obviously hold. Notice that the matrix $Q_i = \left[\vec{q}_{i1}\ \vec{q}_{i2}\ \vec{q}_{i3}\right]$ represents the 3×3 transformation matrix from the local coordinate system of the i-th link to the reference frame Oxyz. Accordingly, if $\underset{\sim}{e}_{i+1}$, $\tilde{r}_{ii}$ and $\tilde{r}_{i,i+1}$ denote vectors with respect to the local system of the *i*th link, in the fixed system these vectors will become

$$\vec{e}_{i+1} = Q_i\ \underset{\sim}{e}_{i+1}$$

$$\vec{r}_{ii} = Q_i\ \tilde{r}_{ii} \quad \text{and} \quad \vec{r}_{i,i+1} = Q_i\ \tilde{r}_{i,i+1} \tag{1.2.4}$$

If the i-th joint is a prismatic one, vector $\vec{r}_{ii}$ will become $\vec{r}_{ii} = Q_i\ \tilde{r}_{ii} + q_i\vec{e}_i$. We have thus formed all required vectors with respect to the reference system which belong to the set of kinematic variables.

Dynamic analysis of the mechanism in accordance with Newton-Euler's method comprises the calculation of the inertial forces and moments acting to the links during the motion of the mechanism. The inertial forces are obtained from Newton's law, and the moments from Euler's dynamic equations. Driving moments or forces are determined applying a kinetostatic procedure. This method obviously incorporates many laws of mechanics formulated in terms of recursive relations. The transformation of these recursive relations into nonrecursive yields the elements of dynamic model in a closed form [22]. This derivation will not be repeated here because it is rather complex; only the final expressions for the elements of the dynamic model matrices will be given.

Element (i, k) of the H(q, d) matrix is obtained in the form

$$H_{ik} = \sum_{j=\max(i,k)}^{n} \left[m_j <\vec{e}, \vec{r}>_{ji} \cdot <\vec{e}, \vec{r}>_{jk} + \vec{e}_i J_j \vec{e}_k \bar{\xi}_i \bar{\xi}_k \right] \qquad (1.2.5)$$

with

$$\xi_i = \begin{cases} 0 & \text{when the } i\text{th joint is revolute} \\ 1 & \text{when the } i\text{th joint is a sliding one.} \end{cases}$$

Expression $<\vec{e}, \vec{r}>_{ij}$ represents the vector defined as

$$<\vec{e}, \vec{r}>_{ij} = \left(\vec{e}_j \times \vec{r}_{ij}\right)\bar{\xi}_j + \vec{e}_j \xi_j \qquad (1.2.6)$$

with $\bar{\xi}_j = 1 - \xi_j$.

J_j represents the inertia matrix of the *j*th link with respect to the reference frame Oxyz. Having in mind that the Q_j matrix relates between the *j*th and the reference coordinate frame, one obtains

$$J_j = Q_j^T \tilde{J}_j Q_j.$$

Thus, the inertial part of expression (1.2.5) becomes

$$\vec{e}_i J_j \vec{e}_k = \sum_{\mu=1}^{3} \left(\vec{e}_i \cdot \vec{q}_{j\mu}\right)\left(\vec{e}_k \cdot \vec{q}_{j\mu}\right) J_{j\mu}$$

From the right hand side of expression (1.2.5) one can easily show that the inertia matrix is symmetric and positive definite.

Consider now $C^i(q, d)$ matrices describing centrifugal and Coriolis' effects. Element (k, ℓ) of the matrix C^i can be expressed as

$$C^i_{k\ell} = \sum_{j=\max(i,k)}^{n} \left\{ m_j <\vec{e}, \vec{r}>_{ji} \cdot \left(\vec{e}_\ell \times <\vec{e}, \vec{r}>_{jk}\right) + I^i_{k\ell} \right\} \bar{\xi}_\ell, \text{ for } k \geq \ell \qquad (1.2.7)$$

Similarly to $H(q, d)$ matrix, the inertial part of the above expression may also be written as

$$I^i_{k\ell} = \frac{1}{2} \sum_{\mu=1}^{3} \left[\left(\vec{e}_i \cdot \vec{q}_{j\mu}\right)\vec{\varepsilon}_{\ell k} + \left(\vec{e}_k \cdot \vec{q}_{j\mu}\right)\vec{\varepsilon}_{i\ell} + \left(\vec{e}_\ell \cdot \vec{q}_{j\mu}\right)\vec{\varepsilon}_{ik} \right] \cdot \vec{q}_{j\mu} J_{j\mu} \bar{\xi}_k \bar{\xi}_i \qquad (1.2.8)$$

It was shown in [22] that $C^i(q, d)$ matrix is symmetric and that $C^i_{k\ell}$ =

$= -C^k_{i\ell}$ for $k,i > \ell$, and $C^i_{k\ell}=0$ for $i=k > \ell$ holds.

Gravitational vector g(q, d) is given by the expression

$$g(q, d) = - \sum_{j=i}^{n} m_j <\vec{e}, \vec{r}>_{ji} \cdot \vec{g} \tag{1.2.9}$$

where $\vec{g}$ denotes the vector of gravitational acceleration.

At the end we may conclude that the matrices of dynamic model really depend only on internal coordinates and parameters. To form them, it is necessary to determine the kinematic variables as functions of internal coordinates, and then, by their scalar and vector product, determine the dynamic model matrices.

1.3 Analytical Representation of the Variables of Dynamic Model

In this paragraph we will give a solution to the problem of computer-aided construction of the analytical model of a robot. In order to achieve such a goal two main problems should be considered:

1) How to describe the dependence of an arbitrary model variable on joint coordinates?

2) How to realize the algebraic operations between such functions on a digital computer.

In the preceding paragraph it was shown that the elements of the dynamic model matrices are obtained by using scalar or vector products of vectors from the set of kinematic variables K_i. Dynamic parameters of mechanism $\mathcal{D}_i$ i.e., masses and moments of inertia of manipulator links, figure as the coefficients of proportionality. Let us denote by $\vec{k}_i$ any element from the set of kinematic variables of the ith member, i.e., let $\vec{k}_i$ represent one of vectors $\vec{q}_{ij}$ (j=1,2,3), $\vec{e}_i$, $\vec{r}_{ii}$ or $\vec{r}_{i,i+1}$. Let us assume for a moment that the joints from the first to the i-th joint are revolute, and that all joint coordinates are set to zero. Let us now perform a series of successive rotations around axes $\vec{e}_1,\dots,\vec{e}_i$ by angles $q_1,\dots,q_i$, respectively. After the first rotation, vector $\vec{k}_i$ may be expressed as

$$\vec{k}_i^{(1)} = \vec{k}_{i1}^{(1)} \cos q_1 + \vec{k}_{i2}^{(1)} \sin q_1 + \vec{k}_{i3}^{(1)} \tag{1.3.1}$$

where $\vec{k}_{ij}^{(1)}$ (j=1,2,3) are constants. This expression follows immediately from the finite rotation formula (1.2.3). The corresponding matrix form is

$$\vec{k}_i^{(1)} = \left[\vec{k}_{i1}^{(1)} \; \vec{k}_{i2}^{(1)} \; \vec{k}_{i3}^{(3)}\right]^T \begin{bmatrix} \cos q_1 \\ \sin q_1 \\ 1 \end{bmatrix} \tag{1.3.2}$$

or, simply

$$\vec{k}_i^{(1)} = K_i^{(1)} \mathrm{Rot}(q_1) \tag{1.3.3}$$

where $\mathrm{Rot}(q_1)$ represents the vector $[\cos q_1 \; \sin q_1 \; 1]^T$ and $K_i^{(1)}$ the 3×3 matrix on the right hand side of Equation (1.3.2). The symbol $\mathrm{Rot}(q_1)$ has already been used in the literature with a similar meaning [25]. Clearly, after a series of i successive rotations, vector $\vec{k}_i$ becomes

$$\vec{k}_i^{(i)} = K_i^{(i)} \; \mathrm{Rot}\left(q_1,\ldots,q_i\right) \, , \tag{1.3.4}$$

where vector $\mathrm{Rot}\left(q_1,\ldots,q_i\right)$ contains the products of cosines and sines of angles $q_1,\ldots,q_i$, and $K_i^{(i)}$ the constants. Of course, if one of the degrees of freedom $1,\ldots,i$ is a sliding one, $\mathrm{Rot}\left(q_1,\ldots,q_i\right)$ will not contain cosines and sines of the corresponding joint coordinate. Thus, we conclude that the analytical structure of the kinematic variables can unifoldly be described by functions $\mathrm{Rot}\left(q_1,\ldots,q_i\right)$.

Let us now consider analytical structure of the elements of the dynamic model matrices. As already shown, these elements are obtained by employing scalar or vector products of kinematic vectors. Since the multiplication represents a nonlinear operation, it follows that a dynamic variable can not be presented in the same way as a kinematic variable (1.3.4). For example, a nonlinear operation may yield square cosines and sines which are not contained in vector $\mathrm{Rot}\left(q_1,\ldots,q_i\right)$. This is why we have to introduce a more general form than (1.3.4) is. An arbitrary scalar or vector variable $\underline{v}$ of the dynamic robot model can be presented by the following analytical expression

$$\underline{v} = \sum_{k=1}^{m} \underline{v}_k \left(\cos q_1\right)^{c_{1k}} \cdots \left(\cos q_n\right)^{c_{nk}} \left(\sin q_1\right)^{s_{1k}} \cdots$$
$$\cdots \left(\sin q_n\right)^{s_{nk}} \, q_1^{u_{1k}} \cdots q_n^{u_{nk}} \tag{1.3.5}$$

where $\underline{v}_k$ is a constant, and c_{ik}, s_{ik} and u_{ik} (i=1,...,n) are positive integers. The number of addends in the above sum, m, is not fixed, but depends on the analytical complexity of function $\underline{v}$. Let us introduce a vector of dimension N = 3n:

$$\left(x_1,\ldots,x_N\right)=\left(\cos q_1,\ldots,\cos q_n,\ \sin q_1,\ldots,\sin q_n,\ q_1,\ldots,q_n\right). \tag{1.3.6}$$

Accordingly, we introduced a new set of arguments $x_1,\ldots,x_N$ corresponding respectively to the functions on the right hand side of the Equation (1.3.5), i.e. $x_1 = \cos q_1,\ x_2 = \cos q_2,\ldots,x_N = q_n$. Similarly, let us introduce the vector of exponents appearing in (1.3.5) as

$$\left(\varepsilon_{1k},\ldots,\varepsilon_{Nk}\right)=\left(c_{1k},\ldots,c_{nk},\ s_{1k},\ldots,s_{nk},\ u_{1k},\ldots,u_{nk}\right) \tag{1.3.7}$$

where ε_{ik} (i=1,...,N) are positive integers or zeros. By substituting (1.3.6) and (1.3.7) in (1.3.5), we obtain

$$\underline{v} = \sum_{k=1}^{m} \underline{v}_k\, x_1^{\varepsilon_{1k}} \cdots x_N^{\varepsilon_{Nk}}, \tag{1.3.8}$$

which represents a polynomial defined on the new set of arguments (1.3.6).

Now, we can clearly recognize the difference between the numerical methods, shortly mentioned in Paragraph 1.1., and the analytical method presented here. In a numerical method any kinematic or dynamic variable is considered as a real number (3 reals for a vector variable). For example, a distance vector at any time instant is identified by 3 real numbers, representing the 3 vector components with respect to a given reference frame. Here, this variable is presented by the corresponding polynomial. Although the variable is a symbolic one, we see from (1.3.8) that it can be described by the coefficients and exponents of the polynomial. Suppose that the coefficients $\underline{v}_k$ of the polynomial (1.3.8) represent the components of the vector $v^{(m)}$, i.e.

$$v^{(m)} = \begin{bmatrix} \underline{v}_1 \\ \vdots \\ \underline{v}_m \end{bmatrix} \tag{1.3.9}$$

and that the exponents $\varepsilon_{1k} \cdots \varepsilon_{Nk}$ form the integer matrix

$$E_v = \begin{bmatrix} \varepsilon_{11} & \cdots & \varepsilon_{N1} \\ \vdots & & \vdots \\ \varepsilon_{1m} & \cdots & \varepsilon_{Nm} \end{bmatrix} . \tag{1.3.10}$$

In such a way we obtain the pair

$$v^{(m)} = \left(\begin{bmatrix} \underline{v}_1 \\ \vdots \\ \underline{v}_m \end{bmatrix} , \begin{bmatrix} \varepsilon_{11} & \cdots & \varepsilon_{N1} \\ \vdots & & \vdots \\ \varepsilon_{m1} & \cdots & \varepsilon_{mN} \end{bmatrix} \right) \tag{1.3.11}$$

which uniquely defines the polynomial (1.3.8), i.e. the variable $\underline{v}$. The ith row of matrix (1.3.11)

$$\left(\left[\underline{v}_i \right], \left[\varepsilon_{i1} \cdots \varepsilon_{iN} \right] \right)$$

corresponds to the ith monomial

$$\underline{v}_i \, x_1^{\varepsilon_{i1}} \cdots x_N^{\varepsilon_{iN}}$$

of the polynomial (1.3.8).

The pair (1.3.11) will be referred to as a "polynomial matrix" in text to follow. The vector $v^{(m)}$ will be called the "vector of coefficients" and the matrix E_v - the "matrix of exponents".

We will now present a very important property of the matrix.

If v is an arbitrary kinematic variable of the mechanism, the corresponding matrix of exponents will contain elements which may be either 0 or 1. If v is a dynamic variable of the mechanism, the exponents will then be 0, 1 or 2.

In case of a kinematic variable, this statement is easy to prove, since no square cosines and sines figure in vector $\mathrm{Rot}\left(q_1, \ldots, q_n\right)$ which determines the structure of these variables. The second part of the theorem was proved in [22]. These properties are very important when one writes the computer program, since they show that the exponents of kinematic variables can be stored in a single memory location (one bit) and the exponents of dynamic variables within only 2 bits of a computer memory.

Let us now introduce the basic operations between polynomial matrices. Let $v_1 = \left(v_1^{(m_1)}, E_{v_1}\right)$ and $v_2 = \left(v_2^{(m_2)}, E_{v_2}\right)$ denote two arbitrary vector variables of the model. The following polynomial matrix corresponds to the sum of these two variables

$$S_{v_1+v_2}^{(m_1+m_2)} = \left(\begin{bmatrix} v^{(m_1)} \\ \hline v^{(m_2)} \end{bmatrix}, \begin{bmatrix} E_{v_1} \\ \hline E_{v_2} \end{bmatrix} \right) \tag{1.3.12}$$

Since the following polynomial corresponds to the vector product of variables v_1 and v_2

$$\vec{v}_1 \times \vec{v}_2 = \sum_{k=1}^{m_1} \sum_{\ell=1}^{m_2} \left(\vec{v}_{1k} \times \vec{v}_{2\ell}\right) x_1^{\varepsilon_{1k}^1 + \varepsilon_{1\ell}^2} \cdots x_N^{\varepsilon_{Nk}^1 + \varepsilon_{N\ell}^2} \tag{1.3.13}$$

where ε_{ik}^1 belongs to the matrix of exponents E_{v_1}, and ε_{ik}^2 to matrix E_{v_2}, the polynomial matrix of vector product has the form

$$S_{v_1 \, v_2}^{(m_1 m_2)} = \left(v^{(m_1)} \times v^{(m_2)}, E_{v_1} + E_{v_2}\right)$$

where $v^{(m_1)} \times v^{(m_2)}$ is the $3 \times (m_1 m_2)$ matrix whose rows are vectors $\vec{v}_{1k} \times \vec{v}_{2\ell}$ $(k = 1, \ldots, m_1,\ \ell = 1, \ldots, m_2)$, and $E_{v_1} + E_{v_2}$ the matrix whose rows have the form $\left[\varepsilon_{1k}^1 + \varepsilon_{1\ell}^2 \cdots \varepsilon_{Nk}^1 + \varepsilon_{N\ell}^2\right]$.

The scalar product of two polynomial matrices is defined in a similar way

$$S_{v_1 \cdot v_2}^{(m_1 m_2)} = \left(v^{(m_1)} \cdot v^{(m_2)}, E_{v_1} + E_{v_2}\right) \tag{1.3.14}$$

The operations follow directly from the corresponding polynomial forms. One can easily show that it is possible to define, for polynomial matrices, all operations of a vector space.

Let us now consider the issue of dimensions of a polynomial matrix. It can be seen from (1.3.6) that the arguments of the polynomial which corresponds to variable $\underline{v}$ are interdependent, since $x_i = \cos q_i$ and

$x_{n+i} = \sin q_i$ for $i = 1,\ldots,n$. As a result of trigonometric relation between arguments x_i and x_{n+i}, there appears identities such as

$$x_i^2 = 1 - x_{n+i}^2$$

$$x_i^4 = 1 - 2x_{n+i}^2 + x_{n+i}^4$$

and other. On the other hand, let us consider the polynomial

$$\underline{w} = \sum_{k=1}^{m+1} \underline{w}_k \, x_1^{\xi_{1k}} \cdots x_N^{\xi_{Nk}}$$

and let us assume that the following holds

$$\underline{w}_k = \underline{v}_k, \qquad (k=1,\ldots,m), \qquad \underline{w}_{m+1} = \underline{w}_m$$

$$\xi_{jk} = \varepsilon_{jk} \qquad (j=1,\ldots,N \quad \text{and} \quad k=1,\ldots,m-1)$$

$$\xi_{jm} = \varepsilon_{jm} \qquad (j=1,\ldots,i-1,\ i+1,\ldots,N), \quad {}_{im} = {}_{im} + 2$$

$$\xi_{j,m+1} = \varepsilon_{jm} \quad (j=1,\ldots,n+i-1,\ n+i+1,\ldots,N), \quad \xi_{n+i,m} = \varepsilon_{n+i,m} + 2$$

Having in mind that $x_i^2 + x_{n+1}^2 = 1$, it is easy to recognize that the polynomials of variables $\underline{v}$ and $\underline{w}$ are equivalent. So, they represent the same variable. Thus, we obtain

$$S_v^{(m)} = S_w^{(m+1)}$$

It follows directly therefrom that variable $\underline{v}$ can be represented by two different polynomials, i.e., by two different polynomial matrices. By induction, we conclude that for an arbitrary number $m_\ell > m$ there exists $\underline{v}_\ell$, and the following identity holds

$$\left(v_v^{(m)}, E_v\right) = \left(v_{v_\ell}^{(m_\ell)}, E_{v_\ell}\right)$$

i.e., an infinite number of matrices corresponds to any variable $\underline{v}$. These matrices will be referred to as equivalent analytical matrices. Since the dimensions of equivalent analytical matrices are different, it is necessary to determine the matrix of a minimal dimension

$$S_v^{(m)} = \min_{m_\ell}\left(v_{v_\ell}^{(m_\ell)}, E_{v_\ell}\right) \qquad (1.3.15)$$

The polynomial corresponding to this matrix is the simplest polynomial which describes variable $\underline{v}$ and which may be referred to as a minimal--complexity polynomial. Matrix (1.3.15) may be said to be unique for a given variable if it satisfies the following conditions:

1) None of the elements of the vector of coefficients is equal to zero.

2) There are not two identical rows in the matrix of exponents.

3) There are not two rows which can be compressed into one due to the trigonometric relation $x_\ell^2 + x_{n+\ell}^2 = 1$, for any $\ell \in \{1,\dots,n\}$.

If the first condition is not satisfied, zero elements of the vector of coefficients as well as the corresponding rows of the matrix of exponents can be omitted in order to reduce dimension m. When the second condition is not satisfied, i.e., when two identical rows exist in the matrix of exponents, the corresponding elements in the vector of coefficients can be summed and the reduction in dimensions by 1 performed. The third condition is in some way clumsy for a formal and general definition (see Ref. [22]). Thus, we will explain it by a simple example. Consider a polynomial matrix with the *i*th and *k*th row

$$\left(\left[\underline{v}_i\right], \left[\varepsilon_{1i} \cdots \varepsilon_{Ni}\right]\right)$$

$$\left(\left[\underline{v}_k\right], \left[\varepsilon_{1k} \cdots \varepsilon_{Nk}\right]\right)$$

being

*i*th row = ([2.], [0 1 0 0 1 2 0 0 0])

*k*th rov = ([2.], [0 1 2 0 1 0 0 0 0]).

We see that v represents a scalar variable and that N = 3n = 9. This corresponds to a manipulator with 3 joints and 3 links. Denoting the joint coordinates by q_1, q_2 and q_3, the polynomial corresponding to the *i*th and *k*th row becomes

$$2.\cos q_2 \sin q_2 \sin^2 q_3 + 2.\cos q_2 \cos^2 q_3 \sin q_2 =$$

$$= 2.\cos q_2 \sin q_2.$$

It means that the *i*th and *k*th row can be reduced to one row:

([2.], [0 1 0 0 1 0 0 0 0])

due to the identity $\sin^2 q_3 + \cos^2 q_3 = 1$.

Minimization of the dimension of an analytical matrix, i.e., determination of the simplest polynomial describing a corresponding variable, can easily be automated on a computer. Each mathematical operation intended to give the elements of the dynamic model matrices, should be followed by the dimension reduction of the obtained analytical matrix.

Let us now consider the problem of calculating the obtained analytical matrices so as to achieve a minimal number of floating-point multiplications/additions. It follows from the preceding text that the analytical model reduces to a set of polynomials of N variables. Thus, the problem is how to calculate these polynomials so that the number of floating-point multiplications/additions is the smallest possible. This is a mathematical problem referred to as the problem of optimal factorization of polynomials with several arguments. Here, we will not present the algorithms for optimal factorization of polynomials, but only describe their essence by a simple example.

Consider polynomials P and Q of 3 independent variables x_1, x_2 and x_3, which are to be calculated with a minimal computational effort:

$$P = 0.1\ x_1\ x_2 + 0.7\ x_3 + 0.2\ x_1\ x_2\ x_3$$

$$Q = 0.8\ x_1\ x_2$$

Simple enumeration shows that the calculation of these polynomials requires 8 floating-point multiplications and 2 additions. Performing a partial factorization of the first polynomial:

$$P = x_1\ x_2 \left(0.1 + 0.2\ x_3\right) + 0.7\ x_3$$

and introducing the monomial $R = x_1 x_2$, the calculation reduces to

$$R = x_1\ x_2$$

$$P = R\left(0.1 + 0.2\ x_3\right) + 0.7\ x_3$$

$$Q = 0.8R$$

There are now 5 multiplications to be performed. Structure of the calculation of these polynomials may be represented graphically as follows

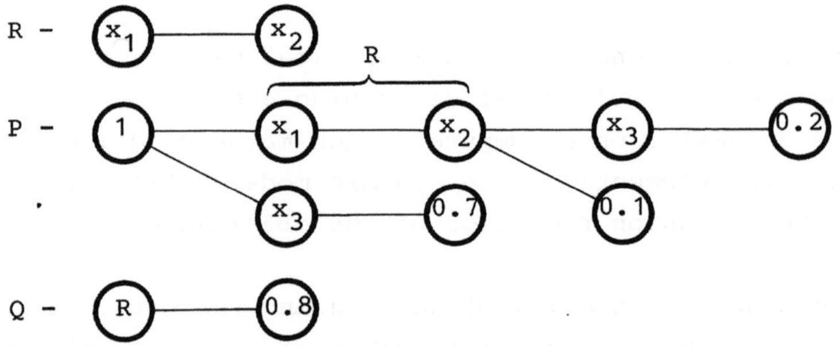

In the above structures, branching stands for the operation of addition, and the branches connecting two nodes for the operation of multiplication.

Now, consider only the structure representing polynomial P. To this structure we can assign two matrices which define it in a unifold way. The first matrix contains the elements corresponding to the elements in nodes, and the second matrix the number of branches originating from corresponding nodes. Thus, for polynomial P, we obtain the matrices

$$E = \begin{bmatrix} x_1 & x_2 & x_3 & c_2 \\ x_3 & c_3 & c_1 & 0 \end{bmatrix}, \qquad V = \begin{bmatrix} 1 & 2 & 1 & 0 \\ 1 & 0 & 0 & 0 \end{bmatrix}$$

where $c_1 = 0.1$, $c_2 = 0.2$ and $c_3 = 0.7$. These matrices describe the structure of the optimal calculation of polynomials. Instead of the symbolic elements (x_i and c_i) in the E matrix, it is more convenient to use the numeric elements. Renaming the constants c_i as

$$c_1 = x_4, \quad c_2 = x_5 \quad \text{and} \quad c_3 = x_6$$

and replacing the elements x_i by their subscripts "i", E matrix becomes

$$E = \begin{bmatrix} 1 & 2 & 3 & 5 \\ 3 & 6 & 4 & 0 \end{bmatrix}.$$

Thus, to each element of the dynamic model matrix, for which we have obtained the polynomial, we associate two matrices which describe how this element can be calculated with a minimal number of floating-point operations. This procedure can be performed by a computer, i.e., is fully automated.

1.4 Construction of Real-Time Program Code

As we have seen in the last paragraph, any polynomial h(x) can be described in terms of the corresponding matrix pair (E, V). Let us now state the question: how to calculate the polynomial h(x), given the E and V matrices. This problem is pointed-out and solved in Ref. [22]. Thus, we will here give only the final result.

Let $X_{i,j}$ denote the argument or the coefficient of polynomial h(x) which corresponds to the (i, j)-th element of matrix E. We suppose that E and V matrices have dimensions $n_r \times n_c$. In addition, let us introduce two auxiliary vectors p and q of dimension n_r. The polynomial can be calculated according to the following algorithm:

<u>1. step</u>: $q(i) = X_{i,n_c}, \quad i=1,\dots,n_r$

<u>2. step</u>: $p(i) = X_{i,n_c-1}\left(q\left(k_{i-1}+1\right)+ \cdots +q\left(k_i\right)\right), \quad i=1,\dots,n_r$

where $k_i = \sum_{j=1}^{i} V\left(j, n_c-1\right), \quad k_o = 1$

⋮

<u>(2ℓ)-th step</u>: $p(i) = X_{i,n_c-2\ell+1}\left(q\left(k_{i-1}+1\right)+ \cdots +q\left(k_i\right)\right), \quad i=1,\dots,n_r$

where $k_i = \sum_{j=1}^{i} V\left(j,n_c-2\ell+1\right), \quad k_o = 1$

<u>(2ℓ+1)-th step</u>: $q(i) = X_{i,n_c-2\ell}\left(p\left(k_{i-1}+1\right)+ \cdots +p\left(k_i\right)\right), \quad i=1,\dots,n_r$

where $k_i = \sum_{j=1}^{i} V\left(j,n_c-2\ell\right), \quad k_o = 1$

⋮

<u>(n_c+1)-th step</u>: $$h(x) = \begin{cases} \sum_{i=1}^{n_r} p(i) & n_c \text{ - odd} \\ \sum_{i=1}^{n_r} q(i) & n_c \text{ - even} \end{cases}$$

As may be seen, the algorithm contains recursive relations each of which comprises one multiplication and a few additions. It is easy to see that these relations describe the calculation of polynomials according to the graphical structures presented in the preceding paragraph. It may also be seen that the analytical matrices, i.e., the polynomials, could be calculated by a computer if these relations were mapped into a series of program statements. It will be shown that even the problem of mapping can be efficiently solved by means of a computer program. The program which does this will be referred to as "expert-program". This is a very important program because it permits fully automated construction of the mathematical model of robot in analytical form. The output of expert-program is also a PROGRAM which is written in a higher or lower-level programming language by the computer itself.

According to the presented algorithm, the basic relation to be generated by expert-program is of the type

$$p_i = x_j\left(q_{i1} + \cdots + q_{in}\right) \;,$$

where i,j,n are given. For example, let i=1, j=2 and n=3. We will present the expert-program output statement corresponding to this expression in FORTRAN and ASSEMBLER for a microcomputer (INTEL 8086 with coprocessor 8087).

1. FORTRAN code

```
P1 = X2*(QI1 + QI2 + QI3)
```

2. ASSEMBLER 8086

```
FLD  QI1  ;  QI1→ST
FADD QI2  ;  ST*QI2→ST
FADD QI3  ;  ST+QI3→ST
FMUL X2   ;  ST*X2→ST
FST  P1   ;  ST→P1
```

where ST denotes the first location of STACK-memory, and → the data transfer.

The generated programs can immediately be translated by appropriate COMPILERs and used for real-time operation, simulation or control synthesis. Notice that, in a general case, the programming language in which expert-program is written does not have to be the same as that of the generated program code. The general block-diagram for the overall program system, including analytical model construction and optimization, is given in Fig. 1.3. The operation of expert program will be illustrated in the next section using the example of STANFORD manipulator of (Fig. 1.4).

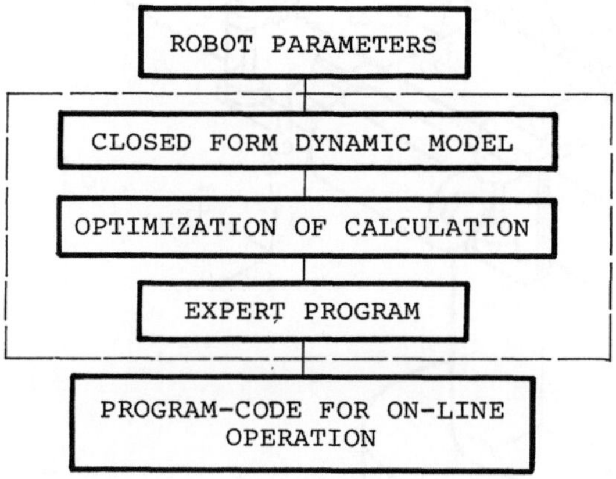

Fig. 1.3. General block-diagram for on-line model generation

1.5 Example

Although the results presented in this book refer to a general n-joint manipulator, manipulator shown in Fig. 1.4. will be used as a reference in illustrating the developed algorithms. This manipulator (Stanford arm) has 6 joints and links in addition to the gripper. Link 1 rotates about vertical axis on the platform, while link 6 is the hand [17, 25]. There are 6 orthonormal coordinate systems $\left(\vec{q}_{i1}, \vec{q}_{i2}, \vec{q}_{i3}\right)$ assigned to mass centers of the links. Fig. 1.4 also shows the unit vectors of joint axes $\vec{e}_i$. Numerical data about geometric parameters, masses and moments of inertia may be found in [25], so they will not be repeated here.

In the text to follow we will consider only the first 3 joints for the sake of clear illustration of the described method. The 6-joint manipulator is considered in Ref. [26]. First, we have to define the manipulator configuration when all joint coordinates are equal to zero (zero-angle configuration). Let us accept the configuration presented in

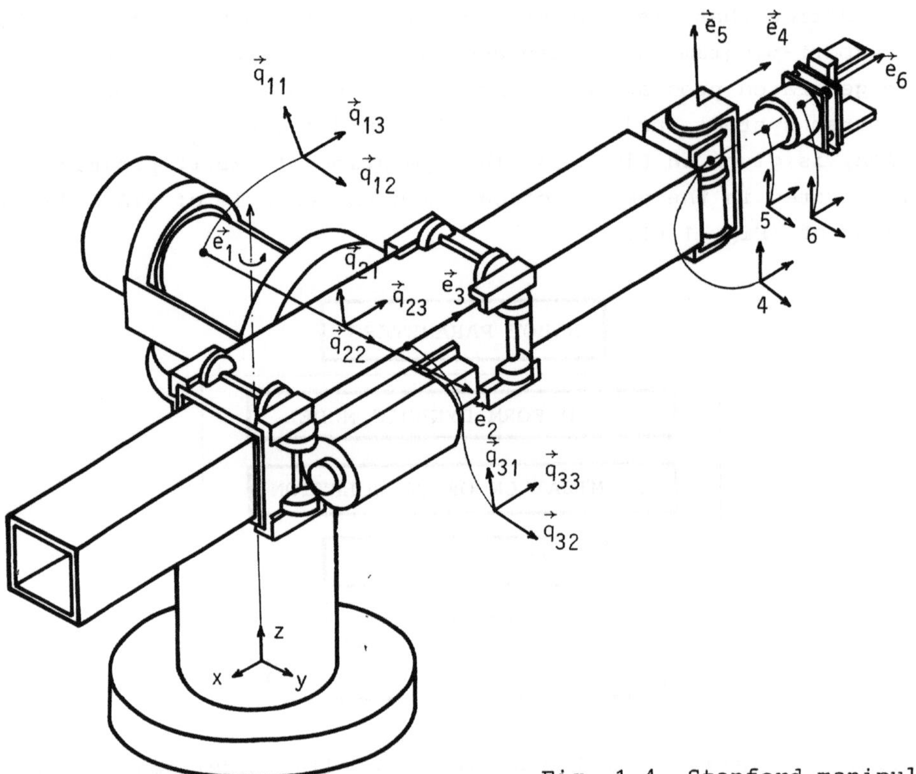

Fig. 1.4. Stanford manipulator

Fig. 1.5. The positive sense of rotation for revolute joints and displacement for the prismatic joint is determined by the direction of the axes $\vec{e}_i$. We can also accept that, at the zero-angle configuration the axes of local coordinate frames are paralled to the axes of the reference frame. The characteristic vectors at this configuration are given in Table 1.1.

Now, we have to determine the characteristic vectors at any desired manipulator configuration $q = \begin{bmatrix} q_1 & q_2 & q_3 \end{bmatrix}^T$. Applying rotations about $\vec{e}_1$ and $\vec{e}_2$ successively, and the translation along $\vec{e}_3$ for displacement q_3, we can derive the analytical expressions for $\vec{e}_i$, $\vec{r}_{ii}$ and $\vec{r}_{i,i+1}$ (i = 1,2,3) as functions of q_1, q_2 and q_3. In the case of a simple robot structure, as in this example, we can obtain these expressions "by hand", i.e. without the aid of a computer. But, in a general case, it is much more convenient to apply the polynomial-matrix algebra, described in preceding sections. Such an algebra is fully "numeric", and convenient for programming. The polynomial matrices corresponding to

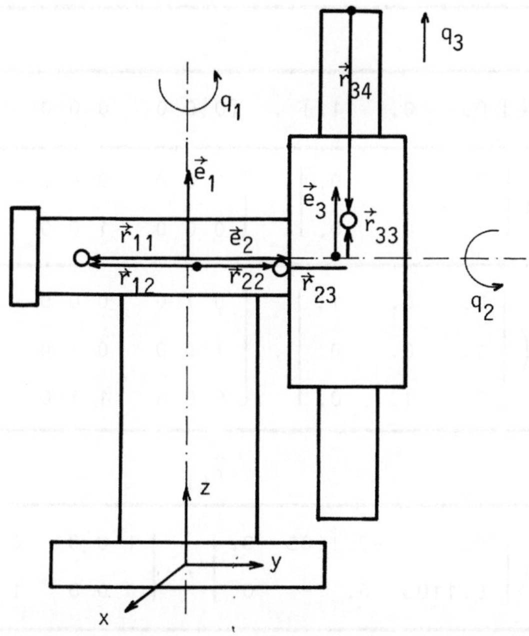

Fig. 1.5. Stanford arm when all joint coordinates are zero

i	$\vec{e}_i$	$\vec{r}_{ii}$	$\vec{r}_{i,i+1}$
1	(0, 0, 1)	(0, -0.1105, 0)	(0, -0.1105, 0)
2	(0, 1, 0)	(0, 0.0475, 0)	(0, -0.1054, 0)
3	(0, 0, 1)	(0, 0, 0)	(0, 0.323, 0)

Table 1.1. Characteristic vectors

the characteristic vectors are given in Table 1.2. The unit vectors $\vec{q}_{ij}$ of local coordinate frames are given in Table 1.3. For clarity, let us explain the relation between the polynomial matrix of $\vec{r}_{33}$ and the analytical expression for $\vec{r}_{33}$. The first row of the polynomial matrix ([0. 0. 1.], [010 000 001]) corresponds to the monomial

$$\begin{bmatrix} 0. \\ 0. \\ 1. \end{bmatrix} x_2 x_9$$

i	$\vec{e}_i$
1	$([0. \quad 0. \quad 1.]\ ,\ [0\ 0\ 0 \quad 0\ 0\ 0 \quad 0\ 0\ 0])$
2	$\left(\begin{bmatrix} 0. & 1. & 0. \\ -1. & 0. & 0. \end{bmatrix} \begin{bmatrix} 1\ 0\ 0 & 0\ 0\ 0 & 0\ 0\ 0 \\ 0\ 0\ 0 & 1\ 0\ 0 & 0\ 0\ 0 \end{bmatrix}\right)$
3	$\left(\begin{bmatrix} 0. & 0. & 1. \\ 1. & 0. & 0. \\ 0. & 1. & 0. \end{bmatrix}, \begin{bmatrix} 0\ 1\ 0 & 0\ 0\ 0 & 0\ 0\ 0 \\ 1\ 0\ 0 & 0\ 1\ 0 & 0\ 0\ 0 \\ 0\ 0\ 0 & 1\ 1\ 0 & 0\ 0\ 0 \end{bmatrix}\right)$
	$\vec{r}_{ii}$
1	$\left(\begin{bmatrix} 0. & -0.1105 & 0. \\ 0.1105 & 0. & 0. \end{bmatrix}, \begin{bmatrix} 1\ 0\ 0 & 0\ 0\ 0 & 0\ 0\ 0 \\ 0\ 0\ 0 & 1\ 0\ 0 & 0\ 0\ 0 \end{bmatrix}\right)$
2	$\left(\begin{bmatrix} 0. & 0.475 & 0. \\ -0.475 & 0. & 0. \end{bmatrix} \begin{bmatrix} 1\ 0\ 0 & 0\ 0\ 0 & 0\ 0\ 0 \\ 0\ 0\ 0 & 1\ 0\ 0 & 0\ 0\ 0 \end{bmatrix}\right)$
3	$\left(\begin{bmatrix} 0. & 0. & 1. \\ 1. & 0. & 0. \\ 0. & 1. & 0. \end{bmatrix}, \begin{bmatrix} 0\ 1\ 0 & 0\ 0\ 0 & 0\ 0\ 1 \\ 1\ 0\ 0 & 0\ 1\ 0 & 0\ 0\ 1 \\ 0\ 0\ 0 & 1\ 1\ 0 & 0\ 0\ 1 \end{bmatrix}\right)$
	$\vec{r}_{i,i+1}$
1	$\left(\begin{bmatrix} 0. & -0.1105 & 0. \\ 0.1105 & 0. & 0. \end{bmatrix}, \begin{bmatrix} 1\ 0\ 0 & 0\ 0\ 0 & 0\ 0\ 0 \\ 0\ 0\ 0 & 1\ 0\ 0 & 0\ 0\ 0 \end{bmatrix}\right)$
2	$\left(\begin{bmatrix} 0. & -1.054 & 0. \\ 1.054 & 0. & 0. \end{bmatrix}, \begin{bmatrix} 1\ 0\ 0 & 0\ 0\ 0 & 0\ 0\ 0 \\ 0\ 0\ 0 & 1\ 0\ 0 & 0\ 0\ 0 \end{bmatrix}\right)$

Table 1.2. Polynomial matrices of $\vec{e}_i$, $\vec{r}_{ii}$ and $\vec{r}_{i,i+1}$

where $x_2 = \cos q_2$ and $x_9 = q_3$. The second row

$([1. \quad 0. \quad 0.], [1\ 0\ 0 \quad 0\ 1\ 0 \quad 0\ 0\ 1]$

and the third row

([0.   1.   0.], [0 0 0   1 1 0   0 0 1])

correspond to

$$\begin{bmatrix} 1. \\ 0. \\ 0. \end{bmatrix} x_1x_5x_9 \quad \text{and} \quad \begin{bmatrix} 0. \\ 1. \\ 0. \end{bmatrix} x_4x_5x_9$$

respectively, with $x_1 = \cos q_1$, $x_4 = \sin q_1$ and $x_5 = \sin q_2$.

i	j	$\vec{q}_{ij}$
1	1	$\left(\begin{bmatrix} 1. & 0. & 0. \\ 0. & 1. & 0. \end{bmatrix}, \begin{bmatrix} 1\,0\,0 & 0\,0\,0 & 0\,0\,0 \\ 0\,0\,0 & 1\,0\,0 & 0\,0\,0 \end{bmatrix}\right)$
	2	$\left(\begin{bmatrix} 0. & 1. & 0. \\ -1. & 0. & 0. \end{bmatrix}, \begin{bmatrix} 1\,0\,0 & 0\,0\,0 & 0\,0\,0 \\ 0\,0\,0 & 1\,0\,0 & 0\,0\,0 \end{bmatrix}\right)$
	3	$([0. \quad 0. \quad 1.], [0\,0\,0 \quad 0\,0\,0 \quad 0\,0\,0])$
2	1	$\left(\begin{bmatrix} 1. & 0. & 0. \\ 0. & 1. & 0. \\ 0. & 0. & -1. \end{bmatrix}, \begin{bmatrix} 1\,1\,0 & 0\,0\,0 & 0\,0\,0 \\ 0\,1\,0 & 1\,0\,0 & 0\,0\,0 \\ 0\,0\,0 & 0\,1\,0 & 0\,0\,0 \end{bmatrix}\right)$
	2	$\left(\begin{bmatrix} 0. & 1. & 0. \\ -1. & 0. & 0. \end{bmatrix}, \begin{bmatrix} 1\,0\,0 & 0\,0\,0 & 0\,0\,0 \\ 0\,0\,0 & 1\,0\,0 & 0\,0\,0 \end{bmatrix}\right)$
	3	$\left(\begin{bmatrix} 0. & 0. & 1. \\ 1. & 0. & 0. \\ 0. & 1. & 0. \end{bmatrix}, \begin{bmatrix} 0\,1\,0 & 0\,0\,0 & 0\,0\,0 \\ 1\,0\,0 & 0\,1\,0 & 0\,0\,0 \\ 0\,0\,0 & 1\,1\,0 & 0\,0\,0 \end{bmatrix}\right)$

Table 1.3. Polynomial matrices of $\vec{q}_{ij}$

This follows from the definition of polynomial matrices (1.3.11). By adding the monomials, we obtain the analytical expression of $\vec{r}_{33}$ as

$$\vec{r}_{33} = \begin{bmatrix} q_3 \cos q_1 \sin q_2 \\ q_3 \sin q_1 \sin q_2 \\ q_3 \cos q_2 \end{bmatrix}$$

which we can easily prove "by hand". It is evident from Table 1.2. that none of the elements of any matrix of exponents exceeds 1.

In order to obtain the analytical expressions for inertia-matrix elements H_{ik}, we have to apply the expression (1.2.5). Obviously, this expression is burdened with a rather large number of scalar and vector products and vector additions. For this reason, it is much more profitable to apply the algebra of polynomial matrices and use the facilities of a digital computer. The obtained polynomial matrices are presented in Table 1.4. Likewise, the elements of $C^i(q, d)$ matrices (1.2.7) describing centrifugal and Coriolis' effects, and the terms of gravitational vector (1.2.9), are given in Tables 1.5. and 1.6. The elements which are not listed in Tables 1.5. and 1.6. can be obtained from the properties of dynamic model matrices. In view of the importance of the properties, we will repeat them once again:

1) Matrices $H(q, d)$ and $C^i(q, d)$, for any superscript $i \in \{1,\dots,n\}$, are symmetric.

2) Given $C^i(q, d)$ and $C^k(q, d)$ matrices, then, for any $k > \ell$ and $i > \ell$, the relation $C^i_{k\ell} = -C^k_{i\ell}$ holds.

Using one of these elements, for example H_{11}, we will illustrate the algorithm for computer-aided optimal calculation of the model matrices described in Paragraph 1.3. As already stated, this algorithm is intended to optimize the number of floating-point multiplications/additions which have to be performed to calculate these elements. The following analytical expression corresponds to element H_{11}:

$$H_{11} = 11.251 + 2.618 \sin^2 q_2 + 0.106 \cos^2 q_2 + 4.250(\sin^2 q_2)q_3^2$$

or in polynomial form

$$H_{11} = 11.251 + 2.618\, x_5^2 + 0.106\, x_2^2 + 4.250\, x_5^2 x_9^2$$

Denoting the coefficients of the polynomial by

i	j	H_{ij}
1	1	$\begin{bmatrix} 11.251 \\ 2.618 \\ 0.106 \\ 4.250 \end{bmatrix}, \begin{bmatrix} 0\ 0\ 0 & 0\ 0\ 0 & 0\ 0\ 0 \\ 0\ 0\ 0 & 0\ 2\ 0 & 0\ 0\ 0 \\ 0\ 2\ 0 & 0\ 0\ 0 & 0\ 0\ 0 \\ 0\ 0\ 0 & 0\ 2\ 0 & 0\ 0\ 2 \end{bmatrix}$
2	1	([-6.498] , [0 1 0 0 0 0 0 0 1])
2	2	$\begin{bmatrix} 2.528 \\ 4.250 \end{bmatrix}, \begin{bmatrix} 0\ 0\ 0 & 0\ 0\ 0 & 0\ 0\ 0 \\ 0\ 0\ 0 & 0\ 0\ 0 & 0\ 0\ 2 \end{bmatrix}$
3	1	([-6.498] , [0 0 0 0 1 0 0 0 0])
3	2	([0.] , [0 0 0 0 0 0 0 0 0])
3	3	([4.25] , [0 0 0 0 0 0 0 0 0])

Table 1.4. H_{ij} polynomial matrices

$$x_{10} = 11.251, \quad x_{11} = 2.618, \quad x_{12} = 0.106 \quad \text{and} \quad x_{13} = 4.250$$

we obtain the form

$$H_{11} = x_{10} + x_{11}x_5^2 + x_{12}x_2^2 + x_{13}x_3^2x_9^2 \tag{1.5.1}$$

whose arguments are now x_i, $i=1,\dots,13$.

We see that the calculation of this polynomial requires 8 multiplications and 3 additions. Using the algorithm desribed in Paragraph 1.3, we can get the matrices which describe the algorithm of optimal calculation of H_{11}, i.e. the calculation of H_{11} with a minimal number of floating-point multiplications/additions. The E-matrix, whose elements correspond to the indices of arguments in (1.5.1), is obtained as

$$E = \begin{bmatrix} 5 & 5 & 9 & 9 & 13 \\ 2 & 2 & 11 & 0 & 0 \\ 10 & 0 & 12 & 0 & 0 \end{bmatrix}.$$

i	k	ℓ	$C^i_{k\ell}$
1	2	2	([6.498] , [0 0 0 0 1 0 0 0 1])
	3	2	([-6.498] , [0 1 0 0 0 0 0 0 0])
	3	3	([0.] , [0 0 0 0 0 0 0 0 0])
2	1	1	$\left(\begin{bmatrix} -2.513 \\ -4.250 \end{bmatrix}, \begin{bmatrix} 0 & 1 & 0 & 0 & 1 & 0 & 0 & 0 & 0 \\ 0 & 1 & 0 & 0 & 1 & 0 & 0 & 0 & 2 \end{bmatrix}\right)$
	3	3	([0.] , [0 0 0 0 0 0 0 0 0])
3	1	1	([-4.250] , [0 0 0 0 2 0 0 0 1])
	2	1	([-0.0027], [0 0 0 0 1 0 0 0 0])
	2	2	([-4.250] , [0 0 0 0 0 0 0 0 1])

Table 1.5. $C^i_{k\ell}$ polynomial matrices

i	g_i
1	([0.] , [0 0 0 0 0 0 0 0 0])
2	([-41.693] , [0 0 0 0 1 0 0 0 1])
3	([41.693] , [0 1 0 0 0 0 0 0 0])

Table 1.6. g_i polynomial matrices

The V-matrix, whose elements represent the numbers of "branches" originating from nodes of the corresponding graph, is obtained as

$$V = \begin{bmatrix} 1 & 2 & 1 & 1 & 0 \\ 1 & 1 & 0 & 0 & 0 \\ 0 & 0 & 0 & 0 & 0 \end{bmatrix} .$$

On the basis of these matrices we can drow the graph of the optimal calculation of H_{11} (Fig. 1.6).

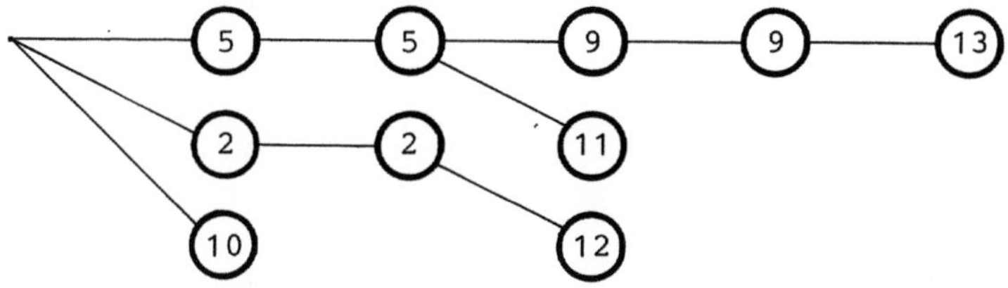

Fig. 1.6. Graph of the optimal calculation of H_{11} element

The following polynomial corresponds to this graph

$$H_{11} = x_5^2\left(x_9^2 x_{13} + x_{11}\right) + x_2^2 x_{12} + x_{10}$$

which is identical to the original polynomial for H_{11}. Enumeration shows that it is necessary to perform 6 multiplications, and this number is reduced by 25% in comparison with the number of operations in the previous polynomial which is not optimized.

Using the algorithm given in Paragraph 1.4, the computer also generates the program code for calculating model matrices in some programming language. For H_{11} element the following FORTRAN program is obtained

```
P1=X9* 0.42500E+01
Q1=X9*P1
P2=X2* 0.10600E+00
P1=X5*(Q1+0.26185E+01)
Q2=X2*P2
Q1=X5*P1
H(1,1)=Q1+Q2+0.11251E+02
```

Once again, let us emphasize that this program code is obtained by a computer, not "by hand", i.e., by a fully automated procedure. The program which generates this code (see Paragraph 1.4) is called EXPERT-PROGRAM.

Finally, for proper illustration of the operation of the developed program system, we will present the program code for calculating all elements of any dynamic model matrix for the 3 degree-of-freedom Stanford manipulator (Fig. 1.7).

```
      X7=Q(1)
      X8=Q(2)
      X2=COS(X8)
      X5=SIN(X8)
      X9=Q(3)
C
      Q1=X2* 0.41693E+02
      G(3)=Q1
      P1=X5*(-0.41693E+02)
      Q1=X9*P1
      G(2)=Q1
      G1)=0.
      Q1=X9*(-0.42500E+01)
      C(3,2,2)=Q1
      Q1=X5*(-0.27495E-02)
      C(3,2,1)=Q1
      Q1=X5*(-0.42500E+01)
      P1=X5*Q1
      Q1=X9*P1
      C(3,1,1)=Q1
      C(2,3,3)=0.
      P1=X9*(-0.42500E+01)
      Q1=X9*P1
      P1=X2*(Q1 -0.25125E+01)
      Q1=X5*P1
      C(2,1,1)=Q1
      C(1,3,3)=0.
      Q1=X2*(-0.64983E+01)
      C(1,3,2)=Q1
      P1=X5*0.64983E+01
      Q1=X9*P1
      C(1,2,2)=Q1
      H(3,3)=0.42500E+01
      H(3,2)=0.
      Q1=X5*(-0.64983E+01)
      H(3,1)=Q1
      P1=X9*0.42500E+01
      Q1=X9*P1
      H(2,2)=Q1+0.25280E+01
      P1=X2*(-0.64983E+01)
      Q1=X9*P1
      H(2,1)=Q1
      P1=X9*0.42500E+01
      Q1=X9*P1
      P2=X2*0.10600E+00
      P1=X5*(Q1+0.26185E+01)
      Q2=X2*P2
      Q1=X5*P1
      H(1,1)=Q1+Q2+0.11251E+02
```

Fig. 1.7. Computer-generated FORTRAN program for the calculation of dynamic model matrices

As may be seen by simple enumeration, the construction of the complete model of this manipulator requires 26 floating-point multiplications and 5 additions to be carried out. The time needed to calculate all elements of the matrices of dynamic model by PDP 11/70 minicomputer is

0.46ms. This time is about 40 times shorter than 20ms, which may be taken as a reference for real-time operation. Consequently, it is possible to construct this model in real time even by microcomputers which operate 40 times slowlier than PDP 11/70. For example, an INTEL 8086/ /8087 - based microcomputer needs about 4ms for the same task.

The same example but for 6 degree-of-freedom Stanford manipulator is given in Ref. [26]. In that case, more than 300 floating-point multiplications is required. It consumes about 5ms on PDP 11/70, which is still convenient for real-time implementation.

At the end, it should be pointed out that for practical application in most cases it is necessary to take into account the dynamics of the first 3 links only. The last 3 links (see links 4, 5 and 6 in Fig. 1.4) are oftenly small compared with the first 3 links, and determine the orientation of the end-effector. Thus, their dynamics is oftenly negligeable comparing to the dynamics of the first 3 links. As we have seen from the previous example, the dominant dynamic effects can be calculated in a few miliseconds on a single up-date 16-bit microcomputer.

References

[1] Uicker J.J., "Dynamic Force Analysis of Spatial Linkages" ASME Journal of Applied Mechanics, pp. 418-424, June, 1976.

[2] Kahn M.E., "The near Minimum Time Control of Open Loop Articulated Kinematic Chains", Ph.D. Thesis, Stanford University, MEMO AIM, 106, 1969.

[3] Voo L.S., Freudenstein F., "Dynamic Analysis of Mechanisms Using Screw Coordinates", ASME Journal of Engineering for Industry, February, 1971.

[4] Yang A.T., "Inertia Force Analysis of Spatial Mechanisms", ASME Journal of Engineering for Industry, February, 1971.

[5] Orlandea N., Berenyi T., "Dynamic Continuous Path Synthesis of Industrial Robots Using Adams Computer Program", ASME Journal of Mechanical Design, No. 5, 1981.

[6] Mahil S.S., "On the Application of Lagrange's Method to the Description of Dynamic Systems", IEEE. Trans. on SMC, Vol. 12, No 6, pp. 877-890, 1982.

[7] Renaud M., "Contribution à L'etude de la Modelisation et de la Commande des Systèms Mècaniques Articulès", Thèse de Docteur--Ingènieur, Toulouse, France, 1975.

[8] Hollerbach J.M., "A Recursive Formulation of Lagrangian Manipulator Dynamics", IEEE Trans. on SMC, Vol. 10, No 11, pp. 730-736, 1980.

[9] Vukobratović M., Potkonjak V., "Contribution to Automatic Forming of Active Chain Models via Lagrangian Form", Journal of Applied Mechanics, No 1, 1979.

[10] Waters R.C., "Mechanical Arm Control", A.I. Memo 549, MIT Artificial Intelligence Laboratory, 1979.

[11] Saridis G.N., Lee C.S.G., "An Approximation Theory of Optimal Control for Trainable Manipulators", IEEE Trans. on SMC., Vol. 9, No 3, pp. 152-160, 1979.

[12] Kane T., Dynamics, New York, Holt, Rinehart and Winston, 1968.

[13] Huston R.L., Kelly F.A., "The Development of Equations of Motion of Single Arm Robots", IEEE Trans. on SMC., Vol. 12, No 3, pp. 259-266, 1982.

[14] Vukobratović M., Stepanenko Yu., "Mathematical Models of General Anthropomorphic Systems", Mathematical Biosciences, Vol. 17, pp. 191-242, 1973.

[15] Walker M.W., Orin D.E., "Efficient Dynamic Computer Simulation of Robotic Mechanisms", Trans. of ASME Journal of Dynamic Systems, Measurement and Control, Vol. 104, No 3, pp. 205-211, 1982.

[16] Luh J.Y.S., Walker M.W., Paul R.P.C., "On-Line Computational Scheme for Mechanical Manipulators", Trans. of ASME Journal of Dynamic Systems, Measurement and Control, Vol. 102, No 2, pp. 69-76, 1980.

[17] Luh J.Y.S., Lin C.S., "Scheduling of Parallel Computation for a Computer-Controlled Mechanical Manipulator", IEEE Trans. on SMC, Vol. 12, No 2, pp. 214-234, 1982.

[18] Aldon M.J., Liègeois A., "Génération et Programmation Automatiques des Equations de Lagrange des Robots et Manipulateurs", Rapport. de Recherche, INRIA.

[19] Vukobratović M., Kirćanski N., "New Method for Real-Time Manipulator Dynamic Model Forming on Microcomputers", Proceeding of First Yugoslav-Soviet Symp. on Applied Robotics, Moscow, February, 1983.

[20] Kirćanski N., "Computer-Aided Procedure of Forming of Robot Motion Equations in Analytical Forms, Proc. of VI IFToMM Congres, New Delhi, 1983.

[21] Renaud N., "An Efficient Iterative Analytical Procedure for Obtaining a Robot Manipulator Dynamic Model", Proc. of First International Symp. of Robotics Research, Bretton Woods, New Hampshire, USA, 1983.

[22] Vukobratović M., Kirćanski N., Scientific Fundamentals of Robotics 4, Real-Time Dynamics of Manipulation Robots, Springer-Verlag, 1985.

[23] Denavit J., Hartenberg R.S., "A Kinematic Notation for Lower Pair Mechanisms Based on Matrices", Journal of Applied Mechanics, pp. 215-221, June, 1955.

[24] Vukobratović M., Potkonjak V., Scientific Fundamentals of Robotics 1, Dynamics of Manipulation Robots, Springer-Verlag, 1982.

[25] Paul P.R., Robot Manipulators: Mathematics, Programming, and control, MIT Press, 1981.

[26] Vukobratović M., N.Kirćanski, "Computer-Assisted Generation of Robot Dynamic Models in an Analytical Form", Journal of Applied Mathematics and Mathematical Applications - Acta Applicandea Mathematicae, Vol. 3, pp. 49-70, 1985.

Chapter 2
Non-Adaptive Control of Manipulation Robots with Variable Parameters

2.1 Introduction

In this chapter we present the synthesis of non-adaptive control of manipulation robots with variable parameters. This book deals with the lowest hierarchical level (the so-called executive level) of manipulation control. The tactical control level which performs distribution of a movement to the motions of each degree of freedom of the robot has been considered in detail in the third book of this series [1].

The executive control level has already been treated in the second book of this series [2]. However, in that book we have treated the control synthesis for manipulation robots with constant and well-known parameters; we have assumed that all parameters of the manipulator are precisely defined. This assumption has allowed us to introduce nominal programmed control which has to be synthesized using the exact and complete model of robot dynamics. This programmed control realizes the desired motion of the robot under ideal conditions when no perturbation acts upon the system. Then, the model of deviation from the nominal trajectory and control has been considered and decentralized control synthesized. Nominal, programmed control compensates for coupling among the subsystems at the nominal level; thus, coupling among subsystems is reduced at the second control level.

In many cases in robotic practice the assumption that the parameters of the system are precisely known is valid. However, in a general case this need not be true, since some parameters of the robot (e.g. payload, clearances, frictions) may be uncertain and variable. On the other hand, calculation of nominal programmed control using a centralized model may be time consuming and cumbersome, because, the models of large-scale mechanical systems may be highly nonlinear and complex. Thus, we have assumed that the calculation of nominal control should be performed off-line, and calculated nominal control and trajectories have to be stored. However, this approach is acceptable in cases when the desired motion is well known in advance, when system parameters are precisely defined and constant and when there are only a few trajectories to be realized (which have to be repeated many times, as it is the common case in industrial robotics). However, if these assumptions are not satisfied the synthesis of nominal programmed control using complete, centralized model is not recommendable.

In this book we shall consider control synthesis for the robotic system with variable parameters. Our aim is to find simple non-adaptive and robust decentralized control capable of withstanding all expected variations of parameters. However, if it is impossible to find such a simple robust control it is necessary to introduce adaptive control.

In this chapter we shall consider the synthesis of non-adaptive control of manipulation robots with variable parameters, and in the next, Chapter 3, we shall consider the synthesis of adaptive control.

In Chapter 1 we have considered the mathematical model of the dynamics of the mechanical part of the robot, i.e. the mathematical model of the robot mechanism. In Paragraph 2.2 we consider the mathematical model of the complete robotic system when actuators dynamics is also taken into account, and we define the control task imposed on the executive control level. In Appendix 2.A we present how we can set mathematical models of actuators and discuss various complexities of these models from the standpoint of control synthesis. In Paragraph 2.3 we present various methods for solving the control tasks which have been considered by other authors, i.e. we shall make a brief survey of non-adaptive control methods for manipulation robots.

As explained above, the centralized nominal control is not useful for the case involving parameter variation. We consider the system as a set of subsystems, each of them being associated to one degree of freedom of the mechanism. For each subsystem we synthesize a local controller which stabilizes the decoupled (free) subsystem (Paragraph 2.4). Then, we directly examine the stability of the whole (coupled) system for the given set of allowable parameters values (Paragraph 2.5). This allows us to find the set of parameter values for which the chosen local controllers are satisfactory, or, vice-versa, we can find the local controllers which stabilize the whole system for the given set of allowable parameter values. If the set of allowable parameter values is given, it may happen that we cannot find unique local regulators which correspond to the system for all the values of the given region of parameters. In this case we have to introduce either global control (Paragraph 2.6) or adaptive control (Chapter 3).

In Volume 2 [2] we have analyzed asymptotic stability of the system around nominal trajectory. Now, when only local controllers are applied, we must directly analyze the practical stability of the whole system around the nominal trajectory. In this chapter we shall apply methods for practical stability analysis of large scale mechanical systems in finite regions around the set of nominal trajectories and for the given region of parameter variation. In Appendix 2.B we shall explain in detail the method for practical stability analysis.

Thus, in this chapter we present the synthesis of robust non-adaptive control which can be used as the executive level of the robot control. The control synthesis for a particular manipulation robot will be presented in Paragraph 2.7.

2.2 Mathematical Model of Manipulation Robots and Control Task Definition

In this paragraph we shall consider the mathematical model of the robotic manipulator system and define the task which has to be accomplished by robot control system.

2.2.1. Mathematical model

The robotic system consists of the mechanical part of the system and actuators. Mechanical part S^M of the robotic system has n degrees of freedom. Let us assume that each degree of freedom is powered by one actuator S^i, $i = 1,2,\dots,n$. D.C. electro-motors, hydraulic servo-actuators, etc. can serve as actuators for robotic systems.

The mathematical model of the mechanical part of the robotic system has been considered in detail in the previous chapter. As stated in Paragraph 1.2 the mathematical model of the mechanical part S^M can be written in the general form [3, 4]:

$$S^M\colon\ P_i = H_i(q,\ d)\ddot{q} + \dot{q}^T C_i(q,\ d)\dot{q} + g_i(q,\ d) \equiv$$

$$\equiv H_i(q,\ d)\ddot{q} + h_i(q,\ \dot{q},\ d) \qquad (2.2.1)$$

where $P_i \in R^1$ is the torque or force acting in the *i*th joint of the mechanism (*i*th d.o.f.); H_i: $R^n \times R^{\ell} \to R^{1\times n}$ is the vector of inertia; C_i: $R^n \times R^{\ell} \to R^{n\times n}$ is the matrix of centrifugal and Coriolis effects, g_i: $R^n \times R^{\ell} \to R^1$ is the gravity moment (force), h_i is defined as: $h_i(q, \dot{q}, d) \equiv \dot{q}^T C_i(q, d)\dot{q} + g_i(q, d)$, so that h_i: $R^n \times R^n \times R^{\ell} \to R^1$ are centrifugal, Coriolis and gravitational forces; $q \in R^n$ is the vector of robot angles (or displacements), $q = (q_1, q_2, \ldots, q_n)^T$, q_i corresponds to the *i*th d.o.f.; $d \in R^{\ell}$ is the vector of parameters of the mechanism (for example, payload, friction coefficients, etc.) which has to belong to the finite region of allowable parameter values D, i.e., $d \in D \subset R^{\ell}$; I denotes set $I = \{i: i = 1, 2, \ldots, n\}$. As we have mentioned in Paragraph 2.1, we shall consider the case when all parameters of the mechanism are not known in advance, or when some of them vary but within the given allowable boundaries (defined by the finite region D). It should be noted, that masses and moments of inertia of actuators must be also taken into account in the model (2.2.1). However the inertia terms are also included in the actuators models so we must substract the terms J_R^i from H_{ii}, where J_R^i is the moment of inertia (mass) of the rotor of the actuator which drives the *i*th joint. The mathematical models of actuators are nonlinear, in the general case. However, satisfactory results can be achieved if we suppose that the models of actuators are linear by state and nonlinear by input. Thus, in order to simplify the control synthesis, we shall adopt the mathematrical models of actuators in the following form:

$$S^i: \dot{x}^i = A^i(\theta^i)x^i + b^i(\theta^i)N(u^i) + f^i(\theta^i)M_i, \quad \forall i \in I \qquad (2.2.2)$$

where $x^i \in R^{n_i}$ is the vector of the state coordinates of the *i*th actuator S^i; n_i is the order of the mathematical model of actuator S^i; A^i: $R^{\ell_i} \to R^{n_i \times n_i}$ is the subsystem matrix; b^i: $R^{\ell_i} \to R^{n_i}$ is the input distribution vector, f^i: $R^{\ell_i} \to R^{n_i}$ is the load distribution vector; $u^i \in R^1$ is the input to actuator S^i; $M_i \in R^1$ is the load acting upon the *i*th actuator (for example, with D.C. motors M_i represents the load acting upon the output shaft of the reducer gear); $N(u^i)$ represents a nonlinear function of input u^i of amplitude saturation type:

$$N(u^i) = \begin{cases} -u_m^i & \text{for} \quad u^i < -u_m^i \\ u^i & \text{for} \quad |u^i| < u_m^i \\ u_m^i & \text{for} \quad u^i > u_m^i \end{cases} \qquad (2.2.3)$$

where u_m^i is the upper bound on input amplitude; $\theta^i \in R^{\ell i}$ is the vector of parameters of the ith actuator (viscous friction coefficient, moment and electromotor constant etc.).

We shall suppose that the parameters θ^i of the actuators are precisely identified and that they may vary very slowly. We also assume that the parameters of actuators must belong to some finite sets of parameters Θ^i, $\theta^i \in \Theta^i \subset R^{\ell i}$.

The order n_i of the actuator model (2.2.2) depends on the complexity of its adopted mathematical model. It has been shown [3] that for D.C. motors and hydraulic actuators (which are most commonly implemented with robotic systems) it is quite acceptable from the standpoint of control synthesis to adopt the third-order models. In Appendix 2.A we shall consider various complexities of actuators models (for D.C. motors and hydraulic actuators). The state vector x^i of the actuator model (2.2.2) depends on the type of actuator and the adopted model. For example, for D.C. motors we can adopt the third-order model with state vector x^i in the form $x^i = (l^i, \dot{l}^i, i_R^i)^T$ where l^i is the output shaft rotation and i_R^i is the rotor current; for hydraulic actuators we can also adopt the third-order model, but the state vector can be adopted as $x^i = (l^i, \dot{l}^i, p^i)^T$, where l^i is now the piston travel and p^i is the fluid pressure drop in the cylinder. The models of D.C. motors and hydraulic actuators have been presented in [2].

Now, we have to establish the connection between the model of the mechanical part of the robot S^M (2.2.1) and the models of actuators S^i (2.2.2). The connection between the motion of the actuator l^i and the angular or linear displacement q_i of the corresponding d.o.f. is, in the general case, nonlinear, i.e. we can write*)

$$q_i = \tilde{g}^i(l^i) \tag{2.2.4}$$

where $\tilde{g}^i: R^1 \to R^1$ is some nonlinear function of l^i. For example, if a rotational d.o.f. of the mechanism is powered by an actuator with a

---

*) It should be mentioned that in the general case one actuator might drive more than one mechanical d.o.f.; for example, two mechanical coordinates might be a complex function of displacements of two actuators: $(q_i, q_j) = g(l^i, l^j)$. For example ASEA manipulators have two actuators driving simultaneously two joints of the mechanism. However, we shall restrict ourselves to the case given by (2.2.4) where mechanical coordinate q_i depends only on l^i.

linear displacement (e.g. hydraulic linear actuator), $\tilde{g}^i$ is then given by cosines formula. If a rotational joint is powered by an actuator with rotational motion the connection (2.2.4) might be trivial: $q_i = l^i$; the same might hold if a linear d.o.f. of the mechanism is powered by an actuator with a linear displacement. Generally, the connection between the mechanism joint coordinate q_i and the state vector x^i of the corresponding actuator S^i can be written in the form:

$$q_i = G^i(x^i) \tag{2.2.5}$$

where $G^i: R^{n_i} \to R^1$.

Similarly, we have to establish the relation between the load M_i acting upon the actuator S^i and torque or force P_i developed in the *i*th d.o.f. of the mechanism. Analogously to relation (2.2.4), we can write that, in the general case, the relation between P_i and M_i is given by nonlinear mapping:

$$P_i = w^i(M_i, q_i) \tag{2.2.6}$$

where $w^i: R^1 \times R^1 \to R^1$ is some nonlinear function of M_i and q_i. As explained above, when the rotational joint of the mechanism is driven by the linear actuator the relation between the load acting upon the actuator M_i and the torque developed in mechanism joint P_i might be given by cosines formula or some other relation which depends on the joint position. For example, if a rotational joint is driven by a D.C. motor or vane hydraulic actuator the relation (2.2.6) might be trivial: $P_i = M_i$, but even in this case the relation (2.2.6) might be complex if some special clutches are implemented. For simplicity, we shall restrict our considerations to the case when relation (2.2.6) may be written in the form:

$$P_i = z^i(q_i) \cdot M_i \tag{2.2.7}$$

where $z^i: R^1 \to R^1$ is some nonlinear function of q_i.

The schematic presentation of the robotic manipulator model is given in Fig. 2.1.

Now, we can obtain the complete model of the robotic system S in the centralized form. In order to form the centralized model of the system, we shall unite the model S^M of mechanical part of the system and models

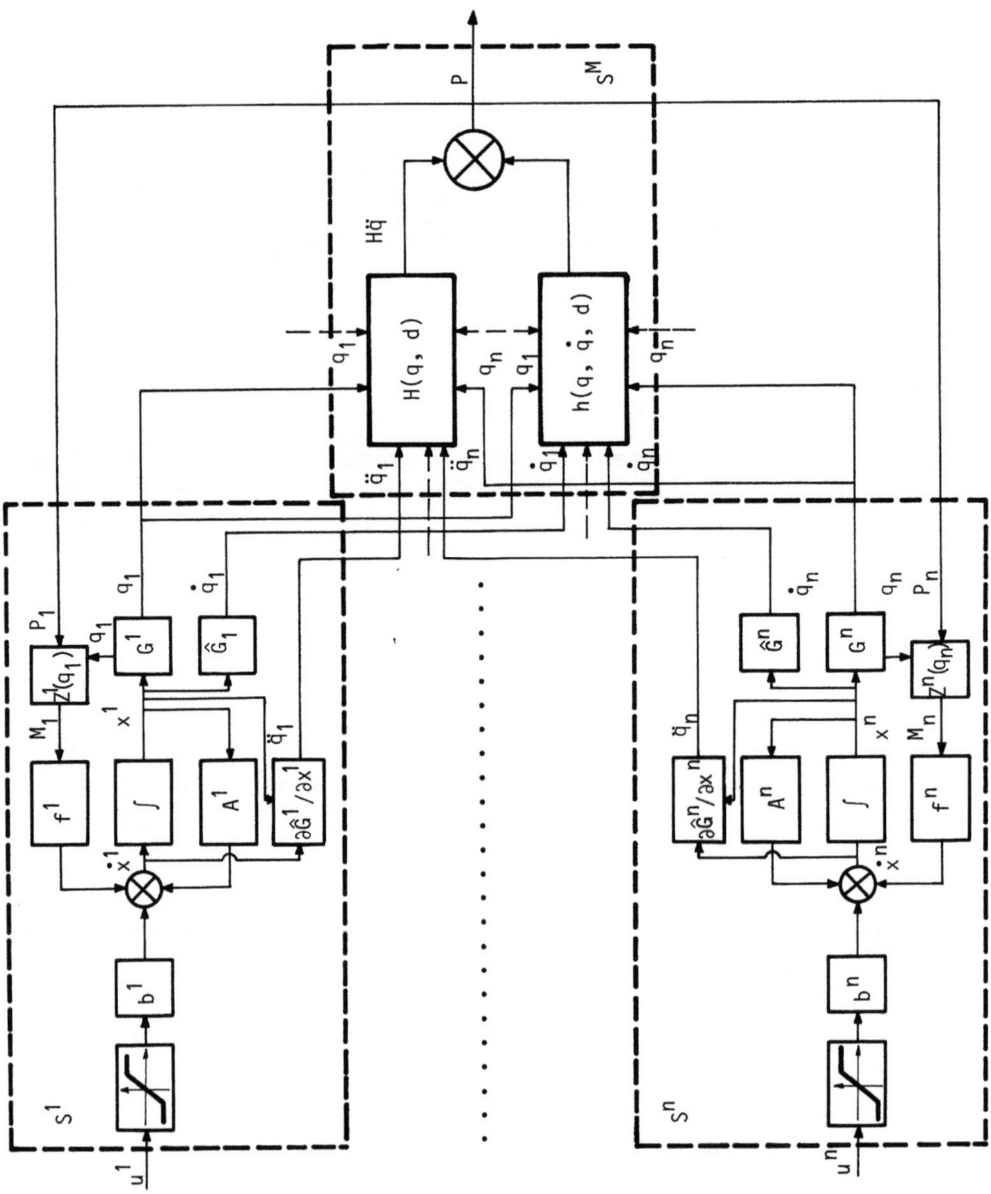

Fig. 2.1. Scheme of the model of the robotic manipulator

of actuators S^i. We get the centralized model in the form:

$$S:\quad \dot{x} = A_D(x,\ \theta,\ d) + B_D(x,\ \theta,\ d)N(u) \qquad (2.2.8)$$

where $x \in R^N$ is the state vector of the robotic system, $x(t) = (x^{1T}(t), x^{2T}(t),\ldots,x^{nT}(t))^T$; N is the order of the complete robotic system:

$$N = \sum_{i=1}^{n} n_i$$

$u \in R^n$ is the vector of inputs, $u(t) = (u^1(t),\ u^2(t),\ldots,u^n(t))^T$; $N(u)$ denotes the vector of nonlinearities: $N(u) = (N(u^1),\ N(u^2),\ldots,N(u^2))^T$; A_D: $R^N \times R^L \times R^\ell \to R^N$ is the vector given by:

$$A_D(x,\ \theta,\ d) = \left[I_N - F(\theta)z'(G(x))\cdot H(G(x),\ d)\tilde{G}(x)\right]^{-1}\cdot\left[A(\theta) + \right.$$

$$\left. + F(\theta)z'h(G(x),\ \hat{G}(x),\ d)\right] \qquad (2.2.9)$$

and B_D: $R^N \times R^L \times R^\ell \to R^{N\times n}$ is the input distribution vector given by:

$$B_D(x,\ \theta,\ d) = \left[I_N - F(\theta)z'(G(x))\cdot H(G(x),\ d)\tilde{G}(x)\right]^{-1}B(\theta) \qquad (2.2.10)$$

In (2.2.9) and (2.2.10) the following notation is used: A: $R^L \to R^{N\times N}$ denotes matrix $A(\theta) = \text{diag}(A^i(\theta^i))$, B: $R^L \to R^{N\times n}$ denotes matrix $B(\theta) = \text{diag}(b^i(\theta^i))$, F: $R^L \to R^{N\times n}$ denotes matrix $F(\theta) = \text{diag}(f^i(\theta^i))$, $H(q,\ d)$ is $n\times n$ inertia matrix defined by $H(q,\ d) = [H_i(q,\ d)]$, and $h(q,\ \dot{q},\ d)$ is the $n\times 1$ vector of centrifugal, Coriolis forces defined by $h(q,\ \dot{q},\ d) = [h_i(q,\ \dot{q},\ d)]$, z': $R^n \to R^{n\times n}$ denotes matrix $z(q) = \text{diag}(z^i(q_i)^{-1})$; $\theta \in \Theta \subset R^L$ denotes the vector of all actuators' parameters $\theta = (\theta^{1T},\ \theta^{2T},\ldots,\theta^{nT})^T$, Θ is the finite set defined by $\Theta = \Theta^1 \times \Theta^2 \times \ldots \times \Theta^n$, L is the total number of parameters:

$$L = \sum_{i=1}^{n} \ell_i$$

Obviously, according to (2.2.5) the vector of mechanical coordinates can be expressed by the state vector x in the following way:

$$q = G(x) = (G^1(x^1),\ G^2(x^2),\ldots,G^n(x^n))^T \qquad (2.2.11)$$

Starting from (2.2.11) we get:

$$\dot{q} = \frac{\partial G}{\partial x}\dot{x} = \hat{G}(x) = (\hat{G}^1(x^1),\ \hat{G}^2(x^2),\ldots,\hat{G}^n(x^n))^T \qquad (2.2.12)$$

where by $\hat{G}^i$: $R^n \to R^1$ we denote $\hat{G}^i = \partial G^i/\partial x^i \cdot \dot{x}^i = \partial \tilde{g}^i/\partial l^i \cdot \dot{l}^i$, since $\tilde{g}^i$ is a function of l^i only, and not of other state variables in x^i. Similarly, we get:

$$\ddot{q} = \frac{\partial \hat{G}(x)}{\partial x} \dot{x} = \left(\frac{\partial \hat{G}^1}{\partial x^1} \dot{x}^1, \frac{\partial \hat{G}^2}{\partial x^2} \dot{x}^2, \ldots, \frac{\partial \hat{G}^n}{\partial x^n} \dot{x}^n\right)^T = \tilde{G}(x) \cdot \dot{x} \qquad (2.2.13)$$

where $\tilde{G}$: $R^N \to R^{n \times N}$ denotes matrix $\tilde{G} = \mathrm{diag}\left(\frac{\partial \hat{G}^i}{\partial x^i}\right)$. Expressions (2.2.12) and (2.2.13) are also used in (2.2.9) and (2.2.10).

Thus, by (2.2.8) the model of robotic manipulator S is expressed in the centralized form. This model corresponds to the situation when the robot is not in mechanical contact with its environment, i.e. when there is no interaction between the robot and environment, so no external forces are acting upon the robot. In this book, we shall restrict ourselves to this case. The problem of interaction between the robot and environment has been treated in [2].

2.2.2. Control task definition

Now, we have to define the control task for manipulation robots. We shall synthesize the control which has to accomplish this control task.

As we have said in the Introduction, we shall consider the lowest - executive level of robot control system. Higher control levels are out of the scope of this book. Higher control levels define the task that the robotic system has to accomplish [5].

A robotic task is naturally specified in terms of its terminal device (manipulator tip) coordinates with respect to world reference frame. These coordinates we shall call external coordinates. The external coordinates $S(t)$ consist of hand position, described by a position vector $p(t)$ of the tip with respect to absolute Cartesian coordinates, and gripper orientation $\psi(t)$, which can be specified in various manners [1]. Here, we shall not discuss the ways of specifying external coordinates: this problem will be briefly presented in Chapter 4, but it has been considered in detail in [1]. The relation between the external coordinates $S(t) = [p^T(t), \psi^T(t)]$ of the manipulator and its joint coordinates $q(t)$ is given by:

$$S(t) = f_s(q(t)) \qquad (2.2.14)$$

where f_s: $R^n \rightarrow R^m$ is a vector function; m is the order of vector S(t) of external coordinates $S(t) \in R^m$. If m=n the manipulator is nonredundant and the relation (2.2.14) is unique: for the given q(t) the unique value of S(t) can be obtained and vice versa, if the inverse vector function is nonsingular. If m<n the robot is redundant and for the given S(t) we cannot find a unique solution for q(t), so we have to introduce some additional criteria to get the unique solution.

Starting from (2.2.14) the control system has to calculate q(t) which corresponds to the given S(t). This problem is solved at the tactical control level which has been considered in [1]. So, the tactical level calculates q(t) and sends it to the executive control level. The executive control level has to generate commands for joint actuators which should ensure realization of joint coordinates, q(t) so the desired external coordinates S(t) will be accomplished.

Thus, our task is to synthesize the control for the executive level which should ensure that the internal coordinates get the values specified by the tactical control level. However, several problems arise concerning the specification of control task at the executive level [6]. The first problem is: must the robot follow some specified path in space, i.e. is it necessary only to place the manipulator terminal device in some specified positions in space $S(t_j)$ or there is some path S(t) in space which has to be followed by the robot? The second problem, closely related to the first one, is: is the work space free from obstacles? A further problem arising is: must the robot follow some specified velocity profile along the given path, i.e. must the velocity of the robot gripper follow some specified trajectory? If the robot gripper has to follow some specified trajectory (and its velocity has to follow some trajectory) the question is: what are the allowable deviations of the real robot state from the specified nominal trajectory? The next question which could be set here is: are all parameters of the manipulator d, θ sufficiently precisely known in advance, or are some of them variable or unknown (for example payload is often variable and cannot be known in advance but its variation must be within certain limits). Depending on how we answer all these questions, we can define various control tasks at the executive level.

Most of the robots that are installed today in industry do not follow any specified path in the space, nor are they capable of withstanding parameter variations. With such robots the control system has to ensure that the robot terminal device passes through some specified points $S(t_i)$ in space. In that case the control at the executive level is reduced to the positional control: the specified points in external coordinates $S(t_i)$ are transformed into corresponding internal (joint) coordinates $q(t_i)$ and then the robot position is controlled from point to point in internal coordinates. Of course, in this case there is no coordination among the motions of robot joints, so the path of the robot hand between the specified points $S(t_i)$ is quite arbitrary.

This is acceptable in many simple tasks in industry when the work space is free. However, in the general case this approach cannot be adopted due to the presence of various obstacles in the work space, and since in many tasks it is necessary to follow the specified trajectory in space; even more, in many complex industrial tasks it is necessary to ensure desired velocity and acceleration of the robot terminal device along a desired trajectory (for example, welding or transfer of liquids). Thus, in modern robotics the requirements upon robotic manipulators performances become more and more severe.

The most general task in robotic practice can be regarded as a task of practical stabilization of the robot around the specified trajectory. Thus, in this book we shall consider such a control task at the executive control level. We suppose that a tactical control level supplies the lowest control level with desired nominal trajectory $x^o(t)$, $\forall t \in T$ for all state coordinates of the robot; here, T denotes the time interval in which the desired trajectory should be realized $T=\{t: t \in (0, \tau)\}$; τ is a specified time period. Naturally, nominal trajectories of state coordinates $x^o(t) = (x^{o1T}(t), x^{o2T}(t), \dots, x^{onT}(t))^T$ correspond to desired trajectories of joint coordinates $q^o(t)$ and joint velocities and accelerations $\dot{q}^o(t)$, $\ddot{q}^o(t)$ and, accordingly, $x^o(t)$ corresponds to desired trajectories $S^o(t)$, velocities $\dot{S}^o(t)$ and accelerations $\ddot{S}^o(t)$ of external coordinates of the robot. Namely, we can state that the nominal trajectory is imposed in external coordinates $S^o(t)$, $\dot{S}^o(t)$, $\ddot{S}^o(t)$ and tactical and executive control levels have to realize it*).

However, in the general case it is not possible to ensure realizations of nominal trajectory without any error in position or velocity or

---

*) It should be mentioned that it is not indispensable to divide the control system into two levels: tactical and executive, as it is assumed in this text. Some authors try directly so control external coordinates (see Paragraph 2.3).

acceleration; on the other hand, some tolerances around trajectory are always allowed. Let us denote by $X_s(t) \subset R^m$ the set of alowable deviations of real external coordinates from nominal trajectory $S^o(t)$; analogously, let us denote by $X_s^v(t)$ and $X_s^a(t)$ the set of allowable tolerances of external velocities and accelerations of the robot, respectively. On the basis of (2.2.14), relation between the external and internal coordinates, we can map the set $X_s(t)$, in the space of external coordinates, into the corresponding set $Q(t) \subset R^n$, in the space of internal (joint) coordinates:

$$\underline{F}_s^{-1}(X_s(t)) \rightarrow Q(t), \qquad \forall t \in T \qquad (2.2.15)$$

where mapping $\underline{F}_s^{-1}$: $R^m \rightarrow R^n$ is assumed to be nonsingular for all points in the set $X_s(t)$, $\forall t \in T$. Similarly, using (2.2.14) we can map the sets of allowable deviations of external velocities and external accelerations $X_s^v(t)$, $X_s^a(t)$ into corresponding sets of allowable deviations of joint velocities and joint accelerations $Q^v(t)$, $Q^a(t)$, $\forall t \in T$. In this way we get the regions of allowable deviations of internal coordinates, velocities and accelerations $Q(t)$, $Q^v(t)$, $Q^a(t)$, $\forall t \in T$ around nominal trajectories of joint coordinates $q^o(t)$, velocities $\dot{q}^o(t)$ and accelerations $\ddot{q}^o(t)$.

Using (2.2.5), relation between the joint coordinates of the robot q_i and state coordinates x^i of the corresponding actuator, we can map the regions $Q(t)$, $Q^v(t)$, $Q^a(t)$, $\forall t \in T$ into the regions $X^{t(i)}(t) \subset R^{n_i}$ $\forall i \in I$ in the subsystems state spaces:

$$\underline{G}^{-1}(Q(t),\ Q^v(t),\ Q^a(t)) \rightarrow X^t(t), \qquad \forall t \in T \qquad (2.2.16)$$

where mapping*) $\underline{G}^{-1}$: $R^n \times R^n \times R^n \rightarrow R^N$ is nonsingular in all points of regions $Q(t)$, $Q^v(t)$, $Q^a(t)$, $\forall t \in T$; $X^t(t) \subset R^N$ denotes the region of allowable deviations of state coordinates $x(t)$ around nominal trajectory $x^o(t)$, $\forall t \in T$, which might be taken in "decoupled" form:

$$X^t(t) = X^{t(1)}(t) \times X^{t(2)}(t) \times \cdots \times X^{t(n)}(t), \quad \forall t \in T \qquad (2.2.17)$$

It should be mentioned that the region $X^t(t)$ is not only defined by the

---

*) Here we assummed that $n_i=3$, $\forall i \in I$, which is commonly the case. If we choose $n_i=2$, it is sufficient to define regions $Q(t)$, $Q^v(t)$. If $n_i>3$, additional restrictions upon the subsystems state coordinates have to be imposed.

allowable deviations of external coordinates about nominal trajectory due to tolerances in tracking the given trajectory; this region is also constrained by the presence of different obstacles in the work space and by various constraints upon the manipulator kinematics. The sets $Q^v(t)$, $Q^a(t)$ are also constrained by the possibilities of the actuators (for more details on imposing the region $X^t(t)$, see Paragraph 4.2).

By these restrictions, the region $X^t(t)$ around $x^o(t)$ is defined to which the system state must belong during the tracking of $x^o(t)$. Perturbations that are acting upon the robotic system can be reduced, in principle, to perturbations of initial conditions type. However, initial error of the robot state can be assumed to be constrained, i.e. we can assume that initial condition x(0) must belong to some finite region (set)$\in X^I$ in the state space $X^I \subset R^N$. Thus, our control task at the executive level is to synthesize the control which will ensure that for $\forall x(0) \in X^I$ it must be satisfied $x(t) \in X^t(t)$, $\forall t \in T$, where $x^o(0) \in X^I$, $x^o(t) \in X^t(t)$, $\forall t \in T$, and $X^I \subseteq X^t(0)$ must be satisfied (see Fig. 2.2).

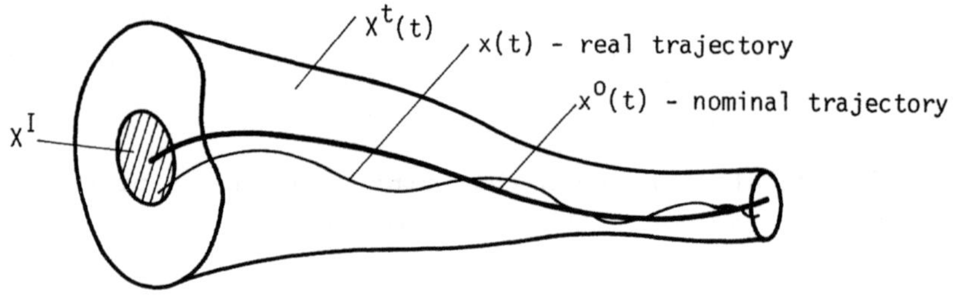

Fig. 2.2. Regions of practical stability of robotic system

This control task can be viewed as a task of practical stabilization of robotic system in the finite time interval, around the given nominal trajectory $x^o(t)$. Similar control has already been considered in our previous book [2]*). However, previously we have assumed that all parameters of the robots are well identified and known in advance. Now, we shall consider the case when all parameters of the robots d, θ cannot be defined in advance or some of them are variable. However, we shall divide the parameters of the robot into two groups: d parameters of the mechanical part of the robot are assumed to be variable and unknown, and we shall assume that their variation is relatively fast;

---

*) Actually, in [2] we have also introduced the region X^F of allowable deviations around terminal point on the trajectory $x^o(\tau)$. However, for the reason of simplicity, we have omitted this region X^F since this can be defined by a proper definition of $X^t(\tau_s)$.

θ parameters of actuators are assumed to vary very slowly. Thus, we shall assume that variation of actuator parameters θ may be neglected and their identification can be performed off-line. So we can synthesize the control assuming that the models of actuators are constant and precisely defined. During robot operation, the control system must occasionally check the parameters of actuators θ to identify their values, and, if they significantly vary, either synthesize new feedback gains or indicate variation of the parameters (see Paragraph 5.4).

On the other hand, some of the parameters of the mechanical part of the robot, may vary significantly (for example, payload). Thus during the synthesis of control we have to take care about the parameter variations. However, in the general case, variations of such parameters are not known in advance. So, we have to synthesize the control which is capable of withstanding all expected variations of parameters. As we have already noted, we assume that $d \in D$, i.e. parameter values must belong to some constrained set D of the allowable values of parameters. Thus, our control task at the executive level can be stated as follows (practical stabilization of robotic system):

(2.2.18) Definition of control task: The control $u(t, x)$ has to be synthesized which will ensure that $\forall x(0) \in X^I$ and $\forall d \in D$ implie $x(t, x(0), d, u(t, x(t)) \in X^t(t)$, $\forall t \in T$ *), where X^I and X^t are finite regions in the state space around prescribed nominal trajectory $x^o(t)$.

Such a definition of control task is sufficiently broad to cover all possible control tasks in robotics (at the lowest control level). Typical industrial tasks such as arc welding, paint spraying, parts assembly, etc. can be included in the above definition. If we have to deal with some simple control tasks it is easy to "reduce" the above statement to suit the desired task; for example, if we have to deal with positional control only, i.e. if the robot does not have to follow some specified path, instead of the nominal trajectory $x^o(t)$ we can put only the given points $q^o(t_i)$ (corresponding to $S^o(t_i)$) and reduce the time-varying region $X^t(t)$ to set of time-constant regions $X^t(t_i)$ around the given points $q^o(t_i)$ which define allowable tolerances in positioning the robot around the points $S^o(t_i)$; the velocities and accelerations of robot are not important in such a case, so the regions $X^t(t_i)$ are restricted with respect to velocity and accelerations by actuators

---

*) For simplicity, in the text to follow we shall denote real state of the robotic system by $x(t)$, instead of $x(t, x(0), d, u(t, x(t))$.

capabilities. On the other hand, if there are some obstacles in the work space of the robot, by the regions X^I and $X^t(t)$ we can define the allowable deviations from the prescribed colision-free trajectory, to avoid collision with obstacles during the tracking of trajectory. It is obvious that the above definition includes the control task which has been considered in [2]; by putting $D = \{d: d=d^o\}$, where d^o are given, known in advance, parameters of the robot, we get the previously considered control task.

Now, our aim is to synthesize the control which can accomplish the above defined task. Since we have already considered this task in the case when the parameters of mechanism are known in advance, we shall pay our attention to the fact that now parameters d are variable and not known in advance. The presence of variable parameters imposes several dilemmas. The first is: can we synthesize unique robust nonadaptive control (with constant gains) which can accommodate the robotic system for all expected variations of parameters or, must we introduce adaptive control? In this Chapter we shall restrict ourselves to synthesizing nonadaptive control for robotic manipulators; we shall examine whether we can determine such nonadaptive control which will satisfy the control task for given (X^I, X^t, τ, D). The second problem is: how complex a control law we must choose in order to satisfy the specified task? Can we adopt decentralized control, as we did in [2, 10], or, must we compensate for coupling and for parameters variations? Can we apply centralized programmed control, as we did before [2, 8]? Can we analyze the stability of the system using the same procedure as in [2, 7, 8]?

First, we shall briefly survey several approaches to control synthesis of robotic systems which have been developed by other authors. Here, we shall also restrict to consideration of nonadaptive control synthesis only (for adaptive control see Chapter 3). Then, we shall present in detail our approach to solving the above stated control task.

Before passing to the survey of nonadaptive control schemes, we have to make two additional remarks concerning the control task definition.

(I) In order to simplify considerations about the robot stability, let us observe particular forms of finite regions X^I and $X^t(t)$ (which is the most commonly encountered). We assume that the regions are given by:

$$X^I = X^{I(1)} \times X^{I(2)} \times \dots \times X^{I(n)}, \quad X^{I(i)} \in R^{n_i},$$

$$X^{I(i)} = \left\{x^i(0): \quad ||\Delta x^i(0)|| < \bar{X}^{I(i)}\right\}, \tag{2.2.19}$$

$$X^{t(i)} = \left\{x^i(t): \quad ||\Delta x^i(t)|| < \bar{X}^{t(i)} \exp(-\alpha^{(i)} t)\right\}, \quad \forall t \in T,$$

where $\bar{X}^{(i)} > \bar{X}^{I(i)} > 0, \alpha^{(i)} > 0$, $\forall i \in I$. Here $\bar{X}^{I(i)}$, $\bar{X}^{t(i)}$, $\alpha^{(i)}$ are real-valued positive numbers, $||\cdot||$ denotes Euclidean norm of the corresponding vector, and $\Delta x^i \in R^{n_i}$ denotes error of the *i*th subsystem state vector from its nominal trajectory $\Delta x^i(t) = x^i(t) - x^{oi}(t)$, $\forall t \in T$, $\forall i \in I$. It is easy, to extend all results to the general case when the regions X^I and X^t are given in some arbitrary form*).

(II) The second remark concerns the robustness of the control synthesized. Namely, we want to synthesize the nonadaptive control which is capable of withstanding all system nonlinearities and parameter variations. Thus, our aim is to find unique control for all control tasks that can be put upon the particular robotic system. Our definition of control task is general; we did not impose any limit upon the regions X^I and X^t and the set of allowable parameters values D, or upon the time duration of the task τ. So, it is possible to impose such a control task which will ensure that the corresponding control is sufficiently robust. However, there may exist some correlation between the regions X^I and X^t, time duration of the movement τ and the set D; for example, if the mass of the payload is larger, then we may demand slower motion of the robot (τ is longer and X^t might be wider) than in the case when the mass of the payload is lower. Thus, in order to ensure the synthesis which is closely related to the requirements for the particular robotic system, we shall modify our definition (2.2.18) of control task. Let us assume that instead of one nominal trajectory $x^o(t)$, $\forall t \in T$, the set of J_1 nominal trajectories $x_j^o(t)$, $\forall t \in T_j$, $j \in J = \{j: j=1,2,\dots,J_1\}$ is given, where $T_\ell = \{t: t \in (0, \tau_j)\}$, τ_j are given time periods (durations of nominal trajectories). To each nominal trajectory $x_j^o(t)$ are associated regions $X_j^I \in R^N$, $X_j^t(t) \in R^N$, $\forall t \in T_j$, and sets of allowable parameter variations along the corresponding nominal trajectory $D_j \subset D$, $\forall j \in J$. Now, we can define the extended control task (at the executive control level):

*) Actually, if the regions X^I and $X^t(t)$ are given in some arbitrary form (e.g. X_1^I and $X_1^t(t)$), we can always find numbers $\bar{X}^{I(i)}$, $\bar{X}^{t(i)}$ and $\alpha^{(i)}$ in (2.2.19) such that $X^I \subseteq X_1^I$ and $X^t(t) \subseteq X_1^t(t)$, $\forall t \in T$.

(2.2.20) Definition of extended control task: The control u(t, x) has to be synthesized which will ensure that $\forall x(0)\in X_j^F$ and $\forall d\in D_j$ imply $x(t)\in X_j^t(t)$, $\forall t\in T_j$, $\forall j\in J$, where the regions X_j^F and $X_j^t(t)$ are finite regions in the state space around the corresponding prescribed nominal trajectory $x_j^o(t)$, $\forall t\in T$, $\forall j\in J$ (i.e. $x_j^o(0)\in X_j^I$ and $x_j^o(t)\in X_j^t(t)$, $\forall t\in T_j$).

In the general case regions X_j^I and $X_j^t(t)$ can be arbitrarily chosen; but, in accordance with what we have said above, we shall restrict to the case when these regions are defined analogously to (2.2.18). So, we can assume that the regions X_j^I and $X_j^t(t)$ are given by:

$$X_j^I = X_j^{I(1)}\times X_j^{I(2)}\times \cdots \times X_j^{I(n)},\quad X_j^{I(i)}\subset R^{n_i},\quad \forall i\in I$$

$$X_j^t(t) = X_j^{t(1)}(t)\times X_j^{t(2)}(t)\times \cdots \times X_j^{t(n)}(t),\quad X_j^{t(i)}(t)\subset R^{n_i},\quad \forall i\in I$$

$$X_j^{I(i)} = \left\{x^i(0):\ ||\Delta x_j^i(0)|| < \bar{X}_j^{I(i)}\right\} \tag{2.2.21}$$

$$X_j^{t(i)} = \left\{x^i(t):\ ||\Delta x_j^i(t)|| < \bar{X}_j^{t(i)}\exp(-\alpha_j^{(i)}t)\right\},\quad \forall t\in T_j$$

where $\bar{X}_j^{t(i)} > \bar{X}_j^{I(i)} > 0$, $\alpha_j^{(i)} > 0$, $\forall i\in I$, $\forall j\in J$. Here, $\bar{X}_j^{t(i)}$, $\bar{X}_j^{I(i)}$, $\alpha_j^{(i)}$ are real-valued positive numbers and $\Delta x_j^i(t)$ denotes the deviation of the *i*th subsystem S^i state vector from the *j*th nominal trajectory, $\Delta x_j^i(t) = x^i(t) - x_j^{oi}(t)$, $\Delta x_j^i(t)\in R^{n_i}$, $\forall t\in T_j$, $\forall j\in J$, $\forall i\in I$. Obviously, $x_j^o(t) = (x_j^{o1T}(t), x_j^{o2T}(t),\ldots,x_j^{onT}(t))^T$.

Although our aim is to synthesize control which will accomodate the extended control task (2.2.20), for the sake of simplicity we shall present control synthesis and stability analysis for the simpler task (2.2.18), and the extension of the results to the case (2.2.20) is trivial. We shall show how we can accommodate task (2.2.20) on an example (see Paragraph 2.7).

2.3 Survey of Non-Adaptive Control Algorithms

In this Paragraph we shall briefly survey various approaches to the synthesis of nonadaptive control for robotic systems. We shall concentrate mainly upon the problems of control synthesis of the executive control level. But, as already mentioned, in some approaches the tactical and executive control levels are undivided so we cannot speak solely about the executive control level but we must also touch some problems concerning trajectories planning and their generation.

The main problem with control of robotic systems is: to what extent it is necessary to include dynamic terms in the control law? Namely, as it has been explained in Chapter 1, the mathematical model of the robotic mechanism S^M (2.2.1) in general case is very complex system of nonlinear differential equations. The problem of on-line computation of robot dynamic model is very difficult. In Chapter 5 we shall discuss computation complexity of the various control laws and dynamic models. Various methods for computing the input torques P by (2.2.1) require various numbers of additions and multiplications to be performed each time the driving torques P are needed (every sampling period). However, the analytical models of robot dynamics, which have been proposed by Vukobratović and Kirćanski (Chapter 1), lead to the fastest computation of robot dynamic models achieved so far. Unfortunately, even in this case computation of driving torques is too complex(for some types of robot structures) to be computed by temporary sixteen-bit microprocessors. There have been made numerous attempts to use simplified models of the robot dynamics in which some terms have been neglected in order to simplify on-line computation of control. We shall mention some of them while discussing various control laws. Usually, centrifugal and Coriolis terms in (2.2.1) have been neglected since these terms are insignificant while the robot approaches its goal position and orientation (since the joint velocities are low during that time). However, if we attempt to ensure precise tracking of fast trajectories, these velocity dependent terms have to be compensated for, too. To implement on-line computation of dynamic model of the robot we have to use complex multiprocessor system. Thus, trade-off between the complexity of control equipment and the performance of the robot has to be made: the more complex law we use the more complex is the controller hardware but the performance of the robot would be better.

One of the dilemmas arising in the synthesis of control for robotic system is whether or not we have to minimize some criterion. Actually, we have defined our control task (2.2.18) (or (2.2.20)) without introducing any numerical criterion. Our control task is functionally imposed. However, in principle we can add some criterion which has to be minimized by the control (which also has to accomplish the given control task (2.2.20))*)

---

*) Obviously, we assume that the criterion (2.3.1) is set so as to be consistent with the control task (2.2.20).

$$J = \int_0^{t_s} \underset{\sim}{L}\ (x(t),\ u(t))dt + \underset{\sim}{g}(x(t_s)) \tag{2.3.1}$$

where time interval t_s is not fixed (but is shorter than τ); $\underset{\sim}{L}$: $R^N \times R^n \rightarrow R^1$ is a scalar, continuous and differentiable function of state and control and $\underset{\sim}{g}$: $R^N \rightarrow R^1$ is the function of the terminal state.

There were a few attempts to solve the control task together with minimization of some criterion (2.3.1). However, most of the authors tried to simplify the problem by synthesizing suboptimal control or avoiding the introduction of any criterion; or, they simplified the model of the robot in order to achieve some acceptable solution. Here, we shall briefly present some of these approaches to control synthesis for robotic systems. We have tried to choose the most representative contributions to the dynamic control synthesis. For clarity of presentation, we have, conditionally, divided all approaches to six directions, as can be seen in Fig. 2.3. Let us note that we have restricted ourselves to dynamic control of manipulation robots, i.e. to such control laws that take into account dynamic effects of the robotic systems. Thus, various kinematic approaches, that are based execusively on kinematic models of the robots are not included in this survey.

2.3.1. Optimal control synthesis

To synthesize the control which will satisfy the given control task (2.2.20) and, at the same time, minimize the criterion (2.3.1) is a very difficult problem. In [2] we have discussed this problem and underlined several reasons for this: (a) complexity of the highly nonlinear model of the robotic system (2.2.8), (b) the choice of the criterion (2.3.1) is often conditional and heuristic, (c) the constraints imposed by the control task (through region $X^t(t)$) are usually severe, so it is difficult to take them into account during optimization procedure, etc. Now, when we have assumed that the parameters of the robot are unknown and variable, the problem of optimization becomes more difficult. However, we shall briefly present a few attempts to minimize some criterion in the control synthesis.

First, let us consider the case when initial $x(0)$ and final $x^o(t_s)$ states of the robot are given (but not the complete trajectory $x^o(t)$). We have to synthesize the trajectory $x^o(t)$ which minimizes some criterion (2.3.1). The search for an optimal solution to the problem stated

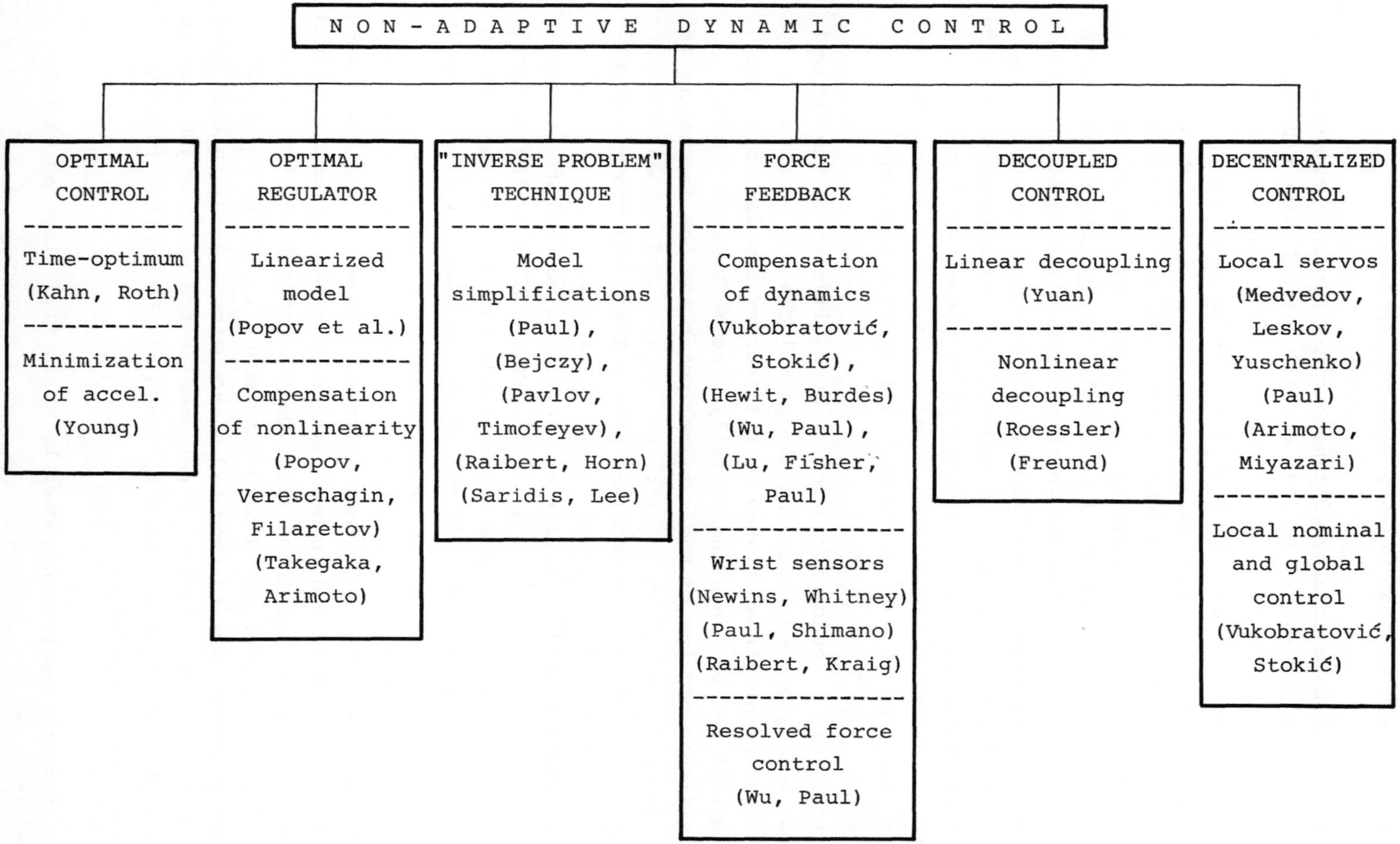

Fig. 2.3. Survey of control strategies

is determined by the minimum principle of Pontryagin.

Kahn and Roth [11] have considered time-optimal control problem: given the robotic system defined by (2.2.8) with the initial state $x(0)$, and the terminal constraint $x^o(t_s)$; find the control $u(t)$ which transfers the state of the system from $x(0)$ to $x^o(t_s)$ in the minimum time, i.e. such that the functional J, defined by (2.3.1), where: $\tilde{L}(x(t), u(t)) = 1$, $\tilde{g}(x(t_s)) = 0.$, is a minimum. Obviously, the control is constrained by (2.2.3). However, it can be shown that the analytical solution to this problem cannot be found even for a particular manipulation robot with three revolute degrees of freedom which has been considered in [11]. Owing to the nonlinearity of the model, only a numerical approach is obtainable which yields the optimal control only as a function of time and does not account for any unexpected disturbances which may act on the system or parameter variations; in addition, the computations must be repeated for each new set of initial and final conditions.

In order to obtain a feedback control an approximation to the optimal control has been proposed [11]. The suboptimal control is obtained by approximating the nonlinear system by a linear system for which the optimal control can be found analytically. The mathematical model (2.2.8) is linearized around the terminal point and the decoupling of the model is performed by neglecting the coupling and compensating only gravitational moments in the terminal point. Thus, the robot's model decouples into n double integrator systems for which analytical solution to the above stated optimization problem is well-known (it has been assumed that $n_i = 2$, $x^i = (q_i, \dot{q}_i)^T$, $\forall i \in I$). A switching surface accounting for the gravity loads on the robot is then obtained and an approximation is made for the effects of the angular velocity terms in the nonlinear system. It has been shown that for a particular robot suboptimal control results in response times and trajectories which are reasonably close to the optimal solutions. However, for more complex manipulation robots and longer distance between the terminal points this solution might be too suboptimal. On the other hand, the suboptimal control for this problem is bang-bang which is hardly acceptable for robotic practice, due to overload of actuators. Also, in this case trajectory of the robot gripper is not predictable which might lead to collision with obstacles; so, this approach can be applied in very limited manipulator applications.

A similar approach has been proposed by Young [12]. Instead of time-

-optimal control, Young adopted criterion (2.3.1) with

$$\underset{\sim}{L}(x(t),\ u(t)) = 0.5\cdot\ddot{q}^T M\ \ddot{q},\quad g(x(t_s)) = 0.$$

where $M \in R^{n\times n}$ is a positive definite matrix, i.e. he wanted to minimize the integral of a quadratic function in acceleration. Similarly to the above mentioned approach [11], here again the robotic system is considered as a set of n double integrator plants (by ignoring the dependance of $\ddot{q}$ on q(t) and $\dot{q}(t)$). Optimal trajectories $q^{oi}(t)$, $\dot{q}^{oi}(t)$, $\ddot{q}^{oi}(t)$, which drive the double integrators from given initial state $x^{oi}(0) = (q^{oi}(0),\ \dot{q}^{oi}(0))^T$ to desired state $x^{oi}(t_s) = (q^{oi}(t_s), \dot{q}^{oi}(t_s))^T$ and minimize (2.2.3), are well known. Now, from (2.2.1) the driving torques $P^o(t)$ are calculated that would drive the system along desired trajectories:

$$P^o(t) = H(q^o(t),\ d^o)\ddot{q}^o(t) + \underset{\sim}{h}(q^o(t),\ \dot{q}^o(t),\ d^o) \tag{2.3.2}$$

where d^o are well-defined parameters. Using (2.2.2) we can calculate "optimal" control. Obviously, this results in open loop control (explicit functions of time), and this control requires on-line calculation of the complete model. Of course, the control (2.3.2) compensates for all nonlinearities of the robot, and the robot's model is formally reduced to n double integrators. However, the obtained control is far from being optimal for the complete nonlinear model of the robotic system. On the other hand, calculation of the complete dynamics might be too complex. Parameter variations cannot be compensated by this control law.

We have shown two attempts to synthesize optimal control for robotic systems. Numerous problems that are encountered, in optimization procedures result in enormous simplifications, which make the obtained control far from optimal. The obtained control laws are too complex even for simple manipulator structures for which they were developed [11, 12]. For more complex robotic structure their on-line imprementation might demand a rather complex multiprocessor system. On the other hand, the control laws are explicit functions of time so they are not robust and cannot withstand parameter variations.

2.3.2. Optimal regulator

The approaches described above were intended for positional control of robots. The problem of tracking some prescribed path in work space is more complex, so approaches by optimal synthesis are not likely to yield an acceptable solution.

An alternative aproach is to calculate (off-line) nominal trajectory by some optimal [1, 13] or suboptimal procedure [1, 14], and then, at the executive level, to track desired path*). In this book, we shall pay attention to various attempts to synthesize control for tracking the given nominal trajectory.

The control for tracking the given nominal trajectory $x^{o}(t)$, $\forall t \in T$ (executive control level only) can be synthesized by minimizing some criterion (2.3.1). The most commonly applied criterion is the standard quadratic criterion where

$$\begin{aligned} \underset{\sim}{L}(x(t),\ u(t)) &= \frac{1}{2}\,[\Delta x^{T}(t)Q(t)\Delta x(t) + \Delta u^{T}(t)\underline{R}(t)\Delta u(t)], \\ \underset{\approx}{g}(x(t_s)) &= \frac{1}{2}\,\Delta x^{T}(t_s)Q_T\Delta x(t_s) \end{aligned} \tag{2.3.3}$$

where $Q(t): T \to R^{N\times N}$, $Q_T \in R^{N\times N}$ are positive semidefinite matrices and $\underline{R}(t): T \to R^{n\times n}$ is a positive definite matrix. Here $\Delta x \in R^{N}$ is the deviation of the state vector from the nominal trajectory $\Delta x(t) = x(t) - x^{o}(t)$, $\Delta u(t) \in R^{n}$ is the deviation of the control vector from the nominal programed control $u^{o}(t)$, corresponding to $x^{o}(t)$ (see [2]) $\Delta u(t) = u(t) - u^{o}(t)$. Interval t_s, and the weighting matrices $Q(t)$, $\underline{R}(t)$, Q_T are chosen to satisfy the conditions of practical stability of the robot ((2.2.18) or (2.2.20)).

If we try to minimize criterion (2.3.1), (2.3.3) using the nonlinear model of the robot (2.2.8) we shall encounter numerous problems; we can find only a numerical solution to this problem resulting in an open--loop control law whose implementation is practically impossible [2]. A common approach in solving this problem is to consider some approximative model of the robot. The approximation that leads to an elegant well-known solution of control is to linearize the model (2.2.8) around the nominal trajectory $\Delta x^{o}(t)$, $\forall t \in T$.

Let us consider the model of deviations of the robot's state from the nominal trajectory $x^{o}(t)$ [2].

---

*) Actually, this approach has been assumed in Paragraph 2.2.2 (when we have spoken about nominal trajectory), but our definitions of control tasks are wide enough to include cases considered in Paragraph 2.3.1, when only terminal points are given.

Starting from the robot's model (2.2.8) and assuming that nominal (programmed) control $u^o(t)$ satisfies:

$$\dot{x}^o(t) = A_D(x^o(t),\ \theta^o,\ d^o) + B_D(x^o(t),\ \theta^o,\ d^o)u^o(t) \qquad (2.3.4)$$

where θ^o, d^o denote some nominal values of parameters $\theta^o \in \Theta$, $d^o \in D$, we get the model of deviation in the form:

$$S:\ \Delta\dot{x} = \bar{A}^o(\Delta x,\ \theta,\ d,\ t) + \bar{B}^o(\Delta x,\ \theta,\ d,\ t)N(t,\ \Delta u), \qquad (2.3.5)$$

where $\bar{A}^o(\Delta x,\ \theta,\ d,\ t)$: $R^N \times \Theta \times D \times T \to R^N$ is the vector function of order N,

$$\bar{A}^o(\Delta x,\ \theta,\ d,\ t) = A_D(x,\ \theta,\ d) - A_D(x^o(t),\ \theta^o,\ d^o) + \left[B_D(x,\ \theta,\ d) - B_D(x^o(t),\ \theta^o,\ d^o)\right]u^o(t),$$

and $\bar{B}^o(\Delta x,\ \theta,\ d,\ t)$: $R^N \times \Theta \times D \times T \to R^{N\times n}$ is the matrix function of dimensions $N\times n$ given by

$$\bar{B}^o(\Delta x,\ \theta,\ d,\ t) = B_D(\Delta x,\ \theta,\ d,\ t) = B_D(\Delta x + x^o(t),\ \theta,\ d)$$

The nonlinearity of the amplitude saturation type of inputs $\Delta u(t)$ is given by $N(t,\ \Delta u) = (N(t,\ \Delta u^1),\ N(t,\ \Delta u^2),\dots,N(t,\ \Delta u^n))^T$, where

$$N(t,\ \Delta u^i) = \begin{cases} -u_m^i - u^{oi}(t) & \text{for } \Delta u^i < -u_m^i - u^{oi}(t) \\ \Delta u^i & \text{for } -u_m^i < u^i + u^{oi}(t) < u_m^i \\ u_m^i - u^{oi}(t) & \text{for } \Delta u^i > u_m^i - u^{oi}(t) \end{cases} \qquad (2.3.6)$$

and $\Delta u = (\Delta u^1,\ \Delta u^2,\dots,\Delta u^n)^T$.

Now, as we said above, we want to consider the linearized model of the robot around the nominal trajectory. Linearization of the deviation model (2.3.5) can be performed analytically [15], or by some numerical procedures for model linearization on a digital computer [16], or by means of various identification methods [2]. The linearized model is obtained in the form:

$$\Delta\dot{x} = \tilde{A}^o(\theta^*,\ d^*,\ t)\Delta x + \tilde{B}^o(\theta^*,\ d^*,\ t)N(t,\ \Delta u), \qquad (2.3.7)$$

where $\tilde{A}^o(\theta^*, d^*, t): T \to R^{N\times N}$ is an N×N matrix the elements of which are continuous functions of time $\tilde{A}^o = [\tilde{a}^o_{ij}]$: $\tilde{a}^o_{ij} = \left.\frac{\partial \bar{A}^o_i}{\partial \Delta x_j}\right|_{\Delta x=0,\ \theta=\theta^*, d=d^*}$, $i=1,2,\ldots,N$, $j=1,2,\ldots,N$, $\tilde{B}^o(\theta^*, d^*, t): T \to R^{N\times n}$ is an N×n matrix whose elements are piecewise continious in the interval T, $\tilde{B}^o(\theta^*, d^*, t) = \bar{B}^o(0, \theta^*, d^*, t)$. θ^* and d^* denote some particular values of parameters $\theta^* \in R^L$, $d^* \in D$ which might coincide with θ^o, d^o.

Popov and co-authors [15] were the first to synthesize an optimal linear regulator for robotic manipulators. It is well known that the optimal control minimizing the criterion (2.3.1), (2.3.3), under the constraint (2.3.7), is obtained in the form:

$$\Delta u(t) = -\underline{R}^{-1}(t)\ \tilde{B}^{oT}(\theta^*, d^*, t)K(\theta^*, d^*, t)\Delta x(t) =$$
$$= D(\theta^*, d^*, t)\Delta x(t) \qquad (2.3.8)$$

where $K(t): T \to R^{N\times N}$ is a positive definite symmetrical matrix of dimensions N×N, which is the solution of the differential matrix equation of Riccati type:

$$-\dot{K}(\theta^*, d^*, t) = K(\theta^*, d^*, t)\tilde{A}^o(\theta^*, d^*, t) +$$
$$+ \tilde{A}^{oT}(\theta^*, d^*, t)K(\theta^*, d^*, t) + Q(t) -$$
$$- K(\theta^*, d^*, t)\tilde{B}^o(\theta^*, d^*, t)\underline{R}^{-1}(t)\tilde{B}^{oT}(\theta^*, d^*, t)\cdot$$
$$\cdot K(\theta^*, d^*, t),\ K(\theta^*, d^*, \tau) = Q_T \qquad (2.3.9)$$

$D(t): T \to R^{n\times N}$ is the n×N matrix of feedback gains. In (2.3.8) it is assumed that the matrix pair $[\tilde{A}^o, \tilde{B}^o]$ is controllable in the interval $(0, t_s)$ and that all state coordinates of the robot S are measured, and we have neglected constraints upon inputs' amplitudes.

Obviously, control (2.3.8) requires time-varying gains in the feedback loops. The implementation of such control is very difficult and demands large memory capacity of the control computer to store time-variable gains, since on-line calculation of $K(\theta^*, d^*, t)$ is difficult to implement.

In order to simplify implementation of control law, a linear time-invariant model of deviation from the nominal trajectory is obtained by "time-averaging" the model (2.3.5). So, we get the approximative model of the robot's dynamics in the form:

$$\Delta\dot{x} = \bar{\tilde{A}}^{o}(\theta^*,\ d^*)\Delta x + \bar{\tilde{B}}^{o}(\theta^*,\ d^*)N(t,\ \Delta u) \qquad (2.3.10)$$

where $\bar{\tilde{A}}^{o}(\theta^*, d^*)\in R^{N\times N}$ is an N×N matrix, and $\bar{\tilde{B}}^{o}(\theta^*, d^*)\in R^{N\times n}$ is an N×n matrix. Instead of criterion (2.3.3) we consider criterion (2.3.1) with:

$$\underset{\sim}{L}(x(t),\ u(t)) = \frac{1}{2}\left[\Delta x^T(t)Q\Delta x(t) + \Delta u^T(t)\underline{R}\Delta u\right]$$
$$\underset{\sim}{g}(x(t_s)) = 0 \qquad (2.3.11)$$

where $Q\in R^{N\times N}$ is a positive semidefinite N×N matrix and $\underline{R}\in R^{n\times n}$ is a positive definite n×n matrix, both time-invariant. We also assume that $t_s\to\infty$. It is well known that the control is now obtained in the form:

$$\Delta u(t) = -\underline{R}^{-1}\bar{\tilde{B}}^{oT}(\theta^*,\ d^*)K(\theta^*,\ d^*)\Delta x(t) = D(\theta^*,\ d^*)\Delta x(t) \qquad (2.3.12)$$

where $K(\theta^*, d^*)\in R^{N\times N}$ is the solution of the matrix equation of Riccati type:

$$K(\theta^*,\ d^*)\bar{\tilde{A}}^{o}(\theta^*,\ d^*) + \bar{\tilde{A}}^{oT}(\theta^*,\ d^*)K(\theta^*,\ d^*) -$$
$$- K(\theta^*,\ d^*)\bar{\tilde{B}}^{o}(\theta^*,\ d^*)\underline{R}^{-1}\bar{\tilde{B}}^{oT}(\theta^*,\ d^*)K(\theta^*,\ d^*)+Q=0 \qquad (2.3.13)$$

and $D(\theta^*, d^*)\in R^{n\times N}$ is the n×N matrix of constant feedback gains. The choice of the weighting matrices Q, $\underline{R}$ has to ensure that the closed--loop linear model of the robot is practically stable.

Three main problems concerning the optimal linear regulator (2.3.12) arise:

(a) It is evident that the linear regulator requires a complex control structure with many feedback loops (N×n). The control scheme is presented in Fig. 2.4. For example, for the manipulator with n = 6 d.o.f., if we take models of actuators of the third order $n_i = 3$, $\forall i\in I$, it follows that we have to implement 6×18=108 feedback loops. Thus, such a control scheme is too complex and unreliable, and is very difficult to maintain.

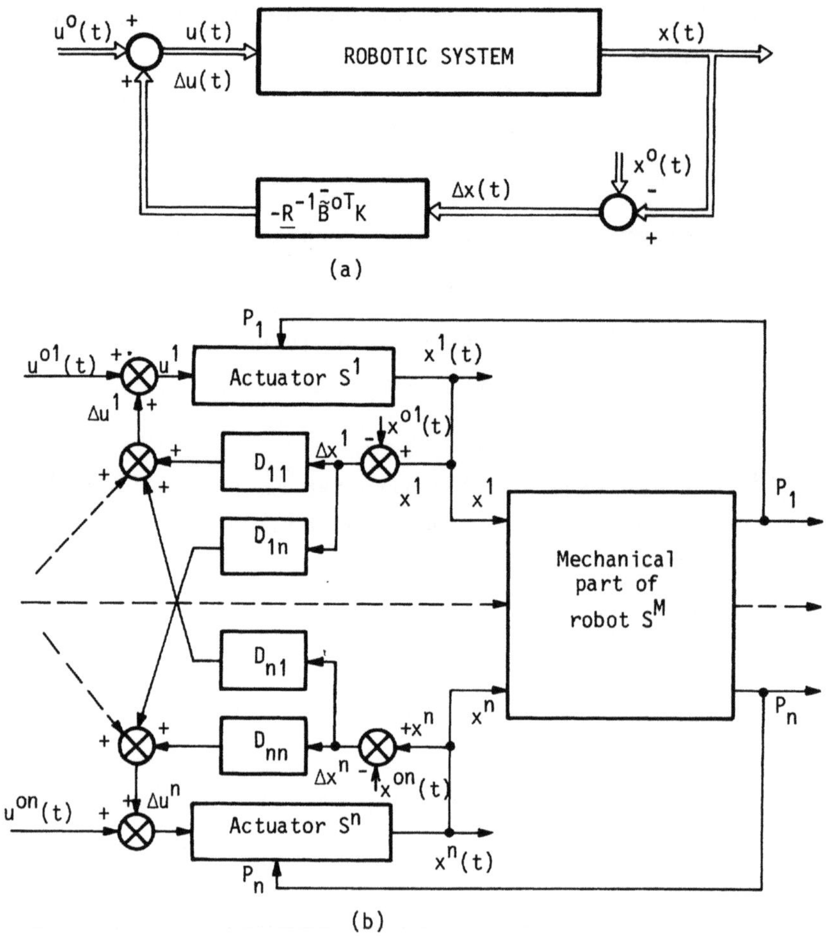

Fig. 2.4. Control scheme of linear optimal regulator
a) global scheme
b) control structure

(b) The second problem concerning the optimal regulator is that it guarantees the practical stability of the linearized model of the robot only. Since robot models are usually highly nonlinear, it is very questionable whether such linear control can accomplish the stated control task for an actual nonlinear model of the robot. In [2] we have shown how we can analyze stability of the nonlinear model of the robot when the linear regulator is applied.

(c) The third problem is the fact that the linear regulator is not robust enough to withstand all parameter variations. We have consistently denoted that the linearized model ((2.3.7) or (2.3.10)) and gains of optimal regulator (2.3.8) or (2.3.11)) depend on the chosen parameter values θ^*, d^*. This means that to each set of parameter values θ^*, d^* there corresponds a gain matrix $D(\theta^*, d^*)$, and it may be difficult to find unique feedback gains D which can withstand all parameter variations $\forall d \in D$. Even more, synthesis of D for given θ^*, d^* is relatively complex for complex robotic manipulators, so it is not easy to perform this synthesis after the parameter values were identified.

Popov, Vereschagin and Filaretov [17] have compensated for nonlinearities of the real robots models, in order to make the control law more adequate for nonlinear models of robots (i.e. to solve the above mentioned problem (b)). To achieve this, they observed the model of the robot (2.3.5) in the form*):

$$\Delta\dot{x} = \tilde{\bar{A}}^o \Delta x + f(\Delta x, \theta, d) + \tilde{\bar{B}}^o N(t, \Delta u) \qquad (2.3.14)$$

where $f: R^N \times \Theta \times D \to R^N$ is a vector function of order N, given by:

$$f(\Delta x, \theta, d) = \bar{A}^o(\Delta x, \theta, d, t) - \tilde{\bar{A}}^o(\theta^*, d^*)\Delta x.$$

In (2.3.14) it has been assumed that $\tilde{\bar{B}}^o = \bar{B}^o(\Delta x, \theta, d, t)$; this assumption is valid in some cases (see Appendix 2.A). We have also assumed that f is time-invariant; this is the case when only the terminal position is set, i.e instead of $x^o(t)$, $\forall t \in T$, $x^o(\tau)$ is given only, and (2.3.14) becomes a model of deviation around given state $x^o(\tau)$. The control minimizing criterion (2.3.1), (2.3.11), with constraint given by (2.3.14), is achieved in the form:

$$\Delta u(t) = -\underline{R}^{-1}\tilde{\bar{B}}^{oT}K\Delta x(t) - \underline{R}^{-1}\tilde{\bar{B}}^{oT}(\tilde{\bar{A}}^o - K\tilde{\bar{B}}^o\underline{R}^{-1}\tilde{\bar{B}}^{oT})^{-1}K\, f(\Delta x, \theta, d) \qquad (2.3.15)$$

i.e. we can state that control is in the form:

$$\Delta u = \Delta u_{lin} + \Delta u_N \qquad (2.3.16)$$

where Δu_{lin} is the linear and Δu_N the nonlinear part of the control law. The matrix K is obtained from (2.3.13) Actually, we should substitute $\tilde{\bar{A}}^o + \partial f/\partial x$ for $\tilde{\bar{A}}^o$ in (2.3.13), but we can assume that in the region

*) For the sake of simplicity we have denoted $\bar{A}^o(\theta^*, d^*)$, $\bar{B}^o(\theta^*, d^*)$ by $\tilde{\bar{A}}^o$, $\tilde{\bar{B}}^o$ etc.

$x^t(t)$ around $x^o(\tau)$, the eigenvalues of the matrix $\bar{\tilde{A}}^o + \partial f/\partial x$ do not differ a lot from eigenvalues of the matrix $\tilde{A}^o$ [17]. Thus, the matrix K can be precalculated.

The control scheme is presented in Fig. 2.5. Obviously it differs from the classical optimal regulator (presented in Fig. 2.4) due to the addition of nonlinear part Δu_N whose role is to compensate for nonlinear effects of robot model. However, the main problem arising here is that such control is very complex. In addition to complex control structure of optimal linear regulator, on-line calculation of the nonlinear term f is demanded here. This means that the complete model of the robot dynamics has to be calculated on-line what might be a very difficult task (see next Paragraph). On the other hand, this nonlinear model depends on parameters d. We have assumed that these parameters might be variable and unknown. Thus, the robustness of such control scheme to parameter variations is questionable.

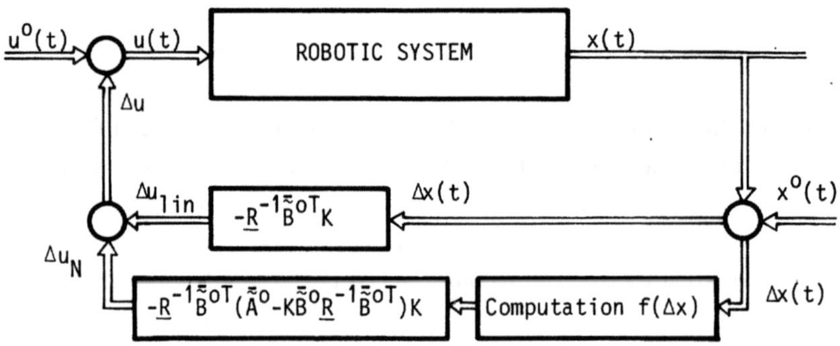

Fig. 2.5. Control scheme - optimal regulator and nonlinear control (after [17])

It should be noticed here that, in deriving the linearized model of the robotic system, we have assumed that nominal programmed control is introduced. However, the linearized model (and optimal regulator (2.3.13), or (2.3.15)) can be applied when nominal programmed control is not introduced; in this case it should be examined whether the optimal regulator can ensure tracking of nominal trajectory, or stability around the terminal point.

A similar idea of compensating for nonlinear effects of robot model by direct on-line calculation of model has also been exploited by several other authors.

For example, Takegaki and Arimoto [18] have applied positional control in the form*):

$$u(t) = G(q^o(\tau)) - K_1(q(t)-q^o(\tau)) - K_2\dot{q}(t) \qquad (2.3.17)$$

where $G(q^o(\tau)$ is an $n\times1$ vector of gravitational forces (moments) in a desired position $q^o(\tau)$), $K_1 \in R^{n\times n}$ is an $n\times n$ matrix of positional feedback gains, $K_2 \in R^{n\times n}$ is an $n\times n$ matrix of damping gains, and $x(t) = (q^T(t), \dot{q}^T(t))^T$. It has been shown that the control (2.3.17) is optimal with respect to some criterion (2.3.1). In this case gravitational forces in the terminal point only are to be calculated on-line, but this is just positional control; the tracking of nominal trajectory demands calculation of some more complex terms in the mechanical model of the robot. On the other hand, it has been shown [18] that this control allows us to avoid the inverse of Jacobian matrix, i.e. the calculation of joint coordinates of the desired position $q^o(\tau)$. Namely, as we have explained in the previous Paragraph a desired position (or trajectory) is usually imposed in external coordinates $S^o(\tau)$; so, if we want to realize the control (2.3.17), we have to solve eq. (2.2.14) for $q(\tau)$, i.e. to calculate the inverse of (2.2.14). It is well known that by differentating (2.2.14) by q we get:

$$\dot{S}(t) = J(q(t))\dot{q}(t) \qquad (2.3.18)$$

where $J = [\partial f/\partial q]$, $J(q): R^n \to R^{m\times n}$ is an $m\times n$ Jacobian matrix. The solution of inverse problem of (2.3.18) might be very complex i.e. the computation of inverse matrix $J^{-1}(q)$ might be too time consuming. So it is recommendable to avoid this calculation. It has been shown [18] that instead of (2.3.17) we can use the control

$$\Delta u = G(S(\tau)) - J^T(K_1(S(t)-S^o(\tau)) + K_2\dot{S}(t)) \qquad (2.3.19)$$

where S(t) is the vector of actual external coordinates of robotic manipulator. Thus, in control law (2.3.19) we have to calculate on-line the Jacobian matrix and not the inverse of this matrix, which is, by far, an easier problem. However, this control with constant gains K_1

---

*) Here, only the model of mechanical part of the robot has been assumed. However, it is easy to extend the results to the general model which includes actuators models.

and K_2 cannot be acceptable for trajectory tracking and when parameter variations have to be taken into account.

Up to now we have presented a few attempts to synthesize control at the executive level by minimization of some criterion (either to calculate the optimal trajectory or just to calculate the optimal control for tracking some given nominal trajectory). We have shown that high nonlinearity of the robot model leads to the conclusion that it is impossible to calculate the optimal control for the exact nonlinear model of the system. Thus, we have either to calculate optimal control using some approximative (linearized) model of the robot or, by adding some nonlinear term, to compensate for nonlinearities in the robot models. In both cases the control is far from being optimal.

2.3.3. "Inverse problem" technique

We have shown that it is impossible to get an acceptable and simple control by standard optimization techniques. Actually, it is necessary to take care about dynamics of the complete robotic system in order to achieve good tracking of a desired trajectory. This means that we have to include the complete dynamic model of the robot in the control synthesis. Then, it is impossible to get a closed-loop solution by minimizing certain criteria. This was the reason why most researchers have attempted to synthesize dynamic control of the robots by some suboptimal approaches. They tried to directly include the mathematical model of robot dynamics in the control scheme.

Paul [19] has investigated the "inverse problem" technique, which was called the "computed torque" technique by Bejczy [20]. A similar approaches has been taken by Pavlov and Timofeyev [21]. Their approaches include on-line computation of the complete model of robot dynamics, i.e. they involve computation of driving torques by eq. (2.2.1) using the measured values of internal coordinates q and velocities $\dot{q}$ of the robot and the computed values of internal accelerations $\ddot{q}^o(t)$. Namely, if the desired trajectory is computed we can obtain $q^o(t)$, $\dot{q}^o(t)$, $\ddot{q}^o(t)$, $\forall t \in T$. It has been shown [21] that the robot is asymptotically stable around the nominal trajectory if the driving torques are computed by:

$$P(t) = H(q, d) \cdot \left[\ddot{q}^o(t) + K_1(q(t) - q^o(t)) + K_2(\dot{q}(t) - \dot{q}^o(t)) \right] + h(q, \dot{q}, d) \tag{2.3.20}$$

where $K_1 \in R^{n \times n}$ is an n×n matrix of position feedback gains and $K_2 \in R^{n \times n}$ is an n×n matrix of velocity feedback gains; K_1 and K_2 must be chosen in such a way, that a trivial solution of the equation

$$\ddot{e} = K_1 e + K_2 \dot{e}$$

is asymptotically stable, where $e \in R^n$. It can easily be shown that the driving torques (2.3.20) also ensure the practical stability of the robot (2.2.18). However only driving torques are computed in (2.3.20). It is necessary to include also the models of actuators (2.2.2), i.e. to calculate inputs u^i that correspond to computed driving torques (2.3.20).

The control scheme is presented in Fig. 2.6. Obviously, this scheme combines a closed-loop controller with "nominal" control signals computed on the basis of the equations of motion. In this scheme compensation is provided for time varying gravitational, centrifugal and Coriolis forces; the feedback gains are adjusted according to the changes in matrix H(q, d) of moments of inertia; an acceleration feedforward term is also included to compensate for changes along nominal trajectory.

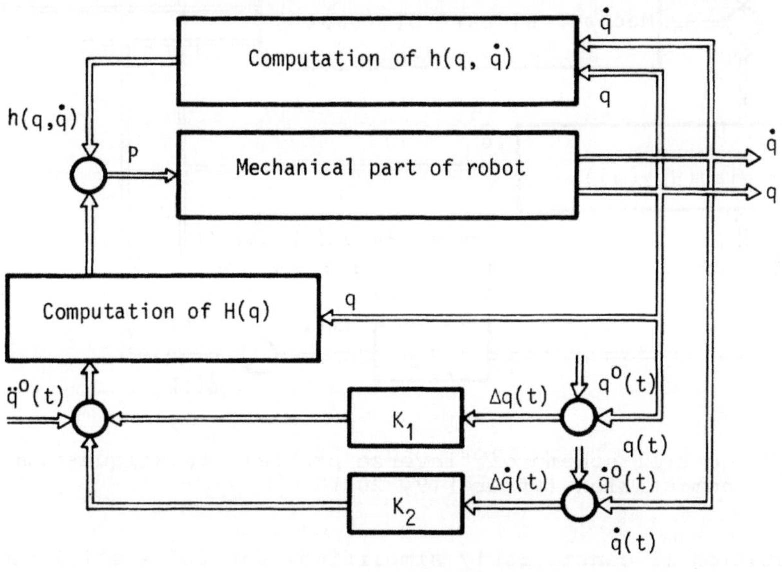

Fig. 2.6. Control scheme of "inverse problem" technique (after [19 - 21])

However, these approaches suffer from several disadvantages. The main problem is that in (2.3.20) computation of the complete dynamic model of robot is required. For complex robot structures this requirement may be very difficult to satisfy. This is the reason why some authors have tried to implement an approximative model of robot dynamics. They have omitted cross-coupling terms of moment of inertia in the matrix H(q, d) and they have omitted centrifugal and Coriolis forces. This means, that the model is reduced to diagonal terms in inertia matrix H(q, d) and to gravity terms, i.e. the control (2.3.20) is reduced to:

$$P_i(t) = \dot{H}_{ii}(q,\ d)\left[\ddot{q}^{oi}(t)+K_1(q(t)-q^o(t))+K_2(\dot{q}(t)- - \dot{q}^o(t))\right]+g_i(q(t),\ d) \quad (2.3.21)$$

where g_i: $R^n \times D \to R^1$ is gravity force (moment) in the *i*th joint. The control scheme is now reduced to the one presented in Fig. 2.7. By this,

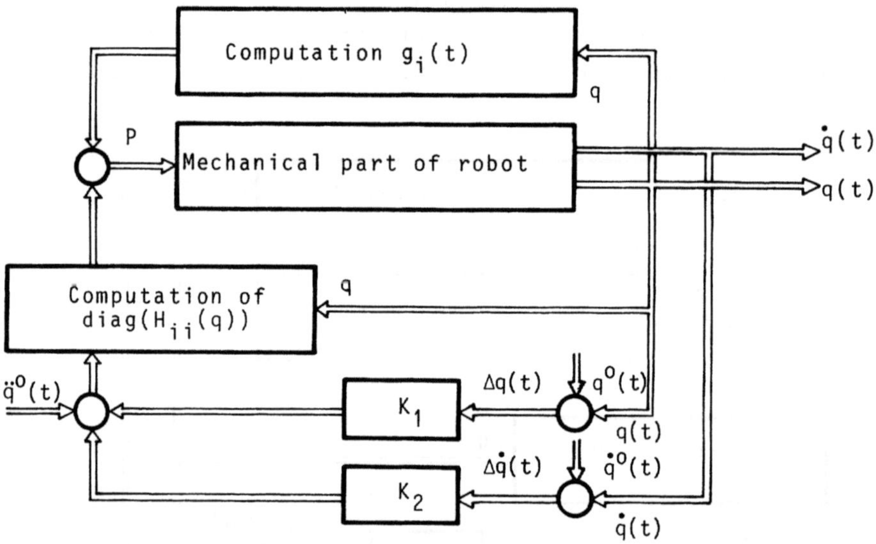

Fig. 2.7. Control scheme of "inverse problem" technique-simplified computation (after [19, 20])

the computation is considerably simplified, but it is still very cumbersome for some types of manipulators. On the other hand, it is questionable whether or not the efficiency of control is lost by these simplifications. Paul [19] has found that in his experiments with the Stanford manipulator, the contribution by the Coriolis and centrifugal terms is relatively insignificant. This is true when the manipulator approaches its goal position and orientation since the joint velocities are low during that time (so-called "fine" motions). However, no general analysis of the robot performance has been presented. Actually, in order to improve the quality of control for both "gross" and "fine" manipulator motions so that they can be executed with higher speed (but without loss in precision), we have to compensate for these velocity dependent terms.

A further reduction of computation time has been done by Bejczy. Bejczy [20] investigated a specific manipulator and found approximations to the diagonal terms in matrix H(q, d) and in gravity terms. These approximations lead to a tremendous reduction of computing time for the control scheme presented in Fig. 2.7. However, these approximations are valid for a specific manipulator only and for relatively slow motion conditions.

Paul [19] suggested that some terms in the dynamic model could be precalculated and stored, so as to reduce the time necessary for on-line calculation.

As we have already claimed, the problem of on-line computation of robot dynamic model is very difficult. Here, we shall not discuss various methods for on-line computation of dynamic model. Let us mention that in [22] one can find a study on the computational efficiency and comparison of various methods of computing the input torques which is based on a recent survey of numerical solution techniques made by Hollerbach [23]. On the other hand, Bejczy and Paul [24] have analyzed some approximations of robot dynamic equations using a symbolic state equation technique. However, the method for forming analytical equations of robot dynamics by computer which has been presented briefly in Chapter 1, leads to by far the fastest computation of robot dynamic models.

Raibert and Horn [25] have used a partial table look-up approach to simplify the computation automatically on a digital computer. Rather than compute the coefficients in (2.2.20) each time they are needed (every sampling period), their approach (called configuration space method) is to look them up in a pre-defined multi-dimensional memory organized by the positional variables q(t) (the so-called configuration space controller). Their control scheme is presented in Fig. 2.8. The disadvantage of this scheme is the requirement for a large memory.

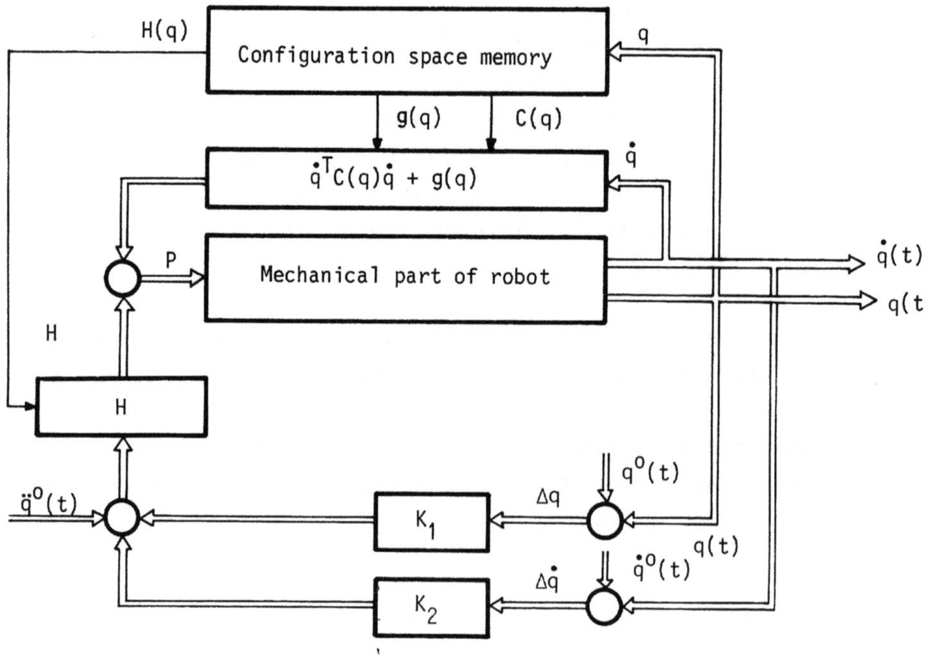

Fig. 2.8. Control scheme of the configuration space controller (after [25])

Thus, it is obvious that the main difficulty with the "inverse problem" technique is on-line computation of the dynamic model of the robot. Actually, the analysis of the complexity of the model that is needed for this control law in order to achieve sufficiently good tracking of nominal trajectory has not been given. However, there are several other problems with this approach. The implementation of control law (2.2.20) (or (2.2.21)) requires knowledge of the complete vector d of mechanism parameters; however, in def. (2.2.18) (or (2.2.19)) we have assumed that parameters d are not known in advance. So, it is questionable whether the control (2.2.20) (if synthesized for one chosen set of parameters d^o) is robust enough to withstand all parameter variations $d \in D$. Thus, the robustness of this control law has not been precisely analyzed.

Timofeyev has extended this approach to adaptive control in the case of unknown and variable parameters of the robot [26]; this approach will be described in Chapter 3. However, he has not analyzed whether non-adaptive control (2.2.20) can be applied to the manipulator with variable parameters.

The next difficulty with the "inverse problem" technique is the choice of gains in (2.2.20). In [21] it has been proved that the robot is stable if the gain matrices K_1 and K_2 are chosen as explained above. However, if we choose full matrices the control structure becomes complex and thus suffers from all disadvantages that were mentioned concerning the centralized linear regulator (Paragraph 2.3.2). Obviously, we can choose gain matrices in a diagonal form. However, the problem with such a choice lies in its suboptimality, i.e. such control may be very suboptimal from the standpoint of energy consumptions. Saridis and Lee [27] have proposed the method for suboptimal choice of the gains; the choice is done taking into account the complete nonlinear model of the robot. However, the method results in choice of full matrices K_1 and K_2.

Thus, there are several problems with the "inverse problem" technique, the main being its complex implementation and difficult maintenance. In addition, no systematic procedure for control synthesis of an arbitrary manipulator (choice of the model complexity, feedback structure and gains, analysis of robustness, etc.) has been elaborated up to now. In our opinion the problem with all of the above mentioned control schemes lies in their centralized approach to control problem; i.e. the robot is considered as a single plant which makes the implementation and maintenance of such control schemes very difficult and inpractical.

There were made few attempts to develop such control algorithms which include compensation for robot dynamics during motion but in which on--line computation of complex terms in the robot model is avoided. The force feedback offers such a possibility.

2.3.4. Force feedback

The forces (moments) that are acting in the robot joints can be directly measured. Thus, by introducing feedback by these forces we can compensate for dynamics of the robot and decouple the robotic manipulator into a set of separate subsystems. Force feedback allows easy compensation for the complete dynamics of the robot. This attractive idea was recognized and elaborated by the authors of this book [2, 7-9, 28, 29] and it will be presented and discussed in Paragraph 2.6.

The force feedback has recently been exploited by several authors. Hewit and Burdess [30] introduced force transducers in the joints of a manipulator, but they also introduced accelerometers which provide information about accelerations $\ddot{q}(t)$. They calculate on-line the matrix of inertia $H(q, d)$. Since by force transducers they measure the complete forces (moments) $P(t)$, from (2.2.1) they can calculate $h(q, \dot{q}, d)$ - gravity, friction, centrifugal and Coriolis forces. So their control scheme is relatively complex (although the computation is shorter than when the complete model has to be computed on-line). The control scheme is presented in Fig. 2.9. They have not analyzed the stability of the robot and they have not discussed whether the whole implemented equipment (transducers, accelerometers, computer for on-line calculation of the inverse of inertia matrix, etc.) is necessary to achieve good tracking of nominal trajectory. On the other hand, the problem of unknown parameters is not solved by this scheme since calculation of matrix $H(q, d)$ which depends on parameters, is also required.

There were made several attempts to include force feedback in servo control of joints of manipulators. Wu and Paul [31] made an experiment on a single-joint manipulator with a force sensor in the joint. Because the force feedback loop was closed around the joint and all the hardware was of analog type, the scheme completely avoided the computational difficulties, and provided a fast response. However, they have not analyzed stability.

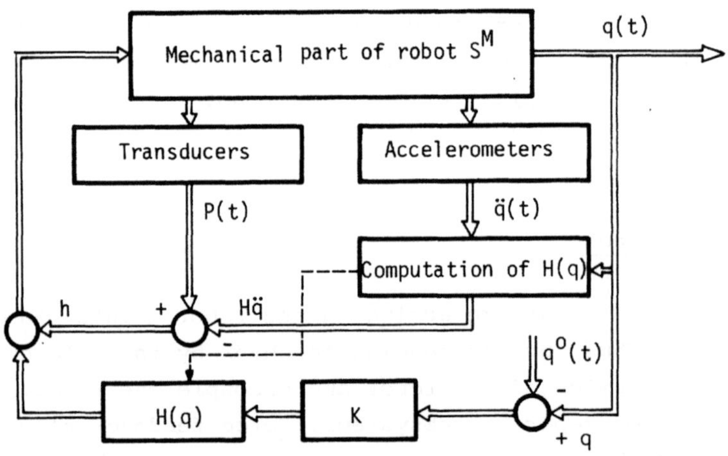

Fig. 2.9. Control scheme with force feedback and acceleration feedback (after [30])

Luh, Fisher and Paul [32] have made an experiment with Stanford manipulator: the first two joints have been redesigned and fabricated to include torque sensors. They analyzed each joint separately; by means of the method of describing functions they analyzed limit cycles of the nonlinear models of separate joints and they eliminated the limits by series compensation. However, the stability of the complete robot has not been analyzed in their paper. This analysis will be presented in Paragraphs 2.5 and 2.6 [2].

All above mentioned attempts concern the implementation of force sensors directly in the joints, i.e. direct force feedbacks around the joints of robot. However, there were many attempts to measure forces in the wrist of manipulator. A force sensing wrist has been suggested by Nevins and Whitney [33]. Paul and Shimano [34] developed a control scheme with sensing wrist so that load forces and moments with respect to the axis of the wrist coordinates could be measured on line. Force controllers employing the sensing wrist were implemented by Craig and Raibert [35]. Their control scheme contained two separate closed loops: one for positional control and the other for force control. However, since the signal from the sensing wrist is referenced to wrist coordinates it is necessary to perform the Jacobian transform to get joint loads every sampling period, i.e. some computational difficulties are present with this solution*). All these attempts mostly deal with application of the force feedback for assembling with manipulators. As we have already stated, we shall not treat assembling tasks in this book, so these and numerous other results from the force compliance will not be discussed here in more detail. We shall limit ourselves to the cases when force feedbacks are used to compensate for dynamics of robots (and not for sensing external forces acting upon the robot as is the case in the insertion process [2]).

The force feedback also offers a possibility to avoid the inverse of Jacobian matrix when the desired trajectory is imposed in external coordinates. Vukobratović and Stokić [2, 36] proposed a dynamic control scheme for the so-called "drink-test" (transfer of a vessel with liquid by a manipulator); we have implemented force transducers at the contact points between the hand and the object and by this information we can approximately solve the dynamic equilibrium of the object during motion,

*) Actually, the relationship beetwen the static wrist forces and static joint torques is given by transpose of Jacobian matrix. In the case of dynamic forces this relation is obviously much more complex (see the text to follow).

i.e. we can achieve the desired orientation of the object along the trajectory. Popov, Vereschagin and Zenkevich [37] also discussed implementation of force feedback for solving various robotic tasks and to avoid the inverse of Jacobian matrix*).

Wu and Paul [38] proposed position control of manipulator in external coordinates which they called resolved motion force control (RMFC). This control scheme adapts the force convergence concept to control the hand forces and (external) position instead of classical joint control. Actually, all methods described in the previous paragraphs assume that at the tactical control level the calculation of joint coordinates is performed and then at the executive level joint coordinates are controlled. Although this book concerns just executive control level, at this point we shall very briefly review some methods for obtaining joint coordinates $q^o(t)$ for imposed external coordinates $S^o(t)$ [38]:

a) Resolved motion position control [39]: In this method $q^o(t)$ is directly obtained from the inverse solution of (2.2.14). However, as we have already said, in the general case eq. (2.2.14) is very complex and may not be solved. If the manipulator is of simple structure then we can obtain $q^o(t)$ from given $S^o(t)$; in addition, joint velocities $\dot{q}^o(t)$ and accelerations $\ddot{q}^o(t)$ can be obtained by numerical differentiation.

b) Resolved motion rate control [40, 41]: In this method the actual manipulator external coordinates $S(t)$ are calculated from (2.2.14) and measured $q(t)$. By comparing actual $S(t)$ to desired nominal coordinates $S^o(t)$ we obtain corrective external rates $\dot{S}(t)$ in order to reduce any position error. Joint velocities are obtained by inverting (2.3.18):

$$\dot{q}(t) = J^{-1}(q(t))\dot{S}(t) \qquad (2.3.22)$$

Then, joint accelerations $\ddot{q}(t)$ are obtained by numerical differentiation.

c) Resolved motion acceleration control [42]: This method calculates corrective external accelerations $\ddot{S}(t)$ (from the measured $q(t)$, $\dot{q}(t)$

---

*) All these attempts concern "mixed" tactical and executive levels, i.e. the same control loop solves both levels.

actual $\dot{S}(t)$, are calculated and compared to desired $\dot{S}^o(t)$). By differentiating (2.3.22) we obtain joint accelerations:

$$\ddot{q}(t) = J^{-1}(q(t))\cdot\left[\ddot{S}(t) - \frac{\partial J}{\partial t}\dot{q}(t)\right] \qquad (2.3.23)$$

where $\partial J/\partial t$ is the derivative of the Jacobian matrix with respect to time.

We have briefly reviewed these methods for obtaining joint coordinates $q^o(t)$, velocities $\dot{q}^o(t)$ and accelerations $\ddot{q}^o(t)$, in order to show complexity of the calculations that have to be performed at the tactical control level and to make a connection with the RMFC method. RMFC is based on the relationship between terminal link forces F and joint torques P, and consists of two parts. The first part is the position control of the terminal link (hand) and calculates the desired forces $F^o(t)$ to be applied to the hand in order to track the desired external trajectory $S^o(t)$. The second part of RMFC is the determination of the joint torques P, to be applied, such that hand has desired forces F^o applied as calculated in the first step. Desired hand forces $F^o(t)$ for correcting the external position and orrientation errors are obtained by closing a simple position-derivative (PD) controller, compensated with the desired external accelerations $\ddot{S}^o(t)$. Actually, if the desired external trajectory $S^o(t)$ is given, we can numerically obtain desired external velocities $\dot{S}^o(t)$ and accelerations $\ddot{S}^o(t)$. The actual external accelerations $\ddot{S}(t)$ are obtained by closing two servo feedback loops*):

$$\ddot{S}(t) = \ddot{S}^o(t) + K_1\Delta S(t) + K_2\Delta\dot{S}(t), \qquad (2.3.24)$$

where $\Delta S(t) = S(t) - S^o(t)$ is the position error, $\Delta\dot{S}(t) = \dot{S}(t) - \dot{S}^o(t)$ is the velocity error, and $K_1 \in R^m$, $K_2 \in R^m$ are constant position and velocity feedback gains. Actual external coordinates S(t) and velocities $\dot{S}(t)$ are obtained by measuring actual joint coordinates q(t) and velocities and by applying (2.2.14) and (2.3.18). The gains K_1 and K_2 are calculated so that the characteristical roots of

$$\Delta\ddot{S}(t) = K_1\Delta S(t) + K_2\Delta\dot{S}(t)$$

---

*) Luh, Walker and Paul [42] used eq. (2.3.24) in their resolved acceleration control scheme to calculate actual external accelerations $\ddot{S}(t)$; then, they used (2.3.23) to calculate corresponding internal accelerations $\ddot{q}(t)$; using calculated $\ddot{q}(t)$ and measured $q(t)$, $\dot{q}(t)$, driving torques P(t) are computed according to the control scheme of "inverse problem" type (Paragraph 2.3.3).

have negative real parts. The desired hand forces $F^o(t)$ to correct for any external position errors can be calculated by

$$F^o(t) = M\,\ddot{S}(t), \qquad (2.3.25)$$

where $M = \text{diag}(m^o, m^o, m^o, I_x^o, I_y^o, I_z^o)$, m^o is the total mass of the load and hand, I_x^o, I_y^o, I_z^o are the moments of inertia on the principal axes of the load and hand (we assume that the principal axes of the load are aligned with the hand's principal axes).

Now, in the second step we have to calculate joint torques $P(t)$ that will ensure realization of $F^o(t)$. If we assume that all members of the manipulator are massless except for the hand and load, the desired hand forces F^o can be resolved into applied joint torques by:

$$P(t) = J^T F^o(t) \qquad (2.3.26)$$

This scheme involves only calculation of the transpose of Jacobian matrix $J(q(t))$. At this point, if the manipulator has no mass except for the hand and load, this scheme works perfectly*). For a manipulator in which the load clearly dominates, (the space shuttle manipulator with a 25000 kg load, for example), the scheme also works well. As the mass of the hand and load approaches the mass of the rest of the manipulator, the above simple control scheme no longer converges as the desired forces to be applied to the hand are reduced, as some portions of the applied joint torques obtained from (2.3.26) are used in accelerating the members of the manipulator.

In order to compensate for these effects, the second part of control scheme - force convergent control - has been developed. Force convergent control adopts the Robbins-Monro approximation method to determine an applied hand force F_a and corresponding applied joint torques such that the actual observed hand force F will converge to the desired hand force F^o obtained from (2.3.25). The actual applied force F at the hand is measured by a multi-element strain gauge force wrist sensor. RMFC is presented in Fig. 2.10. It contains two servos; the outer servo

---

*) It should be mentioned that Krutko and Lakota [43] used practically the same approach; they also neglected the masses of manipulator members and used eq. (2.3.24)-(2.3.26) to calculate driving torques $P(t)$; however, they did not consider the case when the masses of the manipulator are not negligible with respect to load mass and did not use force feedback as in [38].

is the hand position control (2.2.24) and the inner servo is the force convergent control. Actually, the outer servo corresponds to the tactical control level, and the inner servo to the executive control level. Thus RMFC solves both control levels at the same time. Calculation of the inverse of Jacobian matrix and calculation of complicated dynamics of the manipulator are both avoided. However, the convergent rate of force convergent control depends on the structure of manipulator, so it might demand several iterations to achieve good accuracy of the method. Thus, calculation of dynamic model is replaced by an iterative stochastic method which also demands extensive computation. The problem of variable parameters has not been discussed in [38]. However, implementation of wrist force sensor offers a possibility of identify a payload (see Chapter 3), and thus we could easily extend this control scheme to include a variable payload. The robustness of this control scheme has not been analyzed.

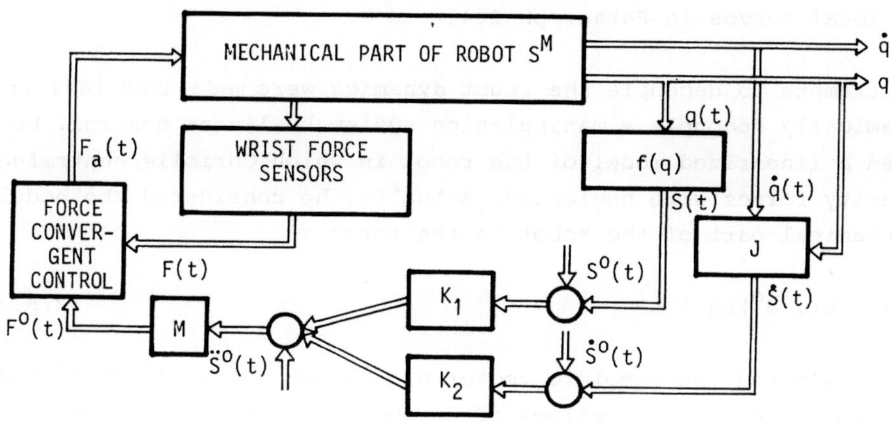

Fig. 2.10. Resolved motion force control scheme (after [38])

Thus, we have presented several control schemes which use force feedback. It is evident that the force feedback offers a good opportunity to simplify control law and to compensate for the robot dynamics. However, there are several drawbacks of implementation of force feedback. The price of the force transducers it not negligible and there are some technical problems regarding the noise appearing at the force sensors. Thus, a trade-off between the complexity and price of control computer and price of the sensor system has to be carefully studied. As we have already said we shall also use the force feedback in our non-adaptive and adaptive control schemes (see Paragraph 2.6 and Chapter 3).

2.3.5. Decoupled control

In all above presented approaches to control synthesis the main problem is to compensate for the influence of robot dynamics. In many control schemes the aim is to decouple the robotic system into the set of decoupled subsystems of lower order which can be controlled separately. Since in most cases the trajectory given in external coordinates is resolved into compatible joint coordinates trajectories, we ussually want to use these joint trajectories as inputs for servos which drive individual joints. Thus, we usually want to control each joint separately, i.e. to treat each joint servo as an independent subsystem. Obviously, this solution is the simplest and the most convenient, from the standpoint of control implementation. We shall discuss the synthesis of local servos in Paragraph 2.4.

A few attempts to decouple the robot dynamics were made. Yuan [44] tried to dynamically decouple a manipulation system by linear control. He observed a linearized model of the robot in which Coriolis, centrifugal and gravity forces were neglected. Actually, he considered the model of the mechanical part of the robot in the form:

$$H(q^o(0),\ d^o)\Delta\ddot{q} = \Delta P \tag{2.3.27}$$

i.e. he neglected the complete vector $h(q,\ \dot{q},\ d)$. In (2.3.27) $d^o \in D$ denotes some chosen nominal values of parameters. The linear models of actuators (2.2.2) were also taken into account. In the model (2.3.27) the coupling among the degrees of freedom of the robot are given by off-diagonal elements of the inertia matrix $H(q^o(0),\ d^o)$ i.e. by the cross-inertia terms. Thus, if we want to decouple the system (2.3.27) we just have to introduce linear control which will compensate for the cross-inertia terms in (2.3.27), i.e. a decoupling compensator has to be chosen in the form:

$$\Delta P = (I+R\cdot Q)\Delta\hat{P} \tag{2.3.28}$$

where $\Delta\hat{P} \in R^n$ is a vector of driving torques of the decoupled model of the robot, $I \in R^{n\times n}$ is the identity matrix and the matrices $R \in R^{n\times n}$, $Q \in R^{n\times n}$ are given by:

$$Q = \begin{bmatrix} 0 & H_{12} & \cdots & H_{1n} \\ H_{21} & 0 & \cdots & H_{2n} \\ \vdots & \vdots & \ddots & \vdots \\ H_{n1} & H_{n2} & \cdots & 0 \end{bmatrix}$$

$$R = \text{diag}\,(H_{11}, H_{22}, \ldots, H_{nn}),$$

where H_{ij} are the elements of matrix H. If we implement control (2.3.28) (Fig. 2.11) we decouple the model (2.3.27) into the set of subsystems:

$$H_{ii}\Delta\ddot{q}_i = \Delta\hat{P}_i, \quad \forall i \in I \tag{2.3.29}$$

each corresponding to one degree of freedom of the robot. Obviously, this is decoupling of the mechanical part of the robot. It is easy to extend (2.3.28) to include linear models of actuators (2.2.1) which are associated to each degree of freedom. Actually, we get the decoupled model of the robotic system (when actuators are taken into account) in the form:

$$\Delta\dot{x}^i = \hat{A}^i\Delta x^i + \hat{b}^i N(\hat{u}^i), \quad \forall i \in I$$

where $\hat{u}^i \in R^1$ is a new input of the decoupled model (corresponding to $\Delta\hat{P}$), and $\hat{A}^i$, $\hat{b}^i$ are the matrices of decoupled robot model given by (assumming $P_i = M_i$):

$$\hat{A}^i = (I_{ni} - f^i H_{ii} T^i)^{-1} A^i, \quad \hat{b}^i = (I_{ni} - f^i H_{ii} T^i)^{-1} b^i, \quad \forall i \in I$$

where by T^i we denote $T^i = \partial\hat{G}^i/\partial x^i$, so that, acc. to (2.2.13), $\ddot{q}_i = T^i\dot{x}^i$. Thus, by implementing the control scheme from Fig. 2.11 we get the model of robot in decoupled form (2.3.29), where $\hat{u}^i$ is input to each decoupled subsystem. Now, we can introduce a local controller for each decoupled subsystem (2.3.29), in the classical linear form

$$\hat{u}^i = k_i^T \Delta x^i, \quad \forall i \in I \tag{2.3.30}$$

where $k_i \in R^{n_i}$ is a local gain vector, which is chosen so as to ensure that the closed-loop local subsystem is stable. Namely, local controllers (2.3.30) can be chosen as local servos for each actuator of the robot, as they are usually implemented with robots in practice. Thus, by control (2.3.28) we compensate for coupling among the degrees of freedom of the manipulator, and we enable each actuator to be independently controlled.

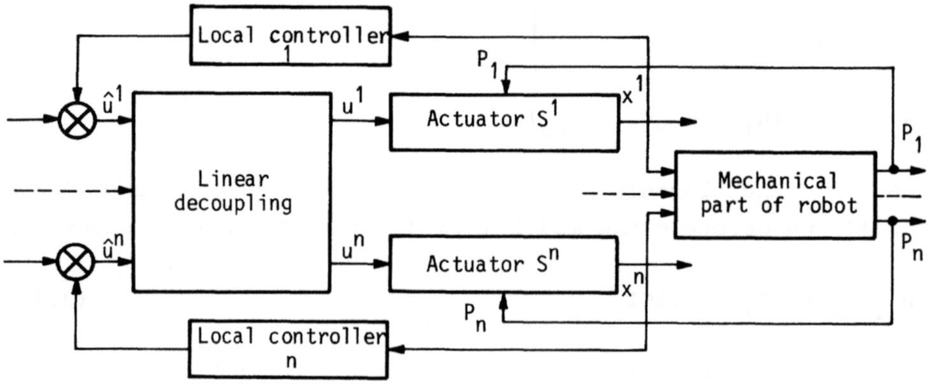

Fig. 2.11. Linear decoupling control scheme (after [44])

The decoupling scheme (2.3.28) is of open-loop type and very simple, and it is directly compatible with the independent joint control which is adopted in most manipulator control systems. However, this scheme suffers from many disadvantages. Since the model used (2.3.27) is very approximative, this control cannot compensate for many dynamical effects. Actually the simplicity and linear form of the control (2.3.28) result from the very rough approximation of the robot model. If the complete nonlinear model of the robot were taken into account the decoupled control would be much more complex. The problem of the effect of parameter variations on decoupling has not been treated in [44]. However, it is obvious that this scheme is very sensitive to parameter variation. This decoupling solution may happen to be structurally unstable.

Roessler [45] applied the nonlinear hierarchical control to decouple robot model. He "divided" the control vector into two terms which correspond to two control levels. At the level of local subsystems, local controllers are synthesized as usual to stabilize local decoupled subsystems. Subsystems in this case correspond to actuators' models*).

*) Actually, Roessler [45] considered the nonlinear models of subsystems, and he linearized them and compensated for nonlinearities by nonlinear local controllers. However, this has no consequence on his decoupled control so we omitted these nonlinear terms for simplicity.

$$\dot{x}^i = A^i x^i + b^i N(u^i) \qquad \forall i \in I \tag{2.3.31}$$

where coupling among actuators (2.2.2), given by $f^i M_i$, has to be compensated for by the global control synthesized at the "coordination" level. This "second part" of control vector is intended to decouple the robotic manipulator into the set of local (subsystems (2.3.31)). This control u^G is proposed in the form:

$$u_i^G(t) = \begin{cases} (b^{iT}b^i)^{-1}b^{iT}f^iM_i(t_{\ell-1}) & \text{for} \quad \kappa_i(t_{\ell-1})>0 \\ (1-\varepsilon)(b^{iT}b^i)^{-1}b^{iT}f^iM_i(t_{\ell-1}) & \text{for} \quad \kappa_i(t_{\ell-1})<0 \end{cases}$$

$$\forall t \in (t_{\ell-1}, t_\ell) \tag{2.3.32}$$

where by $\kappa_i(t_{\ell-1})$ we denote

$$\kappa_i(t_{\ell-1}) = d(f^iM_i(x(t), d))/dt\Big|_{t=t_{\ell-1}}$$

The control (2.3.32) is constant during the interval $(t_{\ell-1}, t_\ell)$. By ε we denote the number which satisfies:

$$||f^iM_i - b^iu_i^G|| < \varepsilon||f^iM_i|| \tag{2.3.33}$$

The number ε determines the extent to which the coupling is reduced by the global control u_i^G. Obviously if $\varepsilon=1$ the system is not decoupled, if $\varepsilon=0$ the system is completely decoupled. The time intervals $(t_{\ell-1}, t_\ell)$ during which the global control is kept constant are determined by "coordination" algorithm: it checks in every sampling interval T_D whether the conditions (2.3.33) are satisfied with the global control (2.3.32) calculated by the moment t_ℓ:

$$||f^iM_i(t_{\ell-1}+rT_D)-b^iu_i^G(t_{\ell-1})|| < \varepsilon||f^iM_i(t_{\ell-1}+rT_D)|| \tag{2.3.34}$$

where $r = 0,1,2,\ldots$. If the condition (2.3.34) is satisfied the control (2.3.32) is kept constant; if not, new global control is calculated for $t_\ell = t_{\ell-1} + rT_D$.

By this control scheme (Fig. 2.12) decoupling of the robot can be achieved. If we choose $\varepsilon=0$, we can totally decouple the robot into the set of subsystems (2.3.31) and then implement local controllers as is usually done in practice. Thus, the control (2.3.32) can compensate for the complete dynamic effects of the robot. However the control (2.3.32) requires the calculation of the complete dynamic model of the robotic system in each sampling interval T_D. This is a very severe condition since the model of robotic manipulator may be very complex. Actually, this control is similar to "the inverse problem" technique described in Paragraph 2.3.3, i.e. "the inverse problem" technique may also be regarded as decoupled control since this control also compensates for the effects of dynamics of the robot (coupling among degrees of freedom).

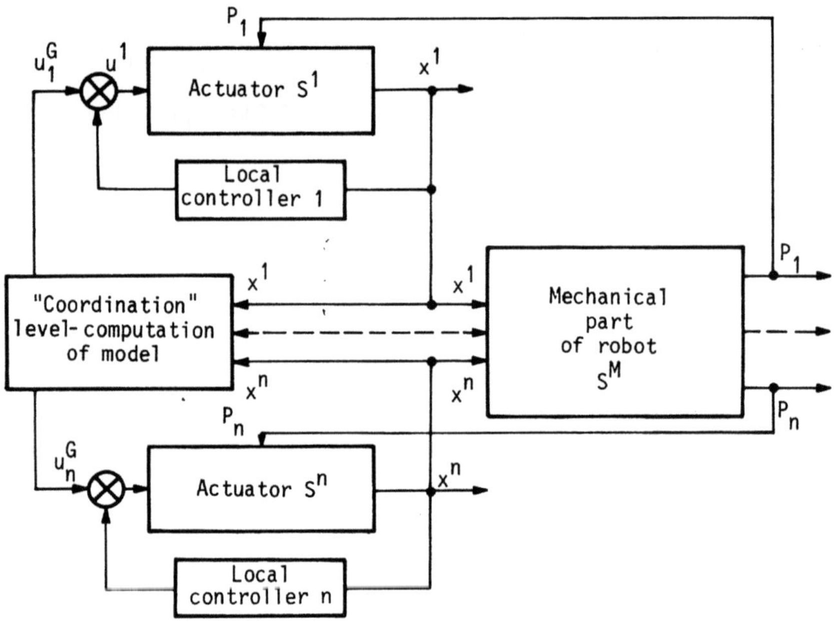

Fig. 2.12. Nonlinear hierarchical control scheme for decoupling of robot (after [45])

However, all problems concerning the implementation of "the inverse problem" technique are also encountered with the nonlinear hierarchical control of Roessler (cumbersome calculation of dynamic model, sensitivity to parameter variations etc.).

Nonlinear decoupling control of robot has also been proposed by Freund [46]. Starting from a very general control strategy for decoupling of nonlinear systems, he attempts to completely decouple the nonlinear model of robot dynamics in external coordinates. However, such control would be extremely complex and very hard to implement. Thus, when dealing with a particular robot the author simplifies the control by neglecting the accelerations in the coupling and he decouples the robot in joint coordinates. In essence, this approach also reduces to "inverse problem" technique. The crucial problem of the robot stability if such simplified controller is applied has not been considered in [46].

As we have already mentioned in previous paragraph force feedback can also be used to decouple dynamics of robotic system. Thus, force feedback can also be regarded as decoupled control of robots.

2.3.6. Decentralized control

Decoupled control presented in previous paragraph is intended to decouple the robotic system into the set of independent subsystems which can be stabilized by local servos. Thus, we arrive to the simplest and most commonly used control in practice-decentralized control.

The decentralized control structure is adopted as our approach to control synthesis in this book. We have already discussed this approach in our previous book [2] and we shall present it in detail in this chapter. Here, we shall briefly survey some results of other authors who have also considered decentralized control of robotic systems.

In this approach to control synthesis the robot is, at once, regarded as a set of decoupled subsystems, each corresponding to a separate joint and coupling among them is neglected. Starting from the model of robot, the robot is considered as a set of local decoupled actuators (2.3.31) in which coupling term f^iM_i is neglected. For each subsystem (2.3.31) a local control is synthesized in order to stabilize free (decoupled) subsystem.

In many applications it has been assumed that local control can stabilize the whole robotic system. This most commonly used approach is effective for positioning of a manipulator and tracking of a relatively slow trajectory. However, if fast trajectory has to be precisely tracked this approach cannot be accepted. Medvedov, Leskov and Yuschenko [47] have analyzed overall system behaviour when only local controllers are implemented. They linearized the robot model around nominal trajectory and analyzed the stability of the linearized model with local controllers in frequency domain. The validity of this analysis is limited by the validity domain of the linearized model.

Paul [48] has presented several servosystem schemes in which compensation for some dynamic effects of the robot is introduced (but only at servosystem level). He presented compensation for the influence of gravity forces and Columb friction, compensation for the velocity and acceleration changes along the trajectory, etc. However, all these improvements have been made at the local level, and their effects might be very limited (this has not been analyzed in [48]).

Arimoto and Miyazaki [49] have proved that PID local controller can be effectively applied for the position control of manipulation robots. They proved the global asymptotic stability of the robot around a target point under the condition of a PID local feedback control scheme. However, the capability of the control to ensure tracking of nominal trajectory has not been considered in [49]. Arimoto and Miyazaki, following the results presented in [18], have modified their PID feedback scheme to suit the case when the target point is described in external coordinates (similarly to (2.3.18)). The asymptotic stability of such a PID sensory feedback scheme is also proved in [49].

In [50] Arimoto and co-authors attempted to extend the results of [49] to tracking of a desired path in space. Actually, they introduced such a local controller which enables the robot to move at a high speed and smoothly stop with high positioning accuracy. However, this scheme ensure the asymptotic stability of positioning, but tracking of some path in space is not reliable.

Thus, the conventional local servos ensure just positioning of the robot even at high speeds. The problem of tracking a desired trajectory by decentralized control, which is very complex, has been studied in [2]. In this book we shall for the first time consider decentralized control synthesis for manipulation robots with variable parameters, and we shall also add some global feedback loops if it is necessary to ensure stability of the robotic system and satisfy a stated control task.

2.3.7. Other approaches

We have briefly discussed some of the most characteristic results in dynamic control of manipulation robots. We have started with the most complex approach (optimal control) and arrived to the simplest (decentralized-joint servo control). The considered approaches are, in our opinion, the most characteristic and the most representative (but not always the most successful). Besides the considered approaches there were many other attempts in dynamic control of robots which should also be mentioned. Albus [51] attempted to control manipulators by control signals directly memorized in the computer memory. Young [52] attempted to synthesize the control for manipulators using the theory of variable structure systems, etc. There are also a few papers dealing with the problem of flexibility of the manipulator. Book, Maizza-Neto and Whitney [53] considered a simple two-beam, two-joint manipulation with distributed flexibility. A more general case was treated in a paper by Truckenbrodt [54] where a manipulator with rigid and flexible elements is properly modelled.

In [55] the preview tracking control algorithm is applied to the trajectory control of robots; the control algorithm consists of the integral control action of the afore predicted deviation. In [56] compensation for the robot dynamics is performed by nonlinear compensator and the control of external coordinates is established. Actually, the control scheme proposed has some similarities to "inverse problem" technique, except for the fact that control in external coordinates is proposed and that compensation for nominal acceleration along trajectory is not introduced.

In the text to follow, we shall present in detail our approach to synthesis of control of manipulation robots which satisfies the stated control task. As already mentioned, we shall first consider the decentralized control for robotic systems and, present stability analysis of the robots with variable parameters if local controllers are applied. Then, we shall also introduce additional global control to compensate for the robot dynamics in the case when the local controllers cannot withstand the influence of coupling between the robot joints. Actually, our aim is to find the simplest control law which can satisfy the given control task. Instead of treating the system as a single plant and introducing at once the centralized and complex control and, then, by various approximations trying to simplify the control algorithm, we shall consider the problem piece-by-piece. We first introduce local controllers and then add some global feedback loops until the desired performance of the system is achieved. In doing this, we shall consider the complete dynamic model of the manipulation robots with no simplifications and neglecting any nonlinear term.

2.4 Synthesis of Local Controllers

We shall start our control synthesis from the classical, simplest and most frequently encountered, in practice, approach via local controllers. In this approach, for each joint and its corresponding actuator, an independent local controller is synthesized which stabilizes the actuator and joint regardless of the rest of the robot. This approach is obviously the simplest possible from the point of view of control information structure; each local controller has the information about the coordinates of the corresponding joint only. This decentralized control structure is schematically presented in Fig. 2.13. The simplicity of such control structure is the reason why it is most commonly used in up-to-day robotic manipulators.

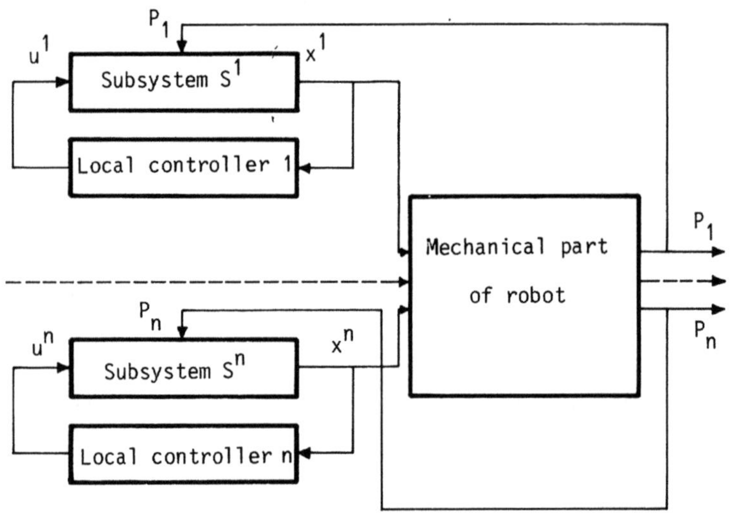

Fig. 2.13. Decentralized control structure

We shall not discuss various possibilities as to how to choose decentralized control structure. We adopt the control structure presented in Fig. 2.13 since it is physically the most appropriate. This means that we assume that each control input u^i has the information about the state coordinates of the corresponding actuator x^i, i.e. only:

$$u^i = \phi_i(x^i), \qquad \forall i \in I \tag{2.4.1}$$

where ϕ_i: $R^{n_i} \to R^1$ is some function of the subsystem state vector x^i.

Here, we shall consider the control task at the executive level as stated in Paragraph 2.2.2. We assume that nominal trajectory $x^o(t) = (x^{o1T}(t), x^{o2T}(t),...,x^{onT}(t))^T$ $\forall t \in T$ is synthesized at the tactical control level using some of the methods for calculating the joint coordinates when the nominal path is given in external coordinates [1]. Thus, we assume that we have $x^{oi}(t)$, $\forall t \in T$, $\forall i \in I$ which we have to track by the control law at the executive level.

There are several possibilities for synthesizing local controllers (2.4.1) for independent manipulator joints. We shall briefly discuss several approaches to the synthesis of local controllers.

Synthesis of decentralized control for large-scale systems has been widely investigated by many authors approaching this problem from the aspect of general systems theory. A very good survey of decentralized control methods for large-scale systems is given in [57].

The first question encountered when attaching this problem is whether the decentralized control has to minimize some criterion (2.3.1) or not. Namely, as we have explained in Paragraph 2.3, we might try to synthesize control in the form (2.4.1) which will minimize criterion (2.3.1) along with satisfying control task (2.2.18). However, numerous problems arise if optimal decentralized control is to be synthesized. In [2] we have analyzed these problems, so we shall not repeat this discussion.

The second question concerning the synthesis of decentralized control is: should we synthesize the decentralized control law (2.4.1) and its parameters using the complete centralized model of the robot (2.2.8), or should we first synthesize local controllers using the approximate decoupled model of the robot, and, then, analyze the stability of the overall system. The first approach has been considered by many authors but mainly for linear large-scale systems. They attempt to synthesize decentralized control (2.4.1) so that the overall linear model has certain properties (e.g. poleplacement). This means that we have at once to determine the decentralized control law and feedback gains which ensure stability of the complete system. Davison [58] considered robust decentralized servomechanism problem, i.e. he attempted to find a decentralized controller such that certain outputs of the system asymptotically track given reference inputs independent of any external disturbances which may affect the system, and independent of any variations in the plant parameters and gains of the system. He found necessary and sufficient conditions for a solution to the problem to exist, and found a complete characterization of all decentralized controllers which solves the problem. However, this approach is very difficult to apply to nonlinear systems. On the other hand, this "centralized" synthesis of decentralized control is not convenient for practical application: a designer can hardly use his own experience about the robot and tune the controller in accordance with his desires, since it is very difficult to think about dynamics of the complete robot as a single plant.

This is the reason why we have chosen the second approach: we first synthesize local controllers for independent (decoupled) subsystems and then check whether or not the overall robot is practically stable with these local controllers. This approach has certain advantages from the point of view of control designer since the synthesis is performed "piece-by-piece" [59]: local controllers are synthesized for low-order subsystems and many classical and well-elaborated methods for the synthesis of controller can be applied. Designer has to think about low order subsystems and synthesize local controllers for each manipulator joint regardless of the complete robot dynamics. Then, the stability of the complete robot is analyzed and if the system is not stable the local controllers have to be chosen again. If we cannot find local controllers which can stabilize overall robot, we have to introduce global feedback loops, i.e. the global control which should compensate for coupling among subsystems.

Thus, we shall first consider the synthesis of local controllers for local subsystems. However the choice of subsystems models is not unique, even if information control structure has already been chosen. As we have already explained above, the control structure (2.4.1) is the most adequate from the physical and practical points of view. However, the model associated to each independent joint of the manipulator has to be chosen. Each joint is driven by its actuator S^i the model of which is given by (2.2.2) where $f^i(\theta^i)M_i$ represents the influence of the manipulator dynamics upon the *i*th actuator. Thus, we can choose the models of decoupled (free) subsystems as:

$$\bar{S}^i: \dot{x}^i = A^i(\theta^i)x^i + b^i(\theta^i)N(u^i), \qquad \forall i \in I \tag{2.4.2}$$

where we have neglected coupling term $f^i(\theta^i)M_i$.

However, M_i representing the coupling among subsystems (2.4.2) is a function of all state coordinates of the manipulator. It is also a function of state coordinates x^i of the subsystem $\bar{S}^i$: Since the relation the mechanism joint coordinate q_i and the state vector x^i is given by (2.2.5) and since P_i is a function of q_i, $\dot{q}_i$, $\ddot{q}_i$ (2.2.1), it is clear that P_i is a function of x^i (relation between M_i and P_i is given by (2.2.7)). For example model (2.4.2) takes into account only the inertia of the actuator: inertia forces of the mechanical part around the *i*th joint are included in coupling term $f^i M_i(x)$. Similarly gravitational term around the *i*th joint which might depend upon x^i is not included in the model (2.4.2). Thus, we have to extract from $M_i(x)$ the part that depends on x^i and associate it to the subsystem model $\bar{S}^i$. If we look at the model of the mechanism dynamics (2.2.1) we can try to extract the terms that depend on x^i; for example, inertia term $H_{ii}(q, d)\ddot{q}_i$, gravity term $G_i(q, d)$ etc. However, in the general case it is not possible to extract the terms that are functions of x^i only, for example, H_{ii} is usually a function of all mechanism joint coordinates q and it is the same situation with gravity term G_i. On the other hand, these terms are, in the general case, highly nonlinear. The models of subsystems $\bar{S}^i$ are linear, except for nonlinearity of the amplitude saturation type upon the input $N(u^i)$. We would prefer to preserve linearity of the subsystems models in order to simplify the synthesis of local controllers*). Thus, we shall extend the subsystems models by constant inertia term $\bar{H}_{ii}\ddot{q}_i$ (similarly as in Paragraph 2.3.5) and constant gravity term $\bar{h}_i q_i$ so that we get the models of the subsystems in the form [2]:

$$\tilde{S}^i: \quad \dot{x}^i = \bar{A}^i(\theta^i)x^i + \bar{b}^i(\theta^i)N(u^i), \qquad \forall i \in I \tag{2.4.3}$$

where $\bar{A}^i \in R^{n_i \times n_i}$, $\bar{b}^i \in R^{n_i}$ are matrices of the subsystem $\tilde{S}^i$ given by:

$$\bar{A}^i(\theta^i) = (I_{n_i} - f^i(\theta^i)\cdot\bar{z}^i\bar{H}_{ii}T^i)^{-1}(A^i(\theta^i) + f^i(\theta^i)\bar{z}^i\bar{h}_i\hat{T}^i) \tag{2.4.4}$$

$$\bar{b}^i(\theta^i) = (I_{n_i} - f^i(\theta^i)\bar{z}^i\cdot\bar{H}_{ii}T^i)^{-1}b^i(\theta^i), \quad \forall i \in I$$

where by $\bar{z}^i$ we denote a constant number estimating the function $z^i(q_i)$ in (2.2.7), T^i is a constant number estimating $\partial G^i/\partial x^i$ in (2.2.13), $\hat{T}^i$ is a constant number estimating $G^i(x^i)$ in (2.2.5). The numbers $\bar{H}_{ii}$ estimate inertia terms $H_{ii}(q, d)$, and constant numbers $\bar{h}_i$ estimate gravity terms in $h_i(q, \dot{q}, d)$, i.e. estimate terms $g_i(q, d)$. In [2] we have already analyzed the introduction of these estimations into subsystems

*) In fact, we can choose nonlinear models of subsystems. However, as we want to synthesize linear controllers we should linearize subsystems models. Thus, we shall start at once with linear subsystems model.

models. We have analyzed the influence of choice of the numbers $\bar{H}_{ii}$ and $\bar{h}_i$ upon the synthesis of control parameters and the suboptimality of decentralized control. We have to choose numbers $\bar{H}_{ii}$ and $\bar{h}_i$ such that

$$\bar{H}_{ii} > \max(H_{ii}(q, d)), \quad \bar{h}_i < \min|\partial g_i(q, d)/\partial q_i|$$

where the maximum and minimum are taken on the sets $x \in X^t$, $d \in D$. Otherwise, if we choose $\bar{H}_{ii} < \max(H_{ii}(q, d))$, then the overshoot might appear in the ith joint when the robot comes in position in which inertia around this joint is greater than $\bar{H}_{ii}$. Namely, if we choose $\bar{H}_{ii} < \max(H_{ii}(q, d))$, and synthesize local gains so that the subsystem is critically damped then the corresponding damping factor might be less than critical in the position which corresponds to $\max(H_{ii}(q, d))$; thus, when robot comes to a position in which inertia around the ith joint is $\max(H_{ii}(q, d))$, then the subsystem is underdamped and overshoot must appear. It is well known that overshoot must not occur in controlling robots under any circumstances. Thus, we shall choose $\bar{H}_{ii}$ and $\bar{h}_i$ as above. It should be noted that we have taken into account only linear dependent member in the Taylor's series of gravity term $g_i(q, d)$, while the rest members are taken into account through coupling term.

The model of subsystem $\tilde{S}^i$ (2.4.3) includes the model of actuator in the ith manipulator joint and the model of the independent ith joint dynamics*):

$$\tilde{P}_i = \bar{H}_{ii} T^i \dot{x}^i + \bar{h}^i \hat{T}^i x^i \tag{2.4.5}$$

where $\tilde{P}_i$ is an estimate of the driving torque in the ith joint. Thus, the models of subsystems (2.4.3) are better approximations of the robot dynamics than models (2.4.2) which take into account dynamics of actuators only. The approximative decoupled model (2.4.3) also takes into account dynamics of the mechanism but using linear decoupled model (2.4.5). Obviously, a more adequate decoupled model would take into account the nonlinear model of the mechanism (in a decoupled form), but, as explained above we want to deal with linear models of subsystems. The coupling among subsystems (2.4.3) is given by $f^i(\theta^i) z^i(q_i) \cdot \bar{P}_i(x, d)$ where $\bar{P}_i$ is given by

---

*) The physical explanation of the model (2.4.5) is obvious: it is assummed that all joints of the robot except for the ith are locked and only the ith joint can rotate with acceleration $\ddot{q}_i$; since $H_{ii}(q, d)$=const for q_j=const, for $j \neq i$, it can be taken $H_{ii}(q, d) = \bar{H}_{ii}$ and $h^i q_i$ is the approximation of the gravity force.

$$\bar{P}_i(x, d) = P_i(x, d) - \tilde{P}_i(q_i, \ddot{q}_i)\cdot\bar{z}^i/z^i(q_i) \qquad (2.4.6)$$

If we compare the coupling among subsystems $\bar{S}^i$ (2.4.2) and the coupling among subsystems $\tilde{S}^i$ (2.4.3) we can see that the coupling in the latter case is considerably reduced for the value of estimation of driving torques $\tilde{P}_i(q_i, \ddot{q}_i)$. Since we shall synthesize local controllers for independent subsystems neglecting the coupling among them, it is obvious that subsystems $\tilde{S}^i$ with reduced coupling would lead to more adequate local controllers regarding the stability of the overall robotic manipulator. Actually, the approximative model (2.4.3) is closer to the real system model than (2.4.2), so the control synthesized using (2.4.3) has a better chance to accommodate the overall system than the control synthesized using (2.4.2).

The next problem is the variation of actuator parameters θ^i. As we have explained in Paragraph 2.2.2, we shall assume that the parameters of the actuators vary relatively slowly, so that there is no need to permanently take care about parameter variation. We shall synthesize local controllers assuming that parameters of the actuators are constant and known in advance. We shall consider the synthesis of local controllers assuming that the values of parameters of the actuators are given $\bar{\theta}^i \in R^{\ell_i}$ so that the models of subsystems $\tilde{S}^i$ (2.4.3) can be written in the form:

$$\tilde{S}^i: \quad \dot{x}^i = \tilde{A}^i x^i + \tilde{b}^i N(u^i) \qquad (2.4.7)$$

where by $\tilde{A} \in R^{n_i \times n_i}$ and $\tilde{b}^i \in R^{n_i}$ we denote $\tilde{A}^i = \bar{A}^i(\bar{\theta}^i)$ and $\tilde{b}^i = \bar{b}^i(\bar{\theta}^i)$. So we shall synthesize local controllers for linear time-invariant subsystems (2.4.7) with constant parameters. From time to time the control system will identify the parameters of the actuators and if they change significantly the controllers gains must be calculated again (and changed). Thus, in the text to follow we shall deal with subsystems models in the form (2.4.7).

Now, we have to define the control task on the subsystems level in accordance with the control task for robotic manipulators (2.2.18), or (2.2.20). As we have explained in Paragraph 2.2.2, the regions of practical stability X^I and X^t are asummed to be in "decentralized" form. Thus, we can decouple control task (2.2.18) into subsystems subtasks. We shall synthesize local controllers for decoupled subsystems (2.4.7) so that the following control task has to be accomplished:

(2.4.8) Local control task (for the ith subsystem): The local control $u_L^i(t, x^i)$ has to be synthesized which will ensure that $\forall x^i(0) \in X^{I(i)}$ implies $x^i(t) \in X^{t(i)}$, $\forall t \in T$, where $X^{I(i)}$ and $X^{t(i)}$ are finite regions around the prescribed nominal trajectory $x^{oi}(t)$.

This definition of local control task corresponds to the control task for robotic manipulator (2.2.18). It is easy to extend this definition to correspond to definition (2.2.20). According to (2.2.19) the regions of practical stability for local subsystems are defined as $X^{I(i)} = \{x^i(0): ||\Delta x^i(0)|| < \bar{X}^{I(i)}\}$ and $X^{t(i)}(t) = \{x(t): ||\Delta x^i(t)|| < \bar{X}^{t(i)} \cdot \exp(-\alpha^{(i)} t)\}$, $\forall t \in T$, where $\bar{X}^{t(i)} > \bar{X}^{I(i)} > 0$, $\alpha_i > 0$, $\forall i \in I$. Our approach is to first synthesize the local controllers which will stabilize the local subsystems in accordance with local practical stability definition (2.4.8) and then analyze if such local controllers can stabilize the overall robotic manipulator according to the control task definition (2.2.18). If the result of the test is negative, we have to choose new local controllers regardless of the local task definition (2.4.8), or, in other words, we must synthesize local controllers with higher gains (or, we redefine local tasks by increasing $X^{I(i)}$, $X^{t(i)}$ and α_i and synthesize local controllers with higher feedback gains).

Before starting to consider various procedures for local control synthesis, we must once again underline the difference between the control strategy presented in our previous book [2] and the control scheme which we shall discuss here. In [2] we have considered the manipulators with constant and known parameters. Thus, we were able to synthesize nominal programmed control $u^o(t)$ using a centralized (complete) model of the manipulator, i.e. we synthesized programmed control $u^o(t)$ to satisfy (2.3.4) where d^o, θ^o are given (defined in advance) values of parameters. Then, we considered the model of deviation from nominal trajectory $x^o(t)$ and nominal control $u^o(t)$ (2.3.5). We considered the approximative decoupled model of the system at this level of deviation from nominal. The form of this decoupled model is analogous to (2.4.7) where Δx^i and Δu^i have to be substituted for x^i and u^i (since the deviations from nominal trajectory $x^{oi}(t)$, and control $u^{oi}(t)$ have been considered). The only difference is that in [2] the coupling among subsystems is given by $f^i(\theta^{io})[z^i(q)\cdot\bar{P}_i(q, d^o) - z^i(q^{oi})\bar{P}_i^o(q^o, d^o)]$ which is less that for subsystems (2.4.7). (The difference is in nominal driving torque $z^i(q^{oi})\bar{P}_i^o(q^o, d^o)$ which is compensated by nominal programmed control $u^o(t)$). Thus, the coupling among subsystems is considerably reduced if the nominal programmed control is applied. However, the application of nominal programmed control synthesized using the centralized model suffers from two main drawbacks:

(1) Synthesis of the programmed control on the basis of centralized model (2.3.4) is very complex, and it can hardly be computed in real time. This is the reason why in [2, 7, 10] we have proposed to synthesize the nominal programmed control off-line and store it in the computer memory. This approach is accepteble in many cases in robotic practice in which the control tasks and operating conditions are well defined in advance. However, in the general case, the task cannot be prepared in advance since all conditions cannot be anticipated. On the other hand, if a complex and rather long control task has to be performed, this approach demands large memory capacity. This approach has the same drawbacks as the approach by Raibert and Horn [25] or Albus [51], although some advantages of our strategy [2] concerning simplicity of the control scheme are evident.

(2) The synthesis of nominal programmed control $u^{o}(t)$ using the centralized model (2.3.4) assumes that all parameters of the robot are defined and precisely known in advance. If this assumption is not satisfied, application of the centralized programmed control is not efficient in general since the nominal control cannot compensate for robot dynamics when the parameters deviate from their nominal values d^{o}, θ^{o} (for which the nominal control has been synthesized).

Since in this book we consider the robotic manipulators with variable parameters the application of centralized nominal control will be omitted. Thus, we shall start at once with the approximate decoupled model of the robot (2.4.7) and directly synthesize local controllers.

We can attack the problem of local control synthesis (i.e. the synthesis of local controller for the subsystem $\tilde{S}^{i}$ (2.4.7) which will satisfy local control task (2.4.8)) by numerous approaches. Namely, we can apply various approaches to control synthesis which have been developed in the classical and modern control theory: optimal servosystem approach [60]; the tuning regulators [61]; the robust servomechanisms approach [62]; classical PID controllers, synthesized by various methods in frequency domain [63] or by root-locus methods [63] and so on; pole placement approach [64], etc. Certainly, we shall not survey various methods for the synthesis of local controllers for linear subsystems. We shall briefly present only two characteristic approaches: a) by minimization of the standard quadratic criterion, and b) by pole placement. In doing this, we shall consider the synthesis of the local controller: a) by complete state feedback b) by addition of integral feedback, c) by output feedback. However, numerous other methods can be applied; the stability analysis of the complete robotic system and introduction of global control are valid regardless of the method applied for local control synthesis.

Note that the local models of subsystems (2.4.7) are nonlinear with respect to inputs due to the presence of nonlinearities $N(u^i)$ of amplitude saturation type. However, in the synthesis of local controller we shall first consider the linear model of subsystem:

$$\tilde{S}^i: \quad \dot{x}^i = \tilde{A}^i x^i + \tilde{b}^i u^i \tag{2.4.9}$$

where input enters also linearly in the model, and afterwards we shall consider the influence of the input amplitude constraint upon the subsystem stability and overall system performance. Thus, we shall start with the local control synthesis for the linear models of subsystems (2.4.9).

2.4.1. Optimal servosystem

Let us suppose that we have to solve the local control task (2.4.8) by minimizing standard quadratic criterion in the form:

$$J_i(x^i(0), x^{oi}(t)) = \int_0^{\tau} [u^i r_i u^i + (x^i(t) - x^{oi}(t))^T Q_i (x^i(t) - x^{oi}(t))] dt \tag{2.4.10}$$

where $r_i > 0$, is a positive number and $Q_i \in R^{n_i \times n_i}$ is a positive definite symmetric matrix. The theory of optimal linear servosystem is well known [60], so we shall not present it here. For the linear subsystem (2.4.9) and performance index (2.4.10) the solution of optimal servo-problem is given by

$$u^i(t) = -r_i^{-1} \tilde{b}^{iT} (\tilde{K}_i(t) x^i - g^i(t)), \quad \forall t \in T \tag{2.4.11}$$

where $\tilde{K}_i: T \rightarrow R^{n_i \times n_i}$ is the positive definite symmetric matrix which is the solution of the Riccati differential equation:

$$-\dot{\tilde{K}}_i(t) = (\tilde{A}^{iT}\tilde{K}_i(t) + \tilde{K}_i(t)\tilde{A}^i) + Q_i - \tilde{K}_i(t)\tilde{b}^i r_i^{-1}\tilde{b}^{iT}\tilde{K}_i(t)$$

$$\tilde{K}_i(\tau) = 0 \qquad (2.4.12)$$

and $g^i: T \to R^{n_i}$ is the $n_i \times 1$ vector which is the solution of the equation:

$$-\dot{g}^i(t) = (\tilde{A}^i - \tilde{b}^i r_i^{-1}\tilde{b}^{iT}\tilde{K}_i(t))^T g^i(t) + Q_i x^{oi}(t), \quad g^i(\tau) = 0, \qquad (2.4.13)$$

The control scheme of optimal linear servosystem (2.4.11) is presented in Fig. 2.14. Obviously, implementation of such a control law is too complex. Differential equations (2.4.12) and (2.4.13) have to be integrated backwards from the time instant τ, so these computations cannot be performed on-line. This means that we have to compute $\tilde{K}_i(t)$, $g(t)$ off-line and store it in the computer memory for each movement. Evidently such a solution is not acceptable in practice, since it demands too large computer memory, and the computational time even in the off-line mode is too long.

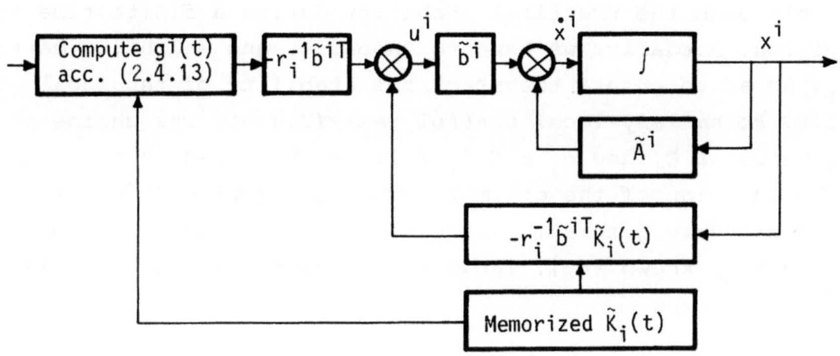

Fig. 2.14. Local, optimal servosystem for tracking desired trajectory

Therefore we shall consider a simplified solution of the optimal servo problem. Let us assume that there exists programmed control $\bar{u}^{oi}(t)$ satisfying:

$$\dot{x}^{oi}(t) = \tilde{A}^i x^{oi}(t) + \tilde{b}^i \bar{u}^{oi}(t), \qquad \forall t \in T \qquad (2.4.14)$$

This means that the desired trajectory x^{oi} is chosen so that such a $\bar{u}^{oi}(t)$ can be found which satisfies (2.4.14). Then, let us consider the model of the deviation of the subsystem state from the nominal trajectory $x^{oi}(t)$ and nominal programmed control $\bar{u}^{oi}(t)$. The model of state deviation is given by:

$$\Delta\dot{x}^i = \tilde{A}^i\Delta x^i + \tilde{b}^i\Delta u^i, \qquad \forall t\in T \tag{2.4.15}$$

where $\Delta x^i(t) = x^i(t) - x^{oi}(t)$ is the vector of dimension n_i which represents the deviation of the actual subsystem state from the nominal state $x^{oi}(t)$ at each moment $t\in T$, and $\Delta u^i(t) = u^i(t) - u^{oi}(t)$ is the scalar, $\Delta u^i \in R^1$, which represents the control which should be added to the nominal programmed control $u^{oi}(t)$ in order to stabilize subsystem (2.4.9). Now, we can consider stabilization of the model of deviation (2.4.15) around its origin $\Delta x^i(t) = 0$, i.e. around the nominal trajectory $x^i(t) = x^{oi}(t)$ and nominal control $\bar{u}^{oi}(t)$. To stabilize subsystem (2.4.15) we shall minimize the criterion:

$$\bar{J}_i(\Delta x^i(0)) = \int_0^\infty (\Delta u^i r_i \Delta u^i + \Delta x^{iT} Q_i \Delta x^i)\exp(2\beta_i t)dt \tag{2.4.16}$$

where $\beta_i > 0$ is the prescribed degree of the exponential stability of free subsystem. Here, we observe the criterion over an infinite time interval, although the practical stability during a finite time interval is desired. Actually, we have to choose β_i and weighting matrices Q_i and r_i, so as to ensure the practical stability of the local subsystem, i.e. to satisfy local control task (2.4.8). The choice of the weighting matrices Q_i and r_i and β_i will be explained in the text to follow. The solution of the optimal regulator problem (i.e. minimization of the standard quadratic criterion (2.4.16) under the constraint (2.4.15)) is well known [60]. The control law minimizing (2.4.16) is given by*)

$$\Delta u_i^L(t) = -r_i^{-1}\tilde{b}^{iT}K_i\Delta x^i(t), \qquad \forall t\in T \tag{2.4.17}$$

where $K_i \in R^{n_i \times n_i}$ is the positive definite matrix which represents the solution of the Riccati algebraic equation

$$K_i(\tilde{A}^i + \beta_i I) + (\tilde{A}^{iT} + \beta_i I)K_i + Q_i - K_i\tilde{b}^i r_i^{-1}\tilde{b}^{iT}K_i = 0 \tag{2.4.18}$$

Now, the control which is to stabilize free subsystems (2.4.9) around the nominal trajectory $x^{oi}(t)$ is given by

$$u^i(t) = \bar{u}^{oi}(t) + \Delta u_i^L(t) = \bar{u}^{oi}(t) - r_i^{-1}\tilde{b}^{iT}K_i\Delta x^i(t), \ \forall t\in T \tag{2.4.19}$$

---

*) Note that we have denoted the control which stabilizes the model of deviation by Δu_i^L in order to underline that it has local information only.

The control scheme of such solution of the local controller is presented in Fig. 2.15. In comparison to the control scheme of optimal servosystem (Fig. 2.13) this control scheme is much simpler and its implementation is considerably easier. However, the control (2.4.19) is evidently suboptimal with respect to the original criterion (2.4.10). Nevertheless, it is more convenient to adopt a suboptimal solution which can relatively easily be implemented. The computation of local nominal programmed control $\bar{u}^{oi}(t)$ can easily be performed on-line, since the orders of local subsystems (2.4.9) are relatively low (see Paragraph 4.2 for details about the computation of local programmed control which satisfies (2.4.14)). The computation of local regulator gains $D^i = -r_i^{-1}\tilde{b}^{iT}K_i$ is performed off-line and the implementation of control (2.4.17) reduces to simple multiplication of the system state deviation from nominal trajectory Δx^i by the gains D_i. However, this solution has some drawbacks regarding its robustness to parameter variations. Thus, we have to consider the synthesis of robust servo problem if we keep in mind the fact that this control should withstand variations of manipulator parameters.

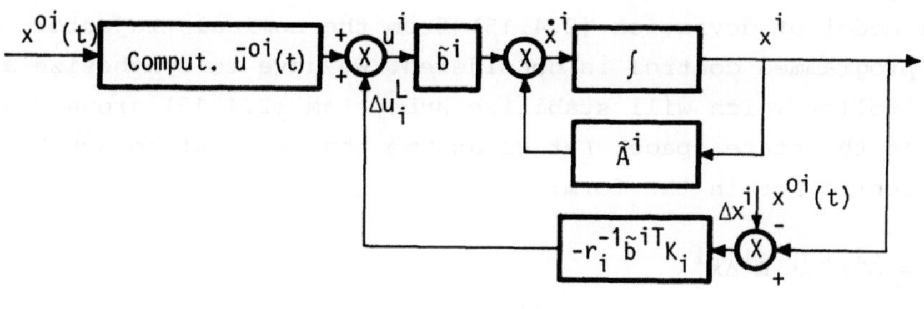

Fig. 2.15. Local optimal regulator and local nominal control

Actually the controller presented in Fig. 2.15 involves only static feedback (but it requires a feedback with respect to the complete subsystem state x^i). In order to achieve a robust controller capable of withstanding parameter variation we have to consider a dynamic feedback controller.

2.4.2. Robust servo-controller

Davison has considered the general robust servomechanism controller [62], i.e. he considered synthesis of a controller which can withstand arbitrarily large perturbations in the plant parameters. Davison has found necessary and sufficient conditions for there to exist a robust controller for a linear, time-invariant, multivariable system (plant) so that asymptotic tracking/regulation occurs independent of input disturbances and arbitrary perturbations in the plant parameters of the system. It has been shown that any robust controller must consist of two devices: 1) a servocompensator, and 2) a stabilizing compensator. The servocompensator is a feedback compensator with error input which depends on the disturbances and reference inputs to the system. The servocompensator is a generalization of the integral controller of clasical control theory. The purpose of the stabilizing compensator is to stabilize the resultant system obtained by applying the servocompensator to the plant.

However, such approach to the robust servomechanism problem is too general and complex. Thus, we shall consider a simplified form of the dynamic robust servo-controller.

First, we shall assume again that the local programmed control $\bar{u}^{oi}(t)$, satisfying (2.4.14), exists and that it is applied to the subsystem $\tilde{S}^i$. Now, the model of deviation (2.4.15) from the nominal trajectory and nominal programmed control is considered. We have to synthesize a robust controller which will stabilize subsystem (2.4.15) around the point $\Delta x^i = 0$ in the state space. Let us assume that we want to synthesize a dynamic controller in the form:

$$\begin{aligned} \dot{z}^i &= \hat{S}^i z^i + \hat{R}^i \Delta x^i \\ \Delta u^i &= \hat{Q}^i z^i + \hat{D}^{iT} \Delta x^i \end{aligned}, \qquad \forall i \in I \qquad (2.4.20)$$

where $z^i \in R^{m_i}$ is the state vector of the *i*th dynamic controller, $\hat{S}^i \in R^{m_i \times m_i}$ is the matrix of the *i*th controller, $\hat{R}^i \in R^{m_i \times n_i}$, $\hat{Q}^i \in R^{1 \times m_i}$ and $\hat{D}^i \in R^{n_i \times 1}$ are gain vectors, m_i is the order of the *i*th controller. The scheme of such a dynamic controller is presented in Fig. 2.16. We have to choose the elements of the matrices $\hat{S}^i$, $\hat{R}^i$, $\hat{Q}^i$ and $\hat{D}^i$ so as to stabilize subsystem (2.4.15) and ensure robustness of the subsystem to parameter variations. Actually, we have to stabilize the subsystem with the dynamic controller by a proper choice of the elements of the corresponding matrices. The augmented subsystem (plant $\tilde{S}^i$ + controller) is given by:

$$\Delta \dot{\hat{x}}^i = \hat{A}^i \Delta \hat{x}^i, \qquad \forall i \in I \qquad (2.4.21)$$

where $\hat{A}^i \in R^{(n_i+m_i)\times(n_i+m_i)}$ is the matrix of the total closed-loop subsystem given by:

$$\hat{A}^i = \left[\begin{array}{c|c} \tilde{A}^i+\tilde{b}^i\hat{D}^{iT} & \tilde{b}^i\hat{Q}^i \\ \hline \hat{R}^i & \hat{S}^i \end{array}\right]$$

and $\Delta\hat{x}^i \in R^{n_i+m_i}$, $\Delta\hat{x}^i = (\Delta x^{iT}, z^{iT})^T$ is the state vector of the augmented subsystem. We have to choose the elements of $\hat{D}^i$, $\hat{Q}^i$, $\hat{S}^i$, $\hat{R}^i$ so as to achieve that the eigen-values of the closed-loop augmented subsystem lie to the left from the line $\lambda = -\beta_i$ in the complex plane, where β_i is the desired stability degree. Namely, we want to achieve that

$$\mathrm{Re}(\lambda_i(\hat{A}^i)) < -\beta_i, \quad i=1,2,\ldots,n_i+m_i \tag{2.4.22}$$

where λ_i (...) denotes the *i*th eigenvalue of the corresponding matrix. Even more, we want to achieve robustness of the plant (2.4.21) to parameter variations, i.e. we want to ensure regulation of the subsystem (2.4.15) when the parameters of the plant are perturbed. Actually, if the parameters of the plant are perturbed so that the subsystem matrices become $\tilde{A}^i \to \tilde{A}^i+\delta\tilde{A}^i$, $\tilde{b}^i \to \tilde{b}^i+\delta\tilde{b}^i$, the subsystem with the dynamic controller (2.4.20) should still be stable and, even more, condition (2.4.22) should still hold. Roughly speaking, we have to choose local controller (2.4.20) so that perturbations of the subsystems parameters cannot

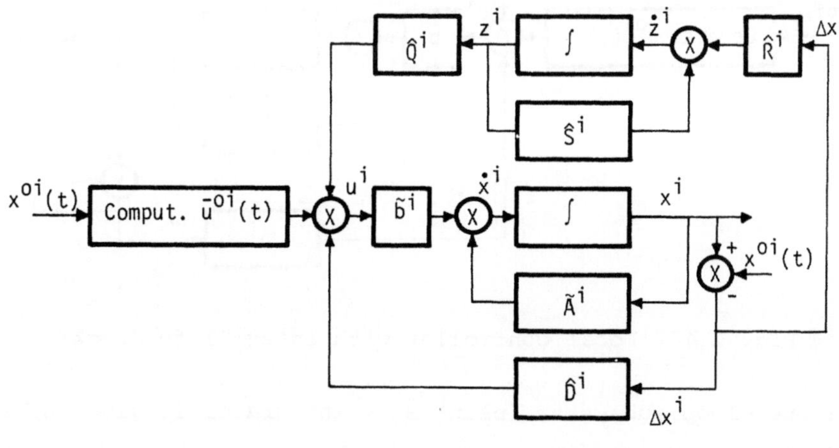

Fig. 2.16. Local dynamic controller

"destroy" subsystem stability. The robustness of the subsystem might require high feedback gains. However, by introduction of dynamic controller we get "more room" to stabilize the system with relatively low gains, by a proper choice of the dynamic part of the controller (by choosing matrices $\hat{S}^i$, $\hat{R}^i$, $\hat{Q}^i$). On the other hand, dynamic controller (2.4.20) might be too complex to be implemented if we choose too high order m_i of the controller. Thus, a trade-off between the controller complexity and its robustness should be analyzed.

Here, we shall consider the simplest dynamic controller, the order of which is $m_i=1$ and $\hat{S}^i=0$. Thus, the synthesis of dynamic controller reduces to choice of the gain matrices $\hat{Q}^i$ and $\hat{D}^i$, so as to stabilize the subsystem matrix $\hat{A}^i$. Thus, the local control is reduced to the local regulator with the addition of the integral feedback loop:

$$\Delta u_i^L = \hat{D}^{iT}\Delta x^i + \hat{Q}^i z^i = \hat{D}^{iT}\Delta x^i + \hat{Q}^i \int_0^t \hat{R}^i \Delta x^i dt, \qquad \forall i \in I \qquad (2.4.23)$$

i.e. the local controller is reduced to a classical PID regulator (assuming that $z^i(0) = 0$). The scheme of such simple dynamic local controller is presented in Fig. 2.17.

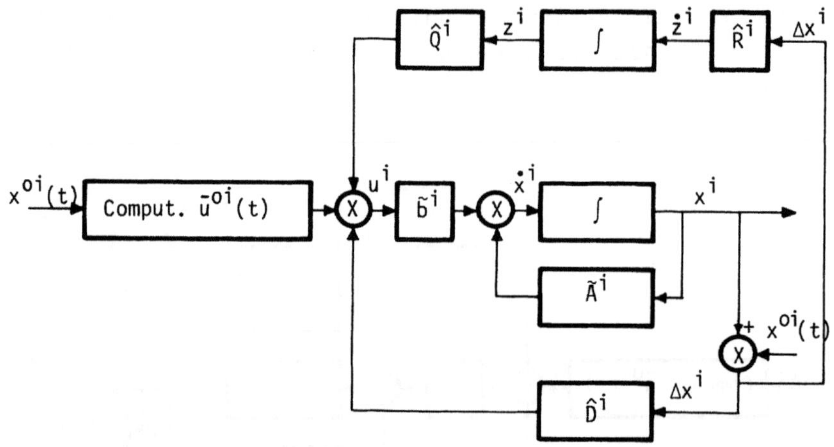

Fig. 2.17. Local controller with integral feedback

The total open-loop subsystem (plant $\tilde{S}^i$ + integrator) is given by

$$\Delta\dot{\hat{x}}^i = \hat{A}_I^i \Delta\hat{x}^i + \hat{b}_I^i \Delta u^i \qquad (2.4.24)$$

where the matrix $\hat{A}_I^i$ and the vector $\hat{b}_I^i$ of the total subsystem are now given by:

$$\hat{A}_I^i = \begin{bmatrix} \tilde{A}^i & 0 \\ \hat{R}^i & 0 \end{bmatrix}, \qquad \hat{b}_I^i = \begin{bmatrix} \tilde{b}^i \\ 0 \end{bmatrix} \tag{2.4.25}$$

and $z^i(t) = \int_0^t \hat{R}^i \Delta x^i dt$, $\Delta\hat{x}^i = (\Delta x^{iT}, z^i)^T$.

The synthesis of the feedback gains $\hat{D}^i$ and $\hat{Q}^i$ has to ensure satisfaction of the nonequality (2.4.22). This can be done either by minimization of the standard quadratic criterion, or by pole placement (or, by some other classical method for stabilization of linear time-invariant system, but, as already mentioned, we shall consider just these two methods). The linear optimal controller has already been presented in the previous Paragraph. Here, we shall extend the results from the previous Paragraph to include the dynamic controller in minimization of standard quadratic criterion.

Instead of the standard quadratic criterion in the form (2.4.16), for the augmented subsystem (2.4.24), (2.4.25) we shall consider the criterion:

$$\hat{J}_i(\Delta\hat{x}(0)) = \int_0^\infty (\Delta u^i r_i \Delta u^i + \Delta\hat{x}^{iT}\hat{Q}_i\Delta\hat{x}^i)\exp(2\beta_i t)dt \tag{2.4.26}$$

where $\hat{Q}_i \in R^{(n_i+1)\times(n_i+1)}$ is a positive definite symmetric matrix, which can be chosen in the form

$$\hat{Q}_i = \begin{bmatrix} Q_i & 0 \\ 0 & \hat{q}^i \end{bmatrix}, \qquad \hat{q}_i \in R^1$$

where Q_i is defined in (2.4.10). Thus, we have to synthesize control Δu^i which should minimize criterion (2.4.26) under the constraint given by the total subsystem (2.4.24), (2.4.25). The solution of this problem is analogous to the solution of the problem considered in the previous Paragraph. The control minimizing (2.4.26) is given by:

$$\Delta u_i^L = -r_i^{-1}\hat{b}_I^i\hat{K}_i\Delta\hat{x}^i = -\hat{k}^i\Delta\hat{x}^i \tag{2.4.27}$$

where $\hat{K}_i \in R^{(n_i+1)\times(n_i\times 1)}$ is the positive-definite solution of the corresponding Riccati algebraic equation:

$$\hat{K}_i(\hat{A}_I^i+\beta_i I)+(\hat{A}_I^{iT}+\beta_i I)\hat{K}_i+\hat{Q}_i-\hat{K}_i\hat{b}_I^i r_i^{-1}\hat{b}_I^{iT}\hat{K}_i = 0 \qquad (2.4.28)$$

In (2.4.27) by $\hat{k}^i \in R^{n_i+1}$ we have denoted the feedback gains of the augmented subsystem $\hat{k}^i=(\hat{D}^{iT}, \hat{Q}^i)^T$. Since $\hat{b}_I^i$ is given by (2.4.25), and $\Delta\hat{x}^i = (\Delta x^{iT}, z^i)^T$, the control (2.4.27) can be written in the form (2.4.23), where the feedback gains $\hat{D}^i$ and $\hat{Q}^i$ are given by:

$$\hat{D}^i = -r_i^{-1}\tilde{b}^{iT}\tilde{K}_i, \qquad \hat{Q}^i = -r_i^{-1}\tilde{b}^{iT}\tilde{k}_i \qquad (2.4.29)$$

where $\tilde{K}_i$, $\tilde{k}_i$ are defined by:

$$\hat{K}_i = \left[\begin{array}{c|c} \tilde{K}_i & \tilde{k}_i \\ \hline \cdots & \cdot \end{array}\right]$$

$\tilde{K}_i \in R^{n_i \times n_i}$, $\tilde{k}_i \in R^{n_i}$. Thus, we again get the standard linear regulator (2.4.17) with the addition of integral feedback loop (2.4.23). Johnson [65] has shown that such a controller can withstand constant perturbations acting upon the subsystem, but it is also more robust to parameter variations than the static controller presented in Fig. 2.15*). Up to now, we have assumed that the information on the complete state vector x^i of the subsystem is available, i.e. that we can measure all state coordinates x^i and implement feedback loops by them. Thus, both static (Fig. 2.15) and dynamic controllers (Fig. 2.17) assume feedback loops by all state coordinates of the subsystems. However, it is not always convenient to measure all state coordinates of the robot. For example, technogenerators are not always available to meassure speeds of the joints, feedbacks by robot currents (if D.C. electro-motors are implemented), or feedback by pressure (if hydraulic actuators are used) is not convenient to be introduced. In these cases, if we still want to apply optimal local regulators we can solve these problems in two ways: by considering output regulators (i.e. trying to minimize standard quadratic local criteria by output feedback) [60], or by introducing observers to reconstruct the subsystem state from the output. Namely, we assume that outputs of the subsystems y^i are measurable:

$$y^i = C^i x^i \qquad (2.4.30)$$

---

*) It should be noted that we might consider subsystem with constant estimation of the gravity term in coupling, and synthesize PID regulator, but the real values of gravity term will be taken into account in stability analysis.

where $y^i \in R^{k_i}$ is the output of the *i*th subsystem, k_i is the order of the *i*th output vector, $k_i < n_i$, $C^i \in R^{k_i \times n_i}$ is the output matrix. Thus, we can minimize criteria (2.4.16) or (2.4.26) by output-feedback, but this usually leads to complex problems regarding the synthesis of feedback gains.

The second approach, by introduction of observer, has already been considered in [2, 66]. Thus, we shall not repeat the synthesis of decentralized observer for robotic systems. Let us note, that we can introduce a local observer for each subsystem $\tilde{S}^i$ in the form of Luanberger's minimal observer [67]. Using these observers we get an estimate $\Delta\tilde{x}^i$ of the subsystem of state vector which we apply to compute local regulator (2.4.17), or (2.4.23) instead of real state Δx^i. Under the assumption that the subsystems are observable by output y^i (which is always satisfied if we assume that joint position is measurable), it has been shown that the subsystem is stabilized by such a controller in which estimation of the subsystem state $\Delta\tilde{x}^i$ is applied instead of real state Δx^i. The control scheme with local observers is presented in Fig. 2.18. Obviously, such local controllers, with local observers, are suboptimal with respect to local criteria (2.4.16). In [2, 66] the stability of the global system is analyzed if local regulators and local observers are applied.

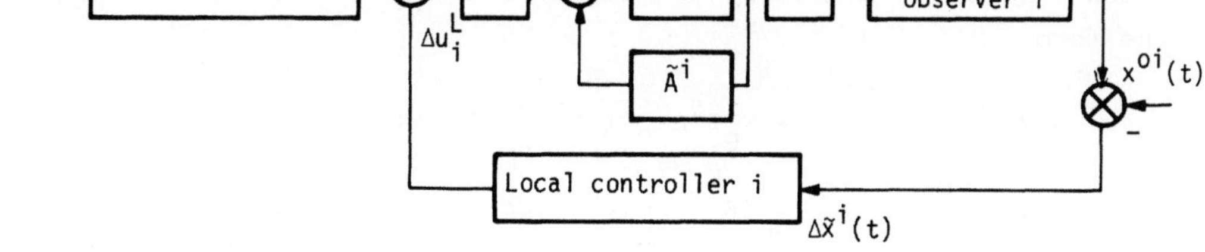

Fig. 2.18. Local controller with local observer

So far we have considered synthesis of the local controller as static or dynamic optimal linear regulators, i.e. by minimization of local standard quadratic criteria. This analytic approach to local control synthesis certainly has some drawbacks: it is relatively difficult to establish a connection between the weighting matrices in the criteria and requirements of the local control task (2.4.8). Thus, the choice of the criteria is to some degree heuristic. However, once the weighting matrices are chosen, the synthesis of local controller is straightforward (in both cases of static or dynamic controller). The problem of choice of the weighting matrices will be considered in Paragraph 2.4.4.

2.4.3. Synthesis of local controller by pole-placement method

The second method that might be applied for synthesis of either static or dynamic local controllers is by pole-placement. This is a well-known procedure for synthesis of control for linear systems. Let us consider the synthesis of dynamic output controller, i.e. let us assume that the output y^i (given by (2.4.30)) of the subsystem is measurable and that we want to introduce dynamic controller of the first order. This means that we shall consider the augmented model of the subsystem (2.4.24), (2.4.25) in which an integrator is added, but we assume that feedback by the output y^i can be implemented, only (together with integral feedback).

We shall assume again that local nominal control $\bar{u}^{oi}(t)$ satisfying (2.4.14) is introduced, and we shall consider the model of deviation from the nominal trajectory $x^{oi}(t)$ and control $\bar{u}^{oi}(t)$ but in its augmented form (2.4.24), (2.4.25).

The idea of the pole-placement method is simple. We want to apply linear feedback control by the subsystem output and by the integral feedback in the form:

$$\Delta u^i = k_p^{iT}\Delta y^i + \hat{Q}^i z^i = k_p^i C^i \Delta x^i + \hat{Q}^i \int_0^t \tilde{R}^i C^i \Delta x^i dt, \qquad (2.4.31)$$

where $\Delta y^i = y^i - y^{oi} = C^i \Delta x^i$, $k_p^i \in R^{k_i}$ is the vector of output feedback gains $k_p^{iT} C^i = \hat{D}^i$, and $\tilde{R}_i C^i = \hat{R}_i$, $\tilde{R}_i \in R^{1\times k_i}$, i.e. we assume that the dynamic part of the controller represents integral of the subsystem output. The problem is to choose feedback gains k_p^i and $\hat{Q}_i$. We observe closed-loop subsystem in the form:

$$\Delta\dot{\hat{x}}^i = (\hat{A}_I^i - \hat{b}_I^i k_I^{iT} \hat{C}^i)\Delta\hat{x}^i, \qquad (2.4.32)$$

where $k_I^i \in R^{(k_i+1)}$ is the vector of feedback gains of the dynamic controller given by: $k_I^i = (k_p^{iT}, \hat{Q}^i)^T$ and $\hat{C}^i \in R^{(k_i+1)\times(n_i+1)}$ is the output matrix of the augmented subsystem defined by:

$$\hat{C}^i = \left[\begin{array}{c|c} C^i & 0 \\ \hline 0 & 1 \end{array}\right]$$

The state vector of the augmented subsystem has been defined above.

The gains k_I^i should be chosen so as to achieve that the poles of the closed-loop subsystem (2.4.32) are placed in desired positions, i.e. we have to choose k_I^i so that the eigenvalues of the closed-loop matrix $(\hat{A}_I^i - \hat{b}_I^i k_I^{iT} \hat{C}^i)$ are in certain prescribed positions in the complex plane. Since the closed-loop matrix of the subsystem (2.4.32) is of dimensions $(n_i \times 1) \times (n_i \times 1)$, it has n_i+1 eigenvalues. However, the number of eigenvalues that can be placed in arbitrary positions depends on the matrix structure and feedback loops introduced, i.e. it depends on the measurable output of the subsystem. Since the structure of the subsystem matrices $\hat{A}_I^i$, $\hat{b}_I^i$ in (2.4.32) is known (see Appendix 2.A), if all state coordinates of the subsystem are measurable (i.e. if $y^i = x^i$, $C^i = I_{ni}$), it is clear that we can place all n_i+1 poles in desired positions. However, if the number k_i of measurable state coordinates (outputs y^i) is less than the subsystem order n_i, then we can place just k_i+1 poles of the subsystem in desired positions in the complex plane. This means, that we can choose k_I^i so that:

$$\lambda_j(\hat{A}_I^i - \hat{b}_I^i k_I^{iT} \hat{C}^i) = -\sigma_1^D, -\sigma_2^D, \dots, -\sigma_{k_i+1}^D \qquad (2.4.33)$$

where $-\sigma_j^D$, $j=1,2,\dots,k_i+1$ are the desired positions of subsystems poles. Obviously these poles might be real or complex (i.e. various combinations of pole types can be imposed). For example if $k_i=2$ one real pole and a pair of conjugate complex poles or three real poles might be set, or two real poles and the real part of the conjugate-complex pair might be prescribed etc. However, the remaining poles of the subsystem (i.e. n_i-k_i poles) cannot be specified in advance and their positions are free. The position of the poles that are not pre-specified, depends on the specified poles σ_j^D. Thus, the problem is how to specify k_i+1 poles of the subsystem so as to achieve that the remaining (nonspecified) poles of the subsystem also lie in some allowable regions in the complex plane.

Actually, the problem of the connection between the requirements in the local control task (2.4.8) and positions of the subsystem poles arises here. This problem will be discussed in the next paragraph. Let us note that one of the obvious constraints upon the placement of the subsystem poles is that they must lie to the left from the line $\lambda = -\beta_i$ where β_i is desired exponential stability degree, i.e.

$$|Re(\sigma_j)| > \beta_i, \qquad j=1,2,\dots,n_i+1 \tag{2.4.34}$$

This means that we have to place all poles of the subsystem far enough in the left part of the complex plane in order to ensure stabilization of the local subsystem (and global system, too). However, the condition (2.4.34) is not always sufficient to satisfy all requirements of local control task (2.4.8) (but this will be discussed in the next paragraph).

Due to the structure of the subsystems matrices $\hat{A}^i_I$, $\hat{b}^i$ and under the assumption that feedback with respect to position of the joint must always be introduced, we may conclude that we can stabilize the local subsystems even if $k_i=1$. However, the stability degree β_i cannot be arbitrarily high when $k_i<n_i$. Here, we shall not discuss various possibilities for pole placement depending on the order of the subsystem output k_i.

Once the output of the subsystem is determined and poles σ^D_j, $j=1,2,\dots$ $\dots,k_i+1$ are specified, the problem is to compute feedback gains k^i_I that satisfy (2.4.33), i.e. to compute k^i_I so that the poles of the subsystem are placed in desired positions. There are many various methods for computing feedback gains, if poles of the system are specified [64]. However, these methods solve this problem in the general case for arbitrary structures of the subsystems matrices of arbitrary order, and for various output matrices. In our case, as we have explained in Paragraph 2.2, the order of the subsystem is at most $n_i=3$, and the structure of the subsystems matrices is fixed (see Appendix 2.A). Thus, the computation of feedback gains if poles of the subsystem are given is very simple and there is no need to apply some general procedure for pole placement. Actually, the feedback gains k^i_I are calculated so as to satisfy the following equation

$$\det(\hat{A}^i_I-\hat{b}^i_I k^{iT}_I \hat{C}^i_i-\sigma I_{(n_i+1)}) = k_a \sum_{j=1}^{n_i+1} (-\sigma^D_j-\sigma) \tag{2.4.35}$$

where $I_{(n_i+1)}$ denotes $(n_i+1)\times(n_i+1)$ unit matrix, k_a is a proportionality coefficient, $-\sigma^D_j$ are desired poles (real or complex). Obviously, eq. (2.4.35) corresponds to the case when $k_i=n_i$, i.e. when all n_i+1 poles of the subsystem can be specified and, thus, n_i+1 gains k^i_I can be determined from (2.4.35). We can write similar equations in the cases if

$k_i < n_i$, and if a smaller number of poles are specified. Thus, the calculation of k_I^i in all these cases is trivial.

In this way we get the control scheme for the ith local subsystem as presented in Fig. 2.19, which is quite similar to the control scheme

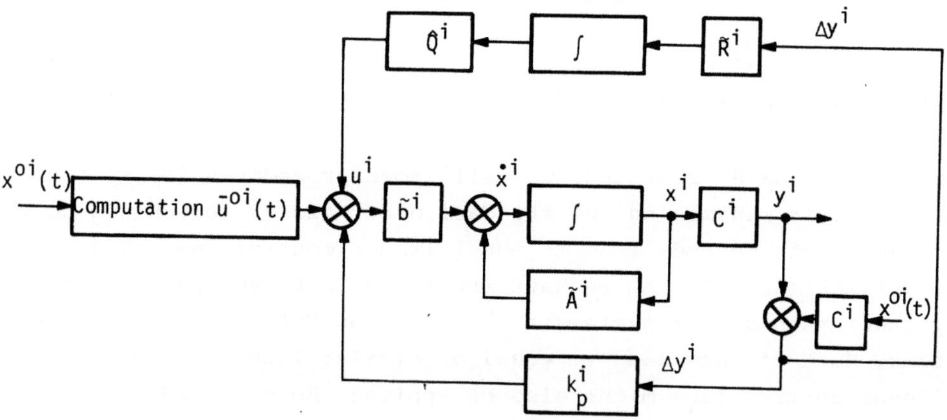

Fig. 2.19. Local dynamic controller with output feedback

in Fig. 2.17 (the optimal regulator with integral feedback loop), except that in the former scheme output feedback is implemented, instead of feedback by the complete state vector. Actually, the only difference between these two control procedures is in the way in which feedback gains are calculated, but the control laws are equal (if $k_i = n_i$).

Two remarks have to be added. First, it is obvious that, if we want to apply the static controller, we may also use pole placement method to compute the feedback gains, but in (2.4.35) we should put matrices $\tilde{A}^i$, $\tilde{b}^i$, C^i instead of $\hat{A}^i$, $\hat{b}^i$, $\hat{C}^i$ and the maximum number of poles that might be specified is just k_i, instead of k_i+1 as in the case of controller with the integral feedback loop. All considerations on pole-placement method stated above can be directly applied to the static controller.

The second remark concerns the application of observer if the order of output of the subsystem k_i is less than the order of subsystem n_i. Namely, instead of applying output feedback (2.4.31) we can apply the local observer to reconstruct the subsystem state from its output, as explained in the previous Paragraph. However, the synthesis of feedback gains can be performed by pole-placement instead of by minimizing the standard quadratic criterion. Thus, the control scheme in Fig. 2.18 can be synthesized using pole-placement method. Obviously, the output feedback in Fig. 2.19 is much simpler to implement than the local observer and complete state feedback (the number of additions and multiplications that have to be performed in each sampling period is by far smaller with the controller in Fig. 2.19 than with the controller in Fig. 2.18), but the performance of the latter is better.

2.4.4. Local control task

Up to now, we have presented two well-known procedures for synthesis of local control: minimizing the standard quadratic criterion and pole placement. Both methods lead to equal linear control laws (2.4.19), or (2.4.20), or (2.4.31). As we have mentioned in Paragraph 2.4, there are many other methods for synthesis of local controllers for linear subsystems. Most of them lead to equal or similar linear control laws, but nonlinear control laws might also be applied. Here, we shall not survey all these methods, since they are well-known and can easily be found in literature. We have briefly presented two above methods in order to demonstrate local control synthesis. However, stability analysis and synthesis of global control which will be presented in the text to follow, can be applied regardless of the method used for local control synthesis and regerdless of the form of the local control law (i.e. they can be applied even with nonlinear local control laws).

Regardless of the method used for local control synthesis, there arises the problem of connection between the imposed local control task (2.4.8) and the parameters that have to be specified in each particular method for control synthesis. Namely, the synthesis of optimal linear regulator requires weighting matrices Q_i, r_i and stability degree β_i in criterion (2.4.16) to be prescribed; pole-placement method requires poles of the subsystem σ_i^D in (2.4.33) to be specified. Similarly, other methods that can be used for local control synthesis also require some data to be specified. The problem is to establish a connection between the stability regions $X^{I(i)}$, $X^{t(i)}$ that are specified in local control task (2.4.8) and data that are required by the chosen method for local control synthesis.

In the general case it is very difficult, to establish an analytic relation between these two sets of parameters. For example, it is difficult to find a relation between the weighting matrices Q_i, r_i in the local criterion and finite stability regions $X^{I(i)}$, $X^{t(i)}$. There are some connections that are evident. For example, it is well known that if the local control is synthesized by minimizing standard quadratic criterion (2.4.16) with prescribed stability degree β_i, then the solution of the closed-loop subsystem (i.e. the subsystem with control (2.4.19)) must satisfy the following inequality:

$$||\Delta x^i(t)|| \leq \Pi_i ||\Delta x^i(0)|| \exp(-\beta_i t), \quad \forall t \in (0, \infty), \ \Pi_i > 0 \qquad (2.4.36)$$

In local control task (2.4.8) it is required that the state of the subsystem satisfies:

$$||\Delta x^i(t)|| < \bar{X}^{t(i)} \exp(-\alpha^{(i)} t), \quad \forall t \in T \qquad (2.4.37)$$

where $\bar{X}^{t(i)} > \bar{X}^{I(i)} > ||\Delta x^i(0)||$. It is obvious that the sufficient conditions to be satisfied are:

$$\beta_i > \alpha^{(i)}, \quad \bar{X}^{t(i)} > \Pi_i ||\Delta x^i(0)|| \qquad (2.4.38)$$

If (2.4.38) are satisfied, (2.4.36) implies (2.4.37). Similarly, if we want to apply pole-placement method, it is obvious that we have to place all poles of the subsystem so that the following condition is satisfied:

$$|\mathrm{Re}(\sigma_j^i)| > \alpha^{(i)}, \quad \bar{X}^{t(i)} > \Pi_i ||\Delta x^i(0)|| \qquad (2.4.39)$$

If (2.4.39) holds, condition (2.4.37) is satisfied.

However, the conditions (2.4.38), (2.4.39) are not necessary for (2.4.37) to be satisfied, since the condition (2.4.37) concerns a finite time interval T, and $\Delta x^i(t)$ is constrained by $\bar{X}^{t(i)} \exp(-\alpha^{(i)} t)$ where $\bar{X}^{t(i)}$ is larger than $||x^i(0)||$. Thus, conditions (2.4.38), or (2.4.39) might be too severe. Actually, the local control can satisfy condition (2.4.37), even if conditions (2.4.38), or (2.4.39) are not met. On the other hand, if the finite regions $X^{t(i)}$ are not specified in the form (2.4.37) the relation between them and the stability degree is not simple. Even if we use conditions (2.4.38), or (2.4.39) the specification of the weighting matrices Q_i, r_i in (2.4.16), or of the poles in (2.4.33) is not unique. Finally, if some other method is used for local control synthesis (e.g. Bode's method in frequency domain, or nonlinear bang--bang control etc.) the relation between the finite regions $X^{I(i)}$, $X^{t(i)}$ and the parameters that have to be specified in the method applied, might be difficult to establish.

It should be noted that in the case of linear subsystems we may solve the above problems in a direct way by some classical analytical approaches. However, we shall establish a general algorithm for solving the local control task which can be used as part of the procedure for control synthesis of robotic systems.

We shall present the general numerical solution of the stated problem. Actually, we shall use the method for practical stability analysis to synthesize the local controller which ensures satisfaction of local control task (2.4.8). First, we shall establish a method for analyzing whether the requirements of the local control task are met by the applied control. Then, if these requirements are not met, we shall iteratively change the control parameters until we reach the specified goal.

Now, the problem is to check whether or not the subsystem $\tilde{S}^i$ with applied control satisfies the conditions of practical stability set in (2.4.8). To analyze the practical stability of the linear subsystem $\tilde{S}^i$ (2.4.9) we shall use the method of Michel [68]. This method can be described as follows.

The subsystem $\tilde{S}^i$ is practically stable with respect to $(X^{I(i)}, X^{t(i)}, \tau)$, as defined by (2.4.8), if there exists a real valued continuously differentiable function $v_i(t, x^i)$ and a real-valued function of time $\psi_i(t)$ which is integrable over time interval T, such that

$$\dot{v}_i(t, x^i) < \psi_i(t), \quad \forall x^i \in \tilde{X}^{t(i)}(t), \ \forall t \in T \tag{2.4.40}$$

$$\int_0^t \psi_i(t')dt' < v_{im}^{\partial X^{t(i)}(t)}(t) - v_{iM}^{\partial X^{I(i)}}(0), \quad \forall t \in T \tag{2.4.41}$$

where:

$v_{im}^{\partial X^{t(i)}(t)}(t)$ denotes $\min\limits_{x^i \in \partial X^{t(i)}(t)} v_i(t, x^i)$

$v_{iM}^{\partial X^{I(i)}}(0)$ denotes $\max\limits_{x^i \in \partial X^{I(i)}} v_i(0, x^i)$

$\partial X(t)$ denotes the boundary of the corresponding region and $\tilde{X}^{t(i)}(t)$ denotes $\tilde{X}^{t(i)}(t) = X^{t(i)}(t) - \bar{X}^{I(i)}\exp(-\alpha^{(i)}t)$.

In (2.4.40) $\dot{v}_i$ denotes the time derivative of function $v_i(t, x^i)$ along the solution of the subsystem $\tilde{S}^i$ (2.4.9) with the chosen local control. The conditions (2.4.40), (2.4.41) are sufficient conditions for the practical stability of subsystem $\tilde{S}^i$ (but not necessary), i.e. if the conditions (2.4.40), (2.4.41) are satisfied then the subsystem $\tilde{S}^i$ is practically stable with respect to $(X^I, X^{t(i)}, \tau)$, but vice versa is not always satisfied (if subsystem $\tilde{S}^i$ is practically stable then conditions (2.4.40), (2.4.41) might not always be satisfied).

The proof of the above stated method for testing the practical stability is given in Appendix 2.B [69]. Here, we shall just explain the application of this method. We shall present how this method might be used for synthesizing the local controllers which ensure local practical stability (2.4.8).

The main problem with the application of the above stated method for practical stability testing lies in the choice of the function $v_i(t, x^i)$ since this choice is not unique and no general recommendations can be given. On the other hand, efficiency of the stability test largely depends on the choice of this function. The method stated gives only sufficient conditions for practical stability. Thus, the test might be conservative: if we make an improper choice of function $v_i(t, x^i)$ the result of the test (2.4.40), (2.4.41) may be negative although the subsystem is practically stable. Thus, the choice of the function $v_i(t, x^i)$ has to be done carrefully in order to ensure validity of the stability test. Otherwise, we might get very restrictive results, i.e. we might choose a local controller with feedback gains too high.

Although there are no general solutions for the choice of functions $v_i(t, x^i)$, we shall suggest one possible choice of these functions. This approach follows the recommendations given by Šiljak [59]. He has shown*) that "the best choice" of these functions (from the standpoint of the test of the overall system) is the one by which the stability degree of the subsystem $\tilde{S}^i$ is precisely estimated; this means that we have to choose function $v_i(t, x^i)$ such that the following condition is satisfied:

$$\dot{v}_i(t, x^i) \leq -\gamma_i v_i(t, x^i), \quad \forall x^i \in X^{t(i)}(t), \quad \forall t \in T \qquad (2.4.42)$$

---

*) Here, we shall not prove this statement, since its proof is not essential for our application. Those who wish to deeply understand this problem are recommended to read [59].

where γ_i denotes $\min|\mathrm{Re}(\sigma_j^i)|$, σ_j^i, $j=1,2,\ldots,n_i$ are the poles of the closed-loop subsystem $\tilde{S}^i$ (i.e. of the subsystem $\tilde{S}^i$ when the local controller is applied). $\dot{v}_i$ again stands for the derivative of function v_i along the solution of the closed-loop subsystem $\tilde{S}^i$. The inequlity (2.4.42) means that by the function $v_i(t, x^i)$ we get the right estimate of the subsystem stability degree γ_i (i.e. the slowest mode of the subsystem $\tilde{S}^i$ must be faster than $||x^i(0)||\exp(-\gamma_i t)$). According to Šiljak [59], if we find such a function $v_i(t, x^i)$, that its derivative along the solution of closed-loop subsystem $\tilde{S}^i$, satisfies the inequality (2.4.42), then this function v_i is the best choice for the stability test (i.e. this choice has the best chance to prove the stability of global system). Thus, we have to find out the function $v_i(t, x^i)$ which, for the given closed-loop subsystem, satisfies the inequality (2.4.42). Obviously, this choice, in the general case, is not trivial. However, in the case of linear subsystems (2.4.9) $\tilde{S}^i$ with the linear local controller, this problem can easily be solved in the following way. Let us choose the function $v_i(t, x^i)$ in the form:

$$v_i(t, x^i) = (\Delta x^{iT} H_i \Delta x^i)^{1/2} \qquad (2.4.43)$$

where $H_i \in R^{n_i \times n_i}$ is a positive definite matrix. The derivative of the function v_i (2.4.43) can be written as:

$$\begin{aligned}\dot{v}_i(t, x^i) &= \frac{\partial v_i}{\partial t} + (\mathrm{grad} v_i)^T \Delta\dot{x}^i = \\ &= \frac{1}{2}\frac{1}{v_i}(\Delta x^{iT} H_i \Delta\dot{x}^i + \Delta\dot{x}^{iT} H_i \Delta x^i)\end{aligned} \qquad (2.4.44)$$

First, we consider the case when the static controller is applied. Let us assume that the local control is given by (2.4.19), i.e. by local nominal control $\bar{u}^{oi}(t)$ and standard quadratic regulator $\Delta u_i^L(t)$. Then, the closed-loop subsystem is given by:

$$\dot{x}^i = \tilde{A}^i x^i + \tilde{b}^i(\bar{u}^{oi}(t) - r_i^{-1}\tilde{b}^{iT} K_i \Delta x^i)$$

Since nominal local control $\bar{u}^{oi}(t)$ satisfies (2.4.14), it can be written:

$$\Delta\dot{x}^i = (\tilde{A}^i - \tilde{b}^i r_i^{-1}\tilde{b}^{iT} K_i)\Delta x^i \qquad (2.4.45)$$

Substituting (2.4.45) in (2.4.44) we get:

$$\dot{v}_i(t, x^i) = \frac{1}{2v_i}\{\Delta x^{iT}[H_i(\tilde{A}^i - \tilde{b}^i r_i^{-1}\tilde{b}^i K_i) + (\tilde{A}^i - \tilde{b}^i r_i^{-1}\tilde{b}^i K_i)^T H_i]\Delta x^i\} \qquad (2.4.46)$$

Since we want to find function $v_i(t, x^i)$ which satisfies inequality (2.4.42), we have to find out the matrix H_i which satisfies the matrix equation [59]:

$$H_i^T(\tilde{A}^i-\tilde{b}^i r_i^{-1}\tilde{b}^{iT}K_i)+(\tilde{A}^i-\tilde{b}^i r_i^{-1}\tilde{b}^{iT}K_i)^T H_i = 2\mathrm{diag}(\sigma_1^i,\sigma_2^i,\dots,\sigma_{ni}^i)H_i$$

$$\leq -2\min_j|\sigma_j^i|H_i \tag{2.4.47}$$

where σ_j^i $(j=1,2,\dots,n_i)$ are the eigenvalues of the closed-loop matrix of the subsystem $(\tilde{A}^i-\tilde{b}^i r_i^{-1}\tilde{b}^{iT}K_i)$. Thus, we have to solve the equation (2.4.47) by the matrix H_i. Since the order of the subsystem n_i is low, it is not too difficult to determine the matrix H_i which satisfies (2.4.47). Obviously, we must first determine the eigenvalues of the closed-loop matrix σ_j^i; neither this is too complex a problem due to the low order of the subsystem.

If we have found the matrix H_i which satisfies (2.4.47), equation (2.4.46) becomes:

$$\dot{v}_i(t, x^i) = \frac{1}{2v_i}(\Delta x^{iT}2\ \mathrm{diag}(\sigma_1^i,\ \sigma_2^i,\dots,\sigma_{ni}^i)\cdot H_i\Delta x^i) \leq$$

$$\leq -\frac{1}{v_i}\min|\sigma_j^i|\ v_i^2 = -\min|\sigma_j^i|v_i$$

assuming that $\sigma_j^i<0$ for $j=1,2,\dots,n_i$.

Evidently, from the last equation it follows:

$$\dot{v}_i(t, x^i) \leq -\gamma_i v_i$$

where γ_i is $\min_j|\sigma_j^i|$ $(j=1,2,\dots,n_i)$. Thus, if we find the matrix H_i which satisfies (2.4.47), then the function $v_i(t, x^i)$ (2.4.43) satisfies the inequality (2.4.42), i.e. it gives "the exact estimate" of the subsystem stability degree. Thus, we have shown how we can determine the function $v_i(t, x^i)$ which has "the best chance" to prove the practical stability of subsystem.

Having chosen the function $v_i(t, x^i)$, let us consider how the conditions (2.4.40) and (2.4.41) can be applied with this particular form of function v_i (2.4.43). From the last inequality, it follows:

$$\dot{v}_i(t, x^i) \leq -\gamma_i\lambda_m^{1/2}(H_i)||\Delta x^i|| \tag{2.4.48}$$

where we have used the well-known inequality:

$$\lambda_m^{1/2}(H_i)||\Delta x^i|| < (\Delta x^{iT}H_i\Delta x^i)^{1/2} = v_i$$

Since the condition (2.4.40) should be satisfied for the region $\tilde{X}^{t(i)}$ defined by $\{x^i: x^i \in X^{t(i)}(t).\text{AND}.||\Delta x^i|| > \bar{X}^{I(i)}\exp(-\alpha^{(i)}t), \forall t \in T\}$, we can write (2.4.48) in the form:

$$\dot{v}_i(t, x^i) < -\gamma_i\lambda_m^{1/2}(H_i)\bar{X}^{I(i)}\exp(-\alpha^{(i)}t) = \psi_i(t) \qquad (2.4.49)$$

i.e. we can determine the function $\psi_i(t)$ as given by (2.4.49). From the elementary theory of matrices it is well-known that:

$$v_{im}^{\partial X^{t(i)}(t)}(t) > \lambda_m^{1/2}(H_i)\bar{X}^{t(i)}\exp(-\alpha^{(i)}t)$$

$$v_{im}^{\partial X^{I(i)}} < \lambda_M^{1/2}(H_i)\bar{X}^{I(i)},$$

By substituting these inequalities in (2.4.41) and taking into account the form of function $\psi_i(t)$ given by (2.4.49), the condition (2.4.41) can be written in the form:

$$\int_0^t \psi_i(t')dt' = -\int_0^t \gamma_i\lambda_m^{1/2}(H_i)\bar{X}^{I(i)}\exp(-\alpha^{(i)}t')dt' =$$

$$= -\gamma_i\lambda_m^{1/2}(H_i)\bar{X}^{I(i)}(1-\exp(-\alpha^{(i)}t))/\alpha^{(i)} < \qquad (2.4.50)$$

$$< \lambda_m^{1/2}(H_i)\bar{X}^{t(i)}\exp(-\alpha^{(i)}t) - \lambda_M^{1/2}(H_i)\bar{X}^{I(i)}, \quad \forall t \in T$$

Thus, to test the practical stability of the closed-loop subsystem $\tilde{S}^i$, we have to check whether or not the condition (2.4.50) is satisfied. In (2.4.50) numbers $\bar{X}^{t(i)}$, $\bar{X}^{I(i)}$ and $\alpha^{(i)}$ are given by the requirements of the local control task (2.4.8), and numbers $\lambda_m(H_i)$, $\lambda_M(H_i)$ and γ_i are determined by the synthesized control. After synthesizing the local control, we have to determine the matrix H_i which satisfies (2.4.47). Then we can determine γ_i which is $\min|\text{Re}(\sigma_j^i)|$, $j=1,2,\ldots,n_i$, and $\lambda_m(H_i)$, $\lambda_M(H_i)$. Then, it is easy to check whether the test (2.4.50) is positive or not, and get the answer as to whether the subsystem is practically stable. Once again we have to underline that, if the test (2.4.50) is not successfull, we cannot conclude whether the subsystem is stable or not; the subsystem may be stable even when the test (2.4.50) is not positive.

In this way, we have made a basis for establishing an algorithm for the synthesis of local control which satisfies local control task (2.4.8). However, before we establish this algorithm, we have to make several remarks and extensions of the tests presented above.

(I) The first remark concerns the solution of the matrix equation (2.4.47). In the special case when the standard quadratic regulator (2.4.19) is applied, we can avoid the problem of solving the equation (2.4.47). Then, we can choose the function v_i as:

$$v_i(t, x^i) = (\Delta x^{iT} K_i \Delta x^i)^{1/2} \tag{2.4.51}$$

where K_i is the solution of the corresponding Riccati equation (2.4.18). Namely, we choose matrix H_i in (2.4.43) as $H_i = K_i$. Since the matrix K_i satisfies equation (2.4.18) it can be written:

$$K_i(\tilde{A}^i - \tilde{b}^i r_i^{-1} \tilde{b}^{iT} K_i) + (\tilde{A}^i - \tilde{b}^i r_i^{-1} \tilde{b}^{iT} K_i)^T K_i =$$

$$= -Q_i - 2\beta_i K_i' - K_i \tilde{b}^i r_i^{-1} \tilde{b}^{iT} K_i = -W_i - 2\beta_i K_i \tag{2.4.52}$$

Then, the derivative of the function v_i (2.4.51) can be written as:

$$\dot{v}_i(t, x^i) = -\Delta x^{iT}(W_i + 2\beta_i K_i)\Delta x^i / 2v_i < -(\frac{1}{2}\frac{\lambda_m(W_i)}{\lambda_M(K_i)} + \beta) v_i$$

$$\dot{v}_i(t, x^i) < -(\frac{1}{2}\frac{\lambda_m(W_i)}{\lambda_M^{1/2}(K_i)} + \beta_i \lambda_m^{1/2}(K_i)) ||\Delta x^i|| \tag{2.4.53}$$

Thus, we get the estimate of the subsystem stability degree as $\gamma_i = (\lambda_m(W_i)/2\lambda_M(K_i) + \beta_i)$, i.e. this form of function $v_i(t, x^i)$ satisfies inequality (2.4.42). Namely, equation (2.4.52) corresponds to equation (2.4.47). Instead of solving equation (2.4.47) to find matrix H_i, we may take the matrix K_i for which we know that it satisfies (2.4.52), and that the function v_i (2.4.51) gives an estimate of the subsystem exponential stability degree. However, it should be noted that this is not "the best estimate" of the subsystem stability degree since in the general case $\lambda_m(W_i)/2\lambda_M(K_i) + \beta_i < |Re(\sigma_j^i)|$ for $j=1,2,\dots,n_i$. Namely the optimal linear regulator places the subsystem poles to the left from the line $Re(\sigma) = -2\beta_i$. Thus, the estimate of stability degree (2.4.53) might be poor. This is the reason why we suggest to choose function $v_i(t, x^i)$ in the form (2.4.43) where matrix H_i satisfies (2.4.47) even in the case when the local optimal regulator is applied. However, we have to solve equation (2.4.47).

Let us state that, if we choose function $v_i(t, x^i)$ as (2.4.51), then, according to (2.4.53), we get function $\psi_i(t)$ in the form:

$$\psi_i(t) = -\left(\frac{1}{2}\frac{\lambda_m(W_i)}{\lambda_M^{1/2}(K_i)} + \beta_i\lambda_m^{1/2}(K_i)\right)\bar{X}^{I(i)}\exp(-\alpha^{(i)}t)$$

In this case, the condition (2.4.41) can be rewritten as:

$$-\left(\frac{\lambda_m(W_i)}{2\lambda_M^{1/2}(K_i)} + \beta_i\lambda_m^{1/2}(K_i)\right)\bar{X}^{I(i)}\frac{1}{\alpha^{(i)}}\left[1-\exp(-\alpha^{(i)}t)\right] < \tag{2.4.54}$$

$$< \lambda_m^{1/2}(K_i)\bar{X}^{t(i)}\exp(-\alpha^{(i)}t) - \lambda_M^{1/2}(K_i)\bar{X}^{I(i)}, \quad \forall t \in T$$

(II) The second remark concerns some additional condition which obviously follows from (2.4.50) (or from (2.4.54)). Namely, for t=0 it is clear that the following relation must be satisfied:

$$\lambda_m^{1/2}(H_i)/\lambda_M^{1/2}(H_i) > \bar{X}^{I(i)}/\bar{X}^{t(i)} \tag{2.4.55}$$

(III) Now, we have to extend the above stability test to include *dynamic* controllers. Up to now we have considered stability of the local subsystem if only *static* controllers are applied. To extend the test, we must note that dynamic controllers increase the order of the closed--loop subsystem. Let us consider the local dynamic controller in the form (2.4.31), i.e. let us assume that the local control is given by:

$$u^i(t) = \bar{u}^{oi}(t) + \Delta u_i^L(t) = \bar{u}^{oi}(t) - k_I^{iT}\hat{C}^i\Delta\hat{x}^i \tag{2.4.56}$$

where $\Delta\hat{x}^i$ is the augmented state vector of the subsystem $\tilde{S}^i$ as explained in connection to (2.4.24), k_I^i is the vector of feedback gains of the dynamic controller, $\hat{C}^i$ is the output matrix of the augmented subsystem (k_I^i, $\hat{C}^i$ are explained in connection with (2.4.32)). We shall again restrict our attention to considering the first order dynamic controller, i.e. the controller which includes just the integral feedback loop in addition to state (or output) feedback loops. In Paragraphs 2.4.2 and 2.4.3 we have also considered this local controller with the integral feedback loop (either a dynamic optimal regulator, or an output dynamic controller synthesized by pole-placement method). This controller increases the order of the subsystem by one only. The closed loop subsystem (i.e. the subsystem with controller (2.4.56)) is given by (2.4.32). Obviously, if we consider the optimal controller with full-

-state feedback, the matrix $\hat{C}^i$ is equal to a unit matrix ($\hat{C}^i = I_{(n_i+1)}$). We have to consider stability of the closed-loop subsystem (2.4.32).

Now, instead of function $v_i(t, x^i)$, which is a function of time and state vector x^i, we have to consider function $v_i(t, \hat{x}^i)$ which is a function of time and state vector of the augmented subsystem $\hat{x}^i$. Let us consider this function in form:

$$v_i(t, \hat{x}^i) = (\Delta\hat{x}^{iT}\hat{H}_i\Delta\hat{x}^i)^{1/2} \tag{2.4.57}$$

where $\hat{H}_i \in R^{(n_i+1)\times(n_i+1)}$ is a positive definite matrix. Using this function we can test the practical stability of the subsystem with the dynamic controller analogously as we have done with the static controller. Let us assume that the matrix $\hat{H}_i$ satisfies the following equation (which is analogous to (2.4.47)):

$$\hat{H}_i^T(\hat{A}_I^i - \hat{b}_I^i k_I^{iT}\hat{C}^i) + (\hat{A}_I^i - \hat{b}_I^i k_I^{iT}\hat{C}^i)^T\hat{H}_i = 2\,\mathrm{diag}(\sigma_1^i, \sigma_2^i, \ldots, \sigma_{n_i+1}^i)\cdot\hat{H}_i \tag{2.4.58}$$

where σ_j^i $(j=1,2,\ldots,n_i+1)$ are the eigenvalues of the closed-loop matrix of the augmented subsystem $(\hat{A}_I^i - \hat{b}_I^i k_I^{iT}\hat{C}^i)$. Then the derivative of the function v_i (2.4.57) along the solution of subsystem (2.4.32) is given by:

$$\dot{v}_i(t, \hat{x}^i) = (\mathrm{grad}\,v_i)^T\Delta\dot{\hat{x}}^i = \frac{1}{2v_i}\Delta\hat{x}^{iT}[\hat{H}_i^T(\hat{A}_I^i - \hat{b}_I^i k_I^{iT}\hat{C}) +$$

$$+(\hat{A}_I^i - \hat{b}_I^i k_I^{iT}\hat{C}^i)^T\hat{H}_i]\Delta\hat{x}^i = \frac{1}{2v_i}\Delta\hat{x}^{iT}2\mathrm{diag}(\sigma_1^i, \sigma_2^i, \ldots, \sigma_{n_i+1}^i)\hat{H}_i\Delta\hat{x}_i$$

$$\dot{v}_i(t, \hat{x}^i) \leq -\gamma_i v_i \tag{2.4.59}$$

where $\gamma_i = \min_j |\sigma_j^i|$, $(j=1,2,\ldots,n_i+1)$.

Now, we have to solve the problem of stability regions for the augmented subsystem (subsystem with the dynamic controller). Namely, the augmented subsystem has one state coordinate more than the original subsystem. As explained in the previous text this state coordinate is defined by:

$$\Delta x_{n_i+1}^i = \int_0^t \tilde{R}^i C^i \Delta x^i dt$$

We shall assume that the initial value of this state coordinate is always equal to zero, i.e. $\Delta x_{n_i+1}^i(0) = 0$, which is a realistic assumption since this is an additional coordinate determined by the control system. Thus, we can write that the region of the initial conditions for the augmented subsystem $\hat{X}^{I(i)}$ is defined by:

$$\hat{X}^{I(i)} = \{\hat{x}^i(0): \ ||\Delta x^i(0)|| < \bar{X}^{I(i)}; \quad \Delta x^i_{n_i+1}(0) = 0.\} \tag{2.4.60}$$

We can estimate the additional state coordinate in the region $X^{t(i)}$ in the following way:

$$|\Delta x^i_{n_i+1}| < (\tilde{R}^i C^i)_M \int_0^t ||\Delta x^i||dt < (\tilde{R}^i C^i)_M \int_0^t \bar{X}^{t(i)} \exp(-\alpha^{(i)}t)dt$$

$$|\Delta x^i_{n_i+1}| < (\tilde{R}^i C^i)_M \bar{X}^{t(i)}(1-\exp(-\alpha^{(i)}t))/\alpha^{(i)} \tag{2.4.61}$$

where $(\tilde{R}^i C^i)_M$ denotes $\max(\tilde{R}^i C^i)_k$, $(k=1,2,\ldots,n_i)$, $(\tilde{R}^i C^i)_k$ is the kth member of the vector $\tilde{R}^i C^i \epsilon R^{1\times n_i}$. Now, the region of allowed states $\hat{X}^{t(i)}$ for the extended subsystem can be estimated as:

$$\hat{X}^{t(i)} = \{\hat{x}^i(t): \ ||\Delta x^i(t)|| < \bar{X}^{t(i)} \exp(-\alpha^{(i)}t), \ |\Delta x^i_{n_i+1}| <$$

$$< (\tilde{R}^i C^i)_M \bar{X}^{t(i)}(1-\exp(-\alpha^{(i)}t))/\alpha^{(i)}\}, \quad \forall t \epsilon T \tag{2.4.62}$$

or, we may estimate it by:

$$\hat{X}^{t(i)}(t) = \{\hat{x}^i(t): \ ||\Delta \hat{x}^i(t)|| < \hat{\bar{X}}^{t(i)} \exp(-\alpha^{(i)}t) +$$

$$+ (\tilde{R}^i C^i)_M \bar{X}^{t(i)}/\alpha^{(i)}\}, \quad \forall t \epsilon T \tag{2.4.63}$$

where $\hat{\bar{X}}^{t(i)}$ is given by

$$\hat{\bar{X}}^{(i)} = \bar{X}^{t(i)} - (\tilde{R}^i C^i)_M \bar{X}^{t(i)}/\alpha^{(i)}$$

Obviously, estimation (2.4.62) is better than (2.4.63) but the latter is more compact and simpler for stability testing.

Starting from (2.4.59) and (2.4.63) we can determine function $\psi_i(t)$, analogously to (2.4.49), which satisfies:

$$\dot{v}_i(t, \hat{x}^i) < -\gamma_i v_i < -\gamma_i \lambda_m^{1/2}(\hat{H}_i)[\hat{\bar{X}}^{I(i)} \exp(-\alpha^{(i)}t) +$$

$$+ (\tilde{R}^i C^i)_M \bar{X}^{I(i)}/\alpha^{(i)}] = \psi_i(t) \tag{2.4.64}$$

where $\hat{\bar{X}}^{I(i)} = \bar{X}^{I(i)} - (\tilde{R}^i C^i)_M \bar{X}^{I(i)}/\alpha^{(i)}$.

The test of practical stability (2.4.41) for the augmented subsystem gets the following form:

$$
\begin{aligned}
&-\frac{\gamma_i}{\alpha^{(i)}}\,\lambda_m^{1/2}(\hat{H}_i)[\hat{\bar{X}}^{I(i)}(1-\exp(-\alpha^{(i)}t))+(\tilde{R}^iC^i)_M\bar{X}^{I(i)}t] < \qquad (2.4.65)\\
&< \lambda_m^{1/2}(\hat{H}^i)[\hat{\bar{X}}^{t(i)}\exp(-\alpha^{(i)}t)+(\tilde{R}^iC^i)_M\bar{X}^{t(i)}/\alpha^{(i)}]-\lambda_M^{1/2}(\hat{H}^i)\bar{X}^{I(i)}
\end{aligned}
$$

Thus, we obtain a test which is analogous to (2.4.50) for the static controller. Using test (2.4.65) we can check the practical stability of local subsystem $\tilde{S}^i$ with the dynamic controller. If the dynamic controller is synthesized by minimization of standard quadratic criterion (Paragraph 2.4.2), the test of practical stability can be written in the form analogous to (2.4.54), using the above explained estimations of the stability region.

(IV) The last remark concerns the amplitude constraints upon the inputs of actuators. The adopted models of subsystems (2.2.2) include the amplitude constraint upon the actuator input of saturation type (2.2.3). However, as we have explained in Paragraph 2.4.1, during the synthesis of local controller we have neglected these input constraints, and have considered the models of subsystems in the form (2.4.9). Thus up to now we have analyzed the practical stability of the local subsystems with unconstrained inputs. Now, we shall take into account the input constraint of amplitude saturation type. This problem has been partially considered in our previous book [2], but we shall here, for the first time present how this problem can be solved concerning the practical stability of the system.

Let us consider the case when the dynamic controller is applied and control is defined by (2.4.56). It is simple to apply the following procedure to the static controller. The amplitude constraint upon the subsystem input (2.2.3) defines an infinite region $X_i(t) \subset R^N$ in the following way:

$$X_i = \{\hat{x}^i: |\bar{u}^{oi}(t) - k_i^{iT}\hat{C}^i\Delta\hat{x}^i| < u_m^i\}, \forall t \in T \qquad (2.4.66)$$

If the state of the subsystems $\hat{x}^i$ belongs to the region X_i, i.e. if $\hat{x}^i \in X_i$, then the input amplitude constraint is not reached and the subsystem behaves as presented above. However, if $\hat{x}^i \notin X_i$, the input amplitude constraint is violated by the desired control and the above analysis of the subsystem stability is not valid. Namely, if the regions $\hat{X}^{I(i)}$ and $\hat{X}^{t(i)}(t)$, $\forall t \in T$ of the practical stability are within the region X_i, i.e. if:

$$\hat{X}^{I(i)} \subset X_i .\text{AND}. \hat{X}^{t(i)}(t) \subset X_i, \qquad \forall t \in T \tag{2.4.67}$$

then the above analysis is valid, and if, the test is positive, we can guarantee the practical stability of the subsystems for the given regions $\hat{X}^{I(i)}$ and $\hat{X}^{t(i)}(t)$, $\forall t \in T$.

However, if the conditions (2.4.67) are not satisfied we have to consider the stability of the subsystem when the input amplitude is saturated, and the desired control cannot be realized for the states which are outside the region X_i. Namely, the poles of the closed-loop subsystem $\sigma_1^i, \sigma_2^i, \ldots, \sigma_{n_i+1}^i$ are the eigenvalues of the matrix $(\hat{A}_I^i - \hat{b}_I^i k_I^{iT} \hat{C}^i)$, only for the states that belong to region X_i. For the states which are not within the region X_i the poles of the closed-loop subsystem move from their positions. However, the subsystem is still exponentially stable but with a stability degree which is less than γ_i $(\min|\mathrm{Re}(\sigma_j^i)|$, $j=1,2,\ldots,n_{i+1})$. In order to determine the stability degree of the subsystem for states which are not in the region X_i, let us apply the procedure explained in [2]. Let us introduce the number λ_i defined as:

$$\lambda_i = \begin{cases} 1 & \text{for} \quad \forall \hat{x}^i \in X_i \\ (u_m^i \pm \bar{u}^{oi}(t)) / |k_I^{iT} \hat{C}^i \Delta \hat{x}^i| & \text{for} \quad \hat{x}^i \notin X_i, \ \forall t \in T \end{cases} \tag{2.4.68}$$

where we take plus or minus depending on the sign of $k_I^{iT} \hat{C}^i \Delta \hat{x}^i$. It is evident that this consideration is valid only if $|\bar{u}^{oi}(t)| < \bar{u}_m^i$, $\forall t \in T$, otherwise the region X_i is empty and we cannot ensure the stability of the subsystem. This means that the nominal trajectory is such that we cannot determine even local nominal control $\bar{u}^{oi}(t)$ which drives a decoupled joint along trajectory, the actuator is too weak for the desired trajectory, or, the trajectory is too fast for chosen actuator (see Chapter 4).

Now, if we introduce λ_i as defined by (2.4.68), we can write the closed-loop subsystem (2.4.32) in the form:

$$\Delta \dot{\hat{x}}^i = (\hat{A}^i - \lambda \hat{b}_I^i k_I^{iT} \hat{C}^i) \Delta \hat{x}^i \tag{2.4.69}$$

This form of the subsystem model includes both cases: if the state $\hat{x}^i$ is within X_i and if it is not (as can be seen from definition of λ_i

(2.4.68)). The poles of the closed-loop subsystem (2.4.69) are given by the eigenvalues of the matrix $(\hat{A}^i-\lambda_i\hat{b}^i_I k^{iT}_I\hat{C}^i)$. Since the number λ_i depends on the state $\hat{x}^i$, it is obvious that the poles of the subsystem depend on the state $\hat{x}^i$ which we observe. In order to determine the exponential stability degree of the subsystem (if the conditions (2.4.67) are not satisfied), we have to determine the number λ_{ig} for which the following relation holds:

$$\lambda_{ig} < |u^i_m \pm \bar{u}^{oi}|/|k^{iT}_I\hat{C}^i\Delta\hat{x}^i|, \quad \text{for} \quad \forall\hat{x}^i\in\hat{X}^{I(i)}, \qquad \forall\hat{x}^i\in\hat{X}^{t(i)}(t) \tag{2.4.70}$$

When we have determined the number λ_{ig} satisfying the relation (2.4.70), we can compute the eigenvalues of the closed-loop subsystem for the regions $\hat{X}^{I(i)}$ and $\hat{X}^{t(i)}(t)$, $\forall t\in T$, i.e. we can compute:

$$\sigma^{iG}_1,\ \sigma^{iG}_2,\dots,\sigma^{iG}_{n_i+1} = \lambda(\hat{A}^i-\lambda_{ig}\hat{b}^i_I k^{iT}_I\hat{C}^i) \tag{2.4.71}$$

Then, we can determine the exponential stability degree γ_{ig} of the sybsystem in the regions $\hat{X}^{I(i)}$, $\hat{X}^{t(i)}(t)$, $\forall t\in T$, as:

$$\gamma_{ig} = \min|\mathrm{Re}(\sigma^{iG}_j)|, \qquad j=1,2,\dots,n_i+1 \tag{2.4.72}$$

Obviously γ_{ig} is less than γ_i (which is valid for linear control mode, i.e. in region X_i) since $\lambda_{ig}<1$.

Now, it is very simple to show that the stability test can be written in the form analogous to (2.4.65) where γ_{ig} is substituted for γ_i. If we choose function $v_i(t,\ \hat{x}^i)$ in the form (2.4.57) we can easily show that the following relation holds:

$$\dot{v}_i(t,\ \hat{x}^i) < -\gamma_{ig}v_i$$

if the matrix $\hat{H}^i$ is chosen to satisfy:

$$\hat{H}^T_i(\hat{A}^i_I-\lambda_{ig}\hat{b}^i_I k^{iT}_I\hat{C}^i)+(\hat{A}^i_I-\lambda_{ig}\hat{b}^i_I k^{iT}_I\hat{C}^i)^T\hat{H}_i = 2\mathrm{diag}(\sigma^{iG}_1,\sigma^{iG}_2,\dots,\sigma^{iG}_{n_i+1})\hat{H}_i \tag{2.4.73}$$

Then, analogously to (2.4.65) we get the following test for the practical stability of local subsystem which takes into account nonlinear constraint upon the input:

$$-\frac{\gamma_{ig}}{\alpha^{(i)}}\lambda^{1/2}_m(\hat{H}_i)[\hat{\bar{X}}^{I(i)}(1-\exp(-\alpha^{(i)}t))+(\tilde{R}^i C^i)_M\bar{X}^{I(i)}t] <$$

$$< \lambda_m^{1/2}(\hat{H}^i)[\hat{\bar{X}}^{t(i)}\exp(-\alpha^{(i)}t)+(\tilde{R}^iC^i)_M\bar{X}^{t(i)}/\alpha^{(i)}]-\lambda_M^{1/2}(\hat{H}_i)\bar{X}^{I(i)} \qquad (2.4.74)$$

Thus, in order to test the stability of the local subsystem if the condition (2.4.67) is not satisfied, we have to determine λ_{ig} in (2.4.70) and then γ_{ig} by (2.4.72) and to check test (2.4.74). The only problem is to determine λ_{ig} which satisfies (2.4.70) since we have to examine the whole regions $\hat{X}^{I(i)}$ and $\hat{X}^{t(i)}(t)$, $\forall t\in T$. However, due to definitions of these regions and to the fact that $\lambda_1<\lambda_2$ if $||\Delta\hat{x}^i||_1 > >||\Delta x^i||_2$ (where λ_1 corresponds to $||\Delta x^i||_1$ and λ_2 to $||\Delta\hat{x}^i||_2$) instead of by (2.4.70) we can determine λ_{ig} by:

$$\lambda_{ig} < |u_m^i \pm \bar{u}^{io}|/|k_I^{iT}\hat{C}^i\Delta\hat{x}^i|, \quad \forall\hat{x}^i\in\partial\hat{X}^{I(i)}, \quad \forall\hat{x}^i\in\partial\hat{X}^{t(i)}(t), \ \forall t\in T \qquad (2.4.75)$$

This means that to determine the number λ_{ig} we have to examine the states along the boundaries of the regions $\partial\hat{X}^{I(i)}$ and $\partial\hat{X}^{t(i)}(t)$, $\forall t\in T$. Obviously, this is by far easier to perform than to examine complete regions $\hat{X}^{I(i)}$ and $\hat{X}^{t(i)}(t)$, $\forall t\in T$.

Now, we can establish the algorithm for iterative synthesis of the local controllers which ensure satisfaction of local control task (2.4.8), for local (decoupled) subsystems. The global flow-chart of the algorithm is presented in Fig. 2.20. By this procedure we can choose local controllers (i.e. compute feedback gains) which ensure the practical stability of the local subsystem in the sense of local control task definition (2.4.8).

The algorithm can be performed according to the following steps: (for the *i*th subsystem)

(1) The local control task (2.4.8) is set, i.e. the regions $X^{I(i)}$ and $X^{t(i)}(t)$, $\forall t\in T$ are set, by defining the numbers $\bar{X}^{I(i)}$, $\bar{X}^{t(i)}$, $\alpha^{(i)}$ and τ. We assume that the nominal trajectory $x^{oi}(t)$, $\forall t\in T$ has already been set, i.e. that the trajectories of all state coordinates for the *i*th subsystem are defined.

(2) Local nominal control $\bar{u}^{oi}(t)$, $\forall t\in T$ is synthesized in order to satisfy (2.4.14); namely, we have to compute $\bar{u}^{oi}(t)$, $\forall t\in T$ so that it drives the decoupled local subsystem $\tilde{S}^i$ along nominal trajectory $x^{oi}(t)$, $\forall t\in T$ if no perturbation is acting upon the subsystem and if its model is perfect; we have to check whether or not the con-

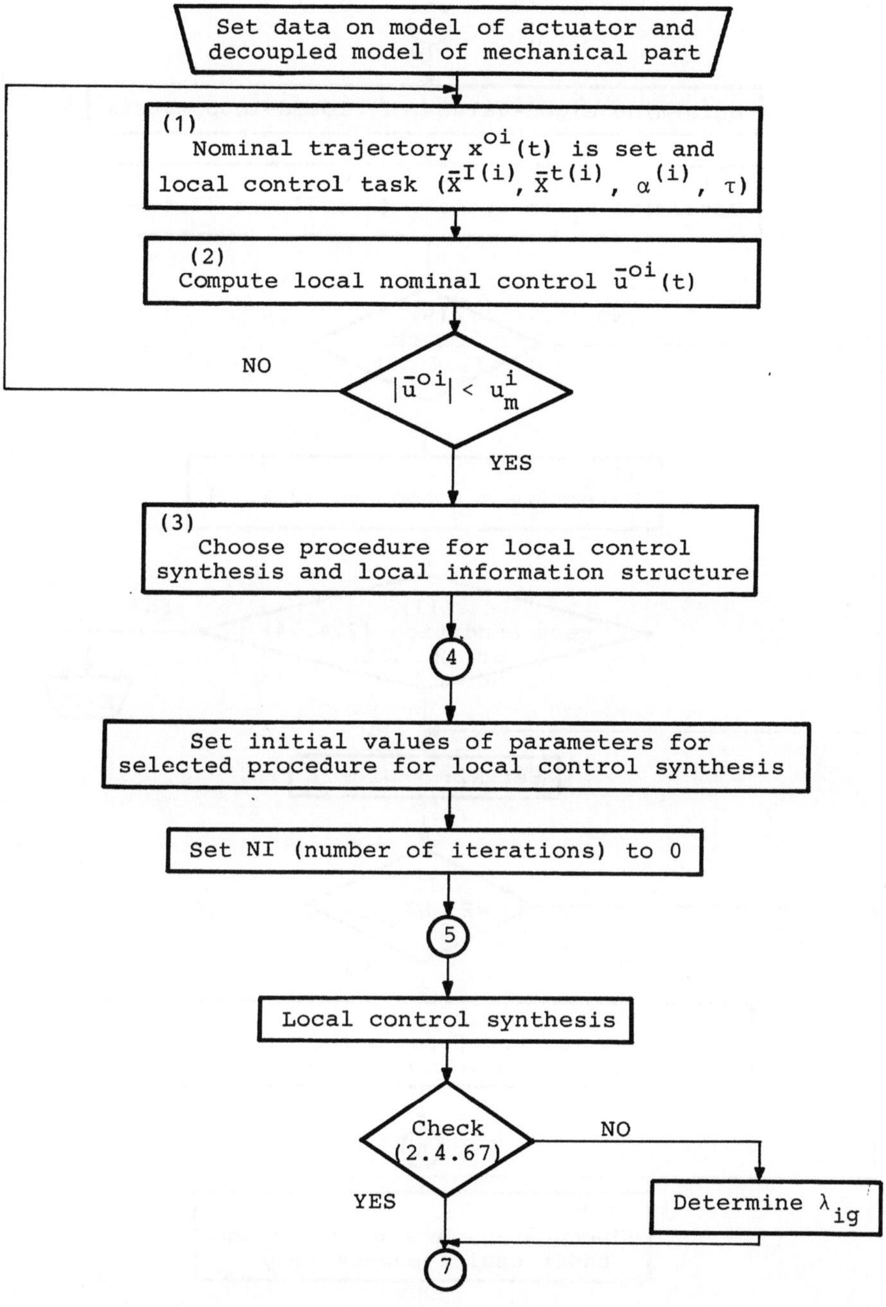

Fig. 2.20. Flow-chart of the algorithm for synthesis of local controller for the ith local subsystem

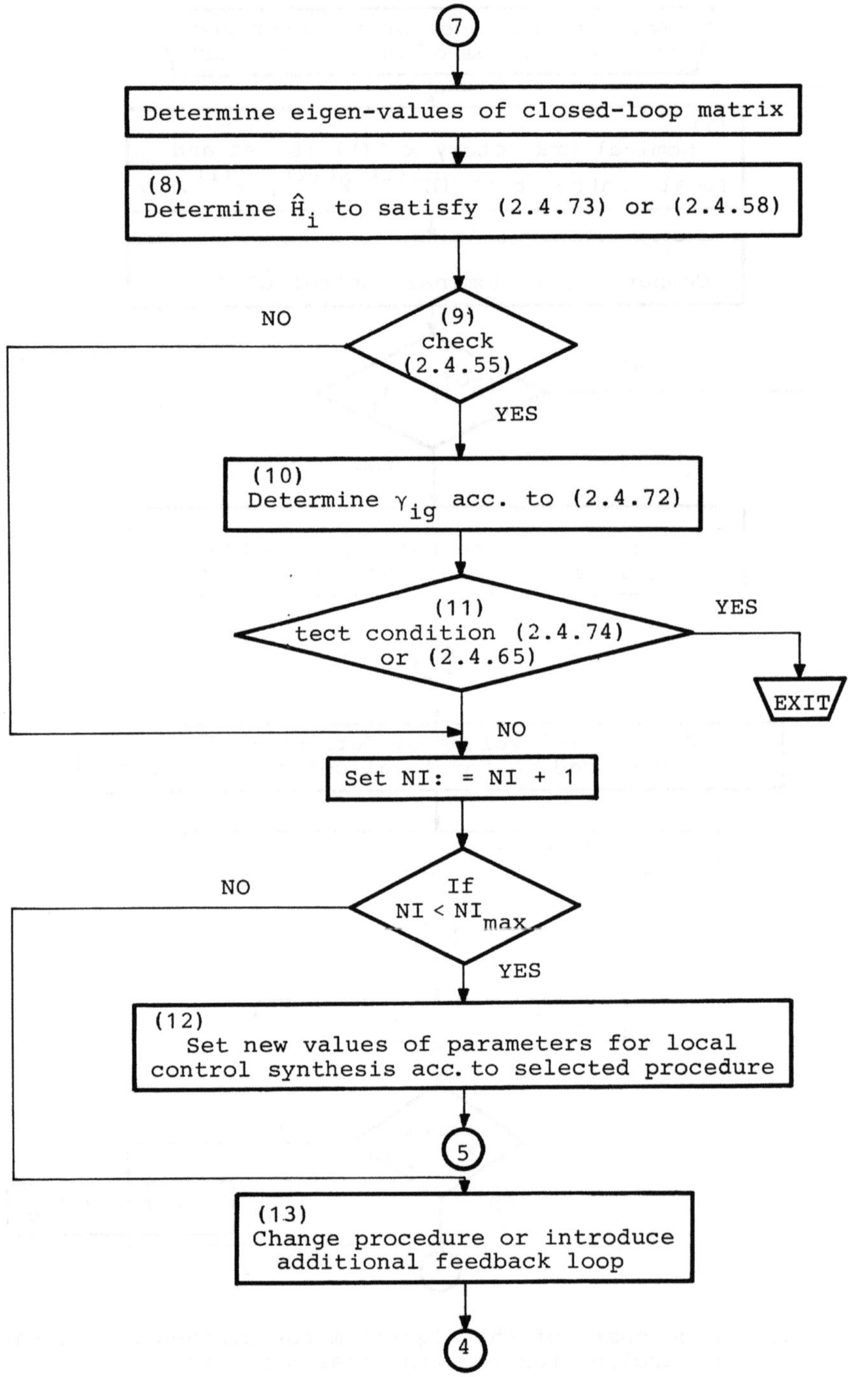
7
Determine eigen-values of closed-loop matrix
(8)
Determine Ĥ_i to satisfy (2.4.73) or (2.4.58)
NO
(9)
check
(2.4.55)
YES
(10)
Determine γ_ig acc. to (2.4.72)
(11)
tect condition (2.4.74)
or (2.4.65)
YES
EXIT
NO
Set NI: = NI + 1
NO
If
NI < NI_max
YES
(12)
Set new values of parameters for local
control synthesis acc. to selected procedure
5
(13)
Change procedure or introduce
additional feedback loop
4

Fig. 2.20. (Cont.)

dition $|\bar{u}^{oi}(t)| < u_m^i$, $\forall t \in T$ is satisfied; if not, we cannot realize the desired trajectory by the chosen actuator and we must select another trajectory, or another actuator (i.e. choose a slower trajectory, or change the actuator)

(3) The procedure for the local control synthesis has to be selected. We must define whether we shall synthesize the local controller by minimization of standard quadratic criterion (i.e. to synthesize the optimal quadratic controller), or by pole-placement method, or by some other method. We must also decide whether we shall introduce feedback loops by complete state vector x^i or by output of the subsystem y^i only. Finally, we have to decide whether a static or dynamic controller will be synthesized, i.e. whether or not integral feedback loop will be introduced. If we decide to synthesize the dynamic controller we must determine region $\hat{X}^{t(i)}(t)$ according to (2.4.63).

(4) Set initial values for the parameters of the local controller which have to be set in the selected procedure. For example, if we have selected to synthesize the local controller by minimization of standard quadratic criterion we have to set weighting matrices Q_i, r_i and prescribed stability degree β_i; in this, condition (2.4.38) may be taken into account. Similarly, if we have selected the pole--placement method for local control synthesis, we must define the desired poles of the closed-loop subsystem (obviously, condition (2.4.39) must be satisfied).

(5) Synthesize the local controller according to the selected procedure. If we have desided to synthesize the local controller by minimization of standard quadratic criterion, we synthesize the controller according to the procedure described in Paragraph 2.4.1 (or, in Paragraph 2.4.2 if we have introduced the integral feedback loop). If pole-placement has been selected we have to compute feedback gains according to the procedure described in Paragraph 2.4.2; obviously, many other procedures may be used for local control synthesis.

(6) Check whether conditions (2.4.67) are satisfied; if not, we have to determine λ_{ig} which satisfies (2.4.75).

(7) Determine the eigenvalues σ_j^i, $j=1,2,...,n_i+1$ of the closed-loop

matrix of the subsystem $(\hat{A}_I^i-\hat{b}_I^i k_I^{iT}\hat{C}^i)$, or σ_j^{iG}, $j=1,2,\ldots,n_i+1$ of the matrix $(\hat{A}_I^i-\lambda_{ig}\hat{b}_I^i k_I^{iT}\hat{C}^i)$; obviously, if we have chosen to apply the static controller we have to determine eigenvalues σ_j^i, $j=1,2,\ldots,n_i$ of the closed-loop matrix $(\tilde{A}^i-\tilde{b}^i r_i^{-1}\tilde{b}^{iT}K_i)$.

(8) Determine the matrix $\hat{H}_i$ which satisfies equation (2.4.73), or (2.4.58) (if conditions (2.4.67) are met); if the static controller has been selected we have to compute matrix H_i which satisfies equation (2.4.47) (as we have already noted, if the standard quadratic regulator has been selected we may avoid this step by choosing the function $v_i(t, x^i)$ as (2.4.51), but some drawbacks of this approach have been recognized).

(9) Check whether condition (2.4.55) is satisfied; if not, we cannot prove the practical stability of the subsystem $\tilde{S}^i$, so we must go to step (12).

(10) Determine the number γ_{ig}, which satisfies (2.4.72), or γ_i which is $\min|\mathrm{Re}(\sigma_j^i)|$, $j=1,2,\ldots,n_i+1$.

(11) Perform the test of practical stability (2.4.74), or (2.4.65); when the static controller is selected we have to perform the test (2.4.50); if the test is satisfied, we can accept the synthesized local controller and be sure that the local control provides the practical stability in accordance with local control task (2.4.8); by this the local controller is synthesized.

(12) If the test of practical stability is not satisfied, we cannot prove that the local subsystem is practically stable. We have to select again the local controller, i.e. to synthesize again feedback gains of the local controller. This means that we have to set new values of parameters which have to be specified in the selected procedure. For example, if we synthesize local optimal regulator we have to select again the weighting matrices Q_i, r_i and prescribed stability degree β_i (obviously, we should try to increase β_i and diagonal elements in the matrix Q_i, or to descrease r_i). Similarly, if pole-placement has been chosen we have to select again the desired poles of the closed-loop subsystem; then we have to go to step (5).

(13) If too many trials to select local controller have been made and we

have not achieved satisfaction of the test of practical stability, then probably we cannot ensure the practical stability of the subsystem by the chosen local controller structure. Then, we must either introduce an additional feedback loop (if we have not already introduced all state feedback loops and integral feedback loop), or select again the procedure for the synthesis of local controller*); thus, we go back to step (4).

Thus, using this procedure we can synthesize local control which ensures the satisfaction of local control task (2.4.8). Obviously this algorithm can easily be implemented by a digital computer to obtain computer-aided synthesis of local controller. This algorithm is a part of general algorithm for computer aided synthesis of control for the manipulation robots which will be presented in Chapter 4.

The critical point in the above presented algorithm is the repeated selection of the parameters that have to be specified in the particular procedure for control synthesis. If the procedure is to be performed completely automatically it is obvious that the specified parameters have to be iteratively changed in such a way as to ensure an increase of subsystem exponential stability degree γ_i. In the case of optimal regulator synthesis, this can be achieved by increasing the prescribed stability degree β_i, or by increasing the diagonal elements of matrix Q_i, or by decreasing r_i. If pole-placement method is used, we have to move the desired poles of the closed-loop subsystem to the left of the complex plane. However, it is questionable how fast this procedure leads to the desired result. If we have chosen output feedback, it may happen that this procedure cannot converge to the desired local controller. Then, as we have explained in connection with step (13) of the algorithm, we must select again the information structure of the local controller (i.e. introduce additional feedback loops). In automatic mode, the user has to specify the number of iterations that is allowed to the algorithm to search for the local controller; if this number of iterations is exceeded, the algorithm should go to re-selection of local information pattern, or the procedure for local control synthesis may be changed. Obviously, various improvements of this algorithm are possible. The algorithm might compare the exponential stability

*) In principle, we can synthesize equal local controllers with various procedures since local subsystems are linear. Thus, there is no need to select again the procedure for control synthesis. However, sometimes one procedure approaches the desired result faster than the order, and thus, this reselection might be effective.

degrees of the subsystem which are achieved in two successive iterations. We may thus conclude now fast the algorithm approaches the desired solution, and decide whether this direction is effective or it should be changed.

The best improvement of the algorithm can be achieved if we include a robot designer in this procedure, i.e. if we establish an interactive algorithm. In this case the designer can by himself choose again the control parameters, according to his own experience and, thus, speed--up the iterative procedure. This will be discussed in detail in Chapter 4.

2.5 Stability Analysis of Manipulation Robots

In the preceding paragraph we have presented synthesis of local controllers for decoupled subsystems of the robotic system. Namely, we have considered the robotic system as a set of decoupled subsystems (each subsystem is associated to a single joint of the robot and its corresponding actuator). We have synthesized a local controller for each subsystem independently from the rest of the system. Our aim is to synthesize a decentralized controller which should stabilize the complete robotic system. The structure of the chosen controller is presented in Fig. 2.13. The following question is posed: can such a decentralized controller, synthesized using the decoupled model of the robot, stabilize the complete robotic system when interactions between the joints are taken into account. In other words, we want to synthesize a decentralized controller which will ensure the practical stability of the robot in accordance with the definition of control task (2.2.18). Up to now, we have synthesized local controllers which ensure satisfaction of local control tasks (2.4.8) for decoupled subsystems (i.e. when interconnections between the joints are neglected). It is obvious that, if the interconnections between joints exist, satisfaction of local control task (2.4.8) is not sufficient to ensure satisfaction of global control task (2.2.18) for the complete robotic system. In this Paragraph we shall present a method for testing the practical stability of the complete robotic system. Using this method we shall establish a procedure for the synthesis of decentralized controller which satisfies the set control task (2.2.18) for the complete robotic system. We shall use the test of practical stability of the complete robotic system, to establish a procedure for iterative improvement of the local controllers.

The model of the robotic system S is given by (2.2.8). During the synthesis of local controllers, in Paragraph 2.4, we have considered the approximate decoupled model of the system in form (2.4.7). For each decoupled subsystem we have synthesized a local controller in form (2.4.19) - a static controller, or in form (2.4.56) - a dynamic controller, where in both cases local nominal control is also introduced. In Paragraph 2.4.4 we have analyzed the local practical stability of the decoupled subsystem if either static or dynamic controller has been implemented. Now, we shall analyze whether the complete model of the robot is stable if local controllers are applied. We have to analyze the stability of the robotic system with the decentralized controller. In case of static local controllers, the model of the closed-loop system is given by:

$$S^i: \quad \dot{x}^i = A^i(\theta^i)x^i - \lambda_{ig} b^i(\theta^i) r_i^{-1} \tilde{b}^{iT} K_i \Delta x^i + b^i(\theta^i)\bar{u}^{oi}(t) + f^i(\theta^i)\cdot M_i, \quad \forall i \in I \qquad (2.5.1)$$

This model is obtained by combining the model of the robot (2.2.2) and static controller (2.4.19), and λ_{ig} is introduced to take into account the amplitude constraint upon the actuators input (λ_{ig} is defined by (2.4.68), but for the static controller).

In Paragraph 2.4.4 the synthesis of local controller which ensures the practical stability of the local decoupled subsystem has been shown, i.e. the local control is synthesized in such a way that the closed--loop subsystems:

$$\tilde{S}^i: \quad \dot{x}^i = \tilde{A}^i x^i - \lambda_{ig} \tilde{b}^i r_i^{-1} \tilde{b}^{iT} K_i \Delta x^i + \tilde{b}^i \bar{u}^{oi}(t), \quad \forall i \in I \qquad (2.5.2)$$

are practically stable in the sense of the local control task (2.4.8).

If we compare decoupled subsystems (2.5.2) with the real system we can recognize that they differ in coupling terms (which are neglected in the approximate decoupled model of the system). If we recall the definition of the decoupled subsystem (2.4.7), i.e. the definitions of matrix $\tilde{A}^i$ and vector $\tilde{b}^i$, we can find out that the difference between the models (2.5.1) and (2.5.2) is given by:

$$\tilde{f}^i(\theta^i)z^i(q_i)\bar{P}_i(q, \dot{q}, \ddot{q}, d) = \tilde{f}^i(\theta^i)z^i(q_i)\cdot[P_i(q, \dot{q}, \ddot{q}, d) - \tilde{P}_i\bar{z}^i/z^i(q_i)] \qquad (2.5.3)$$

where $\bar{P}_i$ is defined by (2.4.6), and $\tilde{P}_i$ is given by (2.4.5), while P_i is the driving torque given by the model of the mechanical part of the robot (2.2.1). Here we have used the relation (2.2.7) between M_i and P_i. By $\tilde{f}^i(\theta^i)$ we denote:

$$\tilde{f}^i(\theta^i) = (I_{n_i} - f^i(\theta^i)\bar{z}^i\bar{H}_{ii}T^i)^{-1}f^i(\theta^i)$$

$\tilde{P}_i$ defined by (2.4.5), represents the decoupled model of the robot mechanism which is also included in the decoupled model of the system (2.5.2). Thus, the difference between the actual model of the robot (2.5.1) and the decoupled model (2.5.2) is practically given by the difference between the real model of mechanism (2.2.1) and decoupled model (2.4.5) (this difference is multiplied by factor $\tilde{f}^i(\theta^i)z^i(q_i)$).

The local controllers ensure the practical stability of the decoupled model of the robot (2.5.2). In order to analyze the stability of the actual model of the robot (2.5.1), we have to investigate the influence of the coupling terms (2.5.3) upon robot stability. However, the model of the coupling term (2.5.3) is given by the model of the mechanical part of the robot (2.2.1), which is, in general case, highly nonlinear as explained in Chapter 1. Thus, the analysis of the practical stability of the robot is related to numerous problems.

Several methods for stability analysis of nonlinear systems have been developed but we shall not survey them here. A very common procedure, as already mentioned in Paragraph 2.3, is to linearize the nonlinear model and then examine the stability of the linearized model. However, the stability of the linearized model of a nonlinear system is only a necessary condition for the stability of nonlinear system. This means that if the linearized model of the system is not stable, the nonlinear system is also unstable. However, vice versa does not hold: if the linearized model is stable, we cannot guarantee the stability of the nonlinear system. Nevertheless, there is a good reason to first examine the stability of the linearized model of the robot. Since the stability analysis of the nonlinear system is often complex and time consuming, and the analysis of the linearized model is much simpler, it is reasonable to first examine the stability of the linearized model. If it is not stable, there is no need to examine the stability of the nonlinear model of the system. In this way we can avoid unnecessary and complex analysis of the nonlinear model. Obviously, if the linearized model of the robot is stable, we must analyze the stability of the nonlinear model, too, in order to guarantee the stability of the robot.

Thus, we shall first briefly present stability analysis of the linearized model of the robot. We have already explained in Paragraph 2.3.2 how we can obtain the linearized model of the system. However, in Paragraph 2.3.2 we have considered the linearized model of the robot if nominal programmed control $u^o(t)$, synthesized using the complete centralized model of the robot (2.3.4), is applied. Let us briefly describe how we obtain the linearized model if decentralized controller (2.4.19) is applied (i.e. if nominal programmed control $\bar{u}^{oi}(t)$ is synthesized at subsystems level).

Let us consider the model of deviation of the state around the nominal trajectory $x^o(t)$, $\forall t \in T$. Starting from the model (2.5.1), we obtain the model of deviation of the state as:

$$\Delta\dot{x}^i = (\tilde{A}^i - \lambda_{ig}\tilde{b}^i r_i^{-1}\tilde{b}^{iT}K_i)\Delta x^i + \tilde{f}^i(\theta^i)\cdot z^i(q_i)\bar{P}_i(q, \dot{q}, \ddot{q}, d) \quad (2.5.4)$$

To obtain (2.5.4) we have employed the fact that local nominal control $\bar{u}^{oi}(t)$, $\forall t \in T$ satisfies (2.4.14). The relation (2.2.7) for connection between M_i and P_i is also applied. Actually, the model (2.5.4) represents the difference between the real model of the robot (2.5.1) with local controllers (2.4.19) and the local "nominal model" (2.4.14).

Now, let us linearize the model of deviation (2.5.4) around the point $\Delta x^i = 0$, $\forall i \in I$, (i.e. around the nominal trajectory in the state space $x^o(t)$, $\forall t \in T$). The complete linearized model is obtained in the form:

$$\Delta\dot{x} = A_L^o(\theta, d, t)\Delta x + 0(\theta, d, t) \quad (2.5.5)$$

where the matrix $A_L^o(\theta, d, t)$: $R^L \times D \times T \rightarrow R^{N \times N}$ is defined as:

$$A^o = \mathrm{diag}[\tilde{A}^i - \lambda_{ig}\tilde{b}^i r_i^{-1}\tilde{b}^{iT}K_i + \tilde{f}^i(\theta^i)\left(\frac{\partial z^i}{\partial q_i}\right)_{q_i = q_i^{oi}} \cdot \left.\frac{\partial G^i}{\partial x^i}\right|_{x^i = x^{oi}} \cdot \bar{P}(q^o, \dot{q}^o, \ddot{q}^o, d) - \bar{z}^i\bar{H}_{ii}\frac{\partial \ddot{q}_i}{\partial x^i} - \bar{z}^i\bar{h}_i\frac{\partial q_i}{\partial x^i})] +$$
$$+ F(\theta)z'(q^o)[(\frac{\partial H(q^o, d)}{\partial q}\ddot{q}^o + \frac{\partial h(q^o, \dot{q}^o, d)}{\partial q})\frac{\partial G(x^o)}{\partial x} +$$
$$+ \frac{\partial h(q^o, \dot{q}^o, d)}{\partial \dot{q}}\frac{\partial \hat{G}(x^o)}{\partial x} + H(q^o, d)\frac{\partial \ddot{q}}{\partial x}]$$

where $\frac{\partial H(q^o, d)}{\partial q}$ denotes a three dimensional matrix n×n×n (a derivative of inertia matrix H(q, d) with respect to q), $\frac{\partial h(q^o, \dot{q}^o, d)}{\partial q}$ is the n×n matrix (derivatives of vector h(q, $\dot{q}$, d) with respect to q), and $\frac{\partial h(q^o, \dot{q}^o, d)}{\partial \dot{q}}$ denotes n×n matrix (derivatives of vector h(q, $\dot{q}$, d) with respect to $\dot{q}$). Matrices F(θ), z'(q) have been defined in relation to the robot model (2.2.8) and vectors G(x), $\hat{G}$(x) are defined by (2.2.11) and (2.2.12), while $\frac{\partial G(x^o)}{\partial x}$ denotes an n×N matrix (derivatives of vector G(x) with respect to x) and the similar holds for $\frac{\partial \hat{G}(x^o)}{\partial x}$. As explained in Paragraph 2.3.2, the main problem in obtaining linearized model (2.5.5) lies in the computation of matrices $\frac{\partial H}{\partial q}$, $\frac{\partial h}{\partial q}$ and $\frac{\partial h}{\partial \dot{q}}$, i.e. in the linearization of the mechanical part of robot model. As we have mentioned, these matrices may be obtained by some numerical procedure [2], or analytically [16] or by means of various identification methods. In (2.5.5) 0(θ, d, t) denotes the term which is not compensated by the local nominal programmed control, and which is given by:

$$0(\theta, d, t) = F(\theta)\cdot z'(q^o)\cdot \bar{P}(q^o, \dot{q}^o, \ddot{q}^o, d) \qquad (2.5.6)$$

The linearized model (2.5.5) differs from the linearized model (2.3.7), just in this term (2.5.6), since in (2.3.7) this term is compensated by nominal centralized control $u^{oi}(t)$ ∀t∈T. Also, in (2.5.5) we have already introduced local static controller (2.4.19).

Now, we have to examine the stability of the linearized model of the robot (2.5.5). If we want to examine the practical stability of the linearized model we can apply the method presented in the previous Paragraph. Namely, in Paragraph 2.4.4 we have examine the practical stability of decoupled linear subsystem. It is obvious that we can apply the same method to analyze the complete linearized model (2.5.5) of the robot. However, since the stability of the linearized model of the robot is only a necessary condition for the stability of the actual model of the robot, there is no need for a precise examination of the practical stability of the linearized model. It is sufficient to test the exponential stability of the linearized model, since afterwards we shall test the practical stability of the nonlinear model of the robot. To test the exponential stability of the linearized model we have to determine the eigenvalues of matrix $A_L^o(\theta, d, t)$, ∀t∈T. Let us denote the eigenvalues of the matrix A_L^o by $\sigma_j(\theta, d, t)$, j=1,2,...,N. They depend on actuator parameters θ, mechanism parameters d, and time t (i.e.

$\sigma_j(\theta^*, d^*, t^*)$, j=1,2,...,N correspond to the eigenvalues of matrix $A_L^o(\theta^*, d^*, t^*)$, for particular values $\theta^* \in \Theta$, $d^* \in D$ and $t^* \in T$). Since the region $X^t(t)$, $\forall t \in T$ of practical stability is defined as exponential shrinkage of subregions $X^{t(i)}(t)$ with exponential degrees $\alpha^{(i)}$, $i \in I$, (see Paragraph 2.2.2), we have to test whether the following condition holds*):

$$\min_j |\mathrm{Re}(\sigma_j(\theta, d, t))| > \max_{i \in I} \alpha^{(i)}, \quad \forall \theta \in \Theta, \forall d \in D, \forall t \in T \qquad (2.5.7)$$

where the minimum on the left side is taken over all eigenvalues σ_j, j=1,2,...,N of the matrix A_L^o and for all allowable values of parameters θ, d and over time interval T. Condition (2.5.7) means that all eigenvalues of the linearized model of the robot (in complex plane) must be on the left from the maximum exponential degree of the finite regions shrinkage $\alpha^{(i)}$. This must hold for all allowable values of parameters and during the desired time period. Thus, we have to test the condition (2.5.7). If it is not satisfied, there is no need to test practical stability of the nonlinear model of the robot, since it is probable that the control (2.4.19) cannot ensure fulfilment of the desired control task (2.2.18), i.e. we may assume that the robot is not practically stable with decentralized controller (2.4.19).

However, if the condition (2.5.7) is satisfied, we may proceed with testing the practical stability of the nonlinear model of the robot, since the satisfaction of condition (2.5.7) is not sufficient to prove the practical stability of the robot. Now, we shall present the method for analysing the practical stability of the nonlinear model of the robot. This method is directly related to the analysis of the practical stability of the local decoupled subsystems, as presented in Paragraph 2.4.4. Actually, the method we are going to present originates from the aggregation-decomposition methods for stability analysis of large-scale systems, established by several authors. As we have already explained in Paragraph 2.4.4, we have used the method for practical stability analysis of large-scale systems developed by Michel [68], but we have modified it to suit the form of the model of the robotic systems [69].

We have to analyze the practical stability of the nonlinear model of the robot (2.5.1) if static local controllers (2.4.19) are applied. We have to test whether these local controllers can accommodate the stated control task (2.2.18).

---

*) Obviously, all eigenvalues $\sigma_j(\theta, d, t)$ of the matrix A_L^o must be on the left side of complex plane.

In Paragraph 2.4.4. we have presented how it is possible to test the practical stability of local decoupled subsystems (2.5.2) if local controllers (2.4.19) are applied. As explained above, the difference between the actual model (2.5.1) and decoupled model (2.5.2) is given by terms (2.5.3). We have to analyze the influence of these nonlinear terms upon the robot stability.

Let us again consider functions $v_i(t, x^i)$ associated to each subsystem $\tilde{S}^i$. Let us consider the time derivative of these functions along the solution of the actual nonlinear model of robot (2.5.1). The derivatives of these functions may be written as:

$$\dot{v}_i(t, x^i)_{(\text{along solution (2.5.1)})} = \frac{\partial v_i}{\partial t} + (\text{grad} v_i)^T \dot{x}^i = \frac{\partial v_i}{\partial t} +$$

$$+ (\text{grad} v_i)^T \dot{x}^i_{(\text{for decoupled subsystem (2.5.2)})} +$$

$$+ (\text{grad} v_i)^T \cdot (\text{coupling term (2.5.3)}) \qquad (2.5.8)$$

The equation (2.5.8) means that the time derivative of the functions v_i may be divided into two parts: the first part concerns the derivative of the state vector for decoupled subsystems (2.5.2) and the second part is related to the difference between the actual model (2.5.1) and decoupled model (2.5.2) (which is given by terms (2.5.2)). The first part has been considered in Paragraph 2.4.4. Now, we have to consider the second part.

Let us write again the terms (2.5.3) in more convenient forms. We may write them in the form:

$$z^i(q^i)\bar{P}_i(q, \dot{q}, \ddot{q}, d, t) = \Delta z^i(t, \Delta q^i)\Delta\bar{P}_i(\Delta q, \Delta\dot{q}, \Delta\ddot{q}, d, t) +$$

$$+ z^i(q^{oi})\bar{P}_i^o(q^o, \dot{q}^o, \ddot{q}^o, d, t) +$$

$$+ \Delta z^i \bar{P}_i^o + z^i(q^{oi})\Delta\bar{P}_i \qquad (2.5.9)$$

where by $\bar{P}_i^o$ we denote the value of $\bar{P}_i$ for $q = q^o$, $\dot{q} = \dot{q}^o$, $\ddot{q} = \ddot{q}^o$, (the so-called nominal "driving torque"*) for arbitrary parameters $d \in D$), and by $\Delta\bar{P}_i = \bar{P}_i - \bar{P}_i^o$ the deviation of "driving torque" $\bar{P}_i$ from its

*) We put driving torque into quotation marks, since P_i differs from the actual driving torque P_i by the value $\tilde{P}_i$ which represents the driving torque of the decoupled model of the mechanism.

nominal value. Similarly, we have written $z^i(q_i)$ as $z^i(q^{oi})+\Delta z^i(t, \Delta q_i)$, where Δz^i denotes the deviation of $z^i(q_i)$ from its nominal value $z^i(q^{oi})$. Further, we may rewrite (2.5.9) in a more compact form:

$$z^i(q_i)\cdot\bar{P}_i = (\Delta z^i(q_i)\cdot\Delta\bar{P}_i+\Delta z^i\cdot\bar{P}_i^o + z^i(q^{oi})\Delta\bar{P}_i) + z^i(q^{oi})\cdot\bar{P}_i^o \quad (2.5.10)$$

Now, we may rewrite the second term in (2.5.8) in the following manner:

$$(\mathrm{grad} v^i)^T\tilde{f}^i(\theta^i)z^i(q_i)\bar{P}_i = (\mathrm{grad} v^i)^T\tilde{f}^i(\theta^i)(z^i(q_i)\Delta\bar{P}_i + \\ + \Delta z^i\bar{P}_i^o + z^i(q^{oi})\Delta\bar{P}_i) + \\ + \mathrm{grad}(v^i)^T\tilde{f}^i(\theta^i)z^i(q^{oi})\cdot\bar{P}_i^o \quad (2.5.11)$$

The aim of this trivial rewriting is to separate the part of coupling which depends on the deviations of state coordinates from the nominal trajectory from the nominal part of coupling which depends only on the nominal trajectory (i.e. on time). Since $\bar{P}_i$ converges to $\bar{P}_i^o$ as q, $\dot{q}$, $\ddot{q}$ converge to nominal values q^o, $\dot{q}^o$, $\ddot{q}^o$, and since Δq, $\Delta\dot{q}$, $\Delta\ddot{q}$ converge to zero as Δx^j converge to zero $\forall j\in I$, we can write:

$$\lim_{\Delta x^j\to 0,\ \forall j\in I} \tilde{f}^i(\theta^i)(\Delta z^i(q_i)\Delta\bar{P}_i+\Delta z^i\bar{P}_i^o+z^i(q^{oi})\Delta\bar{P}_i)\to 0, \\ \forall i\in I,\ \forall t\in T,\ \forall d\in D,\ \forall\theta\in\Theta \quad (2.5.12)$$

In (2.5.12) we have also used the fact that Δz^i converges to zero as Δx^i converges to zero. The relation (2.5.12) means that this part of coupling, which depends on the deviation of state vector from the nominal trajectory, converges to zero as the state vector converges to the nominal trajectory (i.e. the deviation of "driving torques" from nominal should vanish if the state vector approaches nominal trajectory $x^o(t)$, $\forall t\in T$). Obviously, (2.5.12) holds for each set of values of parameters $d\in D$.

Due to (2.5.12), we can find the numbers ξ_{ij} which satisfy the following inequalities:

$$(\mathrm{grad} v_i)^T\tilde{f}^i(\theta^i)(\Delta z^i(q_i)\Delta\bar{P}_i+\Delta z^i\bar{P}_i^o+z^i(q^{oi})\Delta\bar{P}_i) < \sum_{j=1}^{n}\xi_{ij}||\Delta x^j|| \\ \forall(t, x)\in T\times X^t(t),\ \forall i\in I,\ \forall d\in D, \quad (2.5.13)$$

Actually, we can determine the numbers ξ_{ij} so that the sums on the right sides of inequalities (2.5.13) estimate the terms on the left sides. This represents linearization of the nonlinear coupling term, but this linearization holds in the whole region $X^t(t)$, $\forall t \in T$ to which the state of the robot must belong during tracking of nominal trajectory.

Now, we can write the time derivative of function $v_i(t, x^i)$ starting from (2.5.8), (2.5.11) and (2.5.13), in the following manner:

$$\dot{v}_{i(\text{along } (2.5.1))} < \dot{v}_{i(\text{along } (2.5.2))} + \sum_{j=1}^{n} \xi_{ij} ||\Delta x^j|| +$$

$$+ (\text{grad} v_i)^T \tilde{f}^i(\theta^i) z^i(q^{oi}) \cdot \bar{P}_i^o,$$

$$\forall i \in I, \ \forall (t, x) \in T \times X^t(t), \ \forall d \in D, \qquad (2.5.14)$$

The derivative of function $v_i(t, x^i)$ for local subsystem has to satisfy (2.4.40). Along the boundary of the region $X^t(t)$, $\forall t \in T$ (2.5.14) can be rewritten:

$$\dot{v}_{i(\text{along } (2.5.1))} < \psi_i(t) + \sum_{j=1}^{n} \xi_{ij} \bar{X}^{t(j)} \exp(-\alpha^{(j)} t) +$$

$$+ (\text{grad} v_i)^T \tilde{f}^i(\theta^i) z^i(q^{oi}) \cdot \bar{P}_i^o(t, d) =$$

$$= \psi_i'(t, d) \quad \forall x \in \partial X^t(t), \ \forall t \in T, \ \forall d \in D \qquad (2.5.15)$$

In (2.5.15) we have taken into account the fact that for boundary of the region $X^t(t)$, $\forall t \in T$, it holds $||\Delta x^j(t)|| = \bar{X}^{t(j)} \exp(-\alpha^{(j)} t)$, $\forall j \in I$, $\forall t \in T$.

The conditions for the practical stability of the ith subsystem are given by (2.4.40) and (2.4.41). Similarly, we may establish conditions for the practical stability of the complete robotic system. The derivatives of the functions $v_i(t, x^i)$ along the solution of the nonlinear model of the robot (2.5.1) are bounded by functions $\psi_i'(t)$ given by (2.5.15). Analogously to condition (2.4.41), the conditions for the practical stability of the robotic system (2.5.1) can be written as:

$$\int_0^t \psi_i'(t', d) dt' < v_{im}^{\partial X^{t(i)}(t)}(t) - v_{iM}^{\partial X^{I(i)}}(0), \ \forall i \in I, \ \forall t \in T, \ \forall d \in D,$$

(2.5.16)

The proof of this statement is given in Appendix 2.B, so we shall here just rewrite these conditions to show how we can use them to test the practical stability of the nonlinear model of the robot. Introducing relation (2.5.15) for $\psi_i'(t)$ in (2.5.16), we get sufficient conditions for the practical stability of the complete robotic system, if local controllers (2.4.19) are applied:

$$\int_0^t \psi_i(t')dt' + \sum_{j=1}^n \xi_{ij} \frac{\bar{X}^{t(j)}}{\alpha^{(j)}}[1-\exp(-\alpha^{(j)}t)] +$$

$$+ \int_0^t (\text{grad} v_i)^T \tilde{f}^i(\theta^i) z^i(q^{oi}) \bar{P}_i^o(t, d)dt <$$

$$< v_{im}^{\partial X^{t(i)}(t)}(t) - v_{iM}^{\partial X^{I(i)}}(0), \quad \forall i \in I, \forall t \in T, \forall d \in D \qquad (2.5.17)$$

Let us suppose that functions $v_i(t, x^i)$ are chosen as (2.4.43), where matrices H_i satisfy (2.4.47)*). We have shown in Paragraph 2.4.4 that for these functions we may choose functions $\psi_i(t)$ as (2.4.49). Let us introduce the real-valued functions $\rho_i(t, d)>0$ which satisfy:

$$\int_0^t z^i(q^{oi})\bar{P}_i^o(q^o, \dot{q}^o, \ddot{q}^o, d, t')dt' < \rho_i(t, d), \forall t \in T, \forall i \in I \qquad (2.5.18)$$

By introducing $\psi_i(t)$ defined by (2.4.49), and v_i defined by (2.4.43), and $\rho_i(t, d)$ defined by (2.5.18), into (2.5.17), we get these tests in a more convenient form:

$$-\gamma_{ig}\lambda_m^{1/2}(H_i)\bar{X}^{I(i)}(1-\exp(-\alpha^{(i)}t))/\alpha^{(i)} + \sum_{j=1}^n \xi_{ij}\frac{\bar{X}^{t(j)}}{\alpha^{(j)}}[1-\exp(-\alpha^{(j)}t)] +$$

$$+ \frac{\lambda_M(H_i)}{\lambda_m^{1/2}(H_i)}||\tilde{f}^i(\theta^i)||\rho_i(t, d) < \lambda_m^{1/2}(H_i)\bar{X}^{t(i)}\exp(-\alpha^{(i)}t) -$$

$$- \lambda_M^{1/2}(H_i)\bar{X}^{I(i)}, \quad \forall t \in T, \forall i \in I, \forall d \in D \qquad (2.5.19)$$

Thus, to test the practical stability of the nonlinear model of robotic system we have to test the practical stability of decoupled (local) subsystems by examining conditions (2.4.50), and then determine the numbers ξ_{ij} in (2.5.13) and functions $\rho_i(t, d)$ in (2.5.18). Then it is simple to test conditions (2.5.19). Since the conditions (2.5.19) are sufficient, but not necessary for practical stability, if they are not satisfied, we cannot say whether the robot is practically stable or not. Nevertheless, we can use these tests to improve local controllers so as to ensure the practical stability of the robot. If the local

---

*) Actually, H_i satisfies the equation analogous to (2.4.73), but for the static controller. We have already taken into account the amplitude constraint on actuators inputs through λ_{ig} in (2.5.2).

controllers stabilize the decoupled subsystems $\tilde{S}^i$ (which is proved by testing conditions (2.4.50)), but do not satisfy conditions (2.5.19), we may try to compute again local feedback gains and test again the stability of the robot by examining conditions (2.5.19). Thus, we may establish an iterative algorithm for reselection of the local controllers until the conditions (2.5.19) are satisfied. In this way we can develop an algorithm for the synthesis of decentralized controller which will fulfil the required control task (2.2.18) for the actual nonlinear model of the robotic system.

Before we present this algorithm, we have to make a few remarks concerning the test of the practical stability of the nonlinear model of robot.

(I) We have developed the conditions (2.5.19) to test the practical stability of robot if static local controllers (2.4.19) are applied. In Paragraph 2.4.4 we have shown how we can test the stability of decoupled subsystems $\tilde{S}^i$ if dynamic local controllers (2.4.56) are applied. It is very simple to extend the conditions (2.5.19) to include the case when dynamic local controllers are applied. Here, we shall not present extension of the stability test in detail (since it is quite trivial if we take into account the results obtained in Paragraph 2.2.4). We shall just write tests for the practical stability of the robot if dynamic local controllers are applied. Analogously to local stability test (2.4.74), and to test (2.5.19), we can write the conditions for the practical stability of the robot in the form:

$$
\begin{aligned}
& -\frac{\gamma_{ig}}{\alpha^{(i)}}[\hat{\bar{X}}^{I(i)}(1-\exp(-\alpha^{(i)}t)+(\tilde{R}^i C^i)_M \bar{X}^{I(i)}\cdot t]+ \\
& +\sum_{j=1}^{n}\xi_{ij}\{\frac{\hat{\bar{X}}^{t(j)}}{\alpha^{(j)}}[1-\exp(-\alpha^{(j)}t)]+(\tilde{R}^j C^j)_M \frac{\bar{X}^{t(j)}}{\alpha^{(j)}}t\}+ \\
& +\frac{\lambda_M(\hat{H}_i)}{\lambda_m^{1/2}(\hat{H}_i)}||\tilde{f}^i(\theta^i)||\rho_i(t,\ d) < \lambda_m^{1/2}(\hat{H}_i)[\hat{\bar{X}}^{t(i)}\exp(-\alpha^{(i)}t)+ \\
& +(\tilde{R}^i C^i)_M \bar{X}^{t(i)}/\alpha^{(i)}]-\lambda_M^{1/2}(\hat{H}_i)\bar{X}^{I(i)} \qquad (2.5.20)
\end{aligned}
$$

where we have chosen functions $v_i(t,\ \hat{x}^i)$ in the form (2.4.57), such that matrices $\hat{H}_i$ satisfy (2.4.73), γ_{ig} is given by (2.4.72), and the stability regions are defined by (2.4.60) and (2.4.63). Obviously, we have to consider extended subsystems with extended state vectors $\hat{x}^i$, due to the addition of integral feedback loop.

If we apply local optimal regulators (2.4.19), we may, as explained in Paragraph 2.4.4, choose functions $v_i(t, x^i)$ in the form (2.4.51), where K_i is the solution of the corresponding Riccati equation. The tests of practical stability (2.5.19) can be rewritten in this case analogously to (2.4.54).

(II) We have already introduced the numbers λ_{ig} (through numbers γ_{ig}) into conditions (2.5.19) in order to take into account the amplitude constraints upon actuators inputs. If conditions (2.4.67) are fulfilled for one of the subsystems, then, for this subsystem we can take $\lambda_{ig}=1$ and $\gamma_{ig} = \gamma_i$. Thus, by (2.5.19) (or (2.5.20)) we can test the stability in both cases: if the actuators inputs are within the given constraints, and if they reach the amplitude limits.

(III) In book No. 2 of this series [2] we have analyzed the stability of the robotic system around the nominal trajectory when nominal programmed control $u^o(t)$, $\forall t \in T$ is applied, where this nominal control has been synthesized using the centralized nonlinear model of robot (2.3.4). If such nominal control is applied, and assuming that all robot parameters are precisely defined in advance, the system is in equilibrium along the nominal trajectory $x^o(t)$, $\forall t \in T$ (i.e. for $\Delta x(t)=0$ and $\Delta u(t)=0$ it follows that $\Delta \dot{x}(t)=0$, $\forall t \in T$). Thus, we were able to test the asymptotic stability of the robot around nominal trajectory, instead of directly examining its practical stability. The test of the asymptotic stability is simpler than the test of practical stability.

However, in this book we have not introduced nominal centralized control $u^o(t)$, $\forall t \in T$ but only nominal local control $\bar{u}^{oi}(t)$, $\forall t \in T$, which satisfies (2.4.14). The reasons for this have been explained in Paragraph 2.4. We are not able to examine practical stability by testing the asymptotic stability of the system as we did in [2]. Here, for the first time, we directly examine the practical stability of the robot.

Even more, we are in a position to examine whether the control synthesized can withstand parameter variations. Namely, the tests (2.5.19), or (2.5.20) take into account variable robot parameters (θ parameters of actuators and d parameters of the mechanical part of the robot). We have to test conditions (2.5.19) for each allowable value of parameters θ or d, and if the tests are satisfied for all parameter values we can guarantee that the chosen local regulators are robust enough to withstand all parameter variations. It should be noted that up to now we have not been able to test stability of the robot if its parameters are variable. Here, for the first time, we can test robustness of the control applied to robotic systems.

(IV) We have mentioned several times that the above-presented conditions for the practical stability of the robot, are only sufficient and not necessary. We want to underline once again that this is the reason why this method may be conservative. It may happen that the tests (2.5.19), or (2.5.20), are not satisfied, but, actually, the robot may be stable with the control applied. This may lead to synthesis of too strong local controllers and unacceptable conclusions. Moreover, it may happen that, due to conservatism of the method, we cannot find the decentralized controller which can stabilize the robot and accommodate all allowable parameter variations, although it actually exists. However, the main source of conservatism of the method lies in determination of the numbers ξ_{ij} which satisfy (2.5.13). If we ensure that the numbers ξ_{ij} are good estimations of the interactions between the subsystems, we may expect that the control synthesized using this method is quite acceptable and that all conclusions that follow from these analyses are valid.

Now, we shall establish the algorithm for synthesis of the decentralized control which stabilizes the robotic system around the given nominal trajectory $x^o(t)$, $\forall t\in T$, for all allowable parameters of the mechanism and actuators. The algorithm uses the above presented tests of the practical stability of the nonlinear model of the robot. The aim of this algorithm is to synthesize the decentralized controller which satisfies control task (2.2.18). A brief flow-chart of this algorithm is presented in Fig. 2.21. The algorithm includes the algorithm, shown in Fig. 2.20 for the synthesis of local controllers which stabilize local (decoupled) subsystems.

The algorithm can be performed according to the following steps:

(1) The global control task (2.2.18) is set, i.e. the regions X^I and $X^t(t)$, $\forall t\in T$ are set, by defining the numbers $\bar{X}^{I(i)}$, $\bar{X}^{t(i)}$, $\alpha^{(i)}$ for all n degrees of freedom (actuators) and time interval τ; also, the sets of allowable parameters Θ and D have to be defined; nominal trajectory $x^o(t)$, $\forall t\in T$ is given.

(2) Set initial values of the actuator parameters $\theta = \theta_o\in\Theta$.

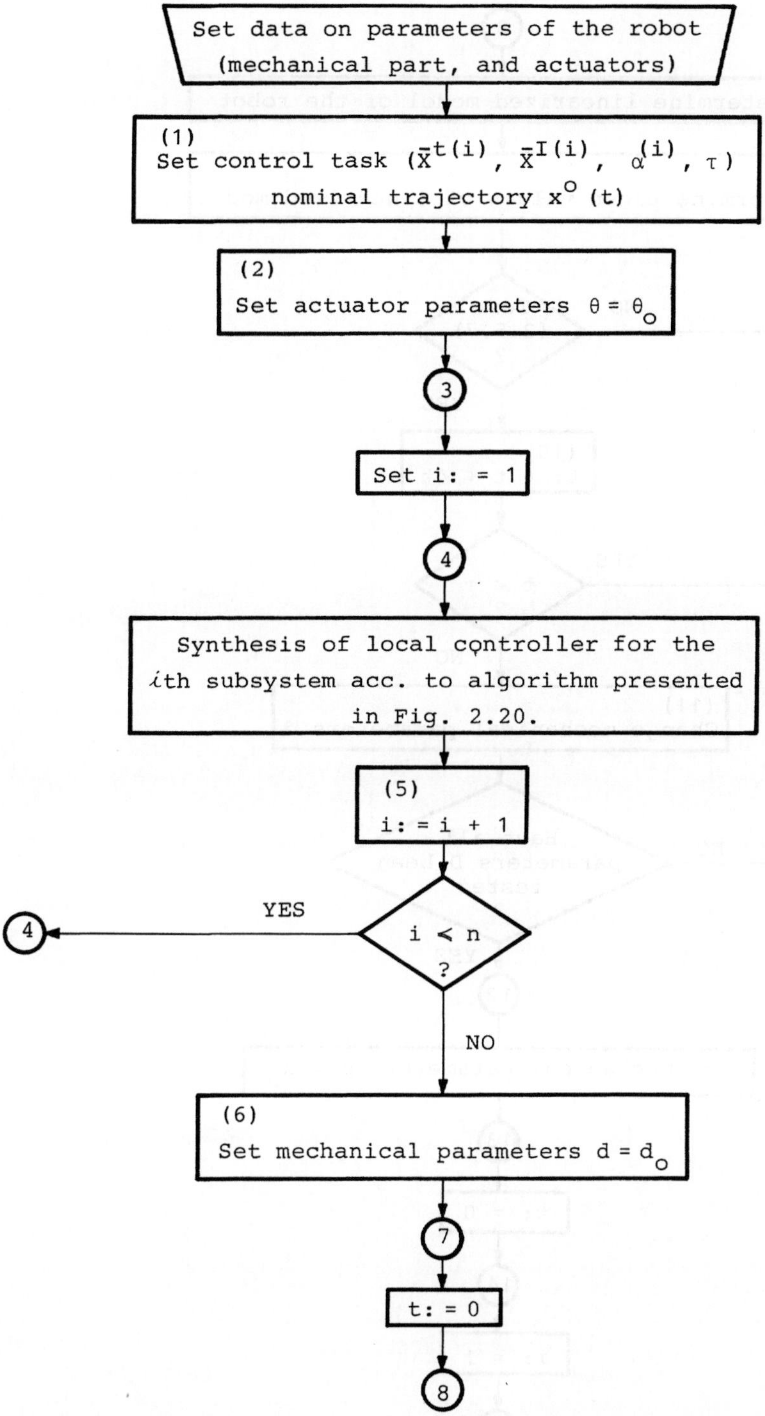

Fig. 2.21. Flow-chart of the algorithm for synthesis of decentralized controller on the basis of practical stability analysis

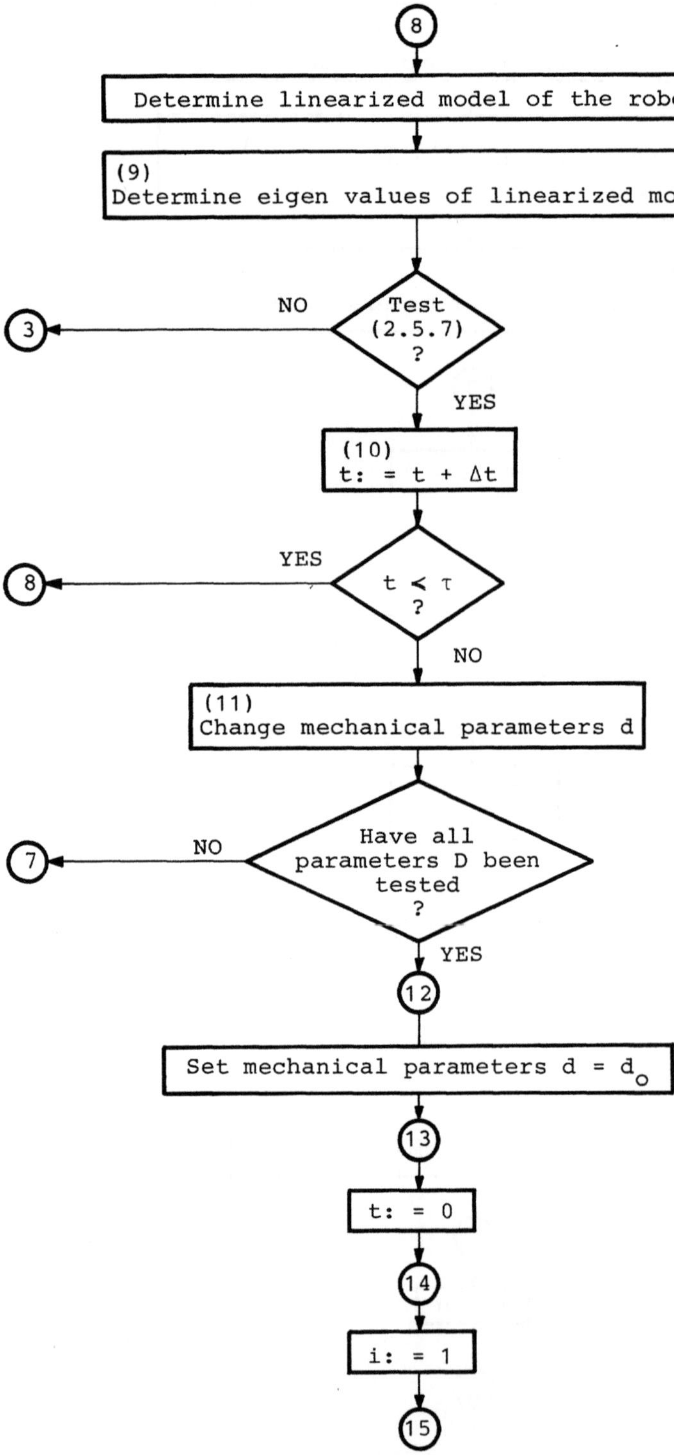
8
Determine linearized model of the robot
(9)
Determine eigen values of linearized model
NO
3
Test (2.5.7) ?
YES
(10)
t: = t + Δt
YES
8
t < τ ?
NO
(11)
Change mechanical parameters d
NO
7
Have all parameters D been tested ?
YES
12
Set mechanical parameters d = d_o
13
t: = 0
14
i: = 1
15

Fig. 2.21. (Cont.)

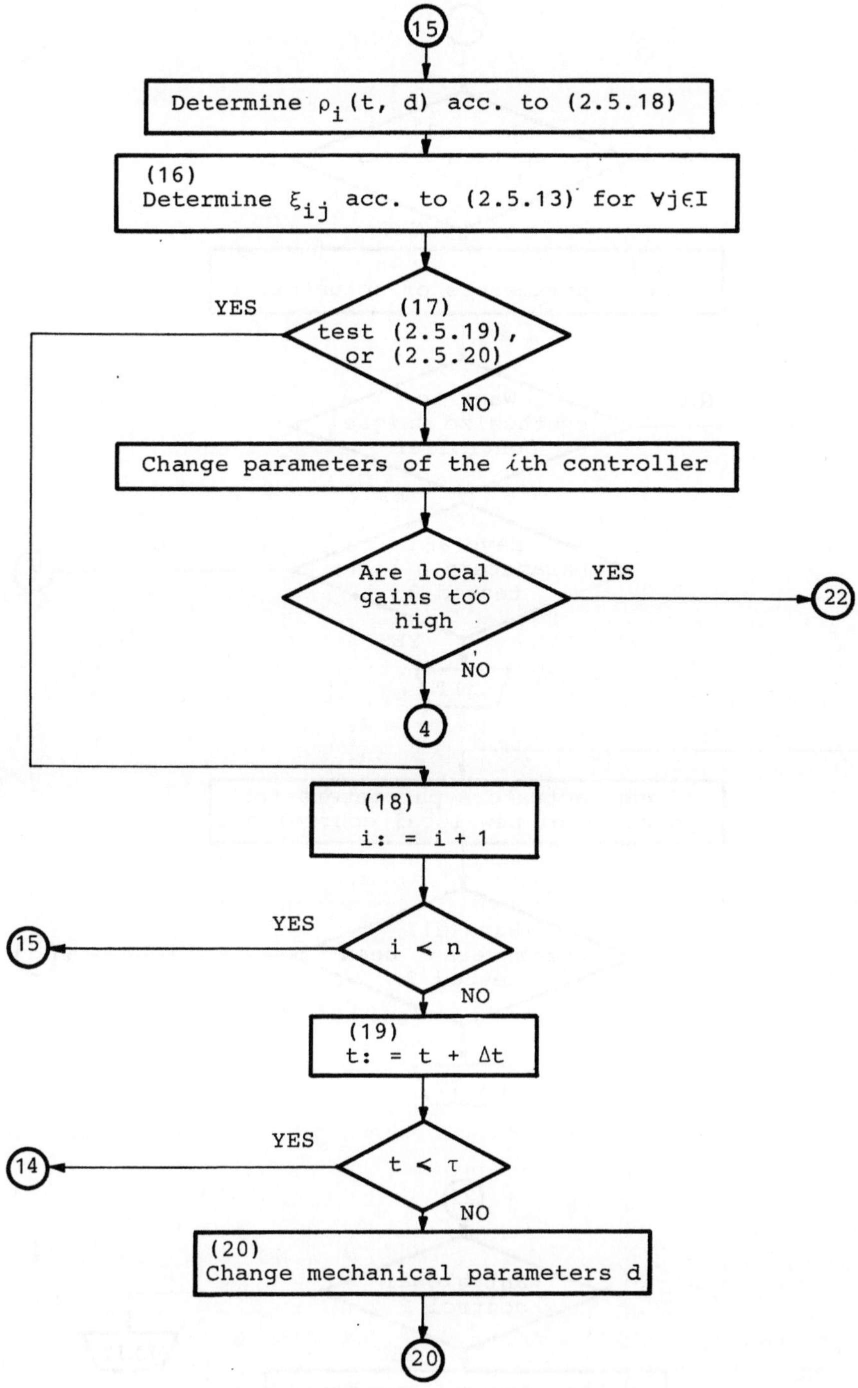
15
Determine $\rho_i(t, d)$ acc. to (2.5.18)
(16)
Determine ξ_{ij} acc. to (2.5.13) for $\forall j \in I$
YES
(17)
test (2.5.19),
or (2.5.20)
NO
Change parameters of the ith controller
Are local
gains too
high
YES
22
NO
4
(18)
i: = i + 1
YES
15
i < n
NO
(19)
t: = t + Δt
YES
14
t < τ
NO
(20)
Change mechanical parameters d
20

Fig. 2.21. (Cont.)

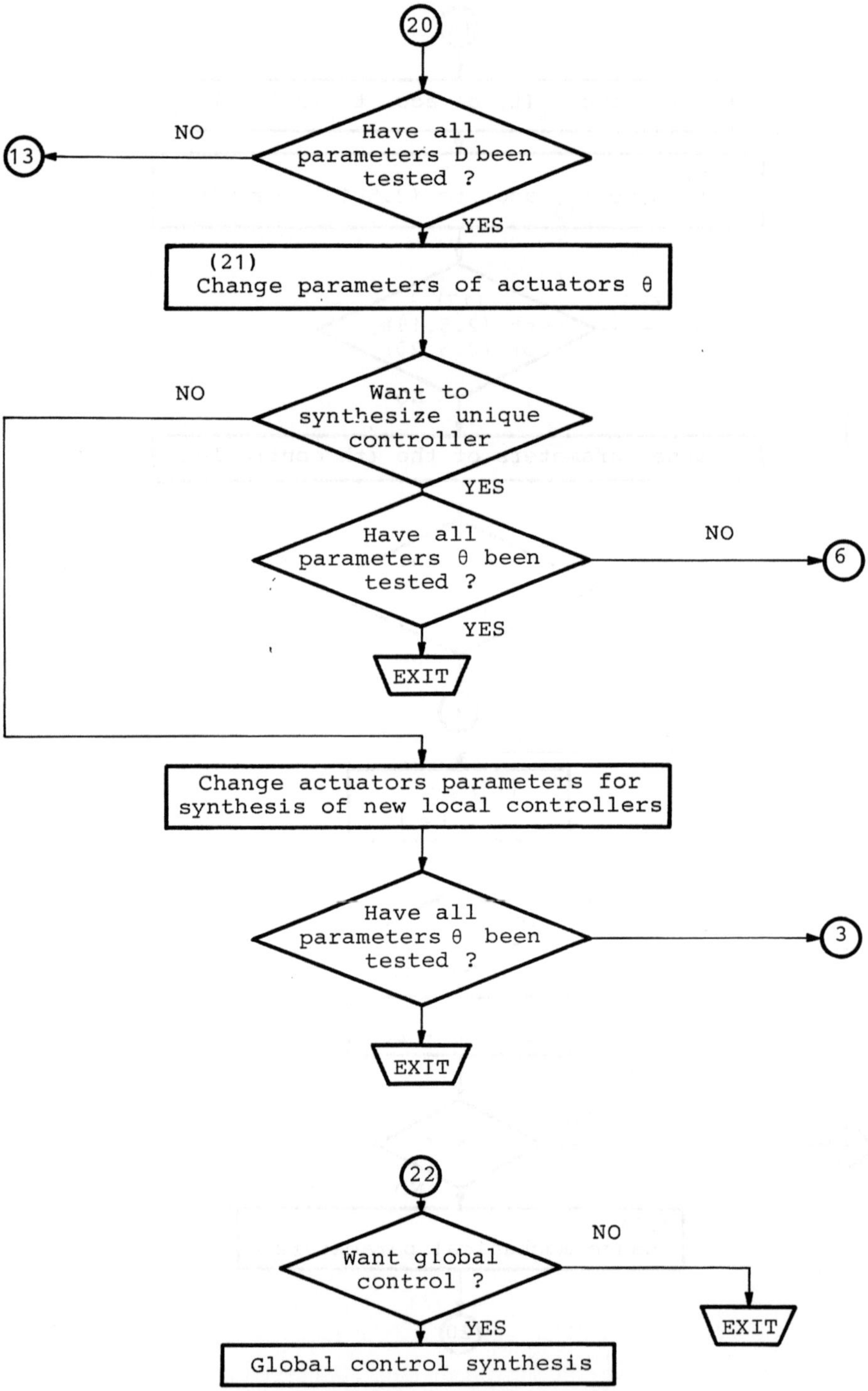
20
NO
Have all parameters D been tested ?
13
YES
(21)
Change parameters of actuators θ
NO
Want to synthesize unique controller
YES
Have all parameters θ been tested ?
NO
6
YES
EXIT
Change actuators parameters for synthesis of new local controllers
Have all parameters θ been tested ?
3
EXIT
22
Want global control ?
NO
EXIT
YES
Global control synthesis

Fig. 2.21. (Cont.)

(3) Set index i to 1 (i=1) - (subsystem index).

(4) Synthesize the ith local controller so as to stabilize the local decoupled ith subsystem using the algorithm presented in Fig. 2.20; in this step the complete algorithm for the local controller is used; as the output of this step we obtain local feedback gains and nominal local control which ensure the practical stability of the local subsystem (2.4.7) - where the coupling among subsystems is not taken into account.

(5) Increase index i by one; if i is smaller than or equal to n - go back to step (4) and synthesize local controller for the next subsystem; if i is larger than n go to the next step; at the end of this step local controllers are synthesized for all subsystems.

(6) Set initial values of the parameters of the mechanical part of the robot $d = d_o \in D$.

(7) Set initial time instant (t=0.).

(8) Determine the linearized model of the complete model of the robot according to (2.5.5); for this purpose we have to determine matrices $\partial H/\partial q$, $\partial h/\partial q$ and $\partial h/\partial \dot{q}$ using the algorithm for automatic linearizaiton of the mechanical part of the robotic system; we determine these matrices for the nominal values of coordinates q^o, $\dot{q}^o$ for the time instant t and parameters d.

(9) Determine the eigenvalues of the matrix A_L^o of the linearized model of robot; test the condition (2.5.7); if this condition is not satisfied, go back to step (3) and choose again the local controllers (increase the stability degree, or move the desired poles of closed-loop subsystems to the left in the complex plane); if the condition (2.5.7) is met, go to the next step.

(10) Increase time instant by Δt, $t := t+\Delta t$, where Δt is the desired time interval in which we want to examine system stability; check whether $t>\tau$, if yes, go to the next step (this means that we have analyzed the stability of the linearized model over the whole desired time interval T); if $t<\tau$, go back to step (8).

(11) Change parameters of the mechanical part of the robot $d \in D$; check

whether we have analyzed the stability of the linearized model for allowable values of mechanism parameters D; if yes, go to the next step; otherwise, go to step (7).

(12) From this step we start to analyze the stability of the nonlinear model of the robot; set initial values of the parameters of the mechanical part of the robot $d = d_o \in D$.

(13) Set initial time instant (t=0.).

(14) Set index i to 1 (i=1).

(15) Determine the number $\rho_i(t, d)$ such that (2.5.18) is satisfied for the ith joint of the robot.

(16) Determine numbers ξ_{ij} that satisfy inequality (2.5.13) for all $j \in I$. This is the most critical step in the algorithm. We have to carefully determine these numbers in order to make the analysis less conservative. A numerical procedure should be developed which searches along the complete finite region $\tilde{X}^t(t)$, $\forall t \in T$, to find maximum values of the coupling between subsystems. In this way we ensure a good (linear) estimation of the robotic system.

(17) Test condition (2.5.19), or (2.5.20) for the ith subsystem depending on whether we have chosen static local controller (2.4.19) or dynamic local controller (2.4.56); if the condition is not satisfied we have to change the ith local controller; thus, we should change parameters of the ith controller so as to increase the stability degree of the ith local subsystem; then, we should go back to step (4) and synthesize again the ith controller; however, we should constrain the stability degree of subsystems; in other words, we have to avoid too high local feedback gains; thus, we have to test whether the local gains (local stability degree) reach the imposed limits; if yes, we cannot find the acceptable local controller which can satisfy test of practical stability (2.5.19), or (2.5.20) and we must stop the algorithm; if local gains are within the given limits, go back to step (4) and try with a new local controller for the ith subsystem; if the test (2.5.19), or (2.5.20) is satisfied (for the ith joint) go to the next step of the algorithm.

(18) Increase index i by one (i: = i+1); test whether $i<n$; if yes, go back to step (15); if $i>n$ go to the next step.

(19) Increase time instant for Δt (t: = $t+\Delta t$); test whether $t<\tau$; if yes go back to step (14); if $t>\tau$, go to next step (this means that we have tested the practical stability of the robot over the complete time interval T).

(20) Change parameters of the mechanical part of the robot $d\in D$; check whether we have analyzed the practical stability of the nonlinear model of the robot for all allowable values of parameters $d\in D$; if yes go to the next step; otherwise, go back to step (13).

(21) Change parameters of the actuators $\theta\in\Theta$; in principle, we may try to synthesize unique local controllers which stabilize the robotic system for all allowable parameters of the actuators $\theta\in\Theta$; in that case we should preserve the already synthesized local controllers and go back to step (6) and test the practical stability of the robot for new values of parameters θ, but with old parameters of controllers; we have to check whether such controllers can accommodate all parameter variations; however, in general case, it is difficult to find unique local controllers which can stabilize the robotic system for various parameters of mechanism d and for various parameters of the actuators θ; on the other hand, as we have explained in Paragraph 2.4 the actuator parameters usually vary slowly and there is no need for synthesizing unique control for all allowable actuators parameters; it is sufficient to synthesize several local controllers corresponding to various values of actuator parameters and, from time to time, identify these parameters and if necessary, change, local feedback gains; in that case we should go back to step (2) and synthesize new local controllers for new values of actuators parameters θ; in this step we have to check whether all allowable actuators parameters have been already tested; if yes, we may terminate the algorithm.

This algorithm can be used to synthesize the decentralized controller (static or dynamic, with complete state feedback or with output feedback), which should satisfy control task (2.2.18): ensure the practical stability of the robot around given nominal trajectory $x^{o}(t)$, $\forall t\in T$. We obtain *unique* local controllers which accommodate all nonlinearities of the model and all expected parameter variations. This algorithm can be easily implemented by a digital computer to obtain computer-aided synthesis of decentralized controller for robotic system (see Chapter 4).

There are few evident numerical problems with the above algorithm, which have already been mentioned: search over finite region $X^t(t)$, $\forall t \in T$, to compute numbers ξ_{ij} satisfying (2.5.15), repeated synthesis of local controllers (how to define new parameters required in local control synthesis) etc. As already mentioned in Paragraph 2.4.4, the interaction with robotic system designer throughout the execution of the algorithm is of great importance. In our opinion, the completely automatic synthesis of control for robotic system without any interaction with designer is not recommendable. We suggest the development of an interactive algorithm, which should utilize designer's experience as much as possible (see Chapter 4). The designer should decide whether the algorithm should continue to iteratively search for the decentralized controller, which can accommodate the imposed control task (2.2.18), or the iteration should be stopped, and try to solve the problem by some different control. Also, the designer might be "included" in the loop to directly change the parameters of the local controllers in an appropriate way to achieve the practical stability of the robot and, thus, speed up the algorithm.

One of the problems connected with this synthesis is the decision about how high local feedback gains should be allowed. Due to the structure of the robotic system it is always possible to find local controllers which can stabilize the robot for constant parameters [59]. The problem is whether we could synthesize unique decentralized control which is robust enough to withstand all parameter variations. However, regardless of the problem of robustness of the decentralized controller, we have to answer the following question: shall we try to stabilize the robot with arbitrarily high local feedback gains, or introduce some additional feedback loops in order to satisfy the imposed control task. Namely, stabilization of the robotic system may require very high local feedback gains, because of the strong influence of coupling between subsystems which has to be compensated by a high stability degree of the subsystems. In other words, in order to satisfy conditions (2.5.19), if numbers ξ_{ij} (estimation of coupling) are large, we must increase γ_{ig} (estimation of the local subsystem stability degree). This can be achieved by higher local feedback gains. However, there are several drawbacks concerning the high feedback gains:

(a) In addition to feedback signals high feedback gains also amplify the noise that often appears in every system (noise due to chattering, vibrations, elastic modes of the robot, errors due to truncation of A/D and D/A convertors, etc.). This amplification of noise may lead to robot instability. Namely in the model of the robot considered up to now (Paragraph 2.2.1) we have not included all these effects, so the stability of the nonlinear model (2.5.1) cannot guarantee the stability of the actual robot (if these effects are too strong). For example, the model of the mechanical part of the robot (2.2.1) does not include the elastic modes of the mechanism, since we considered the mechanism as an open chain consisting of rigid links (see Chapter 1). If low gains are applied, this model is appropriate for most cases (if the links are sufficiently rigid, as is the case with most robots used in industrial practice today). However, if very high feedback gains are applied, this assumption is not valid any more: high amplification of weak elastic effects may cause high chattering of the robot and the elastic modes might become predominant. Thus, the rigid body model of robot mechanism is inappropriate in such regimes, and the above presented stability analysis is not valid.

(b) Too high local gains may lead to high suboptimality of the control with respect to a chosen criterion. We have shown in [2] how it is possible to estimate the suboptimality of the decentralized control (if nominal programmed control is applied). Here, we shall not discuss this problem in detail. We shall just remember that in [2] we have shown that by introducing additional (global) feedback loop we can reduce suboptimality of the decentralized controller. Actually, it is evident that too high local feedback gains can require too high energy consumption and that they are suboptimal from the standpoint of the required power supply.

For the above reasons, it is recommenable to avoid too high local gains. Evidently, by introducing additional feedback loops we can stabilize the robot with lower local gains. By this, we abandon the decentralized control structure and introduce global control. However, the problem is: how high local feedback gains may we allow, or, in other words, at which point should we break the above mentioned algorithm for decentralized control synthesis and introduce global control? This problem is difficult to solve in general case without considering more appropriate models of robots for high-gain regimes (i.e. the models that include elastic modes, the vibrations of robot basement, noise, etc.) and without considering control suboptimality. Both problems are out of the scope of this book, but, in our opinion, this decision should be left to the robot designer. He should, according to his own experience, decide whether he will try to find unique local controllers which satisfy the stated control task (2.2.18), or introduce additional global control.

2.6 Global Control Synthesis

If the unique decentralized controller which stabilizes the robotic system in a desired manner and which is robust enough to withstand all allowable parameter variations, cannot be determined, or if too high local feedback gains are required, we can introduce global control. The aim of the global control is to compensate for the influence of coupling among subsystems, i.e. to compensate for the dynamic interactions between joints of the robot.

The local controllers, synthesized in the previous Paragraph, stabilize local decoupled subsystems (i.e. decoupled joints and corresponding actuators). If the coupling between the subsystems (2.5.3) is weak in comparison with the local stability degree, the local controllers can withstand the influence of coupling. However, in case of strong coupling, we must introduce additional control loops to compensate for the coupling and ensure stability of the robot. In doing this we should try to preserve simplicity of the decentralized control structure, i.e. we should try to synthesize global control as simple as possible and introduce only those feedback loops which are necessary to achieve good tracking of desired trajectory.

Global control might be introduced in several ways. We shall first discuss the general form of global control law that follows from the analysis of the stability of the robotic system. The coupling term in the time derivative of function $v_i(t, x^i)$ is given by $(\text{grad}v_i)^T\tilde{f}^i(\theta^i)\cdot$ $\cdot z^i(q_i)\bar{P}_i(d, x)$. If we want to compensate for this term in equation (2.5.4) we may introduce control in the form [2, 70, 71]:

$$\Delta u_i^G = -k_i^G[(\text{grad}v_i)^T\tilde{b}^i]^{-1}(\text{grad}v_i)^T\tilde{f}^i(\theta^i)z^i(q_i)\bar{P}_i^*(d, t, x) \quad (2.6.1)$$

where $k_i^G \in R^1$ is the global gain (which has to be chosen) and $\bar{P}_i^*(d, t, x)$: $D \times T \times R^N \to R^1$ is the term which corresponds to term $\bar{P}_i(d, t, x)$ and the implementation of which will be discussed in the text to follow. If we consider the derivative of function v_i along the solution of the nonlinear model (2.5.1) and if we assume perfect (ideal) global control in which $P_i^*(d, t, x) = \bar{P}_i(d, t, x)$, $k_i^G = 1$, and if we neglect constraints upon the input of the subsystem we get:

$$\dot{v}_{i(\text{along}(2.5.1),\ (2.6.1))} = \dot{v}_{i(\text{along}\ (2.5.2))} + (\text{gradv}_i)^T\tilde{b}^i\Delta u_i^G +$$

$$(\text{gradv}_i)^T\cdot\tilde{f}^i(\theta^i)z^i(q_i)\cdot\bar{P}_i(t, d, x) = \dot{v}_{i(\text{along}\ (2.5.2))} \quad (2.6.2)$$

This means that, in an ideal case, by global control (2.6.1) we may achieve perfect compensation of coupling. In this case robotic system behaves as if it were perfectly decoupled to a set of independent subsystems-joints. This means that, in case of perfect compensation of coupling, the stability of the robot is proved by the stability of the decoupled subsystems.

Unfortunately, this perfect decoupling is impossible to achieve for several reasons. First, we cannot implement function $\bar{P}_i^*(d, t, x)$ such that perfectly coincides with real coupling $\bar{P}_i$, since the model of the system is not perfect and the parameters of the mechanical part of the robot d are not known in advance. Thus, in practice it is impossible to compute perfectly the driving torques in robotic joints. Second, real actuator inputs are constrained by amplitude. The control law (2.6.1) might require very high control signals: if $(\text{gradv}_i)^T\tilde{b}^i$ is a small value, the control signal might be very high and violate the amplitude limit upon the actuator input. In that case the control (2.6.1) cannot compensate for complete coupling even if $\bar{P}_i^*$ perfectly coincides with real coupling $\bar{P}_i$.

Actually, we have to limit the upper amplitude of global control, i.e. the value of $(\text{gradv}_i)^T\tilde{b}^i$ - since it might happen that $(\text{gradv}_i)^T\tilde{b}^i = 0$ which would require an infinite control signal. Thus, we may define the region $X^\varepsilon(t) \subset X^t(t)$, $\forall t \in T$, in the state space as:

$$X^\varepsilon(t) = X^{\varepsilon(1)}(t) \times X^{\varepsilon(2)}(t) \times \cdots \times X^{\varepsilon(n)}(t)$$

$$X^{\varepsilon(i)}(t) = \{x^i\colon (\text{gradv}_i)^T\tilde{b}^i < \varepsilon_i .\text{AND}. x^i \in X^{t(i)}(t)\}, \quad \forall t \in T \quad (2.6.3)$$

where $\varepsilon_i > 0$ are real-valued numbers which have to be chosen in the process of control synthesis. Instead of control (2.6.1), we have to apply the global control in the form:

$$\Delta u_i^G(t) = \begin{cases} -k_i^G[(\text{grad}v_i)^T\tilde{b}^i]^{-1}(\text{grad}v_i)^T\tilde{f}^i(\theta^i)z^i(q_i)\bar{P}_i^*(t,\ d,\ x) \\ \qquad \text{for } x^i \in X^{t(i)}(t).\text{AND}.x^i \notin X^{\varepsilon(i)}(t) \\ -k_i^G \cdot \varepsilon_i^{-1}(\text{grad}v_i)^T\tilde{f}^i(\theta^i)z^i(q_i)\bar{P}_i^*(t,\ d,\ x),\ x^i \in X^{\varepsilon(i)}(t) \end{cases} \tag{2.6.4}$$

Evidently, the global control (2.6.4) cannot perfectly compensate for the coupling between the subsystems in the region X^ε even if $\Delta\bar{P}_i^* = \Delta\bar{P}_i$.

Although the global control cannot perfectly decouple the robotic system in reality, this control is still capable of reducing the influence of coupling upon the stability of the robot. However, the efficiency of the global control mostly depends on the choice of function $\bar{P}_i^*$. In the text to follow we shall discuss three possible implementations of the global control:

(1) Force feedback can be used as global control. The coupling among subsystems is represented by driving torques (forces) acting around joints' axes. These torques or forces can be directly measured if we introduce force transducers in the joints. In this way we can get complete information about the coupling at each subsystem (joint), and theoretically, compensate for the total influence of coupling between the subsystems [2, 70, 71]. Namely, by measuring the forces in the joints we get the information on driving torques $P_i(d,\ x)$. If we consider subsystems without introducing the aggregate model of the mechanism (2.4.5), i.e. if we assume that $P_i^* = 0$, the coupling term is defined by $\tilde{f}^i(\theta^i)z^i(q_i)P_i$. By measuring P_i we can obtain the information about the complete (actual) coupling between the joints of robot and if we implement function $P_i^*(d,\ t,\ x) = P_i(d,\ x)$ in the global control (2.6.4) we can compensate for the complete influence of the robot dynamics upon its stability (obviously, this holds only if $x \in X^t(t)$ and $x \notin X^\varepsilon(t)$, $\forall t \in T$).

The control scheme with decentralized controller and global control with force feedback is presented in Fig. 2.22 (under the assumption that global control is introduced in all the joints of the robot).

This solution has some adventages:

(a) The information control structure is simple. By introducing force feedback as global control, we increase the number of

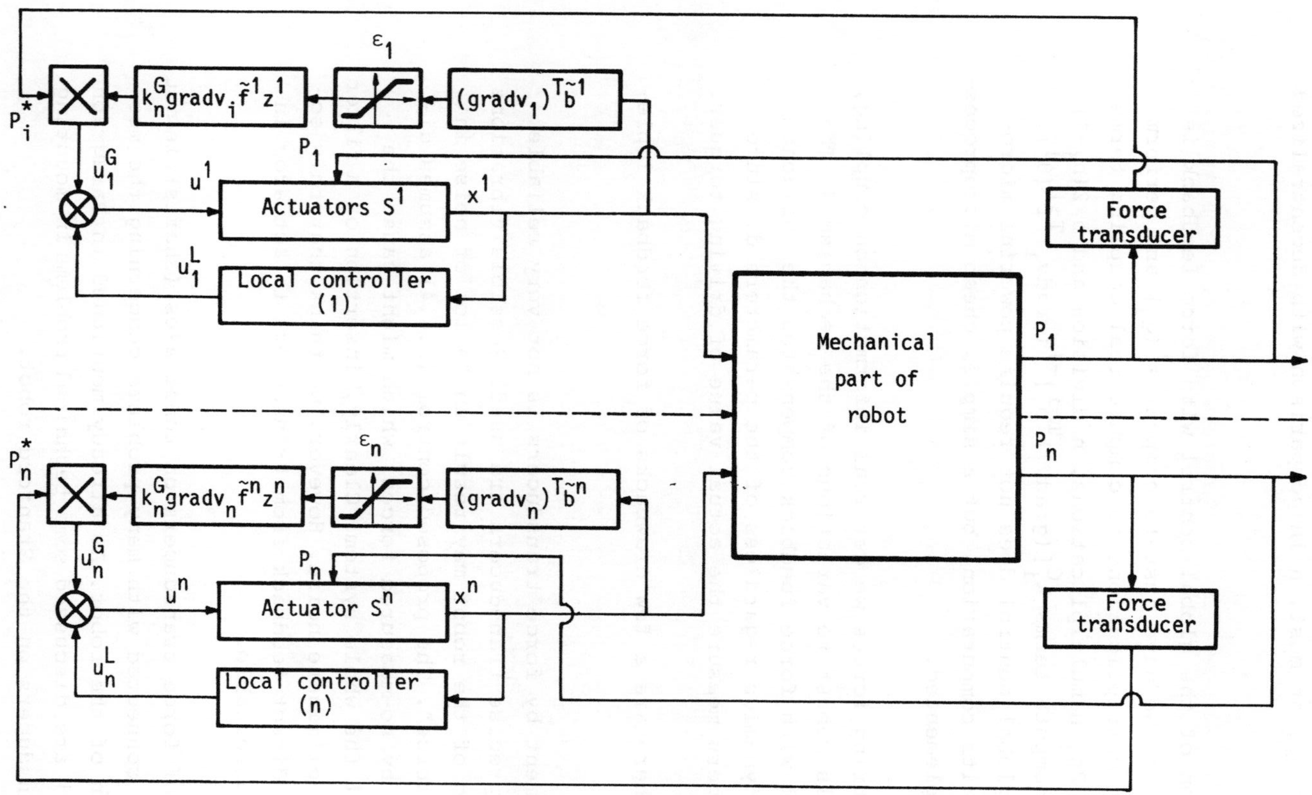

Fig. 2.22. Control scheme with global control implemented by force feedback

feedback loops by, at most, n in comparison with decentralized control.

(b) The computation of the global control with force feedback is extremely simple. We have just to compute $z^i(q_i)$ and perform no more than n multiplications to compute real coupling terms $z^i(q_i)\cdot P_i$ and $2n_i \times n$ multiplications, n division and $n \times 2(n_i-1)$ additions to compute terms $k_i^G[(\text{gradv}_i)^T\tilde{b}^i]^{-1}(\text{gradv}_i)^T\tilde{f}^i(\theta^i)$. Thus, such a global control does not require powerful microprocessor for its computation, but a simple, cheap microprocessor may be implemented.

(c) Since by measuring forces we get real information on coupling, this control is robust to variations of the mechanism d. The global control with force feedback compensates the influence of the robot dynamics regardless of the parameters d, since force transducers measure the actual value of driving torques.

Unfortunatelly, there are a few drawbacks of force feedback implementation:

(a) Force measurement by force transducers is not very reliable even if very precise transducers are used. Possible vibrations and chattering of the robot may result in "a lot of noise in the measured force". The proposed control (2.6.4) assumes direct feedback by so-measured forces, which might cause the instability of the whole system. Clearly, insertion of a filter might help to eliminate noise. However, we think that this solution with a direct feedback from transducers to actuator input might be unreliable.

(b) The mounting of force transducers on robot axes (shafts) is not simple and is connected with many problems concerning the mechanical design of the robot. As already mentioned in Paragraph 2.3.4, in [32] are discussed some technical problems in mounting the force transducers on the Stanford robot.

(c) The price of force transducers is not negligible. Since highly precise transducers are required to obtain accurate information on forces in the joints, their price may happen to be compatible with the price of microprocessors that would be needed to compute torques (if the global control is implemented by on-line computation of the robot driving torques-see the text to follow). Thus, the benefits of introducing force feedback as the global control should be carefully studied.

(2) The second possible implementation of global control is by on-line computation of the robot dynamics using its mathematical model (2.2.1). We can compute the driving torques acting in robot joints, and, in that case, function $\bar{P}_i^*(d, t, x)$ in (2.6.4) represents the computed driving torque in the ith joint. If the parameters of the robot d were precisely known in advance, and if the model of the robot dynamics were sufficiently accurrate, we should achieve the perfect compensation of coupling. However, these two assumptions are rarely satisfied in practice. On the other hand, as we have stated for several times, the driving torques are, in general case, very complex functions of all state variables. Thus such a computation of the driving torque might be very cumbersome and time consuming, and it might require a powerful multiprocessor system to achieve a sampling period compatible with the dynamics of the robot. This solution of the global control leads to a very complex information control structure, so the simplicity of the decentralized structure is lost. Actually, by this implementation of global control we face the same problems as those listed for the "inverse problem" technique (Paragraph 2.3.3):

(a) complexity of the information structure,

(b) complex computation requiring a powerful control multiprocessor system,

(c) sensitivity of the control to parameter variations.

The control scheme with global control which utilizes the computed driving torques is presented in Fig. 2.23.

We can simplify the computation of coupling by using the approximate model of the robot dynamics. In Paragraph 2.3.3 we have already mentioned several possible approximation models of the robot dynamics. Here we shall list some of the approximate models which may be used to compute global control:

(a) The simplest approximate model includes just gravity forces (moments) in the robot joints, which have to be compensated by global control in order to reduce static errors of local controllers. Thus, the functions $\bar{P}_i^*$ are given by:

$$\bar{P}_i^*(x, d^*) = g_i(q, d^*) \tag{2.6.5}$$

where $g_i(q)$ is the gravity moment (force) acting around the ith joint (for particular values of parameters d^*).

(b) A more complex model includes on-line computation of diagonal elements in the inertia matrix $H(q, d)$ (i.e. the eigen-inertia factors around each joint of the robot)*). Thus, the functions $\bar{P}_i^*$ are given by:

$$\bar{P}_i^*(x, d^*) = H_{ii}(q, d^*)\ddot{q}_i + g_i(q, d^*) \tag{2.6.6}$$

where H_{ii} is the ith diagonal element in the inertia matrix $H(q, d^*)$.

(c) The next approximate model of the robot dynamics includes the complete inertia matrix. In addition to the diagonal elements we should compute in real time cross-inertia terms, i.e. off-diagonal elements in inertia matrix $H(q, d)$. The functions $\bar{P}_i^*$ that have to be computed are given by:

$$\bar{P}_i^*(x, d^*) = H_i(q, d^*)\ddot{q} + g_i(q, d^*) \tag{2.6.7}$$

where by $H_i(q, d^*)$ we denote the ith row in the inertia matrix $H(q, d^*)$, $H_i \in R^n$.

(d) A more complex model of the robot dynamics also includes the centrifugal forces. Thus, the computed functions $\bar{P}_i^*$ include the following terms:

$$\bar{P}_i^*(x, d^*) = H_i(q, d^*)\ddot{q} + g_i(q, d^*) + \dot{q}^T C^i(q, d^*)\dot{q} \tag{2.6.8}$$

---

*) It should be noted that these inertia factors and gravity forces might be included in the model of subsystems as the aggregate model (2.4.5). However, we have assumed inertia factors $\bar{H}_{ii}$ to be constant and the gravity term linear by $x^i(\bar{h}^i q_i)$. Here, the nonlinear inertia and gravity terms are computed for global control.

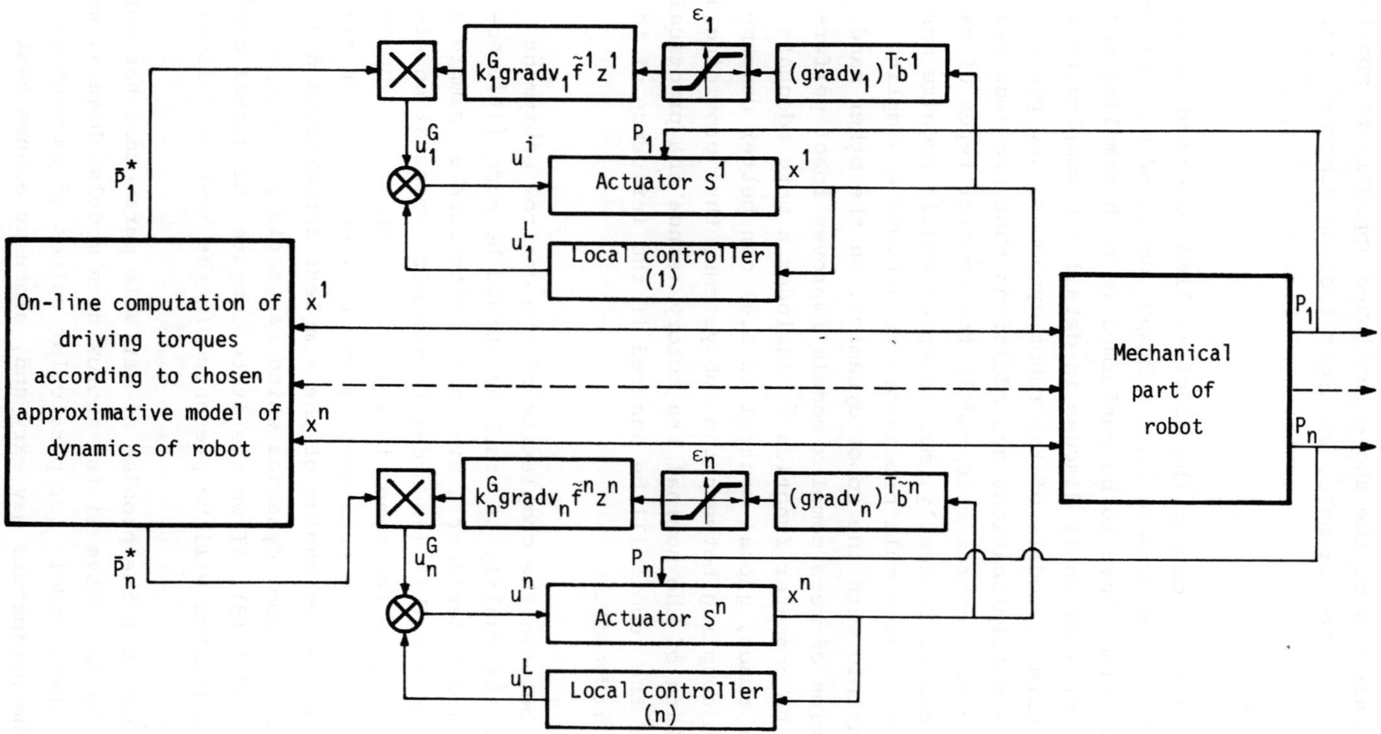

Fig. 2.23. Control scheme with global control implemented by on-line computation of the robot dynamics

where $C^i(q, d^*)$ denotes the n×n "matrix of centrifugal forces".

Various combinations of the above mentioned approximate models might be applied. For example, we might include diagonal inertia elements $H_{ii}(q, d^*)$ and centrifugal forces $\dot{q}^T C^i(q, d^*)\dot{q}$ in the computed model.

Evidently, the more complex the model applied, the more computational efforts we have to make (i.e. a larger number of multiplications and additions have to be performed in each sampling period). In Chapter 5 we shall discuss in detail the complexity of various approximate models of the robot dynamics, and present the number of multiplications and additions that are required to compute various approximate models for several types of manipulation robots. Evidently, more complex models require more complex and expensive multiprocessors to achieve a sampling period compatible with the robot dynamics. On the other hand, the application of more complex models improves robot performances. If the computer function $\bar{P}_i^*$ includes a more adequate model of the robot, global control (2.6.4) can better compensate for the coupling between the subsystems, thus providing a better tracking of the nominal trajectory (since the practical stability of the robot will be ensured if the influence of the coupling is reduced).

A trade-off between the complexity of the control equipment required and the quality of tracking should be made [10]. Actually, the robot designer's aim is to synthesize as simple a control law as possible (in order to minimize computation efforts) ensuring, at the same time, satisfaction of the imposed control task. To solve this problem we shall establish an algorithm for iterative choice of the simplest approximate dynamic model of the robot dynamics which can satisfy the imposed control task (2.2.18), if we use it to compute the global control. This algorithm will be presented in the text to follow.

We should note that the problem of variable parameters has not been solved by the above listed approximate models. Namely, we can compute these models for particular values of parameters $d^* \in D$, but the parameters may vary and, since we assume that their variations are not known in advance, we cannot compensate for these variations. However, we can still partially reduce the influence of the robot dynamics upon its performance by computing on-line approximate models even with constant parameters d^*. This will be explained in the text to follow.

(3) The third possible implementation of the global control which we shall consider here is called "robust global control" [72]. This global control has the following form:

$$\Delta u_i^G = -k_i^G[(\text{grad}v_i)^T\tilde{b}^i]^{-1}\cdot\bar{u}_m^i \tag{2.6.9}$$

where $\bar{u}_m^i$ is some constant (maximum) value, which has to be chosen in the process of control synthesis. Actually, the value $\bar{u}_m^i$ might be chosen to satisfy.

$$\bar{u}_m^i > \max|[(\text{grad}v_i)^T\tilde{f}^i(\theta^i)z^i(q^i)\bar{P}_i^*(t,\ x,\ d)]| \tag{2.6.10}$$

where the maximum is taken over region $\forall x\in X^t(t)$, $\forall t\in T$, $\forall d\in D$, $\forall\theta\in\Theta$. However, since the actuators' inputs are constrained by (2.2.4), the global control is also constrained by amplitude, so we cannot always reach the condition (2.6.10). The control scheme with the global control (2.6.9) is presented in Fig. 2.24.

The main advantage of this form of global control is its extreme simplicity and the fact that it does not depend on mechanism parameters. However, since this global control actually has the form of "bang-bang" control law, it suffers from all the disadvantages of "bang-bang" control:

(a) chattering of control signals which might produce oscillatory motion of the robot and its unstability (due to the presence of elastic modes of the robot which are not included in its model (2.2.1));

(b) high suboptimality of such control since it permanently sends the maximum signal regardless of the value of the coupling between the subsystems which may be less;

(c) the energy consumption required by this control law might be very high.

To prevent chattering of the control around the nominal trajectory, the control (2.6.9) is modified in [72]:

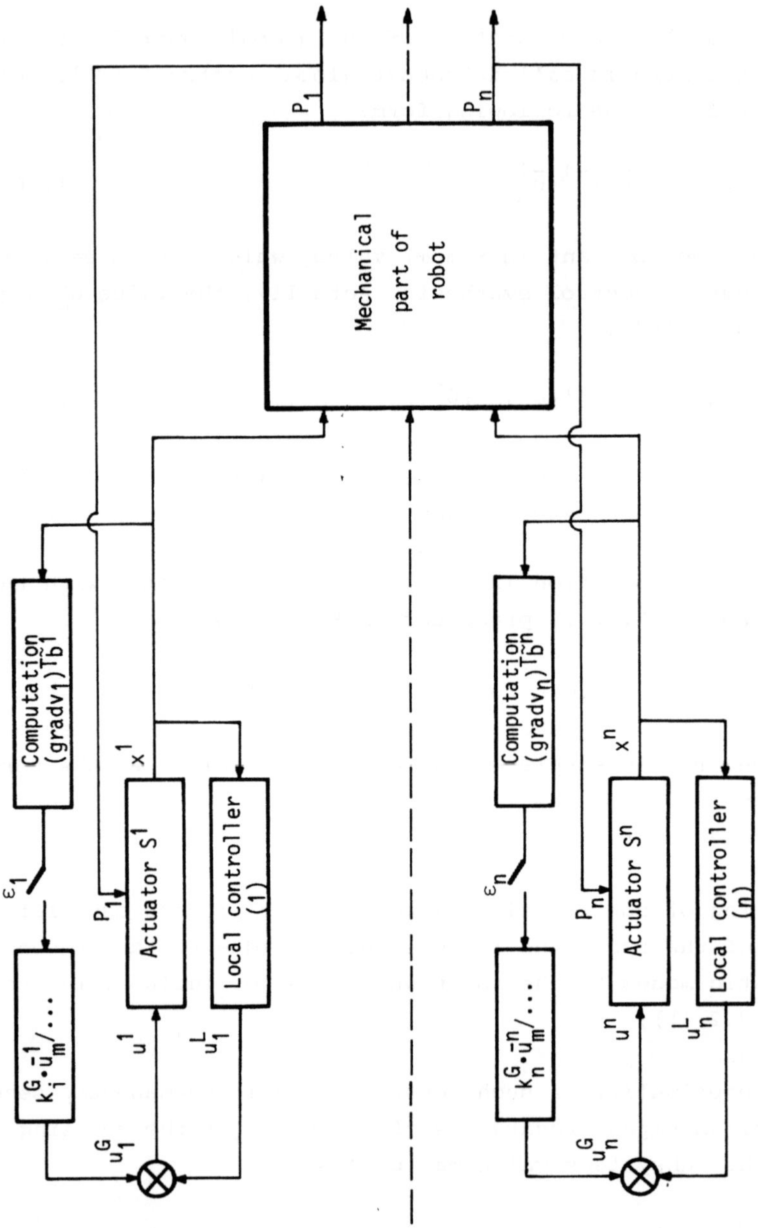

Fig. 2.24. Control scheme with "robust global control"

$$\Delta u_i^G = \begin{cases} -k_i^G[(\text{grad}v_i)^T\tilde{b}^i]^{-1}\bar{u}_m^i & \text{for} \quad (\text{grad}v_i)^T\tilde{b}^i > \varepsilon_i \\ 0 & \text{for} \quad (\text{grad}v_i)^T\tilde{b}^i < \varepsilon_i \end{cases} \tag{2.6.11}$$

where $\varepsilon_i > 0$ is an arbitrary number which should be chosen in the process of control synthesis. However, the choice of the number ε_i is very difficult; if we choose a small number ε_i, chattering of the control signal might still appear; on the other hand, if ε_i is large, it is questionable whether this control law can stabilize the robot and ensure tracking of the nominal trajectory (since the coupling between subsystems is not compensated for by the global control (2.6.11) in the region $X^\varepsilon(t)$, $\forall t \in T$). Thus, this control law, although very simple and robust to parameter variations, may result in poor tracking of nominal trajectory*).

Having presented three possible implementations of global control, we shall now describe how we can analyze the stability of the robot with various forms of global control.

Let us consider the stability of the nonlinear model of the robot (2.2.2) if the control in the form:

$$u^i = \bar{u}^{oi}(t) + \Delta u_i^L(\Delta x^i) + \Delta u_i^G(\Delta x^i, \bar{P}_i^*(d^*, t, x)) \tag{2.6.12}$$

is applied. If the local control is taken as (2.4.19) the nonlinear model with the control (2.6.12) can be written as:

$$\Delta\dot{x}^i = (\tilde{A}^i - \lambda_{ig}\tilde{b}^i r_i^{-1}\tilde{b}^i K_i)\Delta x^i + \tilde{b}^i N_G(t, \Delta x^i, \Delta u_i^G) + $$

$$+ \tilde{f}^i(\theta^i)\cdot z^i(q_i)\cdot\bar{P}_i(t, x, d) \tag{2.6.13}$$

where $N_G(t, \Delta x^i, \Delta u_i^G)$ is the constraint upon the global control amplitude:

$$N_G(t, \Delta x^i, \Delta u_i^G) = \begin{cases} u_m^{iG}(t, \ x^i) & \text{if} \quad \Delta u_i^G > u_m^{iG} \\ \Delta u_i^G & \text{if} \quad -u_m^{iG} < \Delta u_i^G < u_m^{iG} \\ -u_m^{iG} & \text{if} \quad \Delta u_i^G \leqslant -u_m^{iG} \end{cases} \tag{2.6.14}$$

---

*) Actually, the control (2.6.11) does not compensate for the influence of the robot dynamics along nominal trajectory, so it cannot ensure the practical stability of the robot.

with $u_m^{iG}(t, \Delta x^i)$ standing for $u_m^{iG} = \pm u_m^i - \bar{u}^{oi}(t) - \Delta u_i^L(\Delta x^i)$.

To analyze the stability of the robot, let us consider the derivative of function $v_i(t, \Delta x^i)$ (introduced in Paragraph 2.4.4) with respect to the solution of model (2.6.13). As we have written in (2.6.2), the time derivative of function $v_i(t, x^i)$ is given by:

$$\dot{v}_{i(\text{along } (2.6.13))} = \dot{v}_{i(\text{along } (2.5.2))} + \\ + (\text{grad} v_i)^T \tilde{b}^i N_G(t, \Delta x^i, \Delta u_i^G) + \\ + (\text{grad} v_i)^T \tilde{f}(\theta^i) \cdot z^i(q_i) \cdot \bar{P}_i(t, d, x) \quad (2.6.15)$$

Analogously to (2.5.9), we shall divide the function $\bar{P}_i^*(t, d, x)$ into two parts*):

$$\bar{P}_i^*(t, d^*, x) = \bar{P}_i^{o*}(t, d^*, x^o(t)) + \Delta\bar{P}_i^*(t, d^*, \Delta x) \quad (2.6.16)$$

where $\bar{P}_i^{o*}$ denotes the value of function $\bar{P}_i^*$ for nominal coordinates $x^o(t)$, $\forall t \in T$, and $\Delta\bar{P}_i^*$ the difference between $\bar{P}_i^*$ (for actual state coordinates x) and $\bar{P}_i^{o*}$ (for nominal state coordinates $x^o(t)$). Let us substitute (2.6.16) in (2.6.4), and consider coupling term and global control term in (2.6.15):

$$(\text{grad} v_i)^T \tilde{b}^i N_G(t, \Delta x^i, \Delta u_i^G) + (\text{grad} v_i)^T \tilde{f}^i(\theta^i) z^i(q_i) \bar{P}_i(t, d, x) =$$

$$= \begin{cases} (\text{grad} v_i)^T \tilde{f}^i(\theta^i) z^i(q^{oi}) \cdot (\bar{P}_i^o - k_i^G \bar{P}_i^{o*}) + (\text{grad} v_i)^T \tilde{f}^i(\theta^i) \cdot [z^i(q_i) \cdot \\ (\Delta\bar{P}_i - k_i^G \Delta\bar{P}_i^*) + \Delta z^i(q_i)(\bar{P}_i^o - k_i^G \bar{P}_i^{o*})] \text{ for } x^i \in X^{t(i)}(t) . \text{AND}. x^i \notin X^{\varepsilon(i)}(t) \\ (\text{grad} v_i)^T f^i(\theta^i) z^i(q^{oi}) [P_i^o - k_i^G (\text{grad} v_i)^T \tilde{b}^i \cdot \bar{P}_i^{o*} / \varepsilon_i] + \\ + (\text{grad} v_i)^T \tilde{f}(\theta^i) \cdot \{z^i(q_i) [\Delta P_i - k_i^G (\text{grad} v_i)^T \tilde{b}^i \Delta P_i^* / \varepsilon_i] + \\ + \Delta z^i(q_i) [\bar{P}_i^o - k_i^G (\text{grad} v_i)^T \tilde{b}^i \cdot \bar{P}_i^{o*} / \varepsilon_i]\} \text{ for } x^i \in X^{\varepsilon(i)}(t) \end{cases} \quad (2.6.17)$$

where we have neglected (for simplicity) the amplitude constraint upon global control (2.6.14). Now, analogously to what we have done in Paragraph 2.5, we can consider separately two parts of coupling: "nominal

---

*) Obviously this consideration does not hold for global control (2.6.9). It is very simple to establish stability test for this global control.

coupling" and the deviation of coupling from the nominal value. This second part of coupling together with the corresponding part of global control can be estimated by:

$$\sum_{j=1}^{n} \xi_{ij}^{*} ||\Delta x^j|| > \begin{cases} (\text{gradv}_i)^T \tilde{f}^i(\theta^i)[z^i(q_i)(\Delta P_i - k_i^G \Delta P_i^*) + \\ +\Delta z^i(q_i)(\bar{P}_i^o - k_i^G \bar{P}_i^{o*})] \text{ for } x \in X^t(t) .\text{AND}. x^i \notin X^{\varepsilon(i)}(t) \\ (\text{gradv}_i) f^i(\theta^i)\{z^i(q_i)[\Delta \bar{P}_i - k_i^G (\text{gradv}_i)^T \tilde{b}^i \Delta P_i^* / \varepsilon_i] + \\ +\Delta z^i(q_i)[\bar{P}_i^* - k_i^G (\text{gradv}_i)^T \tilde{b}^i \bar{P}_i^{o*}/\varepsilon_i]\} \\ \qquad \text{for } x \in X^t(t) .\text{AND}. x^i \in X^{\varepsilon(i)}(t) \end{cases} \quad (2.6.18)$$

where $\xi_{ij}^{*} > 0$ are constant numbers. The relation should hold for $\forall d \in D$ and $\forall t \in T$. It should be noted that it is always possible to determine numbers ξ_{ij}^{*} satisfying (2.6.18) since ΔP_i^* also satisfies (analogously to (2.5.12)):

$$\lim_{\Delta x^j \to 0, \forall j \in I} \Delta P_i^*(t, \Delta x, d^*) \to 0, \quad \forall d^* \in D, \ \forall t \in T \quad (2.6.19)$$

In (2.6.18) we have not included the nonlinear constraint upon global control (2.6.14), but, this constraint has to be taken into account when numbers ξ_{ij}^{*} are determined.

Considering the "nominal coupling" and its corresponding part of the global control, analogously to (2.5.18) we may write:

$$\rho_i^*(t, d) > \begin{cases} \int_o^t z^i(q^{oi})[\bar{P}_i^o(t', d) - k_i^G \bar{P}_i^{o*}(t', d)]dt', \\ \int_o^t z^i(q^{oi})[\bar{P}_i^o(t', d) - k_i^G \min\limits_{x^i \in X^{\varepsilon(i)}(t)} (\text{gradv}_i) ||\tilde{b}^i|| \cdot \bar{P}_i^{o*}(t', d^*)/\varepsilon_i]dt' \end{cases} \quad (2.6.20)$$

We have to determine the function $\rho_i^*(t, d)$ so that both inequalities (2.6.20) are satisfied.

Now, if we substitute (2.6.17) and (2.6.18) into (2.6.15) we get:

$$\dot{v}_{i(\text{along } (2.6.13))} < \dot{v}_{i(\text{along } (2.5.2))} + \sum_{j=1}^{n} \xi_{ij}^{*} ||\Delta x^j|| +$$
$$+ (\text{gradv}_i)^T \tilde{f}^i(\theta^i) z^i(q^{oi}) \cdot (\bar{P}^o - k_i^G \cdot \bar{P}_i^{o*}) \quad (2.6.21)$$

If we consider the state of the robot satisfying $x \in \partial X^t(t)$, and take function $v_i(t, x^i)$ in the form (2.5.43), (2.5.47) we get:

$$\dot{v}_{i(\text{along }(2.6.13))} < -\gamma_{ig}\lambda_m^{1/2}(H_i)\bar{X}^{I(i)}\exp(-\alpha^{(i)}t) + \sum_{j=1}^{n}\xi_{ij}^{*}\bar{X}^{t(j)}$$

$$\cdot\exp(-\alpha^{(j)}t) + (\text{grad}v_i)^T\tilde{f}^i(\theta^i)z^i(q^{oi})(\bar{P}^o - k_i^G\cdot\bar{P}_i^{o*}) = \psi_i'(t, d),$$

$$\forall x\in\tilde{X}^t(t),\ \forall t\in T,\ \forall d\in D \qquad (2.6.22)$$

To test the practical stability of the robot, we have to test condition (2.5.16) for all subsystems. Thus, taking into account relation (2.6.20), we get the stability test in the form:

$$-\gamma_{ig}\lambda_m^{1/2}(H_i)\bar{X}^{I(i)}(1-\exp(-\alpha^{(i)}t))/\alpha^{(i)} + \sum_{j=1}^{n}\xi_{ij}^{*}\cdot\frac{\bar{X}^{t(j)}}{\alpha^{(j)}}[1-\exp(-\alpha^{(j)})] +$$

$$+\frac{\lambda_M(H_i)}{\lambda_m^{1/2}(H_i)}||\tilde{f}^i(\theta^i)||\rho_i^{*}(t,d) < \lambda_m^{1/2}(H_i)\bar{X}^{t(i)}\exp(-\alpha^{(i)}t) -$$

$$-\lambda_M^{1/2}(H_i)\bar{X}^{I(i)},\quad \forall t\in T,\ \forall i\in I,\ \forall d\in D \qquad (2.6.23)$$

If conditions (2.6.23) are satisfied, we can guarantee that the robot is practically stable with control (2.6.12) i.e. that it satisfies control task (2.2.18). Clearly, conditions (2.6.23) are sufficient but not necessary for practical stability. We may use tests (2.6.23) for the synthesis of global control which can stabilize the robot. Actually we can determine the simplest global control which should satisfy the stated control task. To achieve this, we shall establish an iterative algorithm for the synthesis of global control. Before establishing this algorithm we have to make several remarks concerning the global control and analysis of the practical stability of the robot if global control is applied.

(I) Tests (2.6.23 correspond to static local controllers (2.4.19). By analogy, we can write these conditions for dynamic local controllers (2.4.56), if we choose functions $v_i(t, \hat{x}^i)$ in form (2.4.57). Of course, control (2.6.1) must take into account the fact that the subsystems are extended and that functions v_i also include an additional state coordinate.

(II) In conditions (2.6.23) we have introduced numbers γ_{ig} which take into account amplitude constraints upon the actuators inputs. If conditions (2.4.67) are not satisfied for some of the subsystems, it means that a local control signal reaches the amplitude constraint in the region $X^t(t)$. This, in turn, means that $u_m^{iG}(t, \Delta x^i)$ in (2.6.14) may be zero, and this leads to conclusion that there is "no room left for global control signal". Nevertheless, even in this case application of global control may be effective. Since the coupling is a nonlinear function of robot state, it may happen that the maximum coupling is not achieved for $x \in \partial X^t(t)$ but for some other $x \in X^t(t)$, $\forall t \in T$. Thus, although the global control signal may be zero for $x^i \in \partial X^{t(i)}(t)$, it may compensate for the maximum coupling and, thus, reduce numbers ξ^*_{ij} in (2.6.18) in comparison to ξ_{ij} in (2.5.13). It must be remembered that in determining numbers ξ^*_{ij} in (2.6.18) and functions $\rho^*_i(t, d)$ in (2.6.20) we must take into account amplitude constraints upon global control (2.6.14), i.e. for each $x \in X^t(t)$, $\forall t \in T$ we must test (2.6.14) and then determine the global control signal and, for this control signal, determine numbers ξ^*_{ij} and functions $\rho^*_i(t, d)$.

(III) The robustness of the above presented global control laws has to be carefully studied. The control law (1) with force feedback is obviously robust to parameter variations since it uses information on actual forces measured on the robot. However, problems arise when we want to apply global control law (2) to a robot with variable parameters. As we have already noted, we may compute the driving torques using the approximate model of the robot dynamics for some particular values of parameters $d^* \in D$. Evidently, if the parameters of the robot differ from d^*, the global control cannot compensate for influence of the corresponding forces (which are taken into account in the robot model). However, we may still expect that such global control can reduce the influence of coupling for all allowable parameter variations. For example, let us assume that a parameter d_1 varies between d_{1min} and d_{1max} and that the cross-inertia element H_{ij} linearly depends on d_1 ($H_{ij} = k'd_1+k''$). If we compute this factor for the parameter value d_{1min} ($H^*_{ij}=k'd_{1min}+k''$) and use the so-computed term for global control ($\Delta u^G_i \sim H^*_{ij}\ddot{q}_j$), then we may reduce the influence of this term (it reduces to $[k'(d_1 - d_{1\,min})]$ for all allowable parameter values, although we compute it for only one particular value. It should be noted that the values of parameters should be chosen so as to minimize the numbers ξ^*_{ij} in (2.6.18) and functions ρ^*_i in (2.6.20). The algorithm which we shall present below iteratively searches for such d^* for which the global control can accommodate all parameter variations and ensure practical stability for $\forall d \in D$.

(IV) The form of global control (2.6.1) follows from equation (2.6.2), i.e. from the condition to reduce the influence of the coupling in the time derivative of functions $v_i(t, x^i)$ (or, in other words, to reduce numbers ξ^*_{ij}). This form actually takes into account the dynamics of the actuators through the factor $[(\text{grad}v_i)^T\tilde{b}^i]^{-1}(\text{grad}v_i)^T\cdot$ $\cdot\tilde{f}^i(\theta^i)$. The computation of this terms is not complex but it requires $2n_i$ multiplications, $2(n_i-1)$ additions and one division. We may desire to use a simpler form of the global control and to neglect the dynamics of the actuators in the global control. If we consider the second-order model of actuator $n_i=2$ (see Appendix 2.A), then vectors $\tilde{b}^i$ and $\tilde{f}^i$ have forms $\tilde{b}^i=(0, \tilde{\tilde{b}}^i)^T$ and $\tilde{f}^i=(0,\tilde{\tilde{f}}^i)^T$. If functions $v_i(t, x^i)$ are of form (2.4.43), then $\text{grad}v_i=(H^i_{11}x_1+$ $+H^i_{12}x_2,\ H^i_{21}x_1+H^i_{22}x_2)^T/2v_i$ where H^i_{kj} are the elements of the matrix H^i. In this case the global control (2.6.4) reduces to:

$$\Delta u_i^G = -k_i^G\tilde{\tilde{f}}^i(\theta^i)/\tilde{\tilde{b}}^i\cdot z^i(q_i)\bar{P}_i^*(t, x, d^*) \tag{2.6.24}$$

and there is no need to introduce the region $X^\varepsilon(t)$, $\forall t\in T$. Obviously, control (2.6.24) is much simpler than (2.6.4). Actually, in (2.6.24) we have neglected the delays in actuators which always exist (although they may be negligible if we consider relatively slow motions - see Appendix 2.A).

A compromise between control laws (2.6.4) and (2.6.24) has been suggested in [2] as:

$$\Delta u_i^G = k_i^G\tilde{\tilde{f}}^i(\theta^i)/\tilde{\tilde{b}}^i\ \text{sgn}(\Delta u_i^L(\Delta x^i))\cdot z^i(q_i)\cdot\bar{P}_i^*(t, x, d^*) \tag{2.6.25}$$

where $\text{sgn}(\Delta u_i^L(\Delta x^i))$ denotes the sign of the corresponding value, i.e.

$$\text{sgn}(\Delta u_i^L(\Delta x^i)) = \begin{cases} +1 & \text{if} \quad \Delta u_i^L(\Delta x^i)>0 \\ -1 & \text{if} \quad \Delta u_i^L(\Delta x^i)<0 \end{cases}$$

In [2] we have explained why we have chosen the global control of form (2.6.25).

Obviously, both forms of global control, (2.6.24) and (2.6.25), can be tested for practical stability using the same procedure as we have described above for control (2.6.4).

(V) We can estimate the suboptimality of control (2.6.12) with respect to a chosen criterion, as we have done in [2] for the case when nominal programmed control, synthesized with the complete centralized model of the robot, is applied. However, this is out of the scope of this book, but it is evident that the introduction of global control may reduce the suboptimality of the control compared with the suboptimality of the local controllers.

We shall now briefly establish the algorithm for synthesizing the global control which stabilizes the robotic system around the given nominal trajectory for all allowable parameters of the mechanism and actuators. The algorithm is intended to determine the simplest global control which satisfies stability test (2.6.23). Actually, we have to choose the form of global control; the form of approximate model $\bar{P}_i^*(t, x, d^*)$ (or to choose control laws (1) or (3)) and to determine the global gains k_i^G and numbers ε_i. A brief flow-chart of the algorithm is presented in Fig. 2.25. It includes the algorithm for the synthesis of decentralized controller presented in Fig. 2.21. Actually, this algorithm represents one step in the algorithm for global control synthesis.

The algorithm can be performed according to the following steps:

(1) The synthesis of decentralized control is performed acc. to the algorithm presented in Fig. 2.21. If it is possible to determine a unique decentralized controller which satisfies control task (2.2.18) and if the obtained local feedback gains are not too high, there is no need to synthesize global control. If it is impossible to synthesize adequate local control we should introduce global control. Let us assume that for the jth subsystem (joint) it is impossible to find adequate local controller, so we want to introduce the global control for this subsystem, while for all subsystems $i<j$ we have found local controller which satisfy practical stability of the system.

(2) We have to decide which form of the global control we want to implement. If the algorithm should make this decision automatically, then we may start with the simplest form of global control (2.6.24). If this form has already been tested, the algorithm should choose form (2.6.25). If this form has already tested, the algorithm should choose the most complex form (2.6.4).

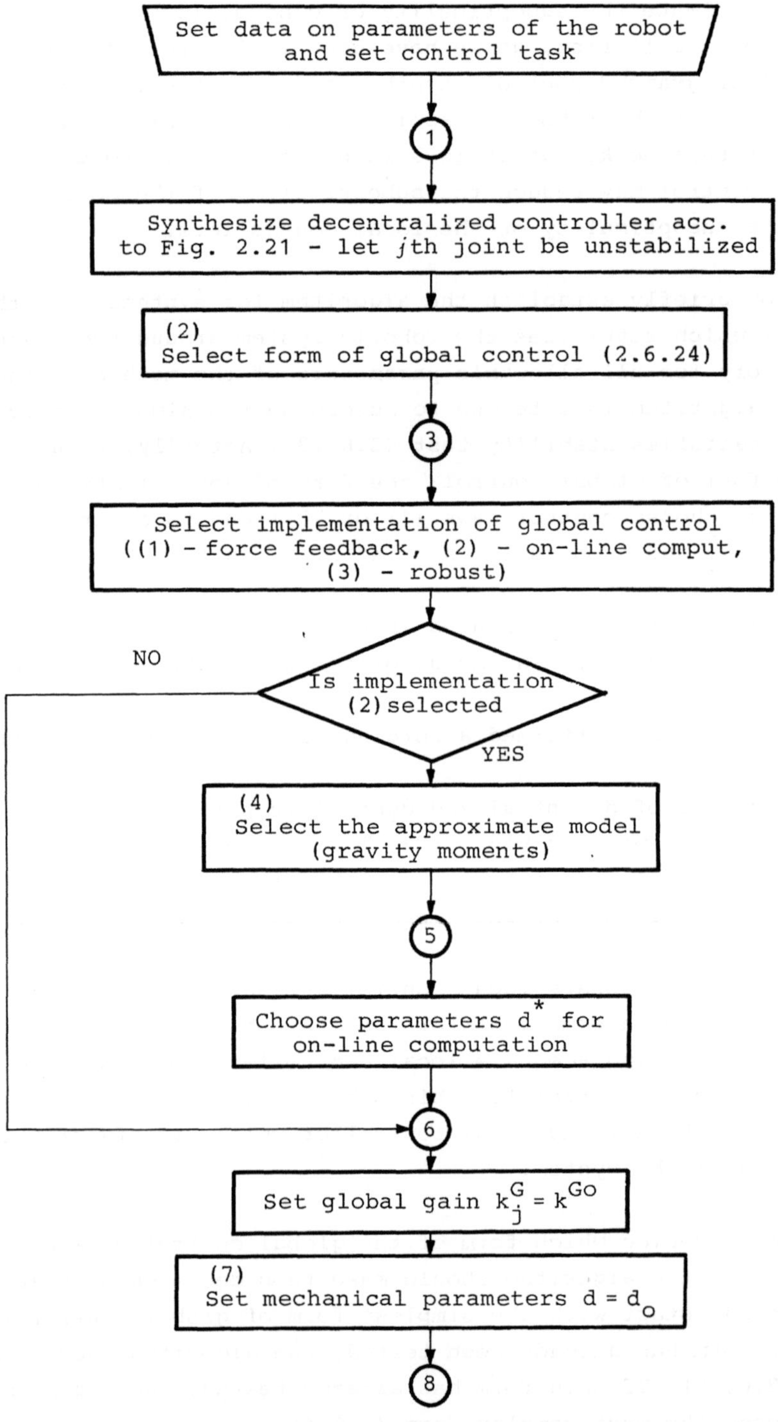

Fig. 2.25. Flow-chart of the algorithm for global control synthesis

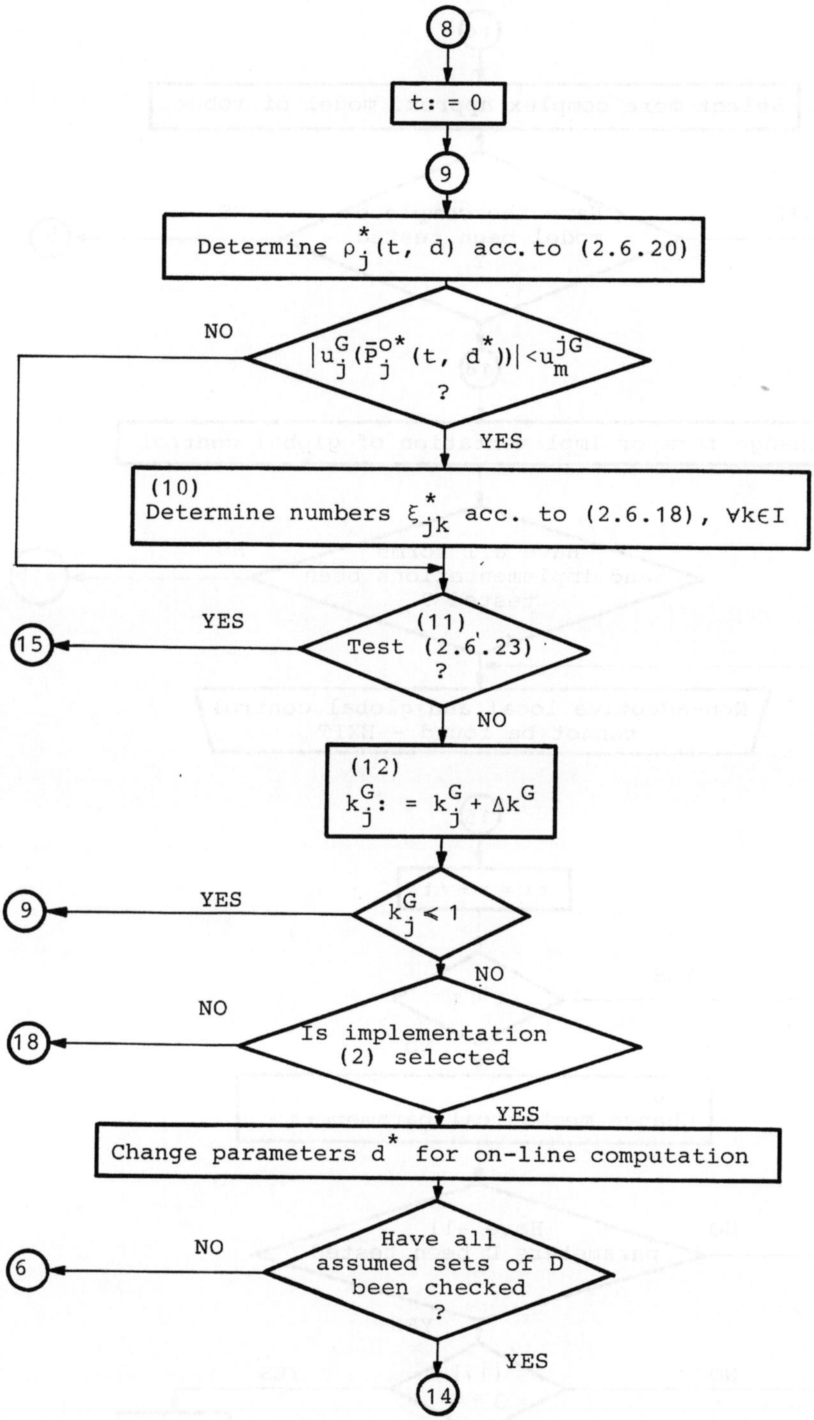
8
t: = 0
9
Determine $\rho_j^*(t, d)$ acc. to (2.6.20)
NO
$|u_j^G(\bar{P}_j^{o*}(t, d^*))| < u_m^{jG}$?
YES
(10)
Determine numbers ξ_{jk}^* acc. to (2.6.18), $\forall k \in I$
YES
15
(11)
Test (2.6.23) ?
NO
(12)
$k_j^G: = k_j^G + \Delta k^G$
9
YES
$k_j^G < 1$
NO
NO
18
Is implementation (2) selected
YES
Change parameters d^* for on-line computation
NO
6
Have all assumed sets of D been checked ?
YES
14

Fig. 2.25. (Cont.)

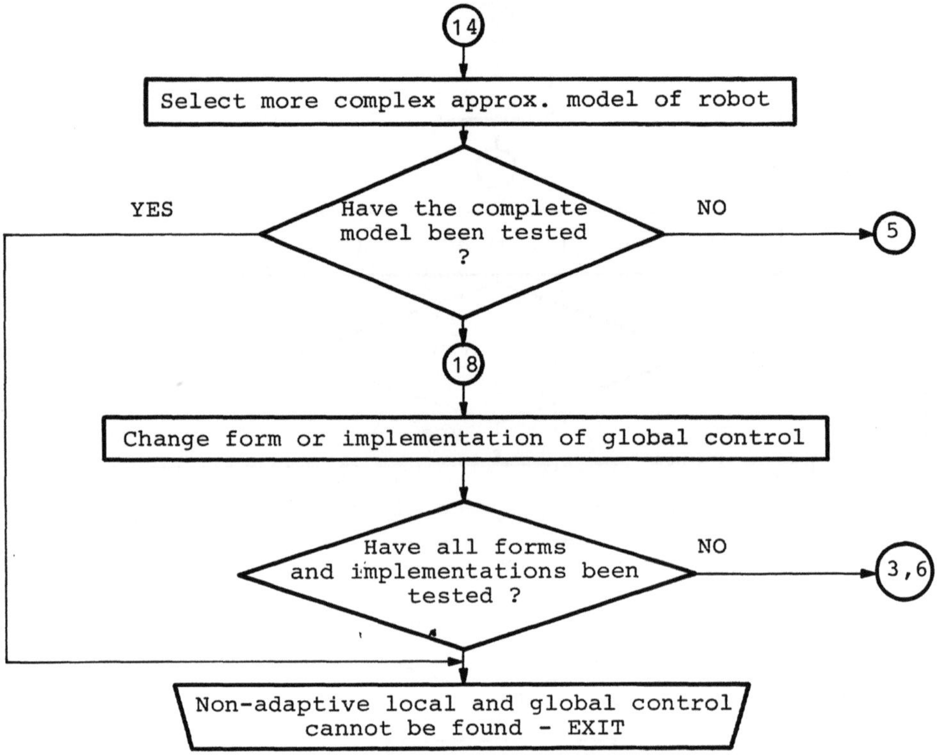
14
Select more complex approx. model of robot
YES
Have the complete model been tested ?
NO
5
18
Change form or implementation of global control
Have all forms and implementations been tested ?
NO
3,6
Non-adaptive local and global control cannot be found - EXIT

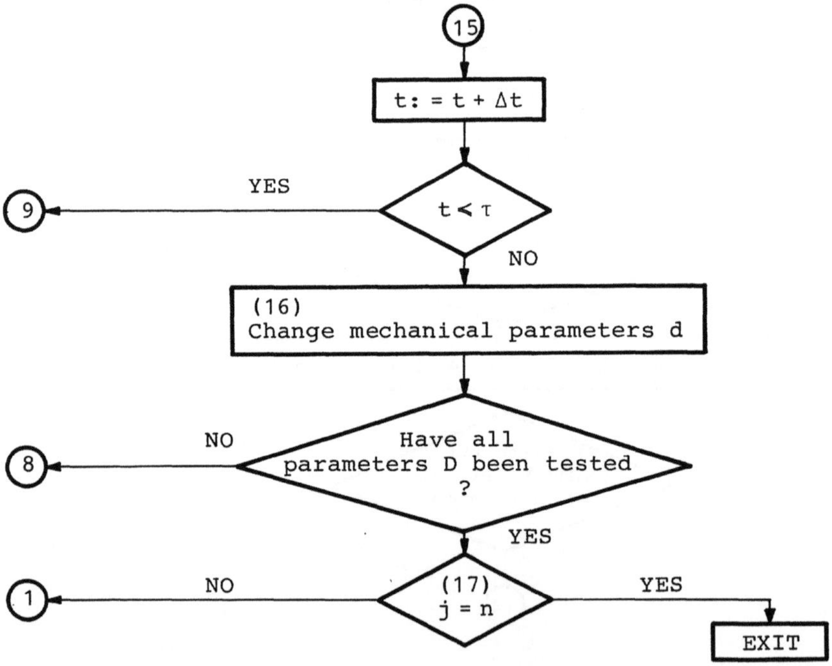
15
t: = t + Δt
YES
9
t < τ
NO
(16)
Change mechanical parameters d
NO
8
Have all parameters D been tested ?
YES
NO
1
(17)
j = n
YES
EXIT

Fig. 2.25. (Cont.)

(3) Choose the form of function $\bar{P}_j^*$: actually the algorithm has to decide which among the three above presented implementations of the global control will be chosen. In principle, the algorithm can automatically check all three implementations, but in practice it is better to leave this decision to the robot designer. We shall assume that we have chosen one of the three possible implementations. Obviously, the algorithm can be repeated three times to check all possible implementations.

(4) If implementation (2) with on-line computation of the coupling $\bar{P}_i^*(x, d^*)$ has been selected, the algorithm has to choose the approximate model of the robot dynamics which will be used to compute global control. The algorithm starts with the simplest approximate model (2.6.5) which includes just gravitational moments.

(5) Choice of the values of parameters $d^* \in D$ has to be made. For these values, the approximate model $\bar{P}_j^*(x, d^*)$ will be computed in the global control (if type (2) implementation has been selected).

(6) The global gain k_j^G is set to an initial value k_j^{Go}.

(7) From this step we start the stability analysis of the nonlinear model of robot with a decentralized controller and global control. Set the initial values of the parameters of the mechanical part of robot $d=d_o \in D$.

(8) Set the initial time instant (t=0.).

(9) Determine the number $\rho_j^*(t, d)$ which satisfies (2.6.20). In doing this, it should be checked whether the global control with "nominal coupling" $\bar{P}_j^{o*}(t, d^*)$ exceeds the constraint upon the amplitude of global control (2.6.14). If yes, it means that just "nominal coupling" exhausts the allowable amplitude of global control signal and then there is no need to determine the numbers ξ_{jk}^* (but ξ_{jk} may be needed for the stability test).

(10) Determine numbers ξ_{jk}^* that satisfy inequality (2.6.18) for the jth subsystem and for all $k \in I$. We must again take care about the constraint upon the global control amplitude (2.6.14), and determine the number ε_j and region $X^{\varepsilon(j)}$ as defined by (2.6.3), in order to ensure that the global control signal (2.6.4) is beyond the amplitude constraint (2.6.14).

(11) Test the condition (2.6.23) for the jth joint. If the condition is not satisfied we have to change the global control by changing either global gain k_i^G or function $\bar{P}_j^*$. So, if the condition (2.6.23) is not met, the algorithm goes to step (12). If the condition (2.6.23) is satisfied, go to step (15).

(12) Increase the global gain k_j^G by a chosen increment Δk^G. Test if $k_j^G<1$; if yes, go back to step (9); if not, we should not increase global gain k_j^G over 1; thus, the algorithm passes to the next step.

(13) Change parameter values d^* for which the approximate model $\bar{P}_j^*(x, d^*)$ is computed. We should depict several sets of parameter values $d^* \in D$ for which we should try to compute efficient global control (since there is no sense in exploring an infinite number of possible parameter values in the allowable parameter region D). If all predicted sets of parameters have already been examined, the algorithm passes to the next step; if not, it goes back to step (6) (of course, this holds if type (2) implementation has been selected).

(14) Change the approximate model $P_j^*(x, d^*)$ for global control; the algorithm takes a more complex model than in the previous iteration according to the listed possible approximate models (2.6.5)-(2.6.8). If the algorithm has already examined all possible approximate models and tried to stabilize the robot even with the complete dynamic robot model and the stability test has not been satisfied, this means that we cannot determine unique non-adaptive local and global control which can stabilize the robot along the desired trajectory and for all allowable parameters of the mechanism. In this case we have to stop this algorithm and implement adaptive control (see Chapter 3). Obviously, if the choice of the global control form and implementation is left to the algorithm, it should select the next possible global control form or the next possible implementation and go back to step (3) or step (6). If the algorithm has not examined all assumed approximate models yet, it has to select the next more complex model and go back to step (5).

(15) Increase time instant by Δt ($t := t+\Delta t$); test if $t<\tau$; if yes, go back to step (9); if $t>\tau$, go to the next step.

(16) Change the parameters of the mechanical part of robot $d \in D$; check

whether we have analyzed the practical stability of the nonlinear model of robot for all allowable values of parameters $d \in D$; if not, go back to step (8).

(17) Check if $j=n$; if yes, it means that the algorithm has already synthesized either local control or local and global control for all robot joints and, thus, the imposed control task (2.2.18) is solved; if $j<n$, the algorithm goes back to step (1) and tries to synthesize local controller for the next $(j+1)$th joint.

It should be noted that in this algorithm we have not considered the variation of actuator parameters θ. As we have already explained, this problem can be treated in two ways. The first is to try to synthesize unique decentralized and global controller which can withstand all allowable parameter variations. In this case we should introduce an additional loop to test stability of the robot with selected global control for various actuator parameters. The alternative approach is to synthesize a few decentralized and global controls for various actuator parameters and change control parameters whenever actuator parameters are changed. The latter approach is essentially adaptive control. However, since we have assumed that the variation of actuator parameters is slow, there is no need to implement such adaptive control on-line; it is sufficient to change control parameters in some time periods.

Although the above algorithm is prepared to be implemented on a digital computer and to be run fully automatically, it is obvious that the interaction with the robot designer might significantly speed up the solution (convergence of the algorithm). Actually, designers experience might be of great help especially in the synthesis of global control, since the designer might directly select the most appropriate approximate model knowing the robot performance. This interaction with the user will be discussed in Chapter 4.

2.7 Example

In order to illustrate the efficiency of the control synthesis presented, we shall consider an example of a particular industrial manipulator. Manipulator UMS-3B of semianthropomorphic type, with 6 d.o.f., is presented in Fig. 2.26. Data on nominal parameters (masses, moments of inertia, lengths of links) are given in Table 2.1. All manipulator joints (d.o.f.) are powered by hydraulic actuators (linear for the first three d.o.f. - "Knapp" - 2.9. 40125 - and vane actuators - "Knapp" ROTAC. D-10-250-1. for the three d.o.f. of gripper), the models of which are given by (2.2.2). The orders of subsystems S^i are $n_i = 3$ and subsystems state vectors are $x^i = (\ell^i, \dot{\ell}^i, p^i)$ where ℓ^i is the piston position, $\dot{\ell}^i$ is the piston speed, p^i is the pressure. The connections among the angles of manipulator q_i and the piston positions ℓ^i are linear $q_i = c_i \ell^i$ for all d.o.f. except for the i=2 where $\ell^2 = (a + b\cos(q_2 + c))^{1/2} + d$. The elements of the actuator model matrices $A^i = [a_{ij}]$ and $b^i = [b_j]$ are given in Table 2.2.

The control task is imposed as follows: $L_1 = 3$ nominal trajectories $x_\ell^o(t)$ are given, for $\tau_1 = \tau_2 = 1$ s and $\tau_3 = 0.6$ s. Nominal trajectories are presented in Fig. 2.27. They correspond to manipulator motion during a particular task of transfer of various objects. We assume that all parameters of the manipulation system are constant except for the mass m_p and moment of inertia J_p of the objects which are transferred by the manipulator. Thus, the regions of the allowable values of variable parameters are given by: $D_1 = \{d: m_p = 0, J_p = 0.\}$ $D_2 = \{d: m_p \in (0., 20 \text{ kg}), J_p \in (0., 0.006 \text{ kgm}^2)\}$, $D_3 = \{d: m_p = 10 \text{ kg}, J_p = 0.003 \text{ kgm}^2\}$. The parameters of practical stability regions are given by: $\bar{X}_\ell^{I(i)} = 0.01$, i=1, 2,3, $\bar{X}_\ell^{I(i)} = 0.1$, i=4,5,6, $\bar{X}_\ell^{t(1)} = 0.02$, $\bar{X}_\ell^{t(i)} = 0.04$, i=2,3, $\bar{X}_\ell^{t(i)} = 0.4$, i=4,5,6, $\alpha_\ell^{(i)} = 3.$, $\forall i \in I$, $\forall \ell \in L$. Nominal trajectories $x_\ell^o(t)$, $\forall t \in T$, are so imposed that $u_\ell^o(t)$ can be calculated which satisfy (2.4.14).

The synthesis of local controllers is performed by an iterative procedure set on a digital computer. We have synthesized the local optimal regulators. In this procedure the weighting matrices in (2.4.16) are varied and the conditions are tested for all imposed nominal trajectories and all allowed parameter values. The algorithm cannot find unique weighting matrices for which local controllers can accommodate all three nominal trajectories and all assumed parameter variations. Thus, we had to introduce global control in the form of force feedback (2.6.4). The algorithm iteratively increases global gains k_i^G, $\forall i \in I$ and tests the conditions of practical stability, in order to find out the smallest global gains for which the system S is practically stable round all $x_\ell^o(t)$ and for all $d \in D_\ell$, $\forall \ell \in L$. The synthesized local and global gains are presented in Table 2.3. In order to verify the results obtained we have simulated dynamics of the manipulator during tracking of all three nominal trajectories for the perturbations of the initial conditions type. We choose initial conditions on the bounds of the regions $X_\ell^{I(i)}$.

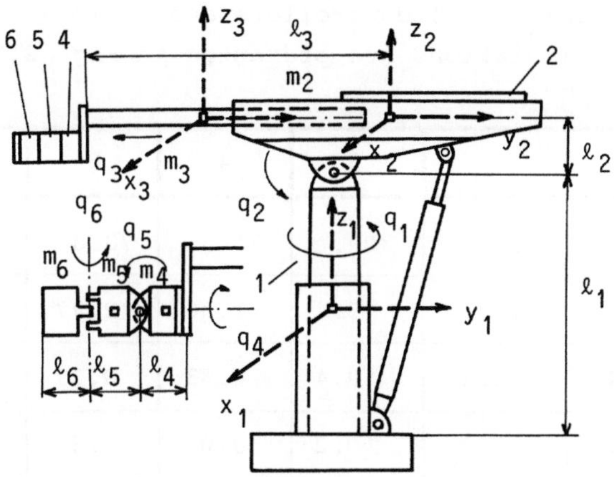

Fig. 2.26. Manipulator UMS-3B with 6 d.o.f.

Link	1	2	3	4, 5	6
Mass m_i (kg)	-	27.8	22.8	2.33	0.33
Length ℓ_i (m)	1.2	0.142	1.14	0.14	0.26
J_{ix} (kgm^2)	-	2.98	1.21	0.004	0.0007
J_{iy} (kgm^2)	-	-	-	0.004	0.0009
J_{iz} (kgm^2)	0.322	3.701	1.21	0.004	0.0009

Table 2.1. Parameters of the mechanism

i	a^i_{22}	a^i_{23}	a^i_{32}	a^i_{33}	b^i_3	f^i_2
1,2	-11.32	47.5	-1122.	-66.18	74.9	-1.885
3	-9.77	41.04	-850.	-49.6	56.1	-1.885
4,5,6	-166.	800.	-300.	-80.	800.	-330.

Table 2.2. Parameters of actuators

We simulate tracking by only local controllers and by local and global control. The results of simulations are presented in Fig. 2.28.

i	1	2	3	4	5	6
k_1^i[mA/m]	1707.	986.5	309.	71.5	73.8	71.2
k_2^i[mA/m/s]	196.2	113.3	5.	1.36	2.97	1.15
k_3^i[mA/bar]	0.46	0.42	0.4	0.33	0.29	0.35
k_i^G	0.10	0.2	0.2	0.0	0.2	0.1

Table 2.3. Local $k^i = (k_1^i, k_2^i, k_3^i)^T$, global k_i^G gains

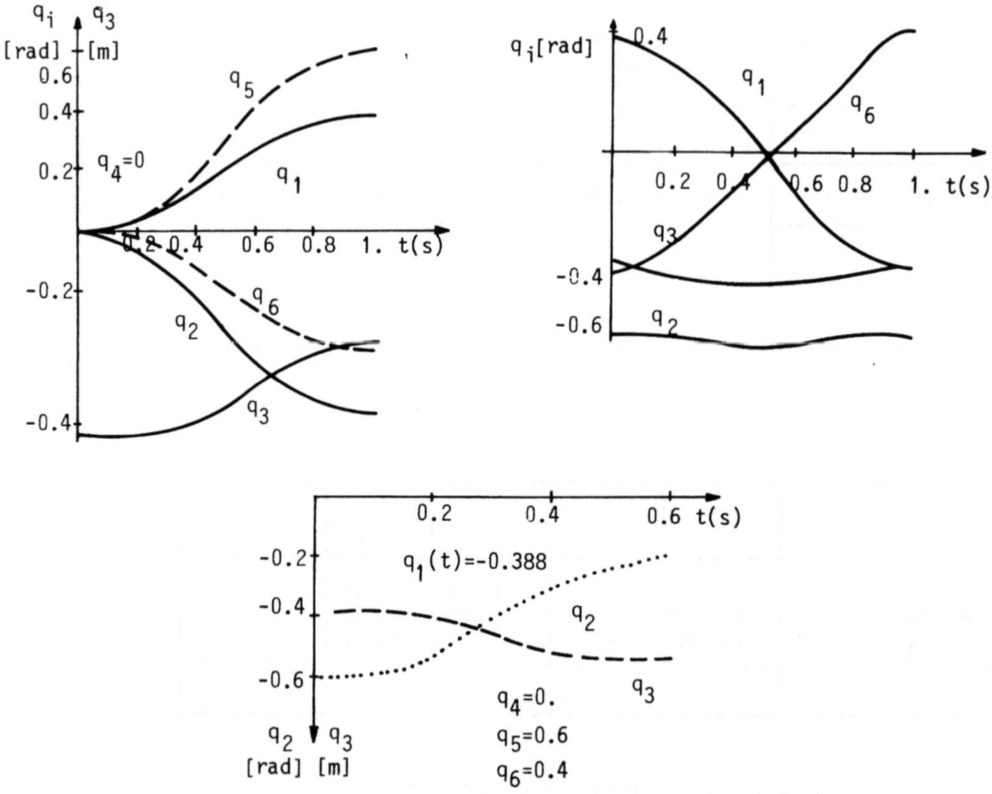

Fig. 2.27. Nominal trajectories

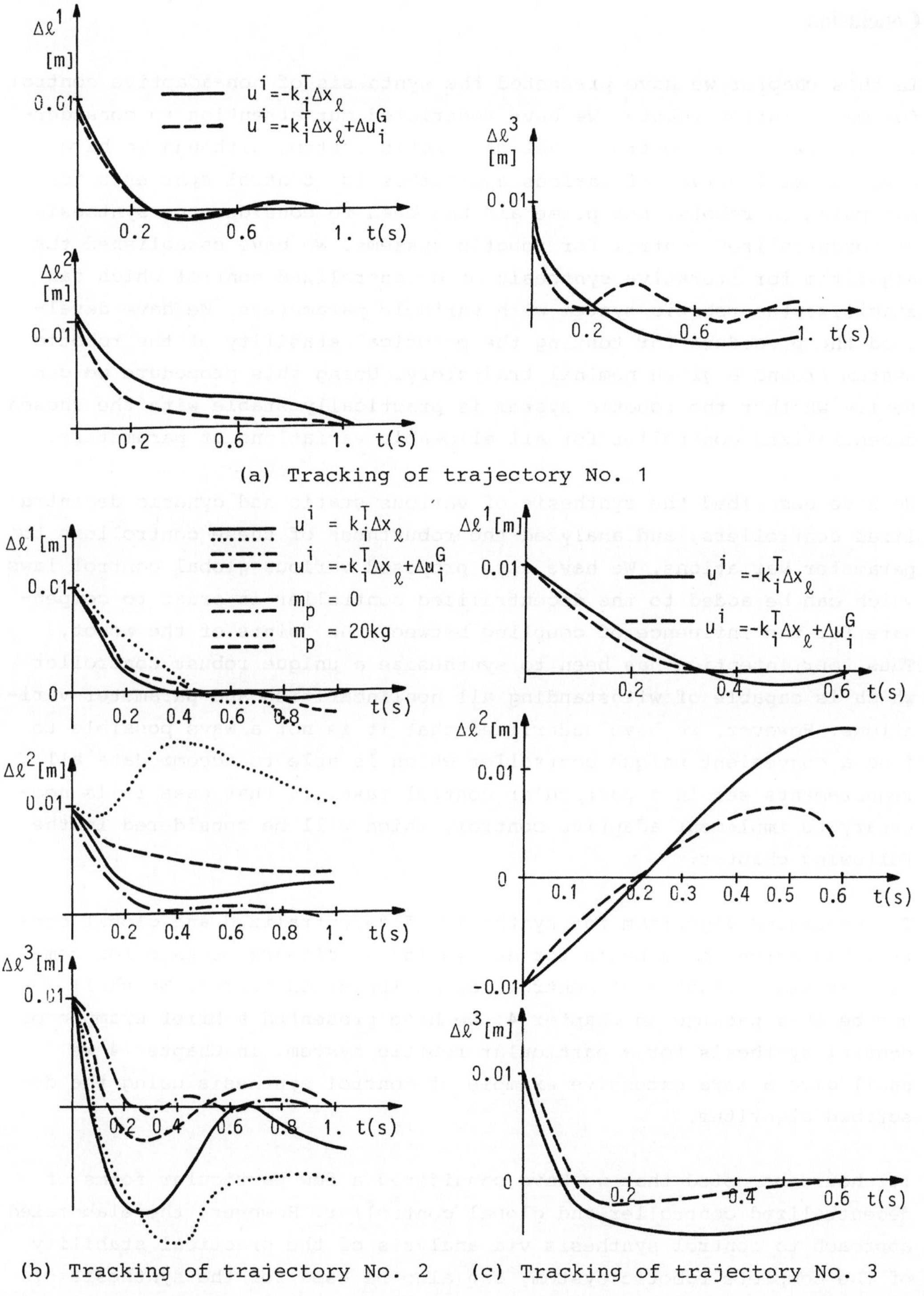

Fig. 2.28. Tracking of nominal trajectories

Conclusion

In this chapter we have presented the synthesis of non-adaptive control for manipulation robots. We have restricted our attention to considering the executive control level of robotic system. Although we have given a brief survey of various approaches to control synthesis for manipulation robots, our prime aim has been to consider the synthesis of decentralized control for robotic systems. We have established the algorithm for iterative synthesis of decentralized control which can stabilize the robotic system with variable parameters. We have developed the procedure for testing the practical stability of the robotic system around a given nominal trajectory. Using this procedure we can verify whether the robotic system is practically stable with the chosen decentralized controller for all allowable variations of parameters.

We have described the synthesis of various static and dynamic decentralized controllers, and analyzed the robustness of these controllers to parameter variations. We have also proposed various global control laws which can be added to the decentralized controller in order to compensate for the influence of coupling between the joints of the robot. Thus, our intention has been to synthesize a unique robust controller which is capable of withstanding all nonlinearities and parameter variations. However, we have underlined that it is not always possible to find a convenient unique controller which is able to accommodate all requirements set in a particular control task. In that case it is necessary to implement adaptive control, which will be considered in the following chapter.

The presented algorithm for synthesis of decentralized and global control has served as a basis for developing a software package for computer-aided synthesis of control for manipulation robots. We shall describe this package in Chapter 4. We have presented a brief example of control synthesis for a particular robotic system. In Chapter 4 we shall give a more extensive example of control synthesis using the described algorithm.

It should be noted that we have considered a few particular forms of decentralized controller and global controller. However, the elaborated approach to control synthesis via analysis of the practical stability of the complete robotic system, can also be used for the synthesis of various other control laws (e.g., nonlinear decentralized control,etc.).

References

[1] Vukobratović K.M., Kirćanski V.M., Scientific Fundamentals of Robotics, 3, Kinematics and Trajectory Planning, Monograph, Springer-Verlag, Berlin, 1985.

[2] Vukobratović K.M., Stokić M.D., Scientific Fundamentals of Robotics, 2, Control of Manipulation Robots: Theory and Application, Monograph, Springer-Verlag, Berlin, 1982, also in Russian, Nauka, 1985.

[3] Vukobratović K.M., Potkonjak V., Scientific Fundamentals of Robotics, 1, Dynamics of Manipulation Robots: Theory and Application, Monograph, Springer-Verlag, Berlin, 1982.

[4] Vukobratović K.M., Legged Locomotion Robots and Anthropomorphic Mechanisms, Monograph, Institute Mihailo Pupin, Beograd, (in English), 1974, also publish by Mir, Moscow, (in Russian), 1976.

[5] Albus S.J., McLean R.C., Barbera J.A., Fitzgerald L.M., "Hierarchical Control for Robots in an Automated Factory", Proc. of the 13th ISIR, pp. 13-29 ÷ 13-43, Chicago, April, 1983.

[6] Luh Y.S.J., "An Anatomy of Industrial Robots and Their Controls", IEEE Trans. on Automatic Control, Vol. AC-28, No 2, pp. 133-152, February, 1983.

[7] Vukobratović K.M., Stokić M.D., "Simplified Control Procedure of Strongly Coupled Complex Nonlinear Mechanical Systems", (in Russian), Avtomatika and Telemechanika, No 11, also in English, Automatica and Remote Control, Vol. 39, No 11, 1978.

[8] Vukobratović K.M., Stokić M.D., "Contribution to the Decoupled Control of Large-Scale Mechanical Systems", Automatica, No 1, January, 1980.

[9] Vukobratović K.M., Stokić M.D., "One Engineering Concept of Dynamic Control of Manipulators", Journal of Dynamic Systems, Measurement and Control, Trans. of the ASME, Vol. 103, No 2, pp. 108--118, June 1981.

[10] Vukobratović K.M., Stokić M.D., "Is Dynamic Control Needed in Robotic Systems, and if so to What Extent?", International Journal of Robotic Research, Vol. 102, June, 1982.

[11] Kahn M.E. Roth B., "The Near Minimum Time Control of Open Loop Articulated Kinematic Chains", Trans. of the ASME, Journal of Dynamic Systems, Measurement and Control, September, pp. 164-172, 1971.

[12] Young D.K.K., "Control and Optimization of Robot Arm Trajectories", Proc. IEEE Milwaukee Symp. on Automatic Computation and Control, pp. 175-178, April, 1976.

[13] Vukobratović K.M., Kirćanski V.M., "A Method for Optimal Synthesis of Manipulation Robot Trajectories", Trans. of ASME, Journal of Dynamic Systems, Measurement, and Control, Vol. 104, No 2, pp. 188-193, 1982.

[14] Vukobratović K.M., Stokić M.D., "Engineering Approach to Dynamic Control of Industrial Manipulators, Part I: Synthesis of Dynamic Nominal Regimes", (in Russian), Mashinovedeniya AN USSR, No 3, 1981.

[15] Popov E.P., Vereschagin A.F., Ivkin A.M., Leskov A.S., Medvedov V.S., "Synthesis of Control System of Robots Using Dynamic Models of Manipulation Mechanisms", Proc. of VI IFAC Symp. on Automatic Control in Space, Erevan, USSR, 1974.

[16] Vukobratović K.M., Kirćanski M.N., "Computer-Oriented Method for Linearization of Dynamic Model of Active Spatial Mechanisms", Journal of Mechanism and Machine Theory, Vol. 17, No. 1, 1982.

[17] Popov E.P., Vereschagin A.F., Filaretov F.V. "Synthesis of Quasi-optimal Nonlinear Feedback Control System of Manipulator", (in Russian) Teknicheskaya kibernetika, No 6, pp. 91-101, 1976.

[18] Takegaki M., Arimoto S., "A New Feedback Method for Dynamic Control of Manipulators" Trans. of the ASME, Journal of Dynamic Systems, Measurement, and Control, June, pp. 113-125, Vol. 102, 1981.

[19] Paul R.C., Modeling, Trajectory Calculation and Servoing of a Computer Controlled Arm, A.I. Memo 177, Stanford Artificial Intelligence Laboratory, Stanford University, Sept. 1972, also in Russian, Nauka, Moscow, 1976.

[20] Bejczy K.A., Robot Arm Dynamics and Control, Technical Memorandum 33-669, Jet Propulsion Laboratory, February, 1974.

[21] Pavlov A.V., Timofeyev V.A., "Calculation and Stabilization of Programmed Motion of a Moving Robot-Manipulator", (in Russian), Teknicheskaya kibernetika, No 6, pp. 91-101, 1976.

[22] Vukobratović K.M., Kirćanski M.N., Scientific Fundamentals of Robotics, 4, Real-time Dynamics of Manipulation Robots, Monograph, Springer-Verlag, Berlin, 1984.

[23] Hollerbach M.J., "A Recursive Langrangian Formulation of Manipulator Dynamics and a Cooperative Study of Dynamics Formulation Complexity", IEEE Trans. on Systems, Man and Cybernetics, Vol. SMC-10, pp. 730-736, November, 1980.

[24] Bejczy K.A., Paul P.R., "Simplified Robot Arm Dynamics for Control", Proc. of IEEE Conf. on Automatic Control, pp. 261-262, 1981.

[25] Raibert H.M., Horn P.K.B., "Manipulator Control Using the Configuration Space Method", The Industrial Robot, Vol. 5, No 2, pp. 69-73, June, 1978.

[26] Timofeyev V.A., Ekalo V.Yu., "Stability and Stabilization of Programmed Motion of Robots-Manipulators", (in Russian), Avtomatika and Telemechanika, No 10, pp. 148-156, 1976.

[27] Saridis N.G., Lee G.S.C., "An Approximation Theory of Optimal Control for Trianable Manipulators", IEEE Trans. on Systems, Man, and Cybernetics, Vol. SMC-9, No 3, March, 1979.

[28] Vukobratović K.M., Stokić M.D., Hristić S.D., "A New Control Concept of Anthropomorphic Manipulators", Proc. of Second Conference of Remotely Manned Systems, Los Angeles, June, 1975.

[29] Vukobratović K.M., Hristić S.D., Stokić M.D., "Algorithmic Control of Anthropomorphic Manipulators", Proc. of V Inter. Symp. on Industrial Robots, Chicago, Illinois, September, 1975.

[30] Hewit R.J., Burdess S.J., "Fast Dynamic Decoupled Control for

Robotics, Using Active Force Control", Mechanism and Machine Theory, Vol. 16, No. 5, pp. 535-542, 1981.

[31] Wu H.C., Paul P.R., "Manipulator Compliance Based on Joint Torque Control", Proc. 19th IEEE Conf. Decision Control, Albuquerque, NM, Vol. 1, pp. 88-94, December, 1980.

[32] Luh Y.S.J., Fisher D.W., Paul C.P.R., "Joint Torque Control by a Direct Feedback for Industrial Robots", IEEE Trans. on Automatic Control, Vol. AC-28, No 2, February, 1983.

[33] Nevins L.J., Whithey E.D., "The Force Vector Assembler Concept", Proc. of the I International Conf. on Robots Manipulator Systems, Udine, Italy, September, 1973.

[34] Paul P.C.R., Shimano E.B., "Complience and Control" Proc. of Joint Automatic Control, San Francisko, CA, pp. 694-699, 1976.

[35] Raibert H.M., Craig J.J., "Hybrid Position/Force Control of Manipulators", Journal of Dynamic Systems, Measurement and Control, Trans. of the ASME, Vol. 103, No 2, pp. 126-133, 1981.

[36] Vukobratović K.M., Stokić M.D., "Dynamic Control of Manipulators via Load-Feedback", Journal of Mechanism and Machine Theory, Vol. 17, No 2, pp. 107-118, 1982.

[37] Popov E.P., Vereschagin F.A., Zenkevich S.L., Manipulation Robots: Dynamics and Algorithms, (in Russian) Series "Scientific Fundamentals of Robotics", Nauka, Moscow, 1978.

[38] Wu H.C., Paul P.R., "Resolved Motion Force Control of Robot Manipulator", IEEE Trans. on Systems, Man, and Cybernetics, Vol. SMC--12, No 3, May/June, 1982.

[39] Paul P.R., "The Mathematics of Computer Controlled Manipulator", Proc. of JACC, Vol. 1, pp. 124-131, 1977.

[40] Whitney E.D., "Resolved Motion Rate Control of Manipulators and Human Prostheses", IEEE Trans. on Man-Machine Systems, Vol. MMS--10, No 2, pp. 47-53, June, 1969.

[41] Whitney E.D., "The Mathematics of Coordinated Control of Prostheses Arms and Manipulators", Trans. of ASME, Journal on Dynamics Systems, Measurement, and Control, December, 1972.

[42] Luh Y.S.J. Walker W.M., Paul P.R., "Resolved-Acceleration Control of Mechanical Manipulators", IEEE Trans. on Automatic Control, Vol. AC-25, No. 3, pp. 468-474, June, 1980.

[43] Krutko P.D., Lakota N.A., "Construction of Algorithms for Control of Motion of Manipulation Robots on the Basis of Solution of Inverse Dynamic Task", (in Russian), Tehnicheskaya kibernetika, No 1 pp. 52-58, 1981.

[44] Yuan S-C.J., "Dynamic Decoupling of a Remote Manipulator System", IEEE Trans. on Automatic Control, Vol. AC-23, No 4, pp. 713-717, 1978.

[45] Roessler J., "A Decentralized Hierarchical Control Concept for Large-Scale Systems", Proc. of the II IFAC Symp. on Large-Scale Systems, pp. 171-179, Toulouse, 1980.

[46] Freund E., "Fast Nonlinear Control with Arbitrary Pole-Placement for Industrial Robots and Manipulators", Int. Journal Robotic Research, 1(1), pp. 65-78, 1982.

[47] Medvedov B.S., Leskov G.A., Juschenko S.A., Control Systems of Manipulation Robots, (in Russian), Nauka, Moscow, 1978.

[48] Paul P.R., Robot Manipulators: Mathematics, Programming, and Control, The MIT Press, Cambridge, 1981.

[49] Arimoto S., Miyazaki F., "Stability and Robustness of PID Feedback Control for Robot Manipulators and Sensory Capability", First Int. Symp. of Robotic Research, Bretton-Woods, New Hampshire, USA, 1983.

[50] Miyazaki F., Arimoto S., Takegaki M., Maeda Y., "Sensory Feedback Based on the Artificial Potential for Robot Manipulators", Preprints of 9th IFAC World Congress, Vol. 6, pp. 27-32, Budapest, July, 1984.

[51] Albus S.J., "A New Approach to Manipulator Control: The Cerebellar Model Articulation Controller (CMAC)", Trans. of the ASME, Journal of Dynamic Systems, Measurement, and Control, pp. 220-227, September, 1975.

[52] Young K.K.D., "Controller Design for a Manipulator Using Theory of Variable-Structure Systems", IEEE Trans. on Systems, Man and Cybernetics, Vol. SMC-8, 1978.

[53] Book J.W., Maizza-Neto O., Whitney E.D., "Feedback Control of Two Beam, Two Joint Systems With Distributed Flexibility", Journal of Dynamic Systems Measurement and Control, Trans. of the ASME, Vol. 97, pp. 424-431, December, 1975.

[54] Truckenbrodt A., "Modelling and Control of Flexible Manipulator Structure", Preprints of IV CISM-IFToMM Symposium on Theory and Practice of Robots and Manipulators, pp. 110-120, Warsaw, 1981.

[55] Yushimoto K., Wakatsuki K., "Application of the Preview Tracking Control Algorithm to Servoing of Robot Manipulator" First Int. Symp. of Robotic Research, Bretton-Woods, New Hampshire, USA, 1983.

[56] Hanafusa H., Yoshihiko Y., "Autonomous Trajectory Control of Robot Manipulators", First Int. Symp. of Robotic Research, Bretton. Woods, New Hampshire, USA 1983.

[57] Sandell M.R., Varaiya D., Athans M., Safonov G.M., "Survey of Decentralized Control Methods for Large-Scale Systems", IEEE Trans. on Automatic Control AC-23, pp. 108-128, 1978.

[58] Davison J.E., "The Robust Decentralized Control of a General Servomechanism Problem", IEEE Trans. on Automatic Control AC-21, pp. 14-24, 1976.

[59] Šiljak D.D., Large-Scale Dynamic Systems: Stability and Structure, North-Holland, New York, 1978.

[60] Athans M., Falb L.D., Optimal Control, McGraw-Hill, New-York, 1966.

[61] Davison J.E., "Decentralized Robust Control of Unknown Systems Using Tuning Regulators", IEEE Trans. on Automatic Control, Vol. AC-23, No 2, pp. 276-288, 1978.

[62] Davison J.E. "The Robust Control of a Servomechanism Problem for Linear Time-Invariant Multivariable Systems", IEEE Trans. on Automatic Control, Vol. AC-21, No 1, pp. 25-34, 1976.

[63] D'Azzo J.J., Houpis C.H., Feedback Control System Analysis and Synthesis, McGraw-Hill Book Company, New York, 1966.

[64] Chen C.T., Introduction to Linear System Theory, Hort, Rinehard and Winston, New York, 1970.

[65] Johnson D.C., "Accomodation of External Disturbances in Linear Regulator and Servomechanism Problems", IEEE Trans. AC-16, pp. 552--554, 1971.

[66] Stokić M.D., Vukobratović K.M., "Decentralized Regulator and Observer for a Class of Large Scale Nonlinear Mechanical Systems", Journal of Large Scale Systems, 5, pp. 189-206, 1983.

[67] Luanberger D.G., "An Introduction to Observers", IEEE Trans. on Automatic Control, Vol. AC-16, No 6, 1971.

[68] Michel N.A., "Stability, Transient Behaviour and Trajectory Bounds of Interconnected Systems", Int. Journal of Control, Vol. 11, No 4, pp. 703-715, 1970.

[69] Stokić M.D., Vukobratović K.M., "Practical Stabilization of Robotic Systems by Decentralized Control", Automatica, Vol. 20, No 3, pp. 353-358, 1984.

[70] Vukobratović K.M., Stokić M.D., "Significance of the Force Feedback in Realizing Movements of Extremities", IEEE Trans. on Biomedical Engineering, December, 1980.

[71] Vukobratović K.M., Stokić M.D., "Contribution to Suboptimal Control of Manipulation Robots", IEEE Trans. on Automatic Control, June, 1983.

[72] Cvetković V., Vukobratović K.M., "One Robust Dynamic Control Algorithm for Manipulation Systems", The Int. Journal of Robotic Research, Vol. 1, No 4, pp. 15-28, 1982.

[73] Vukobratović K.M., Stokić M.D., "Choice of Decoupled Control Law of Large Scale Mechanical Systems", Journal of Large Scale Systems, 3, 1981.

[74] Vukobratović K.M., Stokić M.D., Kirćanski M.N., "Towards Nonadaptive and Adaptive Control of Manipulation Robots", IEEE Trans. on Avtomatic Control, Vol. AC-29, No 9, pp. 841-844, 1984.

[75] Vukobratović K.M., Stokić M.D., "Suboptimal Synthesis of Robust Decentralized Control for Large Scale Mechanical Systems", Automatica, Vol. 20, No 6, pp. 803-807, 1984.

Appendix 2A

Analysis of the Influence of Actuator Models Complexity on Manipulator Control Synthesis

In this appendix we shall briefly analyze the influence of the actuator model on manipulator control synthesis. In Paragraph 2.2.1 we have chosen the models of the actuators driving robot joints in linear form (2.2.2) (with nonlinearity upon the input of amplitude saturation type). However, the problem arising is the order of these models which should be selected so as to achieve adequate representations of a real process. On the other hand, higher-order models require a longer computing time, larger memory capacity and may lead to a larger numerical error. Thus, we have to make a trade-off between the complexity of models and their practical justifiability.

We shall discuss the control synthesis for robotic systems for various degrees of complexity of actuator models.

System behaviour with two types of actuators has been studied: electromechanical and hydraulic.

A d.c. motor with a constant magnetic field controlled by rotor current has served as an electromechanical actuator. Differential equations describing the system are [1]:

$$L_r\dot{i}_r + R_r i_r + C_E\dot{q} = u$$
$$-C_M i_r + J_r\ddot{q} + B_c\dot{q} = -M \qquad (2.A.1)$$

where i_r is the rotor current (A), u is the voltage at motor poles (V), R_r is the rotor resistance (Ω), L_r is the rotor inductance (H), q is the rotational angle of motor output shaft (rad), C_M is the constant of proportionality of moments (Nm/A), C_E is the constant of proportionality of electromotive force (V/rad/sec), J_r is the inertial moment of motor (kg m^2), B_c is the coefficient of viscous-friction (Nm/rad/s), M is the external torque load of motor (Nm).

If we accept $x_i = (q_i, \dot{q}_i, i_R^i)^T$ to be the state vector and present the model of motor in the form (2.2.2)

$$A^i = \begin{bmatrix} 0 & 1 & 0 \\ 0 & -(B_c/J_r) & C_M/J_r \\ 0 & -(C_E/L_r) & -(R_r/L_r) \end{bmatrix} \quad f^i = \begin{bmatrix} 0 \\ -(1/J_r) \\ 0 \end{bmatrix} \quad b^i = \begin{bmatrix} 0 \\ 0 \\ 1/L_r \end{bmatrix}. \tag{2.A.2}$$

If we neglect inductance L_r and viscous friction B_c and accept $x^i = (q_i, \dot{q}_i)^T$ to be the state vector, the system reduces to a second-order system given by

$$A^i = \begin{bmatrix} 0 & 1 \\ 0 & -\frac{C_E C_M}{J_r R_r} \end{bmatrix} \quad f^i = \begin{bmatrix} 0 \\ \frac{1}{J_r} \end{bmatrix} \quad b^i = \begin{bmatrix} 0 \\ \frac{C_M}{J_r R_r} \end{bmatrix} \tag{2.A.3}$$

A hydraulic actuator consists of servovalves and cylinder and may be described by the following system of eqns [2, 3]

$$\begin{aligned} Q &= A_c \cdot \dot{l} + C_{tc} \cdot p_d + \frac{V_u}{4} \dot{p}_d \\ F_c &= A_c p_d = m_t \cdot \ddot{l} + B_c \dot{l} + F_t \\ Q &= Q' - k_c \cdot p_d \\ k_q' \cdot i &= C_1 Q' + C_2 \dot{Q}' + \ddot{Q}' \end{aligned} \tag{2.A.4}$$

where Q' and Q are the theoretical and real flows, respectively (m^3/s), A_c is the piston area (m^2), C_{tc} is the $(C_{kc}+C_{sc})/2$, C_{kc}, C_{sc} are the coefficients of internal and external leakage, respectively ($m^3/s/N/m^2$), p_d is the pressure differential between two piston sides (N/m^2), V_u is the cylinder working capacity (m^3), β is the coefficient of compressibility of fluid $(m^2/N)^{-1}$, m_t is the piston mass (kg), l is the piston displacement (m), B_c is the coefficient of viscous friction (Ns/m), F_t is the force of external load (N), k_c is the slope of servovalve characteristic in the working point ($m^3/s/N/m^2$), k_q' is the coefficient of servovalve ($m^3/s^3/mA$), C_1 and C_2 are the characteristics of servovalves ($1/s^2$) and ($1/s$), respectively.

If we accept the state vector in the form $x^i = (l^i, \dot{l}^i, p_d^i, Q'^i, \dot{Q}'^i)^T$, matrix A^i and vectors b^i and f^i are given in the form:

$$A^i = \begin{bmatrix} 0 & 1 & 0 & 0 & 0 \\ 0 & -\frac{B_c}{m_t} & \frac{A_c}{m_t} & 0 & 0 \\ 0 & -\frac{4\beta A_c}{V_u} & -\frac{4\beta(k_c+C_{tc})}{V_u} & \frac{4\beta}{V_u} & 0 \\ 0 & 0 & 0 & 0 & 1 \\ 0 & 0 & 0 & -C_1 & -C_2 \end{bmatrix} \quad b^i = \begin{bmatrix} 0 \\ 0 \\ 0 \\ 0 \\ k_q \end{bmatrix} \quad f^i = \begin{bmatrix} 0 \\ -\frac{1}{m_t} \\ 0 \\ 0 \\ 0 \end{bmatrix} \tag{2.A.5}$$

Since servovalve bandwidth is wide enough to allow its modes to be neglected, the system may be reduced to a third-order system of the form

$$A^i = \begin{bmatrix} 0 & 1 & 0 \\ 0 & -\frac{B_c}{m_t} & \frac{A_c}{m_t} \\ 0 & -\frac{4\beta}{V_u}A_c & -\frac{4\beta}{V_u}(k_c+C_{tc}) \end{bmatrix} \quad b^i = \begin{bmatrix} 0 \\ 0 \\ \frac{4\beta k_q}{V_u C_1} \end{bmatrix} \quad f^i = \begin{bmatrix} 0 \\ -\frac{1}{m_t} \\ 0 \end{bmatrix} \tag{2.A.6}$$

if the state vector is given by $x^i = (l^i, \dot{l}^i, p_d^i)^T$.

Two mechanical configurations, UMS-1 and UMS-3B have been tested [4]. Figure 2.A.1 shows the minimal configuration (3 d.o.f) of UMS-1 manipulator, and Table 2.A.1 presents its mechanical characteristics.

Mass concentration at the very tip of the third link served for as faithful as possible imitation of load transfer by a gripper; D.C. electromotors produced by Globe Industries Division of TRW Inc., 102A200 type, whose parameters are given in Table 2.A.2 were selected for actuators.

Such a movement was considered that the tip of minimal configuration moved along a straight line between points A and B defined by internal angles according to A(0; 1.1; 0.5), B(0.08; 0.94; 1.25). Velocity time history was triangular. The absolute value of acceleration was 4.9 (m/s^2).

At the stage of nominal regimes, the trajectories of internal angles, velocities and accelerations were obtained.

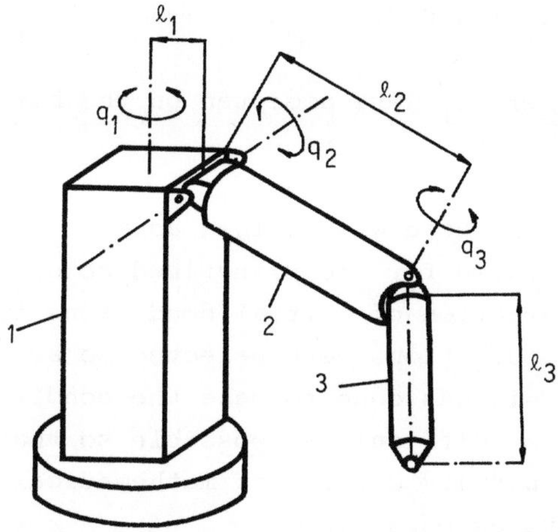

Fig. 2.A.1. UMS-1 manipulator (minimal configuration)

Link	1	2	3
Mass	15	4.7	10
Length	0.11	0.334	0.35
$J_{ix}(kgm^2)$	-	0.000623	0.000623
$J_{iy}(kgm^2)$	-	0.001246	0.00124
$J_{iz}(kgm^2)$	0.0092	-	-

Table 2.A.1. Parameters of mechanism (for UMS-1)

$L_r(H)$	$B_C(\frac{Nm}{rad/s})$	$J_r(kgm^2)$	$C_M(\frac{Nm}{mA})$	$C_E(\frac{V}{rad/s})$	$R_r(\Omega)$
0.01	1.6	1.52	4.31	7	2.45

Table 2.A.2. Parameters of actuators (for UMS-1)

Local feedback gains, used at the stage of perturbed regimes, were synthesized for (according to expression (2.4.17)):

$$Q_i = \begin{bmatrix} 10 & & 0 \\ & 10 & \\ 0 & & 0.1 \end{bmatrix}, \quad r_i = 0.5, \quad \beta_i = 2.5, \quad \forall i \in I$$

and the following values were obtained

$$k_1 = 48.14; \quad k_2 = 6.042; \quad k_3 = 0.194$$

The values for Q_i, r_i and β_i were accepted on the basis of analysis described in Paragraph 2.5.

The movement being simulated was defined as follows: nominal trajectories were first generated for the prescribed conditions, and system behaviour with perturbation of initial conditions type was under observation. These perturbations were selected so as to load the actuators to a maximum. This was done to make the conditions imposed to the manipulation system as difficult as possible so that possible effects due to different complexity degrees of mathematical model of actuator would be as prominent as possible.

Two degrees of complexity of the mathematical model of electromechanical actuator were tested: second and third-order models. Two kinds of nominal trajectories were generated for a particular velocity of the tip of manipulator: for higher and lower complexity degrees of actuator models. Movement simulation was then performed on the basis of each nominal trajectory, applying first the second-order model and then the third-order one.

At the initial moment, only the deviation of angular coordinates Δq_i was accepted as the perturbation, while the remaining two coordinates in the state vector at the beginning of the movement were assumed to have nominal values. The following initial errors were assumed: $\Delta q_1(0) = 0.395$ (rad), $\Delta q_2(0) = 0.17$ (rad), $\Delta q_3(0) = -0.27$ (rad).

The length of the path of the tip of minimal configuration was 292 (mm), and the deviation of the tip from point A at the initial moment was 160 (mm).

Figure 2.A.2 presents the nominal trajectories of driving torques and voltage at electromotor poles, while Figs. 2.A.3 and 2.A.4 show the tracking of nominal trajectories when actuator models of different complexity degrees were used.

Norm of deviation was formed combining the deviations of generalized coordinate and velocity from the nominal in the form

$$C^i = \sqrt{\Delta q^{i2} + 0.1\Delta \dot{q}^{i2}}$$

It is presented as a diagram in Fig. 2.A.5(a-d).

For comparison, these diagrams also show deviation norm when the acceleration of tip is 1.5 (m/s^2) (solid lines) so that the highest velocity of the tip of minimal configuration is 0.6 (m/s). The increase in movement velocity obviously affects considerably the deviation of actual coordinates from the nominal during the movement.

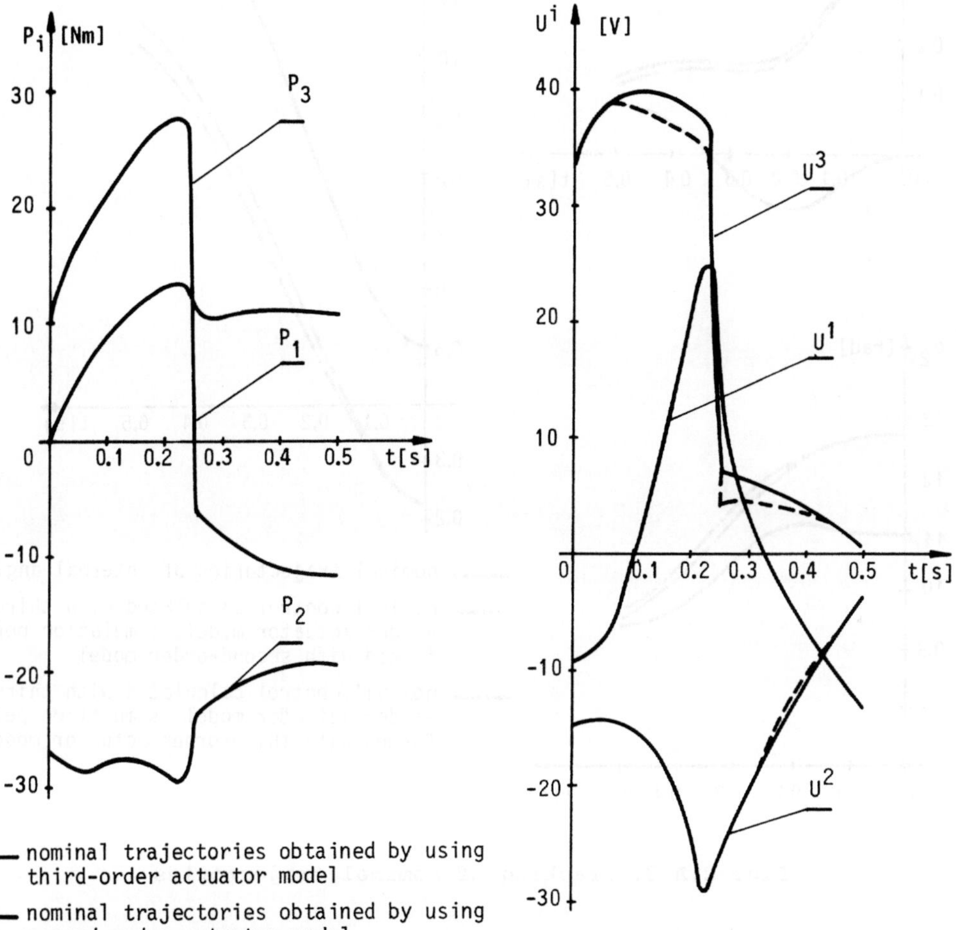

—— nominal trajectories obtained by using third-order actuator model

– – nominal trajectories obtained by using second-order actuator model

Fig. 2.A.2. Driving torques and voltage of electromotor inputs

The second set of simulation results was obtained for UMS-3B (Fig. 2.26) manipulator with minimal configuration consisting of three links connected by two rotational and one linear joint.

Mass was concentrated at the tip of the third link for more faithful simulation of the movement of a manipulator with a spraygun.

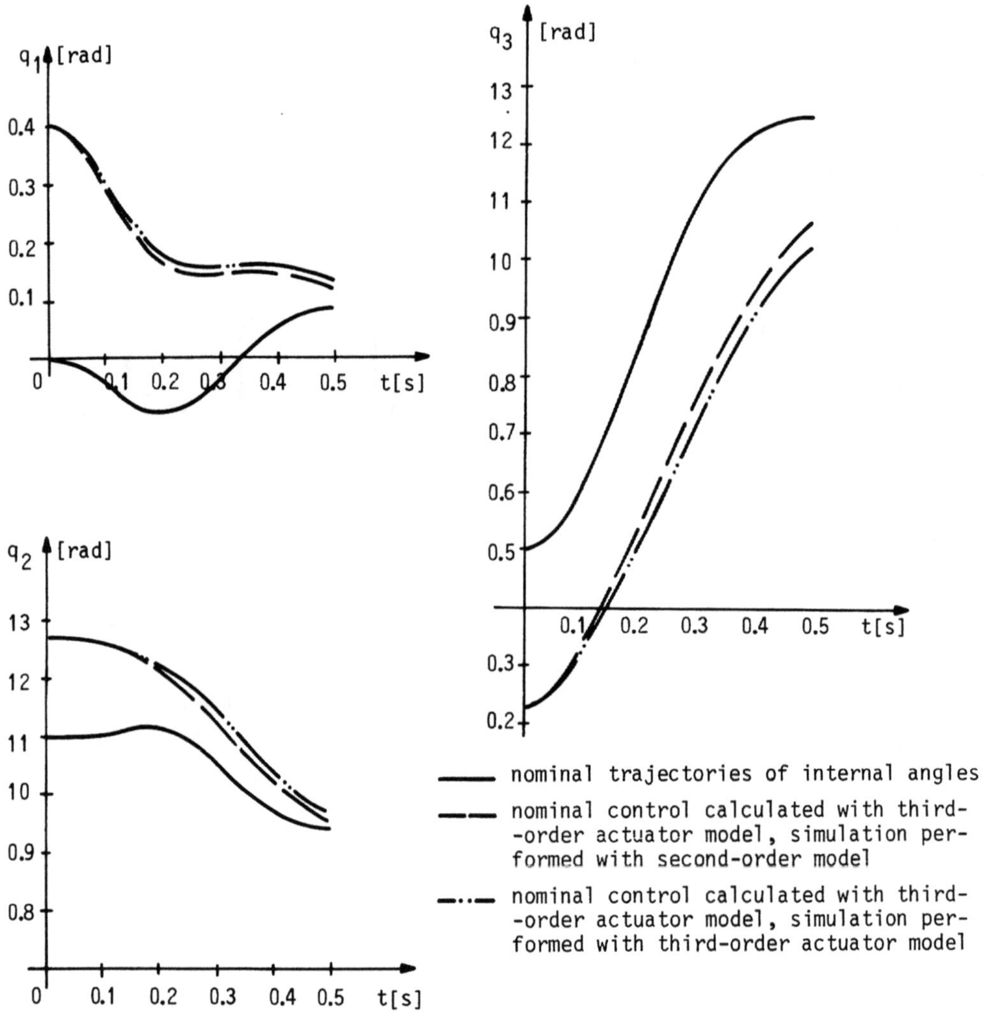

Fig. 2.A.3. Tracking of nominal trajectories

A movement similar to that of UMS-1 was considered. The tip of minimal configuration moves along a straight line between points A and B, with triangular velocity time history. Points A and B are defined by: A(0; 0; -0.68), B(0.4; -0.64; -0.4); the acceleration of tip is 4.9 (m/s^2), and its maximum velocity is 1.68 (m/s).

Feedback gains were synthesized in the same way as for UMS-1, but the following values were accepted for

$$Q_i = \begin{bmatrix} 0.1 & & 0 \\ & 100 & \\ 0 & & 0.1 \end{bmatrix}, \quad r_i = 5, \quad \beta_i = 2.5$$

so, the gains obtained were: $k_1 = 89.2$, $k_2 = 1.5$ and $k_3 = 0.11$.

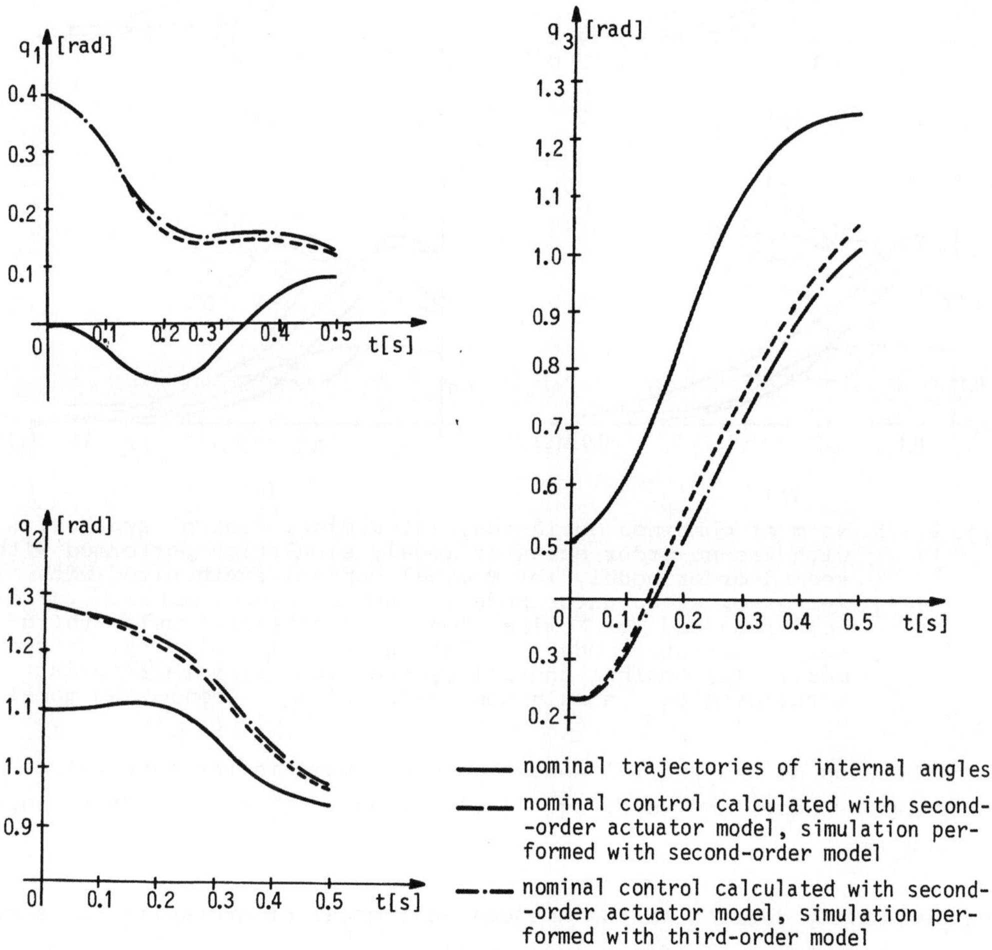

Fig. 2.A.4. Tracking of nominal trajectories

In principle, the simulation was performed in the same manner as for UMS-1. The trajectories of internal angles, velocities and accelerations were first calculated at the level of nominal regimes and then tracked in the presence of perturbation of initial conditions type.

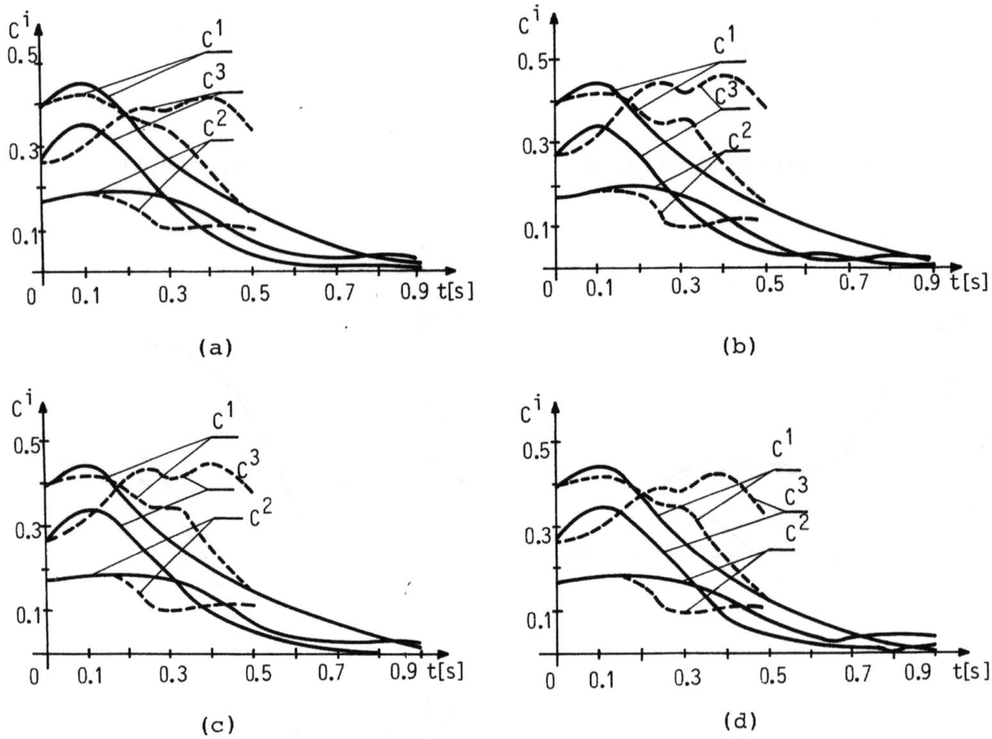

Fig. 2.A.5. Norm of combined deviation, (a) Nominal control synthesized with second-order actuator model, simulation performed with second-order model, (b) Nominal control synthesized with second-order actuator model, simulation performed with third-order model, (c) Nominal control synthesized using third-order actuator model simulation performed with third-order model, (d) Nominal control synthesized using third order actuator model, simulation performed with second-order model

Perturbations at the initial moment were accepted in the same way as in the previous case, and were: $\Delta q_1 = 0.415$ (rad), $\Delta q_2 = 0.25$ (rad), $\Delta q_3 = -0.22$ (m).

Two complexity degrees of the mathematical model of hydraulic actuator were tested: third and fifth-order model.

Nominals were synthesized using the third-order model only, while simulation was performed with both third and fifth-order models.

Figure 2.A.6 shows nominal forces and currents, while Fig. 2.A.7 presents the tracking of nominal trajectories of internal angles upon the simulation of movement with initial positional error.

Finally, Fig. 2.A.8 presents the total deviation during tracking. A point worth mentioning is that diagrams obtained by applying third - and fifth-order models coincide practically, so they are not drawn twice. Solid lines denote the error in the case when the tip of minimal configuration moved with the acceleration equal to 1.5 (m/s^2) to which a maximum velocity of 0.87 (m/s) corresponds.

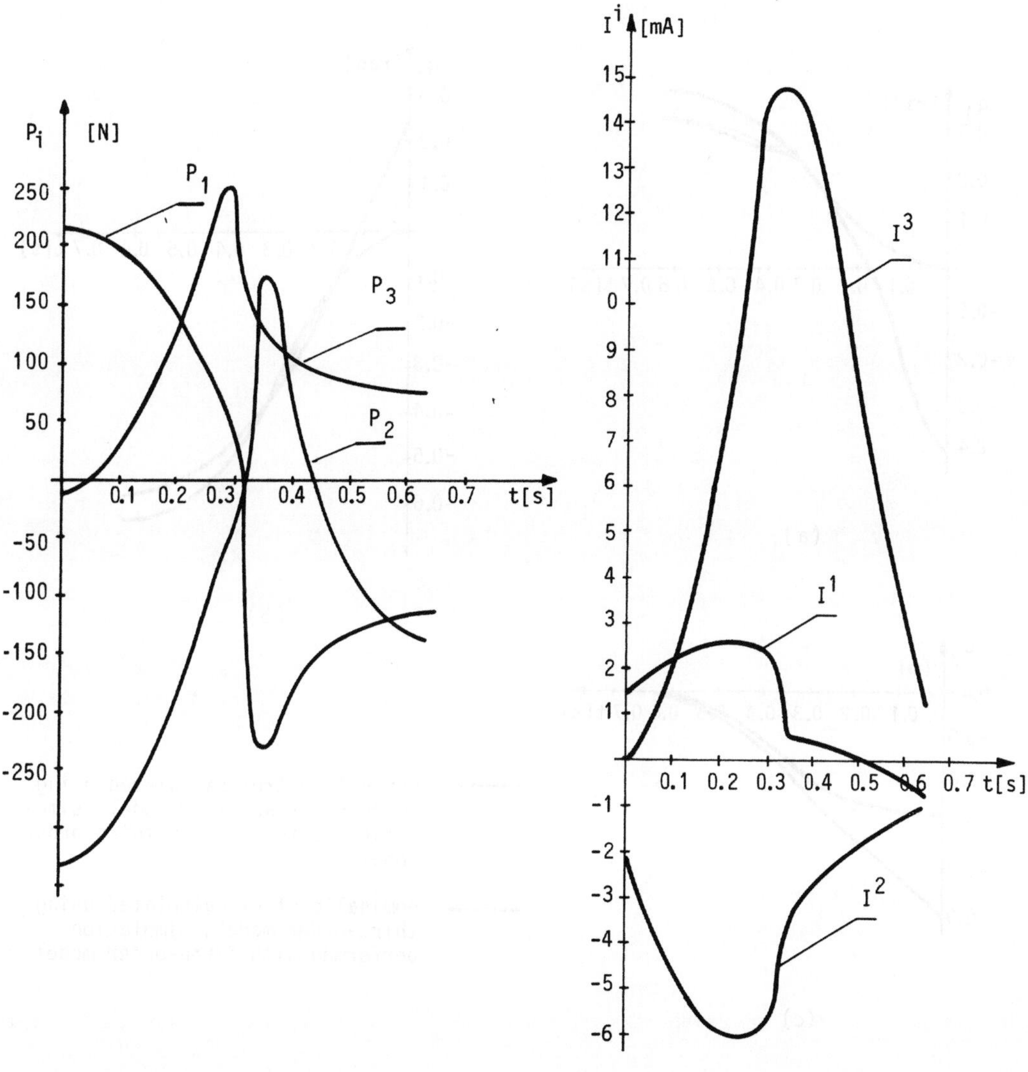

Fig. 2.A.6. Nominal forces and currents

A question of the degree of actuator model complexity which should be taken into account maintaining at the same time the quality of the tracking of nominal trajectories by manipulation robots arises in exact modelling of manipulation mechanisms. The result presented in this appendix has given a sufficiently meritorious answer to such a question and the following conclusion may be reached: as far as conventional operating speeds of manipulation robots are concerned, it is enough to consider second-order models of electromechanical actuators and third--order models of electrohydraulic actuators.

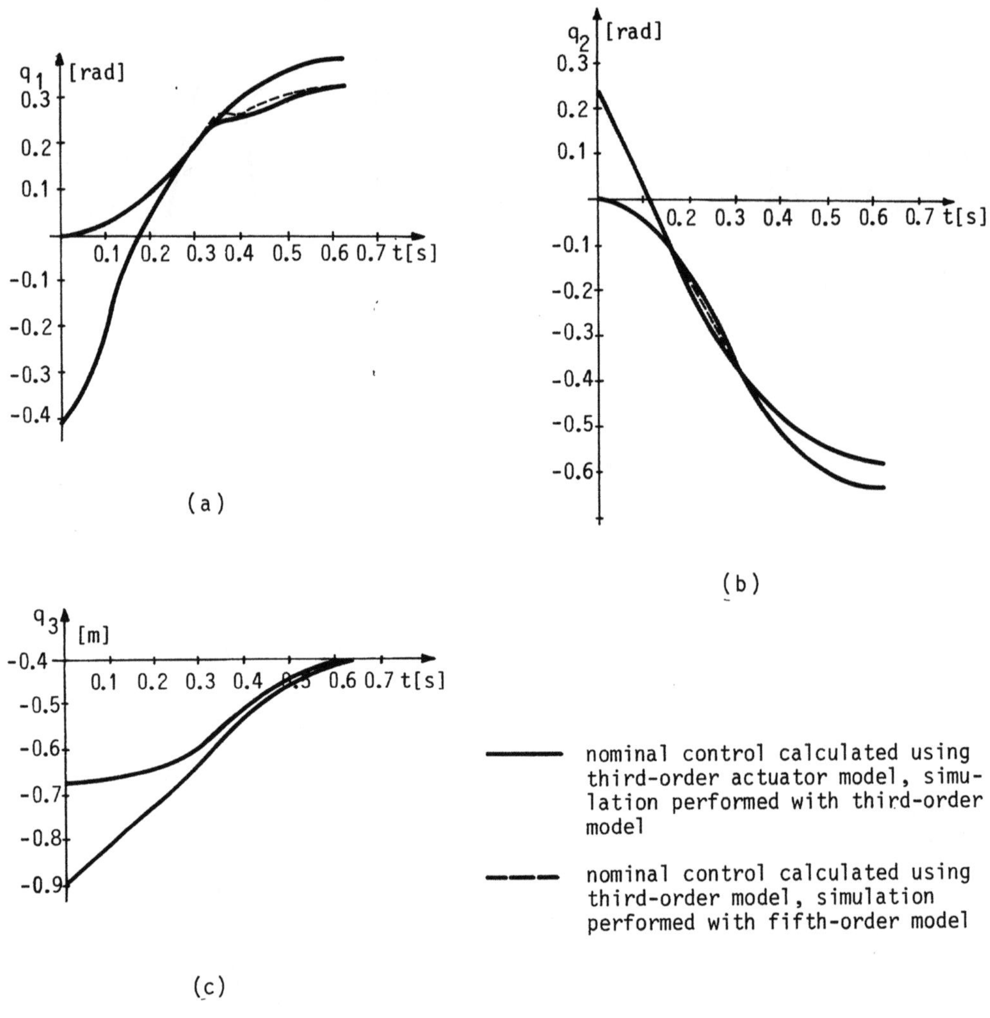

Fig. 2.A.7. Tracking of nominal trajectories of internal angles

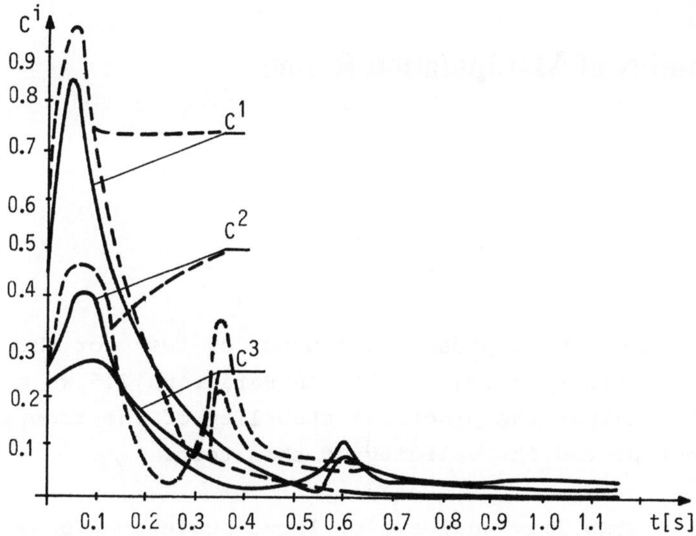

Fig. 2.A.8. Norm of combined deviation vs time

[1] Merrit E.N., Hydraulic Control Systems, Wiley, New York, 1971.

[2] Kuleshov V.S. and Lakota N.A., Dynamics of Control Systems of Manipulators, (in Russian), Energiya, Moscow, 1971.

[3] Vukobratović M., Hristić D. and Stokić D., "Dynamic Control of Industrial Manipulators and its Application", The Industrial Robot, No. 2, 1981.

[4] Borovac B., Vukobratović M., Stokić D., "Analysis of the Influence of Actuator Model Complexity on Manipulator Control Synthesis", Mechanism and Machine Theory, Vol. 18, No. 2, pp. 113-122, 1983.

Appendix 2B
Practical Stability of Manipulation Robots

In this Appendix we shall present the proof of test for the practical stability of robotic system (2.5.17). In Paragraph 2.5 we have presented how we can analyze the practical stability of the robotic system, but we have not proved the validity of this test.

The methods for stability analysis of large-scale nonlinear systems are generally based on two approaches: via Lyapunov first method and approach via input-output stability [1]. These two approaches are in essence parallel [2], but both have certain advantages and disadvantages. Here, we shall not survey various methods for stability analysis of large-scale systems. There are a number of very good surveys on various topics concerning the stability of large-scale systems (see [1-5]). We have chosen the approach via Lyapunov method for stability analysis of robotic systems. Actually, we shall consider the method for practical stability analysis of large-scale systems proposed by Michel [6].

We want to analyze the stability of the system the model of which is given as a set of subsystems:

$$\dot{x}^i = \bar{A}^i x^i + \bar{b}^i u^i + \bar{f}^i(x^i)\bar{P}_i(d, x), \qquad \forall i \in I \tag{2.B.1}$$

where $x^i \in R^{n_i}$ is the state vector of the ith sybsystem, $\bar{A}^i \in R^{n_i \times n_i}$, $\bar{b}^i \in R^{n_i}$, $\bar{f}^i$: $R^{n_i} \to R^{n_i}$ are corresponding matrices and vectors, $u^i \in R^1$ is the scalar input to the ith subsystem, $\bar{P}_i$: $R^{\ell} \times R^n \to R^1$ is the scalar coupling acting upon the ith subsystem which is a function of the parameters $d \in R^{\ell}$ and the state of the complete system $x(t) = (x^{1T}(t), x^{2T}(t), \ldots$ $\ldots, x^{nT}(t))^T$, $x \in R^N$; n_i is the order of the ith subsystem, n is the number of subsystems, ℓ is the order of the parameter vector d, and the order of the complete system is given by

$$N = \sum_{i=1}^{n} n_i$$

The set I is defined as $I = \{i: i=1,2,\dots,n\}$.

We have to analyze whether the system (2.B.1) is practically stable around the nominal trajectory $x^o(t)$, $\forall t \in T$ where T is the given time set $T = \{t: t \in (0, \tau)\}$ with τ being the defined time duration. The practical stability of the system is defined by (2.2.18). Thus, we have to explore whether the system (2.B.1) is practically stable with respect to $(X^I, X^t(t), D, T)$.

Decomposition-aggregation methods for stability analysis are always performed in two steps:

(1) first the stability of the local (decoupled) subsystem is analyzed,

(2) using the results of the first step and by estimating the coupling between the subsystems, the stability of the global system is analyzed.

First, we shall present the practical stability of local (decoupled) subsystems: then, we present the proof of the method for analysis of robotic system if coupling is taken into account; finally, we shall give an example of practical stability analysis for a particular manipulation robot.

Practical stability of local subsystems

We shall prove the test for practical stability of local subsystem. We consider local (decoupled) subsystem in which coupling is neglected:

$$\dot{x}^i = \bar{A}^i x^i + \bar{b}^i u^i(t, x^i) \tag{2.B.2}$$

Here, we have assumed that control for the *i*th subsystem has already been synthesized as a function of t and subsystem state x^i. Thus, we shall analyze local stability for an arbitrary local control law.

The practical stability of local subsystem is defined by (2.4.8).

The following statement has to be proved:

If there exist a real valued, continuously differentiable function $v_i(t, x^i)$ and a real-valued function of time $\psi_i(t)$ which is integrable over time interval T, such that:

$$\dot{v}_{i(\text{along solution of (2.B.2)})} < \psi_i(t), \qquad \forall x^i \in \tilde{X}^{t(i)}(t) \qquad (2.B.3)$$

$$\int_0^t \psi_i(\lambda)d\lambda < v_{im}^{\partial X^{t(i)}(t)}(t) - v_{iM}^{\partial X^{I(i)}}(0), \quad \forall t \in T \qquad (2.B.4)$$

then the subsystem (2.B.2) is practically stable with respect to $(X^{I(i)}, X^{t(i)}, T)$. In (2.B.4) $v_{im}^{\partial X^{t(i)}(t)}(t)$ denotes $\min\limits_{x^i \in \partial X^{t(i)}(t)} v_i(t, x^i)$ and $v_{iM}^{\partial X^{I(i)}}(0)$ denotes $\max\limits_{x^i \in \partial X^{I(i)}} v_i(0, x^i)$. $\partial X(t)$ denotes the boundary of the corresponding region, and $\tilde{X}^{t(i)}(t) = X^{t(i)}(t) - \bar{X}^{I(i)} \exp(-\alpha^{(i)} t)$.

The test defined above has been used in Paragraph 2.4.4 (inequalities (2.4.40), (2.4.41)).

We have to prove that if the inequalities (2.B.3), (2.B.4) hold and if $x^i(0) \in X^{I(i)}$, then the solution of the subsystem (2.B.2) must satisfy $x^i(t) \in X^{t(i)}(t)$, $\forall t \in T$. Let us prove this statement by contradiction. Let us assume that there is at least one initial state $x^i(0) \in X^{I(i)}$ such that the solution of the subsystem (2.B.2) for this initial state and chosen control $u^i(x^i)$ reaches the boundary of the region $X^{t(i)}(t)$, i.e. let us assume that $\exists x^i(0) \in X^{I(i)}$ implies $x^i(t_1, x^i(0)) \in \partial X^{t(i)}(t_1)$. Here t_1 is the first time instant for which $x^i(t)$ reaches the boundary of the region $X^{t(i)}(t)$.

We may write:

$$v_i(t, x^i(t)) = v_i(0, x^i(0)) + \int_0^t \dot{v}_i(\lambda, x^i(\lambda, x^i(0)))d\lambda \qquad (2.B.5)$$

If the inequality (2.B.3) holds, it follows:

$$v_i(t, x^i(t)) < v_i(0, x^i(0)) + \int_0^t \psi_i(\lambda)d\lambda \qquad (2.B.6)$$

If the inequality (2.B.4) is valid, from (2.B.6) if follows:

$$v_i(t, x^i(t) < v_i(0, x^i(0)) + v_{im}^{\partial X^{t(i)}(t)}(t) - v_{iM}^{\partial X^{I(i)}}(0)$$

Since $v_i(0, x^i(0)) < v_{iM}^{\partial X^{I(i)}}(0)$, it follows:

$$v_i(t, x^i(t)) < v_{im}^{\partial X^{t(i)}(t)}(t). \tag{2.B.7}$$

The inequality (2.B.7) holds for $\forall t \in T$. If t_1 is the first time instant for which x^i reaches the boundary of the region $X^{t(i)}(t)$, then for this instant it also holds that:

$$v_i(t_1, x^i(t_1)) < v_{im}^{\partial X^{t(i)}(t_1)}(t_1) \tag{2.B.8}$$

However, due to definition of $v_{im}^{\partial X^{t(i)}(t_1)}(t_1)$, the inequality (2.B.8) can be valid only if $x^i(t_1, x^i(0)) \notin \partial X^{t(i)}(t_1)$. Therefore, if the inequalities (2.B.3), (2.B.4) are fulfilled there is no such moment $t_1 \in T$ for which $x^i(t_1, x^i(0)) \in \partial X^{t(i)}(t_1)$. Since we assume that $X^{I(i)} \subseteq X^{t(i)}(0)$, i.e. $\forall x^i(0) \in X^{t(i)}(0)$, it follows that the state of the subsystem must belong to region $X^{t(i)}(t)$ and it cannot reach the boundary of this region $\partial X^{t(i)}(t)$ if the inequalities (2.B.3), (2.B.4) are valid. Thus, the conditions (2.B.3), (2.B.4) are sufficient to provide the practical stability of the subsystem (2.B.2) with respect to $(X^{I(i)}, X^{t(i)}(t), T)$.

For those not familiar with the notion of time derivative of function along the solution of corresponding subsystem, we have to denote that this means:

$$\dot{v}_i(t, x^i)_{(\text{along solution of (2.B.2)})} = \frac{\partial v_i}{\partial t} + (\text{grad } v_i)^T \dot{x}^i =$$

$$= \frac{\partial v_i}{\partial t} + (\text{grad } v_i)^T (\bar{A}^i x^i + \bar{b}^i u^i(t, x^i)) \tag{2.B.9}$$

i.e. we assume the derivative of function v_i for such values of x^i which are solutions of the subsystem (2.B.2).

As we have already stated in Paragraph 2.4.4, the main problem of this test lies in the choice of the function $v_i(t, x^i)$. However, we have discussed this problem and shown that for linear time-invariant subsystems (2.B.2) we can select functions $v_i(t, x^i)$ in the form (2.4.57), where $\hat{H}_i$ satisfies (2.4.58). We have shown that this choice ensures an effective test of the practical stability of the subsystem.

Practical stability of global system

We have presented above the analysis of the practical stability of local decoupled subsystems in which the coupling between subsystems has been neglected. The second step in stability analysis of the complete interconnected system has to be presented now. We have to prove the test of the practical stability of the robotic system (2.B.1) with respect to the definition of practical stability (2.2.18). The relation between the regions of practical stability of local subsystems ($X^{I(i)}$, $X^{t(i)}(t)$) and the regions of global system (X^I, $X^t(t)$) has been established in Paragraph 2.2.2.

In order to test the practical stability of the global system, we have to estimate the coupling between subsystems. Namely, since the coupling $\bar{f}^i(x^i)\bar{P}_i$ (d, x) is a complex nonlinear function of the system state x and parameters d, we have to determine a time function which gives the boundary of the coupling. Actually, we have to determine function $\varphi_i(t, d)$ which satisfies:

$$(\text{grad } v_i)^T \bar{f}^i(x^i)\bar{P}_i(d, x) < \varphi_i(t, d), \quad \forall x \in \tilde{X}^t(t), \ \forall t \in T, \ \forall d \in D \qquad (2.B.10)$$

Since in robotic systems the coupling between subsystems are driving torques (forces) acting in the joints, the coupling must be limited if the system state belongs to a finite region in the state space and if parameters d are also finite values. Thus, it is always possible to determine functions $\varphi_i(t, d)$ which satisfy inequalities (2.B.10). Actually, functions $\varphi_i(t, d)$ are time estimates of the coupling.

Now, we have to prove the following statement:

Let each subsystem (2.B.2) be practically stable with respect to ($X^{I(i)}$, $X^{t(i)}(t)$, T) which is proved by tests (2.B.3), (2.B.4). If the following inequalities are valid for all subsystems:

$$\int_0^t \psi_i(\lambda)d\lambda + \int_0^t \varphi_i(\lambda, d)d\lambda < v_{im}^{\partial X^{t(i)}(t)}(t) - v_{iM}^{\partial X^{I(i)}}(0), \quad \forall t \in T, \ \forall d \in D \qquad (2.B.11)$$

where functions φ_i: $T \times D \to R^1$ satisfy inequalities (2.B.10), then the global complex system (2.B.1) is practically stable with respect to (X^I, $X^t(t)$, T, D).

We have to prove that if (2.B.11) holds, and if $x(0) \in X^I$, the solution of the complex system (2.B.1) must satisfy $x(t, x(0), d) \in X^t(t)$, $\forall t \in T$, $\forall d \in D$. We shall prove this statement by contradiction. Let us assume that (2.B.3), (2.B.10) and (2.B.11) are valid, but the complex system is not practically stable. If the system is not practically stable, then there is at least one initial state $x(0)\in X^I$ and $\exists d\in D$, such that the solution of (2.B.1) for this initial state and chosen control $u(x) = (u^1(x^1), u^2(x^2),\ldots,u^n(x^n))^T$ reaches the boundary of the region $X^t(t)$. Let us assume that $\exists x(0)\in X^I$ and $\exists d\in D$ imply $x(t_1, x(0), d)\in \partial X^t(t_1)$, where $t_1\in T$ is the first moment for which $x(t)$ reaches the boundary of the region $X^t(t)$. Let us assume that the state of the jth subsystem ($j\in I$) reaches the boundary of the corresponding region $X^{t(j)}(t)$, i.e. that

$$x^j(t_1, x(0), d)\in \partial X^{t(j)}(t_1), \quad x(0)\in X^I, \qquad \exists d\in D \tag{2.B.12}$$

Since we have assumed that the practical stability has been proved for each decoupled subsystem by testing inequalities (2.B.3), (2.B.4), this means that we have selected corresponding functions $v_i(t, x^i)$. For all subsystems we may write:

$$v_i(t, x^i) = v_i(0, x^i(0)) + \int_0^t \dot{v}_i(\lambda, x^i(\lambda, x(0), d))d\lambda, \forall i\in I \tag{2.B.13}$$

Let us consider the derivative of the function v_i along the solution of the interconnected subsystem (2.B.1):

$$\dot{v}_i(t, x^i)_{(\text{along solution of (2.B.1)})} =$$

$$= v_i(t, x^i)_{(\text{along solution of (2.B.2)})} +$$

$$+ (\text{grad } v_i)^T \cdot \bar{f}^i(x^i)\bar{P}_i(d, x), \quad \forall i\in I \tag{2.B.14}$$

Since we have assumed that for free subsystems (2.B.2) inequalities (2.B.3) are valid, and that function $\varphi_i(t, d)$ satisfying (2.B.10) may be found, we may write:

$$\dot{v}_{i(\text{along solution of (2.B.1)})} < \psi_i(t) + \varphi_i(t, d),$$

$$\forall i\in I, \ \forall x\in \tilde{X}^t(t), \ \forall t\in T, \ \forall d\in D \tag{2.B.15}$$

If we substitute (2.B.15) into (2.B.13), we get:

$$v_i(t, x^i) < v_i(0, x^i(0)) + \int_0^t \psi_i(\lambda)d\lambda + \int_0^t \varphi_i(\lambda, d)d\lambda,$$

$$\forall i\in I, \ \forall x\in \tilde{X}^t(t), \ \forall t\in T, \ \forall d\in D \tag{2.B.16}$$

Let us consider function v_j at t_1, the first moment for which the jth subsystem reaches the boundary of the region $X^{t(j)}(t)$. From (2.B.16) it follows:

$$v_j(t_1, x^j) < v_{jM}^{\partial X^{I(j)}}(0) + \int_0^{t_1} \psi_j(\lambda)d\lambda + \int_0^{t_1} \varphi_j(\lambda, d)d\lambda$$

$$\forall x\in\tilde{X}^t(t), \forall t\in T, \forall d\in D \qquad (2.B.17)$$

We have assumed that for the jth subsystem inequalities (2.B.4) and (2.B.11) also hold. By substituting these inequalities into (2.B.17), we get:

$$v_j(t_1, x^j) < v_{jM}^{\partial X^{I(j)}}(0) + v_{jm}^{\partial X^{t(j)}(t_1)}(t_1) - v_{jM}^{\partial X^{I(j)}}(0) =$$

$$= v_{jm}^{\partial X^{t(j)}(t_1)}(t_1) \qquad (2.B.18)$$

(2.B.18) can be valid only if $x_j(t_1, 0, x(0, d)) \notin \partial X^{t(j)}(t_1)$. However, this contradicts the original assumption (2.B.12). Therefore, it follows that $x^j(t, x(0), d)$ must belong to region $X^{t(j)}(t)$, $\forall t\in T$. Clearly, this holds for all subsystems and for all $x^i(0)\in X^{I(i)}$ and $\forall d\in D$. Thus, it follows that if the conditions (2.B.11) are valid, the complex system must be practically stable with respect to $(X^I, X^t(t), T, D)$. This completes the proof of the above statement.

Obviously, we may introduce functions $\psi_i'(t, d)$ which satisfy:

$$\psi_i(t) + \varphi_i(t, d) = \psi_i'(t, d) \qquad (2.B.19)$$

and by substituting in (2.B.11) we get inequality (2.5.16) which has been used in Paragraph 2.5.

It should be mentioned that the test (2.B.11) might be very conservative, since we have estimated the coupling terms by time functions $\varphi_i(t, d)$. However, in Paragraph 2.5 we have shown that we can choose this function in the following way:

$$(\text{grad } v_i)^T\bar{f}^i(\theta^i)z^i(q_i)\bar{P}_i(x, d) < \sum_{j=1}^{n} \xi_{ij}||\Delta x^j|| + (\text{grad } v_i)^T\bar{f}^i(\theta^i)$$

$$z^i(q^{oi})\bar{P}_i^o(t, d) < \sum_{j=1}^{n} \xi_{ij}\bar{X}^{t(j)}\exp(-\alpha^{(j)}t) + (\text{grad } v_i)^T\bar{f}^i(\theta^i)z^i(q^{oi}) \cdot$$

$$\cdot P_i^o(t, d) = \varphi_i(t, d), \quad \forall x\in\tilde{X}^t(t), \forall t\in T, \forall d\in D \qquad (2.B.20)$$

Thus, (2.B.20) determines the functions $\varphi_i(t, d)$ which estimate the coupling terms. By substituting these functions in (2.B.11) we get conditions (2.5.17) (or, (2.5.19)) which are suitable tests of the practical stability of the complete robotic system.

In the above considerations we have not assumed any particular form of local control law. Evidently, if we choose local control laws as explained in Paragraph 2.4.4, we get the test of local stability in the form (2.4.50), and the test of the complex system is obtained in the form (2.5.17) (or, (2.5.19)). However, the tests (2.B.3), (2.B.4), (2.B.11) might be used for arbitrary local control laws. Similarly, if we introduce global control (2.6.4), we can obtain the stability tests (2.6.23), starting from (2.B.3), (2.B.4) (2.B.11), as has been shown in Paragraph 2.6.

Numerical example

Finally we shall give an example of practical stability analysis for a particular manipulation robot. We have chosen a robot with very simple structure for which we can obtain the tests of practical stability in analytical form.

Let us consider the stability analysis for the "cylindrical" manipulation system UMS-2 shown in Fig. 2.B.1. Here we shall consider only the so-called minimal configuration of the manipulator (three degrees of freedom, n=3), while the gripper is not taken into account. This simplifies the stability analysis. The manipulator is powered by d.c. electro-motors, the models of which are given by (2.2.2) The matrices of the models have got the form (2.A.2) ($n_i=3$, $\forall i \in I$).

The order of the complete system is N=9.

The model of the mechanical part of the system S^M (2.2.1) in this particular case has the form

$$S^M:\quad P_i = H_i \ddot{q}_i + h_i \qquad (2.B.21)$$

where

$$H_1 = J_{z1} + J_{z2} + J_{z3} + m_3(q_3+\ell^3)^2,$$

$$h_1 = 2m_3(q_3+\ell^3)\dot{q}_1\dot{q}_3$$

$$H_2 = m_2 + m_3,$$

$$h_2 = (m_2+m_3)g$$

$$H_3 = m_3,$$

$$h_3 = -m_3(q_3+\ell^3)(\dot{q}_1)^2$$

where m_i and J_{zi} are the masses and the moments of inertia of the corresponding links of the manipulator, and ℓ^3 is the length of the third link if $\ell^3 = 0$. We assume that parameters m_1, m_2, J_{z1}, J_{z2}, ℓ^3 are fixed, except for m_3 and J_{z3} which can vary between m_3^o to $\bar{m}_3$ and J_{z3}^o to $\bar{J}_{z3}$, since these parameters include mass and moment of inertia of the load carried by the manipulator, so these parameters are not known in advance. Thus, the finite region of the allowable parameter values is given by $D = \{d: m_1 = m_1^o, m_2 = m_2^o, J_{z1} = J_{z1}^o, J_{z2} = J_{z2}^o, \ell^3 = \ell^{3o}, m_3 \in (m_3^o, \bar{m}_3), J_{z3} \in (J_{z3}^o, \bar{J}_{z3})\}$, where $d = (m_1, m_2, J_{z1}, J_{z2}, m_3, J_{z3})$ and m_1^o, m_2^o, J_{z1}^o, J_{z2}^o, ℓ^{3o} are fixed values.

Let us consider the control task stated as described in Paragraph 2.2. The nominal trajectories of the angles, velocities and accelerations of the manipulator are given by

$$q^{oi}(t) = \begin{cases} \ddot{q}^{oi}_{max}\dfrac{t^2}{2} + q^{oi}(0), & t\in(0, \tau/2) \\ \ddot{q}^{oi}_{max}(\tau t - \dfrac{t^2}{2} - \dfrac{\tau^2}{4}) + q^{oi}(0), & t\in(\tau/2, \tau) \end{cases} \qquad (2.B.22)$$

where $\ddot{q}^{oi}_{max}$ are constant accelerations. The nominal trajectories of robot currents are given by

$$i_r^{oi}(t) = \begin{cases} (J_r^i\ddot{q}^{oi}_{max} - F^i\ddot{q}^{oi}_{max}t)/C_M^i, & t\in(0, \tau/2) \\ [-J_r^i\ddot{q}^{oi}_{max} - F^i\ddot{q}^{oi}_{max}(\tau-t)]/C_M^i, & t\in(\tau/2, \tau). \end{cases}$$

The nominal local programmed control $\bar{u}^{oi}(t)$ can be calculated from (2.4.14). The nominal driving torques corresponding to $q^{oi}(t)$, $\forall t\in T$ can be calculated according to (2.B.21)

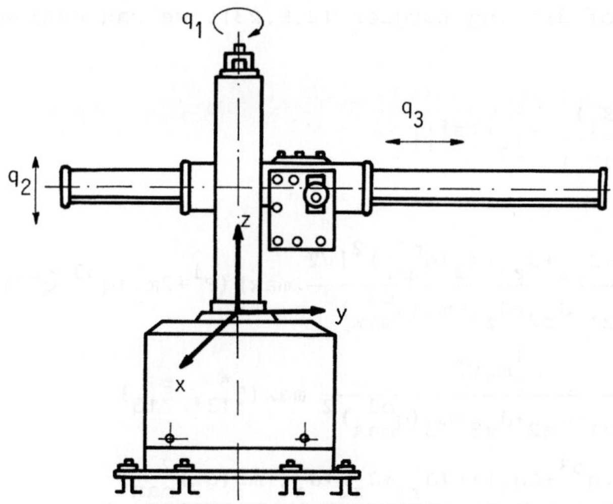

Fig. 2.B.1. Manipulator UMS-2

$$P_1^o = \begin{cases} [J_{z1} + J_{z2} + J_{z3} + m_3(\ell^3 + \ddot{q}_{max}^{o3}\frac{t^2}{2})^2]\ddot{q}_{max}^{o1} + \\ \quad + 2m_3(\ell^3 + \ddot{q}_{max}^{o3}\frac{t^2}{2})\ddot{q}_{max}^{o3}\ddot{q}_{max}^{o1}t^2, \quad t\in(0, \tau/2) \\ -\{J_{z1} + J_{z2} + J_{z3} + m_3[\ell^3 + \ddot{q}_{max}^{o3}(\tau t - \frac{t^2}{2} - \frac{\tau^2}{4})]^2\}\ddot{q}_{max}^{o1} + \\ \quad + 2m_3[\ell^3 + \ddot{q}_{max}^{o3}(\tau t - \frac{t^2}{2} - \frac{\tau^2}{4})] \times \\ \quad \times \ddot{q}_{max}^{o3}\ddot{q}_{max}^{o1}(\tau - t)^2, \quad t\in(\tau/2, \tau) \end{cases}$$

$$P_2^o = \begin{cases} (m_2+m_3)\ddot{q}_{max}^{o2} + (m_2+m_3)g, & t\in(0, \tau/2) \\ -(m_2+m_3)\ddot{q}_{max}^{o2} + (m_2+m_3)g, & t\in(\tau/2, \tau) \end{cases} \tag{2.B.23}$$

$$P_3^o = \begin{cases} m_3\ddot{q}_{max}^{o3} - m_3(\ell^3 + \ddot{q}_{max}^{o3}\frac{t^2}{2})(\ddot{q}_{max}^{o1}t)^2, & t\in(0, \tau/2) \\ -m_3\ddot{q}_{max}^{o3} - m_3[\ell^3 + \ddot{q}_{max}^{o3}(\tau t - \frac{t^2}{2} - \frac{\tau^2}{4})](\ddot{q}_{max}^{o1})^2(\tau - t)^2, & t\in(\tau/2, \tau) \end{cases}$$

First, the local control (2.4.19) for each subsystem $\tilde{S}^i$ should be synthesized. Then, the conditions (2.4.54) for practical stability of the local subsystems should be checked. After that the numbers ξ_{ij} in (2.5.13) should be determined. Starting from the model (2.B.21) and nominal values of driving torques (2.B.23), we can estimate the numbers ξ_{ij} as

$$\xi_{ij} = \frac{\lambda_M(K_i)}{\lambda_m^{1/2}(K_i)} \tilde{\xi}_{ij}||\bar{f}^i|| \tag{2.B.24}$$

where

$$\tilde{\xi}_{11} = \frac{[J_{z1}+J_{z2}+J_{z3}+m_3(q^{o3}_{max})^2]\sqrt{2}}{J_r^1+J_{z1}+J_{z2}+J_{z3}+m_3(q^{o3}_{max})^2} \max[(F^i+2m_3(q^{o3}\cdot\dot{q}^{o3})_{max}),\ C_M^i]$$

$$\tilde{\xi}_{13} = \frac{J_r^1 m_3\sqrt{2}}{J_r^1+J_{z1}+J_{z2}+J_{z3}+m_3(q^{o3}_{max})^2} \max(\xi^*_{13},\ \bar{\xi}_{13})$$

$$\xi^*_{13} = \frac{\max(2q^{o3}+\Delta q_3)\cdot[(J_{z1}+J_{z2}+J_{z3}+m_3(q_3)^2_{max}]}{J_r^1+J_{z1}+J_{z2}+J_{z3}+m_3(q_{3min})^2} \times$$

$$\times [(\frac{F^1}{J_r^1}(\dot{q}_1)_{max} + \frac{C_M^1}{J_r^1}(i_r^1)_{max}) + 2(q_3\dot{q}_1\dot{q}_3)_{max}] + [\max(2q^{o3}+\Delta q_3)\times$$

$$\times (\frac{F^1}{J_r^1}(\dot{q}_1)_{max} + \frac{C_M^1}{J_r^1}(i_r^1)_{max}) + 2(\dot{q}_1\dot{q}_3)_{max}]$$

$$\bar{\xi}_{13} = 2[(q^{o3}\Delta\dot{q}_1)_{max} + (q^{o3}\dot{q}^{o1})_{max}]$$

$$\tilde{\xi}_{22} = \frac{(m_2+m_3)\sqrt{2}}{m_r^2+m_2+m_3} \max(F^2,\ C_M^2)$$

$$\tilde{\xi}_{31} = \frac{m_3 m_r^3}{m_r^3 + m_3}(q^{o3})_{max}[2(\dot{q}^{o1})_{max}+(\Delta\dot{q}_1)_{max}]$$

$$\tilde{\xi}_{33} = \frac{m_3\sqrt{2}}{m_r^3+m_3} \max(m_r^3(\dot{q}_1)^2_{max},\ F^3,\ C_M^3)$$

where $(q^{oi})_{max}$ and $(q^{oi})_{min}$ denote maximum and minimum over the interval T, and $(q_i)_{max}$ denotes maximum of $q^{oi}(t) + \Delta q_i(t)$, for $|\Delta q_i| < \bar{X}^{t(i)}\exp(-\alpha^{(i)}t)$, $\forall t\in T$.

Now, by calculating the integrals of P_i^o over time we can calculate the functions $\rho_i(t)$ satisfying (2.5.18), e.g. for i=2

$$\rho_2(t) = \begin{cases} (m_2+m_3)\ddot{q}^{o2}_{2max}t+(m_2+m_3)gt, & t\in(0, \tau/2) \\ -(m_2+m_3)\ddot{q}^{o2}_{max}(t-\tau)+(m_2+m_3)gt, & t\in(\tau/2, \tau) \end{cases}$$

and, similarly, for $\rho_1(t)$, $\rho_3(t)$. By introducing the expressions for ξ_{ij} and $\rho_i(t)$ into (2.5.17), we obtain the connection among local controls, parameters of the manipulator and nominal trajectories and the parameters of the imposed finite regions of practical stability.

From this connection we can iteratively calculate the local controllers which should satisfy particular conditions of practical stability for the practical domain of parameters variation of this manipulator. On the other hand, if the local controllers are already chosen we can estimate either the regions of practical stability of the manipulator around the given nominal trajectory with such controllers, or the domain of parameters variation for which these controllers ensure practical stability.

Let us consider the latter case. The parameters of the manipulator UMS-2 are given in Table 2.B.1 while those of the chosen actuators (d.c. motors of IG 2315-P20 type) are given in Table 2.B.2 (elements of the matrices of actuator models). Let us consider the nominal trajectory given by (2.B.22) where $\ddot{q}^{o1}_{max}$ = 1.57 rad s^{-2}, $\ddot{q}^{o2}_{max}$ = 0.15 m s^{-2}, $\ddot{q}^{o3}_{max}$ = 0.3 m s^{-2} and τ = 2 s. The nominal trajectories are given in Fig. 2.B.2 and the computed nominal driving torques corresponding to m^o_3 and J^o_{z3} are given in Fig. 2.B.3. The regions of practical stability are imposed as described in Paragraph 2.2 where $\bar{X}^{I(1)} = 0.1$, $\bar{X}^{I(2)} = \bar{X}^{I(3)} = 0.01$ and $\alpha^{(i)} = 5$, $\forall i\in I$, and $\bar{X}^{t(i)}$ are chosen to satisfy $(\lambda_m(K_i)/\lambda_M(K_i))^{1/2} > (\bar{X}^{I(i)}/\bar{X}^{t(i)})$.

The local controllers are chosen first. Since $\alpha^{(i)} = 5$ we choose $\beta_i=10$, $\forall i\in I$ and weighting matrices in (2.4.16) as given in Table 2.B.3. Local gains are calculated and also given in Table 2.B.3. It can easily be checked whether the conditions of practical stability for decoupled subsystems are satisfied. The numbers $\tilde{\xi}_{ij}$ in (2.B.24) are evidently functions of J_{z3} and m_3, and for the values of other parameters, as given in Tables 2.B.1 and 2.B.2 those functions are

$$\tilde{\xi}_{11} = \frac{(m_3 2.37) + 0.355 + (4.23J_{z3})}{0.12 + J_{z3} + 0.5625\,m_3}$$

$$\tilde{\xi}_{13} = \frac{0.048m_3}{0.12+J_{z3}+0.2025m_3}\left[\frac{2.56J_{z3}+(1.85m_3)+2.1}{0.12+J_{z3}+m_3 0.2025} + 3.84\right]$$

$$\tilde{\xi}_{22} = \frac{29.61 + m_3 4.23}{1.028 + 0.004m_3}$$

$$\tilde{\xi}_{31} = \frac{m_3 2.325}{1 + (m_3 0.0025)}$$

$$\tilde{\xi}_{33} = \frac{m_3 4.23}{1 + (m_3 0.0025)}$$

For $m_3=5.6$ and $J_{z3}=J^o_{z3}=0.320$ these numbers get the values

$\tilde{\xi}_{11}=4.28$, $\tilde{\xi}_{13}=1.18$, $\tilde{\xi}_{22}=50.7$, $\tilde{\xi}_{31}=12.8$, $\tilde{\xi}_{33}=23.4$

Link	1	2	3
Mass (kg)	10.0	7.0	5.6
Length (m)	0.38	0.02	0.45
J_{xi} (kgm^2)	-	-	-
J_{yi} (kgm^2)	-	-	-
J_{zi} (kgm^2)	0.029	0.055	0.320

Table 2.B.1. Manipulator parameters

i	a^i_{22}	a^i_{23}	a^i_{32}	a^i_{33}	b^i_3	f^i_2
1	-2.0	20.0	-1000.0	-450.0	2000.0	-29.0
2	-3.0	0.28	-10^5	-450.0	2000.0	-0.004
3	-3.0	0.13	-10^5	-450.0	2000.0	-0.0025

Table 2.B.2. Actuator parameters

By calculating the functions $\rho_i(t)$ for these values of parameters we will see that the condition (2.5.17) is not fulfilled for the first subsystem. Therefore, we have to reselect local control for the first subsystem, or to introduce global control. In the first case, we can

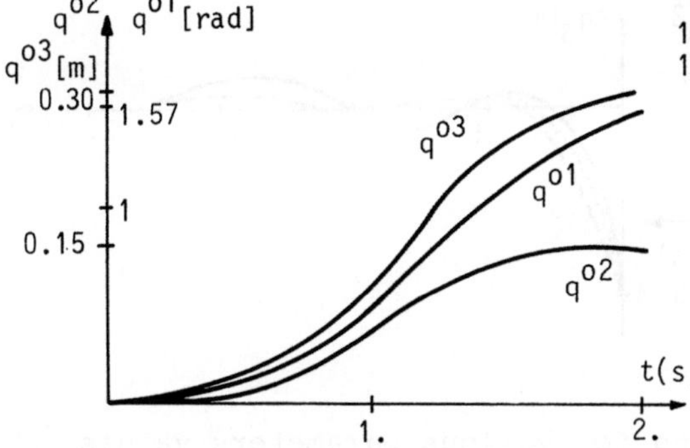

Fig. 2.B.2. Nominal trajectories

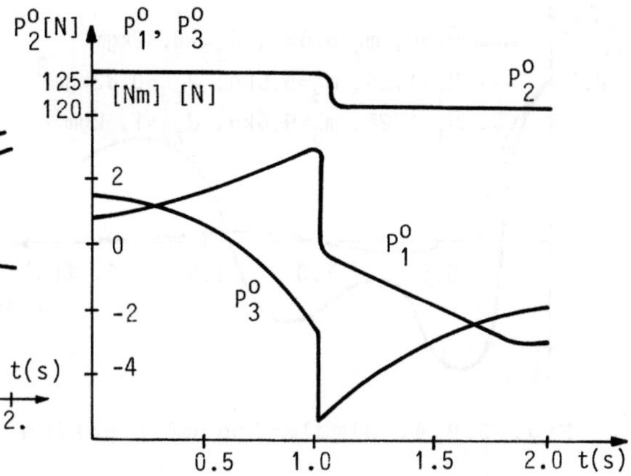

Fig. 2.B.3. Nominal driving torques

rearrange the distribution between the local subsystem $\tilde{S}^1$ and load P_1 (Paragraph 2.4). In the matrices of the local subsystem $\tilde{S}^1$ we introduce $J^1_{r_3} + \bar{H}_1$ instead of J^1_r, where $\bar{H}_1$ is chosen as $\bar{H}_1 = J_{z1} + J_{z2} + J^o_{z3} + m^o_3(\ell^3 + q^{o3}(0))^2 = 1.25$. Thus, the values of elements of subsystem matrices in Table 2.B.2 change (e.g. f^1_2 is now 0.778). The numbers $\tilde{\xi}_{11}$ and $\tilde{\xi}_{13}$ also change so that

$$\tilde{\xi}_{11} = \frac{(m_3 2.37) - 4.93 + 4.23 J_{z3}}{J_{z3} + 0.5625 m_3 + 0.12}$$

$$\tilde{\xi}_{13} = \frac{0.048 m_3}{J_{z3} + 0.2025 m_3 + 0.12}\left[\frac{2.56 J_{z3} + 1.85 m_3 - 1.1}{J_{z3} + 0.2025 m_3 + 0.12} + 3.84\right].$$

$$Q_i = \begin{bmatrix} 0.01 & & \\ & 100.0 & \\ & & 100.0 \end{bmatrix} \qquad r_i = 100.$$

For $\bar{H}_1 = 0.$

$$r_i^{-1} \bar{b}^{iT} K_i = (13.9,\ 1.3,\ 0.94)^T, \qquad \text{for } i=1$$
$$= (406.0,\ 76.0,\ 0.8)^T, \qquad \text{for } i=2$$
$$= (1174.0,\ 202.0,\ 0.76)^T, \qquad \text{for } i=3.$$

For $\bar{H}_1 = 1.25$

$$r_1^{-1} \bar{b}^{1T} K_1 = (23.37,\ 3.75,\ 0.91)^T$$

Table 2.B.3. Local regulator gains

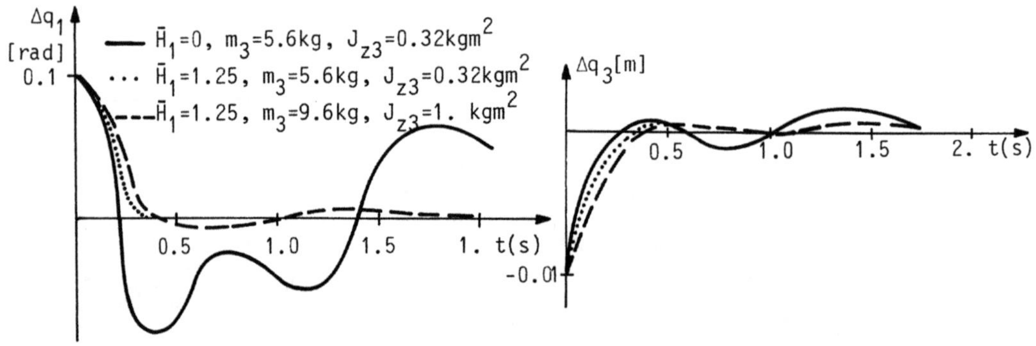

Fig. 2.B.4. Simulation of tracking for various parameters values

The local gains with reselected subsystem model are also given in Table 2.B.3. It can be shown that the system is practically stable with such local regulators for parameter variation $m_3 \in (5.6,\ 9.6)$(kg), $J_{z3} \in (0.320,1)$ (kgm^2).

This has also been verified by digital simulation. The dynamics of the manipulation system of Fig. 2.B.1 during tracking the nominal trajectories of Fig. 2.B.2 has been simulated on a digital computer. The results of digital simulation are shown in Fig. 2.B.4. The deviations of mechanism coordinates from the nominal trajectories Δq_i (for the first and the third degree of freedom) versus time are shown for two sets of values of parameters m_3 and J_{z3}. Initial conditions are chosen on the boundary of the regions $X^{I(i)}$ i.e. $\Delta q_1(0) = 0.1$ (rad), $\Delta q_2(0) = 0.01$ (m), $\Delta q_3(0) = 0.01$ (m) and $\Delta \dot{q}_i(0) = 0$, $\Delta i_r^i(0) = 0$, $\forall i \in I$. The results show good tracking for all parameter values, i.e. the conditions of practical stability are satisfied. This means that the proposed simple control (2.4.19), consisting of local nominal control $\bar{u}^{oi}(t)$ and local regulators (2.4.17), can provide the practical stabilization of this particular manipulator for a relatively wide range of parameter variations. There is thus no need to introduce global control in this particular case.

Figure 2.B.4. also shows the results of tracking of nominal trajectories by the local control when $\bar{H}_1$ is taken to be zero (regulators gains shown in Table 2.B.3). As already stated above, in this case the system is not practically stable.

[1] Voronov A.A., "State-of-the-Art and Problems in Stability Theory", (in Russian), Avtomatika and Telemechanika, No. 1, 1983.

[2] Araki M., "Stability of Large-Scale Nonlinear Systems: Quadratic--order Theory of Composite Systems Method Using M-matrices", IEEE Transactions, AC-23, 129-142, 1978.

[3] Sandell Jr. N.R., Varaiya P., Athans M., Safonov G.M., "Survey of Decentralized Control Methods for Large Scale Systems" IEEE Trans., AC-23, 108-128, 1978.

[4] Vidyasagar M., Input-Output Analysis of Large-Scale Interconnected Systems, Springer-Verlag, New York, 1981.

[5] Michel N.A., Miller K.R., Qualitative Analysis of Large Scale Dynamic Systems, Academic Press, New York, 1977.

[6] Michel N.A., "Stability, Transient Behaviour and Trajectory Bounds of Interconnected Systems", Int. Journal of Control, Vol. 11, No.4, pp. 703-715, 1970.

Chapter 3
Adaptive Control Algorithms

3.1 Introduction

In this chapter we shall present the theoretical background of various adaptive robot control algorithms. This subject is relatively new in robotic research. Within the past six years, only a handful of people have been actively working on this subject. Nevertheless, this area will surely be one of the most interesting in the nearest future, because the classical controllers cannot always satisfy the stability conditions, even if designed to be robust with respect to parametric and state disturbances (see Chapter 2). Thus, the adaptive control algorithm should be considered as an up-grade over the classical control approach. The adaptive control algorithms are often much more complex in numerical sense than nonadaptive laws. Also, it is more difficult to prove the stability of the overall system. But, the adaptive controllers offer more opportunities, especially when the robot works in ambient conditions which are not completely known in advance. This is the case, for example, when the payload mass is not predefined. Of course, this does not mean that the robot controllers should always be designed to be adaptive. On the contrary, in our opinion, the adaptive algorithms should be employed only when simple classical controllers cannot achieve desirable performances.

Within adaptive control theory there are two fundamental approaches. The first is Learning Model Adaptive Control (LMAC), in which an improved model of the plant is obtained by on-line parameter estimation techniques, and is then used in the feedback control. The well-known self-tuning control strategy belongs here. The second approach in adaptive control theory is called Model Referenced Adaptive Control (MRAC). The controller is adjusted so that the closed-loop behavior of a system matches that of a preselected model according to some criterion.

Within the self-tuning control theory there are many approaches based on different estimation techniques: least squares, extended least squares, maximum likelihood, etc. According to the control synthesis procedure, the self-tuning regulators can be divided into: minimum variance controllers, extended minimum variance controllers, and pole-zero placement regulators, [1-9]. The feasibility of least squares/extended minimum variance control in robotic applications is examined by Koivo and Guo [10]. The application of least squares pole zero placement in robotics is elaborated by Leininger [11, 12]. We shall discuss these results in detail in Paragraph 3.2.1 within the scope of centralized robot control strategy. PID self-tuning local regulators will be described with the scope of decentralized control of manipulators in Paragraph 3.3.1.

In this chapter we shall also discuss several basic concepts within model - reference control theory: local parametric optimization theory, methods based on Lyapunov functions and methods based on hyperstability theory [13-19]. As will be shown in the text to follow, there have been several attempts towards the application of these results to robotic devices. The local parametric optimization technique has been used by Dubowsky [20-22], and Lyapunov functions approach has been tested by Arimoto and Takegaki [23, 24]. A particularly interesting concept based on hyperstability and positivity [25-27] will be presented in Paragraph 3.2.2. It should be pointed out that these methods are applied within the centralized control strategy. The decentralized control structure based on hyperstability has been elaborated by Kirćanski and Vukobratović [28]. Let us consider now the results of Dubowsky and Arimoto in more details.

One of the first contributions in adaptive robot control is given by Dubowsky and DesForges in 1979. They developed a model-referenced-adaptive control system based on steepest descent method in order to minimize a cost function of the error between the model and the system. They defined the error between the response of the model and the system by the vector

$$e(t) = y(t) - x(t)$$

where y is the model state vector, and x is the system state vector. In this method, a scalar cost function is formulated as

$$V(e) = \frac{1}{2} e^T Q e$$

where Q is called the adaptive gain matrix. The objective of the algorithm is to drive e(t) to zero, and thereby match the system response to that of the model. Let θ be the system parameter vector including adjustable gains. Then, according to the steepest descent method this parameter vector should be varied according to the law

$$\dot{\theta} = - k \frac{\partial V}{\partial \theta} = -k \frac{\partial e^T}{\partial \theta} Qe \qquad (3.1.1)$$

where k is a positive real. This formula represents the classical gradient algorithm. Since $\partial e/\partial \theta$ cannot be determined, a series of approximations must be introduced. It turns out that the sensitivity equations of reference model take part in the algorithm. Hence, using the obtained parameter vector θ, the feedback gains are calculated.

The advantages of the method are:

- it is computationally less burdensome than the methods which evaluate a nonlinear robot model,
- it has good noise rejection properties, and
- it is tested experimentally on an industrial robot [22].

There are also some undesirable properties which should be pointed out:

- the gradient algorithm built into the adaptation algorithm may negatively influence the overall system stability, and
- the criterion V(e) penalizes only the output error. As the amplitudes of input signals are not penalized, the adaptation mechanism may impose excessively large amplitudes of control signals, which cannot be realized.

Finally, it should be mentioned that the discrete - time version of this method is given in Ref. [21], and the multivariable case in Ref. [22]. Especially interesting are the experimental results obtained with a laboratory rotary positioning device (2 degrees of freedom) and with an industrial robotic manipulator, PUMA 500. The experiments show an expressive significance of adaptive robot controllers, particularly when high precision/high velocity tracking should be realized with different payloads.

Takegaki and Arimoto [23] have also considered the applicability of model reference adaptive control theory in robotics. They considered a linear centralized control law with feed-forward compensation of acceleration and gravitational effects. Then the following problem is posed: how to change the coefficients within the control law in such a way as to drive the output error to zero. For this purpose, similarly to Landau's theory [13-19], the Lyapunov function approach is applied. Thus, both the control law and the adaptation mechanism are obtained in a simple form, suitable for implementation. But, it is not quite clear how the gravity compensation affects the tracking quality, especially when weights of payloads vary over a wide range. If the payload mass (and inertias) is unknown, the gravitational forces cannot be compensated with a nonadaptive feed-forward term. Thus, the adaptation mechanism at the level of perturbation equations should take over this compensation. The same problem appears with some other adaptive algorithms [29, 30]. An attempt to improve the described control strategy was made by Arimoto and associates in 1984, [24], but the mentioned problem remained unsolved.

In Paragraph 3.2.2 we will present the robot control strategy based on hyperstability theory. Starting from the theory developed by Popov, Landau and others [13-19], Balestrino and associates applied it to robotic systems. However, before that Horowitz and Tomizuka presented an interesting attempt to apply hyperstability theory to robotics. They start from the nonlinear robot model

$$P = H(q)\ddot{q} + \dot{q}^T C(q, d)\dot{q} + g(q) \tag{3.1.2}$$

where H, C and g represent dynamic model matrices, described in Chapter 1. Then, they suggest the identification of H and C elements (they neglect gravitational effects) by using a specific adaptation mechanism based on Popov's inequality [13]. Here, the reference model is defined as a set of n linear, decoupled second-order systems (n double integrators), intended to decrease dynamic interaction between subsystems. However, in order to compensate for gravitational effect, the authors had to add an outer-loop PID controller. The evaluation of the algorithm on a 3-degree-of-freedom manipulator has been performed by Anex and Hubbard [31]. The experiments have shown that the basic algorithm must be slightly changed in order to cope with disturbances due to Coulomb friction, gravitational loading and actuator saturation. The algorithm was tested on low velocities because of the torque limitations of actuators. The experiments were not performed at higher joint rates at which adaptive control must offer significant improvements over the performance available from classical control methods.

The good features of the approach result from the fact that the adaptation mechanism is derived from the condition of overall system stability. Except for this, the control structure is based on a nonlinear dynamic robot model. Thus, the decoupled control is easy to achieve. But, the basic problem with this approach is the following: the dynamic effects are estimated without using any knowledge about the system dynamics. According to this approach it is necessary to identify H and C matrices, as if nothing about them were known ("black-box system"). Fortunately, most dynamic effects can still be calculated on line, because many parameters of a robot are mainly known and vary only slightly. For this reason, it would be more convenient to estimate only the unknown and highly variable parameters, as is the payload mass.

Another interesting attempt to introduce adaptive control strategy in robotics can be found in Lee's papers [29]. Here, the adaptive control is introduced at the level of linearized perturbation equations in the vicinity of a nominal joint trajectory. Lee suggests on-line calculation of Newton-Euler's equations for feed-forward computation of nominal control signals. A recursive least-squares identification scheme is used to identify the system parameters in the linearized perturbation equations and an optimal (one step ahead) adaptive self-tuning controller is designed to minimize the position and velocity errors along the trajectory. An extension of the idea to resolved motion rate and acceleration control is given in Ref. [30]. But, there is one problem with this approach which is still unresolved. Let us first suppose that the parameters of a robotic system are exactly known. Then, it is obvious that the identification of the linearized model is not necessary. We can use the method for linearized model calculation, which is also based on Newton-Euler's equations [32]. On the other hand, if we suppose that some parameters are unknown (for example, workpiece mass and inertias), then the nominal control cannot be calculated exactly. Thus, it is necessary to introduce an adaptive algorithm at the nominal level as well. The adaptive feed-forward compensation is not discussed in Ref. [29, 30].

Another interesting concept of adaptive robot control has been developed by Timofeev and associates [33-35]. As will be shown in Paragraph 3.2.3, this strategy is based on a quasi-gradient estimation algorithm and nonlinear feedback loops. Thus, it belongs to the class of indirect adaptive control laws. The unknown parameters are first estimated, and then fed to the controller. The controller as well as the estimator use the entire nonlinear robot model in on-line operation. For this reason, although a high quality tracking can be expected, its numerical complexity makes it very unsuitable for implementation.

Finally, we shall present an indirect decentralized adaptive control approach, which represents a trade-off between numerically burdensome but high performance and simple robust controllers suitable for implementation on low-cost microcomputers. The main difference between this and the previously described approach is in the following: here, a set of a few unknown parameters is estimated. Actually, this set includes the parameters of payload (its mass and inertias). The parameter estimation is based on an efficient quasigradient algorithm and the robot sensitivity model [36-39]. This model relates the driving torques/ forces of actuators and the mass (inertias) of a payload. Vukobratović and Kirćanski [40] have shown that the sensitivity model contains much fewer numerical operations than the entire dynamic model. The estimated parameters then influence the decentralized controller gains. The feedback gains are obtained from the stability analysis of the entire system for different parameters of payload. That is, the adaptive controller increases position and velocity feedback gains when manipulating payloads with increased mass and inertias, and vice versa. This concept will be illustrated by several examples.

3.2 Centralized Adaptive Control of Robot Manipulators

In this section we shall describe several adaptive control strategies. based on centralized control structure. As explained in Chapter 2, within the centralized control structure the plant to be controlled is considered as an unique multivariable system that includes the model of both robot arm and actuators. We shall pay special attention to self-tuning control, reference model-following control and a specific indirect centralized adaptive algorithm.

3.2.1. Self-tuning control strategy

There are many structures of self-tuning regulators differing in parameter estimation technique and control algorithms. But, it is usually assumed that the process to be controlled can be described by the stochastic system [1-9]

$$A(q^{-1})y(t) = B(q^{-1})u(t-t_d)+C(q^{-1})e(t) \tag{3.2.1}$$

where u and y are input and output signals, and $\{e(t)\}$ is a distrubance which represents a sequence of independent random variables. Further, $A(q^{-1})$, $B(q^{-1})$ and $C(q^{-1})$ are polynomials in the backward shift operator q^{-1}. In (3.2.1) t denotes the sampling instant, the sampling interval T is normalized to be one unit, and t_d is a positive integer specifying the time delay. Notice that $u(t-t_d)$ is equivalent to $q^{-t_d}u(t)$. Generally, the autoregressive model (3.2.1) is multivariable with u and y representing input and output vectors, respectively. Then the coefficients A and B represent the matrices whose elements are polynomials in q^{-1}.

Almost all parameter estimation algorithms for linear systems have been based on this model [1-9]. This model is linear with constant coefficients which should be estimated. On the other hand, the robot model is a highly nonlinear system. Thus, we shall not start our presentation with such an approximation, but with the nonlinear discrete model. We shall try to present a theory which is "compatible" with nonlinear robotic systems. But it should immediately be pointed out that such a theory is quite new, published in the past few years (for example, [41-43]). These results give a clear theoretical background necessary to explain various phenomena related to parameter vector dimensionality, noise influence, prediction error model design and others. We believe that these results will prove to be very applicable in the near future, regardless of enormous numerical complexity.

Nonlinear estimation

Parameter estimation techniques for nonlinear systems depend critically on the choice of model structure. The classical model structure used in nonlinear systems identification has been the functional series expansion of Volterra or Wiener [42]. Most of these expansions require a very large number of coefficients to characterize the process (several hundreds for a simple quadratic nonlinearity in cascade with a first-order linear system). The reason for this lies in the fact that these expansions map past inputs into the present output:

$$y(t) = \sum_{i=1}^{\infty} V_{k_i}(u(i),\ldots,u(t)) \tag{3.2.2}$$

where V_{k_i} is a homogeneous polynomial of degree i. This expansion involves lagged inputs only and thus requires a large number of coefficients. Utilizing results from automata theory to obtain a nonlinear difference equation model, Billings and Leontaritis [41] derived the following representation

$$y(t) = F_*[y(t-1),\ldots,y(t-n_y),\ u(t-1),\ldots,u(t-n_u)] \qquad (3.2.3)$$

where $F_*[\cdot]$ is some nonlinear function of u and y. Supposing that the degree of nonlinearity does not exceed ℓ, autoregressive model (3.2.3) can be represented as polynomial [42]

$$y(t) = \sum_{i=1}^{s} \theta_i V_i + \sum_{i=1}^{s} \sum_{j=1}^{s} \theta_{ij} V_i V_j + \ldots$$

$$+ \underbrace{\sum_{i=1}^{s} \sum_{j=1}^{s} \cdots \sum_{n=1}^{s}}_{\ell \text{ times}} \theta_{ij\ldots n} V_i V_j \cdots V_n \qquad (3.2.4)$$

where $V_1 = y(t-1),\ldots,V_{n_y} = y(t-n_y)$, $V_{n_y+1} = u(t-1),\ldots$, $V_s = u(t-n_u)$, and $s = n_y+n_u$. Introducing such polynomial expansion, we obtain the linear dependence of y(t) on parameters θ.

Assuming that the system output y(t) is corrupted by zero mean additive noise e(t) to yield the measured output signal

$$z(t) = y(t) + e(t) \qquad (3.2.5)$$

and substituting in (3.2.4), we obtain

$$z(t) = F_*^{\ell'}[z(t-1),\ldots,z(t-n_y),\ u(t-1),\ldots,u(t-n_u),$$

$$e(t-1),\ldots,e(t-n_y)] + e(t) \qquad (3.2.6)$$

we see that, although the model is linear in the parameters, the inclusion of lagged outputs introduces cross-product terms between the noise and the process input-output signals. In linear identification it is usually assumed that the internal noise can be translated to be additive at the output. The superposition principle does not apply here.

Before proceeding to parameter estimation, let us return to robotic systems. The model of a robot arm powered by actuators is the nonlinear multivariable system (2.2.8). Assuming that the state-vector x is measurable, y(t) = x(t), and applying Euler's expansion, we obtain the discrete model

$$S: \quad y(t)=y(t-1)+TA_D(y(t-1),\ \theta,\ d)+TB_D(y(t-1),\ \theta,\ d)u(t-1) \quad (3.2.7)$$

where T is the sampling period, and u is the constrained input vector: $|u_i| < U_m^i$. Matrices A_D and B_C are nonlinear with respect to y(t-1). It was shown in Chapter 1 that the nonlinearities are of sine/cosine, square sine/cosine and simple quadratic type. Approximating the degree of nonlinearity by a positive integer ℓ, we obtain the model (3.2.4) with $n_y=1$, $n_u=1$. As y(t) in Eq. (3.2.7) represents an n-dimensional vector, parameters θ on the right-hand side of (3.2.4) are obviously matrices of appropriate dimensions. In order to obtain a clearer insight into the model structure, let us fix $\ell=3$ and rewrite (3.2.7) as

$$S: \quad y(t) = h+A_D^{(1)}y(t-1)+A_D^{(2)}y^2(t-1)+B_D^{(1)}y(t-1)u(t-1) + $$
$$+ A_D^{(3)}y^3(t-1)+B_D^{(2)}y^2(t-1)u(t-1) \quad (3.2.8)$$

or concisely

$$y(t) = F_*^3[y(t-1),\ u(t-1)] \quad (3.2.8')$$

with h being a constant term due to gravity effects. Here, $A_D^{(1)}$ is an N×N dimensional matrix, A_D^2 is an $N\times((N(N+1))/2)$ dimensional matrix, etc.

Let us consider in more details the robotic system representation (3.2.8). We see that the present output y(t) depends on input/output pair at the time instant t-1. Here y involves joint coordinates and velocities (and perhaps some variables corresponding to actuators. However, accepting second-order models for actuators, the mathematical model of a robot manipulator may be written in the joint coordinate space as follows:

$$\ddot{y} = A(y,\ \dot{y}) + B(y)u \quad (3.2.9)$$

where $y\in R^n$ represents a joint coordinate vector, $A\in R^n$ and $B\in R^{n\times n}$. Following the procedure for obtaining nonlinear autoregressive model

(3.2.8), we shall see that y(t) depends on y(t-1), y(t-2) and u(t-2). Now, although the dimension of output vector is reduced ($y \in R^n$ while in (3.2.8) it was at least 2n-dimensional), the number of unknown coefficients is obviously not decreased. For a 6-degree-of-freedom robot, there are more than 2 thousand scalar parameters.

The parameter estimation of a robotic system represented by nonlinear autoregressive model (3.2.8) is a part of self-tuning control strategy. Introducing the prediction error vector $\varepsilon(t) = y(t) - \hat{y}(t)$, and formulating (3.2.8) into a prediction error model, we obtain the model:

$$y(t) = F^3[y(t-1), u(t-1), \varepsilon(t-1)] + \varepsilon(t) \tag{3.2.10}$$

which is the basis of parameter estimation algorithms. Expanding Eq. (3.2.10) and regrouping terms yields

$$y(t) = F^3_{yu}[y(t-1), u(t-1)]+F^3_{yu\varepsilon}[y(t-1), u(t-1), \varepsilon(t-1)]+\varepsilon(t) \tag{3.2.10a}$$

where $F^3_{yu}[\cdot]$ is a function of y and u only, and $F^3_{yu\varepsilon}[\cdot]$ represents all the cross product terms involving $\varepsilon(t)$. Separating out the unknown parameters gives

$$y(t) = \psi^{3T}_{yu}(t)\theta_{yu}(t-1)+\psi^{3T}_{yu\varepsilon}(t)\theta_{yu\varepsilon}(t-1)+\varepsilon(t) \tag{3.2.10b}$$

or simply

$$y(t) = \psi^3_{yu}(t)\theta_{yu}(t-1)+\xi(t) \tag{3.2.10c}$$

where $\xi(t)$ is highly correlated with the elements of $\psi^3_{zu}(t)$. For the autoregressive nonlinear robot model (3.2.8), we have

$$\psi^{3T}_{yu}(t) = [y(t-1), u(t-1), y^2(t-1), y(t-1)u(t-1), y^3(t-1), y^2(t-1)u(t-1)] \tag{3.2.11}$$

$$\theta_{yu}(t-1) = [\theta_1, \theta_2, \theta_{11}, \theta_{12}, \theta_{111}, \theta_{112}]^T \tag{3.2.12}$$

Because of the high correlation of $\xi(t)$ with $\psi^3_{zu}(t)$, we cannot directly apply the least squares algorithm, since it would yield biased estimates. Thus, we must use extended least squares algorithm based on the model (3.2.10b), i.e. the prediction model:

$$y(t) = \psi^T(t)\theta(t-1)+\varepsilon(t) \tag{3.2.12}$$

with $\psi^T(t) = [\psi^{3T}_{yu}(t), \psi^{3T}_{yu\varepsilon}(t)]$ and $\theta(t) = [\theta_{yu}(t)\ \theta_{yu\varepsilon}(t)]^T$. Now, we can apply the algorithm [41]:

$$\hat{\theta}(t+1) = \hat{\theta}(t)+P(t)\psi(t+1)(\lambda(t+1) + \psi(t+1)^T P(t)\psi(t+1))^{-1}\varepsilon(t+1) \tag{3.2.13}$$

with

$$P(t+1) = (P(t) - \frac{P(t)\psi(t+1)\psi(t+1)^T P(t)}{\lambda(t+1)-\psi(t+1)^T P(t+1)\psi(t+1)})/\lambda(t+1)$$

$$\lambda(t+1) = \lambda_o\lambda(t)+(1-\lambda_o)$$

$$\varepsilon(t) = y(t+1)-\psi(t+1)^T\hat{\theta}(t)$$

where $\lambda(t)$ is a variable forgetting factor.

The main disadvantage of the extended least squares algorithm (3.2.13) is the need to include noise or prediction error terms in the estimation error. The number of entries in $\hat{\theta}(t)$ is enormously large (even several thousands) for a typical manipulator. In an attempt to limit the dimension of the vector $\hat{\theta}(t)$ an interesting suboptimal least squares algorithm has been developed in [41]. Here, instead of immeasurable noise-free output y(t), we use its estimate $\hat{y}(t)$ recursively computed from

$$\hat{y}(t) = \psi^T_{\hat{y}u}(t)\hat{\theta}_{yu}(t-1). \tag{3.2.14}$$

The parameter estimation further proceeds as in (3.2.13) except for the following meaning of $\psi(t)$ and $\theta(t)$:

$$\psi(t)^T = \psi^T_{\hat{y}u}(t)$$
$$\theta(t) = [\theta_{yu}(t)]. \tag{3.2.15}$$

Let us drow now some conclusions from the previous theory. First, least squares parameter estimation algorithms for highly nonlinear systems such as robot manipulators have been developed in the most recent literature. The estimation methods are principally the same as those for linear systems, but the problem of model structure is much more complex. It is shown that for a typical robot it is necessary to estimate more than a thousand coefficients. Although this theory is not applied in robotics yet, we have presented it because of its consistence and clearness. Apart from that, the algorithms which will be described in the text to follow, are special cases of this theory. These special cases are obtained by including certain approximations with respect to the actual plant. These approximations, however, simplify the control structures, which is important for the application on low-cost microcomputers within robot control units.

Linear model estimation

The first and a very common approximation is the model linearization about a reference trajectory [10, 29, 30]. Using the Taylor's series expansion on (2.2.8) about the nominal trajectory and assuming that the higher order terms are negligible, the associated linearized perturbation equations for this control system can be obtained

$$\delta\dot{x} = \left.\frac{\partial A_D(x, \theta, d)}{\partial x}\right|_{x=x^o} + \left.\frac{\partial B_D(x, \theta, d)}{\partial x}\right|_{x=x^o} u^o \, \delta x + + B_D(x^o, \theta, d)\delta u \quad (3.2.16)$$

where $\delta x(t) = x(t) - x^o(t)$, $\delta u(t) = u(t) - u^o(t)$, $x^o(t)$ and $u^o(t)$ are nominal state and input vectors. Here, u^o and δu are constrained in amplitude (see (2.3.6)). Using the same notation as in (2.3.7), we obtain

$$\delta\dot{x} = \tilde{A}_D(x^o, \theta, d)\delta x + B_D(x^o, \theta, d)\delta u \quad (3.2.17)$$

where $\tilde{A}_D$ represents the Jacobian of $A_D(x, \theta, d) + B_D(x, \theta, d)u$, evaluated at the nominal states $x^o(t)$. Discretizing (3.2.17) with the sampling period T, we obtain the following discrete-time linear model

$$y(t) = F(t-1)y(t-1) + G(t-1)u(t-1) \quad (3.2.18)$$

with $u(t) \in R^n$ being a piecewise constant control input vector over the time interval between any two consecutive sampling instants, y(t) is the perturbed state vector $y = \delta x$. Here we suppose that the state variables are measurable. This is quite a realistic supposition with robotic systems. Still, the estimation of the matrices F and G may be computationally awkward because of high dimensions. Supposing that 3 states for any subsystem are measured, we obtain a $(3n)\times(3n)$ dimensional F matrix, and a $(3n)\times n$ dimensional G matrix. Notice that for $n=6$, even 432 parameters are to be estimated. For this reason, it is convenient to follow the model (3.2.9) given in joint coordinate space. The corresponding linearized model becomes

$$\delta\ddot{y} = A_1(t)\delta\dot{y}+A_2(t)\delta y+B(y^o(t))\delta u \tag{3.2.19}$$

where $A_1 \in R^{n\times n}$ and $A_2 \in R^{n\times n}$ are the Jacobians of the right-hand side of (3.2.9) with respect to y and $\dot{y}$, evaluated at the nominal states. Here, $y \in R^n$ is the joint coordinate vector of manipulator, and n - the number of joints. Now, we can apply Euler's method and discretize the linearized model (3.2.19)

$$y(t) = A_1 y(t-1) + A_2 y(t-2) + B_2 u(t-2) + e(t) \tag{3.2.20}$$

For simplicity, the symbol $y(t)$ is used instead of $\delta y(t)$. Matrices A_1, A_2 and B_2 are $n\times n$ - dimensional, with unknown elements, and $e(\cdot)$ represents the modeling error.

Let us note that the model (3.2.20) represents a special case of autoregressive model (3.2.1), on which almost all the parameter estimation algorithms for linear systems [1-9] are based. Introducing the linear backward shift operator q^{-1}, model (3.2.20) becomes

$$[I-A_1q^{-1}-A_2q^{-2}]y(t) = B_2q^{-2}u(t) + e(t) \tag{3.2.21}$$

This is a special case of the model (3.2.1).

Model (3.2.20) can be rewritten in the form:

$$y(t) = [A_1 \quad A_2 \quad B_2]\begin{bmatrix} y(t-1) \\ \hline y(t-2) \\ \hline u(t-2) \end{bmatrix} + e(t) \tag{3.2.22a}$$

or, simply, as

$$y(t) = \theta_{yu}^T \psi(t-1) + e(t) \tag{3.2.22b}$$

with $\theta_{yu}^T = [A_1 \mid A_2 \mid B_2]$ and $\psi(t-1)^T = [y(t-1)^T, y(t-2)^T, u(t-2)]^T$. We see that θ_{yu} comprises $3n^2$ parameters. For a 6-degree-of-freedom robot it corresponds to 108 parameters. This is 1 or even 2 orders of magnitude less than for a nonlinear autoregressive robot model.

Let us point out an essential difference between the nonlinear autoregressive model (3.2.6) and the linear autoregressive model (3.2.20) as far as noise is concerned. The cross-product terms between the noise and the process input-output signals are characteristic for the nonlinear model. The superposition principle is applicable here and results in the additive character of noise. But it does not mean that a classical least squares method is directly applicable. This is a good and simple method, but its main drawback is that it gives biased estimates unless the output y(t) is directly measurable and noise-free. Otherwise, the extended least squares algorithm must be used. But the extended prediction model results in an extended parameter vector, similar to θ in (3.2.12). In most robot manipulators the measurement of joint coordinates can be considered as noise-free. Joint coordinate sensors are most often high-precision and high-quality digital encoders. Thus, we shall make the following assumption: measurement noise is negligible. We can now apply the well known classical least squares scheme to the model (3.2.22b). Thus, the recursive scheme follows

$$\hat{\theta}_i(t+1) = \hat{\theta}_i(t) + P(t+1)\psi(t)[y_i(t+1) - \hat{\theta}_i^T(t)\psi(t)] \tag{3.2.23}$$

$$P(t+1) = \left(P(t) - \frac{P(t)\psi(t)\psi^T(t)P(t)}{\lambda+\psi^T(t)P(t)\psi(t)}\right)/\lambda \tag{3.2.24}$$

where λ denotes the forgetting factor $(0<\lambda\leq 1)$, $\hat{\theta}_i(t)$ - the estimate of the ith row of matrix $[A_1 \mid A_2 \mid B_2]$, and y_i is the output of the ith robot subsystem. Here, for simplicity, λ is taken to be a constant. It could also be time-varying as in (3.2.13). The use of forgetting factor λ is very common when tracking slowly time-varying system parameters. Now, we must impose the second assumption: variation speed of parameters is lower than the adaptation speed. This assumption is made to simplify the identification scheme and it needs to be verified experimentally. Theoretically, it cannot be proved.

Extended minimum variance self-tuning control

In the preceding text we pointed out that the parameter estimation represents the basis for self-tuning regulators. A block diagram of the entire control structure is presented in Fig. 3.1. The methods belonging to the self-tuning structures can be classified into 3 categories

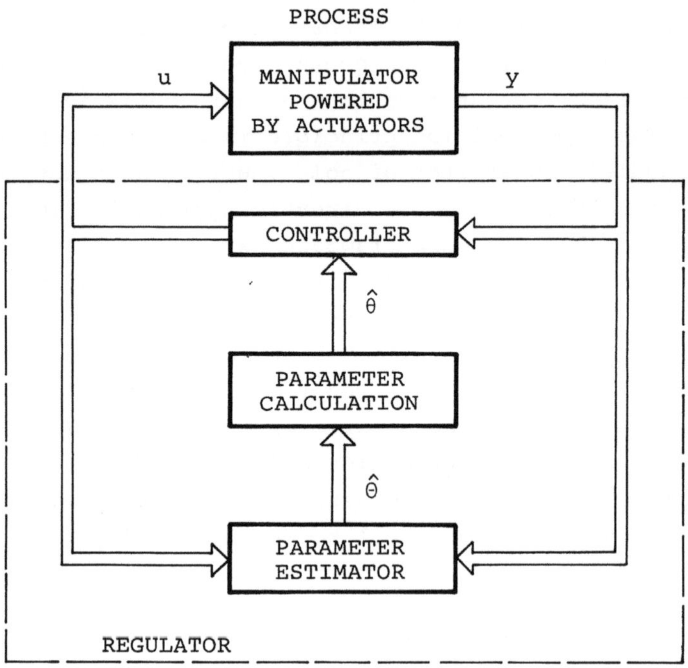

Fig. 3.1. Block diagram of the self-tuning regulator

[1 - 12]:

1) Minimum variance control
2) Extended minimum variance control
3) Pole-zero placement control.

Generally, any of these controllers is of the form [1]:

$$u(t) = \frac{G(q^{-1})}{F(q^{-1})} y(t) \tag{3.2.25}$$

where

$$F(q^{-1}) = 1 + f_1 q^{-1} + \cdots + f_\ell q^{-\ell}$$
$$G(q^{-1}) = g_1 + g_2 q^{-1} + \cdots + g_m q^{-m+1}. \tag{3.2.26}$$

The regulator parameters

$$v = [g_1 \cdots g_m \; f_1 \cdots f_\ell]^T \tag{3.2.27}$$

should be computed from the estimated prediction model parameters. Assuming that the prediction model (3.2.22b) is reasonably good, a regulator can be obtained by applying any design method to (3.2.22b). That would yield from a simple linear to complicated nonlinear expressions whose evaluation is far more time consuming than the updating of the parameter estimates [1].

Minimum variance controllers (MVC) as well as extended MVC are based on Linear quadratic Gaussian theory. They involve solving the Riccati equation following from the minimization of the performance index

$$V = \lim_{N\to\infty} E\{\frac{1}{N} \sum_{i=t}^{N} [y^2(i) + \zeta u^2(i)]\} \tag{3.2.28}$$

This is obviously computationally awkward and difficult for real-time implementation. There are, however, special cases when the calculations can be considerably simplified. When there is no penalty on the control, $\zeta=0$, the criterion (3.2.28) reduces to the variance of the output. The corresponding controllers are called minimum variance controllers. This procedure is essentially a pole placing algorithm where the controller places poles to cancel system zeros. The resulting control is, however, erratic and often with excessively large amplitudes.

Extended MVC includes penalization of both error and input norms (see papers of Clarke and Gawthrop [44, 45]). This approach was also followed by Koivo [10]. For multivariable linear prediction model (3.2.22):

$$y(t) = \hat{\theta}_{yu}^T \psi(t-1) + e(t) \tag{3.2.29}$$

we introduce the performance index

$$J(u) = E\{\Delta y(t+1)^T Q \Delta y(t+1) + u(t)^T R u(t)\} \tag{3.2.30}$$

where $\Delta y(t) = y(t) - y^o(t)$, $y^o(t)$ - joint coordinate vector at nominal trajectory, E{•} - mathematical expectation conditioned on the available measurements at time <t-1, Q>0 is a symmetric n×n matrix, and R>0 is a control weighting matrix. Notice that the main difference between (3.2.28) and (3.2.30) lies in the fact that (3.2.30) includes only one step evaluation, while (3.2.28) takes into account input/output variance accurring at time t, t+1,...,N for N→∞. This simplification leads to the simple control law [10]

$$u(t) = -R^{-1}B_o^T\Omega(\hat{y}(t+1|t-1)-y^o(t+1)) \qquad (3.2.31)$$

with recursive relations

$$\hat{y}(t+1|t-1) = \hat{\theta}_{yu}^T(t-1)\hat{\psi}(t|t-1)$$

and $\hat{\psi}(t, t-1) = [\hat{y}(t|t-1), y(t-1), y(t-2), u(t-2)]$.

Here, $\hat{y}(t+k|t-1)$ means the k step ahead predicted value of y. In practical applications the control law (3.2.31) could result in a closed--loop unstable operation if unknown robot parameters are far from the initial guess and/or are fast time varying compared to adaptation speed. The following remark may be made which applies to optimal control approach in general: many iterations in selection of Q and R matrices compound the design problem. According to the simulation results of Stanford manipulator [10], there exists also the following serious problem: estimated parameters change erratically during the first part of the trajectory (in about 0.3s) producing abrupt variations in control signals (input voltages to DC motors) and erratic movements of robot arm (Fig. 3.2). Thereby, is should be kept in mind that the time evaluations shown in Fig. 3.2 are obtained after some trial-and-error iterations concerning initial guess and performance index weighting factors. Interference between links flexibility and erratic control is the second problem, that generally burdens the application of EMV self--tuning controllers.

The self-tuning approach based on pole-zero placement is presented in many papers devoted to adaptive control of linear systems (see, for example, [46]). Leininger [11, 12] examined their applicability to robotic systems. But, the conclusions drawn for extended minimum variance approach practically hold for pole-zero placement control as well. The difference is in that we impose the closed-loop poles instead of weighting matrices. On the other hand, this procedure is described for single-input, single-output linear systems only. This procedure will be the basis for PID local controllers within the scope of decentralized adaptive control strategy, which will be described in Paragraph 3.3.

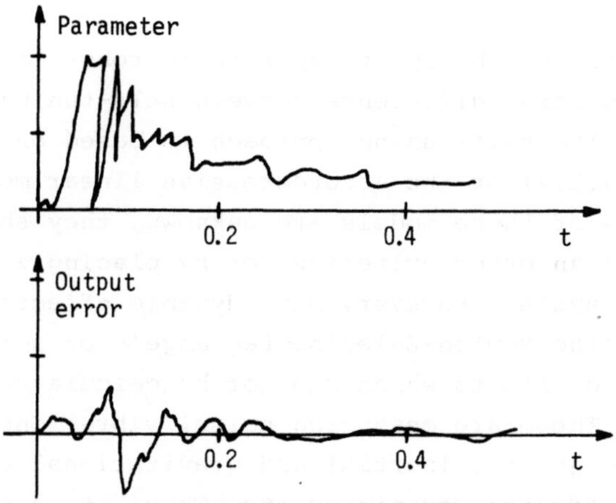

Fig. 3.2. Example of self-tuning action

3.2.2. <u>Centralized reference model following control</u>

There are 3 basic approaches to the design of model reference adaptive systems [13]:

1) Local parametric optimization theory

2) Lyapunov functions

3) Hyperstability and positivity concepts.

The first approach is explained in more details in the introduction to this chapter. This is chronologically the first approach developed within the scope of linear system theory. It includes the well known gradient method - the steepest descent algorithm. An interesting application of this method in robotics is given by Dubowsky and DesForges [20]. The obtained results appear to be very simple and practical. But these methods have a general drawback: nothing is said about the stability of the resulting adaptive system. This approach as well as the approach by Lyapunov functions [47, 48] will not be considered in this book. According to the results from general system theory, one can say that the stability-based approach, and in particular the use of hyperstability and positivity concepts, is the most successful approach to the design of model reference adaptive systems [13]. The application of the theory to centralized robot models is given in Ref. [26, 49].

Before proceeding to the theory of hyperstable robot controllers, let us point out an essential difference between self-tuning and hyperstable regulators. The self-tuning approach is based on the nonlinear polynomial model (3.2.4) or the autoregressive linear model (3.2.1). As the coefficients of these models are unknown, they should be estimated by minimizing an error criterion, or by placing zeros or poles of the closed-loop system. However, many dynamic effects can be computed on-line by using Newton-Euler's, Lagrange's or some other method. There are still some effects which can not be calculated due to their stochastic nature. These are measuring noise, vibrations due to elasticity of links and joints, inertial and gravitational effects due to the influence of different workpieces etc. Thus, it is quite natural to compensate the deterministic effects by "on-line" model computation, and to compensate the stochastic effects by introducing the adaptive control loops, too. Such a control structure can be obtained by combining the hyperstability theory and model reference adaptive control. First, we shall derive a suitable robot reference model in the sequel. Then, the structure of both nonadaptive and adaptive control terms will be presented.

In order to obtain a suitable centralized reference model, let us consider the models of subsystems. Each subsystem is assigned to a manipulator degree-of-freedom, describing the dynamical behaviour of the corresponding actuator and the transmission between it and the joint. Thus, let us consider the subsystem model S^i $(i=1,\dots,n)$, defined by (2.2.2). Denoting by x^{io} the n_i - dimensional state vector of the ith subsystem on the nominal trajectory, and by $u_i^o \in R$ the nominal imput signal, we obtain

$$S^i:\quad \dot{x}^{io} = A^i(\theta^i)x^{io}+b^i(\theta^i)u_i^o+f^i(\theta^i)P_i^o$$

where P_i^o represents the nominal driving torque (or force) of the ith actuator. As P_i^o depends on x^{io}, we can extract the corresponding terms from the manipulator model

$$S^M:\quad P^o = H(q^o,\ d)\ddot{q}^o+h(q^o,\ \dot{q}^o,\ d)$$

and adjoin them to subsystem models. Thus, the diagonal elements of matrix $H(q^o, d)$ should be presented as

$$H_{ii}(q^o, d) = \bar{H}_{ii}(d) + \varepsilon_H(q^o, d)$$

with $\bar{H}_{ii}(d)>0$, $\varepsilon_H = H_{ii}-\bar{H}_{ii}$. The ith element of vector $h(q^o, \dot{q}^o, d)$ can be presented as

$$h_i(q^o, \dot{q}^o, d) = \bar{h}_i(d)q_i^o + \varepsilon_h(q^o, \dot{q}^o, d)$$

with $\varepsilon_h = h_i-\bar{h}_i q_i^o$. Subsystem model S^i now becomes

$$S^i: \quad \dot{x}^{io} = \bar{A}^i(\theta^i, d)x^{io} + \bar{b}^i(\theta^i, d)u_i^o + \bar{f}^i(\theta^i, d)\Delta P_i \qquad (3.2.32)$$

where $\bar{A}^i(\theta^i, d) = \bar{C}^i(\theta^i, d)(A^i(\theta^i) + f^i(\theta^i)\bar{h}(d)T_1^i)$

$$\bar{C}^i(\theta^i, d) = (I_{n_i} - f^i(\theta^i)\bar{H}_{ii}(d)T^i)^{-1},$$

$$\bar{b}^i(\theta^i, d) = \bar{C}^i(\theta^i, d)b^i(\theta^i),$$

$$\bar{f}^i(\theta^i, d) = \bar{C}^i(\theta^i, d)f^i(\theta^i),$$

with $T_1^i \in R^{1\times n_i}$ and $T^i \in R^{1\times n_i}$ being the transformation matrices defined as

$$T_1^i x^i = q_i \quad \text{and} \quad T^i \dot{x}^i = \ddot{q}_i.$$

Here, ΔP_i represents the difference between the actual and the approximated value of driving torque (force) of the ith actuator

$$\Delta P_i = P_i - \bar{H}_{ii}T^i\dot{x}^i - \bar{h}_i T_1^i x^i.$$

The model (3.2.32) includes both the actuator parameters and inertial and gravitational loads. These loads depend on manipulator configuration and are time-varying. Denoting by $\bar{d}$ an average value of parameter vector, the nominal control can be approximately evaluated from the free subsystem S^i (3.2.32):

$$\dot{x}^{io} = \bar{A}^i(\theta^i, \bar{d})x^{io} + \bar{b}^i(\theta^i, \bar{d})u_i^o \qquad (3.2.33)$$

with $\bar{A}^i$ and $\bar{b}^i$ being time invariant matrix and vector, respectively.

The set of subsystems (3.2.33) represents actually n independent linear time-invariant second- or third-order systems. These subsystems are decoupled and thus very useful for control synthesis. If we wish to control the nonlinearly coupled system so that it behaves as a set of linear, decoupled subsystems, it is quite natural to accept (3.2.33) for the reference model. To underline the introduction of reference model, we shall use the following notations

$$A_M^i = \bar{A}^i(\theta^i, \bar{d})$$
$$b_M^i = \bar{b}^i(\theta^i, \bar{d}) \qquad (3.2.34)$$

or

$$S_M^i: \quad \dot{x}^{io} = A_M^i x^{io} + b_M^i u_i^o. \qquad (3.2.35)$$

In the case of second-order subsystems, (3.2.35) becomes

$$\ddot{q}_i^o = -a_i^* \dot{q}_i^o - f_i^* q_i^o + b_i^* u_i^o \qquad (3.2.36)$$

with $a_i^* = a_i/\mathcal{L}_i$, $f_i^* = f_i \bar{h}_i/\mathcal{L}_i$ and $b_i^* = b_i/\mathcal{L}_i$, where $\mathcal{L}_i = 1 + f_i \bar{H}_{ii}$. Here, the coefficients a_i, f_i and b_i are determined from the second-order model of the actuator without adjoint inertial and gravitational load: $\ddot{q}_i = a_i \dot{q}_i + b_i u_i + f_i P_i$. Substituting $P_i = \bar{H}_{ii} \ddot{q}_i + \bar{h}_i q_i$ into it, we get (3.2.36). The matrices of the reference model (3.2.35) are now

$$A_M^i = \begin{bmatrix} 0 & 1 \\ -f_i^* & -a_i^* \end{bmatrix}, \qquad b_M^i = \begin{bmatrix} 0 \\ b_i^* \end{bmatrix} \qquad (3.2.37)$$

If we join together the subsystems (3.2.35), we obtain the centralized reference model

$$S_M: \quad \dot{x}^o = A_M x^o + B_M u^o \qquad (3.2.38)$$

For second-order subsystems, we have

$$A_M = \left[\begin{array}{c|c} 0 & I_n \\ \hline A_{21}^M & A_{22}^M \end{array}\right] \quad \text{and} \quad B_M = \left[\begin{array}{c} 0 \\ \hline B_2^M \end{array}\right] \qquad (3.2.39)$$

with $A_{21}^M = -\text{diag}(f_i^*)$, $A_{22}^M = -\text{diag}(a_i^*)$ and $B_2^M = \text{diag}(b_i^*)$.

The entire manipulator model that includes second-order subsystems can be represented by

$$S:\quad u = \hat{H}(q,\ \theta)\ddot{q} + \hat{h}(q,\ \dot{q},\ \theta) \tag{3.2.40}$$

with $\hat{H}$ and $\hat{h}$ obtained by using simple transformations upon H and h. This model can also be presented in canonical form

$$\dot{\xi} = A(\xi,\ \theta)\xi + B(\xi,\ \theta)u \tag{3.2.41}$$

with $\xi^T = [q^T \mid \dot{q}^T]$.

Let us first suppose that the parameter vector θ is constant and known. Then, we can apply the centralized control

$$u = \hat{H}(q,\ \theta)[\ddot{q}^o + D(\xi-\xi^o)] + \hat{h}(\xi,\ \theta) \tag{3.2.42}$$

with $D \in R^{2n\times 2n}$ being the feedback gain matrix. Further, we shall suppose that this matrix is equal to A_M in (3.2.39). The model (3.2.42) now becomes

$$u = [0 \mid \hat{H}(\xi,\ \theta)](B_M u^o + A_M\xi) + \hat{h}(\xi,\ \theta) \tag{3.2.43}$$

where u^o satisfies the reference model (3.2.38). It is easy to show that $\hat{h}(\xi,\ \theta)$ can be presented as

$$\hat{h}(\xi,\ \theta) = [\hat{Q}_2(\xi,\ \theta) \mid \hat{Q}_1(\xi,\ \theta)]\xi \tag{3.2.44}$$

where $\hat{Q}_1$ and $\hat{Q}_2$ are appropriate n×n matrices. Thus

$$\hat{h}(\xi,\ \theta) = \hat{Q}_{21}(\xi,\ \theta)\xi, \qquad \hat{Q}_{21} \in R^{n\times 2n}. \tag{3.2.45}$$

Substituting this in (3.2.43), we get

$$u = ([0 \mid \hat{H}(\xi,\ \theta)]A_M + \hat{Q}_{21}(\xi,\ \theta))\xi + [0\ \ \hat{H}(\xi,\ \theta)]B_M u^o$$

or simply

$$u = K_p(\xi,\ \theta)\xi + K_u(\xi,\ \theta)u^o \tag{3.2.46}$$

with $K_p(\xi,\ \theta)$ and $K_u(\xi,\ \theta)$ being determined by $\hat{H}$ and $\hat{Q}_{21}$ and by reference model matrices A_M and B_M. The control law (3.2.46) ideally compensates for system nonlinearity and makes it decoupled. The system model in the space of $e=x-x^o$ becomes

$$\dot{e} = A_M e \tag{3.2.47}$$

where A_M is a diagonal matrix.

Suppose now that θ is unknown. Replacing the actual value of θ by a constant "average" quantity $\bar{\theta}$, we obtain the control law

$$u = K_p(\xi, \bar{\theta})\xi + K_u(\xi, \bar{\theta})u^o \tag{3.2.48}$$

It is apparent that the asymptotic stability (3.2.47) does not hold now. Thus, we have to modify (3.2.48) by introducing some adaptive components. Supposing that $\mathcal{L}_p(\xi, e)$ and $\mathcal{L}_u(\xi, e)$ represent the matrices governed by an adaptive mechanism, we can write

$$u = [K_p(\xi, \bar{\theta})+\mathcal{L}_p(\xi, \theta)]\xi+[K_u(\xi, \theta)+\mathcal{L}_u(\xi, e)]u^o \tag{3.2.49}$$

This is the general form of direct, centralized adaptive control law. Here, we are concerned with 2 basic components:

1) a deterministic, dynamic component expressed in terms of matrices $K_p(\xi, \bar{\theta})$ and $K_u(\xi, \bar{\theta})$, and

2) an adaptive component expressed in terms of functions $\mathcal{L}_p(\xi, e)$ and $\mathcal{L}_u(\xi, e)$.

For the computation of the dynamic component, it is very useful to apply the numeric-symbolic method, described in Chapter 1. The adaptive component will be determined using the hyperstability theory. The block diagram of the complete system including reference model (3.2.38), control law (3.2.49) and robot model (3.2.41), is shown in Fig. 3.3. A linear static compensator D is also introduced in this scheme:

$$v = De \tag{3.2.50}$$

where v is the generalized error which will be explained in the text to follow.

Let us now derive the differential equation which satisfies the error

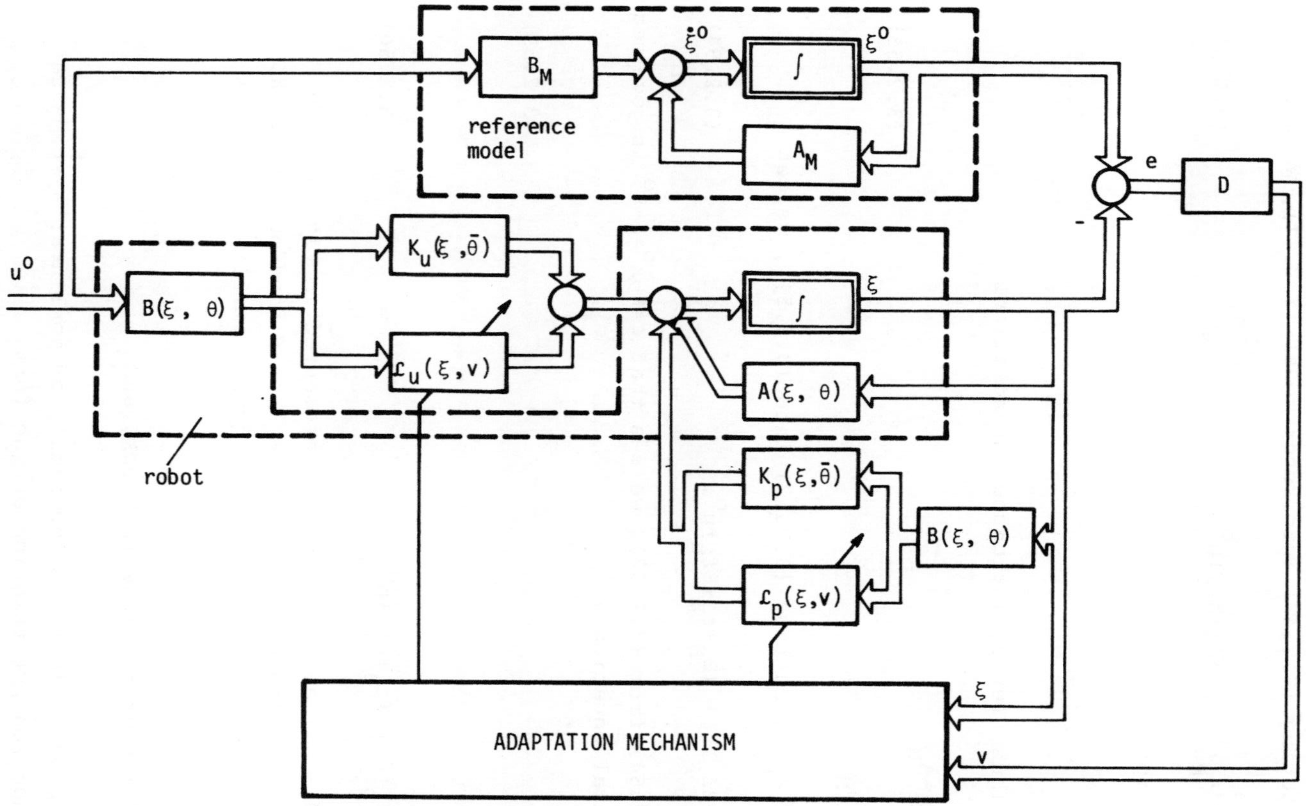

Fig. 3.3. Centrlaized adaptive control scheme

vector e. Substituting (3.2.49) into robot model (3.2.41), we get

$$\dot{\xi} = (A+BK_p+B\mathcal{L}_p)\xi + (BK_u+B\mathcal{L}_u)u^o \quad (3.2.51)$$

In a perfectly compensated system

$$A + BK_p \to A_M, \qquad BK_u \to B_M, \quad (3.2.52)$$

and $\mathcal{L}_p \to 0$, $\mathcal{L}_u \to 0$. Thus, let us introduce the notations

$$\varepsilon_A = A + BK_p - A_M,$$
$$\varepsilon_B = BK_u - B_M \quad (3.2.53)$$

so that $\varepsilon_A \to 0$ and $\varepsilon_B \to 0$. Putting (3.2.53) into (3.2.51), we get

$$\dot{\xi} = (A_M+\varepsilon_A+B\mathcal{L}_p)\xi + (B_M+\varepsilon_B+B\mathcal{L}_u)u^o. \quad (3.2.54)$$

Subtracting (3.2.54) from (3.2.38), we see that $e=\xi-x^o=\xi-\xi^o$ is governed by the differential equation

$$\dot{e} = A_M e - w \quad (3.2.55)$$

where

$$-w = (\varepsilon_A+B\mathcal{L}_p)\xi + (\varepsilon_B+B\mathcal{L}_u)u^o. \quad (3.2.56)$$

The equations (3.2.55) and (3.2.56) are presented in Fig. 3.4. The system shown in this figure consists of a linear feedforward block, and a nonlinear feedback block. Then the hyperstability conditions [13] become:

1) positivity of linear feedforward block, and

2) the feedback block belongs to the family of nonlinear systems satisfying an input/output relation of the form

$$\int_0^{t_1} v^T w \, dt \geq -\gamma_o^2 \quad \text{for} \quad \forall t_1 > 0 \quad (3.2.57)$$

which is known as "Popov's inequality".

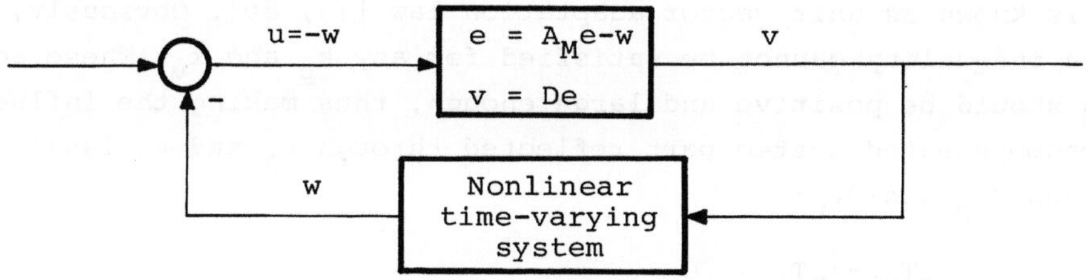

Fig. 3.4. Nonlinear control system

The static compensator D is intended to preserve the positivity of the feedforward block. The condition of positivity is fulfilled if D satisfies the Lyapunov equation

$$A_M^T D + DA_M = -Q \quad (3.2.58)$$

with Q>0.

From the condition 2), one obtains the adaptive components $\mathcal{L}_p(\xi, v)$ and $\mathcal{L}_u(\xi, v)$ as

$$\mathcal{L}_p = k_p(t) v \xi^T$$
$$\mathcal{L}_u = k_u(t) v u^{oT} \quad (3.2.59)$$

where $k_p(t): T \to R^{n\times n}$ and $k_u(t): T \to R^{n\times n}$ are positive real functions. It is apparent that by choosing different forms of functions $k_p(t)$ and $k_u(t)$, we obtain a family of hyperstable adaptive controllers. For example, by choosing $k_p(t)v = k_p\ \mathrm{sgn}(v)$ and $k_u(t)v = k_u\ \mathrm{sgn}(v)$, we obtain

$$\mathcal{L}_p(t) = k_p(\mathrm{sgn}(v))\xi^T$$

$$\mathcal{L}_u(t) = k_u(\mathrm{sgn}(v))u^{oT}$$

where k_p and k_u are positive real constants. The adapttion mechanism (3.2.59) can also be accepted as

$$\mathcal{L}_p = k_p \frac{v}{||v||}(\mathrm{sgn}\ \xi)^T$$
$$\mathcal{L}_u = k_u \frac{v}{||v||}(\mathrm{sgn}\ u^o)^T \quad (3.2.60)$$

which is known as unit vector adaptation law [13, 50]. Obviously, the Popov's inequality cannot be satisfied for any k_p and k_v. These constants should be positive and large enough, thus making the influence of noncompensated system part reflected through ε_A and ε_B less effective than BL_p and BL_u:

$$k_p > c||(B^TB)^{-1}B^T\varepsilon_A|| \qquad (3.2.61)$$
$$k_v > c||(B^TB)^{-1}B^T\varepsilon_B||$$

where the constant c depends on the adaptation mechanism (3.2.59) - (3.2.60).

Finally, let us point out some excellences and shortcomings of the described control strategy. Here, the manipulator model is not considered as an unknown plant, but as a plant whose dynamics is partially known and computable in real-time. Consequently, this strategy offers better transient behaviour compared to that with self-tuning regulators. According to the simulation results [26], "erratic" variations do not occur in control signals and robot movements when starting the learning process, but a smooth adaptation of gains during the time, as shown in Fig. 3.5. The second major advantage of this approach follows from the fact that the adaptation mechanism is based on stability of the entire system. However, the main drawback of this approach is its extremely high numerical complexity.

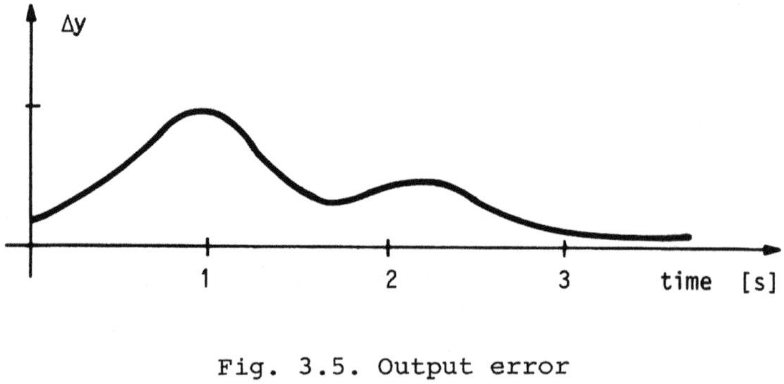

Fig. 3.5. Output error

It originates from the centralized control approach. The complete robot model included in gain matrices $K_p(\xi, \bar{\theta})$ and $K_u(\xi, \bar{\theta})$ must be computed on-line. As a 6-degree-of-freedom robot model computation requires several hundred floating-point multiplications [51, 52], it is difficult to be achieved with a low-cost microcomputer.

3.2.3. Indirect centralized adaptive control

Now we shall examine the indirect adaptive robot control, which consists of two blocks: parameter estimation block and adaptive controller. The adaptive controller is governed by the parameter estimates and output states. A specific indirect adaptive controller for robotic purposes is developed in Ref. [33-35]. It will be shortly presented in the text to follow.

Consider a centralized robot model that includes the model of both mechanical arm and actuators:

$$S: \quad u = \hat{H}(q, d, \theta_a)\ddot{q} + \hat{h}(q, \dot{q}, d, \theta_a) \tag{3.2.62}$$

where d represents the vector of mechanical parameters of robot arm, and θ_a the vector of actuator parameters.

Neglecting the dynamics, of actuators, this model becomes

$$S: \quad u = D_a H(q, d)\ddot{q} + D_a h(q, \dot{q}, d) \tag{3.2.63}$$

where D_a is a diagonal matrix. Let us separate the elements of the vector d into two subvectors

$$d = \begin{bmatrix} \theta_k \\ \hline \theta_d \end{bmatrix} \tag{3.2.64}$$

where θ_k is assigned to kinematical (geometrical) parameters, while θ_d represents the vector of dynamical parameters of links (masses and inertias). Vector θ_d can be represented as

$$\theta_d = [m_1 \cdots m_n \; \underline{J}_1 \cdots \underline{J}_n]^T \tag{3.2.65}$$

where m_i and J_i refer to the mass and the tensor of inertia of the ith segment, respectively.

As shown in Ref. [40, 53], dynamic model matrices H and h depend linearly on θ_d. Thus, the model (3.2.63) can be written as

$$S: \quad u = D_a \phi(q, \dot{q}, \ddot{q}, \theta_k)\theta_d \tag{3.2.66}$$

where D_a and ϕ are $n \times n$ and $n \times n_d$ matrices, respectively.

In the case when we know exactly the parameter vector d, we can apply the centralized nonadaptive control law

$$u = D_a \phi(q, \dot{q}, \ddot{q}^o + D_p(q-q^o) + D_v(\dot{q}-\dot{q}^o), \theta_k)\theta_d \tag{3.2.67}$$

where D_p and D_v are diagonal matrices.

However, θ_d includes the parameters of payload. In this case θ_d is un unknown function of time. Thus, the control law (3.2.67) is applicable only if the parameter vector is estimated on-line. Let us divide the interval $\tau=[t_o, t_f]$ into segments $[t_k, t_{k+1}]$, $k=1,2,\ldots,k_\tau$, and denote the estimate of θ_d at time instant t_k by $\bar{\theta}_d(t_k)$. The estimator is accepted in the form

$$\bar{\theta}_d(t_{k+1}) = \psi(\bar{\theta}_d(t_k)) \tag{3.2.68}$$

then we define a generalized error $v \in R^n$

$$v = v(q-q^o, \dot{q}-\dot{q}^o) \tag{3.2.69}$$

which refers to the state deviation from the reference trajectory. According to Ref. [33-35], the estimator (3.2.68) can be defined as

$$\bar{\theta}_d(t_{k+1}) = \bar{\theta}_d(t_k) + \phi^T(t_k')[\phi(t_k')\phi^T(t_k')]^{-1}D_a^{-1}v(t_k') \tag{3.2.70}$$

where $t_k' \in [t_k, t_{k+1})$ is defined by the condition

$$||v(t_k')|| > \delta \tag{3.2.71}$$

where δ is a given positive real number.

The preceding equations show that the centralized control law should be calculated at any time instant t_k, using the parameter estimate from the time interval $[t_{k-1}, t_k)$. Then we have to test the condition (3.2.71) at least once. Thus, we obtain the time instant t_k'. In the time interval (t_k', t_{k+1}) we have to form the estimate $\bar{\theta}_d(t_{k+1})$ according to (3.2.70). If the condition (3.2.71) is not satisfied for any t_k', then we accept $\bar{\theta}_d(t_{k+1}) = \bar{\theta}_d(t_k)$.

In conclusion, it is interesting to note that the presented concept differs from self-tuning approach because it is based on the dynamic robot model. This method differs from model-following adaptive control, too. Namely, it does not use a reference model to express the control objective. The estimation problem is here solved by using a "quasi-gradient" algorithm. Based on this estimate, the control signals are calculated following the "inverse-control" approach. The numerical complexity of such a procedure is very high. Also, it is obvious that it is unnecessary to estimate such a large number of parameters (3.2.65), because many of them are well-known and constant.

3.3 Decentralized Adaptive Control Strategy for Mechanical Manipulators

The purpose of this section is to provide an overview of decentralized adaptive control algorithms. PID self-tuning local controllers, decentralized reference model-following controllers and a specific indirect adaptive structure will be described. As will be shown, such controllers are very convenient for driving the up-to-date industrial robots. These algorithms are not numerically involved and difficult for real-time applications. Apart from that, they provide for system adaptivity with respect to different payloads and parameter variations.

3.3.1. Self-tuning local controllers

An overwhelming majority of the regulators which are used to drive industrial robots are digital or analog PID, because when properly tuned they generally achieve satisfactory performance. This is undoubtedly true when driving only one joint (or more physically decoupled joints) at a time. As pointed out in Chapter 2, coupling effects and interaction forces between links moving simultaneously may decrease the performance of the overall system and increase the tracking error during following the reference trajectory. The disturbances of unknown magnitude (due to grasping or releasing a payload with unknown mass and moments of inertia, interaction due to flexibility of links etc.) also reduce the quality of tracking.

In this section we shall deal with a possible solution for applications, because of more stringent robot performance requirement and/or the existence of larger modeling uncertainty levels. Supposing that the fixed parameter controllers are inadequate, we shall discuss self--tuning local regulators. Moreover, we shall restrict our attention to PID control structures with the aim to bridge traditional and modern adaptive control concepts.

Let us start with a classical PID regulator (Fig. 3.6)

$$U(s) = K\left[1 + \frac{1}{T_i s} + \frac{T_d s}{1+T_d s/N}\right]E(s) \tag{3.3.1}$$

where K is the gain, T_i and T_d are integral and derivative time constants, N is a positive constant. Notice that the shown PID drives only one robot actuator. Thus, we have one PID controller for each degree of freedom. Off-line tuning of PID parameters may be done utilizing optimization procedures with the simulated subsystem model (actuator with an average inertial load) or using some tuning rules. The main drawback of the first approach lies in uncertainty of model parameters. The simulation might also be time-consuming and numerically involved. The second approach refers to experiments with a real robot. Then, we can apply step-response-based methods [54, 55] or Ragazzini's direct method [55, 56]. However, a designer is forced to tune the regulator parameters at an operating point. In order to cope with variations in subsystem dynamics at different operating points (see Chapter 2) and to satisfy increasingly stringent control objectives, we can apply PID self-tuning local regulators. At the end of this section we shall discuss major advantages as well as some drawbacks of such a control strategy.

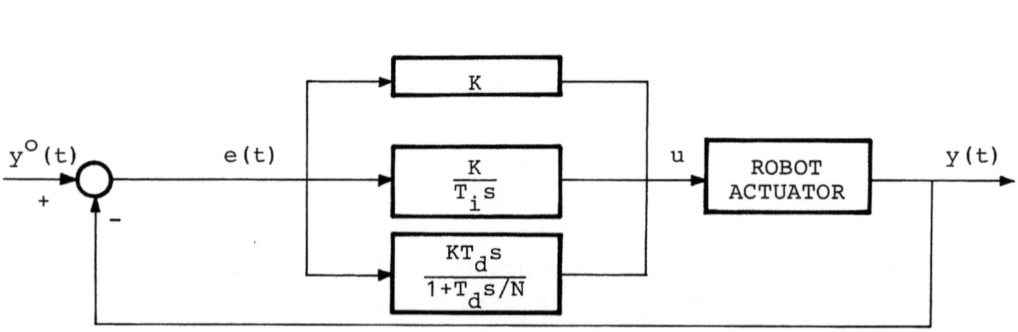

Fig. 3.6. PID controller for one degree of freedom

Differential equation corresponding to classical PID regulator (3.3.1) is

$$\frac{d^2u}{dt^2} + \frac{N}{T_d}\frac{du}{dt} = K(N+1)\frac{d^2e}{dt^2} + \frac{K}{T_iT_d}(NT_i+T_d)\frac{de}{dt} + \frac{KN}{T_iT_d}e \qquad (3.3.2)$$

using Euler's derivative approximation, we obtain the difference equation

$$u(t)+(\gamma-1)u(t-1)-\gamma u(t-2) = r_oe(t)+r_1e(t-1) + r_2e(t-2) \qquad (3.3.3)$$

where the meaning of u(t), u(t-1),... is the same as in Paragraph 3.2.1. Constants γ, r_o, r_1 and r_2 are

$$\gamma = \frac{NT}{T_d} - 1, \qquad r_o = K(\xi(\gamma+1)+N+1)$$

$$r_1 = K(\xi+\gamma-2N-1), \qquad r_2 = r_1 + K(N+1)$$

where $\xi = T/T_i$ (T - sampling period). Equations (3.3.3) can be presented in the following form

$$S(q^{-1})u(t) = R(q^{-1})e(t) \qquad (3.3.4)$$

with

$$S(q-1) = (1-q^{-1})(1+\gamma q^{-1})$$

$$R(q^{-1}) = r_o+r_1q^{-1} + r_2q^{-2}$$

where $e(t) = q^o(t) - q(t)$ represents the tracking error and q^{-1} is the backward-shift operator.

As the plant to be controlled by PID/ST regulator represents a subsystem of a manipulator (one actuator with transmission and an inertial load), it can be described by the following linear time-invariant model:

$$A(q^{-1})y(t) = B(q^{-1})u(t-1) + e(t) \qquad (3.3.5)$$

with

$$\begin{aligned} A(q^{-1}) &= 1-a_1q^{-1}-a_2q^{-2} \\ B(q^{-1}) &= b_o+b_1q^{-1} \end{aligned} \qquad (3.3.6)$$

where a_i's and b_i's are assumed unknown scalar constants. The second order model of the subsystem is quite compatible with overall robot model (3.2.21).

Denoting by $\hat{A}(q^{-1})$ and $\hat{B}(q^{-1})$ the estimates of real polynomials (3.3.6) according to one of least squares algorithms described in Paragraph 3.2.1, and by $\hat{S}(q^{-1})$ and $\hat{R}(q^{-1})$ the corresponding polynomials of the self-tuning regulator (3.3.4), we obtain the closed-loop system scheme shown in Fig. 3.7. After estimating polynomials $\hat{A}(q^{-1})$ and $\hat{B}(q^{-1})$ we

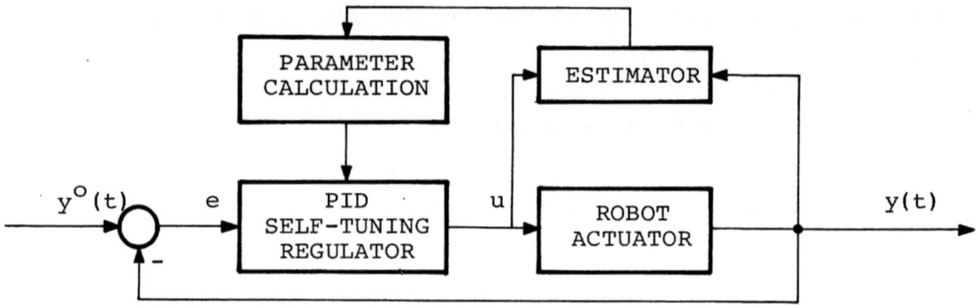

Fig. 3.7. PID self-tuning controller for one robot joint

have to calculate $\hat{S}(q^{-1})$ and $\hat{R}(q^{-1})$. For this purpose, we shall apply the well-known *certainty equivalence* assumption, i.e. the true parameter values will be replaced by their estimated when determining PID parameters. This fundamental ad-hoc hypothesis is implicitly used in Paragraph 3.2.1. The transfer function of the overall system: PID/ST regulator $u(t) = [\hat{R}(q^{-1})/\hat{S}(q^{-1})]e(t)$ together with predicted plant model $y(t) = [\hat{B}(q^{-1})/\hat{A}(q^{-1})]u(t)$ is

$$\frac{y(t)}{y^o(t)} = \frac{\hat{R}(q^{-1})\hat{B}(q^{-1})}{\hat{S}(q^{-1})\hat{A}(q^{-1})+\hat{R}(q^{-1})\hat{B}(q^{-1})} \qquad (3.3.7)$$

Now, we can apply pole-placement method in order to calculate $\hat{S}(q^{-1})$ and $\hat{R}(q^{-1})$. By equating the characteristic polynomial of (3.3.7) with a desired polynomial $C_R(q^{-1})$, we obtain

$$\hat{S}(q^{-1})\hat{A}(q^{-1})+\hat{R}(q^{-1})\hat{B}(q^{-1}) = C_R(q^{-1}) \qquad (3.3.8)$$

where

$$C_R(q^{-1}) = 1 + \sum_{i=1}^{n_c} c_i q^{-1}, \qquad n_c < 4.$$

The polynomial identity (3.3.8) defines a set of 4 linear algebraic equations with 4 unknowns - the regulator parameters. The number of poles to be located in closed-loop is defined by n_c, being the remaining $4-n_c$ poles placed at the origin. A sensible choice for $C_R(q^{-1})$ is

$$C_R(q^{-1}) = 1-2e^{-\rho}\cos\theta q^{-1}+e^{-2\sigma}q^{-2}$$

with

$$\theta = \omega_n T\sqrt{1-\xi^2} \quad \text{and} \quad \rho = \theta\xi/\sqrt{1-\xi^2}$$

where ω_n is the undamped natural frequency and ξ the damping ratio of the corresponding continuous time second-order characteristic polynomial. Finally, the complete control strategy is summarized in Fig. 3.8.

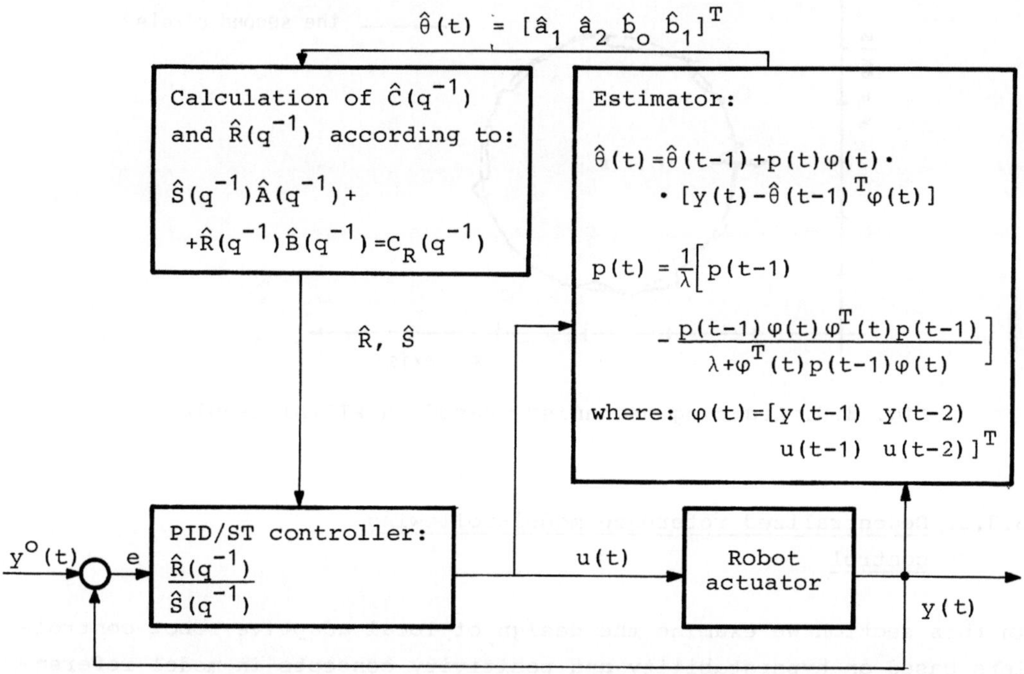

Fig. 3.8. PID self-tuning controller

The simulation of Stanford manipulator controlled by local PID/ST regulators may be found in Koivo's and Leininger's papers [10, 11]. As one could expect, the behavior of the manipulator when starting the learning process depends mostly on the accuracy in initialization of the prediction model parameters. This accuracy determines the degree of "erratic" motion at task start-up. The second problem is related to convergence of estimates. The convergence of parameter estimates and controller gains may not be achieved during the finite time over which the motion takes place. Also, when parameters change abruptly (for example, when grasping a large mass workpiece), the stability of the overall system may fail. On the other hand, the major advantage of PID self-tuning regulators is the attractive "learning mechanism" which could be very useful in repetitive tasks. Then, the last estimates of parameters from the previous run can be used as the initial estimates. Thus, the controller of the robot is "trainable" in repetitive tasks, resulting in a more accurate performance. Fig. 3.9 shows the effect of learning mechanism in "circle drawing" task.

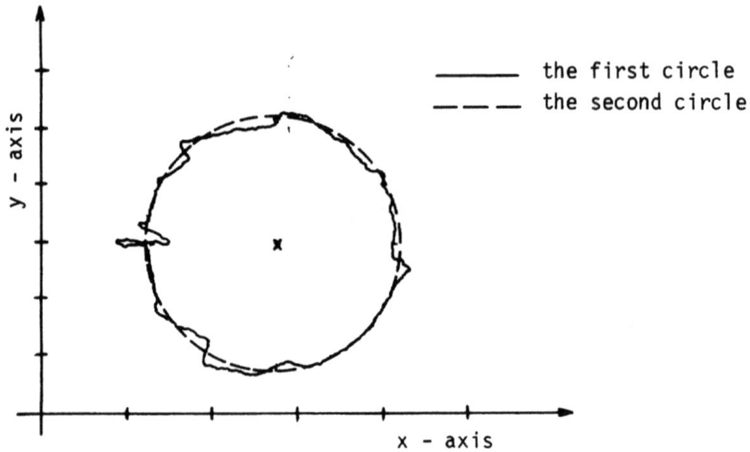

Fig. 3.9. Learning mechanism based on PID/ST regulator

3.3.2. Decentralized reference model-following control

In this section we examine the design of local adaptive robot controllers based on hyperstability and positivity concepts in model reference adaptive systems. Instead of the centralized approach described in Paragraph 3.2.2, here we shall base the control strategy on subsystems assigned to robot degrees of freedom. We shall present a pragmatic approach without formal generalizations and detailed mathematical derivations. In our opinion the algorithm, which will be described in this section, will find its place in robotics applications.

The structure of an adaptive model-following controller for a subsystem S^i is presented in Fig. 3.10. The plant (actuator, reducer and an average inertial and gravitational load) together with a variable-gain controller on one hand, and a reference model on the other hand, work in a parallel manner. Therefore, this system belongs to the family of parallel model-following control systems.

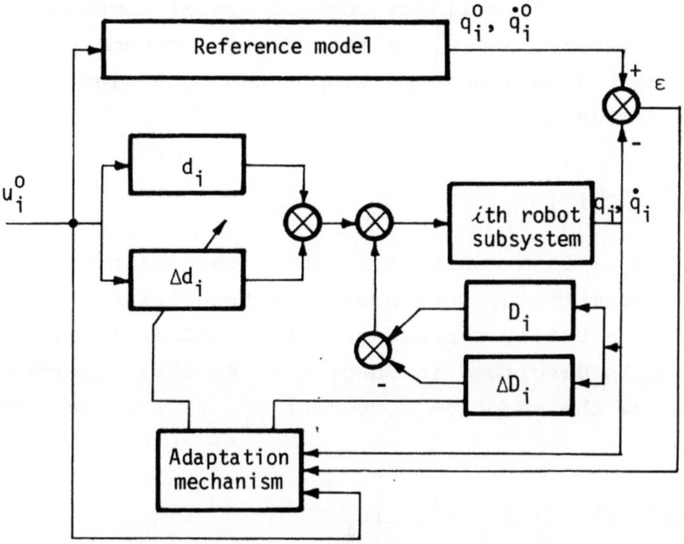

Fig. 3.10. Parallel model-following local controller for driving one degree of freedom of a robot

First, we have to define the structure of the reference model. For this purpose, we can follow the algorithm described in Paragraph 3.2.2. The above method is based on the reference model, whose structure is quite similar to the plant to be controlled. Since, the subsystem model S^i is approximately representable by (3.2.33)

$$S^i: \quad \dot{x}^i = \bar{A}^i(\theta^i, \bar{d})x^i + \bar{b}^i(\theta^i, \bar{d})u_i \qquad (3.3.9)$$

it is convenient to introduce the reference model (3.2.35)

$$S_M^i: \quad \dot{x}^{io} = A_M^i x^{io} + b_M^i u_i^o \qquad (3.3.10)$$

where A_M^i and b_M^i determine a desired dynamical behaviour of *i*th robot subsystem. Substituting $x^i = [q_i \ \dot{q}_i]^T$ in the reference model (3.3.10), we obtain the scalar form $\ddot{q}_i^o = -a_i^*\dot{q}_i^o - f_i^*q_i^o + b_i^*u_i^o$ (Equation (3.3.36)). The nominal joint coordinates, velocities and acceleration (q_i^o, $\dot{q}_i^o$ and $\ddot{q}_i^o$, respectively) are usually calculated at the kinematical level.

Thus, the nominal control u_i^o can be computed from the reference model.

Let us introduce the control in an additive form [13]:

$$u_i = u_i^{NA} + u_i^A \tag{3.3.11}$$

where u_i^{NA} is a non-adaptive linear control signal computed for the nominal dynamic parameters, and u_i^A is the adaptive component. The non--adaptive component should be very simple and convenient for application. Thus, we arrive at

$$u_i^{NA} = -D_i x^i + d_i u_i^o \tag{3.3.12}$$

where $D_i = [d_{i1} \; d_{i2}]$ is a constant feedback gain matrix of dimension 1×2, while the parameter d_i represents the feedforward gain. The expression (3.3.12) actually represents the classical local control structure, which is described in Chapter 2. We shall therefore concentrate on obtaining the adaptive component u_i^A. It will be accepted in a similar form

$$u_i^A = \Delta D_i(e^i, t)x^i + \Delta d_i(e^i, t)u_i^o \tag{3.3.13}$$

where $\Delta D_i(e^i, t): R^2 \times T \to R^{1\times 2}$ is an adaptive feedback gain matrix, and $\Delta d_i(e^i, t)$ a scalar function representing a variable feedforward gain. Let us introduce the error vector $e^i = x^{io} - x^i$, i.e.

$$e^i = \begin{bmatrix} q_i^o - q_i \\ \dot{q}_i^o - \dot{q}_i \end{bmatrix} \tag{3.3.14}$$

The objective of the adaptation mechanism which will generate the time--varying matrix $\Delta D_i(e^i, t)$ and scalar $\Delta d_i(e^i, t)$ is to assure that the state error e goes to zero under certain conditions.

Substituting (3.3.12) and (3.3.13) in (3.3.11), we obtain

$$u_i = (-D_i + \Delta D_i)x^i + (d_i + \Delta d_i)u_i^o \tag{3.3.15}$$

Putting it into (3.3.9), we arrive to

$$\dot{x}^i = [\bar{A}^i - \bar{b}^i D_i + \bar{b}^i \Delta D_i]x^i + \bar{b}^i(d_i + \Delta d_i)u_i^o \tag{3.3.16}$$

This model represents the system parallel to the reference model (see Fig. 3.10). This system is called "parallel adjustable system". Denoting by $A_s(e^i, t)$ and $B_s(e^i, t)$ the matrices of the above model, we obtain

$$\dot{x}^i = A_s(e^i, t)x^i + B_s(e^i, t)u_i^o \qquad (3.3.17)$$

with $A_s \in R^{2\times 2}$ and $B_s \in R^2$. Subtracting the reference model (3.3.10) from (3.3.16), we get

$$\dot{e}^i = A_M^i e^i + w^i \qquad (3.3.18)$$

with

$$w^i = -[A_M^i - \bar{A}^i + \bar{b}^i(D_i - \Delta D_i)]x^i - [b_M^i - \bar{b}^i(d_i + \Delta d_i)]u_i^o$$

Let D_i^o and d_i^o satisfy the equations

$$A_M^i - \bar{A}^i = -\bar{b}^i D_i^o, \quad b_M^i = \bar{b}^i d_i^o \qquad (3.3.19)$$

where $D_i^o \in R^{1\times 2}$ and $d_i^o \in R$. Thus, the vector w^i can be represented as

$$w^i = -\bar{b}^i[(D_i - D_i^o - \Delta D_i)x^i - (d_i^o - d_i - \Delta d_i)u_i^o] \qquad (3.3.20)$$

Now, we have to accept some general form of the adaptation law $\Delta D_i(e^i, t)$ and $\Delta d_i(e^i, t)$. After imposing a desired stability condition, we will obtain the particular forms of adaptation mechanisms. In order to avoid a steady state error, let us introduce a proportional - integral adaptation mechanism. To ensure the asymptotic system stability, we ought to establish a linear compensator in the form [13]:

$$v^i = De^i \qquad (3.3.21)$$

where D represents a 2×2 matrix which will be determined later. The adaptation mechanism will be introduced with respect to the compensator output v^i:

$$\begin{aligned} \Delta D_i(v^i, t) &= \int_o^t \phi_i(v^i, t, \tau)d\tau + \phi_i(v^i, t) + \Delta D_i(0) \\ \Delta d_i(v^i, t) &= \int_o^t \psi_i(v^i, t, \tau)d\tau + \psi_i(v^i, t) + \Delta d_i(0) \end{aligned} \qquad (3.3.22)$$

Now, we can separate the system into 2 parts (as shown in Fig. 3.4):

1) a linear feedforward block comprising the error model (3.3.18) and the linear compensator (3.3.21), and

2) a non-linear feedback block consisting of the model (3.3.20) and the adaptation law (3.3.22).

Next, we can directly apply the hyperstability conditions, positivity of the feedforward block and Popov's integral inequality to the feedback block. From the first condition, it follows that the static compensator must satisfy the condition

$$D(sI-A_M^i)\bar{b}^i = \text{a strictly positive real transfer matrix.}$$

The second condition yields the adaptation mechanism

$$\Delta D_i(v^i,\ t) = \int_0^t (Fv^i)(Gx^i)^T d\tau + (Fv^i)(Gx^i)^T + \Delta D_i(0) \qquad (3.3.23)$$

$$\Delta d_i(v^i,\ t) = \int_0^t (Mv^i)(Nu_i^o)^T d\tau + (Mv^i)(Nu_i^o)^T + \Delta d_i(0)$$

where $F \in R^{1\times 2}$, $G \in R^{2\times 2}$, $M \in R^{1\times 2}$ and $N \in R$ are positive.

Integral terms in (3.3.23) provide memory of the adaptation mechanism, while the proportional terms are introduced in order to accelerate the reduction of the generalized error at the beginning of the adaptation process. The discrete version of the proposed adaptive model-following scheme can be found in Ref. [13].

The action of the proposed controller will be illustrated on an example with direct-current motor speed regulation. First, the motor is regulated by an usual PI controller, and, after some time, the adaptive controller is activated [13]. The action is shown in Fig. 3.11. Some interesting examples are also presented in Ref. [26].

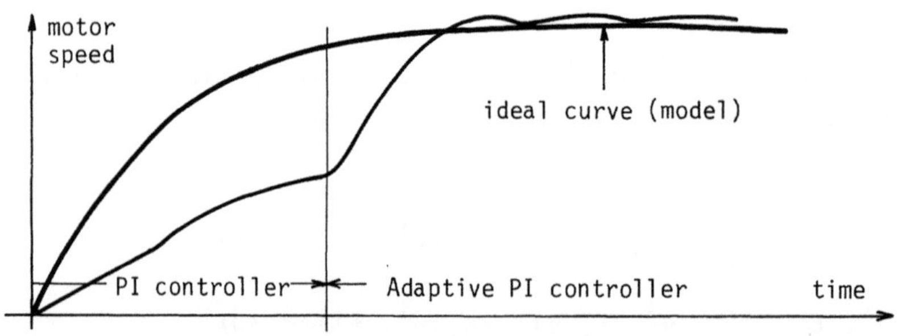

Fig. 3.11. Comparison between classical PI controller action and model-following adaptive controller

3.3.3. Indirect decentralized adaptive control

Having presented adaptive techniques based on various concepts, we will complete the picture by introducing a new adaptive scheme relying on the decoupled control strategy, described in Chapter 2. The goal is to obtain an algorithm which is both simple and stable when manipulating different payloads. From that point of view, the decoupled control strategy is very suitable because of the systematic selection of feedback loops. Note that the set of PID regulators controlling robot degrees of freedom corresponds to local regulators described in Chapter 2. Such a set of regulators represents the simplest control structure, which is applied in most of today's industrial robots. The stability theory related to this as well as to more complex control structures is presented in Chapter 2, too. Thereby, the stability analysis is applicable to any given set of parameters, or to a given range of parameters. However, for some range of parameters, it may appear that there is no fixed-gain-controller which can provide the imposed stability conditions. For instance, if the gains of local controllers are tuned to stabilize the robot carrying a 30 kg workpiece, it may happen that the same stability conditions are not satisfied without a payload or, possibly, with a 60 kg payload. If we still want to stabilize the robot motion with simple controllers, we have to introduce the force-feedback. But the employment of force/torque sensors may be difficult and expensive. The problem can be solved in the following way. First, we determine the gains of local regulators in terms of payload mass and/or inertias.

Then, if we add some recursive parameter estimator, the output of which is the payload mass/inertias, it would not be necessary to introduce the force or torque measurements. The parameters of local regulators would change in accordance with estimates.

We have seen that some algorithms of centralized adaptive robot control involve the estimation of a large number of parameters [33 - 35]. Obviously, this is not necessary, because most of them are well known. There is also a series of quasi-stationary parameters (such as temperature-dependent viscous frictions, static frictions, etc). Thus, we have to separate such parameters which change (in a very wide range) and cannot be prespecified. These are primarily the parameters of workpieces.

In this section we shall describe an indirect adaptive scheme.

Within the indirect adaptive control the procedure is devided into two steps. First, the unknown parameter estimates are generated by using some of the on-line identification algorithms. Thereafter, the obtained estimates are used as inputs to adaptive regulator, which adjusts its coefficients according to the estimates.

Consider the model of a robotic mechanism with the vector of parameters $\theta_p = \bar{\theta}_p+\Delta\theta_p$ in the form

$$P = [0 \mid H(\xi,\ \bar{\theta}_p+\Delta\theta_p)]\dot{\xi}+h(\xi,\ \bar{\theta}_p+\Delta\theta_p)$$

Taking into account the parameter deviation $\Delta\theta_p$, centralized law of nonadaptive control (2.3.20) becomes

$$u = [0 \mid \hat{H}(\xi,\ \bar{\theta}_p+\Delta\theta_p)](\dot{\xi}^o+D(\xi-\xi^o))+\hat{h}(\xi,\ \bar{\theta}_p+\Delta\theta_p) \tag{3.3.24}$$

The state vector ξ can be presented as $\xi = \xi^o+\Delta\xi$, where ξ^o denotes the state vector on the desired trajectory. Denoting by $u^o(\theta_p)$ the nominal control vector obtained from (3.3.24) at the conditions $\xi = \xi^o$ and $\theta_p = \bar{\theta}_p$, the control law (3.3.24) can be presented by

$$u = u^o(\bar{\theta}_p)+[0 \mid \hat{H}(\xi,\ \bar{\theta}_p+\Delta\theta_p)]D(\xi-\xi^o)+\Delta u^N \tag{3.3.25}$$

where Δu^N is the nonlinear control component.

It is shown [40, 53] that the dynamic model matrices are linear with respect to dynamic parameters (masses and inertias of the links). This is a very important property which is suitable for indirect adaptive control synthesis. The control law (3.3.25) now becomes

$$u = u^o(\bar{\theta}_p)+[0 \mid \hat{H}(\xi,\ \bar{\theta}_p)+\hat{S}_H(\xi)\Delta\theta_p]D(\xi-\xi^o)+\Delta u^N \tag{3.3.26}$$

with $\hat{S}(\xi)$ being the sensitivity function valid for both small and large parameter deviations. The computer-aided construction of the sensitivity function for an arbitrary manipulator structure is given in [40]. Following the idea of control decentralization, matrices $\hat{H}$ and $\hat{S}$ can be redistributed to constant parts and nonlinear parts which can be added to Δu^N (3.3.26). Thus, the control law can be significantly simplified.

$$u_i = u_i^o(\bar{\theta}_p)+(\bar{H}_{ii}(\bar{\theta}_p)+\bar{S}_{ii}\Delta\theta_p)D_i(\xi^i-\xi^{io})+\Delta\tilde{u}_i^N$$

where $\bar{S}_{ii}\in R^{1\times n_p}$ and $D_i = [d_i^p \; d_i^v]$. Here we clearly see the nonadaptive component of local control

$$\Delta u_i^{LNA} = \bar{H}_{ii}(\bar{\theta}_p)[d_i^p \; d_i^v](\xi^i-\xi^{io}) \tag{3.3.27}$$

and the adaptive component

$$\Delta u_i^{LA} = \bar{S}_{ii}\Delta\theta_p[d_i^p \; d_i^v](\xi^i-\xi^{io}) \tag{3.3.28}$$

where $\Delta\theta_p$ is not known. For this reason, instead of real value we have to use the estimate $\Delta\theta_p^e$:

$$\Delta u_i^{LA} = \bar{S}_{ii}\Delta\theta_p^e[d_i^p \; d_i^v](\xi^i-\xi^{io}) \tag{3.3.29}$$

When only one parameter is not known, local control can be presented in the form

$$\Delta u_i^L = [D_{i(min)} + \frac{\Delta\theta_p^e}{|\Delta\theta_p|_{(max)}}(D_{i(max)} - D_{i(min)})](\xi^i-\xi^{io}) \tag{3.3.30}$$

where $|\Delta\theta_p|_{(max)}$ represents the largest possible parameter variation, $D_{i(min)}$ and $D_{i(max)}$ - gains of local regulators in the cases of minimal and maximal values of estimated parameters. The values of $D_{i(min)}$ and $D_{i(max)}$ can be obtained by using the stability analysis when the unknown parameter reaches its boundary values (see Chapter 2).

The second part of the control algorithm represents the parameter estimation of $\Delta\theta_p$. For this purpose, the time should be discretized in time intervals $[t_k, t_{k+1}]$. Let us denote by P_k^* the driving torques/ /forces of actuators (k indicates the time instant t_k) which even when the parameter vector changes its value, force the system to follow the nominal trajectory. It is shown [40, 53] that the vector P_k^* can be expressed as

$$P_k^* = [0 \,|\, H(\xi_k^o, \bar{\theta}_p) + S_H(\xi_k^o)\Delta\theta_p]\dot{\xi}_k^o+h(\xi_k^o, \bar{\theta}_p)+S_h(\xi_k^o)\Delta\theta_p \tag{3.3.31}$$

where S_H and S_h do not depend on θ_p. However, in reality the system is out of the nominal trajectory due to parametric or state disturbances. For this reason, real driving torques vector P_k differs from P_k^*. Vector P_k is given by the same expression as P_k^*, except for the state vector ξ_k^o and $\dot{\xi}_k^o$, which are now ξ_k and $\dot{\xi}_k$. Let us denote P_k^o the driving torque vector when the states belong to the nominal trajectory and when $\Delta\theta_p = 0$. Thus the deviation $\Delta P_k = P_k - P_k^o$ becomes

$$\Delta P_k = (S_H(\xi_k)\dot{\xi}_k + S_h(\xi_k))\Delta\theta_p + \Delta P^N(\xi_k, \xi_k^o, \dot{\xi}_k, \dot{\xi}_k^o) \tag{3.3.32}$$

where ΔP^N represents the nonlinear component which is the consequence of the difference of the matrices H and h at the instantaneous states and the corresponding states on nominal trajectory. When the system states under the feedback reaction reach the desired trajectory, i.e. $\xi_k \to \xi_k^o$, then $\Delta P^N \to 0$. The expression enables the derivation of the estimator for the parameter $\Delta\theta_p$. Let us denote by $S_p(\xi_k)$ the matrix

$$S_p(\xi_k) = S_H(\xi_k)\dot{\xi}_k^o + S_h(\xi_k) \tag{3.3.33}$$

Following the quasi-gradient procedure [38, 39], the estimates can be obtained from the recursive algorithm

$$\Delta\theta_p(t_{k+1}) = [I - a_p(t_k)S_p^T(\xi_k)S_p(\xi_k)]\Delta\theta_p(t_k) + p(\xi_k) \tag{3.3.34}$$

where $a_p(t)$ represents a positive real function which determines the transient behaviour during the estimation process, and $p(\xi_k)$ represents the dynamic correction due to the influence of the input variations:

$$p(\xi_k) = a_p(t_k)S_p^T(\xi_k)\Delta P_k \tag{3.3.35}$$

or

$$p(\xi_k) = a_p(t_k)S_p^T(\xi_k)D_a\Delta u_k \tag{3.3.36}$$

with Δu_k being the input variation, and D_a the matrix which depends on the actuator parameters.

A general block diagram of the algorithm is given in Fig. 3.12. The efficiency of the dynamic estimator and the complete adaptive algorithm may be best recognized through numerical examples. We shall present two examples. The first refers to a hydraulic 6-degree-of-freedom manipulator, presented in Fig. 3.13. Manipulator parameters (link lengths, masses and moments of inertia) are given in Table 3.1.

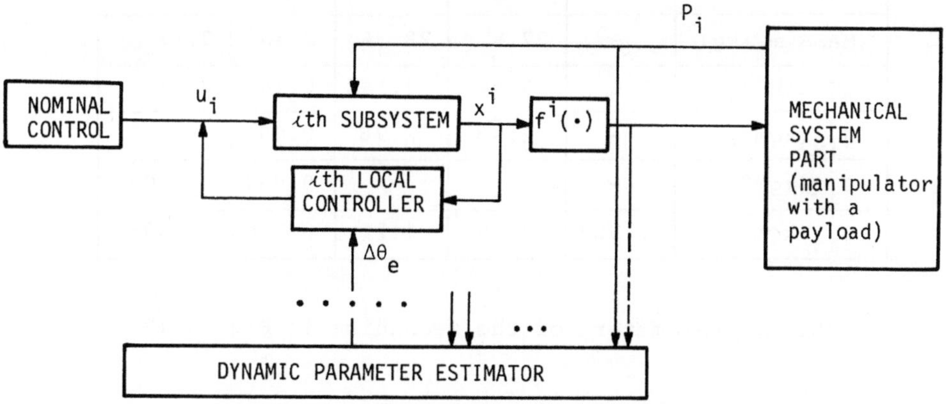

Fig. 3.12. General block-scheme

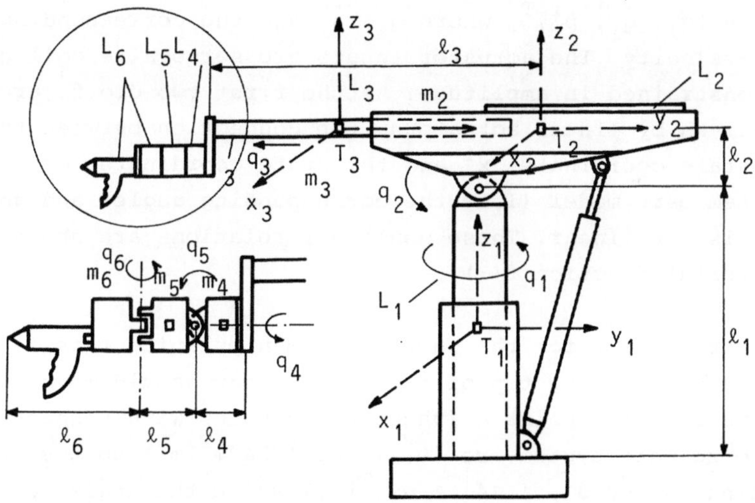

L_i - link i
ℓ_i - length of link i
q_i - joint coordinate i
x_i, y_i, z_i - coordinate frame of link i

Fig. 3.13. Manipulator UMS 3B

LINK	1	2	3	4, 5	6
MASS m_i (kg)	-	27.8	22.34	2.33	0.33
LENGTH ℓ_i (m)	1.2	0.142	1.142	0.14	0.26
J_{ix} (kgm^2)	-	2.98	2.98	0.004	.0007
J_{iy} (kgm^2)	-	-	-	0.004	.0009
J_{iz} (kgm^2)	0.322	3.701	1.21	0.004	.0009

Table 3.1. Parameters of the mechanism in Fig. 3.13.

Hydraulic cylinders, controlled by hydraulic servovalves, are modeled by models of order $n_i=3$. The state vector of the hydraulic actuator is $x^i = [\ell^i, \dot{\ell}^i, p^i]^T$, where ℓ^i is the piston travel, $\dot{\ell}^i$ is the piston velocity, p^i is the oil pressure in the cylinder. The first three manipulator degrees of freedom are driven by means of hydraulic cylinders while the remaining joints are powered by revolute vane actuators. In the second case, the state vector of subsystems S^i (i=4,5 and 6) is taken as $x^i = [q_i, \dot{q}_i, p^i]^T$, where q_i, $\dot{q}_i$ are the corresponding angle and angular velocity. The actuator inputs are servovalve coil currents which are constrained in amplitude. As the first two d.o.f. are revolute, but driven by linear actuators, the connection between the actuator model state coordinates x^i and the state coordinates of the mechanical system part model (i.e. the corresponding angles and angular velocities) is not linear. These nonlinear relations are shown in Fig. 3.12 by vectorial function $f(\cdot)$.

The nominal trajectory for the particular manipulation task is given in the following way: the tip of the manipulator should move along a straight line from the point A (whose coordinates with respect to the reference coordinate system are $[0, 1.14, 1.342]^T$[m]) to the point B (with coordinates $[-0.31, 1.14, 1.65]^T$[m]) while the angles of joints 4, 5 and 6 should be kept constant ($q^4 = 0.$, $q^5 = -1.57$[rad], $q^6 = 0.$). The triangular velocity profile of the manipulator tip is accepted and the time duration of the movement is $\tau = 0.8$ s. The only unknown parameter is the payload mass $\theta = m_p$ which can take values belonging to the region $\Theta = \{m_p: m_p\ (0,\ 10\ kg)\}$.

First we shall try to synthesize non-adaptive control which could withstand all variations of the payload in the assumed range. We have synthesized local controllers for the maximal allowed mass of the payload, θ_d = 10 kg. The local gains are given in Table 3.2. We have simulated the dynamics of the manipulation system (from Fig. 3.13) while tracking nominal trajectory with the synthesized local controllers. If the payload is m_p = 10 kg, the tracking is satisfactory, but when m_p = 0, the tracking is poor, since local gains are too high for the manipulation system without payload. The results of simulation are shown in Fig. 3.14 where $\Delta q_i(t)$ denotes deviations of the joint coordinate i from its nominal value. We have tried to stabilize the system with local contollers synthesized for the mass of the payload θ_d = 5 kg. The tracking of nominal trajectory (see Fig. 3.14) with the local gains given in Table 3.2. is satisfactory for m_p = 5 kg and m_p = 0 kg. The tracking is poor for m_p = 10 kg due to the low gains. This means that we cannot find unique local controllers which are able to withstand all assumed parameter variations.

	SUBSYSTEM	1	2	3	4	5	6
θ_d=0	position gain velocity gain	50.81 10.86	161.77 25.40	154.35 2.30	35.11 0.54	35.09 0.52	35.00 0.35
θ_d=5kg	position gain velocity gain	89.41 19.17	212.89 44.03	154.89 2.65	36.10 2.21	36.10 2.18	35.28 0.87
θ_d=10kg	position gain velocity gain	130.89 28.08	349.16 74.40	154.42 3.01	37.86 4.03	37.83 4.00	35.57 1.37

Table 3.2. Local gains

In order to stabilize manipulation system for all possible payloads we have synthesized adaptive control algorithm as it has been presented before. The local gains have been synthesized for various payload masses (Table 3.2). Fig. 3.15 shows the simulation result of parameter estimation technique. The difference between the real mass step disturbance and the estimated value is quite small. This difference, obviously, depends on constant $a_p(t)$, and the nominal trajectory (velocities and accelerations) of mechanical segments. In this example $a_p(t)$ is substituted by a constant (a_p = 1). The influence of the nominal trajectory itself on the estimated value is rather low. For example, at t $\simeq$ 0.4 s the end-effector acceleration changes from 3.8 m/s^2 influencing the estimated value only about 10 %. Fig. 3.14 shows the tracking of the desired nominal trajectory with adaptive (as well as fixed) control. It can be seen that we now achieve satisfactory tracking of nominal trajectory for arbitrary payload mass in a given range. However, such control is more complex for implementation than the simple robust nonadaptive control law presented above.

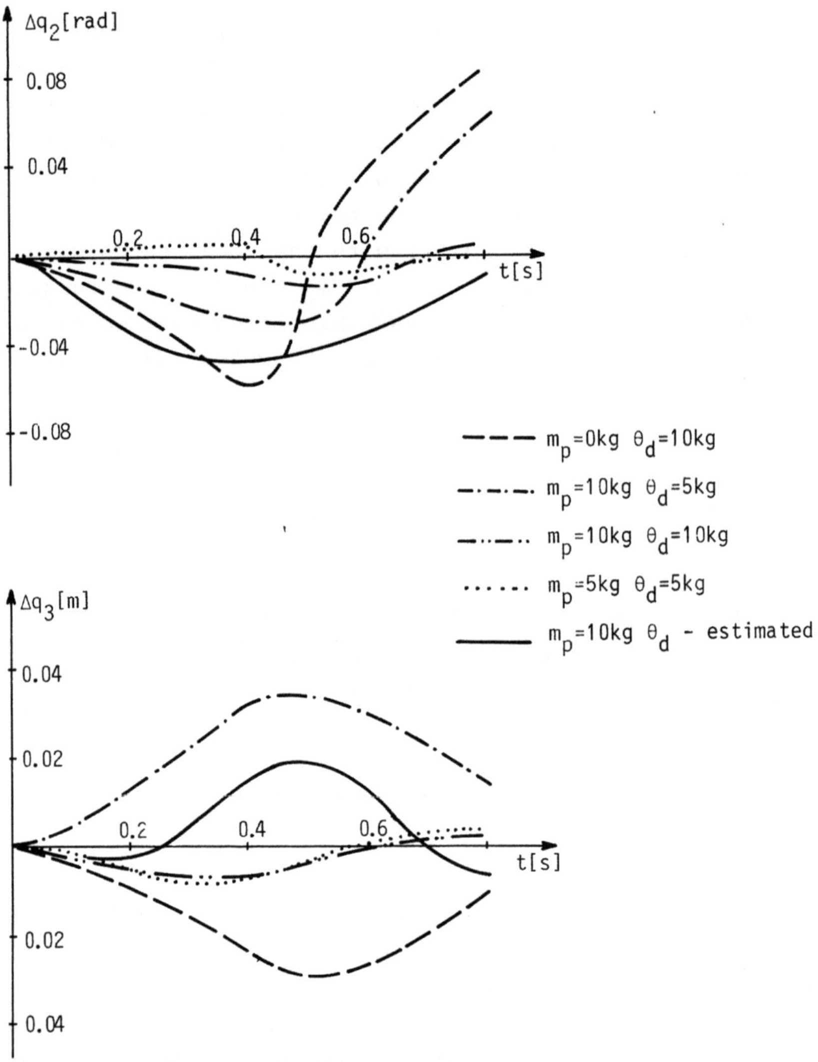

Fig. 3.14. Simulation with fixed and adaptive local regulators

The number of floating-point additions and multiplications that have to be performed in each sampling period for nonadaptive control in this particular example is

$$n_{ADD} = 114, \qquad n_{MUL} = 96$$

and for the identification of payload mass

$$n^e_{ADD} = 28, \qquad n^e_{MUL} = 64.$$

Using the INTEL 8086 microprocessor with 8087 coprocessor, we can achieve sampling period of about 10 ms for nonadaptive and 16 ms for adaptive control.

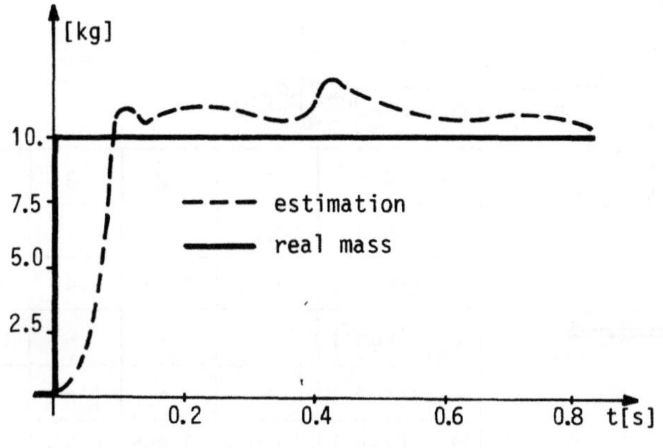

Fig. 3.15. Payload mass estimation

Let us now present the second example. We consider a 6-degree-of-freedom manipulator driven by permanent-magnet DC motors, Fig. 3.16.

Let us consider a straight line trajectory from the initial point $T = T_o(0., 0.45, 0.40)$ [m] to the point $T = T_1(-0.283, 0.45, 0.683)$ [m] in the time interval $t \in [0, \tau]$ with $\tau = 2$s. T denotes a point in the basis of the end-effector (see Fig. 3.16). The velocity profile of the point T along the trajectory is accepted to be triangular. The other three degrees of freedom, which determine the orientation of the workpiece, change from the angular position $(q_4^o, q_5^o, q_6^o) = (0., 1.57, 0.)$ [rad] to $(q_4^1, q_5^1, q_6^1) = (0.4, 0.8, 0.6)$ [rad] (Fig. 3.17). The time-history of driving torques (forces) along this nominal trajectory, is shown in Fig. 3.18. Nominal input signals are shown in Fig. 3.19.

Let us further illustrate the parameter estimation according to dynamic relation (3.3.34). The feedback gains are accepted as $G_{pi} = 10$ and $G_{vi} = 2$ for all subsystems ensuring the practical stability of the manipulation system (with a 1kg workpiece) according to the following conditions: $|q_i(t)| < 0.02$ rad (i=1,4,5,6) and $|q_i(t)| < 0.002$ m (i = 2,3) for $t > 0.6$ s. The simulated manipulation task involves a) gripping an object with the mass equal to 3 kg at time instant t = 0, b) travelling along the prescribed trajectory (Fig. 3.17), c) putting the object off after ≃0.3 s, and d) travelling along the same trajectory to the end of the path. The results of simulation are presented in Fig. 3.20. Obviously, the time of adaptation is approximately 150 ms. It should be noted that the dynamic estimator has "worked" off-line, i.e. it has not affected the control of subsystems.

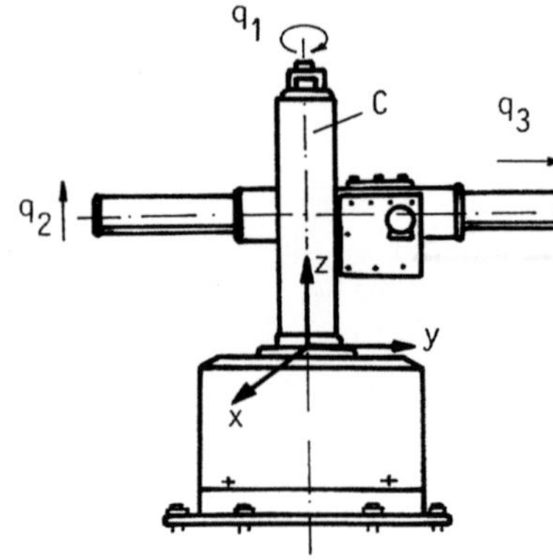

Link - i	1	2	3	4, 5	6
Mass (kg)	10.0	7.0	4.15	0.5	2.
Lingth (m)	0.38	0.02	0.45	0.05	0.2
J_{xi} (kgm^2)	-	-	-	0.01	.0069
J_{yi} (kgm^2)	-	-	-	0.001	.0004
J_{zi} (kgm^2)	0.029	0.055	0.318	0.0015	.0069

Fig. 3.16. Industrial manipulator

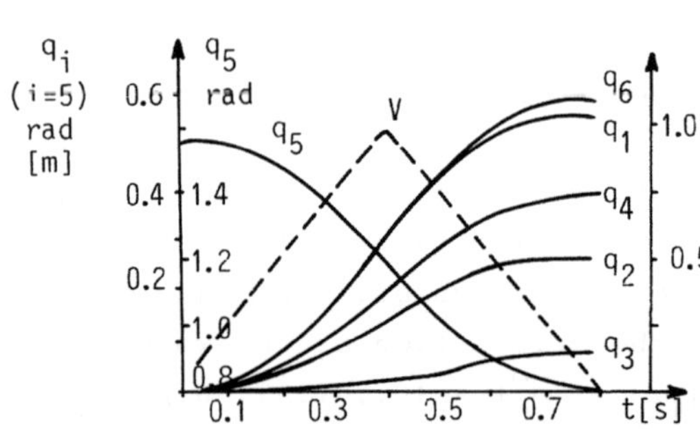

Fig. 3.17. Tip velocity distribution and corresponding joint coordinates (angular for i=1,4,5,6 and linear for i=2,3)

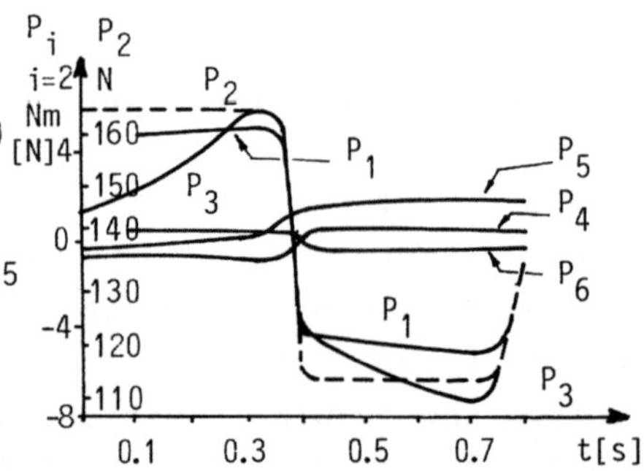

Fig. 3.18. Driving torques (i=1,4,5,6) and forces (i=2,3)

Further, the complete system including the adaptation of all feedback gains proportional to the (on-line) mass estimation is simulated. Gain boundaries are accepted to be $G_{pi}^{min} = 5.$, $G_{pi}^{max} = 20.$, $G_{vi}^{min} = 1.$, $G_{vi}^{max} =$ $= 4$. These gain boundaries correspond to the extreme cases: manipulation without payload and with the payload of 3 kg, ensuring the proposed practical stability conditions. The on-line action of the dynamic

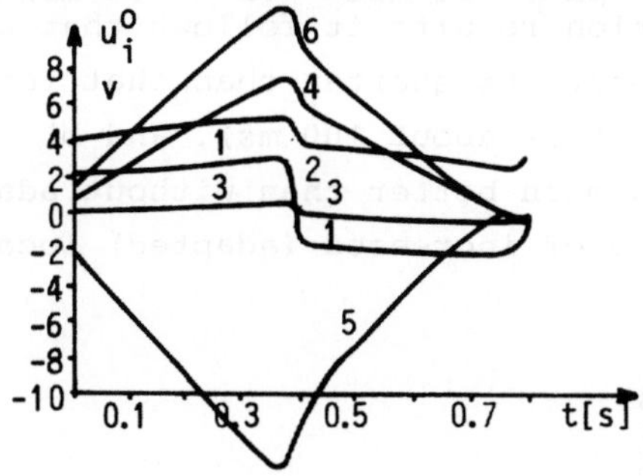

Fig. 3.19. Nominal control signal

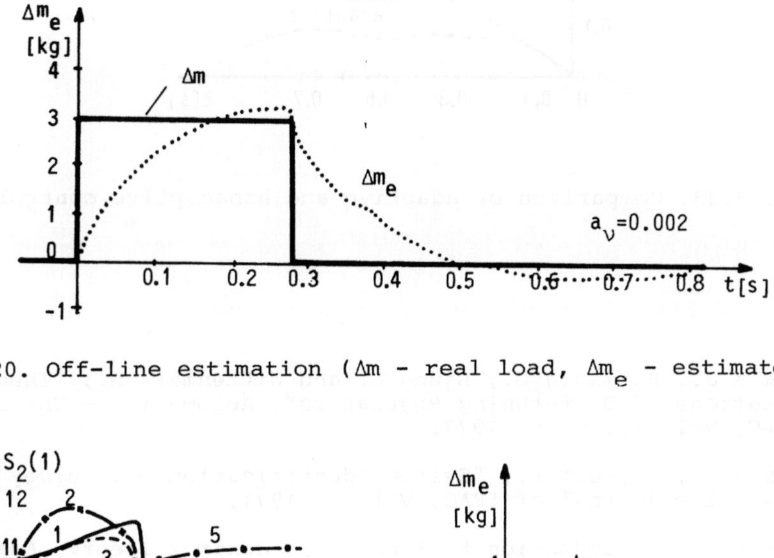

Fig. 3.20. Off-line estimation (Δm - real load, Δm_e - estimated load)

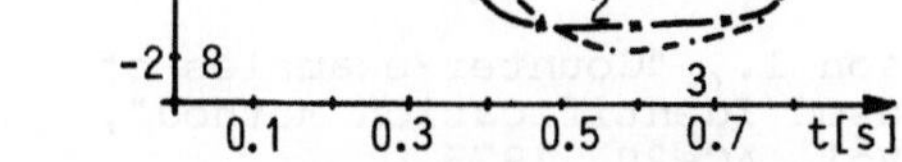

Fig. 3.21. Sensitivity functions on-line generated

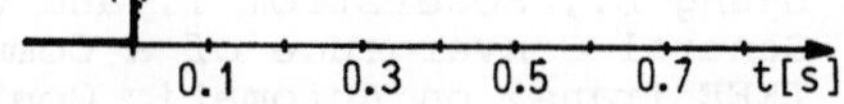

Fig. 3.22. On-line estimation

estimator is represented in Figs. 3.21, 3.22. For that, the gripping of an object (3 kg) occurred at time instant $t=t_o=0$. The sensitivity functions $S_i(t)$, j=1,...,6, formed in real-time by the dynamic estimator are shown in Fig. 3.21. The estimated mass of the manipulated object is shown in Fig. 3.22. Finally, a comparison of adaptive and nonadaptive regulators ($G_{pi} = G_{pi\,min}$, $G_{vi} = G_{vi\,min}$) is shown in Fig. 3.23. From these simulation results it follows that a) the time for on-line adaptation is about 30% shorter than that for non-adaptive control structure (now, it is about 100 ms), and b) the tracking of prescribed trajectory is much better than without adaptation. This is obviously the consequence of increased (adapted) local gains of subsystems.

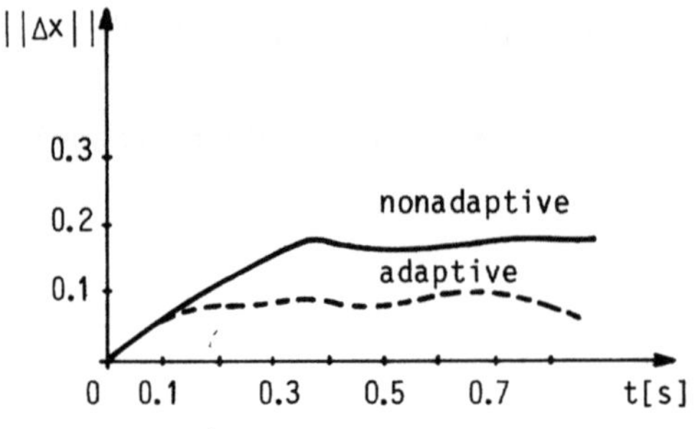

Fig. 3.23. Comparison of adaptive and nonadaptive control

References

[1] Astrom K.J., Borisson U., Ljung L. and Wittenmark B., "Theory and Applications of Self-tuning Regulators", Automatica - The Journal of IFAC, Vol. 13, No 5, 1977.

[2] Astrom K.J., Eykoff P., "System Identification - a survey", Automatica - The Journal of IFAC, Vol. 7, 1971.

[3] Astrom K.J., Introduction to Stochastic Control Theory, Academic Press, New York, 1970.

[4] Astrom K.J., Wittenmark B., "On Self-tuning Regulators", Automatica - The Journal of IFAC, Vol. 9, 1973.

[5] Ljung L., Soderstrom T. and Gustvsson I., "Counter-examples of General Convergence of a Commonly used Identification Method", IEEE Trans. on Automatic Control, Vol. AC-20, 1975.

[6] Ljung L., "On Positive Real Transfer Functions and the Convergence of Some Recursions", IEEE Trans. on Automatic Control, Vol. AC-22, 1977.

[7] Nahorski Z. and Vidal R., "Stabilization of Linear Discrete-time System Using Simultaneous Identification and Control", Int. J. Control, Vol. 19, 1974.

[8] Ljung L., Gustavsson I., Soderstrom T., "Identification of Linear Multivariable systems, Operating Under Linear Feedback Control",

[9] Young P.C., "An Instrumental Variable Method for Real Time Identivication of a noisy process", Automatica - The Journal of IFAC, Vol. 6, 1970.

[10] Koivo A.J., Guo T.H., "Adaptive Linear Controller for Robotic Manipulators", IEEE Trans. on Automatic Control, Vol. 28, No. 2, 1983.

[11] Leininger G., Wang S., "Pole Placement Self-Tuning Control of Manipulators", IFAC Symp. on C.A.D. of Multivariable Technological Systems, W. Lafayette, 1982.

[12] Leininger G., "Self-tuning Control of Manipulators", International Symp. on Advanced Software in Robotics, Liege, Belgium, 1983.

[13] Landau Y.D., Adaptive Control, M. Dekker, New York, 1979.

[14] Landau Y.D., "A Survay of Model Reference Adaptive Techniques. Theory and Applications", Automatica - The Journal of IFAC, Vol. 10, No. 3, 1974.

[15] Courtiol B., Landau Y.D., "High Speed Adaptation System for Controlled Electrical Drives", Automatica - The Journal of IFAC, Vol. 11, 1975.

[16] Tsypkin Ya.Z., Adaptation and Learning in Automatic Systems, Academic Press, New York, 1971.

[17] Popov V.M., Hyperstability of Control Systems, Springer-Verlag, New York, 1973.

[18] Landau Y.D., "A Hyperstability Criterion for Model Reference Adaptive Control Systems", IEEE Trans. Autom. Control, AC-17, No. 2, 1972.

[19] Landau Y.D., "A Generalization of the Hyperstability Conditions for Model Reference Adaptive Systems, IEEE Trans. Autom. Control, AC-17, No. 2, 1972.

[20] Dubowsky S., DesForges D., "The Application of Model Referenced Adaptive Control to Robotic Manipulators", Journal of Dynamic Systems, Measurement, and Control, Vol. 101, 1979.

[21] Dubowsky S., "On the Adaptive Control of Robotic Manipulators: The Discrete Time Case, Proc. 1981 Joint Auto. Cont. Conf., Charlottesville, VA, 1981.

[22] Dubowsky S., "On the Development of High Performance Adaptive Control Algorithms for Robotic Manipulators", 2nd Inter. Symp. on Robotics Research, Kyoto, 1984.

[23] Takegaki M., Arimoto S., "An Adaptive Trajectory Control of Manipulators", Int. J. Control, Vol. 34, No. 2, 1981.

[24] Arimoto S., Kawamura S. and Miyazaki F., "Can Mechanical Robots Learn by Themselves", 2nd Inter. Symp. on Robotics Research, Kyoto, 1984.

[25] Horowitz R., Tomizuka M., "An Adaptive Control Scheme for Mechanical Manipulators - Compensation of Nonlinearity and Decoupling Control", ASME, Winter Annual Meeting, 1980.

[26] Belestrino A., De Maria G. and Sciavicco L., "An Adaptive Model Following Control for Robotic Manipulators", Journal of Dynamic Systems, Measurement, and Control, Vol. 105, 1983.

[27] Kirćanski M.N., "Contribution to Dynamics and Control of Manipulation Robots", Ph. D. Thesis, Beograd, 1984.

[28] Vukobratović K.M., Kirćanski M.N., "An Approach to Direct and Indirect Adaptive Control of Manipulators", Proc. 7th IFAC/IFORC Symp. on Identification and System Parameter Estimation, 1985.

[29] Lee C.S.G., Lee B.H., "Resoved Motion Adaptive Control for Mechanical Manipulators", Journal of Dynamic Systems, Measurement, and Control, Vol. 106, 1984.

[30] Lee C.S.G., "Robot Arm Kinematics, Dynamics, and Control, IEEE Trans. on Computers, Vol. 15, No. 12, 1982.

[31] Anex Jr.R.P., Hubbard M., "Modelling and Adaptive Control of a Mechanical Manipulator", Journal of Dynamic Systems, Measurement, and Control, Vol. 106, 1984.

[32] Vukobratović M., Kirćanski N., "Computer-oriented Method for Linearization of Dynamic Models of Active Spatial Mechanisms", Journal of Mechanisms and Machine Theory, Vol. 16, No. 2, 1981.

[33] Timofeev A.V., Ekalo Yu.V., "Stability and Stabilization of Programmed Robot Movements", (in Russian), Avtomatika i Telemehanika, No. 20, 1976.

[34] Timofeev A.V., "Finite-convergent Local-optimal Algorithms for Solving Inequalities Arrising in Adaptive System Synthesis", (in Russian), Techniceskaya Kibernetica, No. 4, pp. 9-21, 1975.

[35] Liobacevsky B.D., "A Recursive Algorithm of Adaptive Control of Linear Discrete Dynamic Systems", Avtomatika i Telemehanika, No. 3, pp. 83-94, 1974.

[36] Vukobratović K.M., Kirćanski M.N., "An Engineering Concept of Adaptive Control for Manipulation Robots via Parameter Sensitivity Analysis", Bulletin T. LXXXI de L'Academie Serbe des Sciences et des Arts, No. 20, Beograd, 1982.

[37] Vukobratović K.M., Kirćanski M.N., "An Engineering Approach to Adaptive Control Synthesis for Multidegree-of-freedom Manipulation Robots", Proc. of the 3rd IFAC/IFORS Symp. on Large Scale Systems: Theory and Applications, Warsaw, 1983.

[38] Vukobratović K.M., Kirćanski M.N., "An Approach to Adaptive Control of Robotic Manipulators", IFAC Journal - Automatica, Dec. 1985.

[39] Vukobratović K.M., Stokić M.D. and Kirćanski M.N., "Towards Nonadaptive and Adaptive Control of Manipulation Robots", IEEE Trans. on Automatic Control, Vol. AC-29, No. 9, 1984.

[40] Vukobratović K.M., Kirćanski M.N., "Computer Assisted Sensitivity Model Generation in Manipulation Robots Dynamics", Journal of

Mechanisms and Machine Theory, Vol. 19, No. 2, 1984.

[41] Billings S.A., Voon W.S.F., "Least Squares Paramter Estimation Algorithms for Non-linear Systems", Int. J. Systems Sci., Vol. 15, No. 6, 1984.

[42] Volterra V., Theory of Functionals, Glasgow: Blakie, 1930.

[43] Leontaritis I.J., Billings S.A., "Input-output Parametric Models for Non-linear Systems, Part II: Stochastic Non-linear Systems", Int. J. Control, Vol. 41, No. 2, 1985.

[44] Clarke D.W. and Gawthrop P.J., "Self-tuning Controller", Proc. IEE, Vol. 122, No. 9, 1975.

[45] Clarke D.W. and Gawthrop P.J., "Self-tuning Control", Proc. IEE, 126, No. 6, 1979.

[46] Wellstead P.E., Edmunds J.M., Prager D., and Zanker P., "Self--tuning Pole/Zero Assignment Regulators", Int. J. Control, Vol. 80, No. 1, 1979.

[47] Lindorff D.P. and Caroll R.L., "Survey of Adaptive Control Using Lyapunov Design", Int. J. Control, Vol. 18, 1973.

[48] Narendra K.S. and Kudva P., "Stable Adaptive Schemes for System identification and Control", Parts I and II, IEEE Trans. Syst. Man and Cybernetics, Vol. 4, 1974.

[49] Stoten D.P., "The Adaptive Control of Manipulator Arms", Mechanism and Machine Theory, Vol. 18, No. 4, 1983.

[50] Balestrino A., De Maria G. and Sciavicco L., "Hyperstable Adaptive Model Following Control of Nonlinear Plants", Systems & Control Letters, Vol. 1, No. 4, 1982.

[51] Vukobratović M., Kirćanski N., "Computer - Assisted Generation of Robot Dynamic Models in an Analytical Form", Journal of Appl. Mathematics and Mathematical Applications - Acta Applicandae Mathematicae, Vol. 3, 1985.

[52] Kirćanski N., "Computer-Aided Procedure of Forming Robot Motion Equations in Analytical Forms", VI IFToMM Congr. on Theory of Machines and Mechanisms, New Delhi, 1983.

[53] Vukobratović K.M., Kirćanski M.N., Real-time Dynamics of Manipulation Robots, Springer-Verlag, 1985.

[54] Auslander D.M. et al., "Direct Digital Process Control Practice and Algorithms for PM Applications", Proc. IEEE, Vol. 66, 1978.

[55] Ortega R. and Kelly R., "PID Self-Tuners: Some Theoretical and Practical Aspects", IEEE Trans. on Ind. Elect., Vol. IE-31, No. 4, 1984.

[56] Chiu K.Ch. et al., "Digital Control Algorithms: Parts 1, 2 and 3", Instrum. Contr. Syst., Oct., Nov. and Dec. 1973.

Chapter 4
Computer-Aided Control Synthesis

4.1 Introduction

This chapter is dedicated to computer-aided synthesis of non-adaptive and adaptive control for manipulation robots. In Chapters 2 and 3 we have estabilished a theoretical background for the synthesis of control for robotic systems. We have developed algorithms for the synthesis of control at executive control level for an arbitrary type of robotic system and we have underlined, that these algorithms are very suitable for implementation on a digital computer. Thus, the algorithms which have been elaborated in previous chapters are included in the software package for computer-aided synthesis of control for manipulation robots. This software package is developed in the Robotics Department of Mihailo Pupin Institute [1-3].

As we have emphasized in previous chapters, the algorithms for the synthesis of control for manipulation robots can be made considerably faster and more effective if we allow the user to utilize his experience in control design and his knowledge on robotic systems. Thus, such a package has been developed as allows permanent user's parcitipation during the control synthesis. In each step of control synthesis the user can interrupt the algorithm and make a decision on how to continue the synthesis.

In this chapter we shall briefly describe the complete software package for computer-aided synthesis of control for manipulation robots. Since the theoretical background of our approach to control synthesis for robotic systems has been presented in detail in the previous chapters, we shall not explain again the procedures employed to compute control parameters.

We shall especially emphasize the interaction between the package and the user in each step of the algorithm. Actually, the user is enabled to arrange the control synthesis in accordance with his own engineering judgment and his experience about system. The main advantage of our approach to control synthesis over the other approaches (which have been surveyed in Paragraphs 2.3 and 3.1 - 3.3) is the fact that our approach enables the control synthesis to be done step by step (or better to say, "piece-by-piece"): we first synthesize local controllers for decoupled subsystems; then, we analyze the stability of the global robotic system, and then, if necessary, we may introduce global feedback loops. It is obvious that this control synthesis might be performed completely automatically without the participation of the user (save that he has to set requirements i.e. define control task). However, it was recognized a relatively long time ago that the attempts to synthesize control for large-scale systems fully automatically suffer from many drawbacks [4, 5]. Actually, it has been shown that it is very difficult to specify all requirements and all conditions that play certain roles in a specific control task. On the other hand, the user can sometimes find a solution much faster by using his experience. Thus, it is recommendable to avoid a completely automatic synthesis of control and include the user in the control synthesis, leaving all crucial (final) decisions to him. These facts have been taken into account in developing our software package for computer-aided synthesis of control for manipulation robots. Actually, this package can be viewed as an assistive device which can help the user to synthesize the control for a specific manipulator.

In Paragraph 2 we shall describe the computer-aided synthesis of non--adaptive and adaptive control for manipulation robots; we shall specify the data that have to be imposed by the user of the algorithm and describe the interaction between the user and the package. In Paragraph 4.3 we shall present an example of the control synthesis done by the package. We shall describe how we can synthesize control for the specific manipulation system. Finally, in Paragraph 4.4 we shall discuss the possibilities offered by this package to the user.

4.2 Software Package for Computer Aided Synthesis

In this paragraph we shall describe the software package for computer--aided synthesis of control at the tactical and executive control levels for manipulation robots. It is based upon our approach to control synthesis which has been explained in previous chapters. Actually, in this book we have presented control synthesis at the executive control level only, while the synthesis of tactical control level has been discussed in Vol. 3 of this series [6]. However, the synthesis of the executive control level requires a desired movement (trajectories) to be set, so we must include both control levels in this package. We shall briefly explain the synthesis of nominal trajectories at the tactical control level and pay attention to describing the part of the package dedicated to the synthesis of the executive control level.

The software package allows the control synthesis for an arbitrary type of non-redundant manipulation robots. This means that manipulation robots with up to six degrees of freedom are allowed. Actually, this limit is concerned with tactical control level since the solution of the redundancy problem is not included in the package. However, our approach to the synthesis of the executive control level can be applied to redundant manipulation robots, since procedures for the synthesis of local controllers, stability analysis and global control synthesis are not limited with respect to the number of degrees of freedom of the robot.

As we have explained in previous chapters, our approach to control synthesis is based on employing the model of robot dynamics. In order to enable control synthesis for an arbitrary type of manipulation robot, the package includes the algorithm for automatically setting the mathematical model of robot dynamics. As described in Chapter 1, there are various methods for automatic setting of the mathematical models of robot dynamics on a digital computer (see, also books [7, 8]). However, we can divide these methods into two general groups: numerical and analytical. In [7] there were described several numerical methods for automatically setting robot dynamic models. In [8] and in Chapter 1 of this book we have presented our approach to automatically setting the analytical model of robot dynamics. Both approaches (numerical and analytical) have their advantages and disadvantages. The main advantage of the analytical model is a significant reduction of the computer processing time necessary for computing inertia matrix $H(q)$ and vector of gravity, centrifugal and Coriolis forces $h(q, \dot{q})$, once the analytical model has been obtained. Thus, when we obtain the analytical model, control synthesis is much faster since the computer time is highly reduced with respect to numerical models which have to go through all recursive relations at each time-they have to compute H and h. On the other hand, the disadvantage of the method for setting the analytical model of robot dynamics lies in the fact that a long processing time is required to obtain the analytical model for a particular robot. Thus, if we use the analytical approach, it is rather difficult to explore various structures of manipulators and to change parameters or structure of the robot during the control synthesis. The numerical methods for setting dynamical model of the robot do not suffer from this disadvantage: since the mathematical model is assembled each time we have to compute matrices H and h (for given q, $\dot{q}$) quite generally, these methods do not require any pre-computation and preparing when the parameters or structure of the robot change. Thus, these methods are much more convenient if we want to explore various robot structures and parameters. Obviously, these methods take a much longer computation time to synthesize control in comparison with analytical methods.

Because of the above-explained advantage and disadvantage of both approaches, we have decided to include two procedures for setting the mathematical models of robot dynamics in our software package: a numerical approach via D'Alambert principle which has been developed by Vukobratović and Stepanenko [9] and an analytical approach which has been developed by Vukobratović and Kirćanski N. [9]. The user may decide which of these procedures will be employed in particular run. If the parameters and structure of the robot are well-known and defined it is recommendable to employ the analytical method: it will take some period of processing time at the start of the trial to compute the analytical model of robot dynamics, but atterwards the control synthesis will be much faster since this model requires a much shorter processing time. However, if the parameters and structure of the robot are not precisely defined and the user wants to explore various possible structures and parameters of his robot which may still be under design (or, may be redesigned if it suffers from some drawbacks), it is better to employ numerical method for automatic setting of dynamic model of robot. This procedure will take a longer processing time for computing the model matrices, but the variation of robot parameters and structure will not cause any additional time delay (as it would be the case with the analytical method). Obviously, the user can easily combine both methods: he may use the numerical method as long as he wants to vary robot parameters and structure; once he has "fixed" the robot structure and parameters he may pass to the analytical method and obtain the analytical model of his robot. Thus, he can considerably reduce the computation time.

It should be noticed that the above consideration holds for off-line control synthesis (which is actually performed in our package). If the dynamic model is to be used for on-line computation of the control for manipulation robot, then there is no doubt the analytical model will take a much shorter computation time than the numerical, so the analytical approach should be used for real-time control, as it has been explained in Chapter 1. Of course, our package can be employed to obtain the analytical model of a particular robot which will be used in the synthesized controller (assuming that the controller synthesized for a particular control task requires the dynamic model of the robot).

Since we may regard the kinematic model of the robot as a part of the dynamic model, all above considerations hold for kinematic models. In our package we include both the numerical approach to automatic setting of kinematic model and the procedure for automatic setting of analytical kinematic model on a digital computer (see [6]).

A global flow-chart of the package for control synthesis is presented in Fig. 4.1. The order of programming blocks is conditional. The package is organized in such a way that the user can call and access each of the blocks according to his own convenience. In the text to follow we shall briefly present the interaction between the user and each of software blocks.

The algorithm enables the control synthesis for an arbitrary manipulation configuration and arbitrary manipulator types. Thus, the user can synthesize control either for: a) an already built manipulator (evaluation of manipulator), or b) for a manipulator which is under design. In case a) the algorithm can help to improve control for the existing manipulator and determine the equipment necessary for this improvement. In case b) the user can investigate the influence of the choice of various manipulator parameters (link masses distributions, actuator parameters and so on) upon the control synthesis and the performance of the manipulator, in order to find out the best solutions. In both cases the user can determine the simplest control law which satisfies the requirements imposed in a particular manipulation task. The control synthesis can be performed either for a particular pre-determined task (which has to be realized by the manipulator), or, the user can impose some test-task which ensures that the control synthesized is satisfactory for a wide class of tasks.

The interactions between the user and each of software block are basically very similar to one another. Each has two basic modes: the first is "input" mode, and the second is "changing" mode. When the user starts the control synthesis for the first time for his particular manipulation system, he enters the "input" mode. In this mode he has to

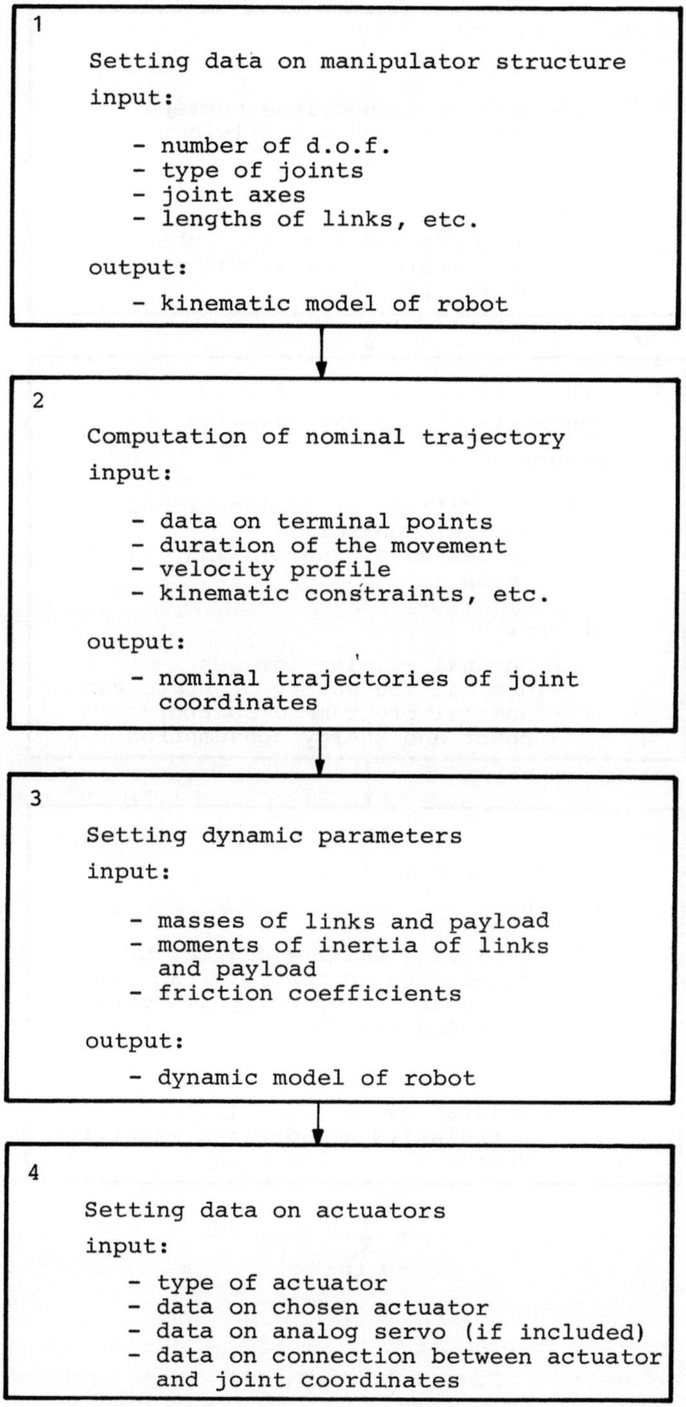

Fig. 4.1. Flow-chart of the software package for computer-aided control synthesis

4

Cont.

- data on connections between actuator load and driving torques around joint

output:

- complete model of the robot (actuators + mechanical part of the robot)

↓

5

Synthesis of nominal dynamics

input:

- centralized or decentralized nominal control
- estimates of inertia and gravity terms

output:

- nominal driving torques
- nominal trajectory of state vector
- nominal programmed control
- power and energy consumption

↓

6

Control task setting

input:

- desired stability degree, or
- tolerances in the terminal points of nominal trajectory (in external coordinates)

output:

- tolerances in joint (internal) coordinates and desired stability degree

↓

(7)

Fig. 4.1. Cont. (1)

(7)

7

Local control synthesis

input:

- local information control structure
- parameters of actuators θ^o
- procedure for local control synthesis
- initial values of the parameters of local controller (weighting matrices, or poles of closed-loop subsystem)
- automatic or interactive synthesis

Synthesis of local controller acc. to algorithm of Fig. 2.20.

---

output:

- local feedback gains

8

Stability analysis of decentralized control

input:

- mode of control synthesis automatic or interactive
- initial value of θ^o and variation $\Delta\theta$
- initial value of d^o and variation Δd

Synthesis of decentralized controller based on the stability analysis of linearized and nonlinear model - Fig. 2.21

If the stability is not guaranteed by decentralized controller:

- go back to (7) and re-select local control (change parameters or procedures or requirements), or
- introduce global control
- change nominal trajectory
- change actuators

(9)

Fig. 4.1. Cont. (2)

(9)

9

Global control synthesis

input:

- automatic or interactive mode of control synthesis
- form of the global control
- implementation of global control (bang-bang global control, force feedback or on-line computation)
- approximate model for on-line computation
- parameters d* for computation
- global gain

Synthesis of global control on the basis of nonlinear model stability analysis - Fig. 2.22

If unique global control cannot be found:

- reselect actuators
- change nominal trajectory and/or tolerances
- introduce adaptive control

output:

- global control law and feedback gains

10

Adaptive control synthesis

input:

- determine the values of parameters for local control synthesis

---

Call blocks (7), (8) for decentralized control synthesis for given parameters

---

- determine transient behaviour during estimation process

Call block (12) for simulation with adaptive control law

---

output:

- variable local gains for adaptive control

Fig. 4.1. Cont. (3)

(11)

11

11

Discrete-time control synthesis

input:

- sampling period

Synthesis of feedback gains in discrete-time domain

- type of microprocessor

output:

- feedback gains in discrete-time domain
- number of additions and multiplications to compute control law
- time required for control computation
- number of μP for control implementation

12

Simulation

input:

- initial conditions
- type of nominal control
- form of local controllers
- form of global control
- adaptive or non-adaptive control
- continuous time or discrete-time control

output:

- deviation of state coordinates, from nominal trajectory
- driving torques developed during tracking
- input signals developed during tracking
- power and energy consumption

Final decision on control law and equipment necessary for its implementation

Fig. 4.1. Cont. (4)

impose all data which are required by the algorithm in the particular step of control synthesis (for example, data on the structure of the chosen manipulator or data on actuators, etc - see the text to follow). All data imposed by the user are memorized in the appropriate files on the corresponding memory unit. Afterwards, if the user wants to change these data he has to enter "changing" mode and he can easily change the previously imposed data for this manipulation system. The conversation between the user and computer is very simple to handle. The algorithm checks all data imposed by the user and detects possible errors. This enables easy synthesis of control for manipulation robots of various types and enables the user to investigate the influence of various manipulator parameters upon the system behaviour [10].

The user can arrange the control synthesis according to his own convenience, as has already been stated. However, some order has to be taken into account; for example, nominal kinematics cannot be synthesized before the user has imposed data on manipulator configuration. The algorithm takes care about this fact, so the user is released of these problems. The user can easily go through the algorithm and iteratively improve the control.

4.2.1. Block for setting data on manipulator structure

The algorithm enables the control synthesis for nonredundant manipulation robots of arbitrary structure. In this block the user sets data on the configuration and geometry of a specific manipulator for which he wants to synthesize the control. The user has to set the following data:

1. The number of degrees of freedom of the manipulator (minimum 3, maximum 6).

2. Type of each joint (revolute or linear).

3. Projections of the joints axes in the internal coordinate systems (each internal coordinate system is connected to one manipulator link, so it is easy to set these data on joint axes' projections).

4. Projections of the links axes in the internal coordinate systems.

5. Lengths of the links (distances between the joint axes).

6. Distances between the joint axis and the corresponding link's center of gravity.

Using these data the algorithm automatically sets the kinematic model of the manipulator. The algorithm also forms a file with the data imposed by the user.

4.2.2. Block for calculating desired kinematic trajectory

The algorithm calculates nominal kinematic trajectories, according to user's desires. The user has to impose the following data:

1. Data on terminal points of each trajectory part. The coordinates of the terminal points can be imposed either in internal coordinates $q \in R^n$ (angles or displacements of each joint of the manipulator) or in external coordinates $s \in R^n$. The following options on external coordinates are available:

   (a) the coordinates of the manipulator tip in the absolute coordinate system (connected to the first joint) and the internal coordinates (angles) of the manipulator gripper,

   (b) the coordinates of the manipulator tip in the absolute coordinate system and the Euler's angles of the last member with respect to the axes of the absolute coordinate system,

   (c) the coordinates of the manipulator tip in the absolute coordinate system and the projections of a unit vector connected to the last member of the manipulator (upon the axes of the absolute coordinate system).

The user has to impose data on the coordinates of the terminal points of each part of desired trajectory. The user may set up to 30 trajectory parts, i.e. 30 points through which the manipulator has to pass.

2. Duration of the movement on each trajectory part (period τ).

3. The profile of the velocity of coordinates between the imposed terminal points. The velocity profile can be triangular or trapezoid. In the latter case the user should impose duration of acceleration

and deceleration.

4. The user can choose whether the manipulator should stop in the imposed terminal point or pass through it at a constant velocity.

5. The user can impose various kinematic constraints upon the internal coordinates of the manipulator, and various obstacles and constraints upon the working space.

The computation of the trajectories of internal coordinates, if external trajectory is defined by terminal points, is performed as follows.

The relation between the external coordinates s and the internal coordinates q is given by:

$$s = f_s(q) \tag{4.2.1}$$

where f_s: $R^n \to R^n$. If the user sets the trajectory in the external coordinates $s^o(t)$, $\forall t \in T$, the algorithm calculates the trajectory in the internal coordinates $q^o(t)$. Namely, using (4.2.1) it is obtained:

$$\dot{q}(t) = J^{-1}\dot{s}(t) \tag{4.2.2}$$

where $J \in R^{n \times n}$, $J = [\frac{\partial f_s}{\partial q}]$ is Jacobian matrix. In (4.2.2) it is assumed that J is a nonsingular matrix. Using (4.2.2) and set $s^o(t)$, $\dot{q}^o(t)$ is calculated and $q^o(t)$ is obtained by numerical integration of $\dot{q}^o(t)$. The Jacobian matrix for each point $q^o(t)$ is obtained from the kinematic model of the robot which is automatically set on the computer using the parameters on the mechanism structure, as explained in the previous block.

The algorithm calculates nominal kinematics so as to ensure the motion of the manipulator tip along a straight line between the terminal points, while the velocity of the tip changes according to the chosen velocity profile. According to our experience, this way of imposing nominal kinematics is quite satisfactory to enable user to synthesize nominal trajectories for most manipulation tasks which can be encountered in industrial practice.

For more details on the synthesis of nominal trajectories using the kinematic model of the robot see book 3 of this series [6]. Obviously, nominal trajectories might be synthesized using the dynamic model of the robot. For example, distribution of the tip velocity might be computed by minimizing the energy required for the movement [6, 11]. Obviously, such an approach requires a much longer processing time than the synthesis based on the kinematic model.

The algorithm forms files with data imposed by the user, and with data on the calculated nominal trajectory. During calculation of the nominal trajectory the algorithm takes care about the imposed constraints and the manipulator kinematic capabilities. A graphical display of the calculated trajectory (internal angles and velocities) is also available.

4.2.3. Block for setting dynamic parameters

In order to set the mathematical model of the manipulator dynamics, the algorithm needs data on the manipulator dynamics, such as:

1. Masses of all links and payload.
2. Moments of inertia of all members (with respect to the main axes of inertia) and of the payload.
3. Data on friction in each manipulator joint.

The user might define allowable variations of all these parameters D, i.e. for each parameter the user might define the minimum and maximum allowable values.

The algorithm automatically sets the dynamic model of the mechanism and forms files with the imposed data the dynamic model is set in form (2.2.1).

Actually, the algorithm computes the matrix $H(q,d)$ and vector $h(q, \dot{q}, d)$ for given $q(t)$, $\dot{q}(t)$ and given parameters d (geometry parameters, masses, moments of inertia, etc.). Each time during the control synthesis when we need the model of dynamics of the robot we have to set the values of $q(t)$, $\dot{q}(t)$ and the algorithm will compute the corresponding matrices H and h. As we have explained above, the user can choose the procedure which will be applied for setting the model: either the numerical or the analytical procedure. In the latter case the package will take some time to prepare the analytical model of the robot at the very start of the control synthesis for a particular robot.

4.2.4. Block for setting data on actuators

The user has to impose data on the actuators for each joint of the mechanism. He can choose the type of each actuator: D.C. electro-motor or hydraulic linear or vane actuator. If he chooses D.C. motor he has to impose the following data (all these data can be picked from the data sheets for the chosen actuator):

1. Viscous friction coefficient (B_C^i),
2. Electro-motor coefficient of the motor (C_E^i),
3. Moment coefficient of the motor (C_M^i),
4. Moment of inertia of rotor (J_r^i),
5. Gear speed and moment ratio (N_r^i),
6. Resistance of the rotor (R_r^i),
7. Inductance of the rotor (L_r^i),
8. Upper and lower amplitude constraint upon the actuator input (u_m^i).

Using these data the package computes the matrices of the time-invariant linear models of actuators S^i. The matrices A^i and vectors b^i, f^i are computed according to Eq. (2.A.2), and the package assumes the models of actuator to be in linear form (2.2.2).

When the user chooses hydraulic actuators, he has to type the following data:

1. Viscous friction coefficient in the cylinder (B_C^i),
2. Piston area (A_C^i),
3. Cylinder (working) volume (V_u^i),
4. Mass of the piston (including the rod mass) (m_t^i),
5. The oil compressibility coefficient (β^i),

6. Gradient of the servovalve flow-pressure characteristic (k_C^i),

7. Proportionality coefficient of the oil flow and servovalve coil current (K_q^i/C_1^i),

8. Upper and lower amplitude constraint upon the actuator input (u_m^i).

Using these data the algorithm computes matrices A^i and vectors b^i, f^i according to Eq. (2.A.6) and assumes the linear time-invariant models of actuators S^i (2.2.2).

In both cases the user might impose the range of all parameters θ (if their variation is expected), i.e. for each parameter the user might define minimum and maximum allowable values.

In both cases the user can choose the order n_i of the model of each actuator. As we have explained in Appendix 2.A., the model of D.C. motor might be taken to be 2 or 3, and the user might select the order he prefers. Obviously, if the user selects the order of the model of D.C. motor to be 2, then the matrices of the model are defined by (2.A.3), and the inductance of the rotor coil is neglected. (Thus, the inductance need not be set). The situation is similar with the hydraulic actuator.

It should also be noted that if the user desires to apply the hydraulic actuator, he might choose between linear and vane actuators. The data required in both cases are as listed above, just the units are different depending on the type of the hydraulic actuator selected.

The package allows a special option to include already implemented analog servosystems.

If the implemented actuators already have analog servosystems*) the user has to set data on feedback gains. The assumed structure of the analog servosystem is presented in Fig. 4.2. The user has to set the following data:

---

*) This situation appears if we have already built the manipulator and implemented local analog servosystems, and now we want to introduce additional control through a microprocessor unit in order to improve robot's performance. Thus, the analog servosystem gains are assumed to have been synthesized previously and the user can type their values.

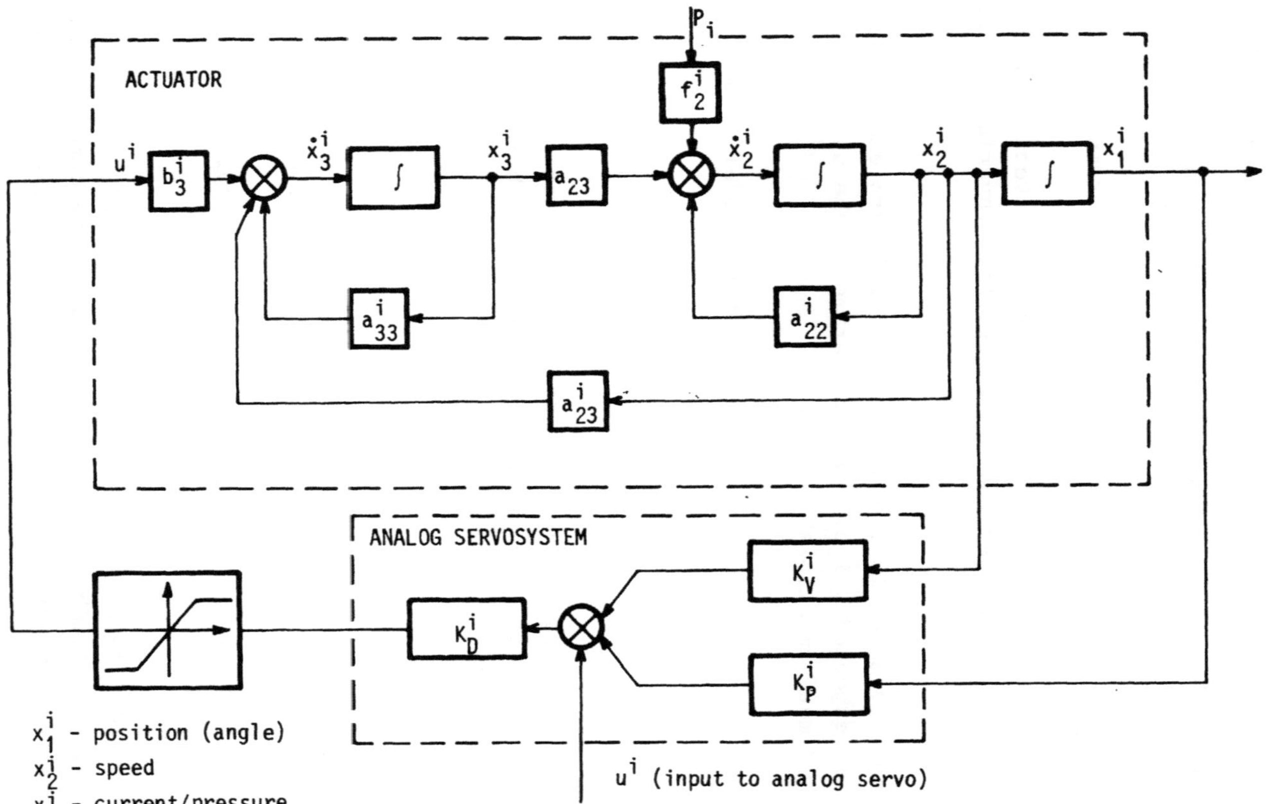

x_1^i - position (angle)
x_2^i - speed
x_3^i - current/pressure
K_P^i - position analog feedback gain
K_V^i - speed analog feedback gain
K_D^i - gain in direct branch

Fig. 4.2. Scheme of the actuator with analog servosystem

1. gain K_D^i in direct branch,

2. gain K_P^i in feedback loop by position,

3. gain K_V^i in feedback loop by speed.

If the analog servosystem exists in the *i*th joint, and the user sets the above gains, the package automatically changes the models of the actuators in order to include the servosystems. Actually, the model of the actuator together with analog servosystem is given by (2.2.2), too, but the matrices A^i, b^i, f^i are changed and get the form (for the third order models of actuators):

- for D.C. motors:

$$A^i = \begin{bmatrix} 0 & 1 & 0 \\ 0 & -B_C/J_r & C_M/J_r \\ -K_DK_P/L_r & -(C_E+K_DK_V)/L_r & -R_r/L_r \end{bmatrix} \quad b^i = \begin{bmatrix} 0 \\ 0 \\ \dfrac{K_D}{L_r} \end{bmatrix} \quad f^i = \begin{bmatrix} 0 \\ -1/J_r \\ 0 \end{bmatrix} \tag{4.2.3}$$

- for hydraulic actuators

$$A^i = \begin{bmatrix} 0 & 1 & 0 \\ 0 & -B_C/m_t & A_C/m_t \\ -K_DK_Pb_3' & -4\beta A_C/V_u-K_DK_Vb_3' & -4\beta(k_C+C_{tc})/V_u \end{bmatrix} \quad b^i = \begin{bmatrix} 0 \\ 0 \\ b_3'K_D \end{bmatrix}$$

$$f^i = (0, \quad -1/m_t, \quad 0)^T, \qquad b_3' = 4\beta K_q/(V_uC_1) \tag{4.2.4}$$

Obviously if the analog servosystems have not yet been synthesized, but still have to be selected by the package, the user cannot impose the above data and the matrices of actuators models remain unchanged.

The user also has to impose the following data:

1. He has to choose the type of connection between the manipulator joint coordinate (angle or displacement) and the coordinate (displacement) of the corresponding actuator. When D.C. motor or vane hydraulic actuators is implemented in rotational joint, or when linear hydraulic actuator is applied in the linear degree of freedom

of the manipulator, this connection is trivial. However, in the opposite case when rotational actuators are applied for linear degrees of freedom or vice versa, this connection may be complex, so the user has to impose the type of connection and the parameters of the chosen connection. These connections are given by relation (2.2.4). There are several types of connections which are included in the package (such as cosines formula, tangens relation etc.) and the user has to depict the one which corresponds to his robot (for each joint he has to select the right type of the connection).

2. The user also has to choose the type of connection between the driving torque in the manipulator joint and the load acting upon the corresponding actuator. The relation between the driving torque and actuator load is defined by (2.2.7). The user has to select among the preassumed possible types of connection which correspond to the connection in each joint of his manipulator.

Obviously, these relations between the joint coordinates and actuator coordinates and the relations between the joint driving torque and load in actuator reflect the mathematical model of the robotic system, as it has been explained in Paragraph 2.2.2. Thus, the load distribution vectors f^i are changed to include relations (2.2.7), so these vector are not constant but become functions of q_i.

The package forms files with all these data imposed by the user. In this way the user has set all the data required to specify the model of the particular robot, and the package can operate with the complete model of the robot when it is needed during the control synthesis.

4.2.5. Block for synthesis of nominal dynamics

In this block nominal dynamics is synthesized in the following manner:

1. Using the calculated nominal kinematic trajectories $q^o(t)$, $\dot{q}^o(t)$ $\forall t \in T$, the package computes nominal driving torques on the basis of the model of the robot mechanism dynamics:

$$P^o(t) = H(q^o(t),\ d^o)\ddot{q}^o(t) + h(q^o(t),\ \dot{q}^o(t),\ d^o) \qquad (4.2.5)$$

where accelerations $\ddot{q}^o(t)$ are obtained by numerical differentiation of the nominal velocity $\dot{q}^o(t)$. The user has to define for which values of the parameters in a given range $d^o \in D$ the nominal driving torques will be computed.

2. If the user has selected that the order of the actuator model is 3, this means that each actuator model has three state coordinates $((\ell^i, \dot{\ell}^i, i_r^i)^T$ - in the case of the D.C. motors, and $(\ell^i, \dot{\ell}^i, p^i)^T$ - in the case of hydraulic actuators, where i_r^i denotes rotor current and p^i denotes pressure difference in the cylinder). Since $q^o(t)$, $\dot{q}^o(t)$ define $\ell^o(t)$, $\dot{\ell}^o(t)$ through set relations (2.2.4), the package computes the nominal trajectory of the third state coordinate of each actuator (let us denote the state coordinates by $x^i = (x_1^i, x_2^i, x_3^i)^T$). Since the matrices A^i are of equal form regardless of whether D.C. motors of hydraulic actuators are selected, the nominal trajectory of the third state coordinate $x_3^{io}(t)$ in both cases is computed as:

$$x_3^{oi}(t) = (\dot{x}_2^{oi}(t) - a_{22}x_2^{oi}(t) - f_2^i(q^{oi}(t))\cdot P_i^o(t))/a_{23}^i \qquad (4.2.6)$$

where a_{kj}^i and f_2^i denote the corresponding elements of the matrices A^i and f^i, respectively.

Obviously, if the user has selected the order of the *i*th actuator's model to be 2, there is no need to compute nominal trajectory of the third state coordinate.

3. The package computes nominal programmed control, i.e. nominal imputs to each actuator which has to be supplied to actuators in order to develop nominal driving torques $P_i^o(t)$ and nominal motion of the robot (i.e. to drive the robot along nominal trajectory $x^o(t)$, $\forall t \in T$). The programmed nominal control is obtained in the form:

- if the order of the actuator model is $n_i=3$

$$u^{oi}(t) = (\dot{x}_3^{oi}(t) - a_{32}^i x_2^{oi}(t) - a_{33}^i x_3^{oi}(t))/b_3^i \qquad (4.2.7)$$

- if the order of the actuator model is $n_i=2$

$$u^{oi}(t) = (\dot{x}_2^{oi}(t) - a_{22}^i x_2^{oi}(t) - f_2^i(q^{oi}(t))\cdot P_i^o(t))/b_2^i \qquad (4.2.8)$$

In Eq. (4.2.7) and (4.2.8) we have taken into account the forms of the actuator model matrices A^i, b^i, f^i.

The nominal programmed control $u^{oi}(t)$ computed as presented above would realize $x^o(t)$ in ideal conditions, i.e. if no perturbation is acting upon the robotic system and assuming that the mathematical model of the robotic system is ideally identified. However, computation of $u^o(t)$ requires to compute dynamic model of the robot, which might be too complex to be implemented on-line as we have explained in previous chapters and which requires perfect knowledge of all parameters of the robot mechanism. Thus, instead of nominal control synthesized using the centralized model of the robotic system, the package might synthesize nominal control using approximative decentralized model (see Paragraph 2.4) in which coupling between the joints is neglected (i.e. in which the dynamics of the mechanism is neglected). Thus, the package might compute the so-called local nominal control $\bar{u}^{oi}(t)$ according to the following relations:

- if the order of the actuator model is $n_i=3$

$$x_3^{oi}(t) = (\dot{x}_2^{oi}(t) - \tilde{a}_{22}^i x_2^{oi}(t))/\tilde{a}_{23}^i$$
$$u^{oi}(t) = (\dot{x}_3^{oi}(t) - \tilde{a}_{32}^i x_2^{oi}(t) - \tilde{a}_{33}^i x^{oi}(t))/\tilde{b}_3^i \quad (4.2.9)$$

- if the order of the actuator model is $n_i=2$,

$$u^{oi}(t) = (\dot{x}_2^{oi}(t) - \tilde{a}_{22}^i x_2^{oi}(t))/\tilde{b}_2^i \quad (4.2.10)$$

where $\tilde{a}_{kj}^i$, $\tilde{b}_j$ denote the corresponding members of the matrices $\tilde{A}^i$, $\tilde{b}^i$ which are defined by (2.4. 7). Actually, $\tilde{A}^i$, $\tilde{b}^i$ are the matrices of the actuator models which include estimation of inertia term $\bar{H}_{ii}\ddot{q}_i$ and estimation of gravity term $\bar{h}_i q_i$, as explained in Paragraph 2.4.

Thus, the user has to make two choices:

a) To choose whether he wants to synthesize nominal control using the centralized model (Eqs. (4.2.7), (4.2.8)), or the decentralized model (Eqs. (4.2.9), (4.2.10)).

b) To choose the estimates of the inertia term $\bar{H}_{ii}\ddot{q}_i$ and gravity terms $\bar{h}_i q_i$ which should be associated to the subsystem model (for each joint).

Actually, the package computes $\min_{t\in T} H_{ii}(q^o(t))$ and $\min_{t\in T} |\partial(g_i(q^o(t))/\partial q_i|$

and the user has to select the part of this value that will be taken in the subsystem model; the user types the part of the inertia estimates that he wants to associate to subsystem model K_I and the package takes $\bar{H}_{ii}$ to be $K_I \min_{t \in T} H_{ii}(q^o(t))$ a similar situation arises with the estimation of the gravity term.

4. The package checks whether the chosen actuators can perform the imposed motion. Namely, the package checks whether the computed nominal control $u^{oi}(t)$ satisfies the amplitude saturation constraint upon the actuator input (2.2.3) for all subsystems and over the desired time interval T. If the computed nominal control for the *i*th actuator $u^{oi}(t)$ at some instant on the trajectory exceed the amplitude bound u_m^i, this means that the chosen *i*th actuator cannot realize the desired nominal trajectory (even in an ideal case if no perturbation is acting upon the system). In that case, the user might decide whether:

   a) to go back to block for input data on actuator parameter and change the *i*th actuator, or

   b) to go back to block for calculation of nominal kinematic trajectory and change the trajectory (often he has to decrease the desired speed of motion by increasing the duration of manipulator motion).

5. The package computes the power and energy demanded to implement the desired nominal trajectory.

The algorithm forms a file with all calculated data on nominal dynamics (nominal angles or displacements, nominal velocities, driving torques, inputs, power and energy consumptions). A graphic display of these data is also available.

4.2.6. Block for setting control task

The user has to impose requirements concerning the quality of tracking the nominal trajectory, i.e. he has to impose the requirements upon the control task. Two ways of imposing the control task are available:

1. The user can directly set the desired degree of stability α of the

manipulation system. In this case the algorithm has to ensure that the poles of the system are to the left from the imposed stability degree α in a complex plane. This means that the slowest response of the system must be faster than exponent of the prescribed stability degree α (i.e. it must be satisfied $||\Delta x(t)|| < ||\Delta x(0)||\exp(-\alpha t)$).

2. The second way is to impose tolerances in the terminal points of the trajectory parts which have been set in block for computation of nominal trajectory. The tolerances have to be imposed in the same type of external coordinates (or internal coordinates) in which the corresponding terminal points have been imposed.

The user sets tolerances in external coordinates so as to impose allowable deviations $\Delta s(t_i)$ from the nominal values for each coordinate where t_i, $\forall i \in I_1$, $I_1 = \{i: i=1,2,\ldots,m\}$ are control instants on the trajectory, $\forall t_i \in T$. In this way we define the regions in manipulator external coordinates space $X_s(t_i)$, $\forall i \in I_1$, which manipulation robot has to satisfy:

$$X_s(t_i)=\{s(t_i): |s^j(t_i)-s^{oj}(t_i)|<\Delta s^j(t_i), \quad \forall j \in I\}, \forall i \in I_1, \quad (4.2.11)$$

where $s = (s^1, s^2,\ldots,s^n)^T$. On the basis of relation (4.2.1) between the external and internal coordinates, the algorithm maps the regions $X_s(t_i)$ from the external coordinates space to the regions $Q(t_i) \subset R^n$ in the internal coordinates space:

$$F_s^{-1}(X_s(t_i)) \to Q(t_i), \qquad i \in I_1 \qquad (4.2.12)$$

Similarly, the user may impose allowable deviations by rates and accelerations in the external coordinates, and then the algorithm determines allowable regions of deviations by rates and accelerations in the space of the internal coordinates $Q^v(t_i)$, $Q^a(t_i)$, $\forall i \in I_1$. If the user does not set allowable deviations by rates and accelerations, the algorithm adopts regions $Q^v(t_i)$, $Q^a(t_i)$, $\forall i \in I$, according to the feasibilities of chosen actuators. Regions $Q(t_i)$, $Q^v(t_i)$, $Q^a(t_i)$, $\forall i \in I$ are thus obtained and mapped by the algorithm, using (2.2.12), into regions $X_s^t(t_i) \subset R^N$ in the state space of the system S, which may be estimated by $X^t(t_i) \supseteq X_s^t(t_i)$ $\forall t \in I_1$ where $X^t(t_i) = X^{t(1)}(t_i) \times X^{t(2)}(t_i) \times, \ldots$ $\ldots, \times X^{t(n)}(t_i)$, $\forall i \in I_1$, $X^{t(j)}(t_i) \subset R^{n_j}$, $\forall j \in I$*). In this way the regions

---

*) Here, we assume that $n_i=3$, $\forall i \in I$, which is the most common case. If we choose $n_i=2$, it is sufficient to define regions $Q(t_i)$, $Q^v(t_i)$.

in the state space to which the system state must belong during tracking of the set nominal trajectories are defined, i.e., $x(t_i) \in X^t(t_i)$, $\forall i \in I_i$.

However, in order to simplify control synthesis we prefer to get stability regions in the form assumed in Para. 2.2.2,

$$X^{t(i)'}(t) = \{\Delta x^i(t): \ ||\Delta x^i(t)|| < \bar{X}^{t(i)}\exp(-\alpha_i t)\}, \quad \forall t \in T \quad (4.2.13)$$

It is very easy to compute the exponential degrees α_i of shrinking the regions $X^{t(i)'}$ so that these regions satisfy:

$$X^{t(i)'}(t_j) \subseteq X^{t(i)}(t_j), \quad \forall t_j \in I_1, \quad \forall i \in I \quad (4.2.14)$$

Thus, the package determines the stability regions in the following way:

a) First, the user has to set allowable deviations $\Delta s(t_j)$, $\forall j \in I_1$ from nominal trajectory in external coordinates and define the allowable regions $X_s(t_j)$, $\forall j \in I_1$ by (4.2.11).

b) The package maps the regions $X_s(t_j)$ from external coordinate space to regions $Q(t_j)$ in the internal coordinate space using (4.2.12).

c) If the user sets allowable deviations by rates and accelerations in the external coordinates, the package maps these regions into regions by rates and accelerations $Q^v(t_j)$, $Q^a(t_j)$, $\forall i \in I_1$ in internal coordinate space, otherwise, the package adopts regions $Q^v(t_j)$, $Q^a(t_j)$ according to the feasibilities of the actuators [10].

d) The regions $Q(t_j)$, $Q^v(t_j)$, $Q^a(t_j)$, $\forall j \in I_1$ define the regions $X_s^t(t_j)$, $\forall j \in I_1$ in the state coordinate system by relations (2.2.11)-(2.2.13).

e) The obtained regions $X_s^t(t_j)$ are "decoupled" by the package; The package defines the regions $X^t(t_j) = X^{t(1)}(t_j) \times X^{t(2)}(t_j) \times \cdots \cdots \times X^{t(n)}(t_j)$, $\forall j \in I$, where $X^{t(j)} \subset R^{n_i}$, $\forall i \in I$ are the regions in the subsystems state space. (Actually, the package defines the largest regions $X^t(t_j)$ which satisfy both $X^t(t_j) \subseteq X_s^t(t_j)$ and $X^t(t_j) = X^{t(1)}(t_j) \times X^{t(2)}(t_j) \times \cdots \times X^{t(n)}(t_j)$, $\forall j \in I_1$).

f) The package determines "the best" estimations of the regions $X^{t(i)}(t_j)$ by the regions $X^{t(i)'}(t)$ defined by (4.2.13); actually, the package has to find out the smallest numbers α_i and largest $\bar{X}^{t(i)}$ so that the region $X^{t(i)'}(t)$ defined by (4.2.13) satisfies (4.2.14).

Thus, the package gets the regions of practical stability $X^t(t)$ defined as in Chapter 2 and, by this, parameters of the control task (2.2.18) are set.

The package forms a file with data on tolerances in external coordinates (as they were imposed by the user) and a file with calculated tolerances in internal coordinates.

4.2.7. Block for local control synthesis

In the previous paragraph we have described that the algorithm automatically "decouples" the stability regions in subsustems state space. In this way the control task (2.2.18) is decouples into local control tasts (2.4.8). Obviously, this decoupling is approximative since the satisfaction of the local control tasks does not guarantee satisfaction of the global control task (2.2.18). Now, the package can synthesize the local controllers so as to satisfy local control tasks (2.4.8), i.e. for each subsystem (actuator) (2.4.7) the package synthesizes the local controller which satisfies (2.4.8). The algorithm for the synthesis of local controller for decoupled subsystem has been described in Paragraph 2.4.4. The package completely implements this algorithm (Fig. 2.20). Naturally, here we shall not repeat description of the algorithm for local control synthesis. We shall just point out the interaction between the user of the package and the algorithm, which is intended to speed-up the procedure, as mentioned in Paragraph 2.4.4.

In this block the user has to make the following decisions:

1) To choose the information control pattern for each local controller, i.e. to choose the local feedback loops that will be introduced for each subsystem (joint); the user has to state for each actuator:*)

   a) Will feedback by speed be introduced, or not?

   b) Will feedback by rotor current (if D.C. motor is applied) or by cylinder pressure (if hydraulic actuator is applied), be introcuced of not?**)

---

*) The package assumes that a positional feedback loop is introduced in each joint which is commonly the case.

**) Obviously, the introduction of the feedback by current/pressure can be done if the user assumes the order of the actuator model to be 3.

c) Will integral feedback (integral of the position error) be introduced or not? (Actually, this question means: shall we apply dynamic or static controller?)

2) To specify parameters of each subsystem-actuator $\theta^{O} \in \Theta$ for which local controller will be synthesized.

3) To choose the procedure for the local control synthesis. The user has to decide whether the package will synthesize the local controller by minimizing local quadratic controller or by pole-placement*): obviously, this choice is connected with the above selection of information control pattern (i.e. the local optimal regulator requires a complete state feedback so that both feedbacks by velocity and current (pressure) have to be introduced).

4) To specify initial values for the parameters of the local controller which have to be set in the selected procedure; if the user has selected to synthesize local optimal controller he has to specify weithting matrices Q_i, r_i and prescribed stability degree β_i in local standard quadratic criterion (2.4.16); if pole-placement has been selected, the user has to specify poles of the closed-loop local subsystem; obviously, if the user does not want to specify these values, the package might adopt them in accordance to local control task specifications.

5) To decide whether the local control synthesis will be performed completely automatically or in the interactive mode; if the user selects the automatic mode, then the package should iteratively re--select local controller until it reaches the specified local control task (2.4.8)**); if the user decides to synthesize local control in interactive mode, this means that the package would ask the user to re-select parameters of the local controller at each itera-

---

*) Our package actually includes several other procedures for local control synthesis (e.g. Bode's method for synthesis in frequency domain, etc.) but, for simplicity, we shall not discuss these well--known methods since the procedure for stability analysis is invariant with respect to the method for local control synthesis.

**) It should be noted that if automatic mode is chosen, even the above listed data (information control pattern, procedure for local control synthesis, parameters of local control etc.) need not be specified by the user, but the algorithm might adopt them starting from the simplest case and iteratively re-choose them. However, this is usually time consuming, so it is much faster if the user can specify even the initial values of these parameters.

tion until the requirements specified in local control task are met.

6. If the automatic mode of local control synthesis has been chosen, the package iteratively searches for the local control which satisfies local control task (2.4.8); the user has to specify:

   a) The maximum number of iterations for searching of local control by increasing the prescribed stability degree β_i (if local optimal regulator is chosen) or by moving the poles of the closed--loop subsystem to the left in the complex plane (if pole-placement method is used); if the specified number of iterations is exceeded without success, the algorithm will pass to change of information pattern.

   b) Feedback loops which might be added in the local controller in order to achieve satisfaction of local control task (e.g. the user should specify whether or not he allows feedback by velocity or by pressure/current).

   c) Sequence of the methods for control synthesis which will be used by the package in searching for an adequate local control (i.e. the user has to specify the method for control synthesis that will be used next, if the preceding one has failed).

7) If interactive mode has been selected, the user is directly included in control synthesis; this means that after each trial the user is asked to:

   a) Re-set the parameters of the controller, i.e. to specify a new value of prescribed stability degree or new weighting matrices, or new values of closed-loop subsystem poles, or

   b) specify new information control pattern if he wants so, or

   c) specify a new method for control synthesis, if the user prefers to try with another procedure for control synthesis.

It should be noted that since we consider linear time-invariant subsystems it is usually rather simple to synthesize local control which satisfies the local control task. Most frequently the user can determine an adequate local controller in one or two iterations (using the package support, of course). However, we have included all above options in order to make the package general and to provide a basis for the next step of control synthesis (linear and nonlinear stability analysis) in which these options are also included (see the text to follow).

4.2.8. Block for stability analysis of decentralized control

In this block of the software package, stability of the overall robotic system is analysed. Actually, this block represents implementation of the algorithm described in Paragraph 2.5 and presented in Fig. 2.21. As with the previous block, we shall not repeat the description of the algorithm. We shall briefly discuss interaction between the user and the package.

As we have explained in Paragraph 2.5, the stability analysis of the overall robotic system is performed in two steps: first, the linearized model of the robot is analyzed and, then, nonlinear analysis of stability is performed. In both steps the user might be directly included in iterative search for a decentralized controller which satisfies the set conditions of stability, or this search might be performed completely automatically. Here we shall list data that are expected by the user in both modes of decentralized control synthesis:

I The user has to choose the mode of control synthesis that will be executed: automatic or interactive.

II If automatic mode has been chosen, the user might impose the following data:

a) Initial values of actuator parameters $\theta_o \in \Theta$ and parameter variations $\Delta\theta$ which will be used to vary parameters of actuators over the imposed region of allowable parameters Θ.

b) Data required for local control synthesis for each decoupled subsystem in automatic mode (see Paragraph 4.2.8).

c) Initial values of parameters of the mechanical part of the robot $d = d_o \in D$ and parameter variations Δd which will be used to vary parameters of the mechanical part of the robot over the imposed region of allowable parameters D in order to examine the stability of the robotic system for $\forall d \in D$.

Obviously, all above data might be automatically chosen by the algorithm, but it seems that their choice is simple and it might considerably speed-up the iteration process of determining the parameters of the local controllers.

III If interactive mode has been chosen then the user is permanently included in searching for the adequate local controllers. In this the user has to impose the following data:

a) All initial data listed above for automatic mode are also included in interactive mode.

b) If the linearized model of the robot does not satisfy the set stability requirements, the user has to specify new parameters for local controllers; the user might determine the local controller that has to be changed in order to stabilize the overall system*); the user might change information control structure in the corresponding local controller in order to improve the performance of global robotic system; the user might change the procedure for local control synthesis if he presumes that it might lead faster to the solution.

c) If the analysis of the practical stability does not guarantee the practical stability of the global system with the synthesized decentralized controller, the user might also specify the parameters of local controllers in the next search; in this case, since the nonlinear stability analysis is performed subsystem by subsystem, it can be easily determined which local controller has to be changed in order to stabilize the nonlinear model of the robot; the local information control structure might also be changed if the user finds that this is worthwhile; the user might also change the method for local control synthesis according to his convenience.

d) If the algorithm cannot find unique local controllers which can accommodate all variations of actuator parameters Θ and parameters of the mechanical part of the robot D, he might try to change parameters of actuators θ^o for which the local control-

*) In automatic mode the algorithm must test the sensitivity of the linearized model to each local controller, i.e. it must change all local controllers in order to find out which of them leads to stabilization of the linearized model (see Paragraph 2.5); however, in interactive mode the user might directly "recognize" the local controller which can improve stability of the overall system.

lers have been synthesized. Similarly, if centralized nominal control is included in the control law, the user might change parameters of the mechanism d^o for which the nominal driving torques are computed (4.2.5). These user's interventions might sometimes help to find unique decentralized control (with or without centralized nominal control) which can withstand all parameter variations.

IV In both modes if too many trials have been made without success, the user has to decide whether he wants to continue searching for decentralized control which satisfies the given control task, or to introduce additional global feedback loops. Namely, as it has been explained in Paragraph 2.5, if the influence of the dynamics of the mechanism is too strong, the satisfaction of the given control task might require very high local feedback gains. We have listed in Paragraph 2.5, some of the drawbacks of "high gain" solution of decentralized controller. It is up to a user to decide whether he wants to continue searching for decentralized controller and "risk" to implement "high gain" local controllers, or to introduce global control. The user should estimate whether the local feedback gains are too high so that they might cause appearance of elastic modes of the robot, or the decentralized controller is still acceptable. Obviously, the user might change the control task if he finds out that the requirements are too hard for a particular robotic system. The user might slow-down the desired trajectory $x^o(t)$ or change the finite regions of practical stability X^I and $X^t(t)$, $\forall t \in T$. The another possibility is to change actuators, i.e. to try to satisfy control task requirements with more powerful actuators which might stabilize the robot even with the decentralized controller only.

As the output of this block, local feedback gains have to be computed, either those which satisfy the stated control task without additional control loops, or the local feedback gains which are acceptable according to the user's opinion but which require introduction of global control in order to satisfy the stated control task. The package forms the file with the computed local feedback gains.

4.2.9. Block for global control synthesis

If the user has decided to introduce global control he has to enter this block and synthesize global control which ensures stability of the overall robotic system. This block is program implementation of the algorithm for global control synthesis which has been described in Paragraph 2.6, the flow-chart of which is presented in Fig. 2.22. Here, we shall briefly discuss interaction between the user and the package.

The list of data and the decisions that might be expected from the user are given below.

I The user has to decide whether the global control synthesis will be performed fully automatically or interactive synthesis will be executed. In automatic mode the user need not set any additional data (except those which he might set during synthesis of local controller - see Paragraph 4.2.8). However, the execution of the automatic mode for global control synthesis might be very time consuming, so it is not recommendable to use this mode. In this block the user's experience about the robot dynamics may be fully utilized.

II If interactive mode has been selected the user might take part in each iteration during searching for adequate global control law and parameter. However, in each step the user may make his own decision or leave to the algorithm to search for adequate solution. Here, we shall list all data that might be imposed by the user, although some of them might be computed by the package.

a) The user might select the form of the global control, i.e. he might select among forms (2.6.24), or (2.6.25), or (2.6.4).

b) The user might select implementation of global control among three possibilities: maximum input amplitude of global control (bang-bang global control), force feedback, or on-line computation of driving torques.

c) If the user has decided to implement on-line computation of the coupling acting upon the corresponding joint (for which the global control is synthesized), he has to select the approximative model of robot dynamics which will be used to compute global control. In Paragraph 2.6, we have listed various approximative models which might be used to compute driving torque acting upon the corresponding joint. In making this decision, the user has to utilize his experience. He may recognize the forces that are significant for the corresponding joint, so that these forces have to be computed on-line. In this way the user may considerably speed-up determination of adequate global control.

d) If the user has decided to implement on-line computation of the coupling, he may determine the parameter values $d^* \in D$ for which the driving torques will be computed. This choice may be very important if we want to find out such global control which will (together with the decentralized controller) withstand all expected parameter variations D. This choice is sometimes very difficult, but the user may find the solution using his experience.

e) The user may also choose the global gain for the particular joint for which the global control will be introduced. Obviously, the package could determine the global gain by iteratively searching for it, but this search might require a long processing time. The user can speed up this process since he may consider the numbers ξ^*_{ij} in (2.6.18) and recognize how the global control changes the interconnections among subsystems. By this he can roughly estimate the global gain and the package may perform just "fine" adjustment of the global gain.

All above listed data may be changed by the user in each iteration. Namely, if the package announces that the robotic system is not practically stable with the selected global control (with previously synthesized decentralized controllers), the user may change any of the above listed data according to his opinion, and the package will test whether the overall robotic system is practically stable.

III In both automatic and interactive mode if the package cannot determine unique decentralized and global control which can withstand all expected parameter variations D, after some predicted number of iterations, the user may decide to stop this procedure and introduce the adaptive controller. Namely, two situations may appear:

a) The package cannot find the global control which can stabilize the robotic system even for parameter values d^* for which the coupling has been on-line computed in global control, then it is very probable that the selected actuators are too weak for the specific robotic manipulator and for the given control task. In that case user may either re-select actuators, or change the control task (i.e. select a slower trajectory and/or require larger tolerances $X^t(t)$, $\forall t \in T$).

b) If the package has found the global control which stabilizes the robotic system for some values of parameters but if the unique control cannot be determined which can withstand all expected parameter variations, then the user should give up searching for non-adaptive control and pass to the synthesis of adaptive control [12].

4.2.10. Block for adaptive control synthesis

The decentralized adaptive control algorithm presented in Paragraph 3.3.3, is implemented in this block of the software package. As explained, the purpose of adaptive control is to introduce a kind of "tuning process" in local gains in accordance with the estimated parameters of a payload. Thus, the user has to impose (Paragraph 4.2.3) the limits of possible payload parameters. For example, for a robot intended for manipulation with up to 60 kg workpieces, the lower bound is m = 0 kg and the upper bound is 60 kg. Of course, if the user wishes to test what will happen when the manipulator is "overloaded", the upper bound might be set to 70 kg or more. The limits of payload moments of inertia should be imposed as well. Then, the local gains corresponding to lower--bound and upper-bound parameters will be automatically determined, as described in Paragraphs 4.2.6 and 4.2.7. The instantaneous gains will be formed to be proportional to the payload parameter estimates (see (3.3.38) - (3.3.30)). The second possibility is to impose more points in which the local gains should be calculated. Then, the function which relates the local gains and the payload parameters will be formed (see Fig. 4.3).

The parameter estimation process is then simulated using (3.3.34). The user should impose the parameter a_p which determines the transient behaviour during the estimation process. The estimation could be realized with or without torque/force measurements. The dynamic correction term $p(\xi)$ in (3.3.34) is then computed using either (3.3.35) or (3.3.36).

The user can simulate the entire process by using the software block for simulation. Thus, the user can get an insight into the quality of both estimation process and tracking (see Figs. 3.14 and 3.15).

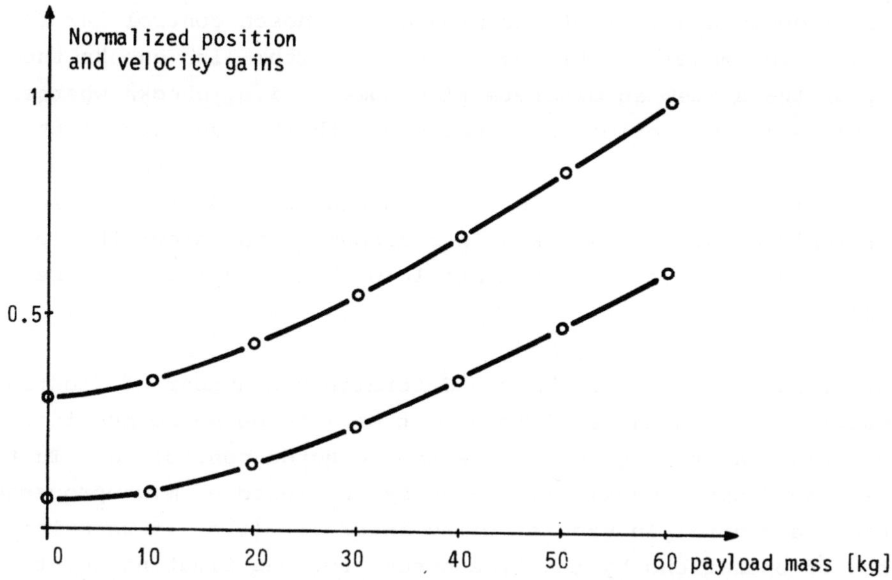

Fig. 4.3. Feedback gains with respect to payload mass

4.2.11. Block for discrete-time control synthesis

The control synthesized in the above described algorithm blocks may be implemented in analog technique or by microprocessors. The latter approach has certain advantages (see Chapter 5). However, microprocessor implementation requires the control synthesis to be considered in discrete-time domain. The control discussed up to now has been synthesized in continuous-time domain. However, the microprocessor implementation introduces delays since the microprocessor requires a period of time to compute the control which will be sent to actuators inputs. Thus, we have to consider the control synthesis in discrete-time domain, i.e. to take into account the sampling period required by the microprocessor to compute the chosen control. This problem has been treated in Vol. 2 of this series [10], and it will also be addressed in Chapter 5.

The algorithm includes a block for the synthesis of control in discrete-time domain. In this block the algorithm synthesizes the parameters of the already chosen control law (i.e. the decentralized and global controller which has been selected in previous blocks) taking into account the sampling period required by the microprocessor. Actually, the user has to select the sampling period and the algorithm computes the parameters (feedback gains) of the previously chosen control law for the discrete-time model of the robot. The algorithm also checks the stability of the system in discrete-time domain, i.e. checks whether the selected sampling period is compatible with the dynamics of the robotic system. In this way the user can verify the performance of the robotic system if the delay in control computation (due to its microprocessor implementation) is taken into account, and select the longest sampling period which is still compatible with the dynamics of the robot [13].

On the other hand, the algorithm can determine the number of floating-point multiplications and additions that have to be performed in each sampling period in order to calculate the selected control law. In this way we get the (approximate) time taken by the selected microprocessor to compute the control in each sampling interval (i.e. if we multiply the number of operations by the time needed for one floating-point multiplication and addition for the particular microprocessor, we obtain the duration of control law computation). Thus, the algorithm can determine the number of microprocessors of the selected type which have to be implemented in order to achieve a desired sampling period for a chosen control law. Obviously, this is an approximate approach, since a considerable processing time is required for data exchange between microprocessors and for some additionals operations. To take this into account, we suggest the user to multiply the above obtained computation time by two. In this way the user can easily select the control equipment necessary to implement various control laws [14]. Evidently, the more complex the control law selected, the more complex end expensive the control equipment required for its implementation. The user is allowed to make a trade-off between control complexity and robot performance. This problem will be discussed in detail in Paragraph 5.3.

4.2.12. Block for simulation

In order to verify the performance of the system with various control laws, the algorithm includes a block for system dynamics simulation. The algorithm enables the user to simulate tracking of the selected nominal trajectory as follows:

1. With specific initial conditions (initial errors) imposed by the user or defined by the algorithm itself (those for which the influence of coupling is the strongest according to stability analysis).

2. With or without nominal control. When the user decides to introduce nominal control he can select:

   a) Nominal control calculated using the complete, exact model of manipulation system [10].

   b) The so-called "decentralized" nominal control - the nominal control using models of actuators only. In this case the calculation of nominal control is much simpler but the dynamics of the mechanism is not taken into account (see Chapter 2).

3. Various forms of local controllers - various information control patterns can be examined.

4. Various forms of global control may be examined by simulation. The user may choose the form of global control which he wants to examine and specify the parameters of the control law. (Obviously, the user should examine the control law which has been synthesized in the above described blocks).

5. The user may simulate the tracking of nominal trajectory by adaptive control. The user has to impose the value of payload parameters and to analyze the estimation process and adjustment of local feedback gains (see Paragraph 4.2.10).

6. The user may examine continuous-time or discrete-time version of the selected control. In the latter case, by simulating the tracking of the nominal trajectory the user can verify the choice of sampling period, i.e. examine whether the chosen sampling period is adequate for a particular robotic system (and selected control law).

As the output of this block the algorithm computes:

1. Deviation of the state coordinates from the nominal trajectory during tracking.

2. The real driving torques developed around the robot joints during tracking the nominal trajectory.

3. The real input signals developed during the tracking of the nominal trajectory by the selected control law.

4. Power and energy consumptions of all actuators for a particular

tracking of the nominal trajectory.

A graphic display of all these values (versus time) is available.

With these results the user can make a final decision on the control law which is the most convenient for his manipulation system and for a particular task. The user can easily analyze the quality of tracking of the imposed nominal trajectory and the energy consumption during this tracking in order to find the best solution.

4.3 Example

In this paragraph we shall present the computer-aided synthesis of control for a specific manipulation robot. The synthesis has been performed using our software package based on the algorithm described in the previous paragraph.

We have selected the manipulation robot GORO-101 with six revolute joints. The robot is shown in Fig. 4.4. To illustrate the computer-aided synthesis of control by our software package, we shall describe the procedure step by step:

1. First, we have to impose data on the geometric parameters of the robot. These data are given in Table 4.1. The geometric structure of the robot is presented in Fig. 4.5.

2. Next, we have to impose data on the dynamic parameters of the robot. These data are given in Table 4.2. We assume that all parameters are fixed and well defined, except for payload parameters which may vary as: $m_p \in (0, 5\text{ kg})$, $J_{px} \in (0., 0.08\text{kgm}^2)$, $J_{py} \in (0., 0.08\text{kgm}^2)$, $J_{pz} \in (0, 0.08\text{kgm}^2)$, where m_p is the mass of the payload and J_{px}, J_{py}, J_{pz} are the moments of inertia of the payload with respect to the main axes of inertia. Thus, the set of allowable parameters may be considered as: $D = \{d: m_p \in (0, 5\text{ kg}), J_{pe} \in (0, 0.08\text{kgm}^2), e = x, y, z\}$ where $d = (m_p, J_{px}, J_{py}, J_{pz})^T$.

3. The nominal trajectory has been synthesized. We have set the terminal points for the nominal trajectory (through which the robot has to pass) and the duration of movement between each two points. We have chosen to specify the coordinates of the robot tip with respect to the absolute coordinate system and internal (joint) coordinates

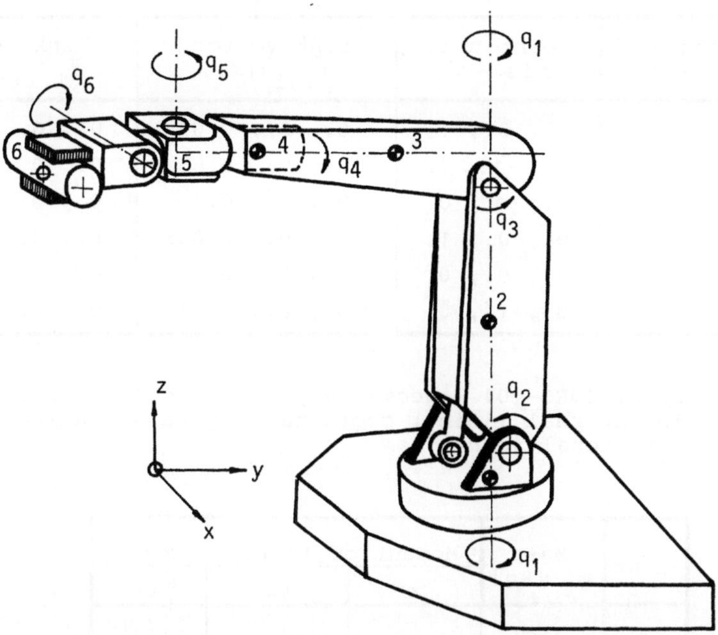

Fig. 4.4. Manipulation system GORO-101

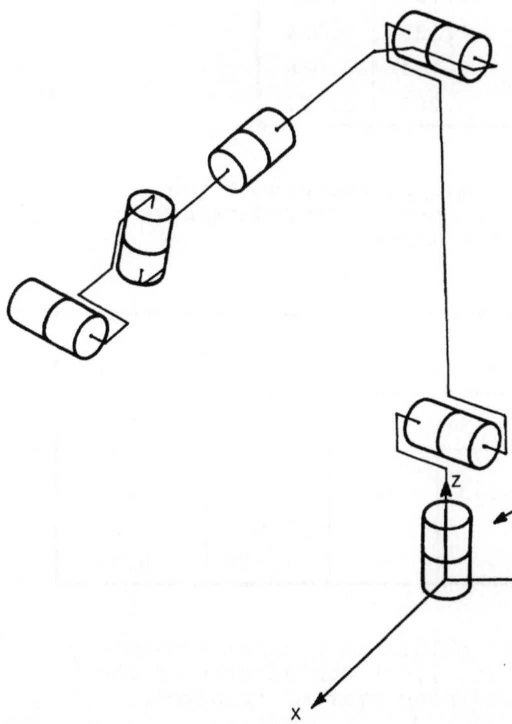

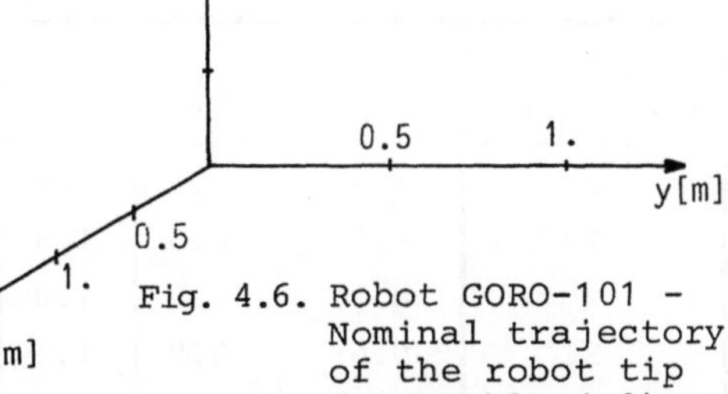

Fig. 4.6. Robot GORO-101 - Nominal trajectory of the robot tip (see Table 4.3)

Fig. 4.5. Robot GORO-101 - Geometric structure

Joint	Type of joint	Joint unit axis - $\vec{e}_i$	Link vector $\vec{r}_{i,i}$ [m],	Link vector $\vec{r}_{i,i+1}$ [m]
1	R	0., 0., 1.	0., 0., 0.05	0., 0., -0.05
2	R	0., -1., 0.	0., 0., 0.55	0., 0., -0.465
3	R	0., -1., 0.	0., 0., 0.2	0., 0., -0.4
4	R	0., 0., 1.	0., 0., 0.008	0., 0., -0.21
5	R	-1., 0., 0.	0., 0., 0.1	0., 0., -0.121
6	R	0., 1., 0.	0., 0., 0.13	0., 0., -0.004

Table 4.1. Robot GORO-101 - geometry parameters (all vectors are in internal (joint) coordinate systems) (R means rotational joint)

Link	Mass m_i [kg]	Moment of inertia [kgm^2]		
		J_{xi}	J_{yi}	J_{zi}
1	210.	-	-	4.57
2	152.	22.17	21.74	5.738
3	67.	7.2	7.19	1.22
4	18.	1.34	1.335	0.054
5	13.	0.194	0.164	0.066
6	35.	0.203	0.205	0.182

Table 4.2. Robot GORO-101 - dynamic parameters of the mechanism (moments of inertia around main axes of inertia of the link)

Point on trajectory	x [m]	y [m]	z [m]	q_4 [rad]	q_5 [rad]	q_6 [rad]	Duration τ[s]
0	1.173	0.	0.8	1.573	0.	0.	-
1	0.9	0.5	1.4	1.573	0.	0.	0.9
2	0.9	0.5	1.4	1.573	0.	0.	0.3
3	0.6	0.9	1.	0.2	0.	1.573	1.2
4	0.6	0.9	1.	0.2	0.	1.573	0.2

Table 4.3. Robot GORO-101 - terminal points on nominal trajectory (external coordinates - (x, y, z) coordinates of the tip w.r. to absolute coordinate system; trapezoid velocity profile)

of the gripper. Also, we have required a trapezoid profile of the tip velocity along the trajectory (between each two given points), and we have specified the duration of acceleration and decelaration. We have selected the mode in which the robot has to stop at each specified terminal point.

Data on the set points on the nominal trajectory are given in Table 4.3. The positions of the robot along the specified nominal trajectory are presented in Fig. 4.6. The algorithm computes the nominal trajectories in joint coordinates that correspond to a desired path of the robot tip. These joint nominal trajectories are given in Fig. 4.7.

4. Next step is to impose data on actuators in the robot joints. The robot GORO 101 is driven by hydraulic actuators. Data on the selected hydraulic actuators are given in Table 4.4. The matrices of actuators models A^i, b^i, f^i are computed as explained in the previous paragraph, and are presented in Table 4.5.

   The connections between the joint coordinates and actuator coordinate are not trivial for the first three joints (since rotational joints are driven by hydraulic actuators with linear motion of pistons). These connections are specified in Table 4.6. The rotational (vane) hydraulic actuators are used for the gripper joints; for these joints, relations between the mechanism coordinates and actuator coordinates are linear.

   Table 4.7. gives the relations between the driving torques around the mechanism joints and the load acting upon actuators.

5. The algorithm computes the nominal driving torques and the nominal programmed control for the given nominal trajectory. The results of these computations are presented in Figs. 4.8 - 4.11. The nominal driving torques around the robot joints are presented in Fig. 4.8 (for $m_p = 0$, $J_{px} = 0.$, $J_{py} = 0.$, $J_{pz} = 0.$). Fig. 4.9 shows the nominal programmed control synthesized using the complete centralized model. (We have not used this nominal control for our controller, but we have computed it in order to check the capability of the selected actuators to realize the chosen nominal trajectory). Fig. 4.10 gives the nominal power required to drive the robot along the desired nominal trajectory. Nominal energy consumptions are presented in Fig. 4.11.

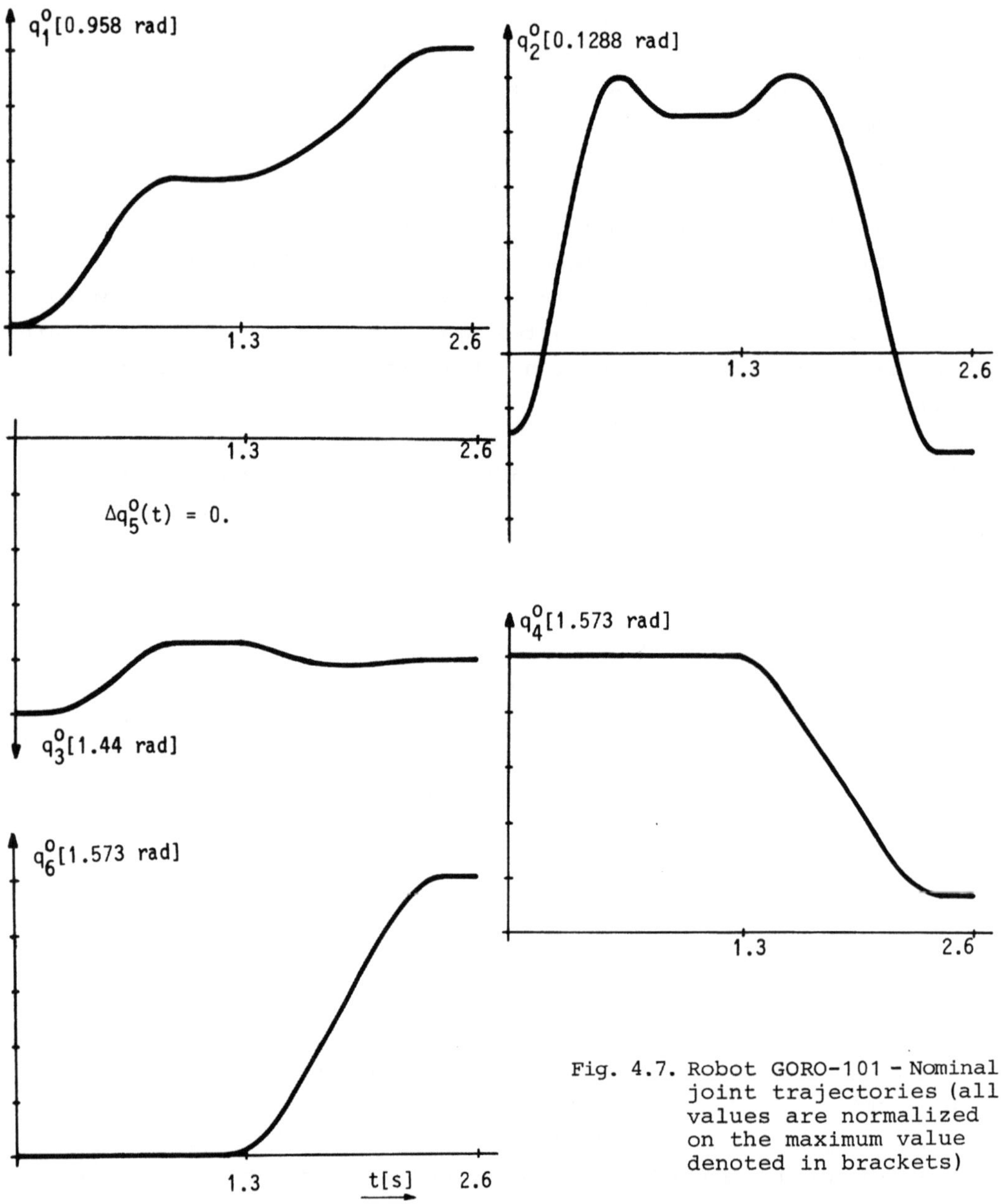

Fig. 4.7. Robot GORO-101 - Nominal joint trajectories (all values are normalized on the maximum value denoted in brackets)

Joint	Piston area [cm^2]	Cylinder volume [cm^3]	Piston mass [kg]	Viscous friction coefficient [N/m/s]	Gradient of servovalve [cm^3/s/N/m^2]	Flow--current coeff. [m^3/s/mA]	Input ampl. constr. [mA]
1	33.	1690.	16.7	30.	0.000107	0.00026	75.
2	25.	1400.	18.4	30.	0.000107	0.00026	75.
3	12.5	1400.	9.20	10.	0.000107	0.00026	75.
4	7.5	300.	0.051	0.5	0.00027	0.00026	75.
5	7.5	300.	0.051	0.5	0.00027	0.00026	75.
6	3.75	250.	0.026	0.5	0.00027	0.00026	75.

Table 4.4. Robot GORO-101 - actuator parameters

Actuator	a_{22}^i	a_{23}^i	a_{32}^i	a_{33}^i	b_3^i
1	-1.79	19.76	-1327.8	-4.305	104.6
2	-1.63	13.58	-1214.3	-5.197	126.29
3	-1.087	13.587	-607.14	-5.197	126.29
4,5	-9.8	1470.6	-1700.0	-61.200	589.33
6	-19.2	1442.3	-1020.0	-73.440	707.20

Table 4.5. Matrices of the actuators models (robot GORO-101)

Joint	a_c^i	b_c^i	c_c^i	d_c^i
1	0.6913	0.2132	0.62	0.93
2	0.583	-0.29	1.86	0.71
3	0.65	-0.31	-0.17	0.75

Table 4.6. Robot GORO-101 - Connection between actuator (ℓ^i) and mechanism coordinate (q_i) $\ell^i=(a_c^i+b_c^i\cos(q_i+c_c^i))^{1/2}-d_c^i$ joint 4,5,6 the connections are trivial

Joint	a_f^i	b_f^i
1	-0.46	-1.029
2	-0.24	0.
3	-0.55	1.29

Table 4.7. Robot GORO-101 - Connection between actuator load and mechanism driving torque ($M_i=P_i a_f^i/\cos(q_i+b_f^i)$)

Point	Tip [m]	q_4 [rad]	q_5 [rad]	q_6 [rad]	Stability degree
0	0.01	0.05	0.05	0.02	-
1, 2	0.002	0.01	0.01	0.01	2.48
3, 4	0.001	0.01	0.01	0.01	2.97

Table 4.8. Robot GORO-101 - Tolerances around points on nominal trajectory (Table 4.3)

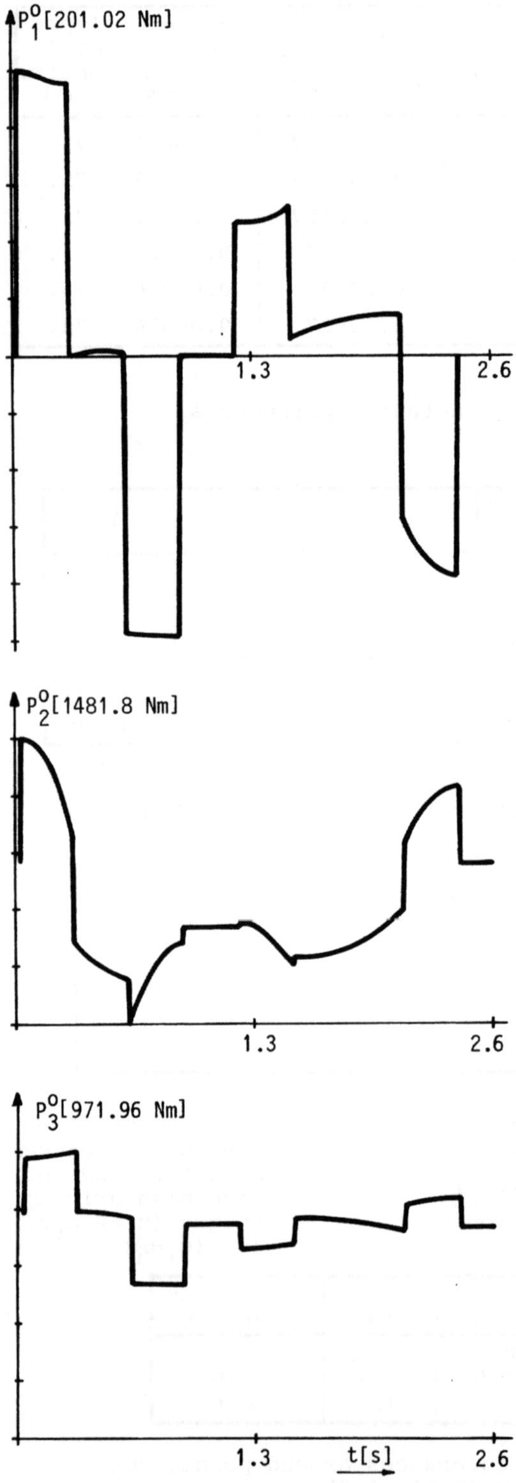

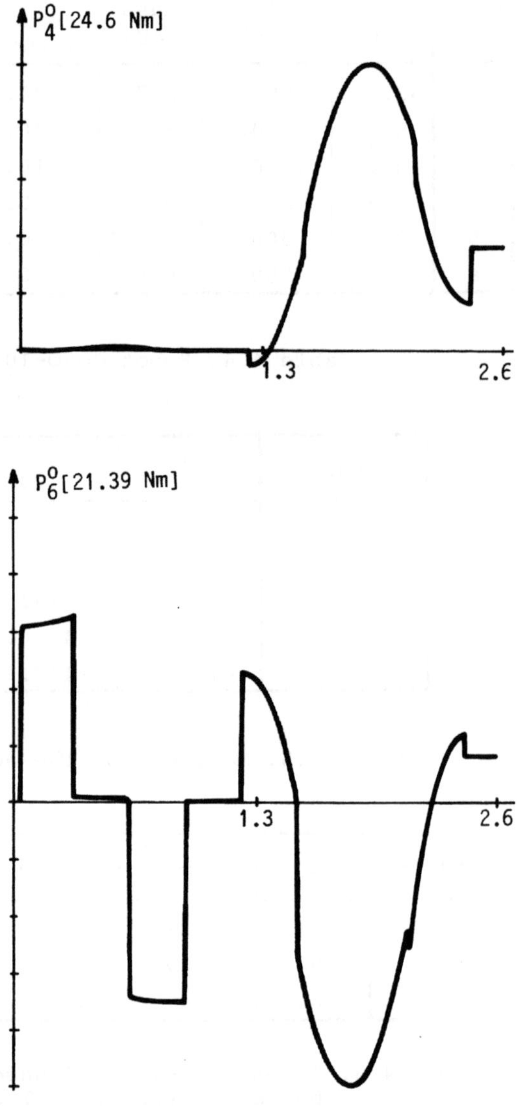

Fig. 4.8. Robot - GORO-101 - Nominal driving torques

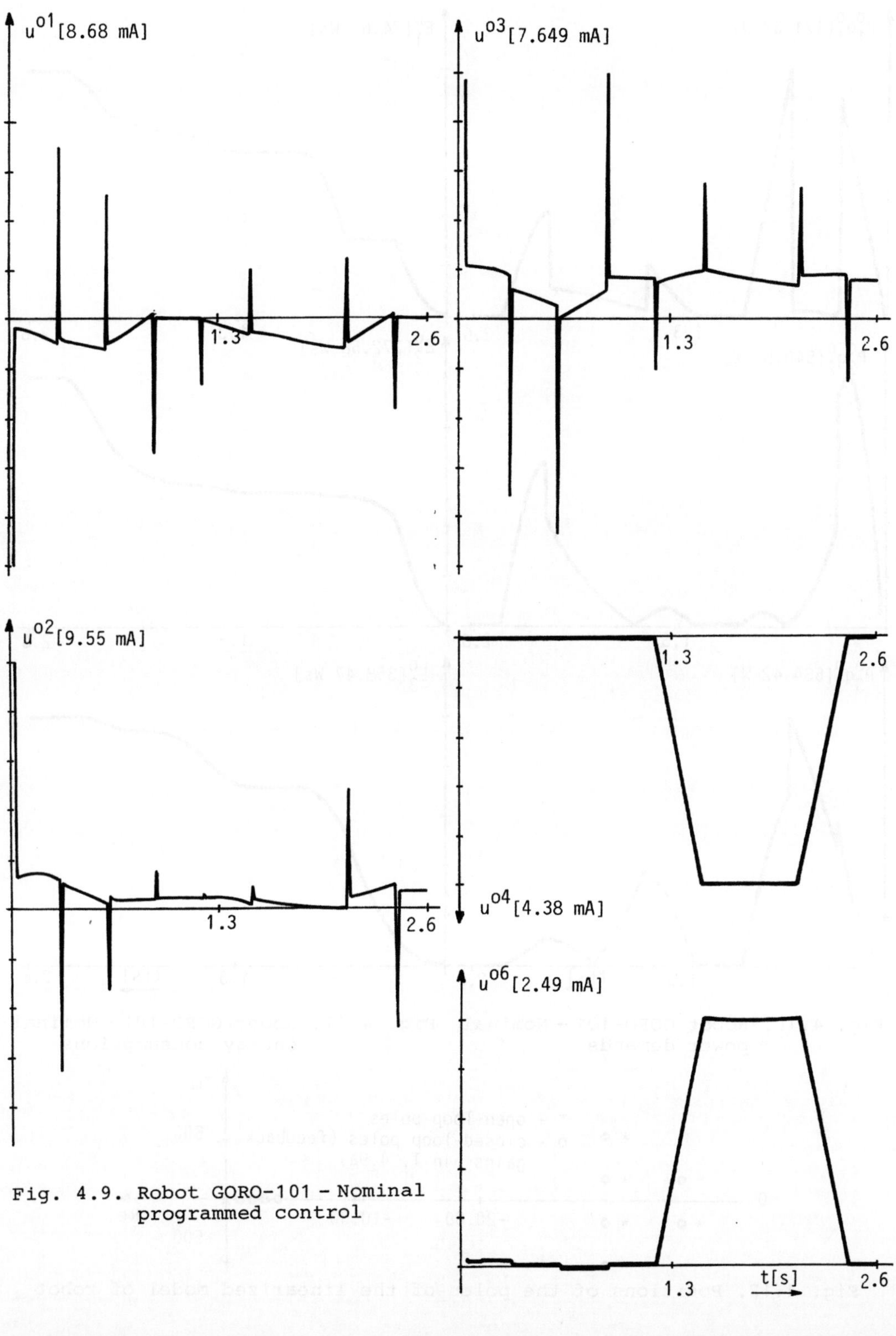

Fig. 4.9. Robot GORO-101 - Nominal programmed control

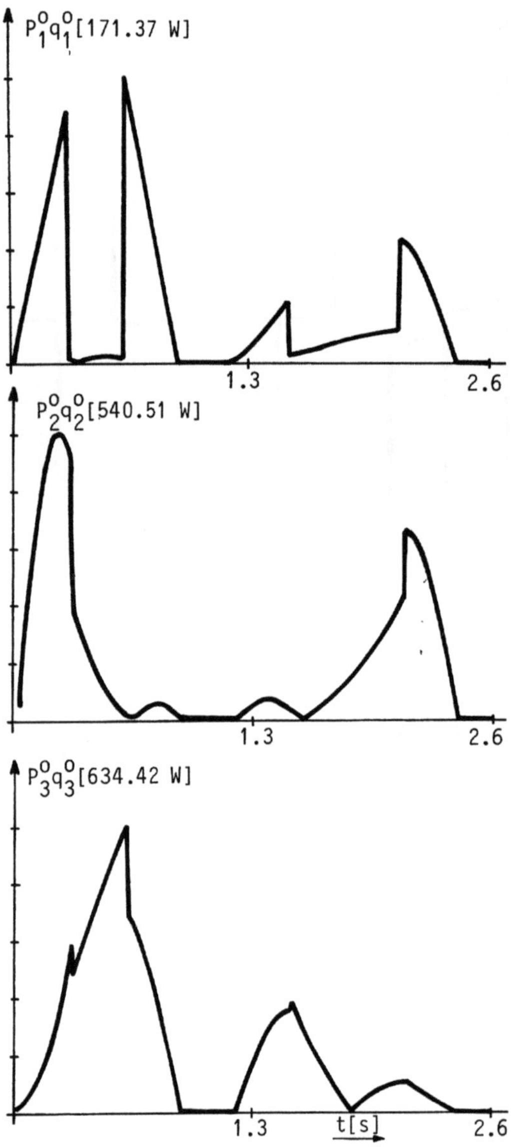

Fig. 4.10. Robot GORO-101 - Nominal power demands

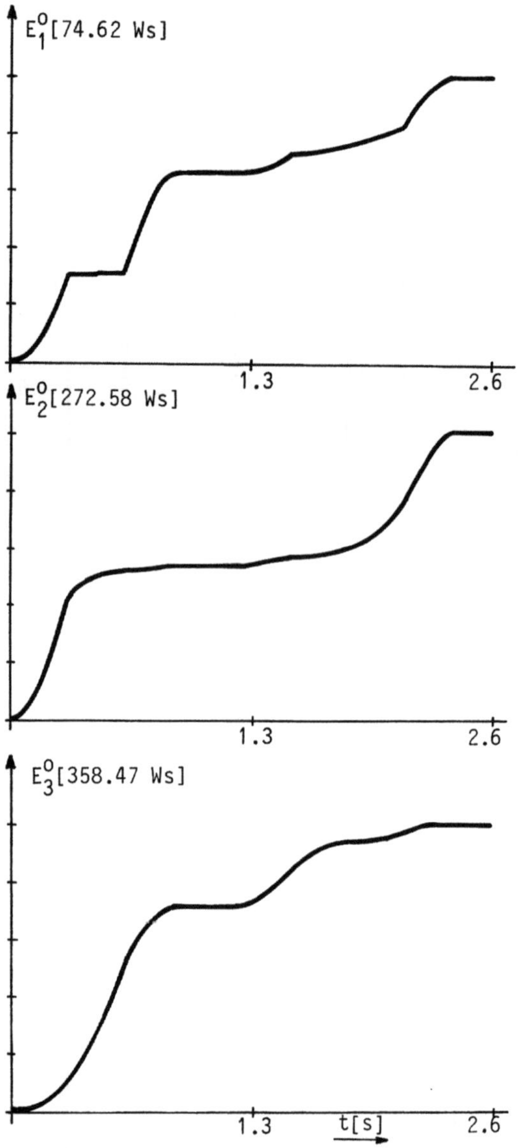

Fig. 4.11. Robot GORO-101 - Nominal energy consumptions

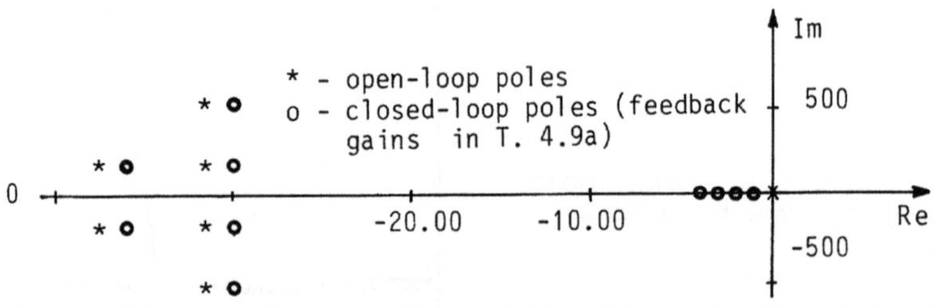

Fig. 4.12. Positions of the poles of the linearized model of robot

6. In the next step we have to specify the control task, i.e. the allowable tolerances around the nominal trajectory. The specified tolerances around the given points on nominal trajectory are given in Table 4.8. The algorithm computes the tolerances in joint coordinates that correspond to the given tolerances around external coordinates and determines the desired stability degree (see Paragraph 4.2.6).

7. Local controllers have to be synthesized next. First we try to synthesize the local controllers by pole-placement. We consider local controllers with various information control structures: (a) with position feedback only, (b) with position and velocity feedback loops, (c) with position, velocity and pressure feedback loop. The results of synthesis are summarized in Table 4.9. The required poles of closed-loop subsystems are given in Table 4.9 for various control structures, together with the obtained feedback gains and poles of the linearized model of the complete robotic system. The positions of the poles of the closed-loop model of the complete robotic manipulators (in the complex plane) are given in Fig. 4.12. The local optimal regulators are also synthesized; the weighting matrices, prescribed stability degrees, obtained local feedback gains and poles of the closed-loop linearized model of the complete robotic system are given in Table 4.10. Stability analysis of the system (next step) shows that we must adopt the local optimal regulators (i.e. feedback by all state coordinates).

8. Next, stability of the nonlinear model has to be analyzed. The package analyzes the practical stability of the robotic system for various values of parameters D. The stability of the system with decentralized controllers synthesized as described in the previous step (and with decentralized nominal control) is analyzed according to the algorithm described in Paragraph 2.5. In Table 4.11 the results of stability analysis are given for decentralized controller with local optimal regulators (Table 4.10). As can be seen from Table 4.11, the stability of subsystems 2 and 5 is not guaranteed with local controllers only. Obviously, the influence of coupling upon these joints is too strong to be withstood by the selected local controllers (although the linearized model is stable). Thus, we may either increase local feedback gains (i.e. increase the prescribed stability degree of local optimal controllers in the corresponding joints) or introduce global control.

Subsystem	Desired poles R_e	I_m	Position feedback gain	Velocity feedback gain	Pressure feedback gain	Poles of linearized closed-loop model R_e	I_m
	1		2	3	4	5	
1	-3. –	0. –	36.63	–	–	-29.8 -35.7	±600. ±281.
2	-3. –	0. –	24.71	–	–	-29.2 -1.35	±277. ±7.8
3	-3. –	0. –	1.22	–	–	-1.03 -0.54	±4.4 ±6.29
4	-3. –	0. –	8.65	–	–	-3.37 -3.14	0 0
5	-3. –	0. –	8.62	–	–	-3.04 -2.98	0 0
6	-3. –	0. –	4.31	–	–	-2.96 -2.35	0 0

a) Positional feedback loop only

Subsystem	1		2	3	4	5	
1	-4. –	0. 15.	113.02	15.18	–	-32.8 -27.	±40. ±14.5
2	-5. –	0. 10.	111.56	11.54	–	-15. -19.4	±31.6 ±16.6
3	-5. –	0. 10.	5.85	0.63	–	-0.7 -3.5	±9.46 ±8.2
4	-12. –	0. 150.	20.3	0.41	–	-20.7 -13.7	
5	-12. –	0. 150.	29.3	0.63	–	-5.12 -5.12	
6	-12. –	0. 150.	14.2	0.65	–	-4.1 -2.3	

b) Position and velocity feedback

Subsystem	1		2	3	4	5	
1	-12. -15.	0. ±7.6	430.	68.	0.36	-157. -119.	±616. ±321.
2	-13. -15.	0. ±20.	871.	155.	0.34	-82. -27.	±328. ±22.
3	-13. -184.	0. 0.	344.	54.8	0.16	-3.3 -6.7	±5.5 ±6.2
4	-13. -157.	0. ±615.	48.	0.37	0.45	-184. -363.	
5	-12. -160.	0. ±722.	45.	0.92	0.17	-32. -13.	
6	-13. -119.	0. ±220.	20.7	0.71	0.25	-12.5 -6.6	

c) Position, velocity and pressure feedback loop

Table 4.9. Robot GORO-101 - Local controllers (pole-placement)

Subsystem	Q_i diag(q^i)	r_i	β_i	K_1^i K_2^i K_3^i	Poles of linearized model of system R_e	I_m
1	1. 0.1 0.1	5.	9.	1030. 131. 0.5	-160. -122. -63.	±615. ±325. ±300.
2	0.1 1. 0.1	0.5	9.5	1750. 231. 0.47	-36. -10. -9.5 -177.	±28. ±9.1 ±9.2
3	1. 0.1 0.1	5.	9.5	723. 79.4 0.175	-40. -18. -164. -18.	
4	0.1 10. 0.1	0.5	9.	58.2 0.389 0.469		
5	0.1 10. 0.1	0.5	9.	55.4 0.133 0.120		
6	0.1 10. 0.1	0.5	9.	39.4 0.771 0.270		

Table 4.10. Robot GORO-101 - Synthesis of local optimal regulators (Q_i, r_i - weighting matrices in the local criteria (2.4.16), β_i prescribed stability degrees $K_1^i=(K_1^i,K_2^i,K_3^i)^T$ - feedback gains of local regulators)

Joint	1	2	3	4	5	6	Stable
1	-.448E+0	.132E-2	.328E-1	.292E-1	.634E-1	.156E+0	Y
2	.951E-3	-.113E+1	.144E+2	.152E-4	.638E-1	.163E-2	N
3	.264E-2	.890E+0	-.566E+1	.481E-3	.159E+1	.719E-2	Y
4	.819E-5	.747E-7	.505E-5	-.101E+3	.352E-3	.652E-2	Y
5	.880E-6	.295E-4	.110E-1	.233E-3	.213E+2	.491E-2	N
6	.370E-3	.200E-4	.527E-4	.107E-1	.603E-1	-.235E+1	Y

Table 4.11. Stability analysis when local optimal regulators are applied (see explanation under Table 4.12)

9. If we decide to introduce global control we have to select its form and implementation. First, we try with on-line computation of coupling using the approximate model which includes just gravity term. However, the results are poor. Then, we try with the approximate model which includes gravity and inertia term. The results are better, but still they do not satisfy the imposed requirements. At last we apply force feedback in joints 2, 3 and 5. The results of practical stability analysis are given in Table 4.12. The robotic system is practically stable for all allowable parameter variations with such unique local and global controllers. The applied control law is presented in Table 4.13. The global gains are determined iteratively as explained in Paragraph 2.6.

10. In order to implement the selected control by microprocessors, we consider the synthesis of feedback gains in time-discrete domain. The results of this synthesis (local feedback gains) for various sampling periods are given in Table 4.14. The analysis of the system performance shows that the longest acceptable sampling period is about 10 ms. The number of additions and multiplications required to compute local control is given in Table 4.15. The processor time which is required for the computation of local control by various microprocessors is also listed in Table 4.15. On the basis of these estimates we can determine the number of microprocessors required to implement the local control and to achieve a sampling period of 10 ms. (Since we have chosen force feedback as global control, which requires just a few additional multiplications and additions, we may neglect the time needed for global control implementation). Obviously, this determination of control equipment is approximate.

11. In the last step of control synthesis we simulate the behaviour of the robotic system with various control laws. The results of simulation are given in Figs. 4.13 - 4.14. Fig. 4.13 presents the results of tracking (deviations of actuator coordinates from nominal trajectories), if local controllers are only (Table 4.10) applied. The tracking is poor, which confirms the results of the above analysis (Table 4.11). Fig. 4.14 shows the tracking with the selected local and global control (Table 4.13) for various values of payload parameters. It can be seen that the tracking is satisfactory for various values of parameters, which means that the unique control is robust enough to withstand all allowable parameter variations.

Joint	1	2	3	4	5	6	Stable
1	-.448E+0	.132E-2	.328E-1	.292E-1	.634E-1	.156E+0	Y
2	.956E-7	-.121E+1	.144E-2	.187E-8	.638E-5	.168E-6	Y
3	.264E-2	.890E+0	-.566E+1	.481E-3	.159E+1	.719E-2	Y
4	.819E-5	.747E-7	.505E-5	-.101E+3	.352E-3	.652E-2	Y
5	.196E-7	.882E-6	.243E-3	.108E-4	-.364E+2	.759E-4	Y
6	.370E-3	.200E-4	.527E-4	.107E-1	.603E-1	-.235E+1	Y

Table 4.12. Stability analysis when local regulators and global control (force feedback in 2 nd and 5th joint) are applied stability matrix G defined by $G_{ij}=-\gamma_i\delta_{ij}+\xi^*_{ij}$ (where δ_{ij} is Kronecker's symbol, γ_i is stability degree of ith local subsystem, ξ^*_{ij} is estimation of coupling from joint j upon the ith joint - see (2.6.18), (-n means 10^{-n}))

Joint	Local nominal	Local	Global
1	$\bar{u}^{o1}(t)$	$-1030.\ \Delta\ell^1$ $-131.\ \Delta\dot{\ell}^1$ $-0.518\ \Delta p^1$	-
2	$\bar{u}^{o2}(t)$	$-1750.\ \Delta\ell^2$ $-231.\ \Delta\dot{\ell}^2$ $-0.47\ \Delta p^2$	$0.97\ (68200\ \Delta\ell^2+7980\ \Delta\dot{\ell}^2$ $+9.\ \Delta p^2)/169\ \Delta\ell^2+9.\ \Delta\dot{\ell}^2\ +$ $+0.1\ \Delta p^2)\cdot P_2$ (measured)
3	$\bar{u}^{o3}(t)$	$-723.\ \Delta\ell^3$ $-79.4\ \Delta\dot{\ell}^3$ $-0.175\ \Delta p^3$	-
4	$\bar{u}^{o4}(t)$	$-58.2\ \Delta q_4$ $-0.389\ \Delta\dot{q}_4$ $-0.469\ \Delta p_4$	-
5	$\bar{u}^{o5}(t)$	$-55.4\ \Delta q_5$ $-0.133\ \Delta\dot{q}_5$ $-0.120\ \Delta p_5$	$0.95\cdot(24\ \Delta q_5+009\ \Delta\dot{q}_5\ +$ $+0.004\ \Delta p^5)/(4.9\ \Delta q_5\ +$ $+0.004\ \Delta\dot{q}_5+0.0017\ \Delta p^5)$
6	$\bar{u}^{o6}(t)$	$-39.4\ \Delta q_6$ $0.771\ \Delta\dot{q}_6$ $-0.270\ \Delta p_6$	-

Table 4.13. Synthesized control laws (local nominal control computed acc. to (4.2.9))

Joint		T=0.03	T=0.02	T=0.01
1	K_1	555.091	684.492	853.196
	K_2	69.318	84.602	104.15
	K_3	0.367	0.413	0.471
2	K_1	876.00	1089.715	1372.214
	K_2	125.59	151.710	185.702
	K_3	0.312	0.352	0.404
3	K_1	105.7	167.934	307.261
	K_2	13.55	20.359	35.314
	K_3	0.043	0.057	0.087
4	K_1	44.33	46.002	47.868
	K_2	-0.05	0.055	0.057
	K_3	0.006	0.001	0.009
5	K_1	44.195	49.09	39.471
	K_2	-0.002	0.246	0.502
	K_3	0.04	0.002	0.062
6	K_1	21.699	19.422	19.221
	K_2	-0.08	0.206	0.257
	K_3	0.024	0.013	0.082

Table 4.14. Local feedback gains synthesized in time-discrete domain for various sampling period

	Number of additions	Number of multiplications
Local nominal control	18	30
Local control	36	18
Total	54	48

μP	Duration [ms]
INTEL-8085	75
INTEL-86/87	2.2
PDP 11/03	12.6
MOTOROLA 6800	∿30.
HP 64000	2.78
LSI-11/2	∿11.56

Table 4.15. Number of additions and multiplications for computation of local control and duration of computation on various microprocessors

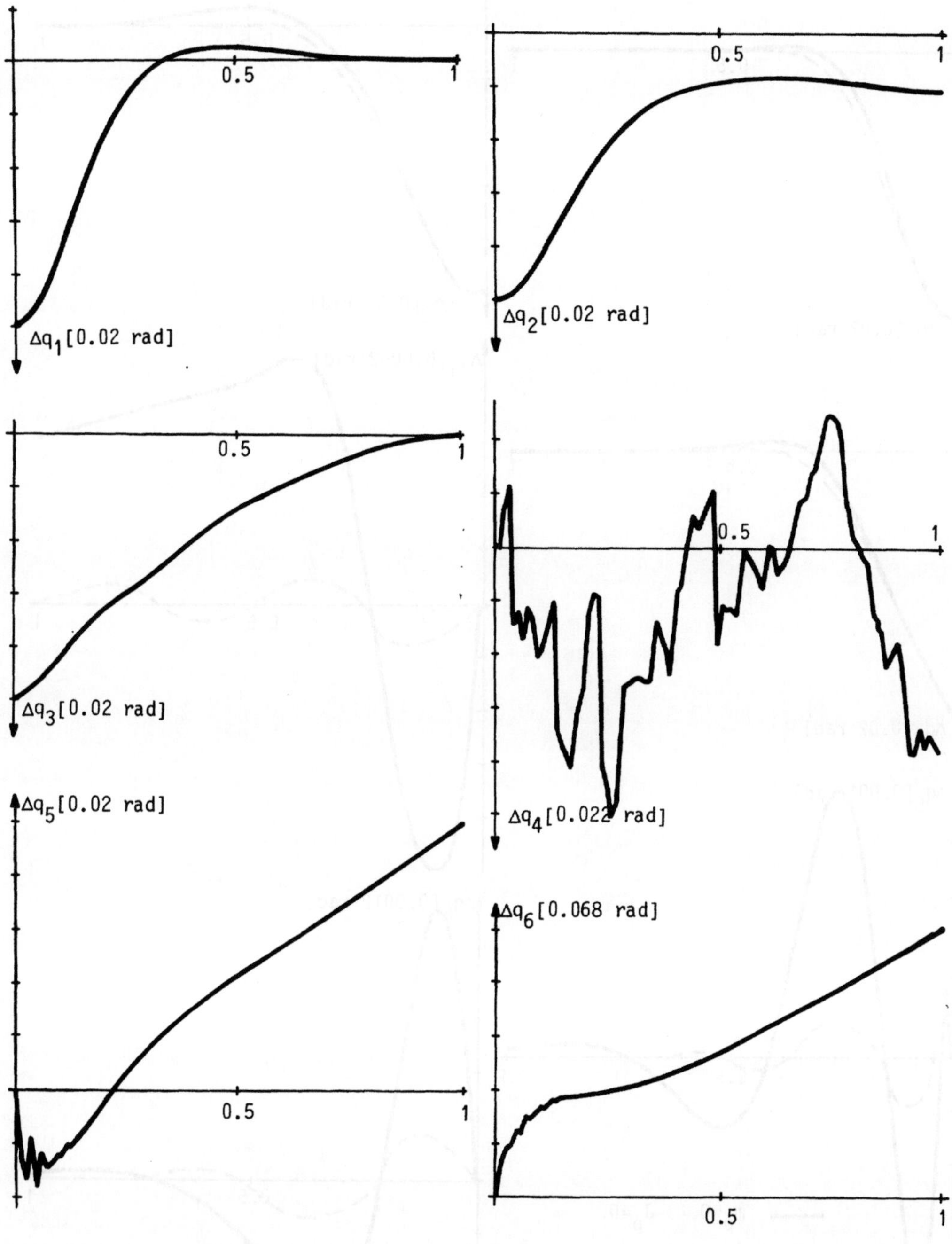

Fig. 4.13. Simulation of tracking of the nominal trajectory with local controllers - deviation of joint angles from nominal trajectory (all values normalized on the maximum value denoted in bracket)

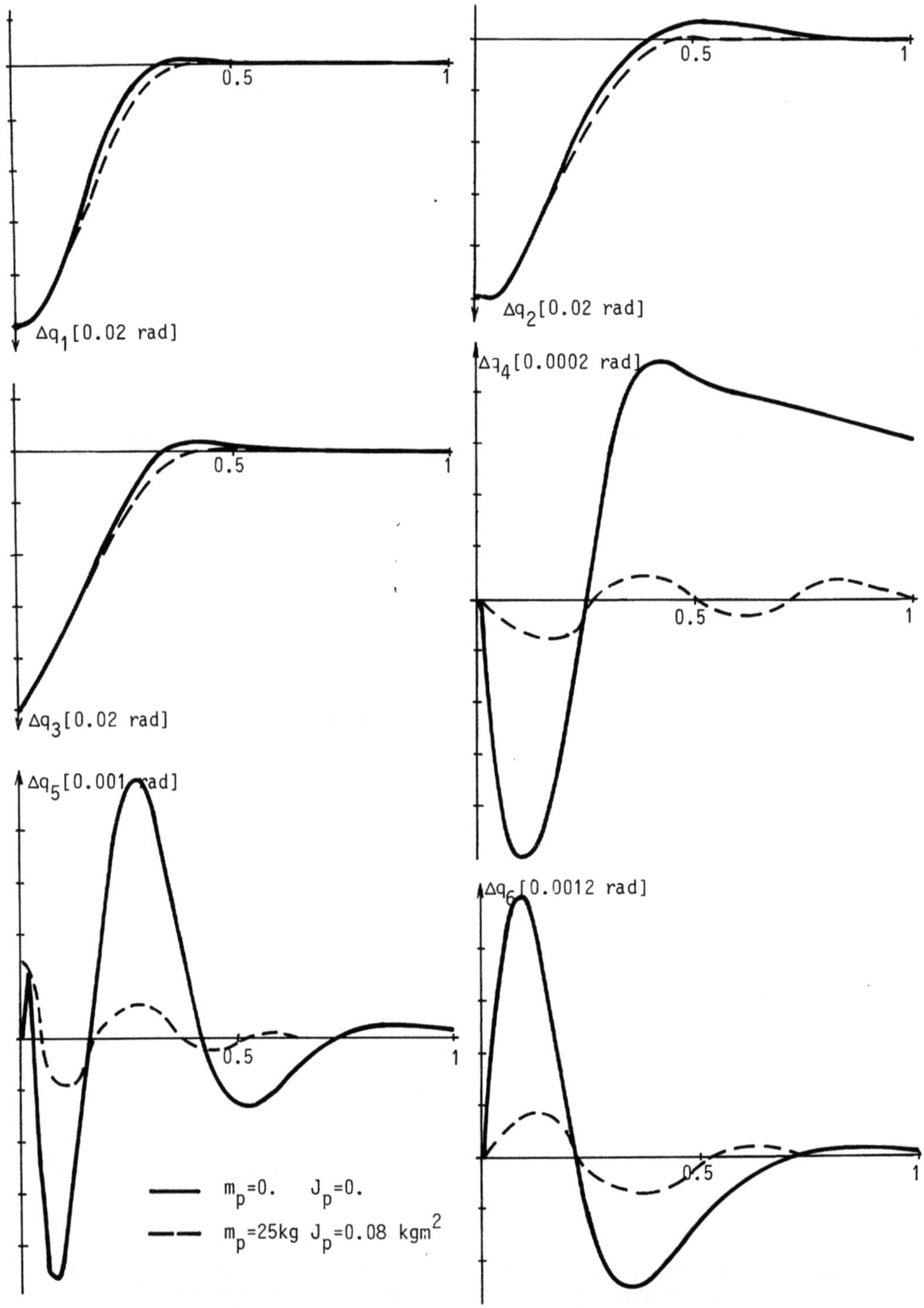

Fig. 4.14. Simulation of tracking of nominal trajectory with local and global control for various payload parameters

Thus, it is not necessary to apply adaptive control in this particular case.

It should be noted that, due to lack of space, we have omitted many intermediate results obtained by the package during the control synthesis (e.g. the iterative selection of local controllers, global control implementation and global gains, etc.), but the results presented here give an insight into the package operation, and show how the package may be used to select the appropriate control law for a particular manipulation robot and a given control task.

Conclusion

In the previous two paragraphs we have briefly described the software package for computer-aided control synthesis of manipulation robots. In Paragraph 4.3 we have described the interaction between the package and the user, and in Paragraph 4.,3 we have presented an example of computer-aided control synthesis for a particular robotic system and control task.

In this paragraph we shall briefly discuss the possibilities offered by this package to the user in order to stress the importance and advantages of computer-aided approach to control synthesis.

The user can easily combine all the above mentioned blocks (Paragraph 4.2) and results according to his desires and examine different control laws. In doing this he can easily use his own experience and understanding of the system. For example, if he knows that some joint is weakly coupled with others (or the coupling is zero) he can omit global feedback loops for this actuator. Similarly, if he knows that the influence of gravity forces upon some degree of freedom is weak the on-line calculation of gravity forces for this degree of freedom is not useful. Thus, the use of designer's experience can significantly speed up the control synthesis and be of great help in determination of the best solution. Practically, the synthesis of control is left to the user's decisions. The above package can be regarded as an assistive device which can help the user to verify his solutions.

The algorithm can help the user to make the following decisions and investigations:

1. To verify whether the particular control task can be performed by the chosen manipulator system from kinematic and dynamic points of view.

2. To choose actuators which can ensure implementation of the given control task.

3. To chosen the simplest control structure and law which can satisfy specific requirements.

4. To determine the dynamic parameters of the manipulator system that have to be taken into account in the controller in order to achieve satisfactory system performance.

5. To determine sensors (feedback loops) which have to be implemented (are tacho-generators necessary or not, should force transducers be used or not, etc.).

6. To determine the complexity of the multiprocessor system which has to be implemented (the number of microprocessors and their capabilities).

7. To calculate the parameters of the chosen control law (local and global gains, sampling period etc.).

8. To examine dynamic performance of a particular manipulation system with various controllers and determine how a change in some dynamic parameters of the manipulator can influence the system performance.

9. To examine the robustness of the selected control and decide whether a non-adaptive control law can be applied, or adaptive control is necessary.

10. To synthesize adequate adaptive control if the expected variations of parameters are too large to be accommodated by robust non-adaptive control.

11. To estimate energy consumptions for the realization of various control tasks.

References

[1] Vukobratović K.M., Stokić M.D., Kirćanski V.M., "A Procedure for Interactive Dynamic Control Synthesis of Manipulators", Proc. of IV CISM-IFToMM Symposium on Theory and Practice of Robots and Manipulators, Warsaw, September, 1981.

[2] Vukobratović K.M., Stokić M.D., "A Procedure for Interactive Dynamic Control Synthesis of Manipulators", Transaction on Systems, Man, and Cybernetics, Sept./Oct. issue, 1982.

[3] Vukobratović K.M., Stokić M.D., Kirćanski M.N., Kirćanski V.M., "Software Package for Computer-Aided Synthesis of Control for Manipulation Robots", Preprints of the 9th World IFAC Congress, Budapest, Vol. 6, pp. 62-67, July, 1984.

[4] Chang K-H., Isomura T., Funakubo H., "The Development of a System to Assist in the Design and Control of Robots", Proceedings of the 14th International Symposium on Industrial Robots, pp. 723--733, Gothenburg, 1984.

[5] Queromes J.G., "Computer Aided Design and Robotics: A Full of Promise Cooperation", Proc. of the 12th ISIR, pp. 185-196, Paris, June, 1982.

[6] Vukobratović K.M., Kirćanski V.M., Scientific Fundamentals of Robotics 3, Kinematics and Trajectory Planning, Monograph, Springer -Verlag, Berlin, 1985.

[7] Vukobratović K.M., Potkonjak V., Scientific Fundamentals of Robotics 1, Dynamics of Manipulation Robots, Theory and Application, Monograph, Springer-Verlag, Berlin, 1982.

[8] Vukobratović K.M., Kirćanski M.N., Scientific Fundamentals of Robots 4, Real-Time Dynamics, Springer-Verlag, Berlin, 1985.

[9] Vukobratović K.M., Stepanenko Y., "Mathematical Models of General Anthropomorphic Systems", Mathematical Biosciences, Vol. 17, pp. 191-242, 1973.

[10] Vukobratović K.M., Stokić M.D., Scientific Fundamentals of Robotics 2, Control of Manipulation Robots: Theory and Application, Monograph, Springer-Verlag, Berlin, 1982.

[11] Vukobratović K.M., Kirćanski V.M., "A Method for Optimal Synthesis of Manipulation Robot Trajectories", Trans. of ASME, Journal of Dynamic Systems, Measurement, and Control, Vol. 104, No. 2, pp. 188-193, 1982.

[12] Vukobratović K.M., Stokić M.D., Kirćanski M.N., "Towards Nonadaptive and Adaptive Control of Manipulation Robots", IEEE Trans. on Automatic Control, Vol. AC-29, No. 9, pp. 841-844, 1984.

[13] Vukobratović K.M., Stokić M.D., Kirćanski V.M., "Contribution to Dynamic Control of Industrial Manipulators", The XI Intern. Symp. of Industrial Robots, Tokyo, 1981.

[14] Vukobratović K.M., Stokić M.D., "Approximative Dynamic Models in Hierarchical Control of Robots Systems", The V IFToMM Symp. on Theory and Practice of Robots Manipulators, Udine, 1984.

Chapter 5
Implementation of Control Algorithms

5.1 Introduction

In previous chapters we have presented the synthesis of non-adaptive control (Chapter 2) and adaptive control (Chapter 3) for the executive control level of manipulation robots. We have also presented (Chapter 4) the algorithm (software package) for computer-aided synthesis of control for robotic systems. In this chapter we shall consider the implementation of various control laws.

In principle, we may consider three basic techniques for control implementation: analog technique, microprocessor-based, and hybrid technique. In the last decade (5-10 years) microprocessor implementation of control has become predominant, thanks to tremendous improvements in microprocessors technology. The implementation of control by digital technique has certain advantages over the classical analog technique. Let us mention some of them: a) The implementation of control by microprocessors is much simpler than that by analog technique. This is especially true if complex control laws which require a lot of multiplications and additions, have to be implemented. For example, if we want to compute the dynamic model of the robotic system for global control, this is very complex to implement by analog technique; on the other hand, on-line computation by microprocessors is much simpler (although it may require several microprocessors to operate in parallel - see Paragraph 5.3). b) The analog control scheme is very difficult to change and move from one system to another. On the other hand, a microprocessor can easily be reprogrammed, so we may use the same hardware for various control systems. Even more, the microprocessor implementation of control allows one to build a general controller for various robotic systems which may automatically be adjusted to each specific manipulation robot. Such a general controller for robotic systems would be very difficult to implement by analog technique. c) The maintenance of microprocessor systems is much more efficient than the maintenance of systems in analog technique. Besides, the microprocessor technique is more reliable and robust to variations of environment conditions.

It is for these and some other reasons that the microprocessor implementation of control is today exclusively used for robotic systems [1 - 4]. It should be underlined that the higher control levels for robotic systems (strategical control level and/or communication with the operator, and tactical control level) require a digital computer for their implementation. It is quite reasonable to implement the executive control level by microprocessors, too. Thus in the text to follow we shall restrict our attention to microprocessor implementation of control for robotic systems.

It should be mentioned that the hybrid (analog/digital) technique might also be used for control implementation. The local servosystems for joint control might be implemented by analog technique, while global control and higher control levels should be implemented by a digital computer. This option will also be briefly considered here (see Paragraph 5.5). However, this mode cannot be used for a general controller for an arbitrary-type manipulation robot, since it is not simple to adjust analog servosystems from one robotic system to another, in contrast to the case when microprocessor implementation (direct digital control) is used for local controllers, too.

As we have mentioned above, the microprocessor implementation of control offers the possibility to develop a general controller which can easily be adjusted to various types of robotic systems. In Paragraph 5.2 we shall briefly explain the concept of the general controller for an arbitrary type of manipulation robot. Obviously, this controller includes higher control levels: robot language for communication with the operator (for task specification) and tactical control level; it also includes the modules for communication with environment and other systems in the process (intended to synchronize the robot with other systems in the process). We shall briefly explain all these modules that are included in the general controller for robotic system. However, our prime interest in this monograph is the executive control level, so in the next few paragraphs we shall exclusively concentrate on the implementation of executive control level in the scope of general controller. In Paragraph 5.3 we shall consider the numerical complexity of various control laws for various robot structures in order to determine the microprocessor equipment (the number of microprocessors) required for the implementation of executive control level. Then, we shall consider the identification of system parameters (Paragraph 5.4) which is required for the implementation of control. In Paragraph 5.5 we shall consider hybrid and microprocessor implementation of executive control level, and present the experimental results of the control implementation for a specific robotic system.

It should be noted that we shall not discuss in detail various implementations of various control laws [1-4] which were mentioned in Chapters 2 and 3; we shall mainly concentrate on our approaches to control of manipulation robots.

5.2 Concept of General Purpose Controller

In this paragraph we shall briefly describe the general purpose controller for arbitrary type of manipulation robot. We shall briefly describe its main design features, and its main software modules. Our intention is to give the reader an insight of the complexity and structure of such modern concept of the controller for robotic system, so that he can understand advantages of direct digital control and application of the control synthesis described in previous chapters.

Most of the existing control systems are intended for use with a particular robot; for example, the most popular system VAL [5] can be used for control of PUMA family robots only, the AML [6] for IBM System/1 robots etc. Recently, some systems that can be applied to various types of robots have been developed and already announced on the market. However, their adjustment to a particular type of robot is still too complex and tedious job to be efficiently accomplished by a customer. Besides, they usually don't perform compensation of dynamic effects, so that good tracking of fast trajectories cannot be achieved. For these reasons, the development of a new general purpose controller UCS-1 was commenced in the Mihailo Pupin Institute, Belgrade [7].

The system is designed to meet two main advantages over existing controllers: dynamic control ensuring tracking of fast trajectories and easy maintenance and adjustment of the system to nonredundant robots of arbitrary type with up to six degrees of freedom.

The specific goals kept in mind during software design were:

- reduction of the run time computation required for calculation of quantities related to the robot dynamic; in order to meet this goal, which has the principal importance in implementing the system on existing microcomputers, the use of an analytical model of the robot is adopted (see Chapter 1 and Paragraph 5.3);

- hardware transportability, i.e. a possibility of adapting a custommer's system to a particular robot and a particular application without the need for intensive training of the user; for this purpose, an interactive procedure for imposing the parameters necessary for the automatic creation of an analytical model and the selection of control algorithm is developed;

- possibility of adapting the robot operation to the robot environment, especially of synchronizing the robot with the external hardware; this condition is essential for the applicability of the robot in most factory sites; in order to achieve this goal, a set of routines for processing input and output signals and for controlling the order of operation are designed;

- possibility of implementating the system on an inexpensive computer system and possibility of operating the system without utilizing mass memories, so that the probability of system faults in factory conditions is decreased;

- reduction of the human effort necessary for programming the robot task; to this end, a specialized programming language RL is designed; the language supports programming the robot in external coordinates, enables to utilize variables of various types, control structures and user-written subroutines;

- robustness of the system, i.e. protection of the system integrity against an unauthorized use and accidental programming errors.

The controller is implemented by two microcomputers based on powerful 16-bit microprocessors, which enable application of on-line kinematics and dynamic direct digital servosystems including on-line computation of robot dynamics. Also, communication with operator and teaching of the robot by robot program language and teaching box are elaborated.

The complete robot control system with controller UCS-1 is presented in Fig. 5.1. Model UCS-1 ensures interfaces to: a general-purpose computer, video terminal/printer, teaching box, and sensory system. The interfaces to actuators (DC motors or hydraulic) are realized by means of direct analog current or voltage signals from D/A converters.

(Obviously, appropriate amplifiers have to be implemented). Interfaces to a general-purpose computer, videoterminal/printer and teaching box are realized by means of serial lines, and to the sensory system by means of digital and analog lines.

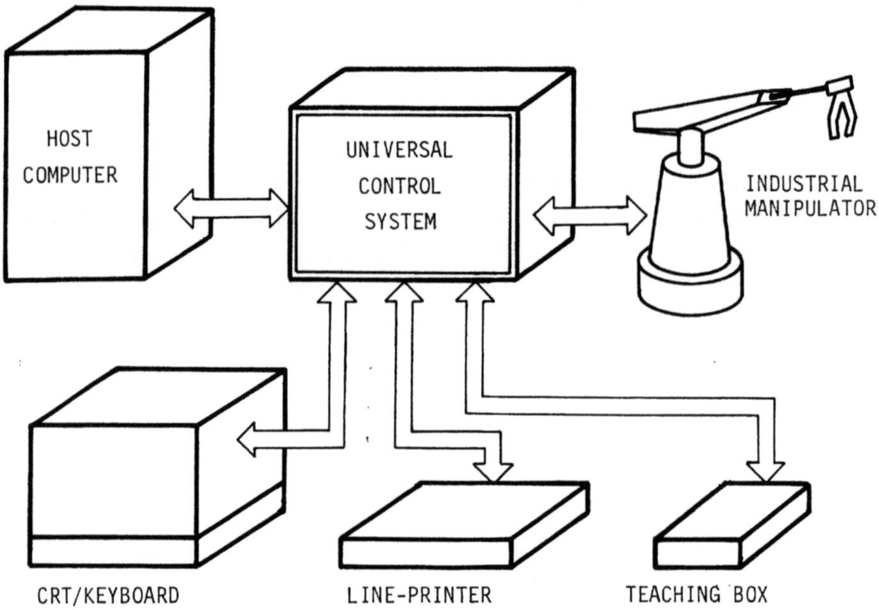

Fig. 5.1. Configuration of general robotic controller

Model UCS-1 contains: 2 microcomputers based on 16-bit microprocessors for processing floating-point operations and calculating various functions, memory (RAM and EPROM), real-time clock, battery back-up system, A/D 12-bit conversion modules, D/A 12-bit conversion modules, digital input/output modules, serial input/output modules, and modules for amplification/attenuation of current and voltage signals.

Controller UCS-1 contains a powerful software support which consists of several interconnected modules:

- software for communication with operator,
- software for initial specification of robot and sensor parameters, i.e. for adjustment of the controller to the particular robot, actuators and sensors system,

- robot programming language,
- program for communication with the teaching box,
- software for on-line robot kinematics, and
- software for direct digital servosystems for tracking trajectories including on-line dynamics.

UCS-1 also contains a number of system routines for servicing discettes/magnetic tape conversion modules, "hardware" - tests, programs for checking the controller's reliability and reactions in emergency situations, etc. The general software organization is presented in Fig. 5.2.

In the text to follow we shall briefly describe some of the modules mentioned above.

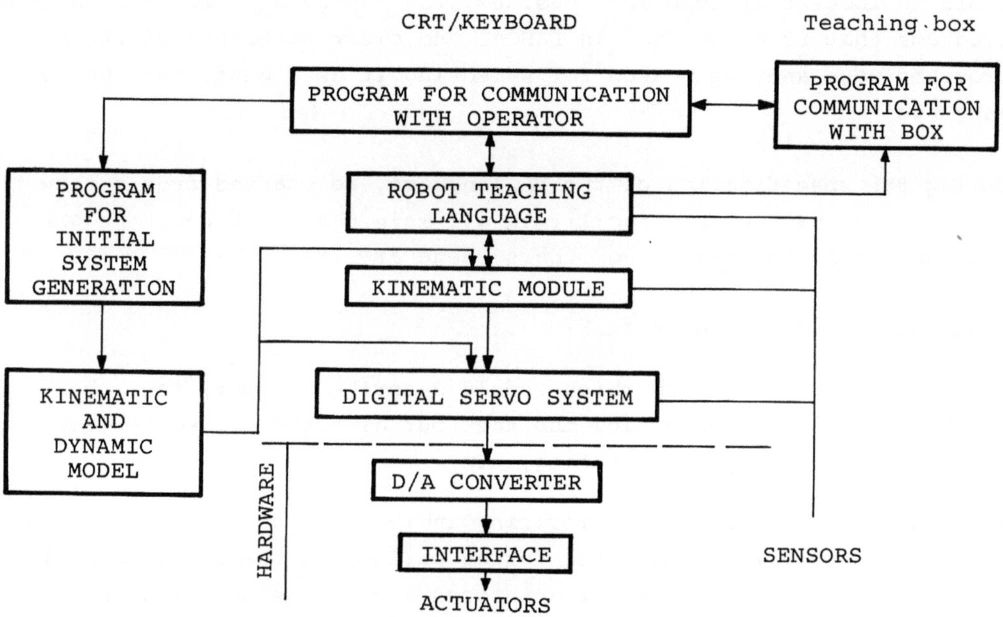

Fig. 5.2. General software organization

1. Software for communication with operator

This module enables communication with the operating system. It allows the operator to call various programs included in the software of the controller, such as: programs for initially setting mechanism parameters, actuators, sensors, programs for teaching the robot, programs of robot tasks, programs for hardware tests, program for adjustment of the system parameters.

2. *Robot programming language*

One of the main objectives stated in design of many robot programming languages was simplicity of use, even for novice programmers unfamiliar with computers and basic programming concepts. We adopted a somewhat different approach; our specific goal was to enable the field engineer, having some experience in programming, to exploit as much as possible the available robot without necessity to learn a new programming language. For this reason we decided to use a PASCAL-like syntax, supposing that the PASCAL is well-known to a majority of system analysis, control and mechanical engineers who are to be the main designers of automated manufacture sites and the main class of users of programming tools in industrial robotics. Besides, the top-down approach in writing programs that is encouraged in PASCAL and clear structure of PASCAL programs were another reason for selecting it as a basis for the RL language.

During the specification of the RL language, we started from a view that the language should facilitate all main phases of robot programming and exploitation; among others these are [8]:

- definition of the robot task;
- writing a robot program which should describe not only the robot behaviour during performing the task but also the procedures for robot teaching, testing, tuning, etc.;
- teaching the robot, i.e. memorizing individual positions and orientations of the robot effector during performing the task, as well as computation of positions, orientations and dimensions of working objects;
- testing the robot program, including eventual reteaching of the positions;
- adjusting the controller parameters in order to meet particular requirements connected to the manipulator mechanical structure and the task to be performed;
- exploitation, which can also include a necessity for occasionally

reteaching particular positions and orientations and adjusting the controller parameters.

The definition of the robot task can be done either in an ad-hoc manner or by using the robot language itself; we decided to encourage the second approach believing that it can speed up the process of writing robot programs and that it can result in more readable programs and thus, programs that are easier to debug, test, tune and expand.

Robot programming language RL is a high level textual language which is implemented in UCS-1 controller in order to simplify communications between the user and the system, i.e. to supply the user with a tool for simply defining particular robot tasks. RL supports the use of program variables, evaluation of logical and arithmetic expressions, use of conditional and repetitive control structures and user-written subroutines. A set of system library subroutines incorporated in the language enables the user to specify manipulator motion, gripper operation, sensor control, synchronization, etc.

Editing, testing and execution of robot language programs are achieved via robot language processor RLP. Robot language processor is a component of UCS-1 software and can be executed in one of the two modes:

- Editor/compiler. In this mode of operation RLP enables interactive creating and editing of a RL program via a terminal keyboard, as well as including sequences of RL instructions generated by the use of the teaching box. During the operation RLP parses input instructions and prepares the RL program for execution. The syntax analysis is performed and diagnostic messages are displayed on the terminal screen immediately after instructions typing.

- Interpreter. In this mode RLP accepts and executes a RL program previously translated into an internal form. RLP permanently monitor the operation of controller and manipulator equipment and informs the user of any hardware or software error detected during the execution.

3. Teaching box

Teaching box represents a "manual programming unit" for quick and efficient programming of the robot. This teaching box is implemented by an 8-bit microprocessor in CMOS technology, so that small size and low weight of the box are achieved. These advantages of the teaching box enable programming of the robot in its close surroundings. The teaching box is connected to controller UCS-1 by a long cable and it consists of two alfanumeric display lines, a keyboard for selecting the execution mode, a keyboard for choosing the execution speed and a keyboard for teaching the robot. The keyboard for teaching the robot includes keys for starting and stopping some procedures, for emergency stop of the robot, for memorizing the robot coordinates, defining the coordinate system in which robot coordinates are specified, for defining duration of some actions, for defining the speed of motion, etc.

In defining some control tasks the operator can set some parts of the task using robot language, and some other by using the teaching box. In this way, maximal flexibility in control task specification is provided as well minimum time for teaching the robot.

4. *Software for initial specification of robot parameters*

A program for initial generation of the system (PIGS) provides flexibility of the controller in the sense of its application to an arbitrary configuration of the robot (with up to 6 degrees of freedom), to various types of actuators and sensors. This is why this program is realized as an interactive program with simple communication with the user. It consists of several modules: program for initial specifications of the parameters of the mechanism, actuators, and sensors, program for kinematic model generation, program for dynamic model generation, program for generating models of the actuators and calculation of the digital servosystems parameters.

Using a simple dialogue between the user and the controller, all above mentioned data are imposed by the operator for a specific manipulation robot, and can easily be changed. The user can also specify the types of sensors which are included in the system, together with numerical data on sensors. The controller UCS-1 supports the following types of sensors: binary sensors, multibit sensors, analog sensors, sensors which have to be elaborated by a host-computer (e.g. camera), etc.

The programs for generating kinematic and dynamic models of the robot automatically form the robot models in the machine language of microcomputers. They form analytic models for a specific manipulation type, according to the parameters of the mechanism which have been set by the user [9].

The program for computing the model of the actuators and for the digital servosystems parameters has to synthesize the gains of digital servosystems on the basis of tolerances imposed by the user (Chapter 4).

All these modules do not depend on the type of the robot, so the controller UCS-1 is general and can easily be "adjusted" from one to another robot type.

5. *Program for robot kinematics*

The program for robot kinematics realizes the commands of the robot program language or teaching box which are concerned with the motion of the gripper. This program enables on-line generation of the trajectories of joint coordinates of the robot according to the user's commands, or according to trajectories imposed by the host-computer. This on-line generation of the joint trajectories if external (gripper) trajectories are given, is achieved by off-line prepared kinematic model of the robot. This model has been generated by the PIGS. Kinematic program is designed to enable generation of joint trajectories for various types of external coordinates, taking into account all constraints in the working space of the robot (obstacles) and/or constraints upon the robot joint drives [10]. This program enables implementation of continual and "point-to-point" trajectories with linear and polynomial interpolation.

6. *Program for direct digital servosystems (DDS)*

Controller UCS-1 includes direct digital servosystems for control of DC electromotors or hydraulic actuators in the manipulator joints. Thus, analog servosystems are not needed for robot control. On the basis of data on actuators and mechanism and on the basis of given tolerances which the robot must satisfy, PIGS computes feedback gains for DDS for all joints of the manipulator(Chapter 2). Implementation of DDS requires feedback by position from the shaft-encoder in the manipulator joint and velocity feedback from tachogenerator. The tachogenerator might be omitted, but this would result in worse tracking of fast trajectories. DDS also includes on-line computation of the dynamics of the robot mechanism for global control. In this way very precise tracking of fast trajectories is achieved, since DDS compensates for dynamic effects (inertia and gravity) during the tracking. Thus, the performances of our DDS are improved in comparison with classical solutions of digital or analog servosystems. This matter has been discussed in more detail in Chapter 2. On-line computation of the dynamic model of the mechanism is achieved by a program for automatic generation of the analytical model of the mechanism dynamics on the basis of initially set data on the robot. This problem will be considered in paragraphs to follow.

DDS are designed to withstand variations of parameters of the mechanism and actuators to some extent (variations with respect to initially specified values). However, the user can adjust servo-gains himself through corresponding commands and programs.

7. Software for execution checks

Besides the standard routines for software errors detection, the controller UCS-1 is supplied with a library of routines for continuous check of the controller performance, during programming of the robot and during test execution. These programs detect all irregularities in the execution of the controller and robot and send appropriate messages. The controller is also supplied with special routines for fast responses in emergency situations. In this way reliability of the controller is ensured and the system is protected from all irregularities in the controller execution which could cause demage on the robot or in the working space of the robot. This makes the use of the controller safe and simple, since the controller is protected from eventual irregular handling and programming.

Since our prime interest in this monograph is the executive control level, in the text to follow we shall concentrate on the problem of implementation of the executive control level. It should be underlined that the key problem in the implementation of general purpose controller is accomplishing on-line kinematics [10] and on-line dynamics which is included in direct digital servosystems. The implementation of local and global (non-adaptive and adaptive) control is the main issue of the next paragraphs. Namely, we shall consider the numerical complexity of various control laws in the executive control level in order to determine the equipment necessary for implementing the general purpose controller. It should be understood that the described general purpose controller includes the control synthesis described in previous chapters.

5.3 Numerical Complexity of Control Laws

In this paragraph we shall discuss one of the most important issues related to the real-time applicability of robot control laws. This issue will be referred to as "numerical complexity" of a control algorithm.

Numerical complexity is quantitatively determined by the number of numerical operations required for the implementation of a control law. The mathematical expressions of control algorithms include algebraic operations between real numbers. The numerical complexity can be expressed by the numbers of floating-point multiplications/divisions and additions/subtractions. These numbers determine the real-time applicability of a control law. Our "reference" law-cost microcomputer will be an up--to-date 16-bit micro provided with a floating-point coprocessor, capable of carrying out over 300 floating-point multiplications and over 300 additions/subtractions in 20 ms sampling time.

We shall see in the text to follow that dynamic effects which are taken into account predominantly determine the numerical complexity of a control law. The compensation of Coriolis and centrifugal forces expecially increases the number of floating-point multiplications/additions. We shall use the described numeric-symbolic method for the evaluation of dynamic effects, because of its computational efficiency.

The numerical complexity of dynamic robot models will be considered in Paragraph 5.3.1. The obtained results apply to centralized control laws as well. Various cases are examined, depending on the dynamic effects which are compensated through the control law.

The numerical complexity of decentralized control laws will be considered in Paragraph 5.3.2. We will determine the number of numerical operations required for the evaluation of both local and global components of control law. Here, the global control will be considered as obtained by force measurement or by the real-time computation of dynamic effects.

In the next paragraph, we will consider some of the adaptive control laws described in Chapter 3. First, we will examine the numerical complexity of the centralized adaptive control strategy based on hyperstability theory (Paragraph 3.2.2). Then, the indirect centralized control (Paragraph 3.2.3) will be examined. The self-tuning control strategy will not be considered, because it does not take into account any dynamic effect of a manipulator. Finally, the numerical complexity of the indirect decentralized adaptive control will be determined.

The number of floating-point multiplications/additions will be determined for several robots with 3 and 6 degrees of freedom. The obtained results should give the answer to the question: which dynamic control laws can be applied in real time on typical up-to-date low-cost microcomputers? For the sake of efficiency, the analytical modelling method is applied. This method is also very suitable for multiprocessing applications.

5.3.1. Numerical complexity of dynamic models

Consider a manipulator with n joints and n links powered by electric or hydraulic actuators. Both types of actuators can be presented by the state-space model (2.2.2):

$$S^i: \quad \dot{x}^i = A^i(\theta^i)x^i + b^i(\theta^i)N(u^i) + f^i(\theta^i)P_i \quad i=1,\dots,n$$

where x^i is an n_i-dimensional state vector of the actuator dirving the joint i,

u^i is the input of the ith actuator,

$N(\cdot)$ is the amplitude saturating function defined as

$$N(u^i) = \begin{cases} u^i_m & u^i > u^i_m \\ u^i & -u^i_m < u^i < u^i_m \\ -u^i_m & u^i < -u^i_m \end{cases}$$

with $u^i_m > 0$ being a given constant,

P_i is the driving torque/force in joint i,

θ^i is the ℓ_i - dimensional parameter vector of the ith actuator, including actuator gain, viscous damping factor, etc.,

A^i is an $n_i \times n_i$ system matrix,

b^i is an $n_i \times n_i$ system matrix,

f^i is an n_i-dimensional load distribution vector.

For example, model matrices describing the dynamics of DC motors are

$$A^i = \begin{bmatrix} 0 & 0 & 0 \\ 0 & -F/J & C_M/J \\ 0 & -C_E/L & -r/L \end{bmatrix}, \quad b^i = \begin{bmatrix} 0 \\ 0 \\ 1/L \end{bmatrix}, \quad f^i = \begin{bmatrix} 0 \\ -1/J \\ 0 \end{bmatrix} \tag{5.3.1}$$

where F - the viscous damping factor, C_M - actuator gain, C_E - back e.m.f. coefficient, r - rotor resistance, L - rotor inductance, and J - rotor moment of inertia. Here, the state vector is $x^i=[q_i\ \dot{q}_i\ i^i]^T$, with q_i being the ith joint angle and i^i the rotor current. Notice that this model is of order 3. Neglecting inductance, we obtain the second--order model

$$A^i = \begin{bmatrix} 0 & 1 \\ 0 & -C_M C_E/rJ \end{bmatrix}, \quad b^i = \begin{bmatrix} 0 \\ C_m/rJ \end{bmatrix}, \quad f^i = \begin{bmatrix} 0 \\ -1/J \end{bmatrix} \tag{5.3.2}$$

with state-space vector $x^i = [q_i\ \dot{q}_i]^T$. When a reducer connects the actuator and the joint, it is necessary to include the reduction ratio into θ^i.

Driving torques/forces P_i are arranged by the dynamic equations of motion of manipulator (see Chapter 1)

$$S_M: \quad P_i = \sum_{j=1}^{n} H_{ij}(q,\ d)\ddot{q}_j + h_i(q,\ \dot{q},\ d), \qquad i=1,\dots,n \tag{5.3.3}$$

where H_{ij} are scalar functions describing the inertial coupling between the degrees of freedom i and j, $q = [q_1 \cdots q_n]^T$ is the vector of joint coordinates, d is an $\underset{\sim}{\ell_i}$- dimensional vector of the mechanical parameters of manipulator and h_i is a scalar function describing gravitational, centrifugal and Coriolis effects. The matrix form of Eq. (5.3.3) becomes

$$S_M: \quad P = H(q,\ d)\ddot{q} + h(q,\ \dot{q},\ d) \tag{5.3.4}$$

where $P = [P_1 \cdots P_n]^T$ is the vector of driving torques for revolute joints or forces for sliding ones, H is an n×n full-rank positive definite inertial matrix and $h = [h_1 \cdots h_n]^T$ is an n vector describing velocity-coupling between links as well as gravitational effects. This vector can be presented in the form (see Eq. (2.2.1)):

$$h = \dot{q}^T C(q,\ d)\dot{q} + g(q,\ d) \tag{5.3.5}$$

where C is an n×n×n matrix, and g is an n vector describing gravitational effects. Quadratic form $\dot{q}^T C(q,\ d)\dot{q}$ represents the n vector $[\dot{q}^T C^1(q,\ d)\dot{q} \cdots \dot{q}^T C^n(q,\ d)\dot{q}]^T$ where C^i are n×n matrices.

Actuator model matrices (5.3.2) indicate that their elements are zero except for $A^i(1,2) = 1$ and $A^i(2,2)$, $b^i(2)$ and $f^i(2)$. Let us introduce the constants a_i, b_i and f_i, such that

$$A^i(2,2) = -a_i, \quad b^i(2) = b_i \quad \text{and} \quad f^i(2) = -f_i$$

Now, the actuator model reduces to $\ddot{q}_i = -a_i\dot{q}_i + b_i u_i - f_i P_i$. The matrix form of the system of n actuators becomes

$$S_A:\quad \ddot{q} = -\mathrm{diag}(a_i)\dot{q} + \mathrm{diag}(b_i)u - \mathrm{diag}(f_i)P \tag{5.3.6}$$

The entire model that consists of S_M and S_A is

$$S_{(2)}:\quad u = \hat{H}(q,\ \theta)\ddot{q} + \hat{h}(q,\ \theta) \tag{5.3.7}$$

where θ represents the vector of mechanical and electrical parameters of mechanism and actuators, and

$$\begin{aligned}\hat{H} &= \mathrm{diag}(b_i^{-1}) + \mathrm{diag}(f_i b_i^{-1})H(q,\ d)\\ \hat{h} &= \mathrm{diag}(a_i b_i^{-1})\dot{q} + \mathrm{diag}(f_i b_i^{-1})h(q,\ \dot{q},\ d)\end{aligned} \tag{5.3.8}$$

Substituting $h = \dot{q}^T C(q,\ d)\dot{q} + g(q,\ d)$ into $\hat{h}$, we obtain

$$\hat{h} = \hat{K}(q,\ \dot{q},\ \theta)\dot{q} + \mathrm{diag}(f_i b_i^{-1})g(q,\ d) \tag{5.3.9}$$

where $\hat{K} = \mathrm{diag}(a_i b_i^{-1}) + \mathrm{diag}(f_i b_i^{-1})\dot{q}^T C(q,\ d)$. To summarize, the model (5.3.7) - (5.3.9) may be represented by the diagram shown in Fig. 5.3. The state-space representation of model (5.3.7) is

$$S:\quad \dot{x} = F(x,\ \theta)x + B(x,\ \theta)u + G(x,\ \theta) \tag{5.3.10}$$

with

$$F = \left[\begin{array}{c|c} 0 & I \\ \hline 0 & -\hat{H}^{-1}(q,\ \theta)\hat{K}(q,\ \dot{q},\ \theta) \end{array}\right] \qquad B = \left[\begin{array}{c} 0 \\ \hline \hat{H}^{-1}(q,\ \theta) \end{array}\right] \tag{5.3.11}$$

$$G = \left[\begin{array}{c} 0 \\ \hline -\mathrm{diag}(f_i b_i^{-1})\hat{H}(q,\ \theta)g(q,\ d) \end{array}\right]$$

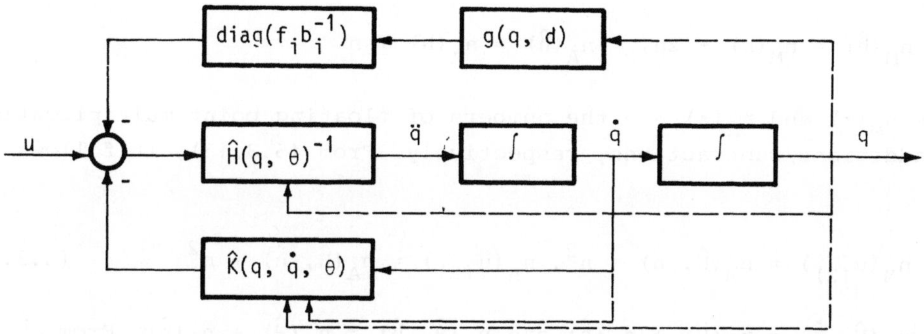

Fig. 5.3. Diagram of the robot model including both the model of mechanical system part and the second-order models of actuators

Under the assumption that the actuators are modelled by third-order systems, the state vector can be taken into the form $x = [q^T\ \dot{q}^T\ p^T]^T$, where q denotes the joint coordinate vector. Vector p is of the form $p = [i^1 \cdots i^n]^T$ (i^j - rotor current of the *j*th actuator for DC motors, and $p = [p^1 \cdots p^n]^T$ (p^j - differential pressure) for hydraulic actuators. Following the derivation of model (5.3.7), one obtains

$$\begin{aligned} \hat{H}\ddot{q} &= -\hat{K}\dot{q} + \mathrm{diag}(a^i_{23}b_i^{-1})p - \mathrm{diag}(f_i b_i^{-1})g \\ \dot{p} &= -\mathrm{diag}(a^i_{32})\dot{q} - \mathrm{diag}(a^i_{33})p + \mathrm{diag}(b_i)u \end{aligned} \tag{5.3.12}$$

with $a^i_{jk} = |A^i(j,k)|$, $b_i = b^i(3)$ and $f_i = f^i(2)$. Matrices $\hat{H}$ and $\hat{K}$ are defined by (5.3.8), (5.3.9) under the condition $a_i = A^i(2,\ 2)$. Now, the robot model may be represented by the diagram shown in Fig. 5.4.

Let us now determine the quantity of floating-point multiplications and additions/subtractions which are to be performed in order to calculate robot model equations. First, we shall suppose that the actuators are modelled by second-order linear time-invariant systems. The input vector, which must be calculated for given q, $\dot{q}$ and $\ddot{q}$, will be denoted by $u_{(2)}$. We see from Eq. (5.3.7) that $u_{(2)}$ can be represented by

$$u_{(2)} = \hat{H}\ddot{q} + \hat{h} \tag{5.3.13}$$

with $\hat{H}$ and $\hat{h}$ determined by (5.3.8). From these expressions, we obtain

$$\begin{aligned} n_M(\hat{H}) &= n_M(H) + n^2, \quad n_A(\hat{H}) = n_A(H) + n \\ n_M(\hat{h}) &= n_M(h) + 2n, \quad n_A(\hat{h}) = n_A(h) + n \end{aligned} \tag{5.3.14}$$

where $n_M(\cdot)$ and $n_A(\cdot)$ are the numbers of floating point multiplications and additions/subtractions, respectively. From (5.3.13), it follows that

$$n_M(u_{(2)}) = n_M(\hat{H}, \hat{h}) + n^2, \; n_A(u_{(2)}) = n_A(\hat{H}, \hat{h}) + n^2 \tag{5.3.15}$$

with $n_M(\hat{H}, \hat{h}) = n_M(\hat{H}) + n_M(\hat{h})$ and $n_A(\hat{H}, \hat{h}) = n_A(\hat{H}) + n_A(\hat{h})$. From (5.3.14) and (5.3.15) we get

$$\begin{aligned} n_M(u_{(2)}) &= n_M(H, h) + 2n^2 + 2n \\ n_A(u_{(2)}) &= n_A(H, h) + n^2 + 2n \end{aligned} \tag{5.3.16}$$

Let us derive the corresponding expressions in the case when the actuators are modelled by third-order systems. From (5.3.12), we see that the input vector $u_{(3)}$ can be expressed as

$$u_{(3)} = \mathrm{diag}(b_i^{-1})\dot{p} + \mathrm{diag}(a_{32}^i b_i^{-1})\dot{q} + \mathrm{diag}(a_{33}^i a_{23}^{i-1})(\hat{H}\ddot{q}+\hat{h}) \tag{5.3.17}$$

Notice that the computation of $\hat{H}\ddot{q} + \hat{h}$ requires $n_M(u_{(2)})$ multiplications and $n_A(u_{(2)})$ additions, given by (5.3.16). Substituting into (5.3.17), we get

$$n_M(u_{(3)}) = n_M(H, h) + 2n^2 + 5n, \quad n_A(u_{(3)}) = n_A(H, h) + n^2 + 4n \tag{5.3.18}$$

We see that the quantity of numerical operations in equations determining the input vector $u_{(3)}$ depends mostly on the number of multiplications and additions necessary to calculate dynamic model matrices H and h.

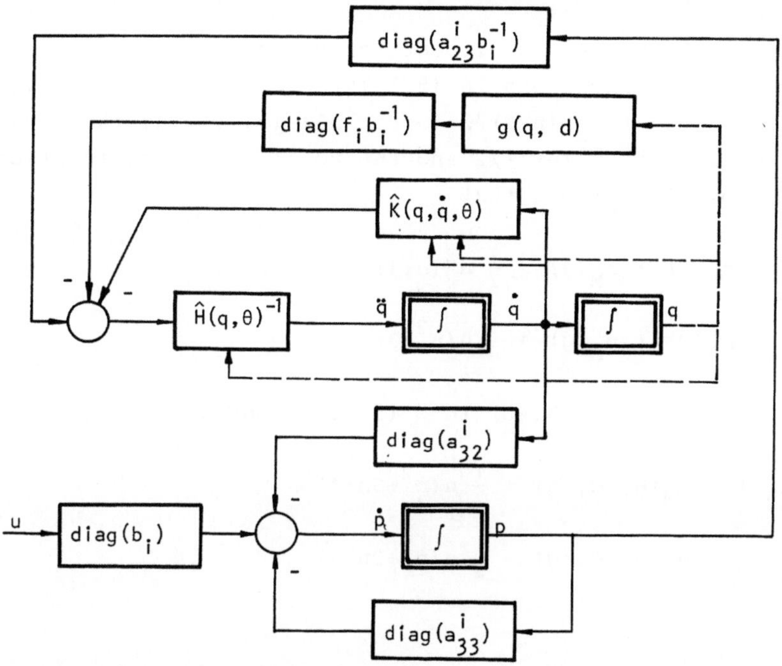

Fig. 5.4. Robot model including both the model of arm and the third-order models of actuators

Depending on the modelling method and the complexity of robot kinematic chain, one obtains different values for n_M (H, h) and n_A(H, h). Let us accept the efficient modelling method described in Chapter 1, and determine n_M and n_A for some typical industrial robots. This method is based on computer-aided generation of analytical expressions for the elements of H, C and g matrices as functions of joint coordinates. To calculate the vector $h = \dot{q}^T C\dot{q} + g$ with a minimal number of numerical operations, we must take into account relations between the elements of C matrices [11]:

$$C^i_{k\ell} = C^i_{\ell k}$$

$$C^i_{k\ell} = -C^k_{i\ell} \quad \text{for} \quad k>\ell \quad \text{and} \quad i>\ell$$

so that $i,k,\ell \in \{1,\dots,n\}$. Therefore

$$h_i = \sum_{\substack{k=1 \\ (k \neq i)}}^{n} C^i_{kk}\dot{q}_k^2 + 2 \sum_{\substack{k=1 \\ (k \neq i)}}^{n} \sum_{\ell=1}^{k-1} C^i_{k\ell}\dot{q}_k\dot{q}_\ell + g_i \tag{5.3.19}$$

with h_i and g_i being the *i*th elements of vectors h and g, respectively. The number of multiplications in (5.3.19) equals $n^2+3n-2(i+1)$, and the number of additions $(n+1)(n+2)/2-i$. For all $i=1,\ldots,n$, the total number of multiplications is $n^2(n+1)/2$ and the total number of additions is $n^2(n^2+3)/2$. Now, it follows that

$$\begin{aligned} n_M(h) &= n_M(C) + n_M(g) + \frac{1}{2}n^2(n+1) \\ n_A(h) &= n_A(C) + n_A(g) + \frac{1}{2}n(n^2+3) \end{aligned} \tag{5.3.20}$$

Finally, substituting (5.3.20) into (5.3.16) and (5.3.18), we obtain

$$\begin{aligned} n_M(u_{(2)}) &= n_M(H, C, g) + \frac{1}{2}n(n^2+5n+4) \\ n_A(u_{(2)}) &= n_A(H, C, g) + \frac{1}{2}n(n^2+2n+7) \end{aligned} \tag{5.3.21}$$

as well as

$$\begin{aligned} n_M(u_{(3)}) &= n_M(H, C, g) + \frac{1}{2}n(n^2+5n+10) \\ n_A(u_{(3)}) &= n_A(H, C, g) + \frac{1}{2}n(n^2+2n+11) \end{aligned} \tag{5.3.22}$$

Let us consider the meaning of these relations on several examples. We shall discuss some commercial industrial robots with 3 and 6 degrees of freedom: a cylindrical robot shown in Fig. 5.5 (we will separately consider a version with 3 links CL-3, and a version with 6 links CL-6), a PUMA-like robot shown in Fig. 5.6 (designated by PU-3), a spherical robot shown in Fig. 5.7 (SF-3), and the Stanford manipulator with 6 joints (ST-6) shown in Fig. 5.8. The number of numerical operations necessary for the computation of dynamic model matrices H, C and g, as well as input vectors $u_{(2)}$ and $u_{(3)}$ is given in Table 5.1. This table also contains the computation time obtained on a typical 16-bit microcomputer. Of course, implementation on more powerful microcomputers (such as MOTOROLA 68000 or INTEL 286) would decrease the computation time 2 to 3 times. From this table we also see that the difference between computation times for $u_{(2)}$ and $u_{(3)}$ is minor compared with total times.

In on-line applications, it is necessary to compute $u_{(2)}$ or $u_{(3)}$ at a sampling frequency preferably not lower than 50 Hz, since the resonance

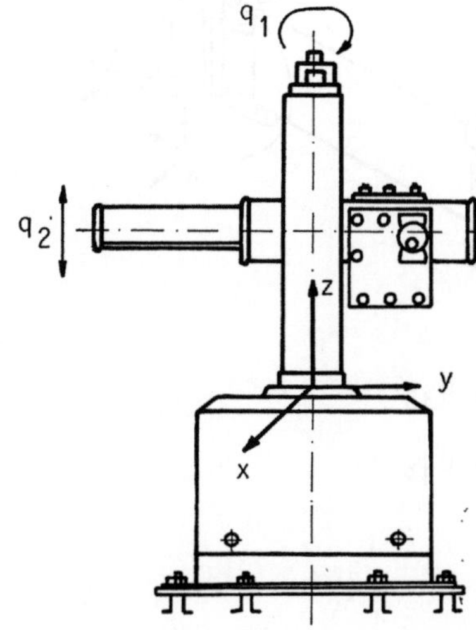

Fig. 5.5. Cylindrical robot (CL)

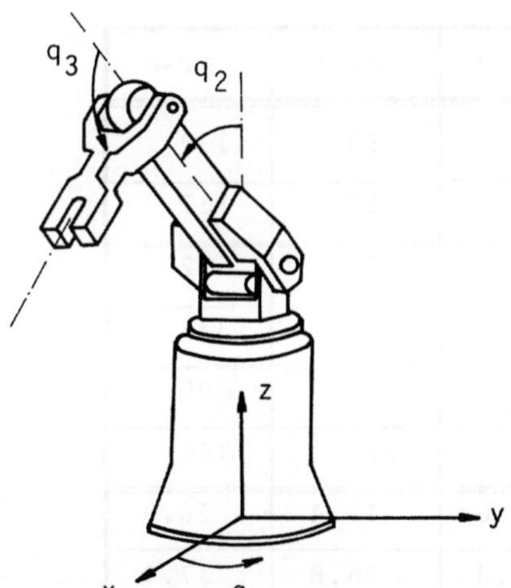

Fig. 5.6. PUMA-like robot (PU)

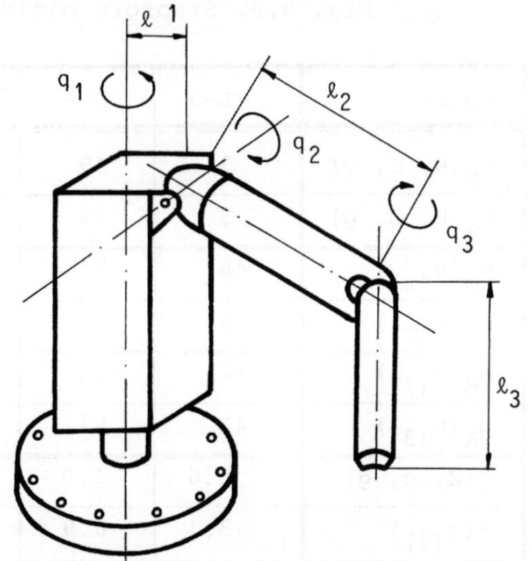

Fig. 5.7. Spherical robot (SF)

frequency of most mechanical manipulators is about 10 Hz. However, the real-time computation (for at most 20 ms) by means of an average 16-bit microcomputer is possible only for 3-degree-of-freedom robots.

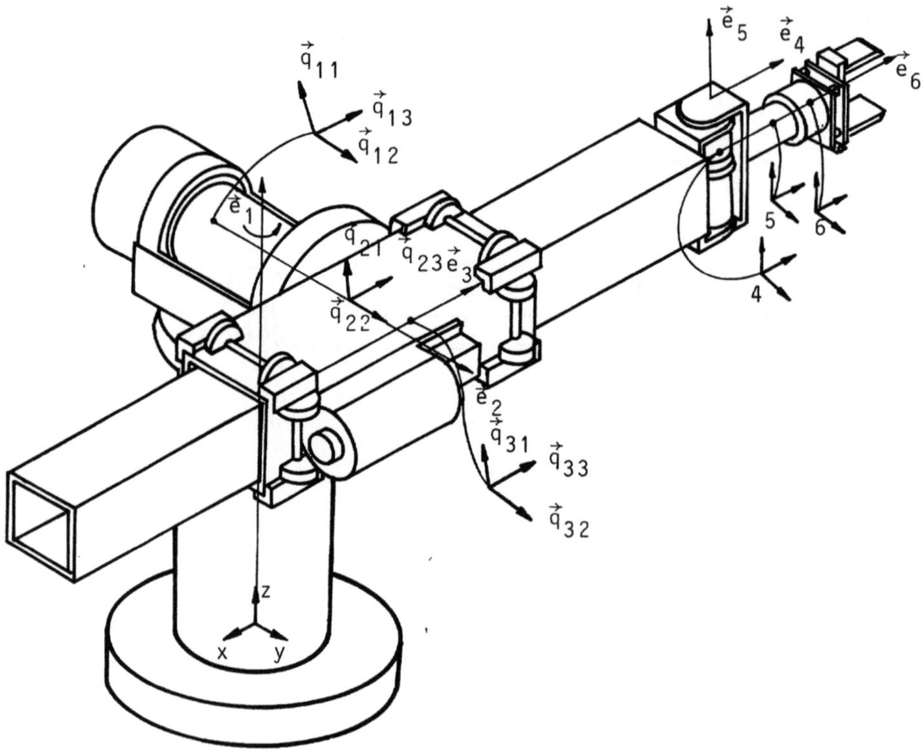

Fig. 5.8. Stanford manipulator (ST)

ROBOT	CL-3	PU-3	SF-3	CL-6	ST-6
$n_M(H, C, g)$	3	49	55	193	372
$n_A(H, C, g)$	3	22	31	80	167
$n_M(u_{(2)})$	45	91	97	403	582
$n_A(u_{(2)})$	36	55	64	245	332
$n_M(u_{(3)})$	54	100	106	421	600
$n_A(u_{(3)})$	42	61	70	257	344
$t(H, c, g)$	0.6	4.0	4.6	12.4	20.8
$t(u_{(2)})$	3.1	6.9	7.4	26.8	37.0
$t(t_{(3)})$	3.7	7.4	8.0	28.0	38.2

Table 5.1. Number of numerical operations and computation time [ms] with microcomputer based on INTEL 8086/8087 at 8 MHz clock

Using more powerful microcomputers, it is possible to reduce the calculation time significantly. However, this makes the price of robot control unit higher.

5.3.2. Numerical complexity of non-adaptive decentralized control laws

Centralized control approach, sometimes called "inverse control structure" or "direct torque method" (see Chapter 2), is implicitly presented in the previous paragraph. For example, both equations (5.3.7) and (5.3.17) may be considered as control laws if the acceleration vector $\ddot{q}$ is computed according to linear feedback structure

$$\ddot{q} = \ddot{q}^{o} + K_p(q-q^{o}) + K_v(\dot{q}-\dot{q}^{o})$$

where K_p and K_v represent n×n gain matrices, and $q^{o} = q^{o}(t)$ is a nominal trajectory in joint-coordinate-space. In the previous paragraph it was shown that the real-time implementation of (5.3.7) or (5.3.17) would require the use of more powerful 16-bit microprocessors. To develop less expensive controllers, it would be justifiable to consider the numerical complexity of decentralized robot control.

Consider the simplest form of decentralized control law (see Chapter 2)

$$u^{i} = u^{oi} + D_i\Delta x^{i} + k_i^{G}\Delta P_i \qquad (5.3.23)$$

where $D_i \in R^{1\times 2}$ includes local gains, $\Delta x^{i} = [\Delta q_i \;\; \Delta\dot{q}_i]^T$, and k_i^G = const is the global gain. Suppose that the manipulator joints include torque sensing capability (or force sensing in sliding joints) by means of strain gauges. For example, Stanford manipulator was redesigned to include force sensors [12]. Manipulators like this one can simply be controlled by (5.3.23). Then the number of floating-point operations necessary to realize (5.3.23) becomes

$$n_M = 3n \quad \text{and} \quad n_A = 6n. \qquad (5.3.24)$$

In some cases, it is not necessary to include force feedback in all subsystems (actuators). Obviously, the practical stability of the entire system can often be achieved by local feedback loops only. For example, it is not necessary to apply force feedback in joints of a cylindrical robot like the one shown in Fig. 5.5. Global control is usually desirable for the joints in which dynamic coupling effects are significant. Taking only necessary feedback loops into account, the number of floating-point operations in control laws (5.3.23) implemented on robots described in the previous section is shown in Table 5.2. We see that the number of numerical operations is drastically decreased compared to that for centralized control (5.3.7). However, the use of force sensors increases the cost of robot system.

On the other hand, the coupling function ΔP_i can be calculated on-line using robot dynamic equations. For this purpose, it is convenient to apply the mentioned analytical method, which is very efficient regarding the numerical complexity. Unfortunately, the exact computation of driving torques implies the use of high-speed microcomputers. In such a way, the advantages of decentralized control would be lost. Thus, with the decentralized control we will take into account only those dynamic effects which are required to be introduced for a given control task.

	ROBOT TYPE					
CONTROL LAW	M/A	CL-3	PU-3	SF-3	CL-6	ST-6
Eq. (5.3.23)	M A	6 9	9 18	9 18	15 27	15 27
Eq. (5.3.25)	M A	6 9	76 54	87 72	230 147	413 234
Approximate vector P	M A	- -	26 16	30 21	78 48	108 65
Eq. (5.3.26)	M A	6 9	35 31	39 36	93 75	123 82
Approximate vector P	M A	- -	23 12	20 14	18 14	55 33
Eq. (5.3.27)	M A	6 9	32 27	29 29	33 41	70 60
Eq. (5.3.28)	M A	6 9	17 18	13 16	15 27	22 30

Table 5.2. Number of floating-point multiplications (M) and additions/subtractions (A) for different control laws

Let us first systematically suppose that the dynamic model is computed exactly. Then, the decentralized control law (5.3.23) becomes

$$u^i = u^{oi} + D_i \Delta x^i + k_i^G(\sum_{i=1}^{n} H_{ij}(x, d)\ddot{q}_j^o + h_i(x, d) - P_i^o) \qquad (5.3.25)$$

Notice that (5.3.25) includes all dynamic effects: inertial, gravitational, centrifugal and Coriolis' effects. The numerical complexity of (5.3.25) is presented in Table 5.2. This table shows that is is possible to implement the control law (5.3.25) "on-line" even for 6-degree-of-freedom robots having relatively simple kinematic chains.

As the next version of decentralized control law we shall discuss the control structure including inertial and gravitational effects

$$u^i = u^{oi} + D_i x^i + k_i^G(\sum_{j=1}^{n} H_{ij}(x, d)\ddot{q}_j^o + g_i(x, d) - P_i^o) \qquad (5.3.26)$$

Here, centrifugal and Coriolis' effects are omitted in the expressions for global control component. Using the proposed analytical method for computing inertial and gravitational forces, we obtain the number of floating-point multiplications and additions given in Table 5.2. The numerical complexity of approximated driving torque vector is also given in this table. Compared to the numerical complexity of the centralized control law, we see that the number of floating-point operations is reduced by about 40%.

A further simplification of global control leads to the elimination of cross-inertial components. Here, only diagonal elements of inertia matrix are taken into account. Then, we have

$$u^i = u^{oi} + D_i x^i + k_i^G(H_{ii}(x, d)q_i^o + g_i(x, d) - P_i^o) \qquad (5.3.27)$$

with P_i^o precalculated according to the expression $H_{ii}(x^o, d)\ddot{q}_i^o + g_i(x^o, d)$. The results for both control vector and approximated driving torques are given in Table 5.2. We see that even for the most complex robot structures the computing time is shorter than 10 ms.

Finally, if we take into account gravitational forces only, we obtain

$$u^i = u^{oi} + D_i \Delta x^i + k_i^G(g_i(x, d) - P_i^o) \qquad (5.3.28)$$

The number of operations is now very small and offers the possibility for implementation on 8-bit microcomputers. The dependence of the number of floating-point multiplications on global control complexity is presented in Fig. 5.9. The computing times measured on INTEL 8086/8087 are given in Table 5.3. Cosine and sine functions of joint coordinates are included, too.

CONTROL LAW	ROBOT TYPE				
	CL-3	PU-3	SF-3	CL-6	ST-6
Eq. (5.3.24)	0.9	2.25	2.25	3.4	3.4
Eq. (5.3.28)	0.6	3.0	2.4	3.4	3.9
Eq. (5.3.27)	0.6	3.5	3.4	4.7	6.9
Eq. (5.3.26)	0.6	3.8	4.1	8.3	9.8
Eq. (3.5.25)	0.6	6.25	7.3	16.3	26.8

Table 5.3. Computing times ms necessary for implementation of various decentralized control laws (INTEL 8086/8087 at 8 MHz)

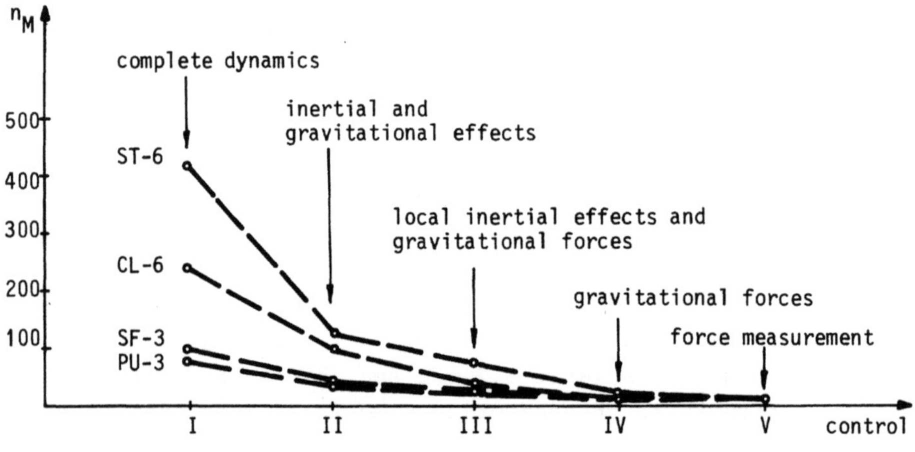

Fig. 5.9. Number of floating-point multiplications versus control law (I - Eq. (5.3.25), II - Eq. (5.3.26), III - Eq. (5.3.27), IV - Eq. (5.3.28) and V - Eq. (5.3.24))

Finally, let us point out the following results. It is shown that for the well-known Stanford arm, it is necessary to implement from 15 to 400 floating-point multiplications depending on the dynamic effects which are compensated. This corresponds to the range of 3.4 to 27 ms on a typical 16-bit microprocessor (for instance, INTEL 8086/8087). Having accepted 20 ms as a maximal sampling period for most robots, we obtain that it is necessary to use 2 processors in a parallel manner. However, if we neglect centrifugal and Coriolis effects, the computational time drops to 10 ms. If the exact nonlinear stability analysis justifies the neglect (as is often the case, except for high-precision/ /high-speed tracking tasks), then the controller may be realized by a single processor unit. Obviously, by the use of powerful microcomputers (which are 2 to 3 times faster), one obtains the possibility to achieve real time evan if entire dynamics is included.

5.3.3. Numerical complexity of adaptive control laws

We described in Paragraph 3.2.2 the centralized reference-model following control based on hyperstability theory. Now, we will consider its on-line applicability on low-cost microcomputers. The numerical complexity of the control structure shown in Fig. 3.3 can be obtained by adding the number of floating-point multiplications/additions for reference model, non-adaptive and adaptive control terms.

To evaluate the reference model (3.2.38):

$$S_M: \quad \dot{x}^o = A_M x^o + B_M u^o$$

using the second-order subsystems, it is necessary

$$n_M(u^o) = 3n, \qquad n_A(u^o) = 2n \tag{5.3.29}$$

multiplications and additions/subtractions, respectively. For the computation of the non-adaptive control term (3.2.49):

$$u = [K_p(\xi, \bar{\theta}) + \mathcal{L}_p(\xi, \theta)]\xi + [K_u(\xi, \theta) + \mathcal{L}_u(\xi, e)]u^o$$

it is necessary to form the dynamic model matrices. Thus, it is convenient to apply the numeric-symbolic method, described in Chapter 1. But, the numbers of floating-point operations are obviously the same as those obtained in Paragraph 5.3.1. These numbers will be denoted by

$$n_M = n_M(u_{NA}) \quad \text{and} \quad n_A = n_A(u_{NA}) \tag{5.3.30}$$

where u_{NA} denotes the non-adaptive component:

$$u_{NA} = K_p(\xi, \bar{\theta}) + K_u(\xi, \bar{\theta})u^o. \tag{5.3.31}$$

Let us consider now the numerical complexity of the adaptive component

$$u_A = \mathcal{L}_p(\xi, v) + \mathcal{L}_u(\xi, v)u^o \tag{5.3.32}$$

using the adaptation mechanism (3.2.60). Taking

$$n_M(||v||^{-1}) = n, \qquad n_A(||v||^{-1}) = n-1$$

we get

$$\begin{aligned} n_M(\mathcal{L}_p) &= 2n^2 + n + 1, & n_A(\mathcal{L}_p) &= n-1 \\ n_M(\mathcal{L}_u) &= n^2 + n + 1, & n_A(\mathcal{L}_u) &= n-1 \end{aligned} \tag{5.3.33}$$

The overall number of operations is

$$\begin{aligned} n_M(\mathcal{L}_p, \mathcal{L}_u) &= 3n^2 + n + 3 \\ n_A(\mathcal{L}_p, \mathcal{L}_u) &= n. \end{aligned} \tag{5.3.34}$$

Notice that $||v||$ includes one square-root. Applying table look-up method, we see that it is necessary to perform at least one multiplication and one addition.

For the complete centralized control law we have

$$n_M(u) = n_M(u^o) + n_M(u_{NA}) + n_M(u_A)$$

$$n_A(u) = n_A(u^o) + n_A(u_{NA}) + n_A(u_A)$$

or

$$\begin{aligned} n_M(u) &= n_M(u_{NA}) + 3n^2 + 4n + 3 \\ n_A(u) &= n_A(u_{NA}) + 3n. \end{aligned} \tag{5.3.35}$$

The numbers of numerical operations for the robot structures shown in Figs. 5.5 - 5.8 are given in Table 5.4. We see that the considered adaptive control law is on-line applicable only for robots with up to 3 degrees of freedom. For a typical 6 degree-of-freedom robot (Stanford arm) it is necessary to use no less than 3 parallel processors.

Number of operations	ROBOT TYPE				
	CL-3	PU-3	SF-3	CL-6	ST-6
$n_M(u_{NA})$	45	91	97	403	582
$n_A(u_{NA})$	36	55	64	245	332
$n_M(u)$	87	133	139	538	717
$n_A(u)$	45	64	73	263	350

Table 5.4. Number of floating-point multiplications/additions for the computation of non-adaptive and adaptive control law

Let us now discuss the class of centralized indirect adaptive control. As described in Paragraph 3.2.3, the indirect control consists of two blocks: parameter estimation block and variable gain block. Using the numeric-symbolic method we shall determine the number of floating-point operations.

The control law (3.2.67):

$$u = D_a\ \phi(q,\ \dot{q},\ \ddot{q}^o+D_p(q-q^o)+D_v(\dot{q}-\dot{q}^o),\ \theta_k)\theta_d$$

is practically the same as the centralized nonadaptive control law (Paragraph 5.3.1). The number of floating-point multiplications and additions will be denoted as

$$n_M = n_M(u), \qquad n_A = n_A(u) \tag{5.3.36}$$

and is given in Table 5.1. The norm of the generalized error $||v||$ requires, at least,

$$n_M(||v||) = n, \quad n_A(||v||) = n-1. \tag{5.3.37}$$

The estimation algorithm (3.2.70)

$$\bar{\theta}_d(t_{k+1}) = \bar{\theta}_d(t_k) + \phi^T(t_k')[\phi(t_k')\phi^T(t_k')]^{-1}D_a^{-1}v(t_k')$$

includes the function ϕ, i.e. the dynamic robot model. Thus

$$n_M(\phi) = n_M(u), \qquad n_A(\phi) = n_A(u). \tag{5.3.38}$$

As $D_a^{-1}v$ can be included into the generalized error v, we shall assume that it does not increase the number of operaitons. Further,

$$n_M(\phi\phi^T) = n^2 n_d, \qquad n_A(\phi\phi^T) = n^2 n_d \tag{5.3.39}$$

where n_d is the number of dynamic parameters. The computation of $(\phi\phi^T)^{-1}v^*$ (with $v^* = D_a^{-1}v(t_k'))$ requires

$$\begin{aligned} n_M((\cdot)^{-1}v^*) &= \tfrac{1}{2}(n^2-1)(n+2) \\ n_A((\cdot)^{-1}v^*) &= \tfrac{1}{2}(n^2-1)n, \end{aligned} \tag{5.3.40}$$

and $\phi^T[(\phi\phi)^{-1}v^*]$ requires

$$n_M(\phi^T(\cdot)) = n n_d, \qquad n_A(\phi^T(\cdot)) = n n_d \tag{5.3.41}$$

additional operations. Summing the expressions (5.3.38) - (5.3.41), we get

$$\begin{aligned} n_M(\bar{\theta}_d) &= n_M(u) + n(n+1)n_d + \tfrac{1}{2}(n^2-1)(n+2) \\ n_A(\bar{\theta}_d) &= n_A(u) + n(n+1)n_d + \tfrac{1}{2}(n^2-1)n \end{aligned} \tag{5.3.42}$$

From (5.3.36) and (5.3.37), we obtain

$$n_M = 2n_M(u) + n(n+1)n_d + \tfrac{1}{2}(n^3+2n^2+n-2)$$

$$n_A = 2n_A(u) + n(n+1)n_d + \tfrac{1}{2}(n^3+n-2)$$

The number of dynamic parameters n_d depends on the number of parameters which describe the dynamics of an isolated link. A link may be described by at least one parameter (mass or moment of inertia), and by at most 10 parameters (mass and 9 terms of inertia tensor). It is often enough to include 4 parameters (mass and the main moments of inertia), or even 3 parameters (mass, longitudinal and transversal moment of inertia). For the last case, we get

$$n_d = 3n. \tag{5.3.44}$$

Then, (5.3.43) becomes

$$n_M = 2n_M(u) + \frac{1}{2}(7n^3+8n^2+n-2)$$
$$n_A = 2n_A(u) + \frac{1}{2}(7n^3+6n^2+n-2) \tag{5.3.45}$$

Taking $n_M(u)$ and $n_A(u)$ from Table 5.1, we obtain the number of floating-point multiplications/additions given in Table 5.5. We see that this control law can be implemented "on-line" for the simplest robot structures only.

	CL-3	PU-3	SF-3	CL-6	ST-6
n_M	221	325	462	1708	2066
n_A	194	232	250	1356	1530

Table 5.5. Number floating-point operations in centralized indirect adaptive control law

Finally, let us consider the numerical complexity of the decentralized indirect adaptive control, described in Paragraph 3.3.3. The local adaptive controllers

$$\Delta u_i^L = [D_{i(min)} + \frac{\Delta\theta_p^e}{|\Delta\theta_p|_{(max)}}(D_{i(max)}-D_{i(min)})](\xi^i-\xi^{io})$$

require

$$n_M(u) = 4n, \qquad n_A(u) = 6n \tag{5.3.46}$$

numerical operations. The number of operations for the estimator (3.3.34) equals

$$n_M(\Delta\theta_p^e) = n_M(S_p) + 2n+1,$$
$$n_M(\Delta\theta_p^e) = n_A(S_p) + 3n \tag{5.3.47}$$

where $n_M(S_p)$ and $n_A(S_p)$ denote the number of operations necessary for the calculation of $S_p(\cdot)$. As shown in [13], we can write approximately

$$n_M(S_p) \approx n_M(P)/n \qquad \text{and} \qquad n_A(S_p) = n_A(P)/n;$$

thus

$$n_M(\Delta\theta^e) = \frac{n_M(P)}{n} + 2n+1$$
$$n_A(\Delta\theta^e) = \frac{n_A(P)}{n} + 3n \tag{5.3.48}$$

where (P) indicates the computation of the complete system dynamics. The estimator (3.3.34), (3.3.36) requires

$$n_M = \frac{n_M(P)}{n} + 3n+1$$
$$n_A = \frac{n_A(P)}{n} + 3n. \tag{5.3.49}$$

These results are also presented in Table 5.6. The estimation with and without force measurement for several typical industrial robots is analyzed. This table includes the computation of sensitivity functions when all of the dynamic effects are incorporated, and the case when the centrifugal and Coriolis effects are neglected. The results show that the number of multiplications is smaller than 150 in all cases. Thus, the real time is easily achievable with our reference microcomputer.

Effects included	M/A	CL-3	PU-3	SF-3	CL-6	ST-6
Inertial, Coriolis gravitational (3.3.35)	n_M n_A	24 31	41 40	46 45	103 87	130 96
Inertial gravitational (3.3.35)	n_M n_A	23 30	28 32	29 34	57 66	59 97
Inertial, Coriolis gravitational (3.3.36)	n_M n_A	27 31	44 40	49 45	109 87	136 96
Inertial gravitational (3.3.36)	n_M n_A	26 30	31 32	32 34	63 66	66 97

Table 5.6. Number of floating-point multiplications/additions in the decentralized indirect adaptive control law

5.4 Parameter Identification

In this paragraph we shall present some practical results devoted to the identification of parameters of robotic actuators. Actually, the idea is to estimate the parameters of robot subsystems, which include not only actuators but also reducers and transmissions. Such driving units are supposed to be integrated with robotic arms. Thus, we can measure joint coordinates and velocities and actuator inputs. In order to estimate the parameters of the *i*th subsystem, we shall suppose that we excite only the *i*th actuator input, producing the motion of the *i*th robot degree of freedom. Further, we shall suppose that the robot subsystems include local analog servoloops. The introduction of analog servoloops is convinient from the standpoint of identification process convergence. However, once the parameters of actuators together with analog servoloops are identified, it is simple to determine parameters of actuators without servoloops if we want to apply direct digital control.

Mathematical model of a servosystem can usually be presented as (see Paragraph 2.4)

$$u^i = D^i(y^i - y^{io}) \tag{5.4.1}$$

where $y^i \in R^{m_i}$ represents the output vector of subsystem S^i, $y^{io} \in R^{m_i}$ is the input vector for the servosystem, and $D^i \in R^{1\times m_i}$ is a gain matrix. The input y^{io} will be denoted by $\bar{u}^i$. Thus, the input vector of the system becomes $\bar{u} = [\bar{u}^{1T} \cdots \bar{u}^{nT}]^T$. For single-input servosystems we can present y^{io} as $y^{io} = [v_i \; 0 \cdots 0]^T$. The corresponding output vector is $y^i = [q_i \,|\, y_r^{iT}]^T$. Now, the model (5.4.1) becomes

$$u^i = [d_i \,|\, d_r^{iT}] \begin{bmatrix} q_i - v_i \\ \hline y_r^i \end{bmatrix} \tag{5.4.2}$$

where $d_i \in R$ is the position gain, and $d_r^i \in R^{m_i - 1}$ is the gain vector corresponding to the remaining coordinates y_r^i. Thus, we obtain

$$u^i = d_i(q_i - v_i) + d_r^{iT} y_r^i. \tag{5.4.3}$$

We see that the actuator input u^i and subsystem input v_i are related by (5.4.3). In the case when there are no analog servoregulators, we have $u^i = v_i$.

Let us introduce the model of mechanical part of the robotic system (i.e. the model of the *i*th joint dynamics) into the model of actuator. This issue has been already considered in Paragraph 2.4. However, for the sake clarity let us briefly repeat this consideration.

Let us consider now the model of the mechanical arm, when only the *i*th joint is moved. Starting from the model

$$P = H(q, d)\ddot{q} + \dot{q}^T C(q, d)\dot{q} + g(q, d)$$

we can extract the differential equation describing the dynamics of the *i*th degree of freedom:

$$P_i = H_r^i(q, d)\ddot{q} + \dot{q}^T C^i(q, d)\dot{q} + g_i(q, d) \qquad (5.4.4)$$

where $H_r^i(q, d)$ represents the *i*th row of the inertial matrix $H(q, d)$, $C^i(q, d)$ is an n×n matrix of Coriolis and centrifugal effects, and $g_i(q, d)$ is the gravitational vector assigned to the *i*th degree of freedom. When changing only the *i*th joint coordinate, the joint velocity vector becomes $\dot{q} = [0 \cdots 0\ \dot{q}_i\ 0 \cdots 0]^T$, and the joint acceleration vector becomes $\ddot{q} = [0 \cdots 0\ \ddot{q}_i\ 0 \cdots 0]^T$. Model (5.4.4) reduces now to

$$P_i = H_{ii}(q, d)\ddot{q}_i + C_{ii}^i(q, d)\dot{q}_i^2 + g_i(q, d) \qquad (5.4.5)$$

where $H_{ii}(q, d)$ represents the (i, i) element of inertial matrix, and $C_{ii}^i(q, d)$ is the *i*th diagonal element of $C^i(q, d)$. But, from Chapter 1 we know that

$$C_{ii}^i(q, d) = 0$$

for $\forall i \in \{1,...,n\}$. Thus, centrifugal and Coriolis effects do not influence the system dynamics when only one joint coordinate is changed.

In the case when q_j = const for $j \neq i$, Eq. (6.2.16) becomes

$$P_i = H_{ii}(q_i, d)\ddot{q}_i + g_i(q_i, d) \qquad (5.4.6)$$

It is obvious that H_{ii} is actually independent of q_i, i.e.

$$H_{ii}(q_i, d) = \bar{H}_{ii} = \text{const.}$$

Thus, we obtain

$$P_i = \bar{H}_{ii}\ddot{q}_i + g_i \tag{5.4.7}$$

Now, let us join together models (5.4.7) and (2.4.2). For this purpose, let us introduce $1\times n_i$-dimensional transformation matrix T^i which maps $\dot{x}^i$ into $\ddot{q}_i$:

$$\ddot{q}_i = T^i\dot{x}^i.$$

Now, the entire model becomes*)

$$\dot{x}^i = A^i x^i + b^i u^i + \bar{H}_{ii} f^i T^i \dot{x}^i + f^i g_i \tag{5.4.8}$$

Notice that f^iT^i is a 3 3 matrix. It should be pointed out that g_i depends on q_i, i.e. x^i. We can use a linear approximation of f^ig_i (see (2.4.5)) and take $f^ig_i = f^i\bar{h}^i\hat{T}^i x^i$ and joint $f^i\bar{h}^i\hat{T}^i$ to A^i. On the other hand, the gravity term g_i can also be approximated by a constant, when the estimation is performed about a single point in the work space. It follows now that

$$\dot{x}^i = W^iA^ix^i + W^ib^iu^i + W^if^ig_i \tag{5.4.9}$$

where $W^i \in R^{n_i\times n_i}$ is given by

$$W^i = (I - \bar{H}_{ii}f^iT^i)^{-1} \tag{5.4.10}$$

Let us include now the local analog servosystems (5.4.3). We suppose that $q_i \in x^i$ and $y_r^i \in x^i$. Then, we can determine a vector $d^i \in R^{n_i}$ such that

$$d_iq_i + d_r^{iT}y_r^i \equiv d^ix^i$$

where d_i and d_r^i are defined by (5.4.3). Substituting into (5.4.3), we obtain the servosystem model

$$u^i = d^ix^i - d_iv_i. \tag{5.4.11}$$

Including (5.4.11) into (5.4.9), we get

$$\dot{x}^i = W^i(A^i+b^id^i)x^i - W^ib^id_iv_i + W^if^ig_i \tag{5.4.12}$$

---

*) We assume that the load acting upon the actuator is equal to the ith joint driving torque, $M_i=P_i$.

Thus, we obtain the model (5.4.12) when the system includes analog feedback gains, and (5.4.9) when the system includes only actuators and transmission. Both models encompass the inertial effects of manipulator arm. These models incorporate some parameters which can be treated as well known, and some which are not exactly known. For example, in the case of DC motor drives the following parameters are exactly known: inductance and resistance of rotor coil, torque gain and back E.M.F. constant, etc. On the other hand, viscous and static frictions are temperature dependent and variable. Translating (5.4.9) and (5.4.12) into discrete time domain and scalar form, we obtain

$$\dot{q}_i(k) = \alpha_i(T, \theta^i)\dot{q}_i(k-1) + \beta_i(T, \theta^i)v_i + e_i(k) \tag{5.4.13}$$

and

$$\dot{q}_i(k) = \alpha_i(T, \theta^i)\dot{q}_i(k-1) + \beta_i(T, \theta^i)\cdot \cdot (v_i - q_i(k-1)) + e_i'(k) \tag{5.4.14}$$

Here, $e_i(k)$ represents the error due to finite sampling time, coupling influence, etc. The coefficients α_i and β_i should be estimated using a method for parameter identification [14, 15, 16]. The estimation procedure should be simple enough to be implementable on microcomputers in real time. In the text to follow we will use the least squares method. The results will be obtained on a real robot, i.e. without using a simulation technique.

Let us consider the evaluation of the system (5.4.13) and (5.4.14) over N sampling intervals (N>>2) and denote the observation vector by $Y_N = [\dot{q}_i(k+1) \cdots \dot{q}_i(k+N)]^T$, and the estimated vector of parameters according to N measurements as $\hat{\theta}_N = [\alpha_i^N \ \beta_i^N]$. The estimation after N+1 measurements $\hat{\theta}_{N+1}$ can be obtained using the estimates $\hat{\theta}_N$ and a term proportional to the difference between the prediction

$$x_{N+1}^T \hat{\theta}_N = [\dot{q}_i(k+N) \qquad u^i(k+N)]^T \hat{\theta}_N$$

in case of model (5.4.13), or

$$x_{N+1}^T \hat{\theta}_N = [\dot{q}_i(k+1) \qquad -q_i(k+N) + v_i(k+N)]^T \hat{\theta}_N$$

for the model (5.4.14), and the measured output $\dot{q}(k+N+1)$:

$$\hat{\theta}_{N+1} = \hat{\theta}_N + K_N(\dot{q}(k+N+1) - X^T_{N+1}\hat{\theta}_N) \quad (5.4.15)$$

The matrix K_N according to the least squares method is

$$K_N = P_N X_{N+1}(1+X_{N+1}P_N X_{N+1})^{-1} \quad (5.4.16)$$

with

$$P_{N+1} = P_N - P_N X_{N+1}(1+X^T_{N+1}P_N X_{N+1})^{-1}X^T_{N+1}P_N \quad (5.4.17)$$

where P_N is a square matrix of dimension corresponding to the numbers of unknown parameters. Let us consider the following example:

Estimation of cylindrical robot parameters

Let us consider an example with a 3-degree-of-freedom cylindrical robot, shown in Fig. 5.5. This robot is powered by DC motors. The rotor shafts are connected to reducers producing either revolute or sliding motion at the outputs. For example, joint 3 is a sliding one (see Fig. 5.10). The actuators are controlled by servosystems which can be modelled by (5.4.11). Here, the state vector of the *i*th subsystem is $x^i = [q_i \ \dot{q}_i]^T$. The servosystems include position and velocity feedback loops. The gain vector can be presented as $d^i = [-a_{pi} \ a_{vi}]$, and $d_i = - a_{pi}$. It holds

$$u^i = -a_{pi}(q_i-v_i) + a_{vi}\dot{q}_i \quad (5.4.18)$$

The measured input-output diagrams of the realized servoregulators are presented in Fig. 5.11. Position gains a_{pi} and velocity gains a_{vi} are thus obtained.

Control of the cylindrical robot is realized by an experimental microcomputer system. Thus, the measurements of robot coordinates and velocities are realized by using A/D converters. The estimation algorithm (5.4.15) - (5.4.17) is implemented in a high-level programming language. First, the estimation of parameters of the subsystem $S^i(i=1)$ is realized. The control $v_i(t)$, joint coordinate $q_i(t)$ and velocity $\dot{q}_i(t)$ during $t\in[0, 5.8s]$ are presented in Fig. 5.12. These data are obtained by measurements combined with computer graphics. The estimation process is illustrated in Fig. 5.13. The curves are normalized to values printed over them. For example, the joint coordinate shown in Fig. 5.12 is normalized to 0.5414 rad. The time is normalized to 5.8 s. We obtain

$\alpha_1 = 0.82$ and $\beta_1 = 0.40$ from Fig. 5.13. The estimation process of parameter β_i during the first 2 seconds is presented in Fig. 5.14. We see

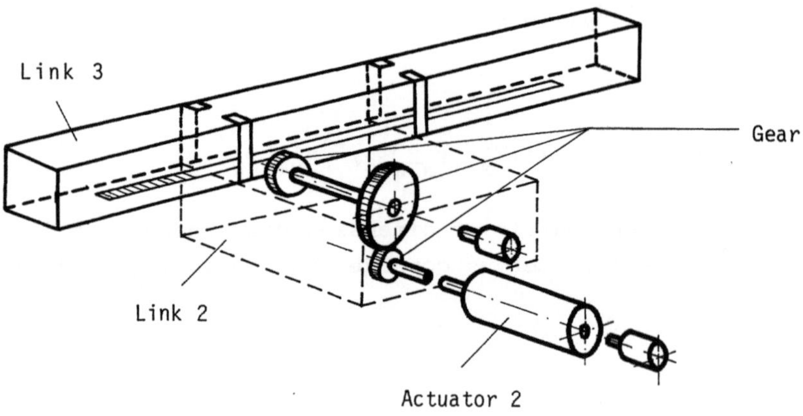

Fig. 5.10. Motor and reducer between the links 2 and 3

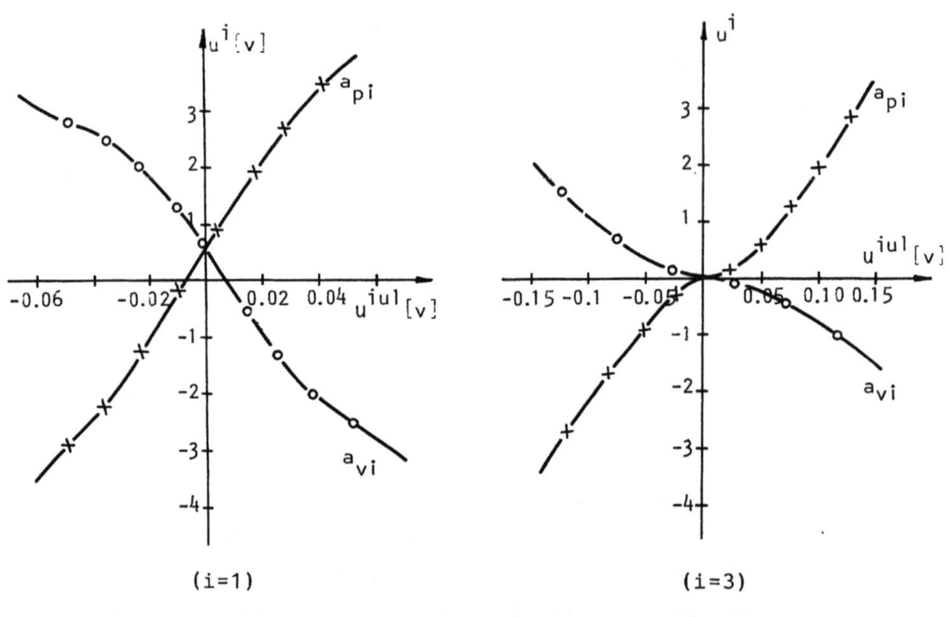

Fig. 5.11. Input-output characteristics of servosystems S^1 and S^3 (a_{pi} is obtained under the conditions $q_i=0$, $\dot{q}_i=0$ and $u^i=v_i$, and a_{vi} under the conditions $q_i=v_i=0$ and $u^i=\dot{q}_i$)

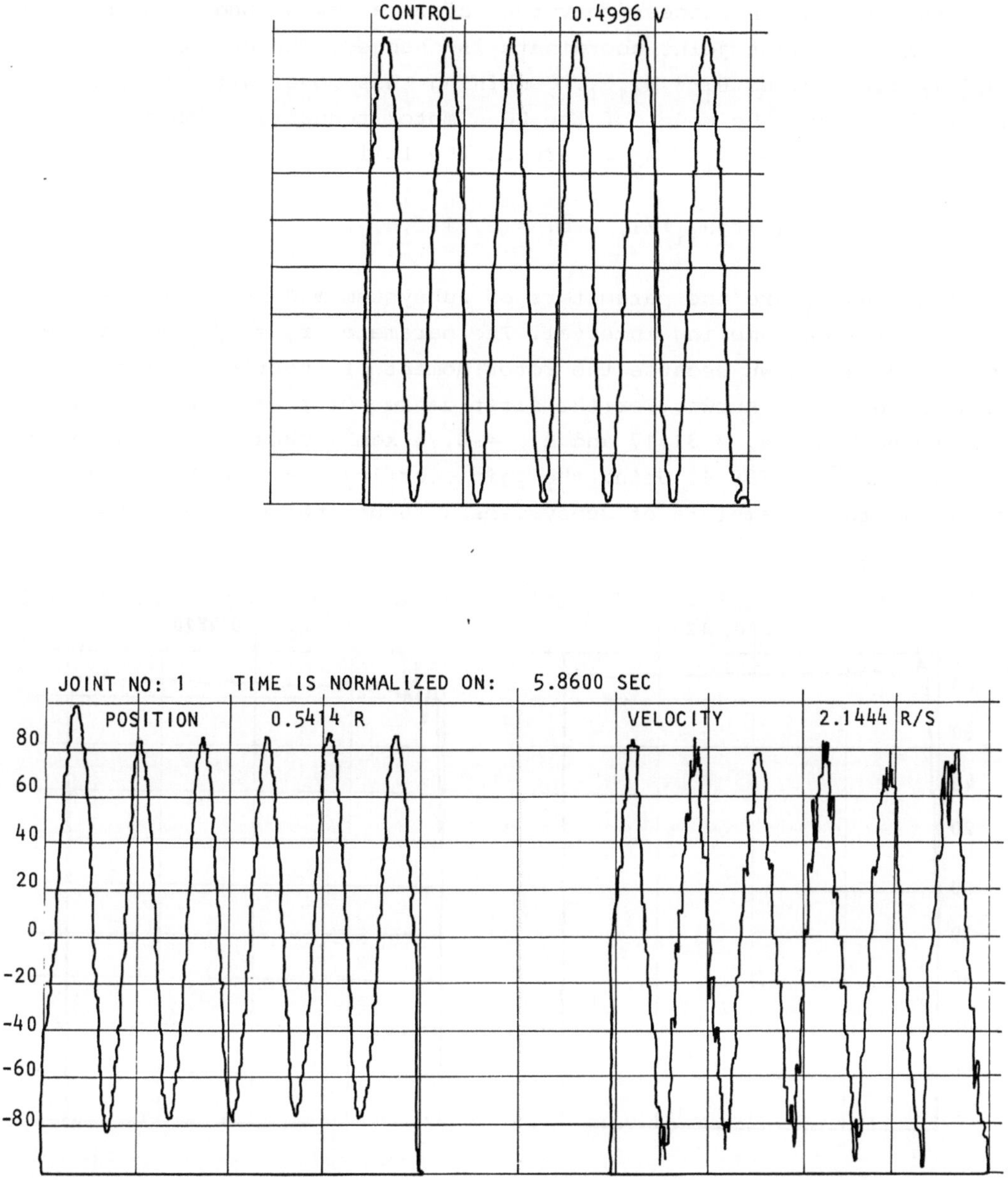

Fig. 5.12. Control $v_i(t)$, joint coordinate $q_i(t)$ and velocity $\dot{q}_i(t)$ for the first degree of freedom

that the estimation process converges after a few seconds. During this time only the first joint coordinate is changed. The dynamic model (5.4.7) now becomes $P_1 = H_{11}\ddot{q}_1$. Combining this model with the servo-system model and the model of the DC - motor/reducer, we obtain that $\bar{a}_i = a_i + a_{vi}b_i$ and $\bar{b}_i = a_{pi}b_i$ are of the following forms:

$$\bar{a}_i = (1-\alpha_i)(1+f_iH_{ii})/T, \qquad \bar{b}_i = \beta_i(1+f_iH_{ii})/T$$

where a_i and b_i are the parameters of subsystem models without servo-systems, T is a sampling interval. The parameter $f_i = 1/J_{ri}N_i^2$ can be considered as known because the rotor moment of inertia and the reduction ratio N_i are known. For the first degree of freedom we have $J_{ri} = 0.000056$ kgm^2, $N_i = 31.17$ and $H_{ii} = 0.76$ kgm^2. Thus, we obtain $\bar{a}_i = 134.7$ and $\bar{b}_i = 299.4$. Using the gain coefficients from Fig. 5.11, we obtain the parameters of subsystems without analog servoloops.

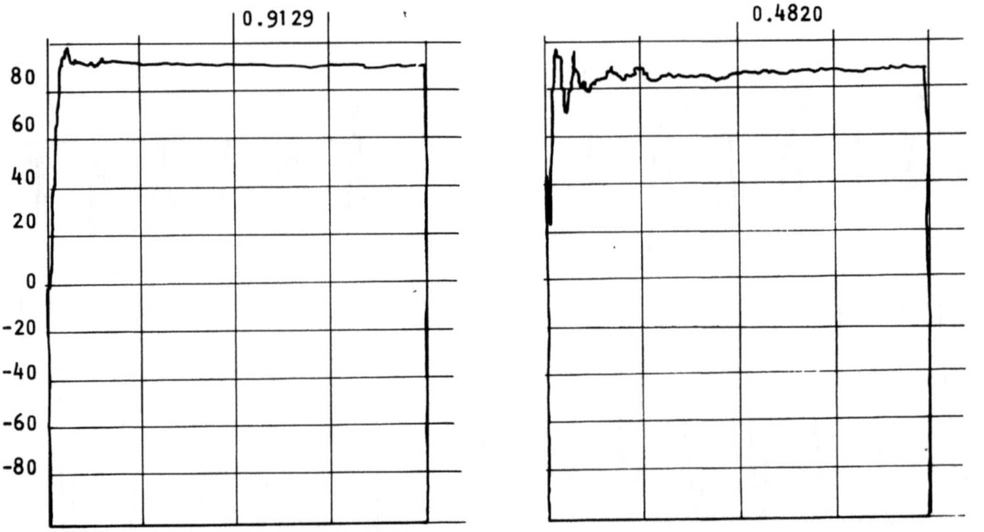

Fig. 5.13. Estimation process of α_1 and β_1

Finally, we will present the results of the estimation of parameters of subsystem 3. The input is excited by triangular voltage signals (2 Hz), as shown in Fig. 5.15. Joint coordinate q_3 and velocity $\dot{q}_3$ are presented in Fig. 5.15. The estimates α_3 and β_3 given in Fig. 5.17.

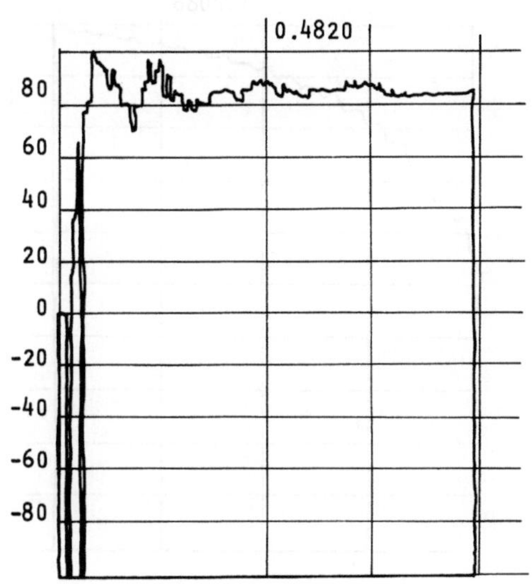

Fig. 5.14. Estimation of β_1 during t=2 s

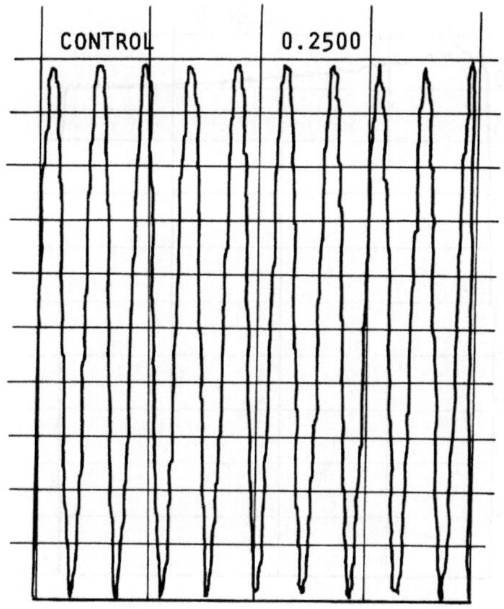

Fig. 5.15. Control $v_3(t)$

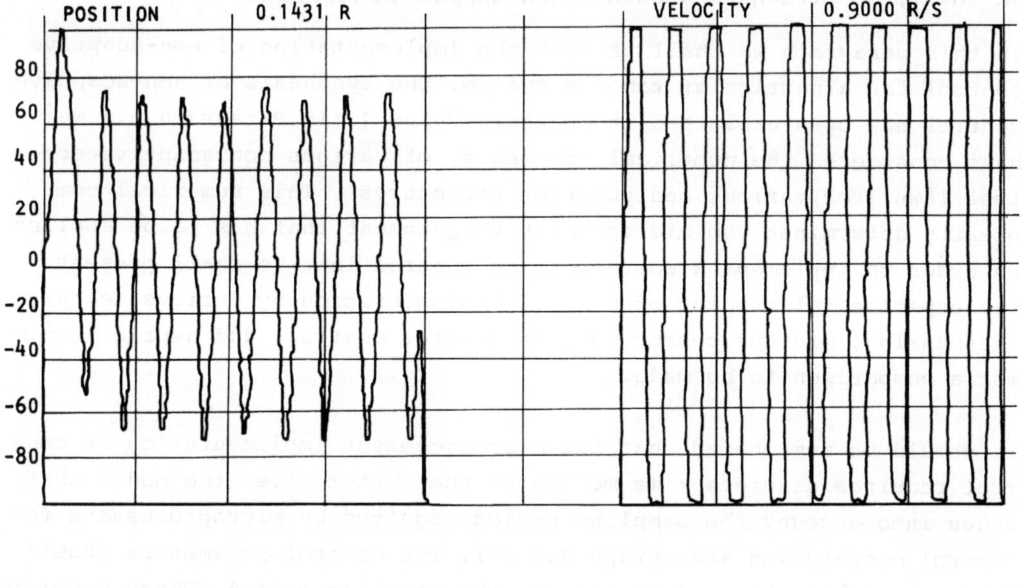

Fig. 5.16. Joint coordinate $q_3(t)$ and velocity $\dot{q}_3(t)$

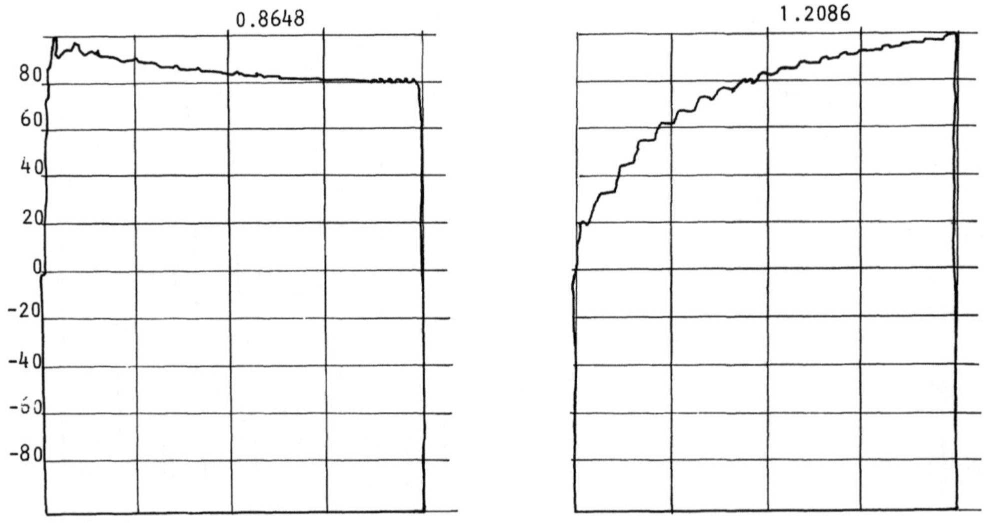

Fig. 5.17. Estimation of α_3 and β_3

5.5 Microprocessor Implementation of Non-Adaptive Control Laws

In this paragraph we shall present the implementation of non-adaptive control for a particular robotic system. The synthesis of non-adaptive control has been explained in Chapters 2 and 4. In Paragraph 5.3 we have considered the numerical complexity of various non-adaptive control laws (for various manipulation structures). This numerical complexity determines the microprocessor equipment that has to be applied in order to implement a corresponding control law. We shall present the experimental results of control implementation by various techniques: analog, microprocessor (direct digital control) and hybrid to permit a comparison to be made.

It should be remembered that the microprocessor implementation of control requires discrete time models of the system, i.e. the model that takes into account the sampling period required by microprocessors for control computation (Paragraph 4.2.11). The control parameters should be synthesized taking into account the sampling period. These problems have already been considered in [17]. Here, we shall briefly list various control forms in the discrete time domain.

The model of actuators (2.4.3) in the discrete time domain can be written as (assuming that $M_i = P_i$):

$$S^i: \quad x^i(k+1) = A_D^i x^i(k) + b_D^i N(u^i(k)) + f_D^i P_i(k), \quad \forall i \in I$$

$$k=0,1,2,\ldots \qquad (5.5.1)$$

where $A_D^i = \exp(\bar{A}^i T)$, $b_D^i = \int_0^T \bar{b}^i e^{\bar{A}^i \tau} d\tau$, $f_D^i = \int_0^T \bar{f}^i e^{\bar{A}^i \tau} d\tau$, $x^i(k) = x^i(kT)$, T is the sampling period and the model of the mechanical part of the robot (2.2.1) can be approximated by:

$$P_i(k) = H_i(q(k))\ddot{q}(k) + h_i(q(k), \dot{q}(k)), \quad \forall i \in I \quad k=0,1,2,\ldots \qquad (5.5.2)$$

The microprocessor (kinematic module) computes the nominal trajectories $q^o(k)$, $k=0,1,2,\ldots,L$ of the joint angles (displacements) in order to perform the motion specified by the operator. The task of the control system is to ensure tracking of the imposed nominal trajectories.

As already explained in previous chapters, the control is taken in one of the following forms [18, 19]:

- nominal centralized control and local control

$$u^i(k) = u^{io}(k) + \Delta u_i^L(k) \qquad (5.5.3)$$

- local (decentralized) nominal control and local control

$$u^i(k) = \bar{u}^{io}(k) + \Delta u_i^L(k) \qquad (5.5.4)$$

- local (decentralized) nominal control and local control and global control

$$u^i(k) = \bar{u}^{io}(k) + \Delta u_i^L(k) + \Delta u_i^G(k) \qquad (5.5.5)$$

The nominal centralized programmed control is synthesized to satisfy:

$$x^{io}(k+1) = A_D^i x^{io}(k) + b_D^i u^{io}(k) + f_D^i P_i^o(k), \quad \forall i \in I \quad k=0,1,\ldots,L$$

$$(5.5.6)$$

where $x^{io}(k) = (q_i^o(k), \dot{q}_i^o(k))^T$; and P_i^o is the nominal driving torque acting upon the *i*th d.o.f., which is calculated from:

$$P_i^o(k) = H_i(q^o(k))\ddot{q}^o(k) + h_i(q^o(k), \dot{q}^o(k)), \forall i\in I, k=0,1,\dots,L \tag{5.5.7}$$

The control satisfying (5.5.6) can be calculated using the minimum inverse of vector b_D^i [20]:

$$u^{io}(k) = (b_D^{iT}b_D^i)^{-1}b_D^{iT}(x^{io}(k+1)-A_D^i x^{io}(k)-f_D^i P_i^o(k)), \quad \forall i\in I \quad k=0,1,2,\dots,L \tag{5.5.8}$$

The local control (2.4.23) in the discrete time domain can be taken as:

$$\Delta u_i^L(k) = \hat{D}_D^{iT}\Delta x^i(k) + \hat{Q}_D^i \sum_{j=0}^{k} \Delta x^i(j), \ \forall i\in I \tag{5.5.9}$$

where $\hat{D}_D^i \in R^{1\times n_i}$ is the feedback gain vector and $\hat{Q}_D^i$ is the integral feedback gain, synthesized in the discrete time domain.

The local nominal control is synthesized to satisfy:

$$x^{io}(k+1) = A_D^i x^{io}(k) + b_D^i \bar{u}^{io}(k), \quad \forall i\in I, \quad k=0,1,2,\dots,L \tag{5.5.10}$$

Similarly to (5.5.8), we can obtain the local nominal control as:

$$\bar{u}^{io}(k) = (b_D^{iT}b_D^i)^{-1}b_D^{iT}(x^{io}(k+1) - A_D^i x^{io}(k)) \tag{5.5.11}$$

The global control ((2.6.1) when the local nominal control is applied) can be taken as:

$$\Delta u_i^G(k) = -K_i^G(x^i(k))\tilde{P}_i(k) \tag{5.5.12}$$

where K_i^G: $R^{n_i} \to R^1$ is the global gain, $\tilde{P}_i(k)$ is the on-line computed driving torque around the *i*th joint. On-line computation of the driving torques using various approximate models (and local control) has been considered in Paragraph 5.3.

In addition to these control laws (which have already been discussed in previous chapters), we shall consider the so-called on-line computation of nominal control in the form:

$$u^{io}(k, x(k)) = (b_D^{iT}b_D^i)^{-1}b_D^{iT}(x^{io}(k+1)-A_D^i x^i(k)-f_D^i\tilde{P}_i(x(k))) \tag{5.5.13}$$

In the text to follow we shall describe microprocessor implementation of the dynamic control for the manipulator UMS-2. We shall present the results of control synthesis which have been obtained using our software package. We shall also present realizations of tracking the nominal trajectories using various control laws and the three above mentioned versions of control implementation: (Ia) when servosystems are implemented by analog techniques, (Ib) when microprocessors are added to improve tracking, and (Ic) when only microprocessors are used for the control implementation.

The manipulation robot UMS-2 is shown in Fig. 5.5. It has five degrees of freedom: two linear and three rotational*). Parameters of the manipulator are presented in Table 5.7 (lengths, masses and moments of inertia of the links). D.C. motors are used as actuators and their paramaters are given in Table 5.8. These parameters have been identified as described in Paragraph 5.4.

The dynamic model of this manipulator is extremely simple so it has been easy to achieve on-line calculation of dynamics. We have used "DIGITAL" microprocessors of PDP 11-03 type. We have found out that it is possible to implement control by two microprocessors only, because of the simplicity of the dynamic model. The block scheme of the three versions of control implementation is presented in Fig. 5.18 [21].

The first microprocessor is used for the synthesis of nominal trajectories and communication with the operator or with higher control levels. In the latter case additional microprocessors or a computer have to be used for the implementation of decision-making levels. The first microprocessor calculates the nominal trajectories in accordance with the operator's requirements. It can calculate nominal trajectories either on-line or off-line and memorize them. It sends nominal angles and velocities at each sampling interval to the second microprocessor.

The executive control level is implemented by the second microprocessor. This microprocessor calculates the nominal programmed control either on-line or off-line using the nominal coordinates and velocities obtained from the first microprocessor. It also calculates local control (5.5.9) and it may calculate global control (5.5.12) by on-line calculation of the driving torques and forces.

We shall not discuss in detail the problems of programming of both

---

*) Actually, the manipulator of Fig. 5.5 has six d.o.f. but the 6th d.o.f. was locked in our experiments.

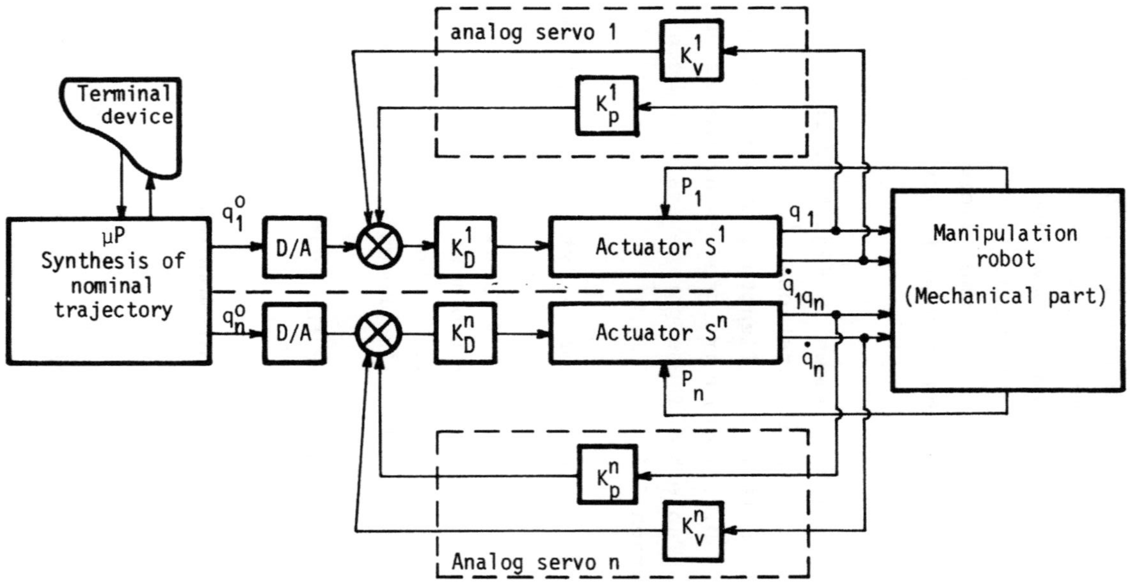

Fig. 5.18. Control scheme (a) analog version

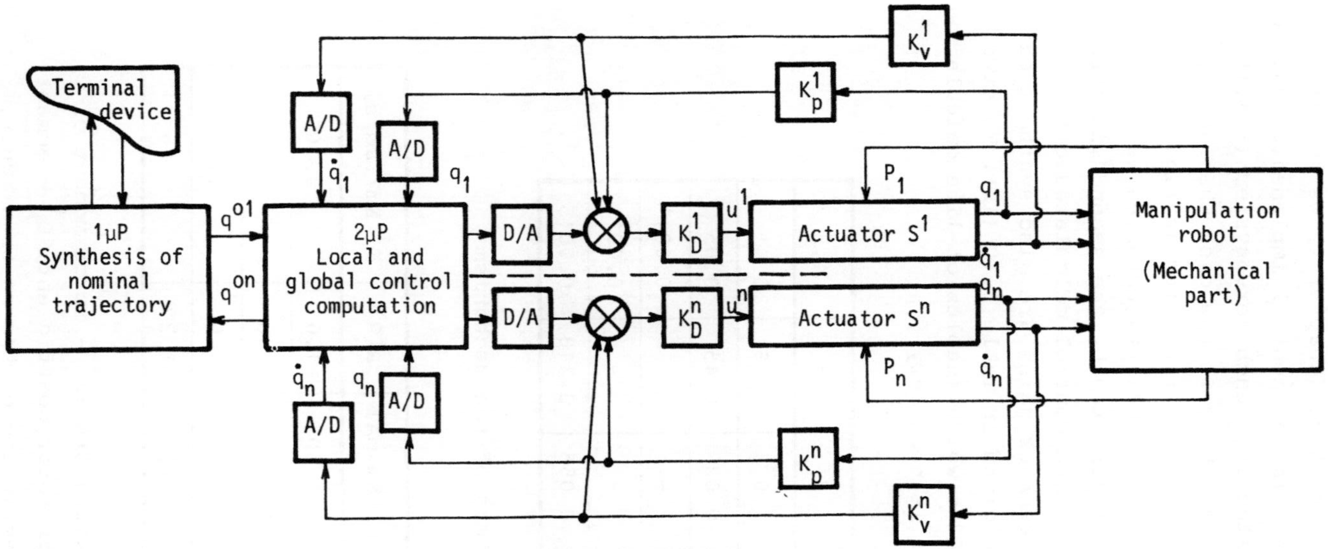

Fig. 5.18(b) Hybrid version

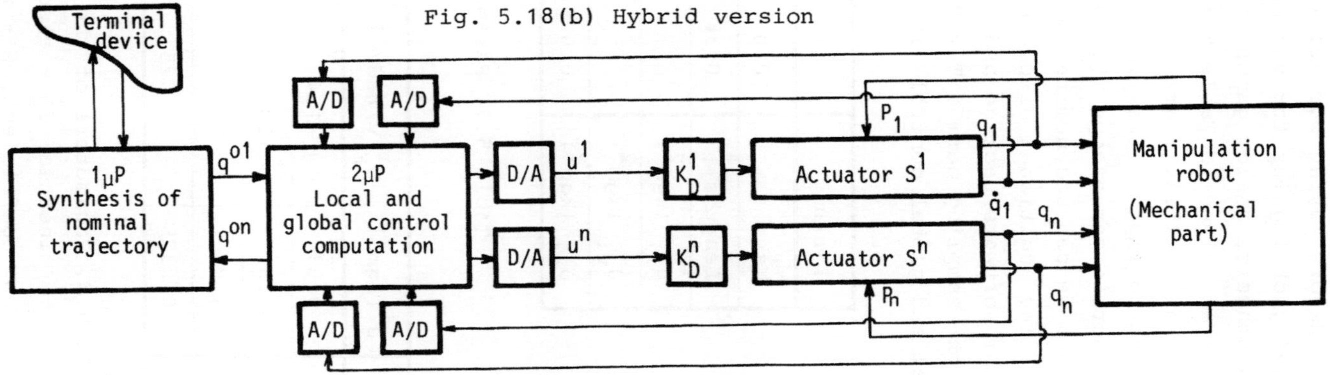

Fig. 5.18(c) Direct digital control

microprocessors. Using our software package (Chapter 4) we synthesize local and global gains for various forms of control implementation. We first synthesize analog gains to stabilize each servosystem (5.4.1). The gains are given in Table 5.9 (Ia). This is the case when analog servomechanisms (5.4.1) are implemented (as presented in Fig. 5.18a). If we want to improve the tracking of nominal trajectories we can add local discrete servoloops (5.5.9) implemented by the second microprocessor and we can add nominal programmed control calculated off-line (5.5.8). The additional discrete feedback gains are also synthesized using our software package and are given in Table 5.10 (Ib). We have chosen the sampling period T = 0.02 s which enables on-line calculation of local and global control (if it is necessary).

Links	1	2	3	4,5
Mass	10.0	7.0	4.15	0.5
Lengths	0.38	0.02	0.45	0.05
J_{xi} (kgm^2)	-	-	-	0.001
J_{yi} (kgm^2)	-	-	-	0.001
J_{zi} (kgm^2)	0.029	0.055	0.318	0.0015

Table 5.7. Parameters of the mechanism

i	J^i[kgm^2]	C_E^i[V/rad/s]	C_M^i[Nm/mA]	R[Ω]	F_D^i[Nm/rad/s]
1	0.03	1.43	1.50	1.6	0.006
2	205.3	120.3	125.4	1.6	40.3
3	74.	72.2	75.5	1.6	1.
4,5	0.0325	0.325	1.36	3.32	2.86

Table 5.8. Parameters of the actuators (J^i - rotor moment of inertia; C_E^i - electromotor coefficient; C_M^i - moment coefficient, R^i - resistance of the rotor circuit, F_D^i - viscous friction coefficient; gear speed and moment ratios are taken into account)

As we have already stated, in this specific case the mathematical model of manipulator dynamics is very simple, so we can achieve on-line calculation of the driving torques by one microprocessor only. Actually, we have calculated on-line driving torques only for the first three degrees of freedom of the manipulator (minimal configuration of the manipulator), since the influence of the gripper dynamics is negligible. So we have introduced global control in the first three degrees of freedom of the manipulator. We have calculated global gains using our software package. The dynamic model of this manipulator is given in Appendix 2.B. The number of multiplications and additions which have to be realized for local and global control is given in Paragraph 5.3.

	1	2	3	4,5
Positional gain [V/rad]	975.	15000.	3037.	50.
Speed gain [V/rad/s]	59.	934.	462.	-

Table 5.9. Analog feedback gains

	1	2	3	4
Positional gain	7.1	3.47	12.2	1.3
Speed gain	0.086	0.064	0.18	-

Table 5.10. Local discrete gain for T = 0.02 s with analog feedback

Fig. 5.19 shows experimental results of tracking the nominal trajectories with various control laws. In order to compare various control laws, we have implemented trackings of the same nominal trajectory with various laws under equal conditions. We have made initial condition errors in the first and third degree of freedom of the manipulator, i.e. we have started the tracking of the nominal trajectories from the initial position of the manipulator which deviates from the nominal initial position by $\Delta q_1(0) = -0.1$ rad and $\Delta q_3(0) = -0.1$ m, where Δq_i denotes deviation of the position (angle) q_i of the ith degree of freedom from its nominal value q_i^o ($\Delta q_i(t) = q_i(t) - q_i^o(t)$). In the remaining degrees of freedom tracking starts from the nominal positions.

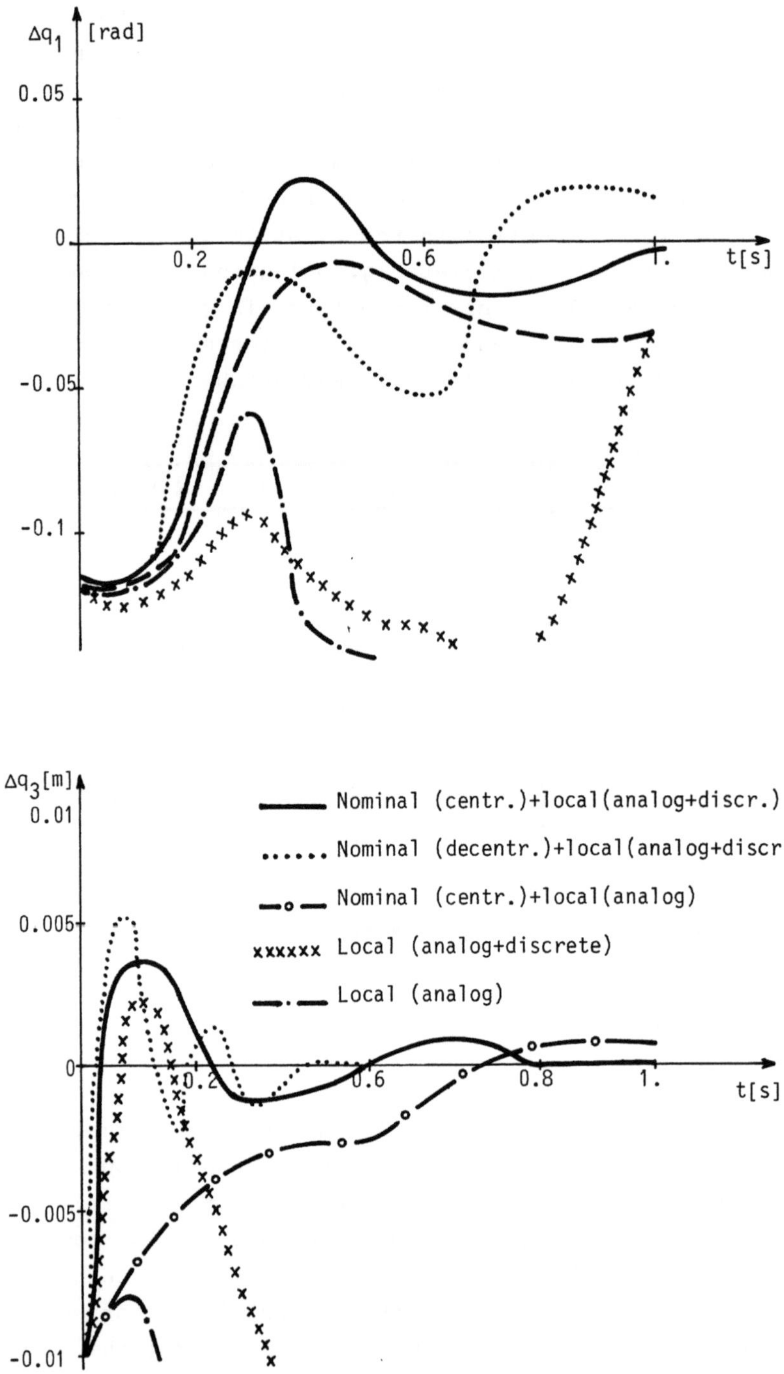

Fig. 5.19. Implementation of tracking of trajectories with discrete and analog control - experimental results

First, the tracking has been realized by analog servosystems only, when the microprocessor sends directly nominal trajectories $q_i^o(k)$ through D/A converters. From Fig. 5.19 it is obvious that the tracking is very poor. In the figures the tracking for the first and third degrees of freedom only is presented, since these two degrees of freedom are coupled. The tracking is very poor since servosystems are not compensated for either dynamics of actuators and mechanism or acceleration along the nominal trajectory.

Then, we have considered the tracking when nominal programmed control $u^{oi}(k)$ is the output from the microprocessor. In this case the computer calculates off-line nominal programmed control and sends it through D/A converters. Obviously the tracking is much better (see Fig. 5.19). In order to improve the tracking we have introduced additional discrete local feedback loops (Fig. 5.18b). In this case, the second microprocessor on-line calculates local control $\Delta u_i^L(k)$, adds it to the nominal control $u^{oi}(k)$ and sends it through D/A converters. The results of tracking are also shown in Fig. 5.19.

We have also considered tracking with decentralized nominal control $\bar{u}^{oi}(k)$ (5.5.11), when the nominal control is calculated using the approximate decoupled model of the manipulator. The results are also presented in Fig. 5.19. We also present the results of tracking when only local control (analog (5.4.1) and discrete (5.5.9)) is implemented.

The next step in the implementation of various control laws has been the omission of the analog servomechanism (Fig. 5.18c). We have implemented discrete controllers (Ic) only to track the same nominal trajectories under the same conditions as before. We have chosen the same sampling period T = 0.02 s. Now, discrete local gains are given in Table 5.11 (when analog servomechanisms are omitted). The results of tracking the nominal trajectory are given in Fig. 5.20. We have implemented both on-line (5.5.13) and off-line (5.5.8) calculation of nominal programmed control. We have realized the tracking with off-line calculated programmed control u^{oi} with local discrete dontrol (5.5.9). Then, we have realized the tracking with nominal control plus local plus global control. Obviously the robot performance is much better in the second case. However, a similar performance can be achieved by on-line calculation of the nominal control (5.5.13). In this case the microprocessor again calculates on-line driving torques in the manipulator joints and then using these torques, the control which should lead the mani-

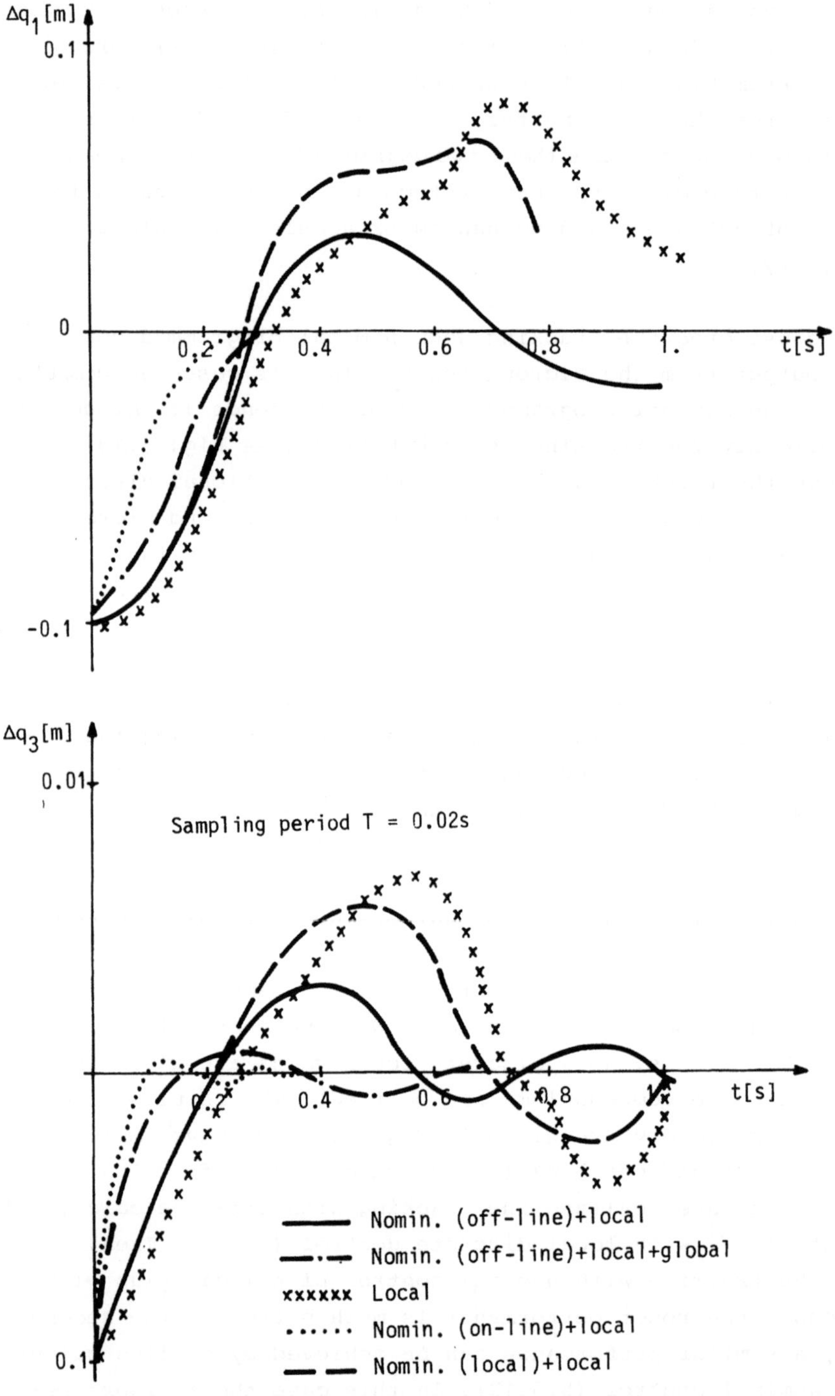

Fig. 5.20. Implementation of tracking of trajectory with discrete control - experimental results

pulator along the nominal trajectory.

	1	2	3	4, 5	T_D[s]
Positional gain	20.07	356.3	355.4	1.3	0.02
	10.0	4.1	100.	0.37	0.06
Speed gain	1.53	7.49	10.4	-	0.02
	4.03	0.28	10.0	-	0.06

Table 5.11. Local discrete gains (when analog servomechanisms are omitted)

We have also considered the case when the nominal control is synthesized using the decentralized model of the robot (3.5.11). If the third degree of freedom is fixed, the tracking of the nominal trajectory for first degree of freedom is the same as in the centralized case (Fig. 5.20). However, if the third degree of freedom is also moving, the tracking is rather poor, since this decentralized control does not take care about the coupling which exists between the first and the third degree of freedom. The results of tracking when only local discrete control (5.5.9) is implemented are also presented. The tracking is poor.

In Fig. 5.21 control signals that are sent through D/A converters for various control laws are presented.

In order to stress the importance of the choice of the sampling period, we have implemented all the above mentioned control laws with the sampling period T = 0.06 s. Local discrete gains (when analog servomechanisms were omitted) are also given in Table 5.11. The experimental results of tracking the same nominal trajectory with various control laws are presented in Fig. 5.22. It can be seen that the robot performance is worse than in the case when the sampling period was shorter. This results from the fact that 0.06 s is too long a period for the manipulator dynamics. The gains have to be rather low in order to keep stability of the robot, and the settling time is thus too long. The control signals are shown in Fig. 5.23.

In order to check the validity of our software package for control synthesis (which we used for the calculation of local and global gains),

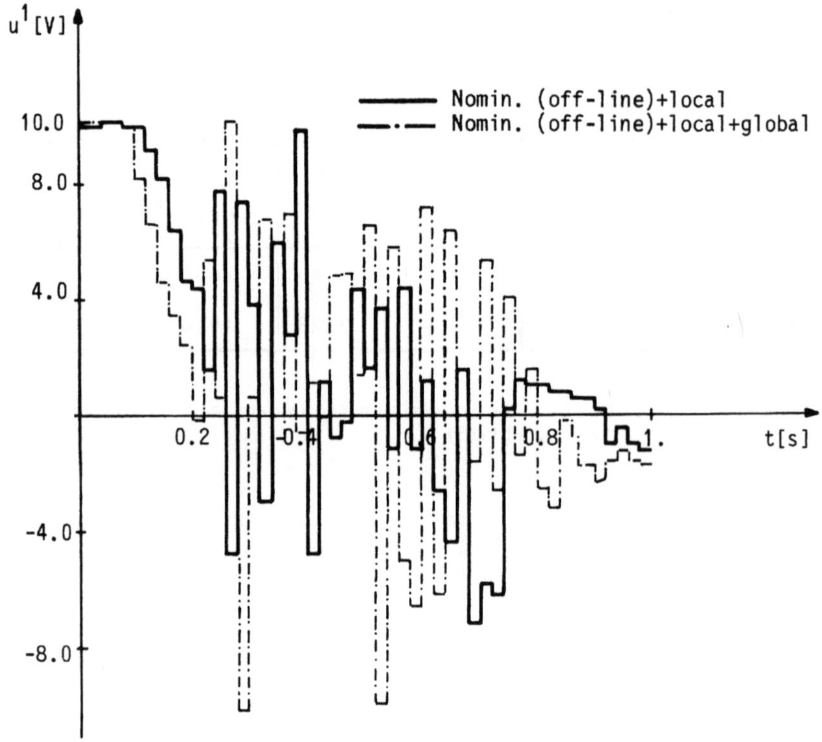

Sampling period T = 0.02s

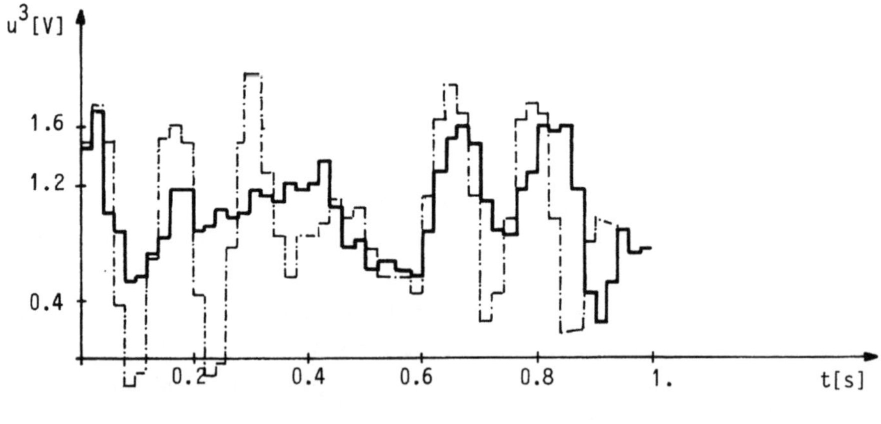

Fig. 5.21. Control signals during tracking of trajectory for UMS-2 - experimental results

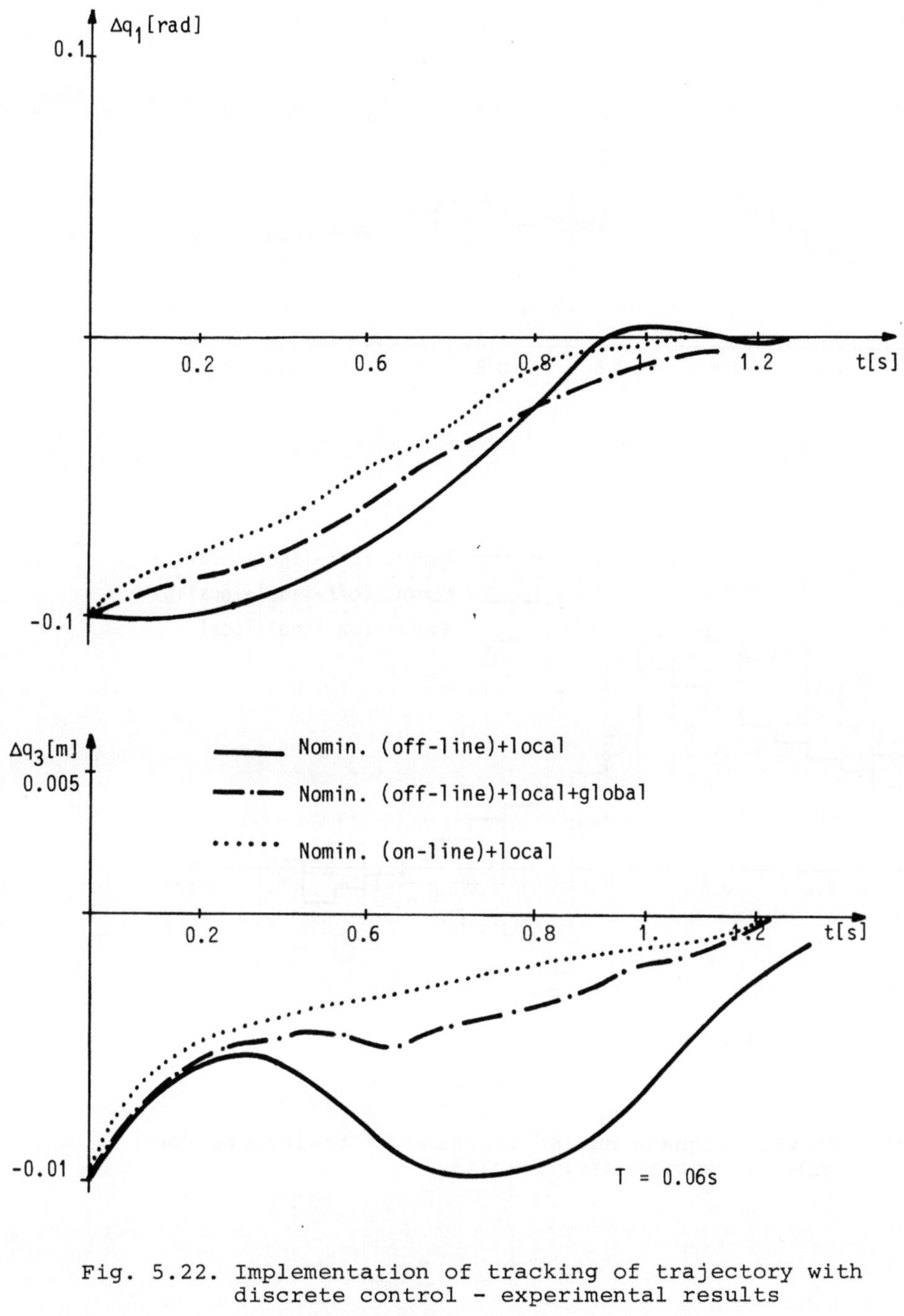

Fig. 5.22. Implementation of tracking of trajectory with discrete control - experimental results

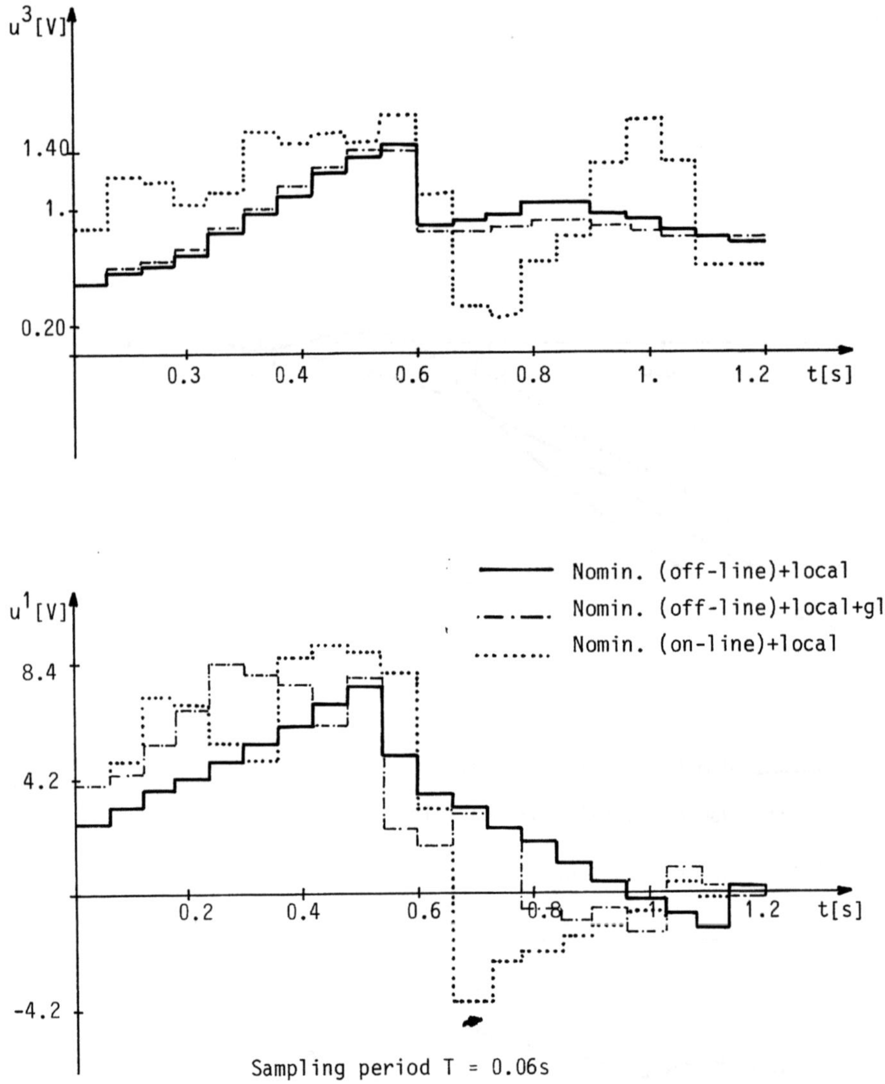

Fig. 5.23. Control signals during tracking of trajectory for UMS-2 - experimental results

we simulated the dynamics of the manipulator during tracking the nominal trajectories with various control laws. The results of simulation are presented in Fig. 5.24 and 5.25. In Fig. 5.24 are presented the results of simulation when discrete control is synthesized with sampling period T = 0.02 s, and in Fig. 5.25 the sampling period is T = 0.06 s. We simulate the robot dynamics under the same conditions as those under which we realized the trackings experimentally. If we compare the results of simulations in Figs. 5.24 and 5.25 with the results of experiment, given in Figs. 5.20 and 5.22, we can see that there is a good agreement between the simulation and real behaviour of the robot. This means that the mathematical model of the robot dynamics used in the package is well stated and that the parameters of the robot are well identified. This is the reason why the feedback gains synthesized using the software package were appropriate for the control implementation.

The results of implementation of various control laws show that a better performance is achieved with the control which takes care about the dynamics of the robot. However, such control is much more complex to be implemented since on-line calculation of the robot dynamics has to be achieved. If we have to ensure precise tracking of a desired trajectory it is necessary to take care about the robot dynamics through either nominal or global control.

If we compare various implementations of the proposed control laws it is obvious that the best results are achieved by analog discrete implementation of the local controllers. However, such implementation is the most complex. Discrete implementation of the controllers is the simplest from the "hardware point of view" (simple microprocessors are necessary for the calculation of trajectory). Discrete implementation is convenient from the point of view of possible changes and robot evaluation, as explained in Paragraph 5.2.

References

[1] Albus S.J., Barbera J.A. and Fitzgerald L.M., "Programming a Hierarchical Robot Control System", Proc. of the 12th. ISIR, pp. 505-517, Paris, June 1982.

[2] Megahed S. and Renaud M., "Minimization of the Computation Time Necessary for the Dynamic Control of Robot Manipulators", Proc. of the. 12th. ISIR, pp. 469-478, Paris, June 1982.

[3] Luh Y.S.J., Walker W.M., Paul C.P.R., "On-line Computational Scheme for Mechanical Manipulators", ASME Trans. J. Dynamic Syst.,

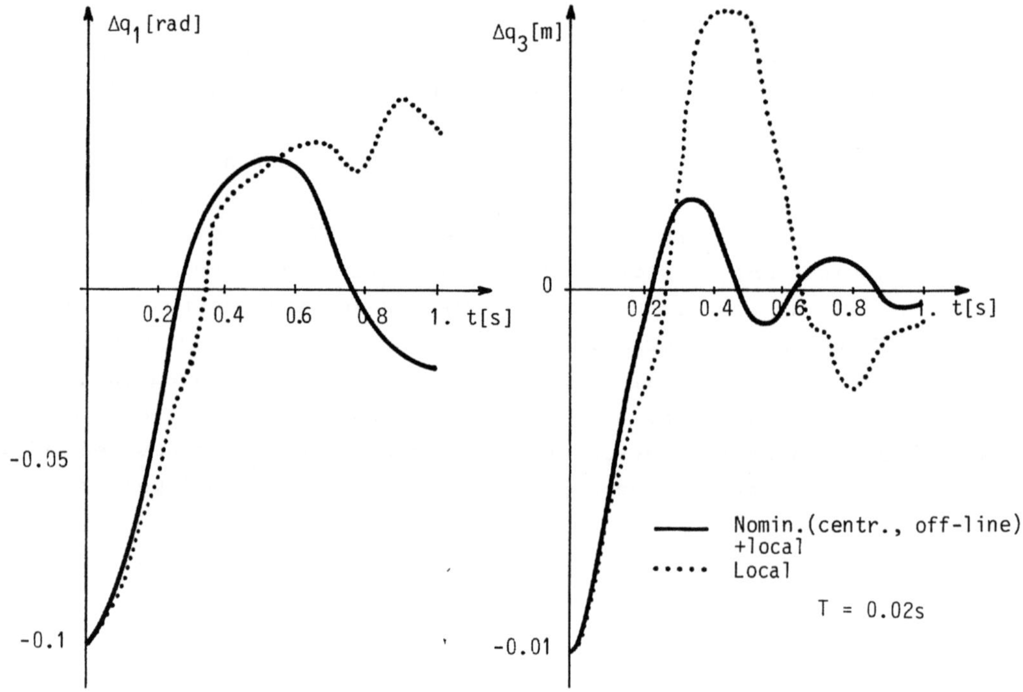

Fig. 5.24. Simulation of tracking of trajectory with discrete control

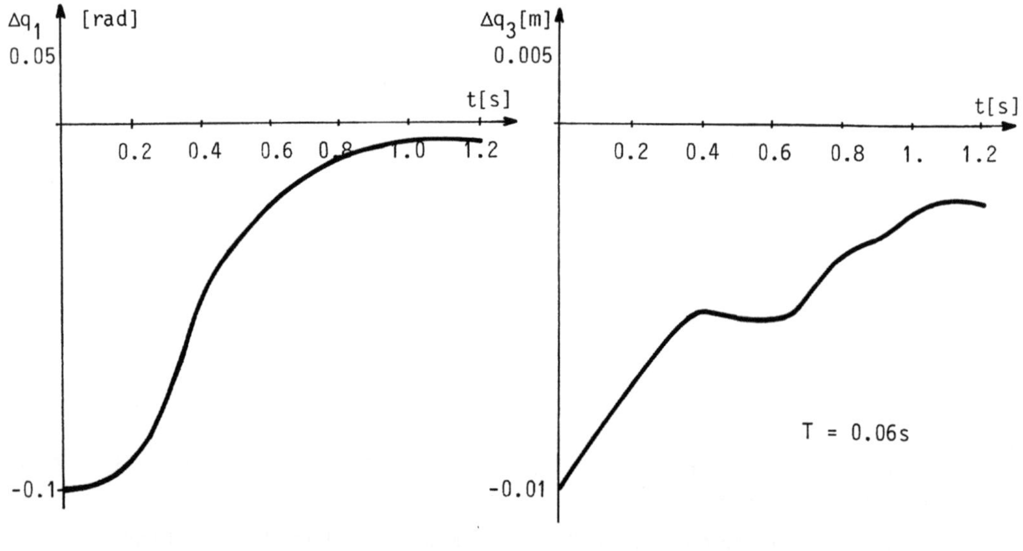

Fig. 5.25. Simulation of tracking with discrete control

Measurement and Contr., Vol. 102, No. 2, pp. 69-76, June,1980.

[4] Luh Y.S.Y., Lin S.C., "Scheduling of Parallel Computation for a Computer-Controlled Mechanical Manipulator", IEEE Trans. on Systems, Man, and Cybernetics, Vol. SMC-12, No. 2, March/April, 1982.

[5] Unimation Inc. "User's Guide to VAL", Version 12, Unimation Inc., Danbury, CT, 1980.

[6] Taylor R.H., Summers P.D., Meyer J.M., "AML: A Manufacturing Language", Robotic Research, Vol. 1, No. 3, pp. 19-41, 1982.

[7] Vukobratović K.M., Kirćanski M.N., Stokić M.D., Kirćanski V.M., Karan B., "General Purpose Controller for Industrial Manipulators", Proc. of the Second Yugoslav-Soviet Symposium on Applied Robotics, Belgrade, pp. 1-15, 1984.

[8] Karan B., Vukobratović K.M., Kirćanski M.N., Stokić M.D., "A Software System for Teaching and Commanding the Industrial Robots", Proc. of the First Symposium on Robot Control, Barcelona, 1985.

[9] Vukobratović K.M., Kirćanski M.N., "Computer Assisted Generation of Robot Dynamic Models in Analytical Form", Acta Applicandae Mathematicae, No. 2, pp. 49-70, 1985.

[10] Vukobratović K.M., Kirćanski V.M., Scientific Fundamentals of Robotics, 3, Kinematics and Trajectory Planning, Monograph Springer-Verlag, Berlin, 1985.

[11] Vukobratović K.M., Kirćanski M.N., Real-Time Dynamics of Manipulation Robots, Scientific Fundations of Robotics, Springer-Verlag, 1984.

[12] Luh Y.S.J., Fisher W.D. and Paul R.P.C., "Joint Torque Control By a Direct Feedback for Industrial Robots", IEEE Trans. on Automatic Control, Vol. AC-28, No. 2, 1983.

[13] Vukobratović K.M., Kirćanski M.N., "Computer Assisted Sensitivity Model Generation in Manipulation Robots Dynamics", Journal of Mechanisms and Machine Theory, No. 1, 1984.

[14] Vukobratović K.M., Kirćanski M.N., "Decentralized Adaptive Control for a Class of Large-Scale Mechanical Systems", III Symp. on Large Scale Systems: Theory, Applications and Impacts, Warsaw, 1983.

[15] Mahmoud M., Singh M., Large Scale Systems Modelling, International Series on Systems and Control, Vol. 3, Perg. Press, 1981.

[16] Hassan M., Singh M., "A two Level Costate Prediction Algorithm for Nonlinear Systems", Automatica - The IFAC Journal, 6, 1977.

[17] Vukobratović K.M., Stokić M.D., Scientific Fundamentals of Robotics 2, Control of Manipulation Robots: Theory and Application, Monograph, Springer-Verlag, Berlin, 1982, also in Russian, Nauka, 1985.

[18] Vukobratović K.M., Stokić M.D., "Is Dynamic Control Needed in Robotic Systems, and if so to What Extent?", International Journal of Robotic Research, Vol. 102, June, 1982.

[19] Vukobratović K.M., Stokić M.D., "One Engineering Concept of Dynamic Control of Manipulators", Journal of Dynamic Systems, Measurement and Control, Trans. of the ASME, Vol. 103, No. 2, pp. 108 - 118, 1981.

[20] Stokić M.D., Timotijević M., "Algorithms of Dynamic Control of Manipulation Robots and its Microprocessor Implementation", The VI IFToMM Congres, New Delhi, 1983.

[21] Vukobratović K.M., Stokić M.D., "Microprocessor Implementation of Dynamic Control for Manipulation Robots", Digital Systems, (to be published), 1985.

[22] Stokić M.D., Vukobratović K.M., Hristić S.D., "Implementation of Force Feedback in Control of Manipulation Robots", International Journal of Robotic Research, (to be published), 1985.

Subject Index

MIX
Papier aus verantwortungsvollen Quellen
Paper from responsible sources
FSC® C105338

If you have any concerns about our products,
you can contact us on
ProductSafety@springernature.com

In case Publisher is established outside the EU,
the EU authorized representative is:
Springer Nature Customer Service Center GmbH
Europaplatz 3, 69115 Heidelberg, Germany

Printed by Libri Plureos GmbH
in Hamburg, Germany